THE ATLAS OF WINTERING BIRDS
IN BRITAIN AND IRELAND

The Atlas of Wintering Birds in Britain and Ireland

Compiled by

PETER LACK

British Trust for Ornithology

Irish Wildbird Conservancy

PUBLISHED BY

T & A D Poyser

© 1986 British Trust for Ornithology

ISBN 0 85661 043 7

First published in 1986 by T & A D Poyser Ltd
Town Head House, Calton, Staffordshire, England
for the British Trust for Ornithology and
the Irish Wildbird Conservancy

British Library Cataloguing in Publication Data
The Atlas of wintering birds in Britain and
    Ireland.
    1. Birds—Great Britain—Migration
    I. Lack, Peter   II. British Trust for
    Ornithology   III. Irish Wildbird Conservancy
    598.252'5'0941   QL698.9

    ISBN 0-85661-043-7

Printed and bound in Great Britain
at The Bath Press, Avon

Contents

Foreword

by JAMES FERGUSON-LEES

Here, in this companion volume to *The Atlas of Breeding Birds in Britain and Ireland* (1976), British and Irish birdwatchers can surely claim to have done it again! Indeed, this new work on winter birds, with its assessments of abundance, may come to be seen as an even greater leap forward in our knowledge of bird distributions. Like its predecessor, *The Atlas of Wintering Birds in Britain and Ireland* has called for an outstanding cooperative effort. Following a pilot survey in 1980/81, 10,000 or more enthusiasts trudged through inhospitable habitats in all weathers during the winters of 1981/82–1983/84, to record the numbers of birds seen in each 10-km square. The whole was supervised by over 100 Regional Organisers marshalled by the National Organiser and backed by a Working Group responsible for the broad planning. Results were stored and analysed on computer, which greatly simplified the production of the maps. Much of the text has been written by over 100 specialists whose names appear at the ends of the individual species accounts; put together by the small editorial team; and illustrated by delightful line drawings contributed by more than a score of artists. Once again, the British Trust for Ornithology and the Irish Wildbird Conservancy have every reason to be proud of a truly creative concerted effort.

Our previous knowledge of winter birds was far poorer than ever it was of breeding species. In winter, birdwatchers have tended to spend much of their time at estuaries, reservoirs and other wetlands. As a result, of course, much was already known about the main concentrations of waterfowl and waders through the monthly Wildfowl Counts (organised by the Wildfowl Trust), the Birds of Estuaries Enquiry (presently funded by the BTO, the Royal Society for the Protection of Birds and the Nature Conservancy Council), and the Wetlands Enquiry (organised for Ireland by the IWC). The general patterns for a good many other species may have been fairly well known and there have, of course, been local surveys in some areas. Ringers also have records over many years from their particular sites and we already had numerous data from gardens in both suburban and rural areas as a result of the BTO's Garden Bird Feeding Survey. But even these components have never before been put together except in general descriptions of distributions by counties and outline maps in field guides, while the detailed winter distributions of, in particular, many landbirds were imperfectly appreciated.

Now we have much clearer pictures, but by no means all the answers. Winter patterns are more fluid and variable than those of the breeding season. We still know too little about how birds use the land in winter. We do not know exactly why birds are where they are, and it is important for conservation to understand the reasons for their selection of particular areas, and their ecology and feeding behaviour throughout the winter months. I believe that this book will make evident some of these gaps in our understanding.

The maps should, and indeed must, become the starting point for many questions. Which are the important areas for birds in winter? Where do birds go in different weather conditions? Where do the thrushes and the finches concentrate? And, to take one specific example, why do Skylarks *Alauda arvensis*, prominent in weather movements, seem less affected by severe conditions and return north early in the year even if it is cold? We have to ponder the reasons for the distributions now recorded. Thus, while the data collected and the resulting maps have more than justified the undertaking, we feel that its potential will not have been realised until it forms a basis for further and more detailed studies. Britain and Ireland are internationally important wintering areas for many species, and we have a duty to other countries to find out all we can.

In the Foreword to *The Atlas of Breeding Birds in Britain and Ireland*, published in 1976, I thought it important to review the history of mapping bird distributions in these islands and elsewhere. The concept of atlases based on grid squares was then still comparatively new. But observers are now familiar with the techniques. Anyone interested in a review of the background to atlas projects is referred to the earlier Foreword, which was to some extent updated by my chapter on 'Distribution maps and bird atlases' in the BTO's Jubilee volume, *Enjoying Ornithology*, edited by Ronald Hickling (1983).

It has been said many times that all atlas fieldwork is fun. It satisfies the competitive and 'ticking' instincts and, since within its framework common birds are of as much interest as rarities, it means that the presence of a Treecreeper *Certhia familiaris*, a Corn Bunting *Miliaria calandra* or even a humble House Sparrow *Passer domesticus* assumes significance when one surveys a square. For the *Breeding Atlas* the aim was to proceed towards proof of nesting in each 10-km square; for the *Winter Atlas* observers were asked to count the birds of each species seen during timed periods of fieldwork.

All atlas fieldwork is easier than is often imagined, because one is working to rules laid down by the organisers as well as within one's own limitations. It quickly generates enthusiasm. Yet, as with its predecessor, this *Winter Atlas* was preceded by years of debate as those with faith in the concept sought to convince the relevant BTO and IWC committees about its practicability. With the success of the earlier project behind us, the new one appeared at first sight comparatively simple to approve and straightforward to plan. But again many doubts were raised. Not least, could the money be found to finance the whole operation? These and many other questions were repeatedly raised.

Moreover, while breeding birds are anchored to a nest and, in many cases, more or less evenly distributed within the available habitat by the requirements of their territories, winter birds come and go, often congregate into flocks of very variable size, and may desert whole tracts of seemingly suitable habitat. Although a winter distribution map for each species, with some indication of numbers, was the main aim, we also hoped to find out more about fluctuations and movements in the course of the winters. This would be poorly shown by plotting presence and absence alone, and so it was doubly important to find some form of quantification. But there were serious doubts about the validity of some of the suggested methods, so these had to be tested and then modified or abandoned after a pilot survey.

The possibility of a *Winter Atlas* was first discussed, at the instigation of Peter Grant, as long ago as 1977, soon after the *Breeding Atlas* was published. A small working party was set up by the Populations & Surveys Committee of the BTO in 1978, meeting for the first time that August and consisting of Peter Grant, Tony Prater, Tim Sharrock, Bob Spencer and myself. But there were still many bridges to be crossed and it was not until the following year that the scheme was finally approved for Britain by the BTO. The main Working Group was then set up, meeting for the first time in May 1980, and a pilot survey was launched in winter 1980/81. The *Breeding Atlas* had taken five years of fieldwork, but with that experience behind us we believed that the *Winter Atlas* could be undertaken in only three. Indeed, it had to, because the costs of such a project on a national scale had escalated.

Most observers sensibly regard Britain and Ireland as a single ornithological unit. From the outset, therefore, the BTO hoped that Ireland would join in this project, and all were delighted when the IWC Council gave its final approval. There were worries about coverage in the remoter parts, as there were for the Highlands and north of Scotland, but in the event these proved foundless. By the end of the third winter, as set out in much greater detail elsewhere (pages 16–18), no less than 94% of the main squares in Britain and Ireland had had timed visits of at least six hours; and two-thirds of the remainder had had visits of at least one hour. In the end, only six of the 3,761 squares with significant land areas had had no timed visits, while the other 95, all on the coast or offshore islands and most in remote parts of Scotland and Ireland, include hardly any land.

Although acknowledgements appear elsewhere, I must take this opportunity of expressing my personal gratitude to, above all, Peter Lack. The organiser of such a survey involving thousands of people has to put an enormous amount of work into basic administration before any analysis can begin. He has to set up the team of Regional Organisers, foster their enthusiasm, encourage them and, if necessary, bully any who seem to be slow in playing their part. By lectures and local meetings, he has to help them enthuse the many observers who will carry out the fieldwork. He has to test methods and discuss them with the highly critical Working Group watching over the whole project throughout. These are not easy tasks, nor is the analysis of the mass of data for the thousands of squares involved, even though the BTO's entry into the computer age has greatly simplified storage, organisation and reference. Peter has also produced the important discussion chapters on the maps, the weather in the three winters, and the patterns and movements of our winter birds. Although it was decided that the individual species texts should, in the interests of speed, be written by others, he had to choose, approach and, as necessary, chase up this team of contributors. As a result of all this, however, the analysis and writing stages through to publication took only two and a half years, as against four for the *Breeding Atlas*.

The Working Group met 18 times for all-day sessions. Its members are listed on page 5, with their periods of service. They include the Director of the BTO and its former Director of Services, a representative of the IWC, the Organiser of the *Breeding Atlas*, two Regional Organisers of this *Winter Atlas*, the publisher of both atlases, and others with special expertise. Richard Nairn, the Director of the IWC, also attended for one meeting when the Republic of Ireland's involvement was still under consideration. Later recruits were Elizabeth Lack, mother of Peter and the chief editor of this volume, and Malgosia Trojanowska who was engaged to help with the last six months of organisation and analysis.

We were particularly fortunate that Elizabeth Lack, barely released from over six years of work with Dr Bruce Campbell on the compilation and editing of *A Dictionary of Birds* (1985), agreed to take on the task of editor, in which she was particularly assisted by Bob Spencer. It is not generally realised how much work is needed to bring a degree of uniformity of presentation and content to the writings of over 100 authors dealing with twice that number of species, while also ensuring that their texts are neither too long nor too short. Elizabeth and Bob have done a remarkable job.

One other member of the Working Group who must be singled out is Trevor Poyser. There are obvious advantages in having the publisher, himself a birdwatcher, on hand for much of the project. He gave valuable advice and practical support, as well as offering a substantial advance against royalties if the money could not be raised in other ways.

I am especially grateful to all the colleagues who have worked together as a team, but of course none of it would have been possible without the thousands who carried out the actual fieldwork and, even more, all the Regional Organisers listed on pages 432–34.

Nor would any of it have been possible if finance had not been found to fund the project, which has cost a total of almost £65,000 in organisation, quite apart from all the money spent personally by the army of individual observers in travelling and correspondence. This time there was no large grant available from a single body. The BTO had the courage to launch the project without secure funding to see it through. That the risk was justified is to a large extent due to the efforts of three people.

Nearly a third of the total sum, over £20,000, was raised by Susan Cowdy and Joy Danter; they wrote hundreds of letters to a whole range of companies and charitable trusts (those which gave money are listed on page 13) and, by organising the Grand National Draws, accounted for £5,765 in the two years when the proceeds were specifically allocated to the *Winter Atlas*. It might be said that they really made the whole thing possible, but hardly less important was the total of some £11,000 raised by Richard Arnold on behalf of the project over four years through the Bardsey New Year Bird Counts. Thus, the work of these three BTO members produced half the total sum.

I am sure that everyone concerned will agree that this remarkable book, a worthy companion to the *Breeding Atlas*, has been well worth the effort. The coverage has certainly been far more complete in the remoter parts of, particularly, Scotland and Ireland than we had dared to hope. It is only human to express satisfaction that the judgement of those of us who, from the outset, strongly backed this project as feasible has been vindicated.

A total of 200 species is mapped, a figure approaching the 218 in the *Breeding Atlas*, though the composition is, of course, rather different. Because on this occasion we were dealing with all birds (not just those actually nesting!), the much higher figure of over 300 species was in fact recorded during the three winters: but this included feral birds and vagrants, with far too few observations to warrant mapping.

The past 25 years have seen considerable changes in some wintering populations. For example, Bewick's Swans *Cygnus columbianus* and Brent Geese *Branta bernicla*, have greatly increased. Such waders as Little Stints *Calidris minuta*, Spotted Redshanks *Tringa erythropus*, Greenshanks *Tringa nebularia* and Common Sandpipers *Actitis hypoleucos* now winter more regularly. The same applies to Blackcaps *Sylvia atricapilla* and Chiffchaffs *Phylloscopus collybita*. Among residents, such natural colonists as Collared Doves *Streptopelia decaocto* (amazing to think how local they still were in 1960!) and Cetti's Warblers *Cettia cetti*, as well as such feral colonists as Ruddy Ducks *Oxyura jamaicensis* and Ring-necked Parakeets *Psittacula krameri*, have considerably increased or have only appeared on the scene. Certain raptors, notably Sparrowhawks *Accipiter nisus* and Peregrines *Falco peregrinus*, have gradually recovered from the more serious effects of organochlorine pesticides in the late 1950s and early 1960s. But many of the fluctuations that take place in numbers and distribution in winter are due not so much to real range changes, as is often the case among breeding birds, but to local or annual changes in habitat conditions, food supplies and weather. Thus, the numbers of Bitterns *Botaurus stellaris* seen away from the breeding areas, the occasional influxes of Rough-legged Buzzards *Buteo lagopus*, the erratic invasions of Waxwings *Bombycilla garrulus*, and the winter populations of Bramblings *Fringilla montifringilla* may all vary greatly from year to year, depending on conditions in Fennoscandia. Our own populations of Kingfishers *Alcedo atthis*, Wrens *Troglodytes troglodytes*, Goldcrests *Regulus regulus*, Long-tailed Tits *Aegithalos caudatus* and, more locally, Dartford Warblers *Sylvia undata* and Bearded Tits *Panurus biarmicus* depend very much on the severity or otherwise of winters here.

Against this knowledge of changes over the past 25 years, it is difficult even to guess what might happen to winter populations in the future. We should look upon this book as the product of an invaluable exercise, which records our knowledge of winter distributions in the early 1980s. We believe that it will be as significant a source of information for conservation as the *Breeding Atlas* has already proved to be, at the same time providing a baseline against which a similar survey may be undertaken in the 21st century.

Where do we go from here? On the international level, our two countries are ready to participate in the ambitious European Breeding Atlas by 50-km squares in 1987 and, after that, the question of repeating our own *Breeding Atlas*, this time with quantification built in, is now being planned. At the end of my chapter in the BTO's Jubilee volume *Enjoying Ornithology*, I speculated whether, following these atlases for the two main seasons, we dared contemplate one for spring and autumn passage. If so, how could such transitory pictures be 'frozen' on to maps? Unrealistic? Possibly—but Britain and Ireland are important staging areas for many northern migrants.

Certainly grid atlases have come to stay. National atlases of breeding birds have now been published in France, Denmark, the Netherlands, Switzerland, parts of Germany and Spain. Most other European countries, Morocco, at least eight sub-Saharan African states, Australia, New Zealand, and sizeable sections of North America have projects at various stages. On a more local level in Britain, at least 18 counties or areas—I know of Kent, London, Hertfordshire, Huntingdonshire, Bedfordshire, Buckinghamshire, Oxfordshire, Devon, Avon, Gwent, Shropshire, Leicestershire, Norfolk, Lincolnshire, Cheshire, Greater Manchester, parts of Yorkshire, and Aberdeen—have at least started fieldwork by tetrads or even 1-km squares, and in some cases have already published. Others are certainly considering the possibility (indeed, this list of those already committed may well be incomplete) and I hope that more will follow suit. Much work is involved: there are 25 2-km squares in each 10-km square, though, theoretically at least, the amount of ground to be covered is the same. But, because the grid is 25 times finer, such surveys show distribution much more precisely. I am sure that many counties would find this a profitable exercise both for breeding and, perhaps later, for winter distributions; we know how much observers enjoy taking part, the results are valuable both to ornithology and to conservation, and, despite the pessimism that will be expressed, just as it was at the national level, all things are possible.

Atlases establish the distribution patterns that form the basis for all studies of ecology and conservation. How birds use the habitats available within the ranges that we have now recorded is the next important question to consider. Much is known about this for breeding species, but for wintering birds the many surprises experienced by observers during fieldwork for the present project show how much we have yet to learn of habitat usage at this season.

Rode, Somerset, October 1985

Introduction and Acknowledgements

After *The Atlas of Breeding Birds of Britain and Ireland* was published in 1976, many people thought that the obvious next step was a similar survey for birds in winter. However, that was much easier said than done. Many difficulties were raised and it was not until the summer of 1980 that the British Trust for Ornithology (BTO) was in a position to go ahead with such a project.

It was proposed to carry out a full-scale Pilot Survey in the winter of 1980/81, initially, and then to start the main survey in the following winter. The Pilot Survey was needed mainly because it was thought essential to have a measure of the abundance of the birds, not just their presence, and because possible methods for assessing abundance had to be tried out.

From an early stage the Irish Wildbird Conservancy (IWC) was involved with the planning and it was hoped that it would co-operate with the BTO in organising the survey so that all of Ireland would be included. The IWC Council gave its final approval and backing to the project in June 1982 after the first winter's fieldwork had shown it to be feasible and useful. Therefore, as was the *Breeding Atlas*, this new atlas of wintering birds has been run as a joint venture by the two organisations.

This is not the first time that such a large scale survey of birds outside the breeding season has been tried. In France fieldwork was carried out in the winters of 1976/77 to 1978/79 on a similar basis to their atlas of breeding birds, and in the Netherlands fieldwork was undertaken from October 1978 to September 1983 for an atlas spanning the whole year on a month to month basis. In Britain too there were two local projects: an atlas of wintering birds based on 2-km squares (tetrads) in Kent (Tardivel, N. 1984. *Winter Bird Survey 1977–80*. Kent Ornithological Society), and a year-round atlas based on 'sites' in NE Scotland.

The present book contains the main results of the major BTO/IWC survey which became known to everyone who took part as the *Winter Atlas*. The book itself has been designed as a companion volume to the *Breeding Atlas*, although there are several obvious and important differences.

In his Foreword James Ferguson-Lees describes the early history and planning of the project. After this Introduction there is a summary of the methods that were used in the field and the procedures used to compile the maps, together with some notes on interpretation, and a short section describing the weather in each of the three winters of the survey.

Following these is a section headed 'Birds in winter: patterns and movements'. This draws some general conclusions from the species maps and points out various features which are common to several species. The distribution of some bird species during winter is not static and, with the aid of maps, some of the differences between the three winters of the survey,

and some of the seasonal changes within a winter are also discussed. Such differences are particularly related to periods of cold weather.

The species maps and their accompanying texts are the main section of the book. The format follows that established in the *Breeding Atlas*, published in 1976: a full page map faced by a page of text.

After the main species texts and maps there is a short section, with maps, dealing with four seabirds and four late summer migrants which were recorded in at least 15 10-km squares. This is followed by a list of all other species, including feral birds, which were recorded on *Winter Atlas* cards and sheets, and lists of scientific names of plants and other animals which are mentioned in the text. Finally, the Appendices contain the details of the Pilot Survey, organisation, methods in the field, methods of analysis and data storage.

A book such as this involves much planning, a large amount of fieldwork and many hours of analysis, compilation, checking and writing before it achieves its final form. Many people have helped in the various stages of the project, and I am very grateful to them all.

First and foremost must be the several thousand observers who contributed the data. These observers were co-ordinated by Regional Organisers, who are listed on p. 432. The Regional Organisers played a major role at several stages. They often undertook fieldwork themselves, and they distributed and collected the cards. The Regional Organisers also checked all original data cards against the computer print-out and later on checked the final data for their squares. All this work was done in their spare time and all did a grand job. However, in fairness, three must be singled out: Ian Forsyth, who organised the whole of Northern Ireland (with help from Joe Furphy and Chris Bailey); and Sean Fleming, for the first two seasons, and Chris Wilson, for the third season and thereafter, who organised work in the Republic of Ireland under the auspices of the IWC. They also had some help with the data checking—these checkers are listed on p. 434.

The project was guided throughout by a Working Group under the chairmanship of James Ferguson-Lees who has also kindly provided the Foreword. The members of the Working Group are listed on p. 5. All played their part but I must mention some in particular. Bob Spencer gave much assistance on many matters while he was Director of Services at the BTO, and subsequently helped in the editing of the text; Raymond O'Connor, as Director of the BTO, helped particularly with the methods and latterly with the general discussion section of the book; and Clive Hutchinson, as representative of the IWC, dealt with all matters relating to Ireland and later read all the text; my mother, Elizabeth Lack, undertook the main burden of editing the text; and Trevor

Poyser quietly and efficiently guided all the planning, design and production of the book itself. Without these two in particular the final production would be a very different thing.

Two members of the BTO staff played major parts in the project. Malgosia Trojanowska, while on a short term contract, provided the bulk of my technical assistance during the middle of 1985. She checked data on the computer files, read texts and liaised with authors and was largely responsible for the compilation of material for the overlays. Secondly, without Elizabeth Murray chaos might well have reigned, particularly in the project's later stages. She organised the secretarial work, kept the necessary records of liaison with authors, minuted all the meetings of the Working Group, read various drafts of the text and, finally, drew the diagrams in the book.

I received considerable help from other BTO staff. Mike Moser read all species texts relating to waders and some other species; Teresa Gregory bravely tackled the unenviable task of typing the manuscript onto the word processor and subsequently dealt with the corrections; Audrey Causer, Liz McHugh and, particularly, Sue Miller and Alana Harrison did much of the initial data preparation and checking of computer files; Dorothy Smallwood and Gill Cracknell helped with the species texts, and Rita Gray, Jeff Kirby and Jane Marchant helped with the proofs.

The species texts were written by 101 authors who are acknowledged individually with their texts. In addition to Bob Spencer and Clive Hutchinson, Ian Forsyth, Joe Furphy, Valerie Thom, Angus Hogg and Ron Youngman kindly read all or most species texts, and staff at the Wildfowl Trust (Malcolm Ogilvie, Myrfyn Owen and/or David Salmon) read those relevant to them. D. Butler, A. R. Dean, L. A. Tucker, Donald Watson and Ron MacDonald helped with certain texts.

The 23 artists whose vignettes enliven the species texts are listed on page 5. They were recruited and organised by Robert Gillmor who also contributed vignettes and drew the jacket illustrations.

The important task of extracting records of rarities was kindly undertaken by Keith Vinicombe. Kieran Grace checked all the Irish records, and maps of less common birds, to ensure that accepted records only are quoted here.

Others who helped with specific matters were: the Irish Forest and Wildlife Service who allowed staff to do fieldwork for the project; the Meteorological Service in Dublin which kindly made available summaries of the weather in Ireland; Helen Aston and Rosemary Balmford who assisted in the preliminary planning stages; Alpha-Numeric Ltd who were responsible for the typing of over 90% of the data from the cards and sheets; Laser-Scan Ltd who produced the final maps in the book; Mike Everett and Richard Porter of the Species Protection Department of the Royal Society for the Protection of Birds, who advised on the treatment of some sensitive species; and Andrew Lack who kindly checked the list of plant names.

Lastly and most importantly I and the BTO must thank all those who raised funds for the project. Susan Cowdy and Joy Danter took on the lion's share; in addition to writing a great many letters they also organised the Grand National Draw each spring which, for two years, was specifically for the *Winter Atlas* fund. Their task was considerably helped by Richard Arnold, who organised the Bardsey Bird and Field Observatory New Year Bird Counts for four years on behalf of the project.

Other funds were generously contributed by: Augustine Trust, Baring Foundation, J. & L. A. Cadbury Charitable Trust, W. A. Cadbury Charitable Trust, Sir Hugh Chance Trust, Conder Trust, W. J. A. Dacombe, Dalgety Ltd, Dulverton Trust, Douglas Heath Eves Charitable Trust, the G. W. Trust, H. Hale, T. Hallam, Idlewild Trust (The Peter Minet Trust), Irish Forest and Wildlife Service, Leverhulme Trust, Marks & Spencer, Mary Snow Trust, Mitchell Trust, Oakdale Trust, Radcliffe Trust, Scottish Ornithologists' Club, Shell Research Ltd, J. Smith (London Marathon), Surbiton Bird Club, and Yapp Education and Research Trust.

To all these people and organisations, and to any I have inadvertently left out, I am very grateful.

ABBREVIATIONS
The following abbreviations are used in the text:

BASC	British Association for Shooting and Conservation (formerly WAGBI)
BOU	British Ornithologists' Union
BTO	British Trust for Ornithology
°C	degrees Celsius
CBC	Common Birds Census
C.I.	Channel Islands
cm	centimetre
g	gram
ICBP	International Council for Bird Preservation
IWC	Irish Wildbird Conservancy
IWRB	International Waterfowl Research Bureau
km²	square kilometre
m	metre
NCC	Nature Conservancy Council
RSPB	Royal Society for the Protection of Birds
WAGBI	Wildfowlers' Association of Great Britain and Ireland (now BASC)
10-km square	10 km × 10 km square (100 km²) of the British or Irish National Grids

Most of the habitat terms used in this book will be found in one or more of the following books.

CRAMP, S. and K. E. L. SIMMONS (eds), 1977. *The Birds of the Western Palearctic*. Vol. 1. University Press, Oxford. (Pages 6–11 contain a glossary of habitat definitions.)

FULLER, R. J. 1982 . *Bird Habitats in Britain*. Poyser, Calton.

POLUNIN, O. and M. WALTERS. 1985. *A Guide to the Vegetation of Britain and Europe*. University Press, Oxford.

RATCLIFFE, D. A. (ed.) 1977. *A Nature Conservation Review: the Selection of Biological Sites of National Importance to Nature Conservation in Britain*. University Press, Cambridge.

The maps

GENERAL

A full account of the different stages of the project including figures and other details is to be found on p. 431. The present chapter gives the essential information needed when considering and interpreting the maps.

From the start this volume was conceived as a companion to *The Atlas of Breeding Birds in Britain and Ireland* (Sharrock 1976), and wherever possible the same conventions have been followed.

The units of distribution are the 10-km squares of the National Grids of Britain and Ireland which are now used in many surveys. Fieldwork in each country was organised by one of the hundred or so Regional Organisers listed on p. 432. The fieldwork occupied the three winters 1981/82 to 1983/84 and, after the Pilot Survey results in 1980/81, it was decided that the middle of November until the end of February would be the winter period for the purposes of the *Winter Atlas*. Actual dates for the survey were 14 November 1981 to 28 February 1982, 13 November 1982 to 28 February 1983, and 12 November 1983 to 29 February 1984, inclusive, giving a grand total of 325 days of fieldwork over the three winters. Records of birds from outside these periods were rejected.

It was decided at an early stage that some form of abundance assessment was essential, as this would make the maps much more useful. After trials of different methods during the Pilot Survey the observers were asked simply to send in counts of the birds they had seen. For compiling the maps, the highest count of each species seen in a square on any one day during the survey period was used.

FIELD METHODS

Two kinds of records were accepted: first, the results of visits made to 10-km squares specifically to do fieldwork for the *Winter Atlas*; and second, any casual records (termed Supplementary Records) of individual species.

For a specific visit, observers were asked to spend a minimum of one hour in a 10-km square and to count the number of birds of each species seen and/or heard. At the end of a visit the total number of birds of each species was recorded on a Visit Card, together with the 10-km square reference, an identifying feature within the square, the date, the time spent in the field and the total number of species recorded. A specimen card is shown in Figure 1.

Only records of birds actually seen or heard were wanted, not those which observers 'knew' to be present. Therefore provision had to be made for the recording of birds at times other than during a special visit. For such records observers filled in a Supplementary Record Sheet (Figure 2). Again, in addition to the number of birds, the 10-km square, an identifying feature and the date were recorded.

The recording of the date of all birds seen meant that separate maps could be compiled for shorter periods than the combined three winters of the survey, for example to show any marked changes resulting from cold weather. Some such maps are included in the next chapter.

S P 9 1
1. Square

16 01 82
Day Mth Year
3. Date

3 15
Hrs Mins
4. Time in field

43
5. Number of species

For Office Use

2. Largest town/village in square
TRING

For Office Use

British Trust for Ornithology
Irish Wildbird Conservancy

WINTER ATLAS PROJECT

VISIT CARD

Please read accompanying instructions carefully before filling in the card. Please return by 31 March to your local organiser. If you have no local organiser, send to:
B.T.O., Beech Grove, Tring, Herts HP23 5NR.

P. C. LACK
7. Name (Block letters)

6. Comments

8. Address
B.T.O.
Beech Grove
Tring
Herts

	Code	Count		Code	Count		Code	Count		Code	Count
Red-throated Diver	RH		Mute Swan	MS		Gadwall	GA		Red-breasted Merg	RM	
Blk-throated Diver	BV		Bewick's Swan	BS		Teal	T	113	Goosander	OS	
Great North Diver	ND		Whooper Swan	WS		Mallard	MA	68	Ruddy Duck	RY	8
Little Grebe	LG	5	Bean Goose	BE		Pintail	PT		Red Kite	KT	
Great Crested Grebe	GG	25	Pink-footed Goose	PG		Shoveler	SV	41	Marsh Harrier	MR	
Red-necked Grebe	RX		White-fronted Goose	WG		Pochard	PO	37	Hen Harrier	HH	
Slavonian Grebe	SZ		Grey-lag Goose	GJ		Tufted Duck	TU	25	Goshawk	GI	
Blk-necked Grebe	BN		Canada Goose	CG	30	Scaup	SP		Sparrow Hawk	SH	1
Fulmar	F		Barnacle Goose	BY		Eider	E		Buzzard	BZ	
Gannet	GX		Brent Goose	BG		Long-tailed Duck	LN		Rough-leg Buzzard	RF	
Cormorant	CA		Egyptian Goose	EG		Common Scoter	CX		Golden Eagle	EA	
Shag	SA		Shelduck	SU		Velvet Scoter	VS		Kestrel	K	2
Bittern	BI		Mandarin	MN		Goldeneye	GN		Merlin	ML	
Grey Heron	H	1	Wigeon	WN		Smew	SY		Peregrine	PE	

Fig. 1 Front of *Winter Atlas* Visit Card (reduced).

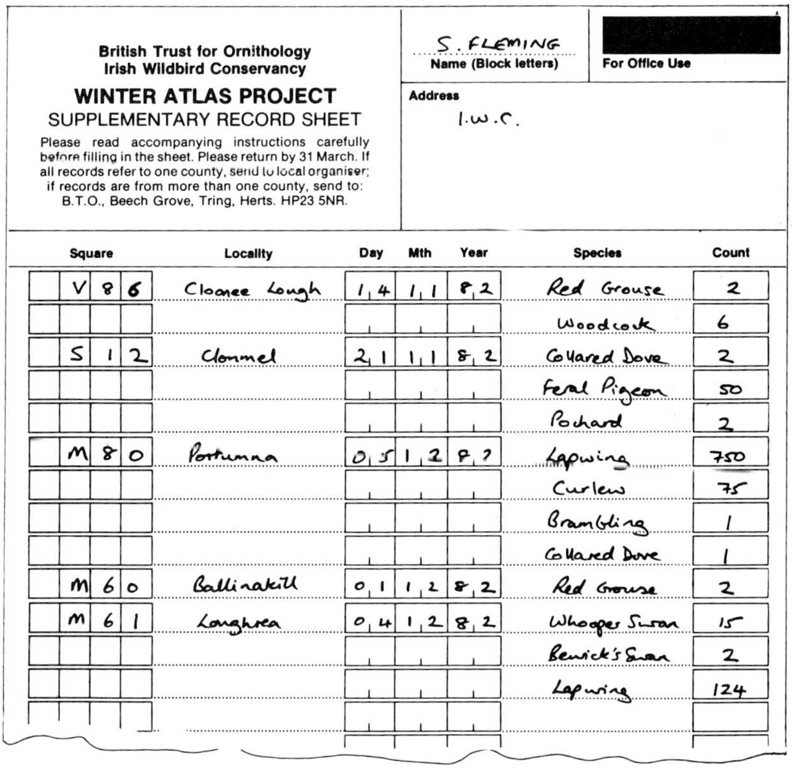

Fig. 2 Upper portion of a *Winter Atlas* Supplementary Record Sheet (reduced).

Observers were asked to record only birds *using* the square. 'Use' of the square included feeding, resting or roosting. Flying birds were recorded where the birds were obviously using the habitat within the square; for example, hunting raptors or movement from one copse to the next, but birds simply flying over the square were not included.

ASSESSMENT OF RELATIVE ABUNDANCE

After analysis and discussion of the results of the Pilot Survey, it was decided to use as the assessment of abundance 'the number of birds seen in a day'. It was further decided that if there was more than one count of a species in a square the highest figure would be used. A 'day' was defined as six hours in the field, this being the longest that most observers would be likely to be able to devote to fieldwork in a day. In fact only about 3.5% of all cards received were for periods longer than this.

All timed counts of more or less than six hours were standardised to this standard 'day length'. This was to permit better comparisons of areas which might have counts of only one or two hour duration with those which had six-hour counts. The standardising procedure adopted was to calculate, for each species, a regression coefficient of number of birds seen on time spent in the field. The data were normalised by putting both axes on a logarithmic scale. With a large number of data points available, even quite weak relationships between numbers of birds and time spent in the field are significant at the usual statistical point of $P = 0.05$. As nearly 200 species were involved, standardisation corrections were only used if the relation was statistically significant at $P < 0.001$.

Many of the commoner land birds came into this category. Most of the rarer species and those which are restricted in habitat preferences have a zero coefficient and no corrections are made. In practice this means that the observer is just as likely to see a rarer or more elusive bird in the first hour of a count as in the sixth; or, similarly, to visit the restricted habitat (*eg* a lake) in the first hour or the sixth. Records are unlikely to accumulate as fieldwork continues. For the commoner land birds, however, this is what does happen, and therefore the coefficient is positive and standardising corrections were needed.

Only counts of more than one hour were treated this way. All data from visits of less than one hour and all Supplementary Records were used directly with no adjustments. The maps for each species plot the largest count in each square, regardless of whether it came from a timed visit or a Supplementary Record.

The species maps use three sizes of dot, the larger dots indicating more birds. The divisions between the different dot values were chosen so that 50% of the dots were in the lowest category, 30% in the middle category and 20% in the highest category, and the divisions were made to the nearest whole number of birds. For common species, a close agreement to the 50 to 30 to 20 percentage split could be achieved, but for the rarer birds there was often a high percentage of '1 bird seen'. For these, the standard division has been followed as nearly as possible, although some species have up to 80% of the dots in the lowest category and a few have even more. In all cases the actual percentage of dots in each level of abundance is given in the table on the text page facing the map.

COVERAGE

The stated aim was to obtain at least one Visit Card, preferably from a visit lasting at least six hours (one standard day), from each 10-km square in Britain and Ireland during the course of the three winters in the survey. The *Breeding Atlas* obtained records from all the 3,862 10-km squares containing land, but about 150 of these have very little. Many of them are on the remote north and west coasts of Scotland and Ireland, and for some the only land is on remote islands. Counts of birds from these squares were not actively sought although any counts that were made were accepted. In the event, 2,746 10-km squares in Britain, 1,010 in Ireland, and all five in the Channel Islands, received a timed Visit of at least one hour. (At the request of the Regional Organiser each of the five main Channel Islands was treated as one 10-km square, as in the *Breeding Atlas*.) This makes a total of 3,761 squares visited. (A few Supplementary Records were received from some of the remaining 101 squares.) Of this total, 94% received at least six hours of timed Visits (93% in Britain, 96% in Ireland and all the Channel Islands). Only six inland squares received no timed visits although Supplementary Records were received from two of them.

On average each 10-km square received 16 visits representing of 47.8 hours of fieldwork. A total of 60,246 Visit Cards was received, amounting to nearly 180,000 hours of timed counts.

The total time spent in the field for each square did vary somewhat in different parts of the two countries. The maps (Figure 3a–d, overleaf) show the distribution of timed Visit Cards received in each winter and in total. These reveal that some areas, for example parts of Scotland and Ireland, were visited less often than other areas, as was to be expected.

The chapter 'Birds in winter' discusses some of the differences within and between the three winters of the survey. For some analyses the winter is divided into 'early' and 'late' periods, the separation being at the turn of the year. Table 1 gives the number of squares receiving timed visits in each of these periods for each winter. In each case the distribution of the squares actually covered was widespread, and there were no large areas which were uncovered in any of them.

INTERPRETING THE MAPS

The minimum requirement for a dot to be plotted on a species map was a record of the species in a square during the course of the three winters. For some of the rarer species this means the maps may give an exaggerated impression of the distribution in any one winter. To take an example, the Great Grey Shrike *Lanius excubitor* was recorded in 238 10-km squares in Britain, and one in Ireland, during the three winters. However, it was recorded in only 71 squares in Britain in 1981/82, in 124 squares in Britain in 1982/83, and in 85 squares in Britain and one in Ireland in 1983/84. It was recorded in only 44 squares in more than one winter. For common and widespread species, such distortions are negligible because the birds occur in most squares anyway.

Another point, again most obvious in (but not exclusive to) the less common species, is that during the course of the winters some individual birds or flocks may move between squares. In such cases the same flock or individual birds may be recorded in more than one square. For example the Marsh Harrier *Circus aeruginosus* was recorded in three squares in the Wexford Slobs area in SE Ireland. All three probably refer to the same individual which wintered there in 1981/82.

A final point is that the uneven total coverage already remarked on could also lead to difficulties when interpreting the maps. Broadly, southern and central England received more visits than elsewhere, and lowland areas received more visits than the upland areas. The use of a square's maximum count as the measure of relative abundance has several advantages (see p. 432) but it does have the weakness that it is potentially biassed when the number of visits is exceptionally high. (It should be added that a mean count, a single count taken at random from all those available, and even a record of presence in the square are also subject to similar difficulties.) To investigate the possibility of bias due to uneven coverage, the counts of each species were tested for correlation with the number of Visit Cards received for each square. Squares which did not record the species were not included. Because sample sizes were up to 3,500, several correlations were statistically significant but negligible in size. For 80% of the species, less than 5% of the variation in abundance was associated with variation in coverage. For these, therefore, over 95% of the variation present was due to the biology of the birds or to the environment of the squares.

In only 16 species (8%) could variation in coverage account for more than 10% of the variation in bird abundance. These species are, from the least to the most affected, Collared Dove *Streptopelia decaocto*, Woodpigeon *Columba palumbus*, Yellowhammer *Emberiza citrinella*, House Sparrow *Passer domesticus*, Goldfinch *Carduelis carduelis*, Robin *Erithacus rubecula*, Mistle Thrush *Turdus viscivorus*, Great Spotted Woodpecker *Dendrocopos major*, Kestrel *Falco tinnunculus*, Dunnock *Prunella modularis*, Moorhen *Gallinula chloropus*, Long-tailed Tit *Aegithalos caudatus*, Magpie *Pica pica*, Wren *Troglodytes troglodytes*, Great Tit *Parus major*, and Blue Tit *P. caeruleus*. Only in the case of the last two species could variation in coverage have accounted for more than 20% of the variation in abundance (27% for Great Tit and 35% for Blue Tit).

Table 1. The number of squares receiving visits of at least one hour, in the 'early' and 'late' periods of each year of the survey.

	EARLY		LATE		COMBINED	
	Britain	Ireland	Britain	Ireland	Britain	Ireland
1981/82	1722	363	1965	479	2177	538
1982/83	1973	470	2154	557	2361	673
1983/84	2032	436	2112	508	2392	608
COMBINED	2531	841	2632	934	2751	1010

NOTES: 'Britain' includes the five Channel Islands. 'Early' is mid November–December; 'late' is January–February.

Fig. 3 The number of Visit Cards received for each 10-km square in: (a) 1981/82, (b) 1982/83, (c) 1983/84, (d) the three winters combined. Small dots represent 1–10 cards, medium dots 11–25 cards, and large dots more than 25 cards.

It will be noticed at once that the species listed above have several features in common. Except for the Moorhen all are land birds. Most are primarily solitary species and only the Woodpigeon, and occasionally the Collared Dove and House Sparrow, occur in large flocks. All are also species which are found mainly in lowland areas containing a mosaic of mixed farmland, woodland and suburban habitat, and that is exactly where the coverage was highest. The correlations with coverage found for these species are thus what one might expect from the species' ecology.

It is also clear that, although there are similarities in the distributions of these species, there are also obvious, and sometimes substantial, differences between them. These differences effectively rule out the possibility of a systematic bias associated with the extent of coverage. See for example the maps for Magpie, Goldfinch and Blue Tit. Differences are particularly obvious in East Anglia, parts of northern England, Scotland, Wales and the southwest peninsula, and in parts of Ireland, *ie* especially away from central southern England where most of them are fairly abundant. In many of these cases too the regional patterns shown can be explained from the known ecology of the species—see relevant species accounts.

In summary, therefore, there is certainly a correlation between the distribution of a small number of species and coverage, particularly for the Great and Blue Tit. It is difficult to assess how much the coverage has affected the maps, because in all relevant cases the distribution patterns are broadly those which might be expected on ecological grounds, but the uneven coverage is not likely to have introduced a major bias.

When writing the species accounts, authors were able to see, if they wished, the distribution map for each of the three winters and for the 'early' and 'late' periods of the winter, as well as the final combined map. A few of the selective maps are reproduced with the species accounts or in the chapter 'Birds in winter: patterns and movements'.

On the maps, all dots are placed centrally in the squares. For some coastal squares with very little land the dot may appear, therefore, to be in the sea.

At the end of each species account there is a table giving some relevant statistics for the maps. The total number of 10-km squares in which each species was recorded is stated, together with the percentage of the total of 3,862 squares which contain land. (Note, though, that the number of squares receiving timed visits during the *Winter Atlas* was 3,761—see above.) The body of the table gives the range of abundance for each size of dot and, separately for Britain and Ireland, the number of squares at each level, and the total; this last includes the Channel Islands.

For those species which breed in Britain and Ireland, the breeding season distribution, as published in the *Breeding Atlas*, is reproduced for comparison in the top right corner of the main winter distribution map. It must be remembered though that, in these inset maps, the size of the dots does not represent relative abundance but denotes possible (small dots), probable (medium dots) and confirmed breeding (large dots). For these species a page reference to the *Breeding Atlas* is given at the end of the text.

The scientific names and order of species follow Voous (VOOUS, K. H. 1977. *List of Recent Holarctic Bird Species*. British Ornithologists' Union, London). This order differs from the order of species in the *Breeding Atlas*. English names follow those in *The 'British Birds' List of Birds of the Western Palearctic* (revised edition 1984).

LITERATURE

References are given at the end of species texts where the work deals extensively with the species concerned, or is referred to specifically. In addition many authors consulted local bird reports where appropriate and not all these are listed.

Certain standard works are referred to frequently in the individual species texts and elsewhere. These are listed here for convenience and to save repetition.

CRAMP, S. and K. E. L. SIMMONS (eds). 1977–1985. *The Birds of the Western Palearctic*. Vols. I–IV. University Press, Oxford. (=*BWP*)

HUTCHINSON, C. D. 1979. *Ireland's Wetlands and their Birds*. Irish Wildbird Conservancy, Dublin.

OWEN, M., G. L. ATKINSON-WILLES and D. G. SALMON. 1986. *Wildfowl in Great Britain*. 2nd edn. University Press, Cambridge.

PRATER, A. J. 1981. *Estuary Birds of Britain and Ireland*. Poyser, Calton.

SHARROCK, J. T. R. 1976. *The Atlas of Breeding Birds in Britain and Ireland*. Poyser, Berkhamsted. (=*Breeding Atlas*)

WITHERBY, H. F., F. C. R. JOURDAIN, N. F. TICEHURST and B. W. TUCKER. 1938–1941. *The Handbook of British Birds*. Vols. I–V. Witherby, London. (=*The Handbook*)

RINGING REPORTS: published annually for the British Trust for Ornithology. They were published with *British Birds* up to 1971 (report for 1969), as a supplement to *Bird Study* from 1972–77 (reports for 1970–75) and subsequently in *Ringing and Migration*.

BIRDS OF ESTUARIES ENQUIRY REPORTS: published annually since 1969 jointly by the British Trust for Ornithology and the Wildfowl Trust as a separate booklet.

IRISH BIRD REPORTS: published annually as a separate booklet until the report for 1975 and subsequently in *Irish Birds*.

SCOTTISH BIRD REPORTS: published annually in *Scottish Birds* until the report for 1979 and subsequently as a special supplement.

The weather in the three winters

The traditional view of winter is of cold weather with frosts and often with snow. There are, however, considerable differences in most climatic variables not only between winters, but also within each winter, and of course between different parts of Britain and Ireland.

This chapter gives a brief description of the weather of the three winters. For Britain the information is taken mainly from the relevant issues of the *Journal of Meteorology*. This journal publishes, for each month, a written summary of the main characteristics, and a table of statistics for stations around the country. For Ireland, similar summaries and tables were kindly made available by the Meteorological Service, Dublin.

The three winters of the survey turned out to be quite distinctive. Although conditions in each winter differed in detail between parts of Britain and Ireland, they were broadly similar and much of Europe experienced similar conditions as well.

THE 1981/82 WINTER
This first winter of the *Winter Atlas* will be remembered chiefly for the prolonged and, at times, record low temperatures during December and January. However, when the fieldwork started on 14th November 1981 conditions were mild and dull. Indeed, November as a whole was warm and dry with mean temperatures a degree or so above the long-term average for the month. Rainfall was below average, and markedly so along the south coast of England. The exception was northern Scotland. Here it was cold and in the northwest also very wet (2.5 times average).

The first week of December continued this fairly mild calm period but everything had changed by 8th. Late on 5th December, a cold front reached Orkney and Shetland and then moved slowly and rather erratically south. By the morning of 8th most of Britain and Ireland was blanketed by quite heavy falls of snow. Only the coastal strip of S England escaped. Several days of severe frosts followed, with record low temperatures of −23°C at Shawbury (Shropshire) and −12.5°C at Mullingar (Co. Westmeath) on 12th. At this time temperatures below −10°C were widespread over central England, and below −4°C over much of Ireland. The cold weather, with snow cover, persisted in many areas until just after Christmas, with especially cold periods from 9–13th and 15–19th December. There were also some further more or less heavy snowfalls during this period. Southwest Britain remained relatively mild, although subject to severe flooding at times, caused by heavy rain and strong winds. Northern and western parts of Ireland had a very dry month in general but the heavy rain hit several parts of the south and east.

In the last few days of December most parts of England, Wales and Ireland became warmer and much of the snow disappeared. In Scotland, although it became a little warmer, most of the snow remained. This lull in the cold was not without its problems, with the melting snow bringing extensive flooding especially in the Severn Valley.

On 7–8th January the cold weather returned to all parts with a vengeance and lasted about ten days. This time low temperatures were more widespread although western central England again had the lowest. In many parts of Scotland the temperature did not rise above freezing for the whole ten-day period.

Blizzards followed the freezing temperatures and all of southern Britain had nearly continual snow, sleet and strong winds for about 36 hours. From 13th January, the anticyclone started moving slowly to the Continent, and by 20th most areas were returning to normal temperatures. Temperatures remained fairly mild for the remainder of the month although the weather was rather unsettled.

In contrast to the record cold in December and January, February was relatively mild, with many parts having average temperatures around 2°C higher than normal. As is to be expected in February, there were one or two colder periods, especially in eastern parts, from about 15th to 24th, but even then very little snow fell and frosts were not continuous.

The 1981/82 winter as a whole was colder than average but this was entirely due to the two ten-day periods of severe weather in December and January. The remainder of the period was mild, and the winter as a whole proved less of a problem to birds than the more prolonged, though less severe, freezing conditions of 1978/79, and much less so than the last really prolonged cold weather of 1962/63.

THE 1982/83 WINTER
The start of the fieldwork (13th November 1982) coincided with the first cold, and very windy, weather of the winter. The first snow fell in England on 14th November. Until then, November had been very mild: indeed for the month as a whole temperatures were a degree or two higher than average in most areas. It was, however, very unsettled, with periods of calm weather alternating with storms and gales which brought rain and snow at times. Except in eastern England rainfall was higher than average.

December was similar, with alternating periods of very mild and quite cold conditions, the latter often accompanied by storms.

In complete contrast to 1982, January 1983 was unusually mild, with temperatures as much as 3.5°C above average over most of England and Wales and 1°C above average in N and W Scotland. It was, however, windy and stormy with rainfall considerably above average (up to 2.5 times) in the west, especially in Scotland, and although eastern parts were drier they did not escape the gales.

The mild January was responsible for the general impression that the winter was exceptionally mild. In fact though, February was fairly cold. Temperatures in central England averaged 2°C or so below normal and the rest of Britain and Ireland was at least 1°C below. Even so, February was generally dry and sunny, especially in the east.

In summary, the winter of 1982/83 was much milder than that of 1981/82 but not as exceptionally mild as it seems to have been remembered. The winds and rain certainly did not make birdwatching pleasant, but any colder spells which did occur were usually short-lived, and in southern England and Ireland there was little snow cover at all.

THE 1983/84 WINTER

November 1983 was in general mild, very dry and comparatively calm although rather overcast—ideal weather for fieldwork in fact. Temperatures were only a degree or so above average, however, and the second half of the month was quite cold at times. Rainfall was down to 25% of normal in places, although sunshine was also well down in central and SW England and in northern Scotland. On the other hand, central Scotland had more sun than usual. The only stormy periods were short-lived.

December was also mild (a degree or so above normal) but, except in a few parts of eastern coastal areas, it was also rather wet with up to 50% more rain than usual. The first major snow of the winter came on 10th in the north but this did not reach southern England.

January was wet and stormy with frequent gales, especially in Scotland and Ireland. There was up to twice normal amounts of rain in many areas and the northern half of Britain had some substantial snowfalls. Ireland, too, had some snow, especially in the northwest. Areas which had snow were also very cold, but southern Britain was milder than usual. There were some colder periods but they were mostly short-lived and there were milder periods in between.

February continued the wet trend, with many parts having slightly above normal amounts of rain, and it was very dull. Temperatures were about normal over most of Britain and slightly above over most of Ireland. As usual, there were some short-lived colder spells and some stormy weather but, on the whole, February 1984 was very much a 'normal' winter month.

The chief memory of the third winter will be the very stormy January, especially in the north where it was also very cold at times, and the mild November and December which meant that some birds remained farther north for a little longer than usual.

Birds in winter: patterns and movements

For many birds, winter is a critical time of year. Although some species which breed in Britain and Ireland avoid the winter by migrating south, many others arrive from breeding grounds farther north and east. Because of the influence of the Gulf Stream, Britain and Ireland are somewhat milder in winter than most of continental Europe at similar latitudes, and this means that many birds are able to remain through the whole period. Indeed these islands are the most northerly wintering grounds in the world for a wide variety of species.

An introduction to the biology of British birds in winter, and their adaptations to survive cold weather, was provided by Spencer (1982), and Elkins (1983) has a general chapter on the subject. There remains, however, relatively little detailed work on birds wintering in Britain and Ireland, apart from studies on wildfowl and waders (see Owen et al 1986, Prater 1981). It is hoped that this book will stimulate people to look at some of the problems more closely. This chapter discusses some of the general results obtained by the *Winter Atlas* but also indicates areas where more research is needed.

EARLY BREEDERS

The fieldwork for the *Winter Atlas* finished at the end of February. This date was decided after the Pilot Survey had shown that several small passerines, such as the Robin *Erithacus rubecula*, Wren *Troglodytes troglodytes* and Dunnock *Prunella modularis*, were detected more frequently from March onwards, probably as a result of increased singing (see p 431). Also many species were known to start quite major migrations in March. Although the 28th February end to the fieldwork avoided most of these problems, some Tawny Owls *Strix aluco*, many Ravens *Corvus corax*, and a few other species are already nesting by then. For some of these species the start of nesting is accompanied by increased displaying and calling and a consequent increase in conspicuousness. The Raven and the Golden Eagle *Aquila chrysaetos*, for example, have obvious display flights. The effect is detectable in some *Winter Atlas* figures. If the number of 10-km squares in which the species was recorded in November and December (early winter) is compared with the number of such squares in January and February (late winter) it is found that a few species show an increase greater than the 4% which could be explained by the increased coverage (see Table 1). Yet among lowland birds the Tawny Owl showed an increase of 13% in the number of recorded squares in late winter, the Corn Bunting *Miliaria calandra* 15%, the Lesser Spotted Woodpecker *Dendrocopos minor* 27% and the Goshawk *Accipiter gentilis* and the Hawfinch *Coccothraustes coccothraustes* 36%; and among highland birds the Dipper *Cinclus cinclus* increased by 16%, the Raven by 21% and the Golden Eagle by 78%. For all these, the extra registrations were randomly distributed throughout the ranges, so the increases were evidently not due to any movement of the populations.

MORTALITY

In marked contrast to the above, some other species showed a reduction in the number of squares in which they were recorded in the late winter. Examples are the Kingfisher *Alcedo atthis*, Grey Wagtail *Motacilla cinerea*, Goldcrest *Regulus regulus* and Stonechat *Saxicola torquata*. The figures in Table 2 show that such reductions are closely correlated with temperature. All these species, except the Goldcrest, suffered greater losses in the cold 1981/82 winter than in either subsequent winter, and in general 1983/84 affected them more than did 1982/83. They were also affected less in Ireland, where conditions are milder than in Britain.

All these four species, especially the Kingfisher and Goldcrest, are well known to be subject to cold weather mortality. For the Kingfisher and Grey Wagtail this mortality and the subsequent recovery are also shown clearly by the BTO's Waterways Birds Survey. Between 1981 and 1982 the population of Kingfishers decreased by 64% and that of Grey Wagtails by 42% (Taylor and Marchant 1983). They then increased by 69% and 43% respectively between 1982 and 1983, and both species increased by 19% between 1983 and 1984 (Taylor 1984, 1985).

The Goldcrest is seen to have been less affected in Britain by the 1981/82 winter than the other species, although it decreased markedly in Ireland (Table 2). The Common Birds Census index for this species, interestingly, shows no significant changes between 1981 and 1982 (Marchant 1983). It appears that, although there were record low temperatures in the

Table 2 The percentage difference in the number of 10-km squares in which four resident land birds were recorded, in the 'late' winter compared with the 'early' winter period.

| | Britain | | | |
	1981/82	1982/83	1983/84	Overall
Kingfisher	−36	2	12	−12
Grey Wagtail	−35	12	−2	−5
Stonechat	−38	16	−8	−6
Goldcrest	−10	5	−15	−5
EXPECTED FROM COVERAGE	14	9	4	4

| | Ireland | | | |
	1981/82	1982/83	1983/84	Overall
Kingfisher	−5	15	0	−2
Grey Wagtail	−6	44	14	14
Stonechat	12	2	17	0
Goldcrest	−13	19	3	3
EXPECTED FROM COVERAGE	32	19	17	11

SPECIES RECORDED

Fig. 4 The number of species (total = 193 species) recorded in
each 10-km square. Blank represents 0–50 species, small dots 51–75 species,
medium dots 76–100 species, and large dots more than 100 species.
Only species with maps in the main section are included.

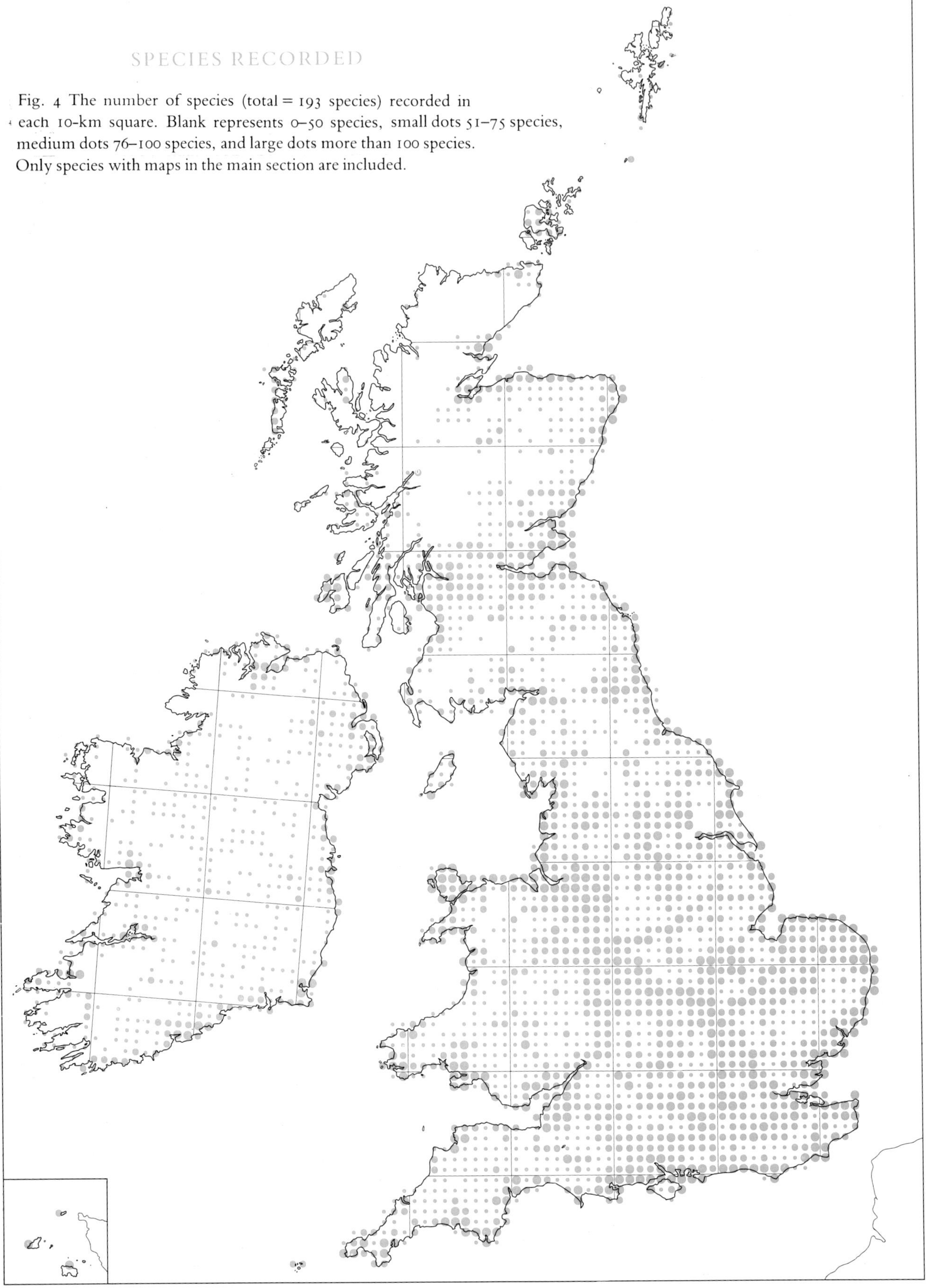

1981/82 winter, there was little glazing on the trees where Goldcrests and some other birds such as Treecreepers *Certhia familiaris* and Long-tailed Tits *Aegithalos caudatus* feed. And neither of these last two species showed a decrease in the CBC index between 1981 and 1982; the index for the Treecreeper actually increased significantly. By contrast, in the 1978/79 winter there was heavy glazing on the trees, and all three species showed marked decreases (Marchant and Hyde 1980).

Another traditional sufferer in cold winters is the Grey Heron *Ardea cinerea*. There are, however, no dramatic differences in the *Winter Atlas* data either between winters or between the early and late winter periods, and this was paralleled by virtually no change being detected in the annual heronries index over the course of the *Winter Atlas* fieldwork (C. M. Reynolds).

All these examples emphasise the point that each cold winter must be treated individually, and that species are likely to be affected in different ways depending on the particular circumstances.

NUMBER OF SPECIES

The two 10-km squares with the highest number of species were TR26 (E Kent including Stodmarsh and the N Kent marshes), which recorded 166 species, and TF74 (NW Norfolk including Titchwell) with 164. These were closely followed by others in the same areas, TR35 (Sandwich and Deal) with 162 and TG04 (Cley and Blakeney) with 159 species. In fact, all the squares with particularly high numbers of species were along the coast in the southeastern quarter of England. The highest total for an inland square was 148 in SK90 (which includes part of Rutland Water), and this was considerably more than the next, ST55 (which includes Chew Valley and Blagdon Lakes) with 133, and SP76 (Northampton, including Pitsford Reservoir) with 132 species. In Ireland the squares with the highest number of species were T02 (Wexford Harbour and part of the Slobs) with 134, and W96 (which includes Ballycotton) with 133. All the remaining Irish squares with more than 100 species were coastal, except for two in the Shannon estuary near the airport. At the opposite extreme several cards were received reporting not a single bird seen during a visit. The longest of these visits was of seven hours and fifty minutes in NN42 (Ben Muic, Perthshire) in December 1981.

The above figures represent the extremes of some more general patterns. Figure 4, p. 22, maps the number of species found in each 10-km square. Four features are particularly obvious. First, there is a marked coastal concentration, although it is somewhat less pronounced where cliffs dominate the coastline. Although this is in part due to the presence of shorebirds, examination of the distribution maps for particular species shows that the pattern applies to some landbird species as well, perhaps most markedly for the Song Thrush *Turdus philomelos*. The second feature is the absence or scarcity of birds on high ground. The mountains of central Scotland are nearly devoid of birds, but even relatively small upland areas, such as Dartmoor and Exmoor, have fewer species and also reduced numbers in many individual species maps. Further, in the map of the Lapwing *Vanellus vanellus*, for example, the line of the Cotswolds can be more or less identified. Thirdly, within the lowlands, numbers of birds and of species are both higher in areas of mixed farming than elsewhere, particularly in the central Midlands of England and northwestwards towards Cheshire. Areas of extensive grassland or intensive cereal management are relatively poor in numbers of species present. Parts of East Anglia do have fairly high numbers of species, but these are the regions with a greater variety of arable crops, rather than the 'prairie' landscape of cereal monocultures. The large urban areas are also low in species numbers.

The fourth obvious feature of Figure 4 is the relative paucity of species in Ireland. Within Ireland the coastal concentration is again apparent, though perhaps less strongly so than in Britain. There are also concentrations towards the south and east of the country, where agricultural land is richer and the crops more diverse, and along the River Shannon, where the floodland hosts many waterfowl during the winter. Areas with extensive peat bogs seem to be particularly unproductive; see for example the maps for Skylark *Alauda arvensis*, Lapwing and Stock Dove *Columba oenas*.

It also appears from the species maps that several widespread species are less common in Ireland than in Britain. To check that this is not due to an artefact, of the methods, the original counts for a variety of species were analysed further. Taking all counts of these species which were between 2.5 and 3.5 hours' duration in Britain and Ireland, it was found that the number of birds seen was also very significantly less in Ireland than in Britain,[*] thus demonstrating that there was a real difference in density of birds recorded.

Figure 4 showed the patterns for all species combined, but this hides some interesting differences between groups. Figure 5 maps the number of predominantly fresh water species in each square. In Britain they are seen to occur in large numbers on the various inland lakes and gravel pits, although many of them are also common along the coast. In Ireland most lakes and other fresh water bodies are to the north and west of a line from about Limerick to Drogheda. Many ducks, especially diving ducks, and grebes are concentrated in this area and largely absent from the south and east (Figure 5), except along the south coast itself and on some reservoirs and lakes near Dublin.

Waders and shorebirds have been extensively surveyed previously, in Britain by the Birds of Estuaries Enquiry (Prater 1981), and in Ireland by the Wetlands Enquiry (Hutchinson 1979). The distribution of waders is summarised in Figure 6 and shows that the highest number of species occurs in coastal areas, particularly in the major estuaries. Away from these, there are marked concentrations along the Essex coast, along the south coast from Poole Harbour to Pagham Harbour and in Lancashire and N Wales. However, all these stretches are really complexes of many small estuaries. Farther north the large concentration of waders on the west coast of the Uists was

* Wilcoxon matched-pairs signed-ranks test P < 0.005.

23

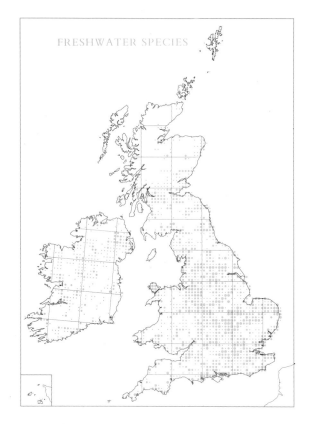

FRESHWATER SPECIES

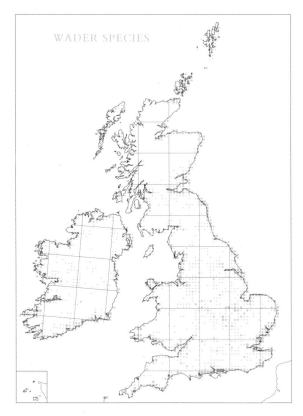

WADER SPECIES

Fig. 5 The number of fresh water species (total = 31 species) recorded in each 10-km square. Blank represents 0–10 species, small dots 11–15 species, medium dots 16–20 species, and large dots more than 20 species.

The species included are Little Grebe *Tachybaptus ruficollis*, Great Crested Grebe *Podiceps cristatus*, Red-necked Grebe *P. grisegena*, Bittern *Botaurus stellaris*, Grey Heron *Ardea cinerea*, Mute Swan *Cygnus olor*, Bewick's Swan *C. columbianus*, Whooper Swan *C. cygnus*, Canada Goose *Branta canadensis*, Egyptian Goose *Alopochen aegyptiacus*, Mandarin *Aix galericulata*, Wigeon *Anas penelope*, Gadwall *A. strepera*, Teal *A. crecca*, Mallard *A. platyrhynchos*, Pintail *A. acuta*, Shoveler *A. clypeata*, Red-crested Pochard *Netta rufina*, Pochard *Aythya ferina*, Ring-necked Duck *A. collaris*, Ferruginous Duck *A. nyroca*, Tufted Duck *A. fuligula*, Goldeneye *Bucephala clangula*, Smew *Mergus albellus*, Goosander *M. merganser*, Ruddy Duck *Oxyura jamaicensis*, Moorhen *Gallinula chloropus*, Coot *Fulica atra*, Kingfisher *Alcedo atthis*, Dipper *Cinclus cinclus*, and Cetti's Warbler *Cettia cetti*.

Fig. 6 The number of wader species (total = 25 species) recorded in each 10-km square. Blank represents 0–5 species, small dots 6–10 species, medium dots 11–15 species, and large dots more than 15 species.

The species included are Oystercatcher *Haematopus ostralegus*, Avocet *Recurvirostra avosetta*, Ringed Plover *Charadrius hiaticula*, Golden Plover *Pluvialis apricaria*, Grey Plover *P. squatarola*, Lapwing *Vanellus vanellus*, Knot *Calidris canutus*, Sanderling *C. alba*, Little Stint *C. minuta*. Purple Sandpiper *C. maritima*, Dunlin *C. alpina*, Ruff *Philomachus pugnax*, Jack Snipe *Lymnocryptes minimus*, Snipe *Gallinago gallinago*, Woodcock *Scolopax rusticola*, Black-tailed Godwit *Limosa limosa*, Bar-tailed Godwit *L. lapponica*, Whimbrel *Numenius phaeopus*, Curlew *N. arquata*, Spotted Redshank *Tringa erythropus*, Redshank *T. totanus*, Greenshank *T. nebularia*, Green Sandpiper *T. ochropus*, Common Sandpiper *Actitis hypoleucos* and Turnstone *Arenaria interpres*.

confirmed by the 1984/85 Winter Shorebird Count (M. E. Moser) and Orkney appears to be richer in wader species than Shetland. The coast of NW Scotland is seen as a particularly poor area, and again this is confirmed by the Winter Shorebird Count. Coasts here are generally very steep and rocky and evidently provide little food.

In Ireland, the number of wader species is high almost all round the coast although numbers of most individual species are highest in the major estuaries. Inland they occur particularly along the floodplain of the River Shannon and this holds large numbers of some species, too, mainly because of the regular winter flooding of the low-lying grasslands. The paucity of waders along the coast of Co. Wicklow

in the east and in the bays of Co. Donegal in the northwest is quite evident. These are areas with many exposed sandy shores which offer little in the way of invertebrate food.

Murton (1971) drew attention to the importance of seed supplies in determining the winter distributions of granivorous birds. Figure 7 (opposite) shows the number of species of seed-eating birds in each square. Several points are apparent. Fewer of these species occur in winter in Ireland than in Britain. This is partly because there is less arable agriculture, but also because a few immigrant seed-eating species occur in Britain only in fairly small numbers along the east coast, and do not reach Ireland very often. Examples are the Shorelark *Eremophila alpestris*, Twite

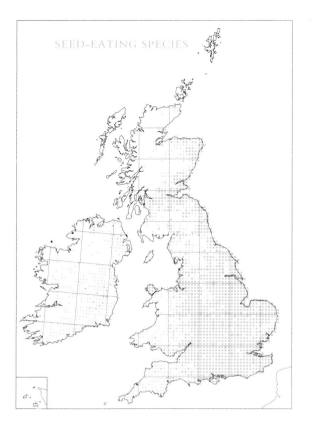

Fig. 7 The number of seed-eating species (total = 23 species) recorded in each 10-km square. Blank represents 0–10 species, small dots 11–14 species, medium dots 15–18 species, and large dots more than 18 species.

The species included are: Red-legged Partridge *Alectoris rufa*, Grey Partridge *Perdix perdix*, Pheasant *Phasianus colchicus*, Rock Dove/Feral Pigeon *Columba livia*, Stock Dove *C. oenas*, Woodpigeon *C. palumbus*, Collared Dove *Streptopelia decaocto*, Skylark *Alauda arvensis*, Shorelark *Eremophila alpestris*, House Sparrow *Passer domesticus*, Tree Sparrow *P. montanus*, Chaffinch *Fringilla coelebs*, Greenfinch *Carduelis chloris*, Goldfinch *C. carduelis*, Linnet *C. cannabina*, Twite *C. flavirostris*, Redpoll *C. flammea*, Lapland Bunting *Calcarius lapponicus*, Snow Bunting *Plectrophenax nivalis*, Yellowhammer *Emberiza citrinella*, Cirl Bunting *E. cirlus*, Reed Bunting *E. schoeniclus* and Corn Bunting *Miliaria calandra*.

Carduelis flavirostris and Lapland Bunting *Calcarius lapponicus*. In Scotland most seed-eating species are found along the east coast and they extend inland only in the central lowlands. Again, this coincides with arable agriculture and the pattern extends south into the northern part of England. Farther south, seed-eaters are scarce in areas of sheep-rearing and on high ground but are otherwise widespread. The east coast concentration seen in the north is still apparent and extends along the south coast west to Southampton, but this is again partly due to the scarcer species noted above. The association with agricultural practice is marked and even occurs within counties, as illustrated by the difference between the eastern and western halves of Dorset. Within Ireland the higher numbers of most of the seed-eating species are in the arable areas, especially where cereal cultivations dominate.

BODY SIZE AND WINTER DISTRIBUTIONS

Figure 8 (a–d) shows the distribution within Britain of birds in four weight classes (0–30 g, 31–300 g, 301–1,000 g and more than 1,000 g). There is a clear pattern between the four maps, with the larger species more prevalent in the northern part of the country and the smaller species more in the southern half. Most larger birds are better able to endure cold weather and shortages of food than are smaller ones (Calder 1974), a factor presumably responsible for these different distributions. Figure 9 (a,b), p. 27, show a similar analysis for Ireland, and it is seen that there are more bigger birds in the west and north of the country and more smaller ones in the east and south. This too reflects the pattern of climate.

SEASONAL PATTERNS

The arrival of winter visitors into Britain and Ireland is spread over several weeks but most have settled by the middle of November. The movements of the landbirds are rather poorly known but those of most wildfowl and waders have been worked out. Many of them leave their Arctic breeding grounds in late summer and spend much of the autumn on the Wadden Sea, moving on to British and Irish estuaries and coasts during November. Other species, particularly certain geese and ducks, stay on the Wadden Sea until the first severe weather, normally in early December. The number of individuals of these species which move into Britain and Ireland seems to depend on the intensity of the cold weather: larger numbers come when the weather is colder. This was apparent in 1981/82 when larger numbers of waterfowl came into Britain and Ireland than in either of the two subsequent winters (see below). By Christmas, nearly all the birds which are going to come to Britain and Ireland have arrived, and their distributions are then relatively static (barring extremely cold weather) until about the middle of March.

If February is mild enough, some species may start to return to their breeding grounds, for example Golden Plovers *Pluvialis apricaria*, some Lapwings and Oystercatchers *Haematopus ostralegus*. This is apparent in the *Winter Atlas* figures. Of the 190 or so 10-km squares recording Oystercatchers which are away from the coast, about 70 were occupied only in late February. Similarly, of the 41 squares recording them in Shetland, where they breed but do not winter in large numbers, 17 squares were occupied only after the middle of February. For the Golden Plover, several of the Visit Cards reporting birds from high ground in late February expressly mentioned that they were birds on their breeding areas. Indeed this species is one for which the breeding and winter maps are almost exact opposites of each other. Such birds will usually vacate these upland areas if the weather becomes colder again.

Altitudinal movements between winter and summer ranges are apparent with some other species. Upland Song Thrushes, for example, move down to the coasts in winter. Comparison of the *Breeding Atlas* and *Winter Atlas* maps for the Meadow Pipit *Anthus pratensis* and for Skylark similarly indicate the abandoning of high ground for the winter.

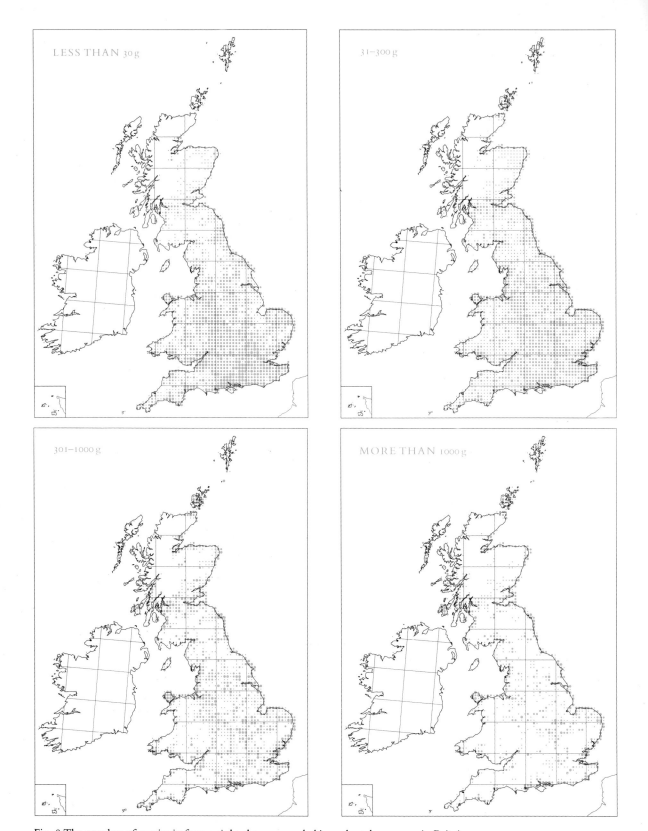

Fig. 8 The number of species in four weight classes recorded in each 10-km square in Britain:
(a) up to 30 g (total = 43 species). Blank represents 0–20 species, small dots 21–25 species, medium dots 26–30 species, and large dots more than 30 species.
(b) 31–300 g (total = 56 species). Blank represents 0–15 species, small dots 16–25 species, medium dots 26–35 species, and large dots more than 35 species.
(c) 301–1,000 g (total = 55 species). Blank represents 0–15 species, small dots 16–20 species, medium dots 21–25 species, and large dots more than 25 species.
(d) more than 1,000 g (total = 38 species). Blank represents 0–10 species, small dots 11–15 species, medium dots 16–20 species, and large dots more than 20 species.

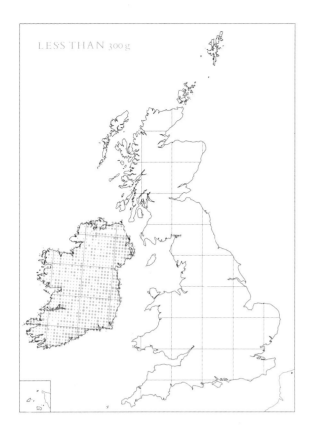
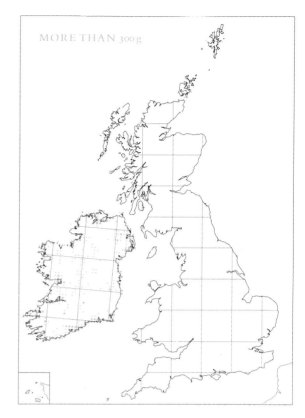

Fig. 9 The number of species of two weight classes recorded in each 10-km square in Ireland:
(a) less than 300 g (total = 84 species). Blank represents 0–20 species, small dots 21–35 species, medium dots 36–50 species, and large dots more than 50 species.
(b) more than 300 g (total = 82 species). Blank represents 0–20 species, small dots 21–30 species, medium dots 31–40 species, and large dots more than 40 species.

Some seabirds, particularly cliff-nesting auks, reappear on the breeding sites in winter especially later on. Many individuals spend perhaps a few hours each day back on the nesting cliffs, with spells of attendance broken by periods of several days in which no birds reappear at all. Birds have regularly been seen on the ledges from December onwards but in recent years such returns have begun progressively earlier with some individuals already present in October (Taylor and Reid 1981). Returning to the ledges probably enables the owners to maintain their claim to particularly good sites within what will be a crowded colony. The earlier return in recent years may be due to the increases in seabird numbers leading to increased competition for prime sites.

PARTIAL MIGRATION

There are two kinds of partial migrants in Britain and Ireland. In the first group some individuals leave Britain and Ireland in the autumn while other individuals remain, and in the second, the breeding population is augmented in the winter by birds from Fennoscandia and other parts of northern and eastern Europe.

A particularly common form of partial migration is for the two sexes to migrate to different extents or to different areas. Thus, although the map for the Chaffinch *Fringilla coelebs* shows it to be present throughout Britain and Ireland during the winter, it hides the different sex ratios in different areas. Males are commoner in northern Britain, and more females are in the south. Reed Buntings *Emberiza schoeniclus* show a similar pattern, with males apparently staying nearer to the breeding grounds, and the less dominant females moving south to milder climates (Prŷs-Jones 1977). Other species which show this are the Pied Wagtail *Motacilla alba*, Song Thrush, Meadow Pipit and Linnet *Carduelis cannabina*.

The Stock Dove and Skylark vacate many northern areas at the start of the winter but return north before the end of the period. For these the moving out appears to be in response more to seasonal changes in food availability than to climate itself. Food supplies are reduced in the north because of the prevalence of spring-sown crops. Farther south, autumn sowing is commoner. For the Stock Dove, O'Connor and Mead (1984) have shown that it is the young birds which are more likely to move, probably because they have a lower social dominance in feeding interactions (Murton *et al* 1964).

This pattern in which the most dominant birds stay nearer the breeding grounds has an important consequence. It enables them (and adult males are normally the most dominant group) to re-establish their breeding territories more readily in the spring and to do so in the best sites, both of which serve to reinforce their dominant status.

COLD WEATHER

Many of the patterns noted in the previous section are intensified by the advent of cold weather. Prŷs-Jones (1977) showed for Reed Buntings that, with colder weather, the male to female ratio increases at ringing stations in southern Britain. This suggests that males are being forced to move farther south, displacing the females from available food sources at times of shortage. Ringing data also suggest that there are regional variations in the extent of movement and consequent changes in numbers depending on the climate. Thus Lapwings and Grey Herons breeding in Scotland and northern England move south or west in greater numbers in cold than in mild winters (Baillie *et al* 1986). The patterns are also apparent in the gross distributions of certain passerines, for example for Redwing *Turdus iliacus* and the Brambling *Fringilla montifringilla*. Their distributions in the cold winter of 1981/82 and in the milder 1982/83 are contrasted in Figures 10 and 11. Other birds showing this effect include Pink-footed Goose *Anser brachyrhynchus*, Fieldfare *Turdus pilaris*, Meadow Pipit, and Siskin *Carduelis spinus*. In very cold weather, especially if there is snow cover as well, ground feeding species

are particularly vulnerable, and large scale movements from Britain south towards Iberia, or west into the milder climate of Ireland, may be apparent. For example, the number of 10-km squares in Britain recording Jack Snipe *Lymnocryptes minimus* in the 'late' winter, after the cold weather of December 1981, was 36% less than in the 'early' period of that winter, despite a 14% increase in coverage. The Woodcock *Scolopax rusticola* similarly decreased by 13% and the Snipe *Gallinago gallinago* by 10%. In Ireland, however, all three species increased between the 'early' and 'late' periods of that winter; Jack Snipe (by 84%), Woodcock (by 18%) and Snipe (by 18%).

The importance of Britain and Ireland as a wintering ground for European birds alters with the severity of the weather, more northern and fewer southern species being present in cold than in mild winters. The influx of wildfowl in cold winters adds to the interest of birdwatchers because the large numbers of commoner species are often accompanied by some relatively rare species. Typical cold weather immigrants present in larger numbers in 1981/82 than subsequently, included Red-necked Grebes *Podiceps grisegena* and Smews *Mergus albellus*. There were also higher numbers of Goosanders *Mergus merganser*, more Red-breasted Mergansers *Mergus serrator* occurred inland, and the other four grebes were more widespread. Even so, all the species mentioned were

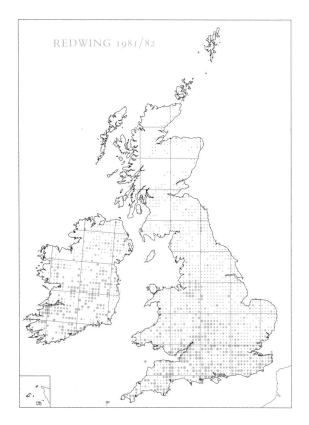
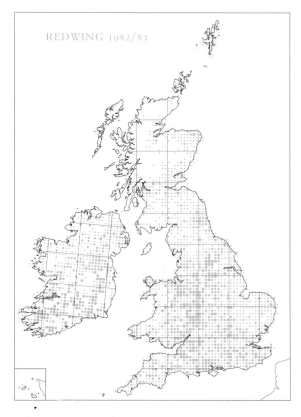

Fig. 10 The distribution of the Redwing *Turdus iliacus* in (a) 1981/82, and (b) 1982/83. Small dots represent 1–130 birds seen, medium dots 131–395 birds seen, and large dots more than 395 birds seen.

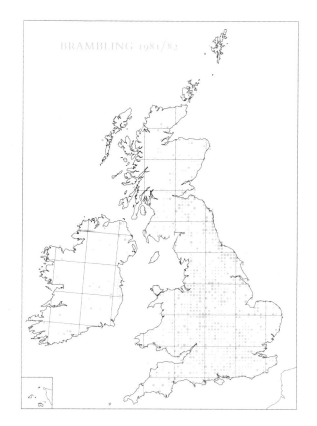

Fig. 11 The distribution of the Brambling *Fringilla montifringilla* in (a) 1981/82, and (b) 1982/83. Small dots represent 1–7 birds seen, medium dots 8–40 birds seen, and large dots more than 40 birds seen.

less numerous than in the more prolonged cold weather of 1978/79 (see Chandler 1981). That wildfowl were generally more numerous in 1981/82 than in the subsequent years was probably due to birds moving across from the Wadden Sea. However, many of these species were also more widely distributed within Britain and Ireland in 1981/82 than subsequently. This was no doubt partly because of the increased numbers, but also because most of the larger reservoirs froze over in the low temperatures, forcing birds into greater use of floods and other moving water which escaped freezing. Further, much of the increase in number of recorded squares occurred in the lowest category of abundance which suggests that the birds were being forced to disperse into smaller flocks. Cold weather immigrants might, of course, need to disperse more widely if existing haunts were filled to capacity by regular winter visitors, but even such species as the Canada Goose *Branta canadensis* and Ruddy Duck *Oxyura jamaicensis*, which are both introduced species from the New World and not subject to any immigration, were more widely dispersed in the cold weather of late 1981/82 than in the other winters.

The effects of cold winters on the Ruddy Duck population are particularly interesting. The species is sedentary in its natural haunts and there is little evidence of any movements over here other than cold weather dispersal. The recent large extension of its British range seems to have been caused mainly by two cold winters. The birds first escaped from the Wildfowl Trust collection at Slimbridge, Gloucestershire, and established a small feral population in north Staffordshire in the early 1960s. The cold of 1978/79 was the first really severe weather that these birds had experienced in Britain and they dispersed widely, looking for unfrozen waters (Vinicombe and Chandler 1982) Although some return movement took place after the thaw in 1979, other birds stayed where they were and bred in the new areas. The 1981/82 winter caused further dispersal, again followed by only a partial return. The map for this species shows that it is now widespread over much of southern and central England. A total of 167 10-km squares was occupied in 1981/82, falling to 112 in 1982/83 and rising slightly to 132 in 1983/84. In Ireland the figures were four, zero, and two squares respectively.

The response of waders to cold weather was generally similar to that of the wildfowl. Of the species mapped, all except Whimbrel *Numenius phaeopus* and Turnstone *Arenaria interpres* were significantly more widespread in Britain in 1981/82 than in 1982/83, and in most cases, the increase occurred mainly in

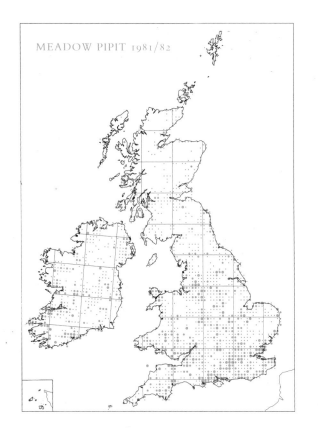
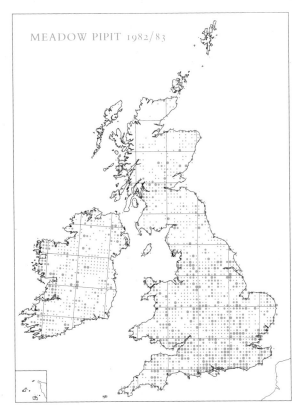

Fig. 12 The distribution of the Meadow Pipit *Anthus pratensis* in (a) 1981/82, and (b) 1982/83. Small dots represent 1–16 birds seen, medium dots 17–43 birds seen, and large dots more than 43 birds seen.

the lowest abundance category. Inspection of the maps reveals no major shifts in geographical distribution between the years and this suggests that, as for the wildfowl, the increase was mainly local dispersal from traditional sites to other parts of the coast or to nearby fields. Interestingly, there were no significant differences between the two years in Ireland, presumably again because of the milder climate there causing less freezing over of the birds' usual feeding sites.

The Bittern *Botaurus stellaris* is another species which becomes more widespread and more abundant in Britain during cold weather, and it closely resembles some of the semi-rarities among wildfowl. The increase appears to be largely due to Continental immigrants but Bibby (1981) found that increased dispersal from the British breeding sites also occurred. In such conditions it may sometimes be seen in some less usual habitats. The *Winter Atlas* records showed the bird present in 127 10-km squares in 1981/82, 32 in 1982/83, and in 74 squares in 1983/84. There were two Irish records in the first winter, none in the second and three in the third winter.

For a number of species Britain and Ireland are at the northern limit of their winter range, and in severe winters they are usually present in lower numbers. Thus, in cold winters, fewer Linnets, Goldfinches *Carduelis carduelis* and Redpolls *Carduelis flam-*

mea remain in Britain and Ireland, and more move south and southwest to France and Iberia. Figure 12 illustrates this for the Meadow Pipit, another species similarly affected.

Another group of species has populations present in Britain and Ireland at all seasons, but the population in winter mostly or completely comprises birds which breed in more northern areas, whereas the summer breeding population spends the winter in warmer areas farther south. The principal examples of this are Chiffchaff *Phylloscopus collybita*, Firecrest *Regulus ignicapillus*, Black Redstart *Phoenicurus ochruros* and Blackcap *Sylvia atricapilla*, although some Chiffchaffs may be residents all the year. Figure 13 shows that proportionately more of these species were seen in warmer than in colder winters. The Chiffchaff and Firecrest, the two which show this to greatest effect, are the smallest species and they also winter in more open countryside than does the Black Redstart. Blackcaps do not show the effect quite as strongly since they make greater use of gardens and garden feeders than do Chiffchaffs and Firecrests. Black Redstarts also make use of urban areas, where they benefit from the warmer microclimate, but they occur mainly along coastal cliffs which also have a milder microclimate.

Cold spells within a winter may produce some visible migration (hard-weather movements) but a

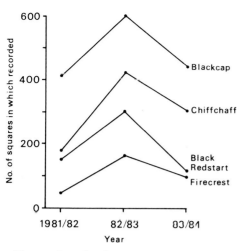

Fig. 13 The number of 10-km squares in which four species were recorded in each winter. Blackcap *Sylvia atricapilla*, Black Redstart *Phoenicurus ochrurus*, Chiffchaff *Phylloscopus collybita*, and Firecrest *Regulus ignicapillus*.

point of particular interest is that there are specific differences in the rate of return. The Lapwing is a classic example of a species which undertakes such movements, but the birds return so quickly following a thaw that few differences are apparent in the *Winter*

Atlas maps for the periods before and after the cold spell of 1981/82 (Figure 14). Most thrushes, too, move south and/or west in cold weather, though to a greater extent in Britain than in Ireland. The Redwing is the smallest of these and therefore potentially the most vulnerable to the cold. Figure 15 (overleaf) illustrates the distribution of this species in the early and late periods of 1981/82. It is clear that, unlike the Lapwing, few, if any, returned to Britain after the New Year, although there were more in Ireland in the later period.

This review of movements and changes in distribution as a result of cold weather over the period of the *Winter Atlas* has concentrated on the larger scale features. The nature of the data precludes a detailed discussion of some of the more subtle changes such as occur on a local scale between habitats, for example the movements of many small birds from open countryside into gardens and suburbia. These movements may be of only a few kilometres but are vital to the survival of the birds concerned. Some of this has been inferred from the BTO's Garden Bird Feeding Survey (Glue 1982). It was found that some species such as the Black-headed Gull *Larus ridibundus* are cold weather specialists, only coming into gardens in severe conditions. There is scope for much more work here, and it would need intensive local surveys to show the full patterns.

On a more local scale still, some individual birds

Fig. 14 The distribution of Lapwing *Vanellus vanellus* in November and December 1981 (left hand map), and in January and February 1982 (right hand map). Small dots represent 1–435 birds seen, medium dots 436–1,500 birds seen, and large dots more than 1,500 birds seen.

of a wide variety of species, (*eg* waders and passerines, residents and immigrants) hold territories for part or all of the winter. But these territories often break down in cold weather, especially at sites where food is abundant and in times of severe shortage. Again there is scope for more research.

IRRUPTIVE SPECIES

Table 3 shows the pattern of invasions during the *Winter Atlas* years by four classic irruptive species—the Waxwing *Bombycilla garrulus*, Crossbill *Loxia curvirostra*, Brambling and Siskin. The data show no common pattern although there are similarities between the Brambling and Siskin. Each probably responds individually to species-specific factors: more information may be found in the individual accounts.

Other less typically irruptive species also appeared irregularly, and in varying numbers, in the three winters. Thus Iceland and Glaucous Gulls *Larus glaucoides* and *L. hyperboreus* were more widespread and in larger numbers in 1983/84 than in either of the two previous winters, and the former also extended farther south in that year. Great Grey Shrikes *Lanius excubitor* had a widespread but scattered distribution throughout England, with small concentrations in the New Forest area and over eastern and central England, but in 1982/83 they were also widespread through central Scotland. There were no less than 48

Table 3 The number of squares in which four irruptive species were recorded in each winter

| | Britain | | |
	1981/82	1982/83	1983/84
Waxwing	130	21	19
Brambling	926	663	1055
Siskin	1033	827	1186
Crossbill	89	158	209
	Ireland		
	1981/2	1982/83	1983/84
Waxwing	8	0	0
Brambling	74	47	123
Siskin	131	76	110
Crossbill	4	3	10

Scottish records that year, against 4 and 12 in the preceding and following years.

A particularly interesting trio of irruptive species is the Hen Harrier *Circus cyaneus*, Short-eared Owl *Asio flammeus*, and Rough-legged Buzzard *Buteo lagopus*. The wintering populations of Hen Harriers and Short-eared Owls in Britain and Ireland include native breeding birds and immigrants from Scandinavia; and both species are commonest in winter in low-

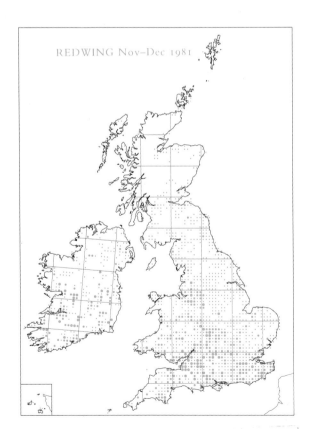

Fig. 15 The distribution of Redwing *Turdus iliacus* in November and December 1981 (left hand map) and January and February 1982 (right hand map). Small dots represent 1–130 birds seen, medium 131–395 birds seen, and large dots more than 395 birds seen.

lying areas, especially marshes and heaths around the Fens and the New Forest. Both species decreased sharply in numbers in 1983/84, compared with the two previous years. The reason is unknown, but fluctuations in the abundance of the small mammals on which they depend for food may have been involved; Rough-legged Buzzards, which are only winter visitors, were also much rarer in that year. Detailed examination of the maps for the different years indicates that the decline was general over the winter range rather than confined to any single area, so the cause may have been simply that fewer arrived from Scandinavia.

Finally, this section would not be complete without mention of the autumn 1982 invasion of Goldcrests and the autumn 1983 invasion of Jays *Garrulus glandarius*. Both invasions continued to have an effect into the following winter. The Goldcrests arrived along the east coast of Britain from Fair Isle south to Norfolk, particularly in the Firth of Forth area in October 1982 (Carrier 1983), and spread across Britain during the winter. Inspection of the maps suggests that the normal winter distribution was affected only in the northeastern parts of Scotland, where Goldcrests were commoner that winter than in either of the other two winters. The invasion of Jays was probably caused by a shortage of acorns in parts of Europe in 1983. It led to a slight general increase in recording frequency but little change in spatial pattern of records during the 1983/84 winter. More details are provided in the species account and by John and Roskell (1985).

References

BAILLIE, S. R., N. A. CLARK and M. A. OGILVIE 1986. Cold weather movements of waterfowl and waders: an analysis of ringing recoveries. Commissioned Report to Nature Conservancy Council. BTO, Tring.

BIBBY, C. J. 1981. Wintering Bitterns in Britain. *Brit. Birds* 74: 1–10.

CALDER, W. A. 1974. Consequences of body size for avian energetics. Pp. 86–144 in PAYNTER, R. A. (ed.) *Avian Energetics*. Nuttall Ornithology Club no. 15.

CARRIER, M. F. 1983. Diary of a mega-fall, Isle of May, October 1982. *BTO News* 124: 8.

CHANDLER, R. J. 1981. Influxes into Britain and Ireland of Red-necked Grebes and other water-birds during 1978/79. *Brit. Birds* 74: 55–81.

ELKINS, N. 1983. *Weather and Bird Behaviour*. Poyser, Calton.

GLUE, D. E. (ed.) 1982. *The Garden Bird Book*. Macmillan, London.

JOHN, A. W. G. and J. ROSKELL 1985. Jay movements in autumn 1983. *Brit. Birds* 78: 611–637.

MARCHANT, J. H. 1983. Bird population changes for the years 1981–1982. *Bird Study* 30: 127–133.

MARCHANT, J. H. and P. A. HYDE. 1980. Bird population changes for the years 1978–1979. *Bird Study* 27: 173–178.

MURTON, R. K. 1971. *Man and Birds*. Collins, London.

MURTON, R. K., N. J. WESTWOOD and A. J. ISAACSON. 1964. The feeding habits of the wood-pigeon *Columba palumbus*, stock dove *C. oenas* and turtle dove *Streptopelia turtur*. *Ibis* 106: 174–188.

O'CONNOR, R. J. and C. J. MEAD. 1984. The Stock Dove in Britain, 1930–1980. *Brit. Birds* 77: 181–201.

PRÝS-JONES, R. P. 1977. *Aspects of Reed Bunting ecology, with comparisons with the Yellowhammer*. D.Phil. Thesis, Oxford University.

SPENCER, R. 1982. Birds in winter—an outline. *Bird Study* 29: 169–182.

TAYLOR, K. 1984. Waterways Bird Survey—1982–83 index results and recent news. *BTO News* 133: 8–9.

TAYLOR, K. 1985. Waterways Bird Survey—1983–84 population changes. *BTO News* 139: 6–7.

TAYLOR, K. and J. H. MARCHANT. 1983. Population changes for waterways birds, 1981–1982. *Bird Study* 30: 121–126.

TAYLOR, K. and J. B. REID. 1981. Earlier colony attendance by Guillemots and Razorbills. *Scot. Birds* 11: 173–180.

VINICOMBE, K. E. and R. J. CHANDLER. 1982. Movements of Ruddy Ducks during the hard winter of 1978/79. *Brit. Birds* 75: 1–11.

Red-throated Diver

Gavia stellata

The Red-throated Diver is the smallest diver, and usually the most plentiful on inshore waters in winter. It figures prominently in weather-induced longshore passage movements of seabirds.

This species is well represented along the east coast of Britain, where it is fairly evenly distributed but with a slight decline in numbers from north to south. Though less abundant, it is also well distributed around the coasts of Ireland, but along the west coast of Britain it is distinctly patchy, numbers being concentrated off the west coast of Scotland and around the northwest coast of Wales. The northwest coast of England has a very low wintering population, numbers only tending to build up there after prolonged periods of onshore winds. A possible explanation of this may be that birds moving south from Scotland in autumn prefer the more direct route (and sheltered lee shore) provided by the east coast of Ireland. The few inland records probably represent either immature birds or those in difficulty, as all divers are essentially maritime in winter.

Throughout the winter season, numbers fluctuate widely in response to weather conditions and other factors which may affect the available food supply. Onshore winds bring birds into the larger bays where rolling seas churn up an abundance of sandeels and small crustaceans which are taken by the divers, as are the sprats, herring and codling that follow them. At other times, and more particularly along fjord coastlines, the latter three species form the bulk of the preferred food supply. The Red-throated Diver is, however, most typically associated with shallow inshore waters and sandy bays, where it also takes numbers of flatfish, which are broken up well by a series of transverse bites before being swallowed. Red-throated Divers are most frequently found singly or in pairs, but parties of from half-a-dozen to a score are not uncommon.

Along the east coast of Britain, stronger onshore winds induce northerly longshore passage, when several hundred birds pass during 2–3 days. Corresponding southerly passage with westerly winds off the west coasts of Britain and Ireland involves fewer birds, but in both cases they are heading towards regions of higher atmospheric pressure, where decreasing winds should give calmer water and better fishing. Such movements apart, there is a general tendency for birds to move further south in severe weather, when more may occur inland.

From late August to mid September, probably some 6,000–7,000 birds move down the west coast of Britain and the coasts of Ireland. These comprise the bulk of some 1,000 breeding pairs (with 300 young) from Britain (an increase since the *Breeding Atlas*), 1,000 pairs from Iceland (*BWP*) and the Faeroes, and an unknown component from Greenland (from where 4 European recoveries are recorded in *BWP*).

A small August dispersal along the east coast of Britain probably represents the Shetland population of about 600–700 pairs (Gomersall *et al* 1984). In mid September further arrivals along the eastern coastline, but mainly in the north, suggest direct immigration from Scandinavia. At this time, large concentrations build up in the Scottish estuaries, as witness over 1,500 in the Moray Firth in early October 1982 (Barrett and Barrett 1985) which was probably the largest western Palearctic concentration so far recorded. The total immigration to the east coast in autumn must number 10,000–15,000 birds, giving a peak total for Britain and Ireland of about 20,000 in early October.

To what extent birds then move on down the coast of France is unknown, and the pattern probably shows considerable seasonal variation, but there are recoveries of Scottish-ringed chicks from Finistère and Vendée (*BWP*) in subsequent winters.

The return passage northwards in spring usually occurs in two distinct phases: a peak in late February/early March, corresponding with the return of British birds to their breeding grounds, and a further passage in April/May presumably involving Scandinavian birds. It seems not unreasonable to estimate a wintering population of the order of 12,000–15,000 birds in Britain and Ireland—a sizeable proportion of the western Palearctic population.

J. D. PARRACK

Total number of squares in which recorded: 695 (18%)

Number (%) of squares

No. of birds seen in a day	Britain	Ireland	TOTAL (incl. C.I.)
1–2	271 (51%)	92 (59%)	364 (52%)
3–7	153 (28%)	47 (30%)	200 (29%)
8+	112 (21%)	18 (11%)	131 (19%)

References

BARRETT, J. and C. F. BARRETT. 1985. Divers in the Moray Firth, Scotland. *Scot. Birds* 13: 149–154.

GOMERSALL, C. H., J. S. MORTON and R. M. WYNDE. 1984. Status of breeding Red-throated Divers in Shetland, 1983. *Bird Study* 31: 223–229.

Breeding Atlas p 30

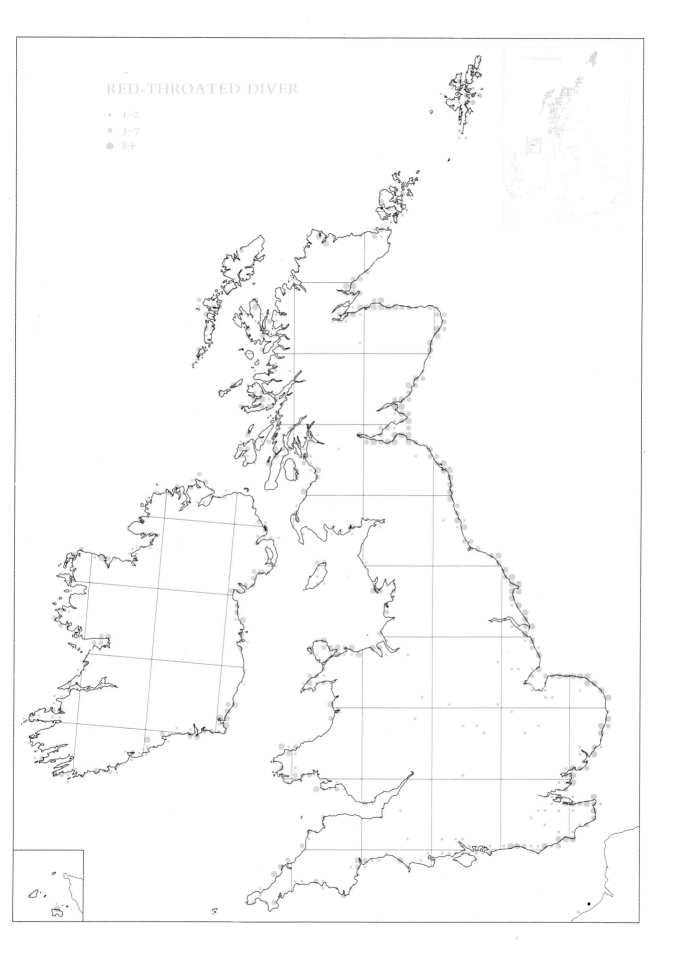

RED-THROATED DIVER

- 1–2
- 3–7
- 8+

Black-throated Diver

Gavia arctica

Being intermediate in size and flight characters between the two other regular wintering divers, the most positive identification feature of the Black-throated Diver is the darkness of the mantle and the white flank patch in all phases of winter plumage. As the extent to which these features can be observed is much dependent on the light, it is arguable that there is an innate tendency for this species to be under recorded. The small, sleek, fast-flying Red-throated Diver G. *stellata*, and the cumbersome, heavy-headed, shallow-beating and slower flying Great Northern Diver G. *immer* are more easily identified.

This said, it still seems clear that this is the rarest of the three divers around the shores of Ireland, western Britain and on inland waters. Birds are very scarce indeed off the Irish coastline apart from the odd one or two in the larger bays, notably Galway Bay. The numbers increase slightly and steadily around the southeast coast of Britain and up the east coast to the Firth of Forth and the Moray Firth. Again, concentration in the larger bays and inlets is noticeable. There is just a suggestion that the northwest coast of England might lie in the 'migratory shadow' of the east coast of Ireland, as with the Red-throated Diver. Peak numbers are found along the fjord coastline of western Scotland, but even here the Black-throated is certainly the rarest of the three during the winter months.

The winter ecology of the Black-throated Diver is similar to that of the Red-throated. Sandeels, crustaceans and flatfish form the preferred food in sandy bays, the normal winter habitat, but elsewhere, and particularly along fjord coastlines, herring and sprats are taken in quantity. The Black-throated is less gregarious than the Red-throated Diver, however, with rarely more than 2 or 3 occurring together except during passage and weather movements.

The extent to which it takes part in longshore weather movements is rather problematical. Suggestions that Black-throated Divers may be under recorded in such movements are supported by counts of beach corpses following oiling incidents. Critical east coast estimates suggest that the Black-throated Diver may occur rather more frequently than the Great Northern Diver off the east coast of Britain, but that Great Northerns may outnumber them by a factor of about 5:1 off western Britain, and about 8–10:1 off the coasts of Ireland.

Though the extent to which British breeders move further south in winter is not known, there seems little doubt that the majority of birds wintering off Finistere and western France are of Scandinavian origin. There are sizeable movements of Black-throated Divers off Finistere in April, and off Cap Gris Nez in October and April (Seabird Bulletins). Numbers reach a peak off the south and Channel coasts of Britain in April, when they may become the most plentiful divers, and this situation is often reflected in more northerly areas, but by this time British birds are back on their breeding grounds.

Assuming the population estimate in the *Breeding Atlas*, of about 150 pairs in the mid 1970s, to have shown a slight decrease, and that 20–30 young are produced, there should be some 250–300 birds available in early September for dispersal, presumably down the coasts of western Britain and Ireland. By the end of that month, immigrants from Scandinavia reaching the east coast of Britain have increased the numbers and suggest a peak autumnal population of about 1,400–1,800 birds. As numbers do not fall greatly following post-autumnal dispersal, it is likely that the wintering population is of the order of 1,300 birds, though this number may drop in late winter, possibly as a result of a moult migration to the Brittany coast.

The main wintering grounds of the western Palearctic breeding population lie in the Baltic area (with possibly some Scandinavian breeders moving to the Black Sea) and down the west coast of Europe. As the seas surrounding Britain and Ireland lie well to the west of this main migration route, they support only a small proportion of the total European stock.

J. D. PARRACK

Total number of squares in which recorded: 316 (8%)

No. of birds seen in a day	Number (%) of squares		
	Britain	Ireland	TOTAL (incl. C.I.)
1	184 (61%)	8 (53%)	192 (61%)
2	58 (19%)	4 (27%)	62 (20%)
3+	57 (19%)	3 (20%)	62 (20%)

References

HOPE JONES, P., J. Y. MONNAT, C. J. CADBURY and T. J. STOWE. 1978. Birds oiled during the Amoco Cadiz incident. *Mar. Pollut. Bull.* 9: 307–310.

Breeding Atlas p 28

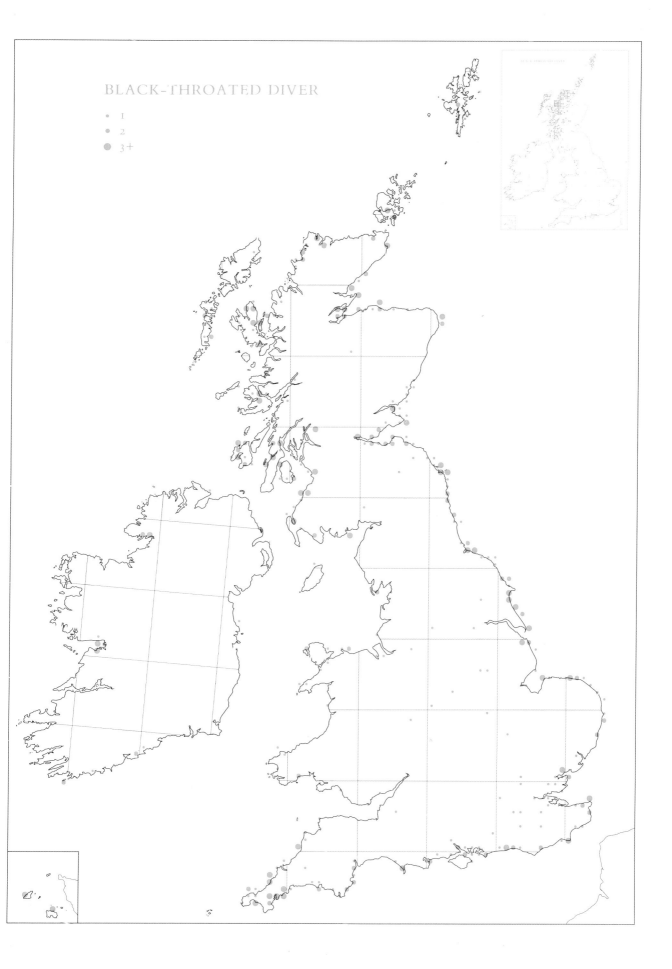

BLACK-THROATED DIVER

- • 1
- • 2
- • 3+

Great Northern Diver

Gavia immer

In addition to being the largest of the divers wintering regularly in the coastal waters of Britain and Ireland, the Great Northern Diver has a characteristically large bill, heavy angular head, and relatively slow, shallow wingbeat. It winters in deeper water and further offshore than the other species, thus creating problems in census work.

The distribution map reflects the northwesterly origin of the wintering population with birds being found off the west coast of Ireland, western Scotland and the Orkney and Shetland Islands. Elsewhere totals are low, suggesting numbers of the order of twice the concentration of wintering Black-throated Divers *G. arctica*, but more evenly distributed. Inland records are also rather more frequent than for Black-throated Divers, a well recognised phenomenon, but none the less surprising in a species that prefers deeper water. It is tempting to postulate migratory overshoot in immature birds as a contributory cause.

In winter the Great Northern Diver occurs off a variety of coastlines, being as much if not more at home among the rocky headlands and tide races of fjord coasts as in the shallow coves and sandy beaches preferred by the other two species. Whereas Red-throated *G. stellata* and Black-throated Divers usually feed within 1–2 km of the shore (and hence within binocular range), the Barretts (1985) found that the Great Northern Diver may be at any distance up to 10 km offshore. Onshore winds that bring herring and codling close inshore to find food, will in their turn attract the Great Northern Divers shorewards to feed on them, and the divers may then become part of longshore movements if the wind strengthens, but as they can fish successfully in calmer, deeper water further offshore, these movements are perhaps less likely to happen than with the other diver species. In shallower waters, crustaceans, cephalopods and flatfish are also taken.

During April, numbers show a peak in the Northern Isles and Scotland, presumably due to birds returning westwards from Scandinavian wintering grounds. At such times, passage flocks may number up to a dozen or more, but, during winter, concentrations are typically smaller, and singles or pairs are more frequently recorded. Numbers in April are high off SW Britain also, as shown by the number of bodies washed up in Cornwall following the 'Torrey Canyon' disaster in 1967, and no doubt these are representative of a similar return movement from the French coast. Considering the extent of the wintering range on the Continent, it seems that there must be a total of at least some 5,000 birds wintering in the western Palearctic, of which about 75% are to be found in British waters.

In recent winters, Heubeck and Richardson (1980) estimated some 300–400 Great Northern Divers around Shetland; numbers are not far short of this figure in Orkney, and there are probably many more in the Outer Hebrides (*Scottish Bird Reports*). Bearing in mind that this could be a considerable underestimate because many occur well offshore, and that Lea (1980) suggested a possible 500 around the Orkney coast alone, there could be a wintering population of at least 1,000–1,500 birds off the Scottish coasts. Allowing another 1,000–1,500 for Ireland, and a similar number for the rest of Britain, gives a wintering total of some 3,500–4,500 birds, making the species about three times as plentiful as the Black-throated Diver.

The origin of such numbers is somewhat puzzling, for the Icelandic population has been estimated at only 100–300 pairs, giving, with birds of the year and a small British summering population, a potential reservoir of no more than 1,000 individuals in all. This suggests a much larger easterly movement of birds from Greenland (or even mainland Canada) than has hitherto been supposed, or else an extremely large ratio of non-breeding birds. At all events, it is clear that the waters around Britain and Ireland support a great proportion of the western Palearctic wintering population.

J. D. PARRACK

Total number of squares in which recorded: 721 (19%)

No. of birds seen in a day	Number (%) of squares		
	Britain	Ireland	TOTAL (incl. C.I.)
1–2	332 (68%)	83 (36%)	416 (58%)
3–5	87 (18%)	72 (31%)	160 (22%)
6+	67 (14%)	77 (33%)	145 (20%)

References

BARRETT, J. and C. F. BARRETT. 1985. Divers in the Moray Firth, Scotland. *Scot. Birds* 13: 149–154.

BOURNE, W. R. P. 1968. Oil pollution and bird populations. The biological effects of oil pollution on littoral communities. *Field Studies* 2 Supp: 99–121.

HEUBECK, M. and M. G. RICHARDSON. 1980. Bird mortality following the *Esso Bernica* oil spill, Shetland, December 1978. *Scott. Birds* 11: 97–107.

LEA, D. 1980. *Seafowl in Scapa Flow, Orkney, 1974–1978*. RSPB, Sandy.

Breeding Atlas p 446

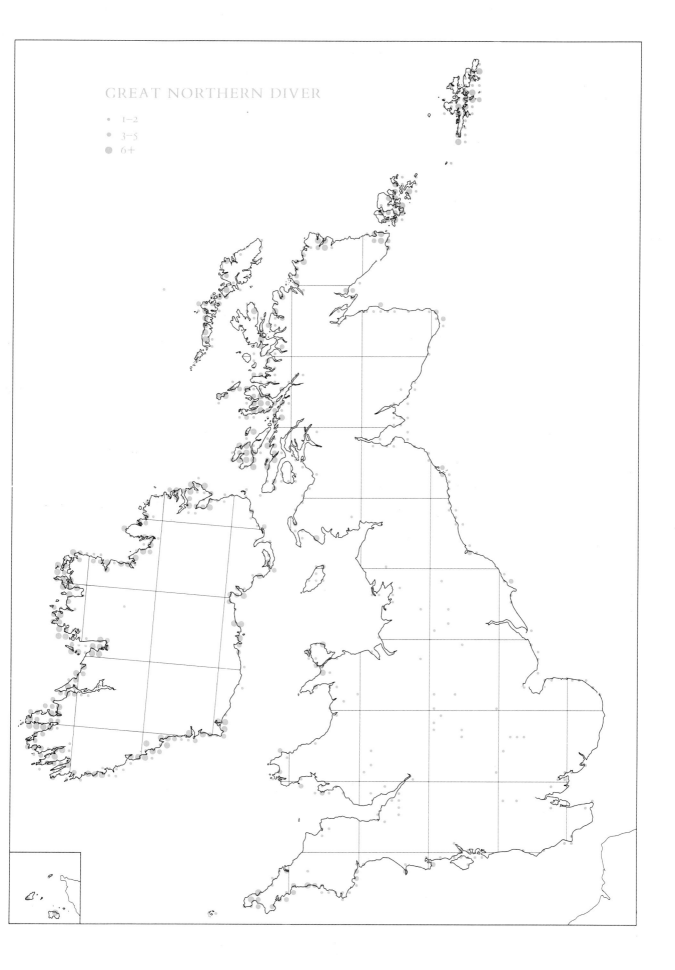

GREAT NORTHERN DIVER

- 1–2
- 3–5
- 6+

Little Grebe

Tachybaptus ruficollis

GBB

The Little Grebe is a widespread and numerous bird but, because of its secretive habits and totally aquatic existence, it is difficult to study, difficult to census and, above all, difficult to trap.

It has been traditionally regarded as largely sedentary in Britain and Ireland, and the winter map is very similar to the one in the *Breeding Atlas*. There are, however, some significant differences (for example, the presence of wintering birds along the S Devon coast). Like the *Breeding Atlas* map, the winter map shows the species' aversion to high ground; in Britain there are relatively few Little Grebes wintering in Scotland and numbers increase generally towards the south and east.

In summer, Little Grebes occur in a wide variety of fresh water habitats. Unlike the Great Crested Grebe *Podiceps cristatus*, there is no evidence of large scale post-breeding moult movements but, in winter, there is a widespread dispersal and migration. At this time, Little Grebes are rather more catholic in their choice of habitat, resorting not only to rivers and streams but also to sheltered brackish or saline coastal environments. Indeed, Prater (1981) estimated that 1,500–2,500 winter around our coasts, mainly in the south. In such situations they become readily visible and often gather into small flotillas when feeding. They often roost together in winter, gathering up to half an hour before sunset and dispersing from an hour or so before dawn (*BWP*). Little Grebes feed mainly on invertebrates (particularly insect larvae) but their diet depends on season and environment and, in winter, fish or molluscs may be far more important (*BWP*).

Although some adults maintain their territories throughout the winter, others, perhaps mainly juveniles, disperse or are forced to move by cold weather. Recent population studies in Avon and Gwynedd, however, clearly demonstrated a widespread autumn exodus from their breeding areas (Vinicombe 1982). At Chew Valley Lake, Avon, only 13% of the August total were on average still present in February, and in some years only 2%. On Anglesey, Gwynedd, in 1976/77, only 43% of the August total remained

by the following January, with 11% having moved to salt water environments; most of the missing 57% were assumed to have left the area. Reasons for this exodus are not clear but, at Chew, it was probably due mainly to the fact that the roach and perch fry, on which Little Grebes feed in autumn, would have grown too big to be exploited by mid winter. Other factors provoking an exodus may include potential winter freezing, a general reduction in aquatic animal life, a more dispersed food supply, caused by higher winter water levels and increased turbidity, making feeding difficult, although it is uncertain how these factors interact. Chew suffers from large seasonal fluctuations in water level, so it is not known whether more ecologically stable wetland environments would generally have such a well marked winter evacuation.

While at least some British birds disperse or migrate, the full extent of the movement is uncertain. South coast areas regularly record a winter influx and 3 mid winter ringing recoveries in northern France may indicate a more extensive southerly migration. In SE England at least, Continental immigrants may partially replace native birds in mid winter. The few ringing recoveries indicate that at least some wintering Little Grebes originate in Denmark, Germany and the Netherlands, and high coastal numbers in Essex and N Kent may confirm a more general Continental immigration, particularly as the highest numbers were recorded in the cold winter of 1981/82.

The *Breeding Atlas* estimated that there were 9,000–18,000 pairs. On average, 75% of pairs breed (pers. obs.) producing an average of 1.73 young per pair (Vinicombe 1982). Assuming that one youngster per pair remains alive in mid winter, a maximum population of 25,000–50,000 birds could be expected. Adding the maximum counts from the *Winter Atlas* data gives a total of just over 11,000. Assuming the *Breeding Atlas* estimate to be of the right order, this large discrepancy would suggest two possibilities: either there really is a widespread winter exodus or, because of their secretive nature, a large proportion of Little Grebes remained unrecorded. Probably both factors contributed. With a huge world range, extending right across Europe, southern Asia and Africa, the British and Irish population must represent only a tiny proportion of the world population.

K. E. VINICOMBE

Total number of squares in which recorded: 1,810 (47%)

No. of birds seen in a day	Number (%) of squares		
	Britain	Ireland	TOTAL (incl. C.I.)
1–3	755 (54%)	212 (53%)	968 (53%)
4–8	377 (27%)	109 (27%)	488 (27%)
9+	273 (19%)	81 (20%)	354 (20%)

References

VINICOMBE, K. E. 1982. Breeding and population fluctuations of the Little Grebe. *Brit. Birds* 75: 204–218.

Breeding Atlas p 38

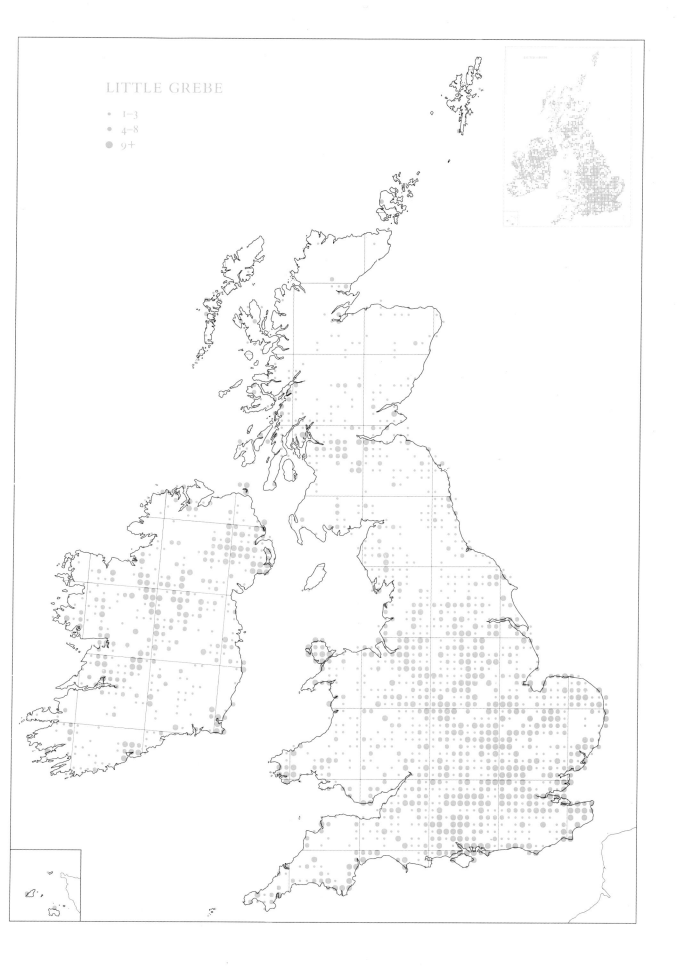

LITTLE GREBE

- 1–3
- 4–8
- 9+

Great Crested Grebe

Podiceps cristatus

GBB

This graceful bird is perhaps our best-known grebe, a joy to watch whether in its ashy winter dress or colourful breeding plumage. Following its severe persecution in Victorian times, the species' recovery in numbers and subsequent expansion are one of the success stories of this century. Its current high population benefits undoubtedly from the creation of man-made habitats such as gravel pits and shallow reservoirs.

The map reveals a broadly similar pattern to that of the *Breeding Atlas*, but the winter records are clearly more numerous and more broadly spread, particularly in England and Wales. Distribution is also more coastal and includes shallow inshore waters and estuaries. Along the sheltered English east coast, records are almost continuous, suggesting regular wintering. In contrast, the rougher coasts of Devon and Cornwall are clearly unattractive to the species.

In England the highest numbers are probably in central England and the Home Counties, where clay and gravel pits, well-stocked with fish by angling societies, provide ideal wintering conditions. In Scotland many breeding sites freeze and are deserted for the hardest part of the winter, the birds returning by February in an 'open' season. Records are largely confined to the Clyde-Forth basin, Tayside and the Firth of Forth. In Wales records are surprisingly widespread and there is marked westward extension of range in winter, particularly in Anglesey and the north. In Ireland winter records closely echo the *Breeding Atlas*. They form a broad diagonal belt from Connaught in the west to S Ulster in the east. Fewer variations in climate may favour a more sedentary distribution. The main difference is that winter records are more coastal and embrace the sheltered estuaries of the south coast.

In winter the species may be found in a variety of aquatic habitats, on deep lakes, slow-moving rivers, estuaries, coastal pools and inshore waters, as well as the shallower lakes, reservoirs and flooded workings which comprise its favoured breeding sites. Generally, it shows a preference for lowland localities. Its food there is chiefly fish, obtained by diving. The grebe pursues its prey under water by foot-propelled swimming. Occasionally birds are trapped by ice or enter underwater culverts in pursuit of fish.

In winter Great Crested Grebes are often solitary when feeding, but will form rafts of up to 100 birds when resting or roosting. Pair-formation begins in mid winter, often prior to occupation of territory. In mild weather, nesting can start as early as January.

After the decline in the 19th century, when the population fell to 42 pairs in England (*BWP*), there has been a sustained recovery during the course of the present century. By 1931 some 1,150 breeding pairs were reported in England and Wales, with at least another 80 pairs in Scotland. In the census of 1965 about 4,500 breeding birds were counted in Britain, which by 1975 had risen to 6,000 birds, and this upward trend has continued in most counties in the 1980s.

Although there has been little extension of geographical range since the 1930s, the species is quick to colonise new sites and in recent years has penetrated the centre of urban London, showing remarkable tolerance of human presence.

The winter population in Britain and Ireland seems likely to be in the region of between 7,000 and 10,000 birds, but, during periods of very hard weather on the Continent, movements may possibly increase the figure to over 20,000 birds. Similarly, during prolonged freeze-ups in Britain, there is dispersal of over-wintering birds southwards to France and westwards to Ireland.

In Europe there has been a comparable increase in breeding populations and a northwards spread into Scandinavia. The populations are dispersive and migratory. Wintering concentrations include counts of 22,000 on the three largest Swiss lakes and 20,000 on the IJsselmeer in the Netherlands. The Finnish and Russian populations normally migrate southeastwards in autumn towards the Black Sea, but Britain and Ireland clearly receive a large influx of winter visitors from western Europe.

K. C. OSBORNE

Total number of squares in which recorded: 1,184 (31%)

No. of birds seen in a day	Number (%) of squares		
	Britain	Ireland	TOTAL (incl. C.I.)
1–3	453 (49%)	132 (50%)	586 (49%)
4–15	285 (31%)	77 (29%)	362 (31%)
16+	181 (20%)	54 (21%)	236 (20%)

References

FULLER, R. J. 1982. *Bird Habitats in Britain*. Poyser, Calton.

HUGHES, S. W. M., P. BACON and J. J. M. FLEGG. 1979. The 1975 census of Great Crested Grebe in Britain. *Bird Study* 26: 213–226.

Breeding Atlas p 32

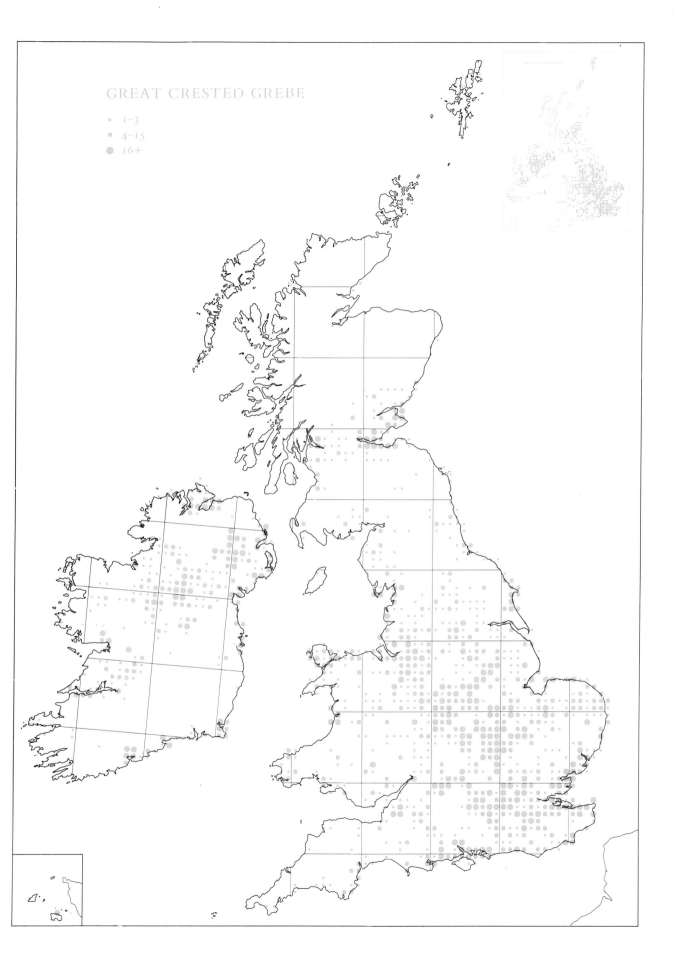

GREAT CRESTED GREBE

· 1–3
· 4–15
● 16+

Red-necked Grebe

Podiceps grisegena

GBB

The Red-necked Grebe, with its diagnostic yellow-based bill, is the only one of the five European grebes that does not breed in Britain or Ireland. Though occasional birds summer, raising hopes of possible future breeding, the nearest breeding area is Denmark.

The winter distribution in Britain during 1981–84 reflects the species' European breeding areas, being most frequent along the east and south coasts from the Firth of Forth to Poole Harbour. They also occur on larger inland waters in south central England and the London area. They are rare in Ireland.

Red-necked Grebes winter for preference in sheltered coastal localities. Flocks of up to 40 have been recorded, particularly on the Firth of Forth, but far smaller numbers are more usual. They feed, by diving, on invertebrates and small fish, the latter predominating in the winter months.

A comparatively small number of Red-necked Grebes winters in Britain, but occasional influxes occur in hard weather. A number of these influxes are listed in *BWP*, and the two most recent (January 1937 and February 1979) were discussed by Chandler (1981). The influxes occurred during easterly winds when the birds appeared suddenly in late January or February, having originated probably from the western Baltic and the Continental North Sea coast. In 1979, the birds were forced to move west by the onset of cold weather on 14th February. Within 3–4 days Red-necked Grebes had appeared at ice-free waters throughout England; the influx continued for 2 weeks, the overall numbers of birds involved being about 500. Their arrival coincided with a similar widespread appearance of Red-breasted Mergansers *Mergus serrator* on inland waters.

The centre of the Red-necked Grebes' distribution during the 1979 influx shifted from southern and southwestern England in the first week, to eastern and northern England and Scotland in the second. In part this was due to the continuing spread of birds, but it appears that during the first week the birds originated from the Continental shores of the southern North Sea, while the more northerly pattern of the second week suggests that additional birds from wintering areas in the western Baltic were involved.

Estimates have been made of about 100 Red-necked Grebes wintering in Britain and Ireland (Chandler 1981), while Prater (1981) recorded an average of 80 or so during 1969–1975. Totals for individual winters of between 120 and 170 are obtained from the *Winter Atlas* survey. Since Red-necked Grebes are fairly conspicuous birds of open water, often remaining at the same locality for several days, if not weeks, most individuals are likely to have been recorded. Indeed, the above totals may well be overestimates for birds will not only have moved about during the winter, but some returning passage birds can arrive as early as late February to swell the numbers (Chandler and Osborne 1977). Generally, no more than 3 appear in Ireland, in some winters none at all.

There do not appear to be any estimates of the European winter population of this species, but taking the total number of breeding pairs given by *BWP*, and assuming an average productivity of one offspring per pair, a potential total of about 10,000 birds may be suggested. In most winters it is probable that a good proportion of these birds will winter in the western Baltic and coastal areas of the North Sea and off SW Norway.

R. J. CHANDLER

Total number of squares in which recorded: 204 (5%)

No. of birds seen in a day	Number (%) of squares		
	Britain	Ireland	TOTAL (incl. C.I.)
1	139 (70%)	4 (100%)	144 (71%)
2	32 (16%)	0 (0%)	32 (16%)
3+	27 (14%)	0 (0%)	28 (14%)

References

CHANDLER, R. J. 1981. Influxes into Britain and Ireland of Red-necked Grebes and other waterbirds during winter 1978/79. *Brit. Birds* 74: 55–81.

CHANDLER, R. J. and K. C. OSBORNE. 1977. Scarce migrants in the London area. *London Bird Rep.* 41: 73–99.

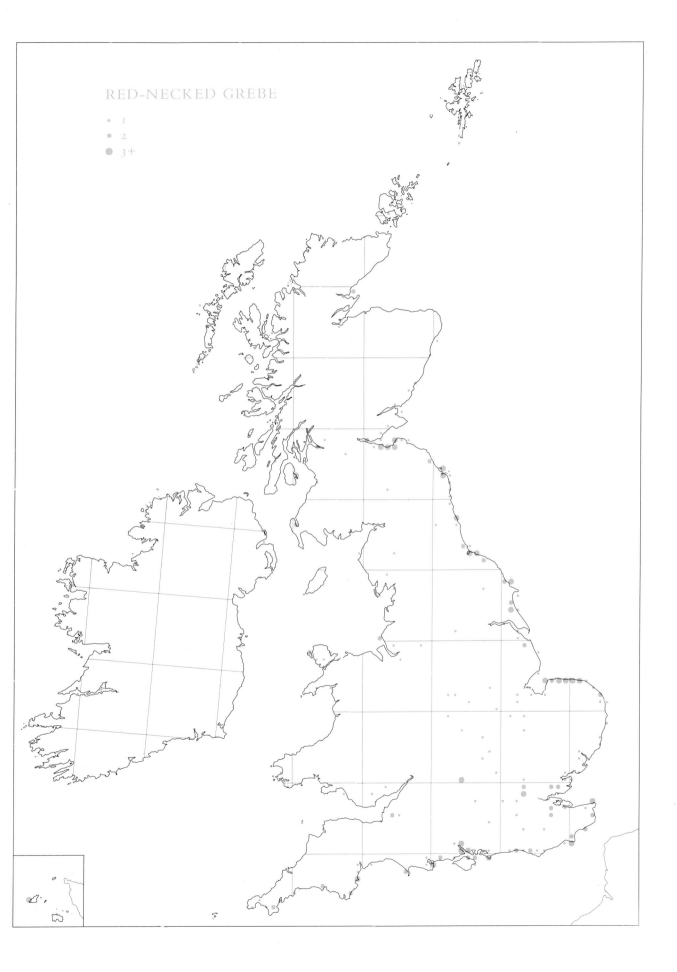

RED-NECKED GREBE

- 1
- 2
- 3+

Slavonian Grebe

Podiceps auritus

The Slavonian Grebe is the most maritime of our grebes, but even so it prefers sheltered coastal waters. It is primarily a winter visitor but, in eastern England, birds which are apparently on passage occur in March–April and September–November. It is probable that many of these passage birds winter no further away than southern Britain and Ireland, for according to *BWP* the winter range seldom extends so far south as the Bay of Biscay.

The map shows that compared with the Red-necked *P. grisegena* and Black-necked Grebes *P. nigricollis* the Slavonian has a more widespread, a more northerly, and essentially coastal distribution. A few traditional localities regularly have numbers of wintering Slavonian Grebes into double figures; these sites include Orkney, the Outer Hebrides, the Dornoch Firth, the south side of the Firth of Forth, the Blackwater Estuary in Essex, and Poole Harbour and the Exe Estuary on the south coast of England. Elsewhere, ones and twos are more usual but increasing numbers have been reported since the 1960s from the London area (Chandler and Osborne 1977), Essex (Cox 1984) and Sussex (Shrubb 1979).

Although the numbers wintering in Ireland have increased significantly since the cold 1978/79 winter, totals are still only in the range 30–50. Wexford Harbour is probably the most important single site, though numbers there have never attained double figures. In winter, food appears to consist mainly of small fish and crustaceans (*BWP*).

The slowly increasing Scottish breeding population which consisted of over 70 pairs in 1983 (*Breeding Atlas*, Hogg 1984), may well account for some of the wintering birds. The species' circumpolar breeding range does however include Iceland, Scandinavia and Russia, and doubtless some of these birds winter at least occasionally in Britain and Ireland. That birds from NW USSR occur is demonstrated by a recovery in Yorkshire in April 1963 of a bird ringed near Vologda in July 1962 (Hudson 1964).

Cold weather movements occur, generally in association with Red-necked Grebes, though the numbers involved (at least inland) are fewer than with the latter species. For example, influxes which occurred in January 1937 and in February 1979 (Chandler 1981), apparently of birds from the nearby Continental coastal areas, involved only 20 inland records on the former occasion and 60 on the latter. Though precise comparisons are difficult, corresponding numbers inland during any one of the winters 1981–1984 probably did not exceed 10–15 birds.

Except perhaps at some of the more remote Scottish coastal localities, most birds, of this comparatively conspicuous species with its traditional wintering sites, will have been recorded during the Atlas years. Slavonian Grebes tend to remain at particular sites for extended periods, so that although there may be some duplication of records over each winter, it is probably sufficient to estimate numbers directly from the yearly maps. These give a total of about 400 birds in Britain, and perhaps 30–40 in Ireland; virtually all occurring in sheltered coastal waters. These numbers are much less than the 670 per year quoted by Prater (1981), which appears excessive.

About 5,000 pairs breed in western Europe (*BWP*), suggesting 15,000 birds as a possible European wintering total.

R. J. CHANDLER

Total number of squares in which recorded: 309 (8%)

No. of birds seen in a day	Number (%) of squares		
	Britain	Ireland	TOTAL (incl. C.I.)
1	163 (58%)	7 (32%)	171 (55%)
2–3	62 (22%)	9 (41%)	72 (23%)
4+	58 (20%)	6 (27%)	66 (21%)

References

CHANDLER, R. J. 1981. Influxes into Britain and Ireland of Red-necked Grebes and other waterbirds during winter 1978/79. *Brit. Birds* 74: 55–81.

CHANDLER, R. J. and K. C. OSBORNE. 1977. Scarce migrants in the London area. *London Bird Rep.* 41: 73–99.

COX, S. 1984. *A New Guide to the Birds of Essex*. Essex Bird Watching and Preservation Society, Ipswich.

HOGG, A. 1984. *Scottish Bird Rep. for 1983*.

HUDSON, R. 1964. Recoveries in Great Britain and Ireland of birds ringed abroad. *Brit. Birds* 57: 583–596.

SHRUBB, M. 1979. *The Birds of Sussex*. Phillimore, Chichester.

Breeding Atlas p 34

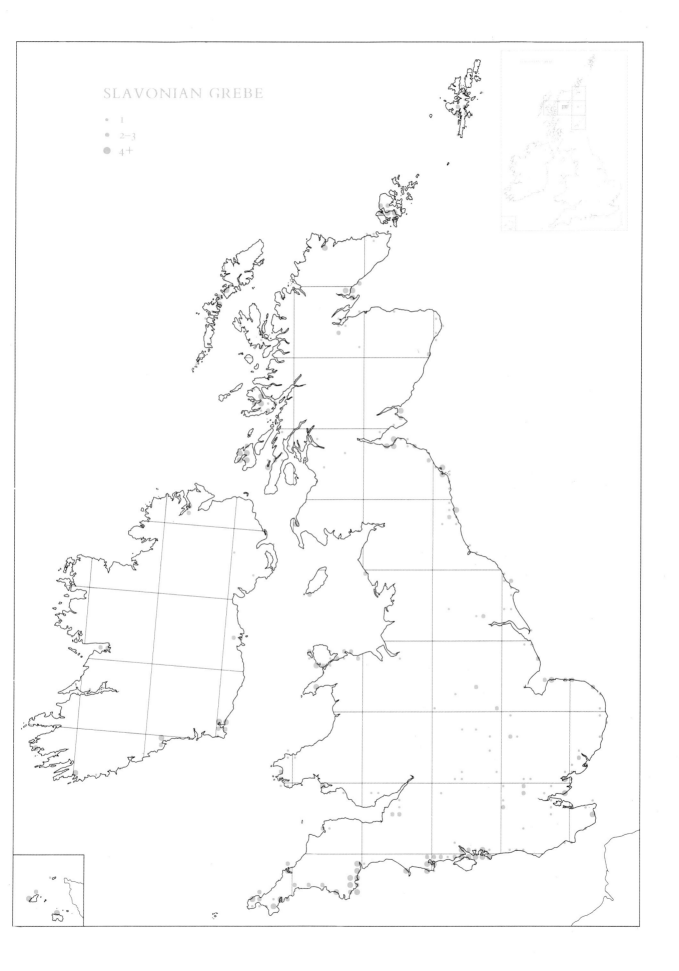

SLAVONIAN GREBE

- 1
- 2–3
- 4+

Black-necked Grebe

Podiceps nigricollis

GBB

A scarce winter visitor, the Black-necked Grebe primarily favours sheltered coastal waters and open inland waters. As a breeding bird in Britain it continues to maintain the 'precarious foothold' that it held during the period of the *Breeding Atlas*; sadly it has not bred in Ireland since 1966.

The winter distribution of the Black-necked Grebe is more southerly and westerly than either the Red-necked *P. grisegena* or Slavonian Grebe *P. auritus*, and the species is clearly less tolerant of cold conditions than are the other two. Only a few localities, which, except Loch Ryan in Scotland, are all in southern England, regularly hold more than three or four birds; amongst these are the London area reservoirs, Langstone Harbour (Hampshire), Poole Harbour (Dorset), the Exe estuary and Torbay (Devon). In Ireland typically no more than six or seven are seen each winter, and only Wexford Harbour is regularly visited by more than two or three individuals, a habit which appears to date only from the 1979/80 winter.

In fresh water environments during the breeding season the Black-necked Grebe is largely insectivorous, obtaining its prey by diving. Little is known of its food during winter (*BWP*), though doubtless an increased proportion of fish is taken.

As a consequence of the comparative rarity and southerly winter distribution of the species, cold weather movements of other water birds include only a few Black-necked Grebes. The species is primarily a passage migrant and only to a lesser extent a winter visitor. The birds disperse from their breeding grounds in mid August (*BWP*), and as can be seen from the London records for the period 1955–74 given in the Figure, there is a marked autumn peak (when flocks of more than 20 may occur), with comparatively low numbers during the winter and a minor peak of returning birds in March. The autumn birds presumably winter further west in Britain and Ireland or further south in Europe, possibly as far as the Iberian peninsula (*BWP*).

The British breeding population can provide very few of the Black-necked Grebes wintering in Britain, which presumably are derived from western Europe,

where breeding occurs sporadically in France, Holland and Denmark, and more commonly further east.

Black-necked Grebes are fairly conspicuous birds frequenting sheltered open water localities, and like Slavonian Grebes they also occur regularly at the same sites in successive years. Thus the number based on the *Winter Atlas* surveys probably gives a reasonably reliable estimate of 120 Black-necked Grebes in Britain and Ireland in winter. This is precisely the same as the total estimated by Prater (1981). It seems probable that autumn numbers in Britain may be considerably greater than this.

The European breeding population fluctuates from year to year, but the total numbers are small, perhaps only 500–1,000 pairs (*BWP* data). Thus the potential European wintering population is probably of the order of only 2,000 birds.

R. J. CHANDLER

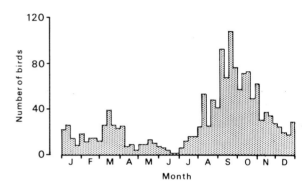

The number of Black-necked Grebes occurring in the London area in seven-day periods during 1955–1974. Data from London Bird Reports, *Nos 20–39.*

Total number of squares in which recorded: 114 (3%)

	Number (%) of squares		
No. of birds seen in a day	Britain	Ireland	TOTAL (incl. C.I.)
1	80 (75%)	2 (40%)	82 (72%)
2	15 (14%)	0 (0%)	16 (14%)
3+	12 (11%)	3 (60%)	16 (14%)

Breeding Atlas p 36

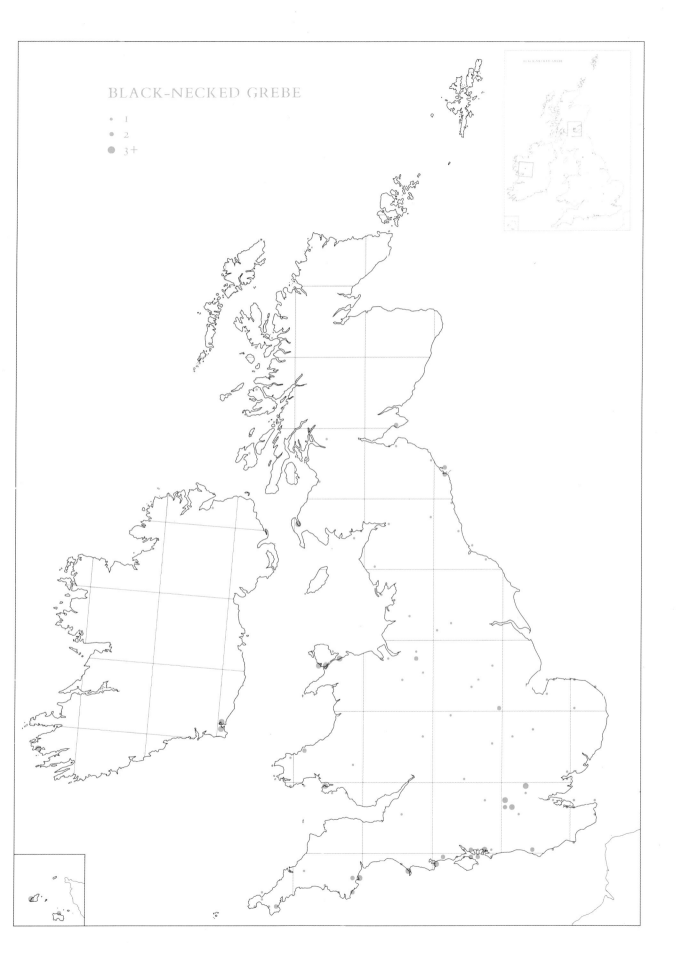

BLACK-NECKED GREBE

- 1
- 2
- 3+

Fulmar

Fulmarus glacialis

On fine still winter days Fulmars may be seen flying around the cliffs, or sitting snoozing on their nest sites either singly or in pairs, occasionally indulging in loud cackling and bowing displays with others who land beside them. Fulmars are the only British seabird which occupy their nest sites throughout the winter, though they do not lay until mid May.

The distribution shown on the map shows a remarkable similarity to the breeding distribution, and confirms that Fulmars are present at breeding sites in winter throughout the British and Irish breeding ranges. There is some indication that in winter small numbers of Fulmars occur on some stretches of the coast where breeding has not yet been confirmed, *eg* East Anglia and Morecambe Bay, but there is no evidence from ringing recoveries that the winter distribution pattern is substantially different from that in the rest of the year.

Fulmars feed entirely pelagically. Fisher (1952) provides lively descriptions of their association with whales and fishermen from the 17th century to the present time. Fulmars were quick to exploit food made available by man and fed voraciously on whale blubbers, fish and fish offal. Indeed Fisher concluded that their increase in numbers and range was a direct consequence of this increased availability of food, especially in winter. Fulmars are still attracted to working trawlers, but also concentrate in oceanographic situations where they find abundant zooplankton, squid, sandeels and other fish, by day and by night.

Macdonald (1980) has shown that breeding Fulmars, their nestlings having fledged in September, return to their nest sites from late October onwards, and by December the breeding population may be fully represented at their breeding cliffs though the birds may be absent for 3 or 4 days at a time. While in the first few years of life Fulmars are truly pelagic in distant oceanic waters, adults, once they have begun to breed, are much more restricted in their movements (Macdonald 1977). Their foraging ranges in the breeding season extend to several hundred kilometres and this probably also applies in winter.

In fine calm weather throughout winter, breeding Fulmars defend their nest territories against intruders, some males holding a second territory close to the nest site. On land, breeding birds are usually seen close to their known nesting sites. In winter, lone female breeders are rarely present on land, the occupants of sites being usually lone males and mated pairs. Males spend rather more time at their sites than do females in winter. Site and mate fidelity are strongly developed and adult Fulmars live, on average, to be over 40 years old.

However, there are more Fulmars at the cliffs than just the local breeders. Macdonald calculated that in winter approximately 77% of the Fulmars settling on land were residents. Among birds flying at the cliffs, but not landing, 35% were breeders from other colonies and the rest young birds which visit breeding colonies for 5 or more years before they start to breed at an average age of about 10 years old. No comprehensive study has yet been done on the pre-breeding component of Fulmar populations.

It is difficult to arrive at an estimate of the total numbers wintering in Britain and Ireland, but it is clear that the entire breeding population could be wintering in British and Irish waters. Based on the estimated breeding population for Britain and Ireland of 305,000 occupied sites in 1969 and 1970 (Cramp *et al* 1974), and a continuing increase of about 7% per annum, the numbers now breeding will be over 600,000 pairs. From Macdonald's figures the proportion of non-breeders in the wintering population associated with cliffs in winter was between 30% and 50%. This leads to an estimate of 1.6–1.8 million Fulmars in British and Irish waters in winter.

G. M. DUNNET

Total number of squares in which recorded: 630 (16%)

No. of birds seen in a day	Number (%) of squares		
	Britain	Ireland	TOTAL (incl. C.I.)
1–37	230 (48%)	83 (56%)	315 (50%)
38–215	134 (28%)	53 (36%)	188 (30%)
216+	115 (24%)	12 (8%)	127 (20%)

References

CRAMP, S., W. R. P. BOURNE and D. SAUNDERS. 1974. *The Seabirds of Britain and Ireland*. Collins, London.

DUNNET, G.M. and J. C. OLLASON. 1982. The feeding dispersal of Fulmars *Fulmarus glacialis* in the breeding season. *Ibis* 124: 359–361.

FISHER, J. 1952. *The Fulmar*. Collins, London.

MACDONALD, M. A. 1977. An analysis of the recoveries of British-ringed Fulmars. *Bird Study* 24: 208–214.

MACDONALD, M. A. 1980. The winter attendance of Fulmars at land in N.E. Scotland. *Ornis Scand.* 11: 23–29.

OLLASON, J. C. and G. M. DUNNET. 1983. Modelling annual changes in numbers of breeding fulmars, *Fulmarus glacialis*, at a colony in Orkney. *J. Anim. Ecol.* 52: 185–196.

Breeding Atlas p 40

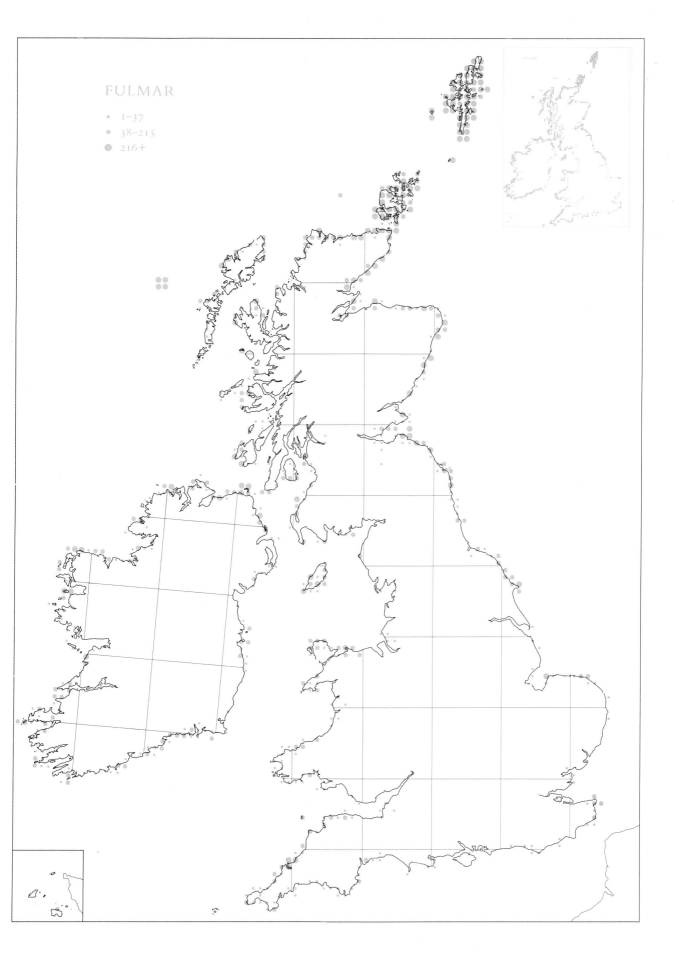

FULMAR

- 1–37
- 38–215
- 216+

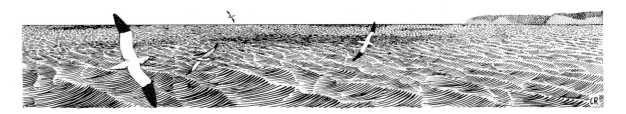

Gannet

Sula bassana

This is perhaps our most spectacular seabird, in appearance and behaviour. In winter, adults can be seen off almost any part of our coastline, singly or in small parties—usually less than a dozen or so. They fly with strong slow wing beats, low over the sea, conspicuously white with black wing tips. If lucky, we may see them plunge-diving to catch mackerel, herring or other pelagic shoaling fish, probably including sandeels. They do not occur on land, except when they attend their breeding colonies.

The main concentration of the larger colonies is round the north and west coasts. After fledging most young migrate southward during August and September, down the Atlantic seaboard, through Biscay, to the tropical waters off West Africa. A few spend their first winter in home waters, but only 1–2% of Gannets seen in the North Sea in winter have immature plumage. Most wintering birds are in full adult plumage and so more than 5 years old. It is thought that most breeding birds remain, highly dispersed, in home waters for the winter months but some certainly move south to warmer waters.

In the North Sea, where most observations have been made, Gannets are seen in small numbers throughout the winter both from ships and from oil installations (North Sea Bird Club 1984). In winter transects in the North Sea they are found in very low densities—0.03–0.13 birds per km^2 (Fulmars *Fulmarus glacialis* are 10–100 times as numerous in winter). They are not attracted to coastlines except to breeding sites in spring and summer, but are regularly seen from the shore. The winter distribution of these Gannet records from the shore is consistent with a sparsely distributed small population in British waters. There is a noticeable increase in numbers from January–March, but although adults are back 'in force' at their breeding colonies in January and February, and final departures from the colonies may be as late as early November, there is only a little sign of concentration of winter records in the vicinity of the colonies.

The breeding population of the Gannet in Britain and Ireland was estimated to be over 140,000 pairs in 1971–74, having increased dramatically over the previous 60 years from about 50,000 pairs (Cramp *et al* 1974). Numbers may have been held down by man's harvesting at some of the main colonies until the late 1880s and early this century. The increase was slow until 1939, more rapid between 1939 and 1949, and the population doubled between 1949 and 1969. Numbers are still growing and now there are prob-

ably more than 150,000 breeding pairs. Not only have numbers increased, but there are now twice as many colonies as there were at the turn of the century, and the breeding range has increased to include both France and Norway.

In winter the numbers of Gannets in British and Irish waters is impossible to estimate precisely but may be slightly fewer than the number of breeders.

G. M. DUNNET

Total number of squares in which recorded: 414 (11%)

No. of birds seen in a day	Number (%) of squares		TOTAL (incl. C.I.)
	Britain	Ireland	
1–3	138 (52%)	66 (45%)	204 (49%)
4–15	80 (30%)	49 (33%)	130 (31%)
16+	45 (17%)	33 (22%)	80 (19%)

References

BLAKE, B. F., M. L. TASKER, P. HOPE JONES, T. J. DIXON, R. MITCHELL and D. R. LANGSLOW. 1984. *Seabird Distribution in the North Sea*. Nature Conservancy Council, Huntingdon.

CRAMP, S., W. R. P. BOURNE and D. SAUNDERS. 1974. *The Seabirds of Britain and Ireland*. Collins, London.

JONES, P. HOPE and M. L. TASKER. 1982. *Seabird Movement at Coastal Sites around Great Britain and Ireland 1978–1980*. Rpt. to Nature Conservancy Council and Seabird Group, Aberdeen.

NELSON, J. B. 1978. *The Gannet*. Poyser, Berkhamsted.

NORTH SEA BIRD CLUB. 1984. *Report for 1983*. Aberdeen.

Breeding Atlas p 48

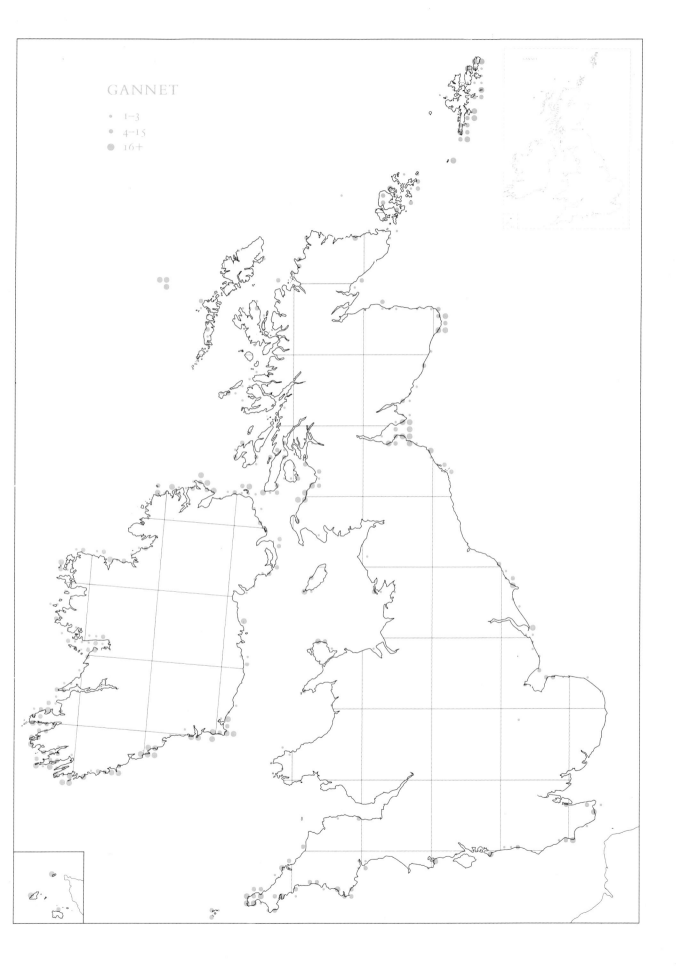

GANNET

- · 1–3
- · 4–15
- ● 16+

Cormorant

Phalacrocorax carbo

This large conspicuous bird is found on coasts, estuaries and inland waters throughout the year. In winter, adults are almost completely black or dark-plumaged, but juveniles and immatures have pale underparts until the end of their second autumn. When roosting on banks, boulders or even trees, it often stands with wings extended.

In Britain and Ireland, Cormorants breed almost exclusively in small (usually less than 50 pairs) coastal colonies mainly on western coasts: there are few on the east coasts of Scotland, England and Ireland. By contrast, winter records are distributed more or less evenly around all coasts, and many others are from inland waters in all but the most mountainous parts of the country. This dramatic difference in distribution results from extensive movements both of immatures and adults. Studies of ringing recoveries have shown movements up to 800 km in the first winter, and while over 70% of these recoveries come from the coast, the others are from up to 65 km from the sea. Cormorants are recorded inland mostly during winter. On the Ythan estuary near Aberdeen, about 170 km from the nearest breeding colony, numbers vary around 10–40 birds during winter, dropping to fewer than 10 in summer, and peaking at about 40–50 in October. Adults and immatures are both present, with immatures arriving a little before the adults. Birds ringed in breeding colonies in Orkney, the Farnes and Dumfries have been recovered on the Ythan. Birds are known to move up to 100 km within the winter season.

Cormorants occur in shallow inshore marine waters, estuaries, rivers and lochs. They are rarely seen from ships, and then only in ones and twos, close to shore. They are present at offshore oil production platforms in the North Sea, mainly from June–December. Because of their non-waterproof plumage they are incapable of being truly pelagic.

Its feeding habits bring the Cormorant into conflict with anglers, fishery managers and fish farmers. For decades it has been regarded as a pest, and persecuted throughout its European range. It fishes by diving from the water surface and is usually sparsely dispersed. They feed entirely on fish, pursuing them underwater in shallow dives, propelled by their large feet. Captured prey are taken to the surface and eaten. Many species of fish are recorded in their diet, and they seem to be remarkably opportunist according to habitat. In estuaries they feed largely on flatfish, but in inland waters trout, salmon, eels and perch are frequently taken. Their status as a pest of natural fisheries is not clear in quantitative terms, but they are unacceptable at fish farms.

The wintering population is almost certainly mainly native: birds breeding in Shetland rarely reach our mainland, though Orkney birds regularly fly over the narrow Pentland Firth to the Scottish mainland. In Britain and Ireland there are approximately 8,000 breeding pairs of Cormorants, which will lead to a wintering population of 20,000–25,000 birds. Elsewhere in western Europe the largest populations are the 14,500 pairs in Norway and 1,500 pairs in the Netherlands. The Cormorant is one of the most cosmopolitan species occurring throughout temperate (and some tropical) parts of the Old World.

G. M. DUNNET

Total number of squares in which recorded: 2,127 (55%)

No. of birds seen in a day	Number (%) of squares Britain	Ireland	TOTAL (incl. C.I.)
1–6	744 (50%)	314 (49%)	1,058 (50%)
7–24	430 (29%)	207 (33%)	640 (30%)
25+	312 (21%)	116 (18%)	429 (20%)

References

BALFOUR, E., A. ANDERSON and G. M. DUNNET. 1967. Orkney cormorants—their breeding distribution and dispersal. *Scot. Birds* 4: 481–493.

BLAKE, B. F., M. L. TASKER, P. HOPE JONES, T. J. DIXON, R. MITCHELL and D. R. LANGSLOW. 1984. *Seabird Distribution in the North Sea.* Nature Conservancy Council, Huntingdon.

COULSON, J. C. and M. G. BRAZENDALE. 1968. Movements of Cormorants ringed in the British Isles and evidence of colony-specific dispersal. *Brit. Birds* 61: 1–21.

MILLS, D. H. 1965. The distribution and food of the cormorant in Scottish inland waters. *Freshw. Salm. Fish. Res.* 35: 3–16.

NORTH SEA BIRD CLUB, 1984. *Report for 1983.* Aberdeen.

SCHAFER, M. M. 1982. *Dispersion and Feeding Ecology of Wintering Cormorants (Phalacrocorax carbo).* Ph.D. Thesis, Univ. of Aberdeen.

Breeding Atlas p 50

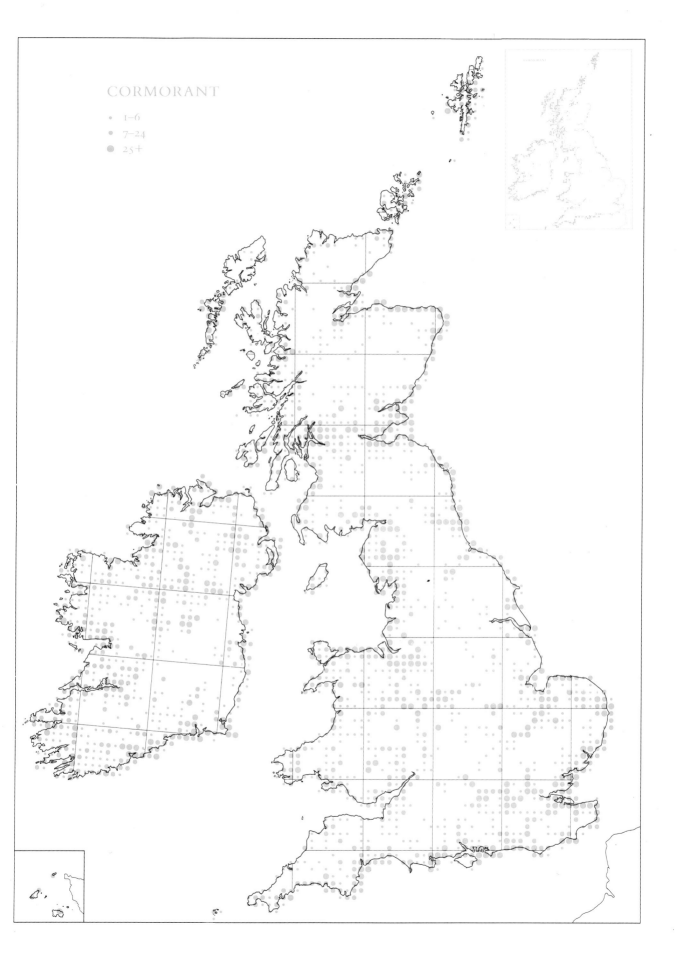

CORMORANT

- 1–6
- 7–24
- 25+

Shag

Phalacrocorax aristotelis

The Shag is the smaller of the two cormorants which occur in Britain and Ireland. It occurs much less frequently inland than the Cormorant *P. carbo* and, even where both occur on the coast, the two species have markedly different food preferences, although both feed mainly on fish.

Because of the very limited movements of most Shags, the pattern of winter distribution closely follows that of the breeding distribution. For example, few Shags are reported in winter on the east coast of Scotland between Wick and Dundee, which reflects the relatively small numbers which nest along a stretch of coastline famous for the numbers of other cliff nesting seabirds. No Shags nest in SE England but, in some winters, there are numerous records in this area.

Very few British or Irish Shags leave the country in winter and there is little evidence of birds arriving from the Continent. In most years, the adults remain within 100 km of their breeding colony; immature birds moving up to 200 km. The birds roost on coastal cliffs and on islands, but the water repellent properties of their feathers is less than that of many other seabirds and they appear to be unable to spend the night at sea.

There are extensive eruptive movements of Shags which take place at irregular intervals, and often result in birds being 'wrecked' (birds being driven inland and stranded in atypical habitats) (Potts 1969). A large proportion of the birds involved in these 'wrecks' are first-year Shags. Some adults are also involved but they occur much less frequently inland. The 'wrecks' are almost always restricted to birds from colonies on the east coasts of Scotland and England. The inland recoveries of Shags ringed on the east coast of Britain chiefly occur between S Yorkshire and Essex, areas with a coastline characterised by low, imprecise shoreline, without extensive cliffs which can be used for roosting. Coulson (1961) has suggested that on stormy nights, usually with strong easterly winds, some of the birds are disturbed from their roost by the rough seas, start to fly in the dark and are drifted inland by the wind. This produces inland records and recoveries of Shags in unexpected places, often many kilometres from the coast, such as in hen runs, house gardens as well as on reservoirs and inland rivers and even on roads. These eruptive movements could also be caused by feeding difficulties brought about by strong and persistent easterly winds. The wrecks usually result in a very high mortality of first-year Shags and in some years over 80% of the young perish. 1983/84 was a wreck year, which accounts for the majority of the inland records on the map, and also those on the southeast coast of England (where Shags are rarely reported in non-wreck years).

The Shag has increased in several parts of Britain and Ireland and new areas are being colonised. On the east coast, they had spread south to the Farne Islands by about 1930 and, in more recent years, have colonised the extensive cliffs between Bempton and Flamborough Head. On the west coast, the increase has been less spectacular, possibly because colonies existed in Wales and SW England throughout this century, and the changes have mainly been represented by local increases rather than by the conspicuous spread of its range. Their study in Ireland is less well documented but numbers are high in S and SW Ireland.

The last complete census of Shags was during Operation Seafarer in 1969–70 when 31,600 pairs were located. As few move into or out of Britain for the winter, and allowing for non-breeding birds and birds of the year, the mid winter population is likely to be between about 100,000 and 150,000.

J. C. COULSON

Total number of squares in which recorded: 1,042 (26%)

No. of birds seen in a day	Number (%) of squares		
	Britain	Ireland	TOTAL (incl. C.I.)
1–10	395 (51%)	130 (49%)	525 (50%)
11–41	200 (26%)	105 (39%)	307 (29%)
42+	176 (23%)	32 (12%)	210 (20%)

References

COULSON, J. C. 1961. Movements and seasonal variation in mortality of Shags and Cormorants ringed on the Farne Islands, Northumberland. *Brit. Birds* 54: 225–235.

POTTS, G. R. 1969. The influence of eruptive movements, age, population size and other factors on the survival of the Shag *Phalacrocorax aristotelis* (L.). *J. Anim. Ecol.* 38: 53–102.

Breeding Atlas p 52

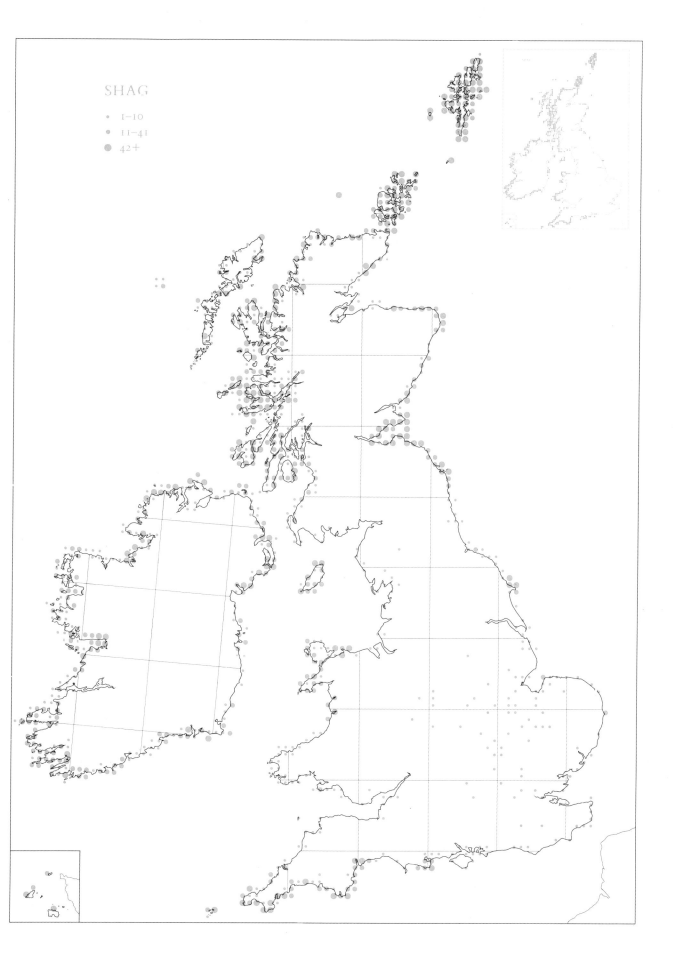

SHAG

- 1–10
- 11–41
- 42+

Bittern

Botaurus stellaris

The unexpected sight of a Bittern standing motionless at a ditchside, or flying briefly in leisurely fashion over a reed bed before dropping to become invisible amongst the innumerable brown stems, always comes as a bonus to the winter birdwatcher. In most years Bitterns are in greater numbers and more likely to be seen in winter than during the summer months.

In a study of their winter distribution and numbers between 1960–79 Bibby (1981) showed that the bulk of the records came from SE England, with the greatest numbers from Norfolk, Kent and Dorset. The *Winter Atlas* confirms this, with more than 50% of all records in the southeast, but with further concentrations on the Humber, the Severn and the coast of S Wales. Bibby showed that the evidence strongly suggests that most of these wintering birds are from mainland Europe, and include adults and juveniles of either sex.

The number of Bitterns wintering in Britain is closely linked with the severity of the weather. There are sporadic occurrences in Ireland. In hard winters more are seen, and more are picked up emaciated or dead, with most records in December and January. Probably most of these birds come from NW Europe, and certainly all the foreign-ringed Bitterns recovered here have come from this area, with birds from Sweden, West Germany, Belgium and the Netherlands.

Except in very hard winters the resident breeding population does not seem to be seriously affected by severe weather but, despite this, numbers of breeding birds are low and the population is declining. Past estimates show that in 1954 the population of breeding birds probably numbered 78–83 pairs, most of them in Norfolk and Suffolk, with less than 10 pairs elsewhere. By 1970 numbers had declined to 68–72 pairs, by a halving since 1954 of numbers in Norfolk from 60 to 27 pairs, though counteracted by increases practically everywhere else. A national survey in 1976 showed a further decline to 45–47 pairs, with decreases no longer confined to Norfolk (Day and Wilson 1978), and the 1983 population numbered only 36–38 pairs.

The causes of this decline are obscure, but it seems probable that pollution, eutrophication, and turbidity caused by a massive increase in boat traffic on the Norfolk Broads, have all played a part. Elsewhere Bitterns have now disappeared as a breeding species from Somerset, Kent and Humberside, and over half the population is now concentrated in only three sites, the reserves of the Royal Society for the Protection of Birds and Nature Conservancy Council at Leighton Moss in Lancashire and Minsmere and Walberswick in Suffolk. In 1983 only a sorry remnant population of 6 pairs could be found on the Norfolk Broads.

Breeding records have been confined to reed beds, but it is not known whether the resident population moves out of these in winter to join wintering Bitterns in other habitats. In mid winter they can turn up almost anywhere, at gravel pits, sewage farms, cressbeds, reservoirs and river systems as well as reed beds. The main foods are fish, especially eels, aquatic invertebrates and small mammals, and the presence of open water during hard weather is probably an important factor in their survival.

The British population is small compared with that of mainland Europe, where, excluding Russia, the breeding population was estimated to be 2,500–2,700 pairs in 1976 (Day 1981), with the highest numbers in the Netherlands (about 500), France (about 400) and Sweden (200–250). In the north of their range (Sweden, Russia and Finland) Bitterns are largely migratory, but in hard winters migrants and resident populations are both affected, and following the severe weather of the 1978/79 winter, breeding numbers in NW Europe as a whole were down by 30–50%. Although a full census of wintering Bitterns has not been attempted, Bibby (1981) says that between 30 and 100 birds are reported away from their breeding areas each winter, with a record 189 in 1978/79. The total winter population in most years is likely to be between about 50 and 150 depending on the severity of the weather.

J. C. DAY

Total number of squares in which recorded: 190 (5%)

No. of birds seen in a day	Number (%) of squares		
	Britain	Ireland	TOTAL (incl. C.I.)
1	167 (91%)	5 (100%)	173 (91%)
2	10 (5%)	0 (0%)	10 (5%)
3+	7 (4%)	0 (0%)	7 (4%)

References

BIBBY, C. J. 1981. Wintering Bitterns in Britain. *Brit. Birds* 74: 1–10.

DAY, J. C. U. 1981. Status of Bitterns in Europe since 1976. *Brit. Birds* 74: 10–15.

DAY, J. C. U. and J. WILSON. 1978. Breeding Bitterns in Britain. *Brit. Birds* 71: 285–300.

Breeding Atlas p 56

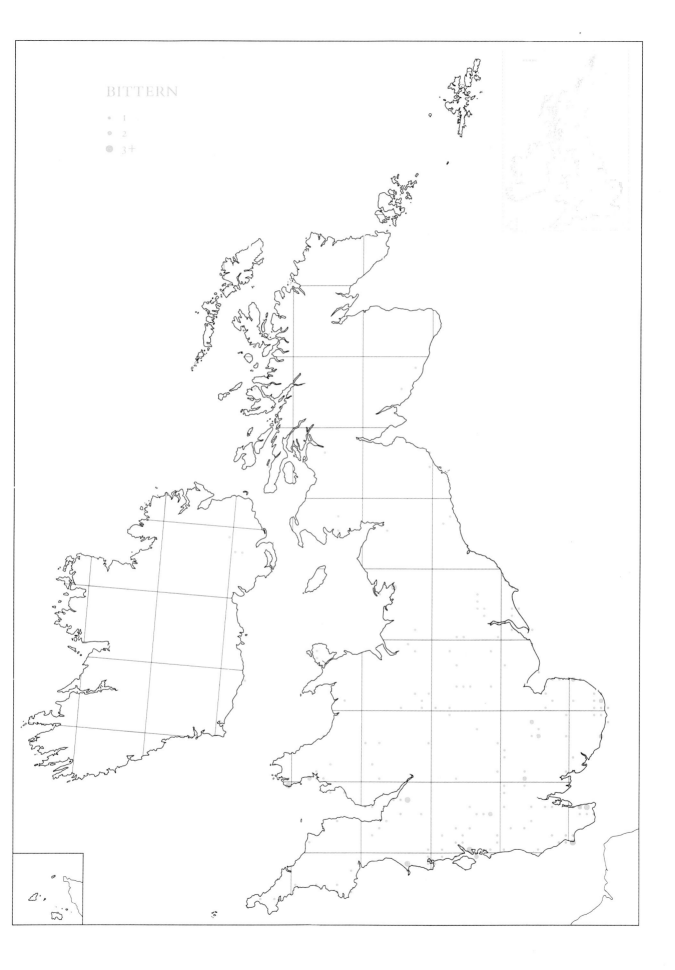

BITTERN

- · 1
- · 2
- · 3+

Grey Heron

Ardea cinerea

The Grey Heron is the largest of European herons. It has the most northern distribution and is resident in Britain and Ireland. An often typical winter sight is that of Grey Herons standing on ice, hunched, with feathers fluffed, but such a scene is misleading for they are well able to cope with most British winters.

The map shows a substantial and widespread population. The only areas with few Grey Herons are those where the January temperature averages less than 3°C, that is, at the higher altitudes and away from the coast in the north of Scotland. Above 3°C other factors must influence abundance, because even in 1981/82, the most severe of the three winters in the *Winter Atlas* survey, there was no increase in numbers in the very mild areas to the far south and west or on the coast. Many Grey Herons return to their breeding colonies by the end of February. The winter map will therefore include some records of birds near breeding sites. Considering that heronries in England and Wales are generally larger than those in Scotland and Ireland, the winter distribution is not inconsistent with the *Breeding Atlas* distribution.

The few behavioural studies of Grey Herons show that they tend to return repeatedly to specific feeding sites; often to areas of running water in streams, ditches and drains, as well as on the verges of rivers, lakes and ponds, in muddy creeks at estuaries and on the seashore itself. Some of these sites will provide insufficient food to sustain a heron. A winter study in Aberdeenshire by Richner (1985) showed that some herons used more than one site. The better feeding sites were rigorously defended and on one occasion during the most severe weather of the 1981/82 winter, an adult bird killed a particularly persistent intruding juvenile.

It can be assumed that Grey Herons will take whatever fish and waterside animals are available in winter. Most larger fishes move into deeper water as the temperature drops and so become less available. Invertebrates are also less active than in summer but small mammals may become more available, particularly in early winter when there are many juveniles and the vegetative cover is decreasing. Birds are known to be taken in winter: there are records of Snipe *Gallinago gallinago* and Water Rail *Rallus aquaticus* being consumed, and an instance of a Chaffinch *Fringilla coelebs*, stalked and seized at a cattle feeding trough.

The most important effect of severe weather is to make many feeding sites unproductive. Freezing temperatures reduce the amount of running water, and ice and drifting snow may cover many feeding sites. Young birds are at a disadvantage because they are less adept at fishing than adults and often occupy poorer feeding sites which become uninhabitable as the winter progresses. The mortality of first winter Grey Herons varies with temperature; over 80% survive the mildest winters but almost none survived the prolonged cold winter of 1962/63 (North 1979). December 1981 and January 1982 were exceedingly cold and many first-winter birds died, though the mortality of older birds was not particularly high. Moreover it seemed that, after the onset of the severe cold, many young birds wandered far afield; recoveries of dead ringed birds were at an average distance of 86 km, more than twice the average usual distance of 36 km for these months (Marquiss *et al* 1983).

The resident breeding population of Britain and Ireland is of the order of 10,000 pairs. Annual production varies but may average about 20,000 young. In most mid winters the Grey Heron population could be about 30,000 birds. This figure is conjectural and does not include the unknown number of immigrants from the northern and western European seaboards, which arrive in late autumn and early winter. Some immigrants from Scandinavia may return to their natal areas in spring.

The Grey Heron is rapidly expanding its range in Europe. Nevertheless the substantial population of Britain and Ireland may be considered important because it is resident. As such it is less vulnerable to persecution, environmental change and pollution, compared to migratory heron and egret populations.

M. MARQUISS

Total number of squares in which recorded: 3,197 (83%)

No. of birds seen in a day	Number (%) of squares		
	Britain	Ireland	TOTAL (incl. C.I.)
1–2	984 (41%)	452 (56%)	1,437 (45%)
3–6	862 (36%)	246 (31%)	1,109 (35%)
7+	541 (23%)	108 (13%)	651 (20%)

References

MARQUISS, M., M. NICOLL and K. BROCKIE. 1983. Scottish Herons and the 1981/2 cold winter. *BTO News* 125: 4–5.

NORTH, P. M. 1979. Relating Grey Heron survival rates to winter weather conditions. *Bird Study* 26: 23–28.

RICHNER, H. 1985. One adult Grey Heron killing another on feeding territory. *Brit. Birds* 78: 297.

Breeding Atlas p 54

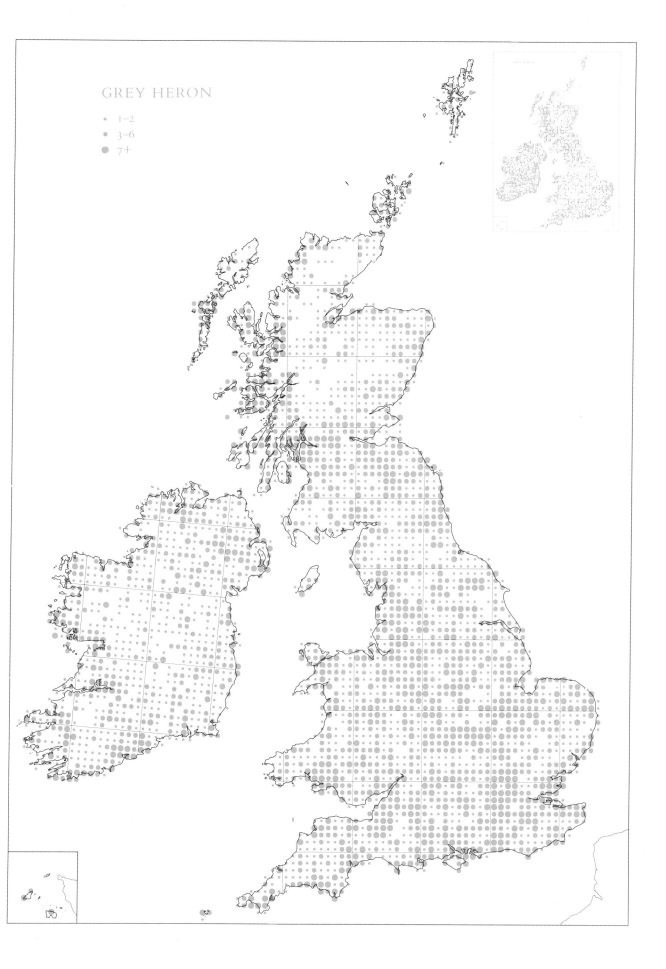

GREY HERON

- · 1–2
- ● 3–6
- ● 7+

Mute Swan

Cygnus olor

Britain's largest bird, adult males can weigh over 15 kg, the Mute Swan is also one of the most familiar. Many pairs and flocks live in city parks and on rivers in town centres and this close proximity to man, coupled with the bird's size and elegance, have given it a special place in the public affection. The relationship is not without conflict, however, with lead poisoning from anglers' weights an extremely serious problem over much of lowland Britain and, on the other side of the coin, alleged damage to riverside farmland by feeding flocks.

The Mute Swan is resident almost throughout Britain and Ireland, avoiding only the higher ground, over about 300 m, and areas lacking any fertile fresh water. Concentrations occur in many lowland river basins, but numbers have been much reduced in recent years in some areas (see below). The species is also especially numerous in the Uists and Benbecula, and well established in Orkney. Most flocks are fairly small, few exceeding 100, the largest, at 500–1,000, being on The Fleet, Dorset.

Breeding and winter distributions are almost identical. Many breeding pairs remain on their territories throughout the year, while immature and non-breeding birds join flocks in highly traditional sites. Severe weather has produced a few records of birds moving into SE England from the near Continent. Except for the most acid or very large, deep, lakes almost all types of water are utilised, including estuaries and coastal lagoons. Natural foods are predominantly submerged aquatic plants, notably *Myriophyllum*, *Potamogeton* and *Chara*, while in brackish and salt water habitats, *Zostera*, *Ruppia* and various green algae form the bulk of the diet. Long association with man has led to many birds becoming more or less dependent upon artificial food supplies, including bread provided by the general public in towns and cities, and grain coming from brewery and distillery outfalls. In a few areas, nearly all in southern England, farmers have complained of agricultural damage, mainly to grass and winter wheat fields lying adjacent to rivers.

Extensive ringing of Mute Swans has revealed mostly short distance movements, tending to follow valleys and watercourses. Some longer movements do occur, mainly associated with the summer moult.

Countrywide censuses of the Mute Swan have been carried out in Britain 1955/56, and including Ireland in 1978 and 1983. At the time of the 1955/56 census the population numbered around 21,000 birds and appeared to be increasing quite rapidly. There was a sharp decline in the early 1960s, brought about by severe winters, followed by a steady recovery. From the late 1960s, however, there was a slow decline overall, but a very marked one in a number of river systems, notably the Warwickshire Avon, the Thames and the Trent. This was eventually identified as being due to poisoning of the swans through ingestion of lead fishing weights (NCC 1981). Subsequent research has confirmed the extent and scale of the poisoning, which is widespread wherever coarse fishing occurs in Britain and Ireland (J. O'Halloran), with an estimated 3,000–4,000 birds dying per annum.

The 1978 census carried out in April/May put the population at around 18,000 birds, while by spring 1983 it had risen slightly to about 19,000 (Ogilvie in press). This means that the winter population is likely to be just under 20,000. The detailed figures have revealed catastrophic declines in some areas, for example from over 1,000 to less than 100 on the Lower Thames in 20 years, being balanced by increases elsewhere, especially in the fly-fishing regions of the country. Substitutes for lead are currently being tested, and it is hoped that lead will be banned by law by the end of 1986.

M. A. OGILVIE

Total number of squares in which recorded: 2,238 (58%)

No. of birds seen in a day	Number (%) of squares		TOTAL (incl. C.I.)
	Britain	Ireland	
1–7	775 (49%)	350 (53%)	1,126 (50%)
8–23	479 (30%)	184 (28%)	663 (29%)
24+	323 (21%)	126 (19%)	449 (20%)

References

ATKINSON-WILLES, G. L. 1981. The numerical distribution and the conservation requirements of swans in northwest Europe. *Proc. 2nd Int. Swan Symp. Sapporo, Japan, 1980*: 40–48. IWRB, Slimbridge.

CAMPBELL, B. 1960. The Mute Swan census in England and Wales, 1955–56. *Bird Study* 7: 208–223.

NCC. 1981. *Lead Poisoning in Swans*. Report of the Nature Conservancy Council's Working Group.

OGILVIE, M. A. 1981. The Mute Swan in Britain, 1978. *Bird Study* 28: 87–106.

OGILVIE, M. A. (in press). The Mute Swan in Britain, 1983. *Bird Study* 33:

RAWCLIFFE, C. P. 1958. The Scottish Mute Swan census 1955–56. *Bird Study* 5: 45–55.

Breeding Atlas p 102

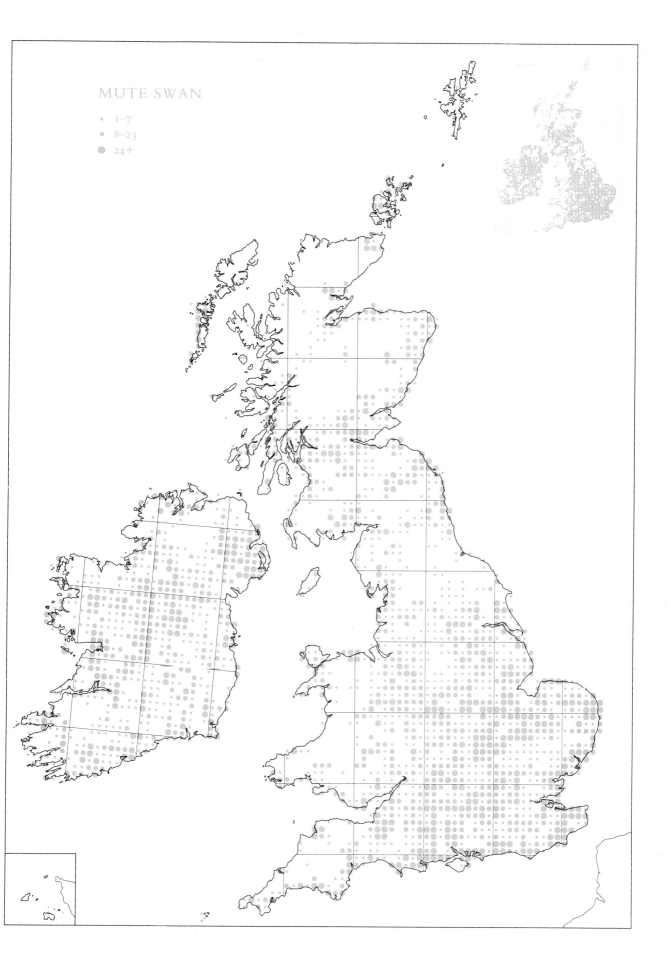

MUTE SWAN

- 1–7
- 8–23
- 24+

Bewick's Swan

Cygnus columbianus bewickii

Bewick's Swan, the smallest and daintiest of our three swans, was separated from the Whooper Swan *C. cygnus* as recently as 1830. There are unsurpassed opportunities for observing Bewick's Swans at close range at Wildfowl Trust establishments at the Ouse Washes and Slimbridge, where large numbers now occur, often in company with the Whooper Swans and Mute Swans *C. olor.*

Bewick's Swans are entirely winter visitors to W Europe. Their distribution in Britain and Ireland during the three *Winter Atlas* years accords well with that established by surveys and censuses organised by the Wildfowl Trust, the International Waterfowl Research Bureau, the Forest and Wildlife Service in Ireland, and the Dutch Bewick's Swan project. Clusters of 10-km squares with 30+ birds show the main haunts established in recent years. In Ireland the three main sites appear on the map, as do the scattered flocks elsewhere. In Wales the only sizeable numbers are on Anglesey. In Scotland, before the 1930s, the species was common. There are generally less than 100 birds now but they have increased recently. There are no records for the Isle of Man.

Traditionally, Bewick's Swans have shown a preference for natural wetland habitats, mainly shallow fresh water lakes and ponds and slow-moving rivers adjacent to extensive grasslands liable to flooding. In Ireland they feed on permanent grassland and, in the past, brackish coastal lagoons appear to have been a favourite haunt (Kennedy *et al* 1954), but these were superseded by flood meadows (callows) and turloughs (temporary winter floods in grassy limestone depressions). Since the early 1970s Bewick's Swans have increasingly taken to foraging also on waste root crops, grain stubbles, and winter cereals.

Bewick's Swans are gregarious outside the breeding season, often occurring in flocks of several hundred, sometimes over 1,000. They mix freely with other swans. Normally they feed by day and roost on water at night. The cygnets accompany their parents during the first winter and often in the second winter too, even if their parents have a new brood.

The increase in numbers wintering at the Ouse Washes, East Anglia, has been spectacular. From a handful in the 1940s the flock grew steadily and topped 1,000 for the first time in 1971. The increase was maintained through the 1970s and 1980s, with the all-time peak so far of 5,227 in February 1985. The Washes are now the most important site in the whole range. The reasons for the increase are thought to be the increased protection given by the RSPB and Wildfowl Trust refuges, and the recent trend to using the abundant food supply on nearby farmland.

The European wintering population of Bewick's Swans is centred on the Netherlands, Britain and Ireland, with small numbers occurring in Denmark, N Germany, Belgium and NW France. A small flock also occurs in S France in the Camargue. The breeding range of this population extends eastwards across the Eurasian tundra from 48°–180°E, with a small outlying western population on the Norwegian/Russian border. Somewhere along this extensive range there is a migratory divide, birds from the eastern part migrating to China, Korea and Japan. The migration to W Europe takes place mainly along the south shore of the Baltic.

Numbers in the past are not very well known, but it is suggested that England saw an increase from a few hundred in the 1950s to over 1,500 by 1970, while over the same period there was a decrease in Ireland from 1,500 to 700–1,000 (Ogilvie 1972). However, there were over 2,000 in Ireland in 1975/76 (Merne 1977) and numbers in Britain increased to probably over 5,000 in 1982/83 (Salmon 1983). A full European census in 1983/84 showed Britain and Ireland to hold 16,000–16,500 birds in winter. Some of the increase is probably due to better coverage and counting.

O. J. MERNE

Total number of squares in which recorded: 581 (15%)

No. of birds seen in a day	Number (%) of squares		
	Britain	Ireland	TOTAL (incl. C.I.)
1–8	222 (53%)	78 (50%)	301 (52%)
9–29	126 (30%)	37 (24%)	163 (28%)
30+	75 (18%)	42 (27%)	117 (20%)

References

BEEKMAN, J.H., S. DIRKSEN and T. H. SLAGBOOM. 1985. Population size and breeding success of Bewick's Swans wintering in Europe in 1983–84. *Wildfowl* 36: 5–12.

KENNEDY, P. G., R. F. RUTTLEDGE and C. S. SCROOPE. 1954. *Birds of Ireland.* Oliver & Boyd, Edinburgh.

MERNE, O. J. 1977. The changing status and distribution of the Bewick's Swan in Ireland. *Irish Birds* 1: 3–15.

OGILVIE, M. A. 1972. Distribution, numbers and migration. In SCOTT, P. and the WILDFOWL TRUST. *The Swans.* Michael Joseph, London.

SALMON, D. G. 1983. *Wildfowl and Wader Counts 1982–1983.* The Wildfowl Trust, Slimbridge.

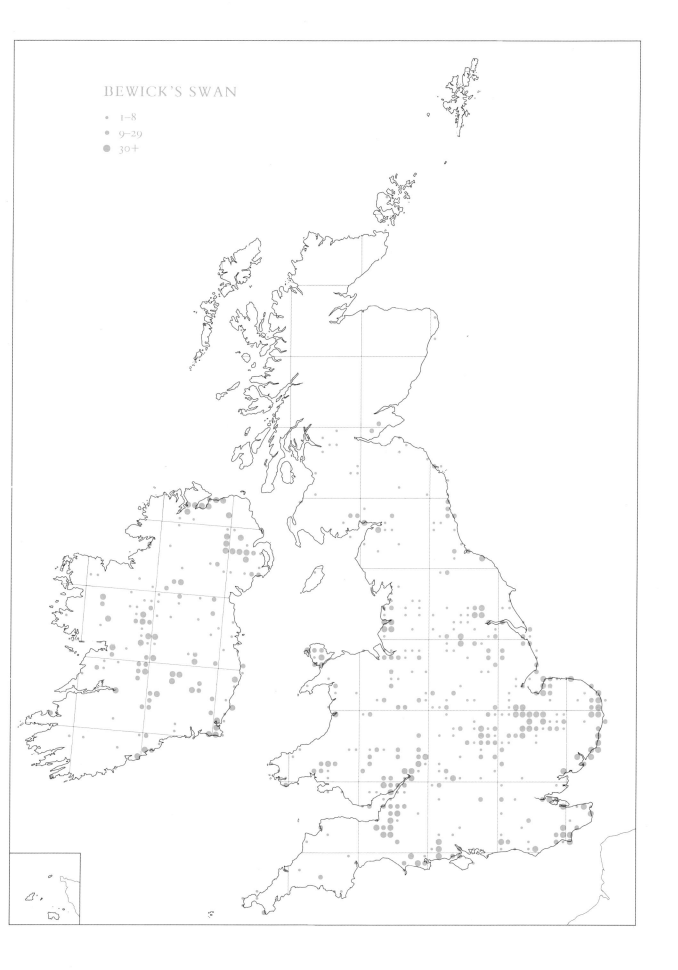

BEWICK'S SWAN

- • 1–8
- • 9–29
- ● 30+

Whooper Swan

Cygnus cygnus

Of the two migratory swans which occur in Britain and Ireland in winter the Whooper Swan is the larger, more majestic, more widespread and better known. It is also here for a longer stay, usually from mid October to mid April. Its distinctive loud 'whooping' calls are evocative of wetlands in winter.

The winter distribution of Whooper Swans in Britain is predominantly a northern one with the great majority of birds occurring north of a line from the Wirral to the Humber. South of this line most of the flocks are small (under 30) with the exception of Anglesey and the Ouse Washes. At the latter, numbers have increased to 223 in recent years (Salmon 1983). The Norfolk Broads, the Kent marshes and the Hampshire Avon also hold higher than average numbers for southern Britain. In Ireland most Whooper Swans winter in the west and north, but there are quite sizeable flocks in the east and south, notably in Wexford where occasionally over 100 occur.

The range of habitats used by Whooper Swans is wider than that of Bewick's Swans as it includes quite small lochs and ponds, often more oligotrophic than those used by Bewick's Swans, and at higher altitudes. They eat a variety of emergent and submergent water plants, and on land they will graze grass and winter cereals. Occasionally they will forage for grass in stubbles and will nibble at waste sugar beet and potatoes. Whooper Swans also feed regularly on intertidal mudflats where eel grass is a favourite food. In Scotland they feed predominantly on farmland. Although occurring occasionally in herds of over 1,000 in a few places, Whooper Swans are usually seen in smaller groups or family parties. The total population in Britain and Ireland is perhaps twice as large as that of Bewick's Swan so the greater number of positive 10-km squares for the Whooper Swan indicates many very small flocks.

Whooper Swans bred in Orkney in the 18th century but less than half a dozen cases of wild birds breeding in Britain are known from this century, though a few birds usually summer in Scotland including some feral breeders at Loch Lomond (*Breeding Atlas*).

Most Whooper Swans wintering in northern Britain and Ireland are probably from the Icelandic breeding population. Of the 45 Whooper Swans ringed on the breeding grounds and recovered here, 44 originated in Iceland and one in Sweden (Spencer and Hudson 1982). In southern Britain they may come from the Continent. There is evidence of winter movement within Britain and Ireland as, for example, when Whooper Swans colour marked on the Solway Firth in Dumfriesshire in November were resighted 280 km southwest on the Wicklow coast later that winter.

Our Whooper Swan population has never been fully censused, but Boyd and Eltringham (1962) recorded about 2,000 in Ireland, about 2,000 in Scotland and about 500 in England and Wales, and estimated the total population to be 5,000–6,000. The Icelandic population has been estimated recently at 10,000–11,000 birds (Gardarsson and Skarphedinsson 1984) and, as only about 800 of these are thought to winter there, the British and Irish wintering population may be much higher than indicated above. At some of the main sites there have been fluctuations in recent years. In 1982 there were marked increases in Shetland, Aberdeenshire and the Ouse Washes, but these may be due to better counting (Salmon 1983).

Besides the Icelandic/British and Irish population Whooper Swans occur right across Eurasia, occupying in the breeding season the taiga zones south of where Bewick's Swans nest. There are about 500 birds in Sweden, of which only a small proportion breed, while in Finland about 80 pairs breed out of a total of about 500 birds. The wintering population in NW Europe (excluding Britain and Ireland) numbers about 14,000 birds, mainly in the Baltic except in severe winters when there is a southerly movement. At least 25,000 winter in the Black and Caspian Seas area (Atkinson-Willes 1981), and 400 have been recorded recently in Greece (Ogilvie 1972).

O. J. MERNE

Total number of squares in which recorded: 1,304 (34%)

No. of birds seen in a day	Number (%) of squares		
	Britain	Ireland	TOTAL (incl. C.I.)
1–9	476 (56%)	177 (39%)	653 (50%)
10–32	248 (29%)	143 (31%)	398 (30%)
33+	125 (15%)	135 (30%)	265 (20%)

References

ATKINSON-WILLES, G. L. 1981. The numerical distribution and the conservation requirements of swans in northwest Europe. *Proc. 2nd Int. Swan Symp. Sapporo, Japan, 1980*: 40–48. IWRB, Slimbridge.

BOYD, H. and S. K. ELTRINGHAM. 1962. The Whooper Swan in Great Britain. *Bird Study* 9: 217–241.

GARDARSSON, A. and K. H. SKARPHEDINSSON. 1984. A census of the Icelandic Whooper Swan population. *Wildfowl* 35: 37–47.

OGILVIE, M. A. 1972. Distribution, numbers and migration. In SCOTT, P. and the WILDFOWL TRUST. *The Swans*. Michael Joseph, London.

SALMON, D. G. (ed.). 1983. *Wildfowl and Wader Counts 1982–1983*. The Wildfowl Trust, Slimbridge.

SPENCER, R. and R. HUDSON. 1982. Report on bird ringing for 1981. *Ringing and Migration* 4: 65–128.

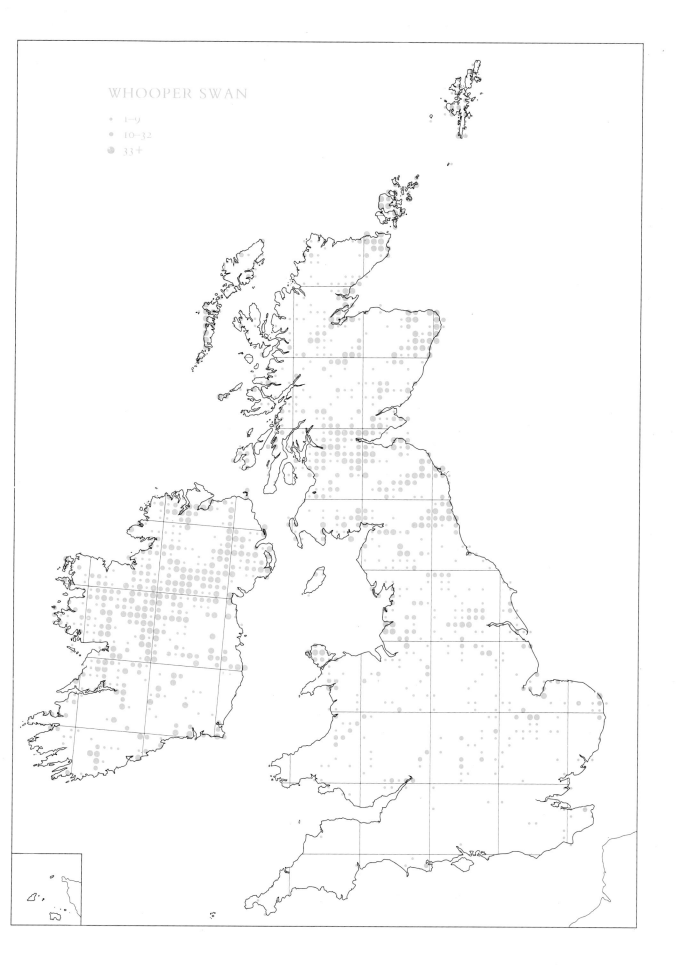

WHOOPER SWAN

- • 1—9
- • 10—32
- • 33+

Bean Goose

Anser fabalis

The status of the Bean Goose has changed considerably in Britain over the last 100 years. In 1886 this species was stated to be 'the common grey goose of the Solway' (Gladstone 1910) and it appears to have been quite numerous in Scotland and N England at that time. Nowadays it is almost a rarity, with only two or three hundred regularly wintering.

Their stronghold now, such as it is, has moved to East Anglia, and especially Norfolk. A flock which inhabits the marshes of the River Yare, between Norwich and Great Yarmouth, has been regular for many years. Numbers have fluctuated, sometimes less than 100 but now reaching 150–200 in mid winter. In February 1982, after a hard-weather influx, there were 329 birds. Elsewhere in Norfolk, especially on the north coast, and on the coastal fringes of Suffolk the Bean Goose appears to be becoming an annual winter visitor in low numbers. Small flocks are regularly recorded on a number of coastal marshes and as many as 120 were seen at one locality in January 1982 (Moore 1983). Similarly the map shows that other parties were recorded along the North Sea coasts of Essex and Kent. However, the winter of 1981/82 was quite severe and more geese than usual appear to have crossed the North Sea to SE England from the Netherlands, where large numbers of Bean Geese winter.

Bean Geese also winter in SW Scotland, in the valley of the River Dee, in Dumfries and Galloway and in the Carron valley. In the 1950s up to 200 were seen in the Dee valley annually, but now their numbers are down to 30–40 per winter (A. D. Watson). In October 1981, there was an influx into N Scotland, and one party of 25 spent the winter on the Black Isle, near Inverness. However, these birds did not re-appear in the two subsequent winters (R. H. Dennis). A few Bean Geese are also seen in some winters in the Severn valley in Gloucestershire, and in Northumberland. No Bean Geese regularly winter in Ireland but small parties occasionally reach there.

The small flocks which have wintered in Britain have shown considerable attachment to quite small areas. Both the Yare and Dee valley flocks have consistently grazed on the same marshes and rough pasture and have used traditional roosts nearby on lakes and rivers. Their winter food consists of a wide range of grasses, clover and cereal grains gleaned from stubble fields and other agricultural crops (*BWP*).

There has been debate as to whether the birds wintering in Britain are a separate population but Ogilvie (1978) considered it probable that they are part of the large group wintering on the other side of the North Sea, principally in Denmark, N Germany and the Netherlands. The British birds probably come from the nearest breeding stock, which is in the northern half of Scandinavia, and a bird ringed in Swedish Lapland was recovered in England in January. In the Carron Valley and Norfolk, birds arrive in November and December, whereas the Galloway flock is sometimes not seen until the New Year. This suggests secondary movement from another wintering area, possibly Denmark (*BWP*). By early March the birds have all returned east.

Between 200 and 300 Bean Geese currently winter in Britain but in a severe winter up to double this number may cross the North Sea. There were over 400 in Norfolk during a cold spell in January and February 1979 (Seago 1980).

The Bean Goose breeds right across the northern part of Europe and Asia, from Norway to the Bering Sea, with a population believed to number at least 250,000. The few wintering in Britain are therefore a tiny fraction of the world population.

MALCOLM WRIGHT

Total number of squares in which recorded: 130 (3%)

No. of birds seen in a day	Number (%) of squares		TOTAL (incl. C.I.)
	Britain	Ireland	
1–3	59 (49%)	2 (22%)	61 (47%)
4–14	39 (32%)	4 (44%)	43 (33%)
15+	23 (19%)	3 (33%)	26 (20%)

References

GLADSTONE, H. 1910. *The Birds of Dumfriesshire*. Witherby, London.

MOORE, D. R. 1983. *Suffolk Birds 1982*. Suffolk Naturalists' Society, Ipswich.

OGILVIE, M. A. 1978. *Wild Geese*. Poyser, Berkhamsted.

SEAGO, M. J. 1980. *Norfolk Bird Report 1979*. Norfolk Naturalists Trust and Norfolk and Norwich Naturalists Society, Norwich.

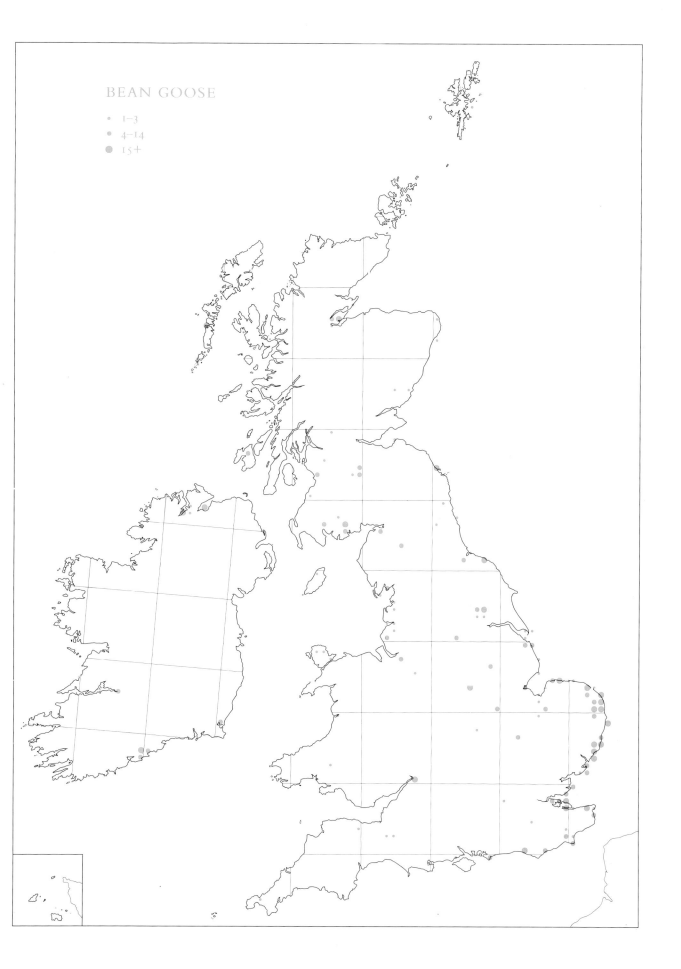

BEAN GOOSE

• 1–3
• 4–14
● 15+

Pink-footed Goose

Anser brachyrhynchus

Large flocks of Pink-footed Geese with their wild, musical cries are a familiar winter sight in E and S Scotland and a few parts of England. To see them at their best one must rise early and watch the great skeins flighting off a large estuary, such as the Tay or Solway, on a frozen, sunlit dawn.

Up to three-quarters of the wintering Pink-footed Geese are found in Scotland. The map shows that their distribution there coincides closely with the areas of lowland farmland, where barley stubbles, potato fields, winter sown cereals and pasture provide them with their winter food. There are strongholds in Aberdeenshire, Perthshire, Kinross, Stirlingshire and the Lothians, and in late winter the Scottish shore of the Solway is an important site. Three areas of England regularly attract Pink-footed Geese, the most important being the coastal belt of Lancashire, especially near the Ribble estuary where numbers have increased dramatically, from 5,000 in the 1960s to 25,000 in some recent years. The low-lying farmland around the Wash and along the N Norfolk coast is once again attracting sizeable flocks of 5,000 or more, but the Humber estuary, formerly a major haunt, now rarely sees more than a few hundred. In the southern half of England and in Wales the Pink-footed Goose is simply a straggler, and some of the records may be due to escapes from wildfowl collections. In Ireland Pink-footed Geese are rare, with only a few wintering regularly on the Wexford Slobs.

Like most of its tribe, the Pink-footed Goose is invariably gregarious outside the breeding season, being found in flocks from a few dozen to several thousand birds strong. Formerly these flocks roosted mainly on the mud flats and sandbanks of estuaries but they have now taken to roosting more on inland fresh water lochs and reservoirs, although some estuaries still have important roosts. This change has probably been a response to shooting pressure. At dawn they flight, usually flying only a few kilometres but sometimes 20 km or more, to feed on farmland and, on the coast, salt marshes. There is a recent trend in some areas to plough in barley stubbles in August–September and resow with barley, winter wheat or oilseed rape before the geese arrive, and this is affecting distribution. The Pink-footed Goose has benefitted from the recent trend to larger farm fields, preferring as it does to feed in as large and open a space as possible.

All the birds which winter in Britain breed in Iceland and E Greenland. The great majority come from Iceland, where more than 10,000 pairs nest in the principal breeding colony of Thjorsarver. East Greenland holds perhaps 1,000 pairs. The geese arrive into E Scotland from mid to late September and there is a gradual movement south through the winter period as food supplies are used up, although Lancashire receives large numbers from October onwards. On occasions, hard weather can force some quite spectacular movements. In February 1982 there were nearly 34,000 in Lancashire. In January 1984 a heavy snowfall made many birds move out of E and SE Scotland and produced a huge influx of at least 25,000 onto the Scottish shore of the inner Solway Firth. Some of these moved on further south within a few days.

The Pink-footed Goose population has been closely monitored by a series of regular winter counts organised by the Wildfowl Trust for the past 35 years. The first census in 1950/51 revealed a total of 30,000 birds and their numbers have increased steadily, to reach 101,000 in November 1983 for Britain and Ireland. The increase has been attributed to more favourable conditions in Britain in winter, where farming changes have led to an increased food supply, especially in E Scotland, and because refuges have been established on many of the more important roosts.

The only other population of Pink-footed Geese breeds in the Svalbard archipelago and winters in the Netherlands. This population currently numbers about 28,000 birds. Thus Britain holds more than 75% of the world's wintering Pink-footed Geese.

MALCOLM WRIGHT

Total number of squares in which recorded: 529 (14%)

No. of birds seen in a day	Number (%) of squares		TOTAL (incl. C.I.)
	Britain	Ireland	
1–23	248 (48%)	13 (100%)	261 (49%)
24–500	161 (31%)	0 (0%)	161 (30%)
501+	107 (21%)	0 (0%)	107 (20%)

References

OGILVIE, M. A. 1978. *Wild Geese*. Poyser, Berkhamsted.

OGILVIE, M. A. 1984 *Greylag and Pink-footed Geese in Britain, November 1983*. The Wildfowl Trust, Slimbridge.

OWEN, M. 1977. *Wildfowl of Europe*. Macmillan, London.

NEWTON, I., V. M. THOM and W. BROTHERSTON. 1973. Behaviour and distribution of wild geese in south-east Scotland. *Wildfowl* 24: 111–121.

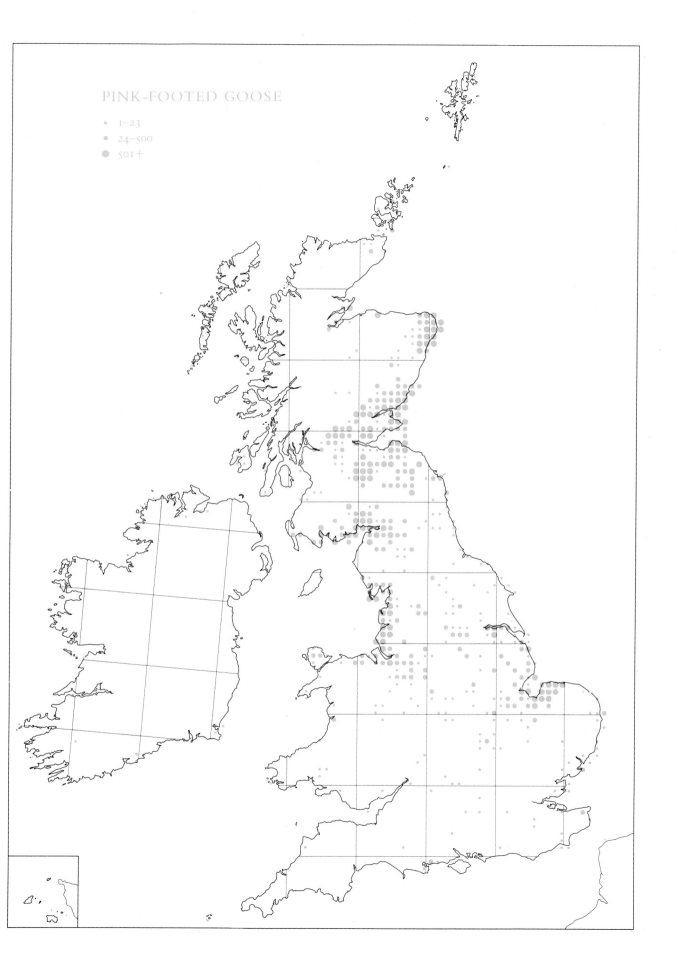

PINK-FOOTED GOOSE

- •   1–23
- •   24–500
- •   501+

White-fronted Goose

Anser albifrons

Two quite distinct subspecies of White-fronted Goose winter in Britain and Ireland, the dark plumaged, orange billed Greenland White-fronted *A. a. flavirostris*, and the paler, pink billed European White-fronted *A. a. albifrons*. The winter map does not separate these populations but *flavirostris* is confined to Ireland, W and N Scotland, and a couple of areas in Wales, while *albifrons* is found in southern England and S Wales. There is virtually no overlap.

The Greenland White-fronted Goose has been the subject of intensive study in recent years, and much is known about its current status and distribution. The map reflects well the overall distribution of Greenland birds and highlights the areas of main concentration. Some 6,000–7,000 spend the winter on the Wexford Slobs: all the other positive Irish squares account for only half that number. The Co. Mayo numbers are probably under-represented on the map. In Scotland, there are over 4,000 on the island of Islay, Inner Hebrides.

The concentration of European White-fronted Geese in the Slimbridge (Gloucestershire) area is clearly indicated, but that of the Swale (Kent) is somewhat obscured by the numerous surrounding records, many of which are probably due to flocks passing through on migration. Probably for this reason, too, the map gives the impression of far larger numbers along the east and south coasts of England than actually occur regularly, a problem with a species whose main arrival and departure times fall within the *Winter Atlas* survey period, and one that is subject to hard weather movements as in 1981/82.

In Ireland, the Wexford Slobs Greenland White-fronted Geese feed on polderland—on improved grassland, stubbles and winter cereals, and potatoes and sugarbeet when available. Elsewhere in Ireland the birds use a variety of habitats including raised and blanket bogs, callows and turloughs, machair, salt marsh, and farmland. There is an increasing tendency to move to improved grasslands. On Islay, the main Scottish haunt of the Greenland White-fronted Goose, the birds also feed on grassland—both *Juncus* infested and improved—and on arable farmland. The European White-fronted Geese feed almost exclusively on grasslands (Owen 1977). They prefer low-lying wet pastures (under constant threat of drainage) bordering coastal marshes or along river valleys. They are much more gregarious than the Greenland birds, often occurring in close flocks of hundreds or even thousands, whereas the Greenland birds spread out. On the Wexford Slobs where the 6,000–7,000 Greenland geese exploit some 2,000 ha of land they split up into 80 or 100 individual flocks.

Greenland White-fronted Geese reach their wintering grounds in October and stay until mid or late April. During this time population levels are usually very constant at most sites, though some wandering within site complexes occurs. In Ireland a colour marking programme is helping to determine the extent of these movements. First arrivals of European White-fronted Geese take place in early October, but relatively few come before December. They leave Britain in March.

The tundra fringe of W Greenland is the breeding area of the Greenland White-fronted Goose. The European birds come from the tundra belt of Eurasia east of 45°E. The number of Greenland birds in Britain and Ireland is currently 16,000–17,000 (Ruttledge and Ogilvie 1979, D. Stroud, J. Wilson, D. Norriss), about 9,000 of which winter in Ireland and 7,200–7,300 in Britain, mainly Scotland (Stroud 1984). The numbers of European White-fronted Geese reaching Britain vary from winter to winter. A high level of about 7,000 was recorded in 1981/82 due to severe weather on the Continent (Ogilvie 1982), while in 1982/83 peak counts at the main sites totalled about 5,500 birds (Salmon 1983). However, up to 13,000 have been recorded in the past—in 1969/70 (Ogilvie 1978).

Britain and Ireland are the wintering grounds for the entire Greenland population, but England and Wales receive only a small fraction of the NW European wintering population which has risen to over 200,000 birds.

O. J. MERNE

Total number of squares in which recorded: 497 (13%)

No. of birds seen in a day	Number (%) of squares		
	Britain	Ireland	TOTAL (incl. C.I.)
1–12	211 (56%)	36 (31%)	248 (50%)
13–64	101 (26%)	48 (42%)	149 (30%)
65+	69 (18%)	31 (27%)	100 (20%)

References

OGILVIE, M. A. 1978. *Wild Geese*. Poyser, Berkhamsted.

OGILVIE, M. A. 1982. Numbers of geese in Britain and Ireland, 1981–1982. *Wildfowl* 33: 172.

OWEN, M. 1977. *Wildfowl of Europe*. Macmillan, London.

RUTTLEDGE, R. F. and M. A. OGILVIE. 1979. The past and present status of the Greenland White-fronted Goose in Ireland and Britain. *Irish Birds* 1: 293.

SALMON, D. G. (ed.). 1983. *Wildfowl and Wader Counts, 1982–1983*. The Wildfowl Trust, Slimbridge.

STROUD, D. A. 1984. Status of Greenland White-fronted Geese in Britain, 1982/83. *Bird Study* 31: 111–116.

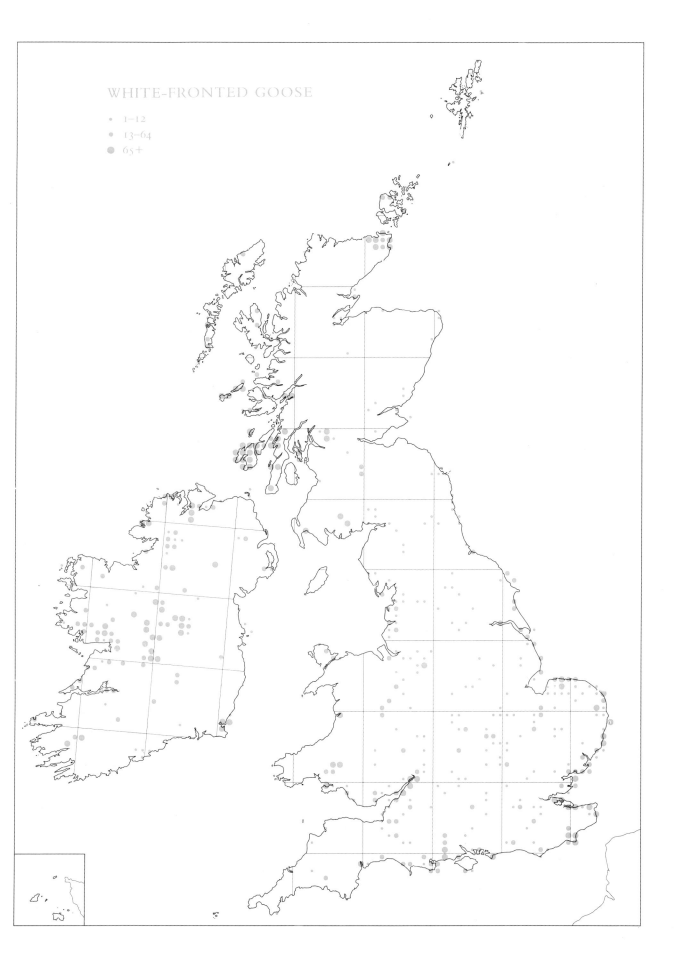

WHITE-FRONTED GOOSE

- • 1–12
- • 13–64
- ● 65+

Greylag Goose

Anser anser

The Greylag Goose is for many people *the* wild goose, our only native breeding goose, and the ancestor of most domestic breeds. It is also the largest of our geese and a large male can weigh as much as 4 kg.

All the Greylags which breed in Iceland come to winter in Britain and Ireland, most of them to Scotland, where the main concentrations are found in the Moray Firth area, Aberdeenshire, the central Southern Uplands, and SW Scotland. South of a line from the Isle of Man to Teesmouth, all the birds are of feral origin, introduced in the last 20 years. The largest feral group, however, established in the early 1930s from Hebrides stock, is in SW Scotland. This numbered over 1,100 in 1971 and is probably larger today. The truly native stock is restricted to the Outer Hebrides, chiefly on South Uist, and the adjacent mainland. Numbers have increased considerably recently, probably reaching 2,000 in 1982. The geese are largely resident, though a few may move to other parts of Scotland or to Ireland, where there has been a clear increase in the last 5 years, with regular wintering flocks in several places. Most of the other Irish records are of feral birds or irregular sightings of wild flocks.

Greylags used to concentrate on British estuaries, eating roots of rushes and sedges, as they do in other parts of their range. In recent times they have moved almost exclusively onto farmland, where they feed on waste grain in the autumn, later moving to potatoes and sometimes swede turnips. Grass forms a substantial proportion of their diet at all times of year and they prefer the young, nutritious leys to permanent or semi-natural pastures. Much less mobile and gregarious than Pink-footed Geese *A. brachyrhynchus,* which are often found in the same areas, Greylags feed within a few kilometres of their roost and gather in flocks of from less than a hundred to a few thousand birds. They often come close to human habitation and are fearless of farm stock; they have been known to feed from troughs or take cut turnips put out for cattle. They roost on estuaries, lakes or even river islands or spits, and their adoption of reservoirs as roosts has enabled them to capitalise on inland farmland in central Scotland.

The movements of Greylags during winter are largely governed by the availability of food. In general most movements are southwards in autumn. Weather is rarely severe enough to cause long distance movements; Greylags will 'sit out' short cold spells, gathering what food they can by grubbing in the snow or browsing on brassicas such as rape or kale. There is a gradual northerly movement before the migrants leave for Iceland in April. Feral flocks show only very local movements throughout the year.

Icelandic Greylags are censused by the Wildfowl Trust each autumn in early November, after all have arrived from the breeding grounds. Numbers in Britain and Ireland have increased markedly since the first census, in 1960, accounted for 26,500 birds. In the 1970s, an average of 65,000 were counted and numbers continued to rise to more than 100,000 in 1984. With annual mortality relatively constant at just over 10%, breeding success largely determines the size of the autumn populations. Relative success has declined as overall numbers have increased; nowadays the proportion of young in autumn flocks rarely exceeds 25% whereas in the 1950s and 1960s it was larger in most years.

The British/Icelandic population is one of several in NW Europe, though most are not as discrete. A population of mixed Scandinavian and central European origin numbers over 100,000 and winters mainly in Spain. Greylag Geese from eastern Europe winter around the Mediterranean, chiefly in N Africa.

M. OWEN

Total number of squares in which recorded: 1,056 (27%)

No. of birds seen in a day	Number (%) of squares		
	Britain	Ireland	TOTAL (incl. C.I.)
1–29	470 (48%)	54 (65%)	525 (50%)
30–250	299 (31%)	21 (25%)	320 (30%)
251 +	203 (21%)	8 (10%)	211 (20%)

References

BOYD, H. and M. A. OGILVIE. 1972. Icelandic Greylag Geese wintering in Britain, 1960–71. *Wildfowl* 23 : 64–82.

NEWTON, I., V. M. THOM, and W. BROTHERSTON. 1973. Behaviour and distribution of wild geese in southeast Scotland. *Wildfowl* 24 : 111–121.

PICKUP, C. H. 1983. *A survey of Greylag Geese* Anser anser *in the Uists, 18 July–28 August 1982.* Unpubl. Rep., NCC.

YOUNG, J. G. 1973. Distribution, status and movements of feral Greylag Geese in southwest Scotland. *Scot. Birds* 7 : 170–182.

Breeding Atlas p 98

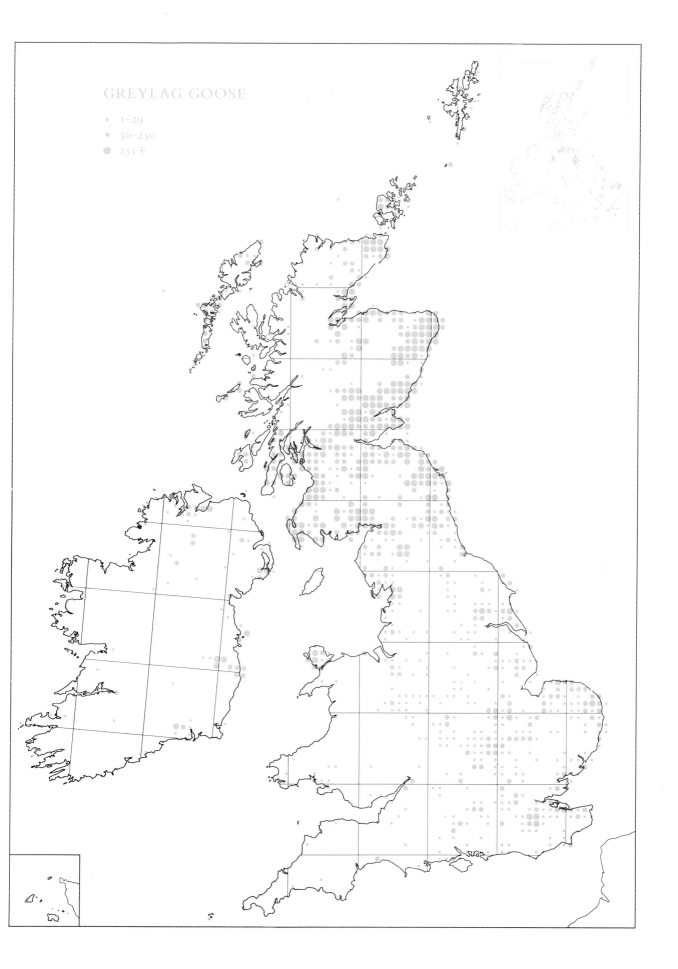

GREYLAG GOOSE

- 1–29
- 30–250
- 251+

Snow Goose

Anser caerulescens

The Snow Goose is only a vagrant to Britain, and even then the number of vagrants is uncertain due to the presence of many birds which have escaped from waterfowl collections and zoos.

It may be that some occurrences of this species in Britain and Ireland, and elsewhere in Europe, are of birds of genuine wild origin, having made a transatlantic crossing. The only positive record of recent years was in the Netherlands in April 1980, when a flock of 18 included a bird which had been ringed in Canada 3 years previously (Blankert 1980). The presence of individuals among flocks of Greenland White-fronted Geese *A. albifrons flavirostris* in Ireland and western Britain has often led to the supposition that these are more likely to be of wild origin than escapes, though the existence of a flock of full-winged Snow Geese, of both colour phases, on the island of Mull in the Inner Hebrides for the past several years does throw some doubt on the matter.

It is quite usual for occasional Snow Geese to be found among flocks of other species of geese, particularly Pink-footed Geese *A. brachyrhynchus* and Greylag Geese *A. anser* in their Scottish and N England wintering grounds, but records of lone birds or small groups account for most of the sightings in the southern half of Britain. There are a great many zoos and waterfowl collections containing full-winged Snow Geese, and as a species they are quite prone to wander. Those based at the Wildfowl Trust at Slimbridge have strayed as far as France during one spell of bad weather, and may also have accounted for sightings on the south coast and in the Thames estuary in recent winters, as well as at reservoirs and gravel pits in the southwest.

The majority of sightings refer to Lesser or Greater Snow Geese, probably indistinguishable to most birdwatchers unless, of course, the bird is of the blue phase of the Lesser. Sightings of the small Ross's Goose *A. rossii* have been made, including a pair (one of which had a colour ring), which lived with Greylag Geese in Scotland during three winters in the 1960s. Each summer they accompanied the Greylag Geese to Iceland, where they attempted to breed in at least two years, though unsuccessfully. There is no doubt about their captive origin, and this perfectly illustrates the problem of regarding any but clearly identifiable individuals, such as the Canadian-ringed bird, as other than escapes from captivity. The map suggests that, apart from the flock on Mull, up to 30 birds may be wandering around Britain each winter, with less than 5 in Ireland.

M. A. OGILVIE

Total number of squares in which recorded: 113 (3%)

No. of birds seen in a day	Number (%) of squares		
	Britain	Ireland	TOTAL (incl. C.I.)
1	62 (56%)	1 (50%)	63 (56%)
2–3	27 (24%)	1 (50%)	28 (25%)
4+	22 (20%)	0 (0%)	22 (19%)

References

BLANKERT, J. J. 1980. Lesser Snow Goose from Canada in Netherlands. *Dutch Birding* 2 : 52.

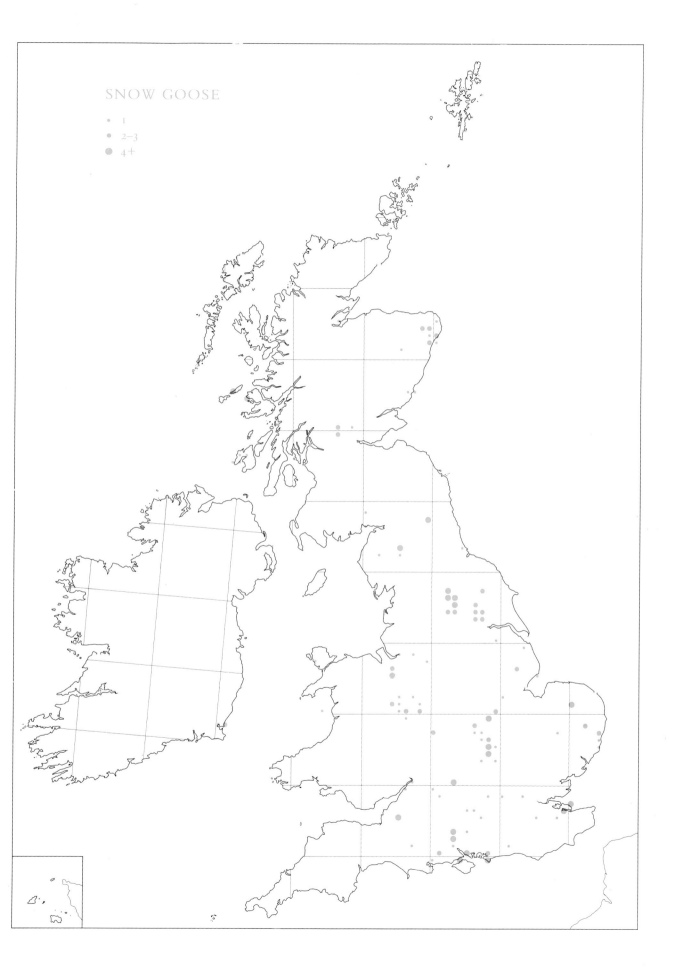

SNOW GOOSE

- 1
- 2–3
- 4+

Canada Goose

Branta canadensis

The Canada Goose was introduced into England about 300 years ago as an ornamental waterfowl. It maintained low numbers, and was relatively scarce away from parks and stately homes until the second world war. Since then, it has increased in numbers and spread through Britain, so that for many people this alien species is the most familiar 'wild' goose.

In Britain, the Canada Goose is very widespread and, during the survey, was recorded in 1,030 10-km squares. This compares with 680 squares in the *Breeding Atlas*. The difference is due largely to an increase in numbers and distribution, rather than a major dispersion away from the breeding sites in winter. Its distribution largely follows the preferred habitat of open standing water in lowlands, although the species is now colonizing upland areas in northern England and central Scotland. In northern Ireland the Canada Goose is confined to the two major localities of introduction. On the Wexford Slobs and on Islay a few apparently truly wild birds occur which include individuals of 'small' races, believed to be from North America. A few hybrids have also been seen.

White-Robinson (1984) has shown that Canada Geese are rather sedentary during late spring and summer, apart from those that undertake the well known moult migration from Yorkshire and the W midlands of England to the Beauly Firth in Scotland. During the winter months the birds become much more mobile, and in Nottinghamshire move freely from lakes to feed in pasture and fields of winter cereals. These may be several kilometres away from the roosts to which they flight back in the late afternoon or evening. In exceptionally hard weather, they may accumulate in substantial flocks in fields where they have easy access to food, such as sugar beet or cereal, and here they sometimes act as a focus for wild geese. Recoveries of British ringed birds overseas reveal that adverse weather may even force some birds out of the country into adjacent, more clement areas.

Estimation of the British population should be straightforward since the birds are large and relatively conspicuous, are frequently vocal, and gather in flocks on or close to open water. Furthermore, in most years there is relatively little movement in or out of Britain and Ireland, so that the population is effectively 'closed'. However, marked individuals have been observed feeding beside more than one lake during a single winter's day, before moving off to roost at yet another. Consequently, rapid counting of a series of lakes may produce dramatically lower but more accurate numbers of geese than a more leisurely survey over several days or weeks, so that any interpretation of numbers has to be made with caution. Adding the maximum counts for each square from *Winter Atlas* fieldwork the total comes to 65,000, but White-Robinson (1984) has shown for a series of 10-km squares in N Nottinghamshire that the maximum count at all known feeding and resting sites was 920 compared with the *Winter Atlas* estimate of 1,870 for the same squares. Since White-Robinson was fairly certain that the real figure was no more than 1,000 birds, this suggests that the *Winter Atlas* figure overestimated the local population by about 90%. Applying this correction to the national figures gives an estimated British population of about 34,000.

Surveys of Canada Geese in Britain and Ireland during the breeding season were undertaken in 1953, 1967, and 1976 (Ogilvie 1976). The results of these counts indicate that the population is growing by about 8.5% per year, a figure close to that estimated by Parkin and McMeeking (1985) for Nottinghamshire. Regular Wildfowl Trust count data, combined with these census results, led to an independent estimate of 30,000–35,000 birds during the winters of Atlas fieldwork (Owen *et al* 1986).

The majority of Europe's Canada Geese is to be found in Britain and Ireland, although there are in excess of 30,000 in Scandinavia (Fadricius 1983). The numbers in western Europe seem insignificant alongside the North American populations which are estimated to exceed 3 million birds (Bellrose 1976).

D. T. PARKIN

Total number of squares in which recorded: 1,030 (27%)

No. of birds seen in a day	Number (%) of squares		
	Britain	Ireland	TOTAL (incl. C.I.)
1–26	491 (49%)	23 (92%)	515 (50%)
27–121	307 (31%)	1 (4%)	308 (30%)
122+	206 (21%)	1 (4%)	207 (20%)

References

BELLROSE, F. C. 1976. *Ducks, Geese and Swans of North America.* Stackpole Books, Harrisburg, Pa.

FADRICIUS, E. 1983. *Kanadagasen i Sverige.* Statens naturvardsverk Nor 1678.

OGILVIE, M. A. 1976. The numbers of Canada geese in Britain, 1976. *Wildfowl* 28 : 27–34.

PARKIN, D. T. and J. M. MCMEEKING 1985. The increase of Canada Geese in Nottinghamshire from 1980. *Bird Study* 32 : 132–140.

WHITE-ROBINSON, R. G. 1984. *The Ecology of Canada Geese in Nottinghamshire, and their Importance to Agriculture.* Ph.D. Thesis, University of Nottingham.

Breeding Atlas p 100

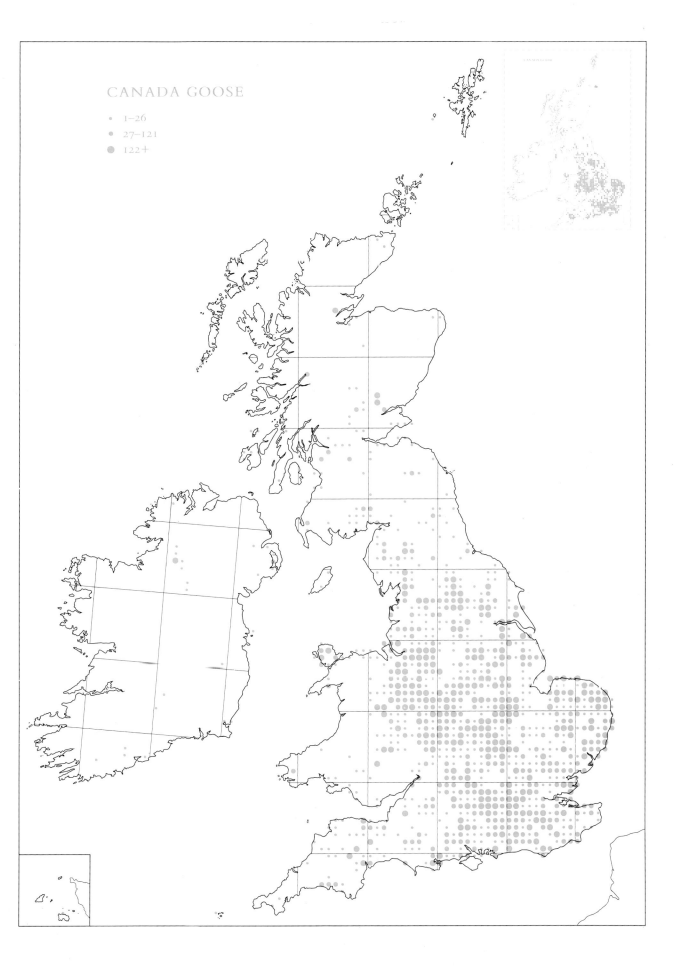

CANADA GOOSE

- 1–26
- 27–121
- 122+

Barnacle Goose

Branta leucopsis

The Barnacle Goose with its black, white and grey plumage is the most attractive of all the geese which winter in Britain and Ireland. The large flocks found on the Solway Firth and on Islay, among other places, provide a splendid wildlife spectacle.

The species is markedly coastal in its distribution, usually frequenting salt marshes or agricultural pastures within 5 km of the sea, and small grass-covered offshore islands, and there are scattered records elsewhere.

There are three separate breeding populations of Barnacle Geese in the world and two of these winter exclusively in Britain and Ireland, using quite different areas. Birds breeding on the eastern coast of Greenland winter on islands off the north and west coasts of Scotland, from the Outer Hebrides to their headquarters on Islay, and on islands off the north and west coasts of Ireland. Their main haunt in Ireland is the Inishkea Islands in Co. Mayo, where up to 2,500 occur. The records of small numbers on the east and south coasts of Ireland, and on Skomer Island off Wales, are probably of wanderers from this Greenland population.

A second, smaller population breeds in the Svalbard (Spitsbergen) group of islands, and these birds winter exclusively on the inner Solway Firth. Their principal stations there are the large area of merse and foreshore protected by the Caerlaverock National Nature Reserve, the adjoining farmland and the large salt marsh of Rockcliffe, in Cumbria.

The third population of Barnacle Geese nests on the islands of Novaya Zemlya and Vaygach, off the Siberian coast, and winters in Holland and West Germany. Small numbers of these birds occasionally cross the North Sea to SE England, especially in a severe winter such as that of 1981/82, and this probably accounts for most of the coastal records on the map between Lincolnshire and Hampshire. Barnacle Geese are commonly kept and bred in waterfowl collections and often escape. The majority of the records from the remainder of England and Wales doubtless arise from this source. Records from central and E Scotland and NE England are usually stragglers from the Spitsbergen population.

Barnacle Geese are very gregarious in their winter quarters, both on the roost and when feeding. At Caerlaverock the whole of the Spitsbergen population sometimes gathers in one flock. The Greenland birds, however, apart from those on Islay, are more scattered, with small flocks on remote, uninhabited islands. Except on the latter, the flocks roost at night in sheltered estuaries, on sandbanks and in sea lochs 1–2 km offshore, and at dawn they flight to nearby merses and pasture to feed. Their food consists of a wide range of natural and cultivated grasses, clover stolons, the seeds and leaves of salt marsh plants and spilt grain from the stubbles.

The Solway birds are resident from October to April and even the severest winters do not cause them to move. The Greenland birds also appear to be faithful to their chosen winter sites but there is some movement between various Scottish haunts and between Scotland and Ireland (*BWP*).

After declining seriously earlier this century all three populations have increased in the last 20 years. The Greenland birds totalled about 11,000 in the 1950s but by 1977/78 had increased to around 33,000. During the same period the numbers wintering on the main haunt, Islay, increased from 3,000 to 24,000 (Ogilvie 1978). More recently there has been some decrease, and in March 1983 there were only 25,000, with 14,000 on Islay. The decrease was due to more intensive shooting of the geese on Islay, to alleviate agricultural damage. Up to the 1930s several thousand Barnacle Geese wintered on the Solway, but by 1948/49 were reduced to under 400 birds, due to heavy shooting pressure and severe wartime disturbance. After being given legal protection throughout its range in the 1950s, and with its wintering grounds safeguarded, numbers have recovered. At the end of the *Winter Atlas* period (1983/84) there were 8,400, and a good breeding season in the following summer took this population to a record 10,500 (C. R. G. Campbell and M. Wright). The Siberian population increased from around 20,000 in the 1950s to 50,000 in 1975/76 and reached about 60,000 in 1983/84. Thus the world population of Barnacle Geese in 1983/84 was about 93,000 birds, of which 33,000 (35%) wintered in Britain and Ireland. Clearly this is a species for which we have an international responsibility.

MALCOLM WRIGHT

Total number of squares in which recorded: 489 (13%)

No. of birds seen in a day	Number (%) of squares		
	Britain	Ireland	TOTAL (incl. C.I.)
1–3	219 (52%)	18 (26%)	237 (48%)
4–31	136 (32%)	18 (26%)	154 (31%)
32 +	65 (16%)	32 (47%)	98 (20%)

References

OGILVIE, M. A. 1978. *Wild Geese*. Poyser, Berkhamsted.

OWEN, M. 1982. Population dynamics of Svalbard Barnacle Geese 1970–1980. *Aquila* 89: 229–247.

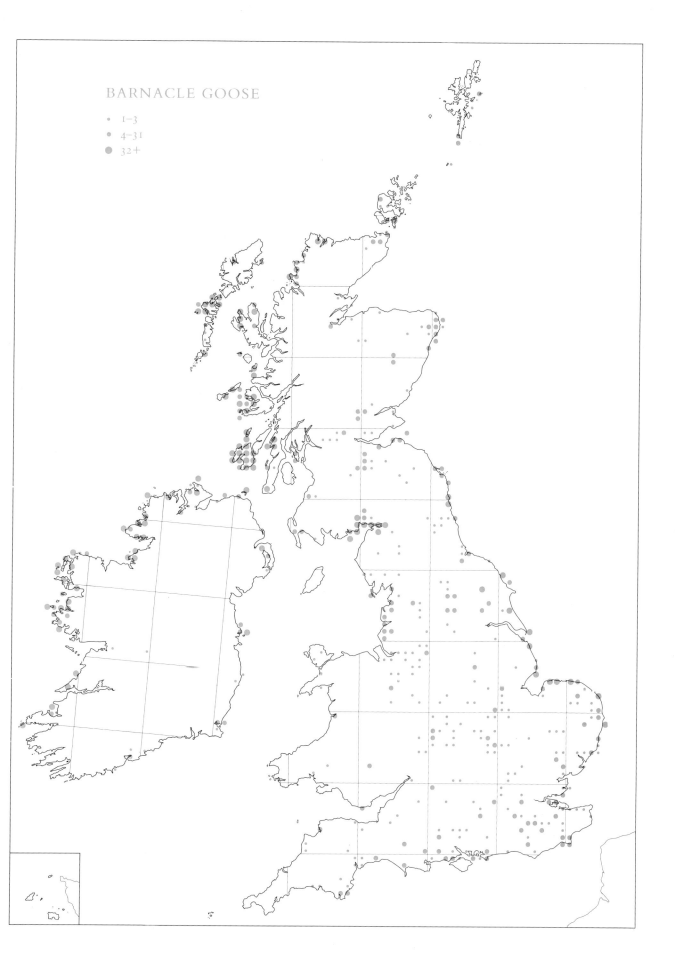

BARNACLE GOOSE

- 1–3
- 4–31
- 32+

Brent Goose

Branta bernicla

The Brent is the smallest of the wild geese wintering in Britain and its distinctive guttural call, increasing tameness and shoreline feeding habit make it an attractive winter visitor.

The distribution is obviously coastal with only a scatter of records from inland waters; indeed, in Ireland there are virtually no inland records at all. Large estuaries and areas of intertidal mudflat with fine sediments are preferred, and many of the gaps between major haunts, in NE and SW Ireland for example, relate to rocky and unsuitable shores where Brent Geese will stay only rarely on passage. NW Scotland is both largely unsuitable and away from major migration routes. The map does not distinguish between the two subspecies present and in fact the winter quarters of three distinct populations are shown here. The major concentrations of the Dark-bellied Brent Goose (*B. b. bernicla*) are in the estuaries of SE England from the Wash to the Solent. These are up to half the world population of the subspecies. The remainder winter on the Continent between Denmark and France. Numbers in the low thousands are found north to the Humber and west to the Burry Inlet, W Glamorgan. Smaller numbers still are to be found north to Lindisfarne, Northumberland, where they overlap with the Light-bellied Brent Goose (*B. b. hrota*). This is the latter's only resort in England although the scattered records in Scotland may relate mainly to this subspecies. Most of the Irish records are also of Light-bellied Brent Geese. The main sites are Strangford Lough, the North Bull in Dublin, and Tralee Bay but there are many lesser ones.

Brent Geese feed on a number of plants in sequence (Charman 1977). Their preference for eel grass is reflected in the autumn concentrations at Foulness, Essex and Strangford Lough where this marine grass is found in abundance. The geese will upend for it at high tide as well as paddling the mud at low tide to expose the rhizomes. By December, this food supply is much depleted and the big concentrations begin to disperse to a wide range of traditionally used estuaries where food selection is more catholic. Until the early 1970s most birds fed on *Ulva*, *Enteromorpha* and salt marsh vegetation, but the very rapid increase in numbers of Dark-bellied Brent Geese caused a shortage of the natural foods and started a new feeding habit on grass and such cultivated crops as barley, wheat and oilseed rape (St Joseph 1977). Up to 40,000 Brents fed inland in 1980 and it now appears that this new food source is preferred. Brent Geese also feed on farmland in Ireland but in very much smaller numbers. From December to March there is little overall change in distribution apart from hard weather movements. In Ireland many birds leave Strangford Lough in December and small parties are found along Irish coasts during the remainder of the winter.

In spring the Light-bellied Brent Geese at Lindisfarne move first to Denmark and then, in May, north to Spitzbergen and perhaps Franz Joseph Land to breed. In a hard winter almost the entire Spitzbergen population may move to Lindisfarne. In 1981/82 there were 1,800 birds. The Irish birds reach Canada and Greenland via Iceland, while the Dark-bellied Brent Geese spend nearly two months along the coasts of the Netherlands, Germany and Denmark before migrating to the Taimyr Peninsula in late May.

Numbers of all 3 populations crashed in the early 1930s, due in part to a disease of eel grass. Except in Scotland (*eg* the Cromarty Firth) most of the original haunts have good numbers again. But only one subspecies (*B.b. bernicla*) has recovered its pre-1930s level, and 45% of the world population is found in Britain in winter. The counts below are from Ogilvie and St Joseph (1976) and Wildfowl Count data.

A. K. M. ST JOSEPH

		B. b. hrota		*B. b. bernicla*	
	Canadian/ Irish Population total	Spitzbergen/ Lindisfarne			
		British total	Population total	British total	Population total
1955/57	6000	—	4000	7400	16500
1963	12000	2000	2000	15200	22800
1973	16000	470	c2000	41000	51800
1983	c12000	610	3400	92600	203000

Total number of squares in which recorded: 421 (11%)

Number (%) of squares

No. of birds seen in a day	Britain	Ireland	TOTAL (incl. C.I.)
1–15	182 (60%)	29 (25%)	213 (51%)
16–330	56 (19%)	67 (59%)	124 (29%)
331 +	65 (22%)	18 (16%)	84 (20%)

References

CHARMAN, K. 1977. The seasonal pattern of food utilization by *Branta b. bernicla* on the coast of south east England. Pp 64–76 in *Technical Meeting on Western Palearctic Migratory Bird Management*. The Wildfowl Trust, Slimbridge.

OGILVIE, M. A. and A. K. M. ST JOSEPH. 1976. Dark-bellied Brent Geese in Britain and Europe, 1955–76. *Brit. Birds* 69 : 422–439.

ST JOSEPH, A. K. M. 1977. The development of inland feeding by *Branta b. bernicla* in southeast England. Pp 132–145 in *Proc. 1st Technical Meeting on Western Palearctic Migratory Bird Management*. The Wildfowl Trust, Slimbridge.

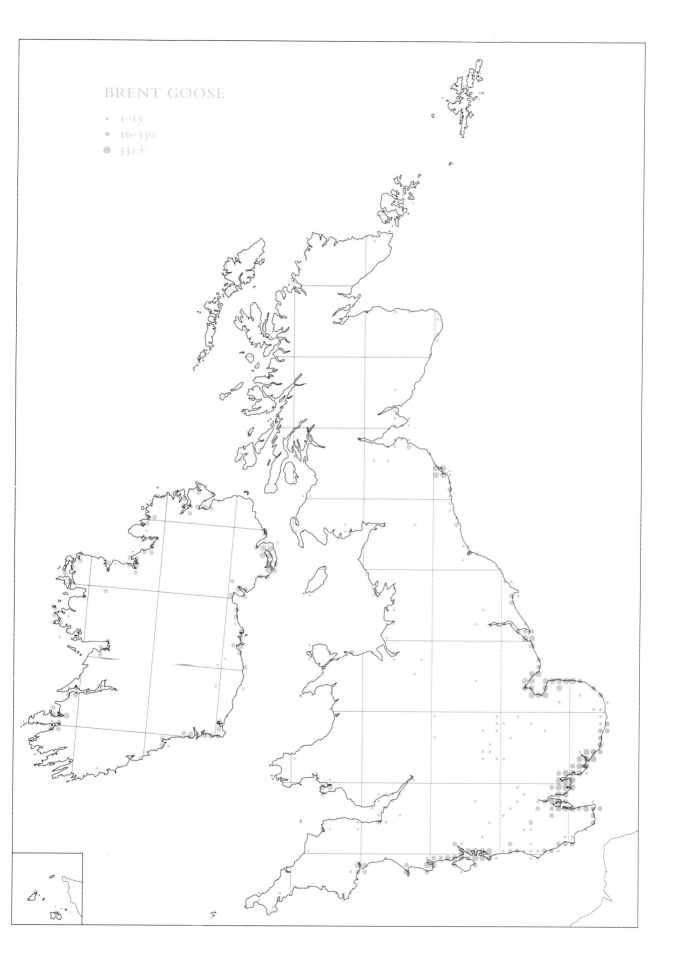

BRENT GOOSE

- • 1–15
- • 16–330
- ● 331+

Egyptian Goose

Alopochen aegyptiacus

The Egyptian Goose was first described in Britain in the Royal Wildfowl Collection at St James's Park, London in 1678. Despite breeding in a feral state for almost 200 years, it remains the least studied of all our introduced species.

The map shows that most records were in Norfolk (as they were in the *Breeding Atlas*), with an overspill into Suffolk. A smaller concentration, along the Dorset/Devon border, was not shown in the *Breeding Atlas*. At Holkham in Norfolk, where late summer concentrations of up to 200 have been recorded in recent years, a maximum of only 30 were found wintering. This suggests autumn dispersal to other areas, probably into Breckland. Apart from those recorded in East Anglia and the West Country, 1–2 Egyptian Geese were found at scattered localities in Yorkshire, Cheshire, Lincolnshire, central England and a few southern counties. There are no records for Ireland.

In England, as in Africa, Egyptian Geese are found almost exclusively on or near fresh water, throughout the year. Their favoured habitats are wooded parkland containing areas of water, pastures and, in Norfolk, broads and breckland meres. On smaller waters breeding pairs often remain together during the winter, while on the larger stretches of water, flocks of over 100 may occur. Adults and young moult at the same time with two peaks of moulting activity in late summer and mid winter. Whilst flightless, they tend to remain on or near large areas of water, to escape predators. They graze by day, feeding mainly on plant leaves, grass and seeds. Like geese, they often feed in pairs or family parties within the larger flocks. In South Africa the larger flocks can be a major source of crop damage, eating and trampling growing shoots (Brown *et al* 1982). This has yet to be reported in England.

During the 19th century, Egyptian Geese which occurred on the Norfolk coast after strong easterly winds, were considered to be genuine wild birds. Even then, however, it was appreciated that they could have originated from the feral population in Holland (Stevenson 1890). Between 1830 and 1880, local wildfowlers on the Northumberland coast were familiar with small wintering parties, which they

referred to as 'Spanish Geese'. There is no evidence from ringing or observations that significant movements of Egyptian Geese occur nowadays within Britain. However, in South Africa, ringing has demonstrated seasonal movements up to 1,100 km, whilst regular wet season trans-Saharan migration occurs from Nigeria and Chad to southern Algeria and Tunisia (Brown *et al* 1982).

Formerly the species was found over most of Africa, the Middle East and southern Europe. Apart from England and the Netherlands, within the western Palearctic it now breeds only in Egypt. The introduced British feral population demonstrates the species' adaptability to new, temperate, lowland habitats. The very slow spread from the favoured East Anglian sites is therefore surprising. Although the first Norfolk record was as long ago as 1808, it was not until 1936 that it was reported in Essex and 1970 before it occurred annually in Kent. The Egyptian Goose was admitted to the British list as a category C species (an established introduction which is self-maintaining) in 1971 and, thereafter, records began to appear in the county bird reports. Since then there has been very little change in the numbers recorded annually in eastern England. Although they survive the winter well, they tend to breed in early spring resulting in poor survival of the young. In Norfolk an average of only 2 young per pair is reared, due to predation by crows and competition with Canada *Branta canadensis* and Greylag Geese *Anser anser* (*BWP*).

As the species is not well recorded in the National Wildfowl Counts, the *Winter Atlas* has provided the first real opportunity to estimate the British population. The total is estimated by using the maximum count for each 10–km square. Using this method 504 Egyptian Geese were recorded, of which 429 were found in Norfolk. This compares with the estimated 1963 total of 300–400 (Atkinson-Willes 1963).

M. P. TAYLOR

Total number of squares in which recorded: 73 (2%)

	Number (%) of squares		
No. of birds seen in a day	Britain	Ireland	TOTAL (incl. C.I.)
1–2	43 (59%)	0 (0%)	43 (59%)
3–9	15 (21%)	0 (0%)	15 (21%)
10 +	15 (21%)	0 (0%)	15 (21%)

References

ATKINSON-WILLES, G. L. 1963. *Wildfowl in Great Britain*. Nature Conservancy Monograph 3. HMSO. London.

BROWN, L. H., E. K. URBAN and K. NEWMAN. 1982. *The Birds of Africa*. Vol. 1. Academic Press, London.

STEVENSON, H. 1890. *The Birds of Norfolk*. Vol. 3. Gurney & Jackson, London.

Breeding Atlas p 96

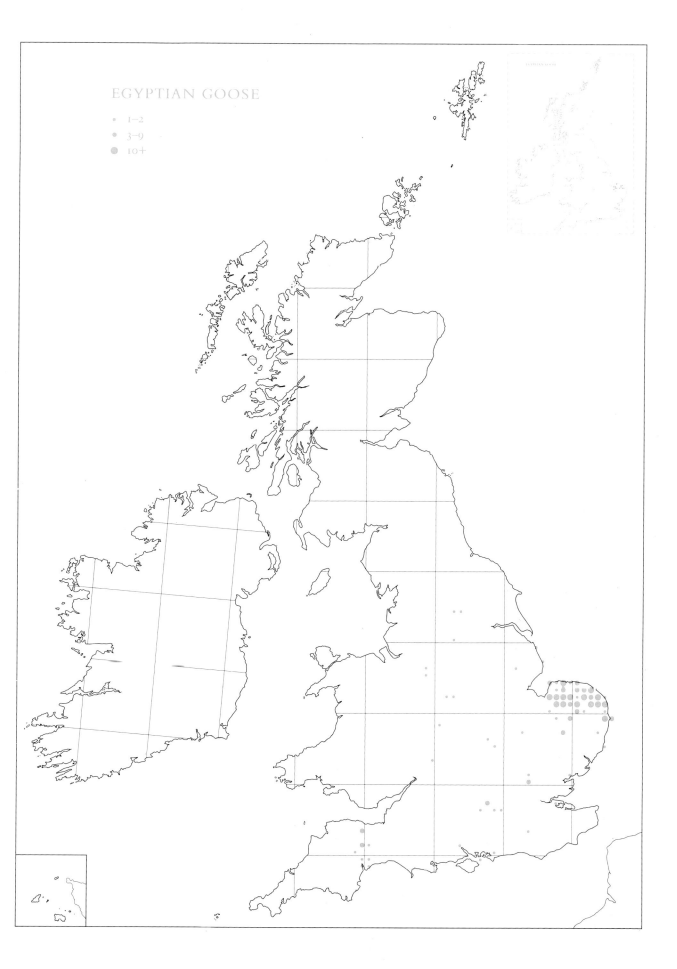

EGYPTIAN GOOSE

- · 1–2
- · 3–9
- · 10+

Shelduck

Tadorna tadorna

The Shelduck is one of the most conspicuous wildfowl occurring on British estuaries in winter. Its large size and contrasting black, white and chestnut plumage make it stand out from other ducks and waders with which it often associates, particularly when it is illuminated by mellow winter sunshine.

The winter distribution is chiefly coastal, with most birds occurring on the muddier estuaries of southern and eastern England, southern Ireland, around the shores of the Irish Sea, and in SW Scotland. Mid winter numbers in Scotland depend partly on the severity of the weather there, some adults returning later from their moulting grounds in colder winters. Shelducks can occur at very high densities on some estuaries, the map does not show the size and character of the concentrations. For example, in some winters up to 4,000 have occurred on the Tees estuary, on only 140 ha of mudflat.

Many of the birds breeding in northern and western Scotland are absent from these areas in winter. Although small numbers of Shelducks in Britain and Ireland nest around pools some tens of kilometres from the coast, in central and southern England they are not as regularly found inland in summer as they are in winter; the map shows a scattering of wintering birds on many reservoirs and gravel pits in England.

On estuaries, Shelducks feed chiefly on areas of more liquid mud, which they sieve through their lamellated bills, extracting a variety of small snails, worms and crustaceans. The most obvious remains found in their guts and faeces are the crushed shells of the snail *Hydrobia ulvae,* but in some estuaries this prey is too scarce to form more than a small proportion of their daily food intake. In such localities Shelducks rely on abundant small polychaete and oligochaete worms. At the coast, birds alter their feeding method according to the stage of the tidal cycle, from scything through the mud at low water to upending in shallow water as the tide covers and uncovers the mudflats. Inland, it is likely that freshwater snails and earthworms are important, but perhaps aquatic plants and algae are also taken.

After breeding, most adult Shelducks from Britain and Ireland move to the German section of the Wadden Sea, where they moult alongside breeding birds from the rest of western Europe. Several thousands remain to moult on the Forth, Humber, Wash and more especially in Bridgwater Bay, but this habit appears to be of relatively recent origin. Moulted birds begin to return to southeastern England in October, and large gatherings also assemble on the Dee estuary and Morecambe Bay. By mid winter, birds have spread northwards and westwards from East Anglia, but others have arrived to replace them. These include not only British and Irish breeding stock but also some immigrants from continental European populations. Thus each estuary tends to be used by a succession of individuals, rather like a winter holiday resort. Birds arrive on their eventual breeding grounds over a period of several months.

After fledging in July, young Shelducks do not follow their parents to the Wadden Sea, but disperse later from their birthplaces. Ducklings hatched on the coast of East Lothian, Scotland, have been seen in the autumn and winter at several sites along the northeast coast of England, and one as far afield as the Camargue, S France, but many move into the upper reaches of the Firth of Forth. Birds from the same brood have been found in several different wintering sites.

In recent winters, 60,000–65,000 Shelducks have been counted in mid winter in Britain, a considerable increase over the 50,000 level recorded regularly up to the early 1970s. This probably results in part from an increase in the breeding population in Britain, but may also reflect more birds moving westwards from the Wadden Sea in response to the more frequent severe winters of recent years. The Irish wintering population is between 6,500 and 8,000 birds. As the whole western European population is of the order of only 120,000–130,000 birds, the importance of the British wintering sites is obvious.

P. R. EVANS

Total number of squares in which recorded: 1,135 (29%)

No. of birds seen in a day	Number (%) of squares		
	Britain	Ireland	TOTAL (incl. C.I.)
1–7	506 (53%)	71 (38%)	579 (51%)
8–80	257 (27%)	72 (38%)	329 (29%)
81 +	183 (19%)	44 (24%)	227 (20%)

References

BRYANT, D. M. and J. LENG. 1975. Feeding distribution and behaviour of Shelduck in relation to food supply. *Wildfowl* 26 : 20–30.

EVANS, P. R. and M. W. PIENKOWSKI. 1982. Behaviour of Shelducks in a winter flock: does regulation occur? *J. Anim. Ecol.* 51 : 241–262.

PATTERSON, I. J. 1982. *The Shelduck: a Study in Behavioural Ecology.* University Press, Cambridge.

PIENKOWSKI, M. W. and P. R. EVANS. 1982. Breeding behaviour, productivity and survival of colonial and non-colonial Shelducks. *Ornis Scand.* 13 : 101–116.

THOMPSON, D. B. A. 1981. Feeding behaviour of wintering Shelduck in the Clyde Estuary. *Wildfowl* 32 : 88–98.

Breeding Atlas p 94

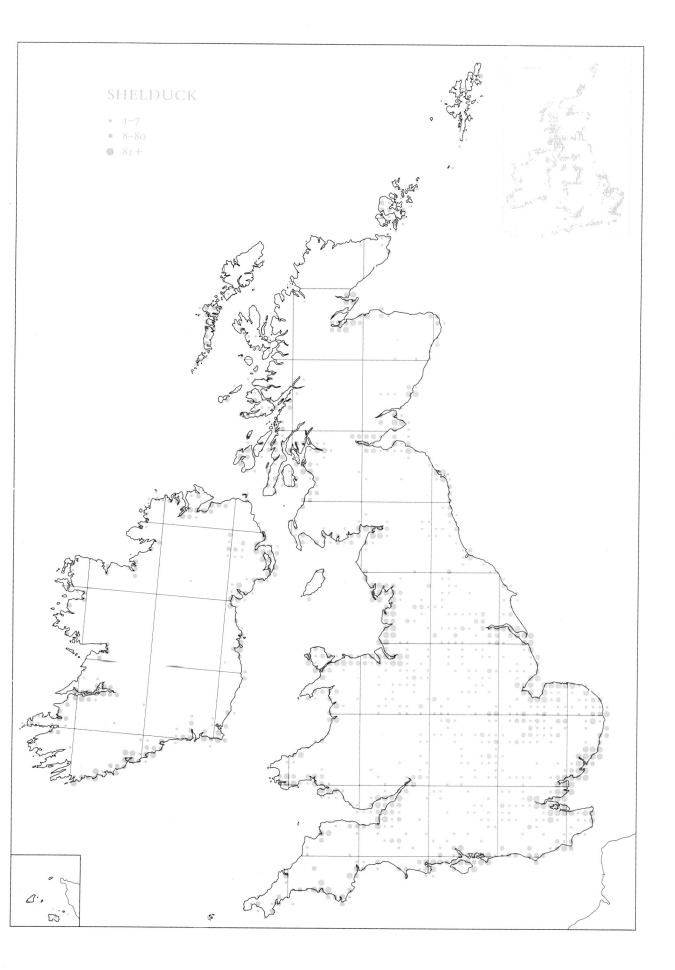

SHELDUCK

- 1–7
- 8–80
- 81+

Mandarin

Aix galericulata

The Mandarin, a native of western USSR, China and Japan, is now an established, although localised, resident maintaining a steady increase both in population and distribution.

The winter map reveals the extent to which the Mandarin has extended its range since the *Breeding Atlas*. As in the breeding season, a significant proportion of the winter population is found centred on Berkshire and Surrey. The records from SW England may be 'the start of something new'. The wooded river valleys of south Devon and Cornwall should be suited to this species but the birds may be recent escapes from wildfowl collections. A few birds are found elsewhere and their presence at two localities on the western fringes of East Anglia may be indicative of new breeding areas. Further north, distribution is sparse. Surprisingly there was only one record from the Eaton Hall, Cheshire, area which held a sizeable population at the time of the *Breeding Atlas*. In Scotland, Perth is the only breeding site, with a population of 60–80. There are occasional records from Ireland.

The indicated level of abundance should be viewed with some caution as the Mandarin is secretive, and is most likely under-recorded due to its preferred habitat of secluded streams or ponds in mature open deciduous woodland, wooded river valleys or parkland, as typified by Windsor Great Park, the Mandarins' stronghold in SE England. Shelter is also a requirement and overhanging rhododendron thickets are especially favoured.

Winter flocking occurs, particularly on larger lakes. Most feeding is at night when the main flocks disperse to their feeding grounds, which may be by ponds and lakes, or in adjoining woodland. The winter diet consists mainly of acorns, chestnuts and beech mast.

Pair formation starts for adult birds in September and continues through the winter, with most birds paired by February. Social play and displays are a feature of the winter months and take many forms, such as small parties of drakes displaying to a single duck, 'pursuit' flights in which a duck may fly around a lake closely followed by a group of young drakes,

or the calling by an unpaired female, just before sunset, which is taken up by other birds in the vicinity.

In Britain, there are only relatively local movements, yet in their natural range (the eastern Palearctic) the species is dispersive and migratory. In central Surrey the birds are absent from the breeding areas from late summer through the winter but return to the same breeding areas each spring (Davies 1985). Little is known, however, about the extent of such movements. *BWP* mentions that individuals .seen occasionally far from nesting areas may be strays from ornamental collections, and it appears that the birds are capable of long-distance movement. Of 2 captive bred birds ringed at Vale de Marais, Channel Islands, on 25 July 1980, one was found at Ottery St Mary, Devon, on 18 December 1980 and the other at Keynsham, Avon, about 25 December 1980. Two others from Norway were shot together in Northumberland in 1962.

Population estimates vary widely, due most likely to under recording, even in its strongholds. A current but speculative estimate of 850–1,000 pairs (Davies 1985) greatly exceeds the estimated population level in the *Breeding Atlas* of 250–400 pairs.

Although the British population increases, there have been reports over the last 20 years of a decline in the Mandarin's status in the eastern Palearctic, although the extent remains undefined at present. Perhaps the continued survival of the species may one day depend on the birds now established in Britain.

K. J. HERBER

Total number of squares in which recorded: 129 (3%)

No. of birds seen in a day	Number (%) of squares		
	Britain	Ireland	TOTAL (incl. C.I.)
1	60 (46%)	0 (0%)	60˙(46%)
2–6	40 (32%)	0 (0%)	41 (32%)
7 +	28 (22%)	0 (0%)	28 (22%)

References

DAVIES, A. 1985. The British Mandarins — outstripping the ancestors. *BTO News* 136 : 12.

JACKSON, E. 1969. Mandarin duck. *Birds of the World*. Part II, Vol 1 : 295–297. IPC Magazine, London.

LEVER, C. 1977. *Naturalised Animals of the British Isles*. Hutchinson, London.

LUBBOCK, M. R. 1981. Waterfowl keeping in England. *American Pheasant and Waterfowl Society Magazine*.

PARR, D. 1972. *Birds in Surrey 1900–1970*. Batsford, London.

SAVAGE, C. 1952. *The Mandarin Duck*. Black, London.

Breeding Atlas p 72

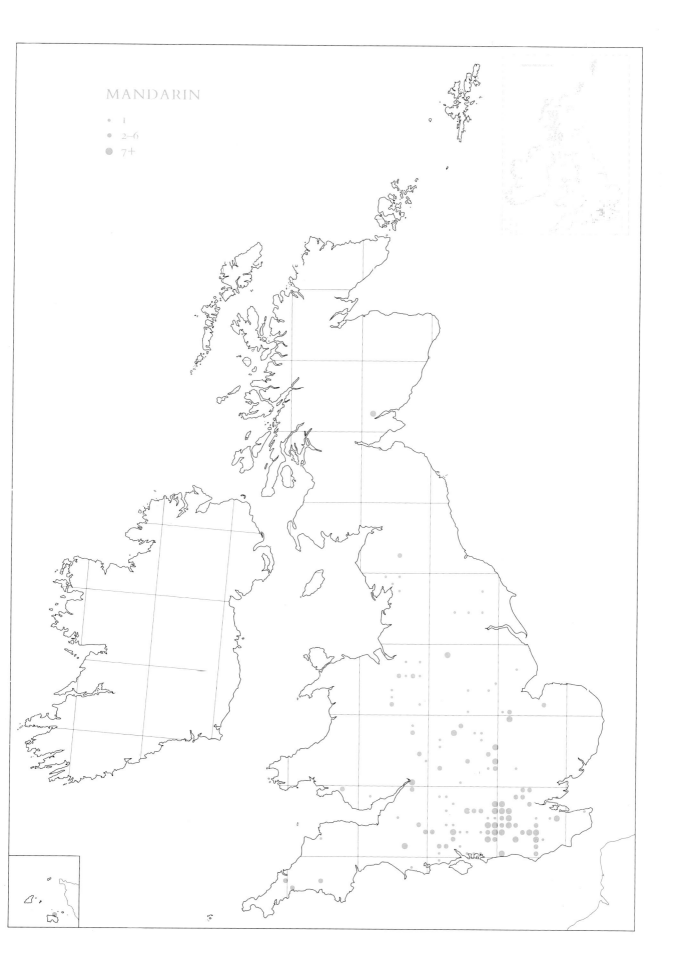

MANDARIN

- · 1
- · 2–6
- ● 7+

Wigeon

Anas penelope

A medium sized, gregarious duck, the Wigeon is a familiar sight around our coasts and its musical whistling a pleasant evocative sound, commonly heard over mudflats or at night as the flock leaves the estuary to feed on nearby marshes or flooded pastures.

The numerical distribution is more coastal than the map suggests. In Britain, in the early 1970s 81% of Wigeons still roosted on the coast and 54% on estuarine habitats, although a move to inland habitats had taken place in this century (Owen and Williams 1976). In Ireland they have always been more of an inland species. Though the major concentrations are on estuaries, they also gather in large numbers in the flooded pastures of the Shannon valley in mid winter. There are 9 sites in Britain holding internationally important concentrations of more than 5,000, but 2 are outstanding: Lindisfarne, Northumberland, with an average peak of nearly 30,000 in October/November has always been important, and the Ouse Washes in East Anglia became so after protection and management of part of the area by voluntary bodies. Both sites have held more than 40,000 Wigeons in some seasons.

The traditional diet of Wigeons was eel grass, algae and grasses gathered on mudflats and saltings, but with the move inland their taste has become more catholic. At the Ouse Washes a wide variety of foods and habitats is used, including stubble grain and winter wheat gathered from the sprouting fields in late winter. The flocks, sometimes numbered in thousands, are often tightly bunched when grazing on land but more spread out on water. Wigeons often feed by picking floating leaves off the water surface or by dabbling in the shallows. In disturbed areas most of the feeding takes place at night, but elsewhere they feed during the day as well. Most birds feed within 8 km of the roost although in a few places they fly up to 15 km (Owen and Thomas 1979).

The movements of Wigeons are complex and not well understood. Birds wintering in Britain and Ireland come from Scandinavia and Siberia, and some from Iceland. Most birds recovered in Iceland in summer come from Scotland and Ireland, but Wigeon ringed in Iceland are sometimes found in later years in continental Europe, so there is some mixing of the stocks. There is some southward and westward movement within Britain and Ireland as the winter progresses and probably a movement into Ireland from Scotland. The peak count is nearly always recorded in January, after a mid winter influx of Continental migrants, which also concentrate on the east coast when there is hard weather in the Netherlands and Germany (Owen *et al* 1986).

Because Wigeons are generally found in large concentrations, they are well covered by Wildfowl Counts. The average maximum in Britain is estimated at about 200,000, with up to 250,000 in some years. There is a less recent estimate of over 100,000 for Ireland (Hutchinson 1979), and the total in NW Europe has been put at about half a million birds (Owen *et al* 1986). The numbers in Britain have shown no trend overall since 1960, but there have been changes in distribution, largely linked to the creation of reserves. Thus there has been a significant increase in numbers on protected sites and a decrease on unprotected areas. This has resulted also in a continuation of the move from coastal to inland habitats.

Britain and Ireland are crucially important wintering areas for NW European Wigeons, jointly holding more than half the total at peak times. Another half a million or so birds, not entirely isolated from the NW European group, winter around the Mediterranean and the Black Sea (Atkinson-Willes 1976).

M. OWEN

Total number of squares in which recorded: 1,885 (49%)

No. of birds seen in a day	Number (%) of squares		
	Britain	Ireland	TOTAL (incl. C.I.)
1–43	750 (53%)	194 (42%)	944 (50%)
44–299	405 (29%)	158 (34%)	564 (30%)
300 +	268 (19%)	108 (24%)	377 (20%)

References

ATKINSON-WILLES, G. L. 1976. The numerical distribution of ducks, swans and coots as a guide in assessing the importance of wetlands in midwinter. *Proc. Int. Conf. Conserv. Wetlands and Waterfowl, Heiligenhafen 1974*: 199–254. IWRB, Slimbridge.

DONKER, J. K. 1959. Migration and distribution of Wigeon *Anas penelope,* in Europe, based on ringing results. *Ardea* 47: 1–27.

OWEN, M., and G. J. THOMAS. 1979. The feeding ecology and conservation of Wigeon wintering at the Ouse Washes, England. *J. Appl. Ecol.* 16: 795–809.

OWEN, M. and G. M. WILLIAMS. 1976. Winter distribution and habitat requirements of Wigeon in Britain. *Wildfowl* 27: 83–90.

Breeding Atlas p 66

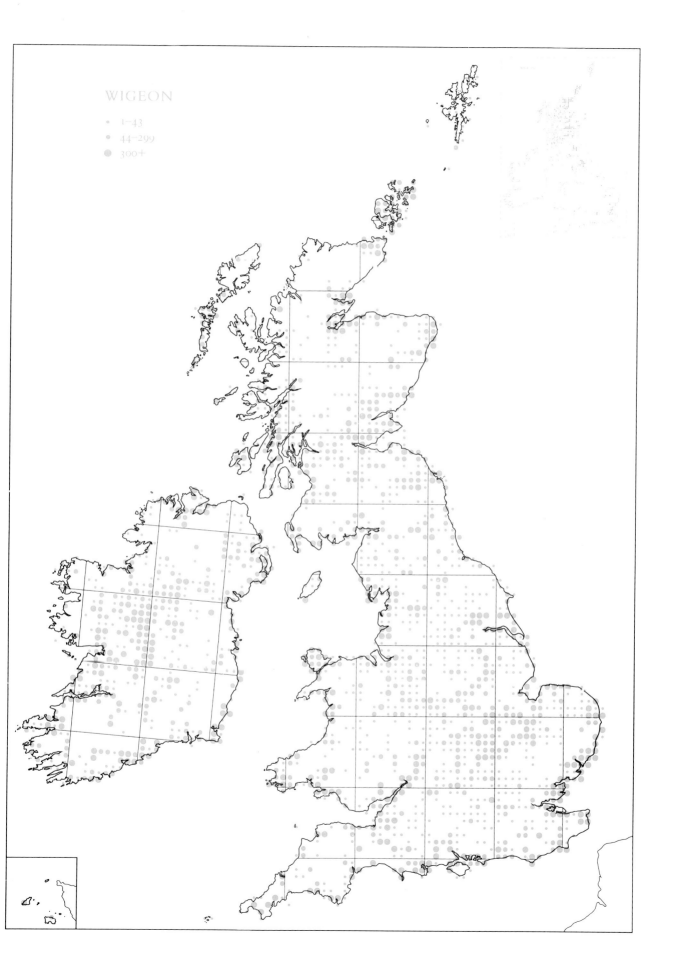

WIGEON

- · 1–43
- · 44–299
- ● 300+

Gadwall

Anas strepera

A predominantly fresh water duck, the Gadwall is commonest on shallow lakes, where it forms small flocks in winter. The leaves and stems of aquatic plants form the bulk of its food, obtained by immersing the head and neck or occasionally by upending. It also grazes land vegetation in some areas.

About 80% of the Gadwalls recorded by the Wildfowl Trust's National Wildfowl Counts are inland (Owen *et al* 1986). Like many other wildfowl they have taken full advantage of the huge numbers of reservoirs and flooded gravel pits which have appeared in the lowlands this century, a process which has probably aided their increase and spread. Apart from the Ouse Washes, floodlands are not used as much by Gadwalls as by other dabbling ducks.

The status of the Gadwall in Britain and Ireland is somewhat complex. The breeding stock originates mainly, if not entirely, from releases and escapes from captivity since the mid 19th century. Ringing has shown the feral population to be largely sedentary, and the map demonstrates that the main wintering areas are still those where releasing was concentrated — East Anglia and the Home Counties. The map gives a wider distribution than that in the *Breeding Atlas*. This is a result partly of continued increase and spread, especially into central England, but also of the species' greater mobility outside the breeding season, and the role of some areas, mainly in the west, purely as wintering grounds. Isolated November records from Scotland and northern England may well refer to passage birds from Iceland. The small but long-established population of unknown origin at Loch Leven (Tayside) and the surrounding region has usually dispersed by late October, apparently to the southwest (Allison *et al* 1974).

Perhaps 20–25% of the British breeding Gadwalls emigrate in winter, to be replaced by a small influx from Iceland, the Netherlands, Scandinavia and central Europe (Owen *et al* 1986). Most Irish wintering birds (numbering probably 300–350, and increasing) are immigrants from Iceland and, to a lesser extent, Scotland and Denmark, the breeding stock being very small. The main Irish site is Ballyallia Lake, Co. Clare, where 180 have been seen (Hutchinson 1979).

The largest concentrations of Gadwalls in Britain are found in autumn in and around East Anglia, presumably comprising the local breeding birds. Although usually at their peak in September and October, these flocks often do not disperse until the early winter.

At Rutland Water, Leicestershire (a 1,260 ha reservoir completed in 1975), an assemblage of 800 in September 1983 increased to 950 in December, much the largest number ever counted in one place in Britain and Ireland. In recent years 200 or more have also been found between November and February at Hickling Broad and Stanford Training Area (Norfolk), the Ouse Washes (Norfolk/Cambridgeshire), Little Paxton Gravel Pits (Cambridgeshire), Slimbridge (Gloucestershire), Hornsea Mere (Humberside) and Martin Mere (Lancashire). The Slimbridge and Martin Mere birds emanate from releases by the Wildfowl Trust between the 1950s and 1970s.

Data from the National and International Wildfowl Counts show that in Britain and Ireland the numbers have increased markedly over the last 25 years, and probably now exceed 4,000, while in NW Europe as a whole they have reached 6,000–7,000 in mid winter (Owen *et al* 1986). If the increase continues a further extension of the range can be expected.

D. G. SALMON

Total number of squares in which recorded: 645 (17%)

No. of birds seen in a day	Number (%) of squares		
	Britain	Ireland	TOTAL (incl. C.I.)
1–5	284 (49%)	32 (53%)	316 (49%)
6–22	183 (31%)	20 (33%)	203 (31%)
23 +	118 (20%)	8 (13%)	126 (20%)

References

ALLISON, A., I. NEWTON and C. R. G. CAMPBELL. 1974. *Loch Leven National Nature Reserve: a Study of Waterfowl Biology*. A WAGBI Conservation Publication.

Breeding Atlas p 64

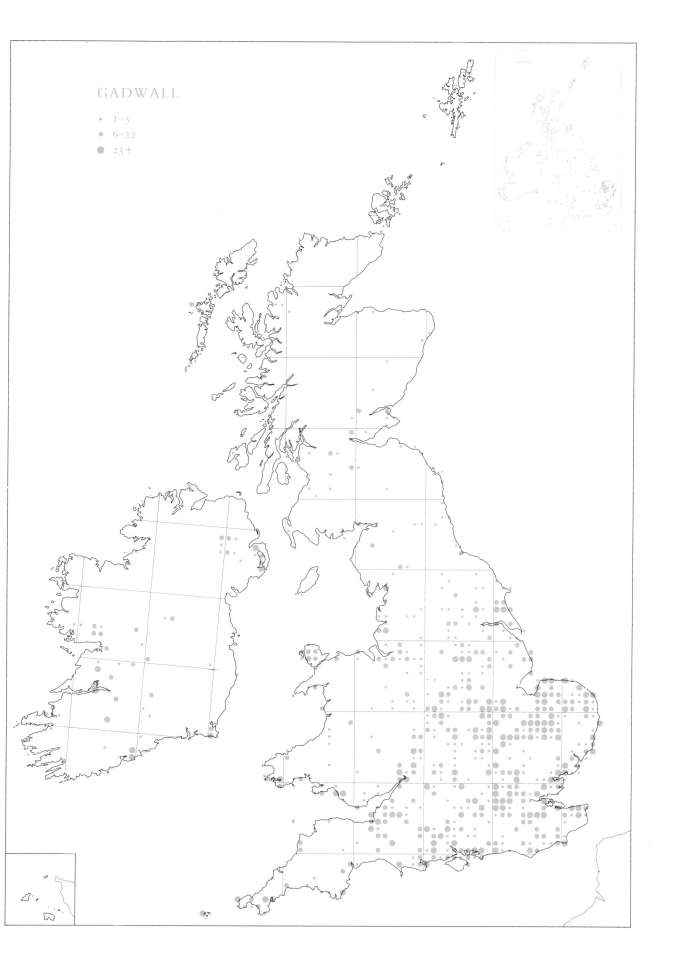

GADWALL

- 1–5
- 6–22
- 23+

Teal

Anas crecca

A tight-packed flock of Teals springing into the air in fast and agile flight accompanied by whistling calls is a familiar sight and sound of winter almost throughout Britain and Ireland. They are one of the most widespread of our ducks, avoiding only mountainous areas, entirely cliff-bound coasts and some inland areas lacking suitable fresh water. Although coastal concentrations are frequent, especially in NW and SE England, there are many inland areas of significance. By far the largest gathering of Teals in Britain is found in the Mersey estuary, with up to 35,000 there in the 1981/82 winter, though dropping suddenly to just over 11,000 in 1983/84, perhaps because of some local change in food availability (Salmon and Moser 1984). Inland floods provide ideal Teal habitat and, where there is adequate protection from shooting and disturbance, flocks of up to 4,000 can occur. However, winter wildfowl counts have revealed that over 40% of wintering Teals in Britain are found in flocks of less than 200 (Owen *et al* 1986).

The winter map is in many ways the reverse of the *Breeding Atlas* map. Several thousand pairs of Teals breed in Britain and Ireland, with boggy upland pools most favoured, though lowland marshy areas are also used. Thus in many areas of Scotland and northern England, where Teals can be found in summer, they tend to be absent in winter.

The Teal is catholic in its food requirements. It is a shallow-water feeder, dabbling at the edges, and upending. Plant seeds, especially small ones, predominate in the diet, particularly those of the commoner species, such as *Polygonum*, *Ranunculus*, *Eleocharis*, *Atriplex* and *Salicornia*, suggesting little selection on the part of the birds. Animal food, which accounts for perhaps 25% of the diet in winter, includes especially chironomid midge larvae and small molluscs. Some feeding occurs on stubble fields in autumn, though weed seeds may be as important as the cereal grains themselves. Teals feed throughout the day where they feel safe, but nocturnal feeding, involving flighting to and from a secure daytime roost, is common in some areas.

The Teals breeding in Britain and Ireland are thought to be relatively sedentary, remaining in the country during normal winters. The immigrants come from a wide breeding range extending from the countries around the Baltic, through to northwestern Siberia. Several thousand Teals also come from Iceland. In common with a number of duck species, females tend to winter further south than males.

Extensive ringing has shown that Teals are highly mobile ducks, reacting quickly to changing environmental circumstances. Thus drought, heavy rainfall, or, particularly, cold weather, will cause them to move to more favourable areas (Ogilvie 1983, and in prep.). Hard weather movements from Britain to Ireland, and south into France and Iberia take place in severe weather of more than a few days' duration.

In Britain there has been a marked increase in the number of Teals counted in winter in the last decade with the 5 year average peak increasing from 64,000 to 88,000 (Owen *et al* 1986). The number of Teals not included in the counts, is probably substantial owing to their widely dispersed nature. The total population estimates in Britain lie between 100,000 and 200,000 of which about 85% are immigrants. For Ireland, Hutchinson (1979) estimated a peak count in normal winters of 30,000–50,000.

Teals breeding and wintering in Britain and Ireland form part of a NW European stock which is thought, from international wildfowl counts, to number at least 200,000 (Scott 1980). In view of the uncertainty surrounding the likely British wintering peak, this can be regarded as a minimum estimate. There is another, much larger population wintering in the Mediterranean-Black Sea region, estimated at around 750,000 (Atkinson-Willes 1976, Scott 1980).

M. A. OGILVIE

Total number of squares in which recorded: 2,522 (65%)

No. of birds seen in a day	Number (%) of squares		
	Britain	Ireland	TOTAL (incl. C.I.)
1–35	916 (49%)	339 (51%)	1,256 (50%)
36–150	570 (31%)	191 (29%)	762 (30%)
151+	365 (20%)	138 (21%)	504 (20%)

References

ATKINSON-WILLES, G. L. 1976. The numerical distribution of ducks, swans and coots as a guide in assessing the importance of wetlands in midwinter. *Proc. Int. Conf. Conserv. Wetlands and Waterfowl, Heiligenhafen*, 1974: 199–254. IWRB, Slimbridge.

OGILVIE, M. A. 1983. *A Migration Study of the Teal (Anas crecca) in Europe using Ringing Recoveries.* Ph.D. Thesis. University of Bristol.

SALMON, D. G. and M. MOSER. 1984. *Wildfowl and Wader Counts 1983–84.* Wildfowl Trust, Slimbridge.

SCOTT, D. 1980. *A Preliminary Inventory of Wetlands of International Importance for Waterfowl in West Europe and Northwest Africa.* IWRB, Special Publ. No. 2, Slimbridge.

Breeding Atlas p 60

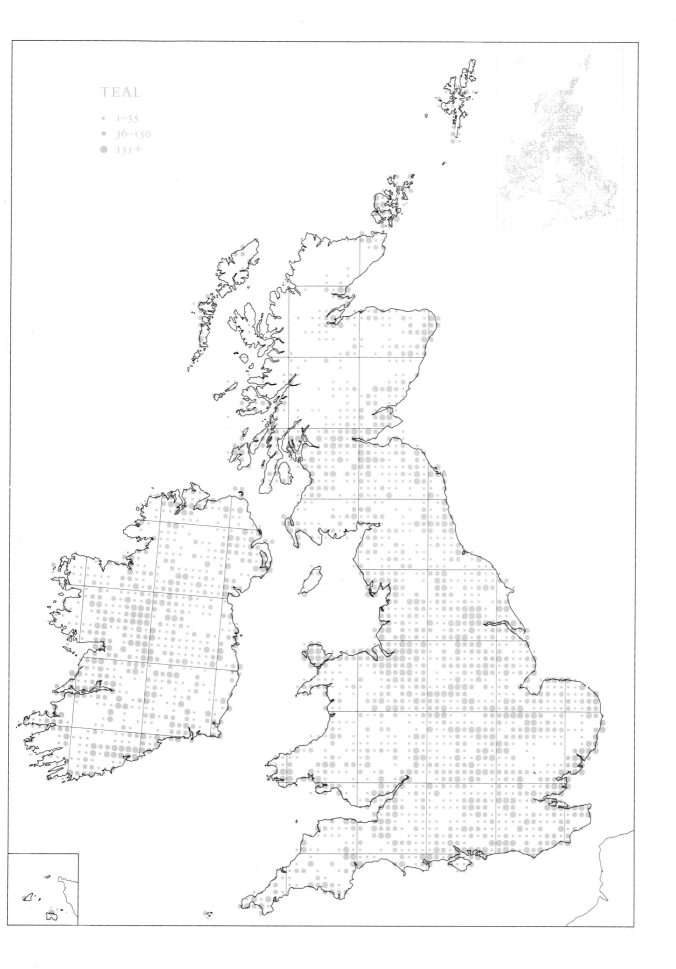

TEAL

- 1–35
- 36–150
- 151+

Mallard

Anas platyrhynchos

So widespread and familiar throughout the world as to be known as 'The Wild Duck' in many languages, the Mallard is, not surprisingly, the most numerous duck in Britain and Ireland. It is highly adaptable and can be found, even in winter, on virtually every kind of wetland, from the smallest pond to the largest reservoir or estuary. It often feeds well away from water, on arable or pasture land.

The map shows how widespread the Mallard is, being absent only from the driest or most mountainous areas. It conceals, however, the paucity of very large concentrations. Only five localities regularly hold over 3,000 Mallards. The same dispersed pattern applies throughout NW Europe, where only one area—the SE corner of the IJsselmeer, the Netherlands—exceeds the qualifying level for international importance of 10,000 (Atkinson-Willes 1976). Not surprisingly, the 10-km squares with over 250 birds in Britain and Ireland are those containing the larger estuaries and enclosed waters. There are relatively few Mallards on the rocky western coasts of Scotland and Ireland.

Food is obtained by every method used by dabbling ducks, though most commonly by upending or immersing the head and neck. Even diving is occasionally recorded where there is a rich underwater food supply. The winter diet consists mainly of vegetable matter, especially seeds. Autumn grazing of stubbles has long been prevalent, and winter feeding on arable crops is now also common, potato and sugar beet being particularly favoured. Mallards are highly tolerant of man and are common in parks and on town rivers and streams, where they frequently rely almost entirely on hand feeding by the public. There are many domestic varieties, which occasionally mix and interbreed with wild birds, resulting in aberrant plumages.

The winter population in Britain and Ireland consists of birds from the large native stock (estimated at approximately 150,000 pairs in the *Breeding Atlas*), supplemented by an influx of winter visitors from Scandinavia and Iceland. There is little emigration by the British breeders and they do not move far within the country in the course of the winter (Boyd and Ogilvie 1961). Immigrants make a small contribution to the Irish winter population, a large proportion of which is resident and sedentary (Hutchinson 1979). Even in hard weather, Mallards are reluctant to move far, and they will 'sit out' short freezing spells.

Estimates of the winter population are difficult to make and vary widely. For Britain, Owen *et al* (1986) have used the National Wildfowl Count data, allowing for the innumerable small waters which are unrecorded, to produce figures of 300,000 for the post-breeding population and 400,000–500,000 for the January peak. They admit, however, that these are still likely to be underestimates, since as many as 500,000 hand reared Mallards may be released on to flight ponds each autumn and 600,000–700,000 shot annually (Harradine 1985). Nevertheless, an annual mortality rate of 48% for adults (Boyd 1962) and the existence of at least a small turnover within the season mean that the true peak population of Mallards in Britain is unlikely to be much in excess of 500,000. There was no discernible trend in the numbers wintering in Britain between 1960 and 1982 (Owen *et al* 1986). Hutchinson (1979) put the Irish total for January at 20,000–50,000, with considerably more in autumn. There are an estimated 4–5 million Mallards in the western Palearctic, with 1,500,000 in NW Europe (Atkinson-Willes 1976).

D. G. SALMON

Total number of squares in which recorded: 3,360 (87%)

No. of birds	Number (%) of squares		
seen in a day	Britain	Ireland	TOTAL (incl. C.I.)
1–55	1,082 (43%)	600 (71%)	1,684 (50%)
56–238	827 (33%)	178 (21%)	1,005 (30%)
239+	598 (24%)	72 (9%)	671 (20%)

References

ATKINSON-WILLES, G. L. 1976. The numerical distribution of ducks, swans and coots as a guide in assessing the importance of wetlands in mid winter. *Proc. Int. Conf. Conserv. Wetlands and Waterfowl, Heiligenhafen, 1974*: 199–254. IWRB, Slimbridge.

BOYD, H. 1962. Population dynamics and the exploitation of ducks and geese. In LE CREN, E. D. and M. W. HOLDGATE, (eds). *The Exploitation of Natural Animal Populations*. Blackwell, Oxford.

BOYD, H. and M. A. OGILVIE. 1961. The distribution of Mallard ringed in southern England. *Wildfowl Trust Annual Report* 12: 125–136.

HARRADINE, J. 1985. Duck shooting in the United Kingdom. *Wildfowl* 36: 81–94.

Breeding Atlas p 58

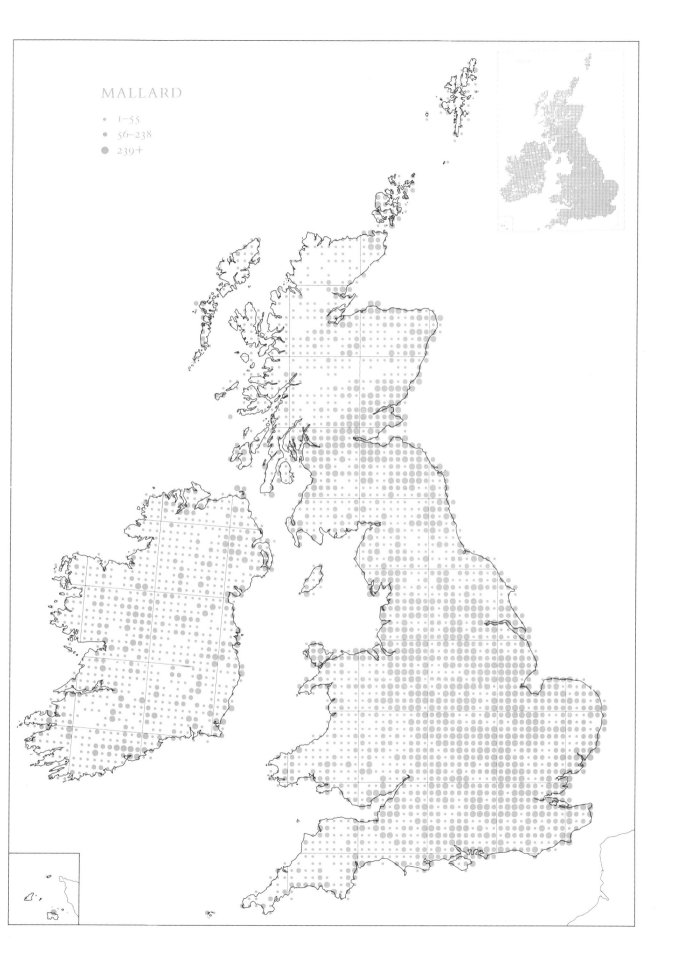

MALLARD

- 1–55
- 56–238
- 239+

Pintail

Anas acuta

CF

The drake Pintail is one of the most striking and elegant of our dabbling ducks, with its pointed tail and chocolate and white head pattern.

The map clearly shows the Pintails' preference for estuaries, especially the larger ones. The only inland squares with over 30 birds are around the Ouse and Nene Washes, apart from a few containing isolated floodlands or large enclosed waters not far from the coast. The courses of rivers lined with gravel workings (such as the Trent) are traced by some of the smaller symbols. Away from the most low lying areas Pintails are virtually absent.

In estuaries small snails of the genus *Hydrobia* are apparently by far the most favoured food, although seeds are also commonly taken (Olney 1965), while on the Ouse Washes seeds, notably of common spikerush, account for over four fifths of the diet. In recent years the arable land around the Washes has also provided food for many of the local Pintails. Cereal stubbles are preferred in the autumn, waste potato and sugar beet thereafter (Thomas 1978, 1981). Field feeding is now common in many other areas.

It is not known where the very small breeding population of Britain and Ireland winters, but from September onwards birds from western Siberia and, to a lesser extent, Scandinavia and Iceland reach our shores. The peak occurs in December in Britain, November or December in eastern Ireland and October or November in western Ireland (Owen *et al* 1986, Hutchinson 1979). Pintails are highly mobile and quickly take advantage of temporary floodwater, yet are extremely concentrated within their NW European range. In Britain, 70–80% of the numbers recorded between November and January by the Wildfowl Trust's National Wildfowl Counts are usually on just 6 sites. The Mersey and Dee estuaries are by far the most important areas.

On the Mersey, the average annual maxima in the Wildfowl Counts (including an occasional October peak) rose from 1,200 in the 1960s to 10,600 in the 1970s and early 1980s, with a maximum of 13,800 in January 1983. On the Dee, a less spectacular

increase began in the mid 1970s, the annual peaks rising from 1,000–2,000 to 5,000–6,000, with the exceptional 11,300 in November 1983. The Dee also holds large numbers for much longer than formerly. These increases, though conforming broadly to the national trend (see below), are particularly marked, due apparently to favourable habitat changes on the south shore of the Mersey and to the creation of reserves in both estuaries.

Movements in response to hard weather are not as clear cut as might be expected, but there are indications that a shift from northern into southern Europe occurred in some recent cold winters (Owen *et al* 1986, International Waterfowl Research Bureau).

The NW European wintering population increased from about 50,000 in the early 1970s (Atkinson-Willes 1976) to 75,000 at the end of the decade (Scott 1980). In Britain there was a parallel increase after a period of relative stability in the 1960s, and the present wintering population exceeds 25,000 (Owen *et al* 1986). The total numbers in Ireland were thought to peak (in November) at about 7,000 in the 1970s (Hutchinson 1979).

D. G. SALMON

Total number of squares in which recorded: 674 (17%)

No. of birds seen in a day	Number (%) of squares		
	Britain	Ireland	TOTAL (incl. C.I.)
1–3	286 (50%)	37 (36%)	324 (48%)
4–29	178 (31%)	38 (36%)	217 (32%)
30+	104 (18%)	29 (28%)	133 (20%)

References

ATKINSON-WILLES, G. L. 1976. The numerical distribution of ducks, swans and coots as a guide to assessing the importance of wetlands in midwinter. *Proc. Int. Conf. Conserv. Wetlands and Waterfowl, Heiligenhafen, 1974*: 199–254. IWRB, Slimbridge.

OLNEY, P. J. S. 1965. The autumn and winter feeding biology of certain sympatric ducks. *Trans. VI Congr. Int. Union Game Biol., Bournemouth, 1963*: 309–322.

SCOTT, D. A. 1980. *A Preliminary Inventory of Wetlands of International Importance for Waterfowl in West Europe and Northwest Africa*. IWRB Special Publication No. 2. IWRB, Slimbridge.

THOMAS, G. J. 1978. *Breeding and Feeding Ecology of Waterfowl at the Ouse Washes, England*. Ph.D. Thesis, Council for National Academic Awards.

THOMAS, G. J. 1981. Field feeding by dabbling ducks around the Ouse Washes, England. *Wildfowl 32*: 69–78.

Breeding Atlas p 68

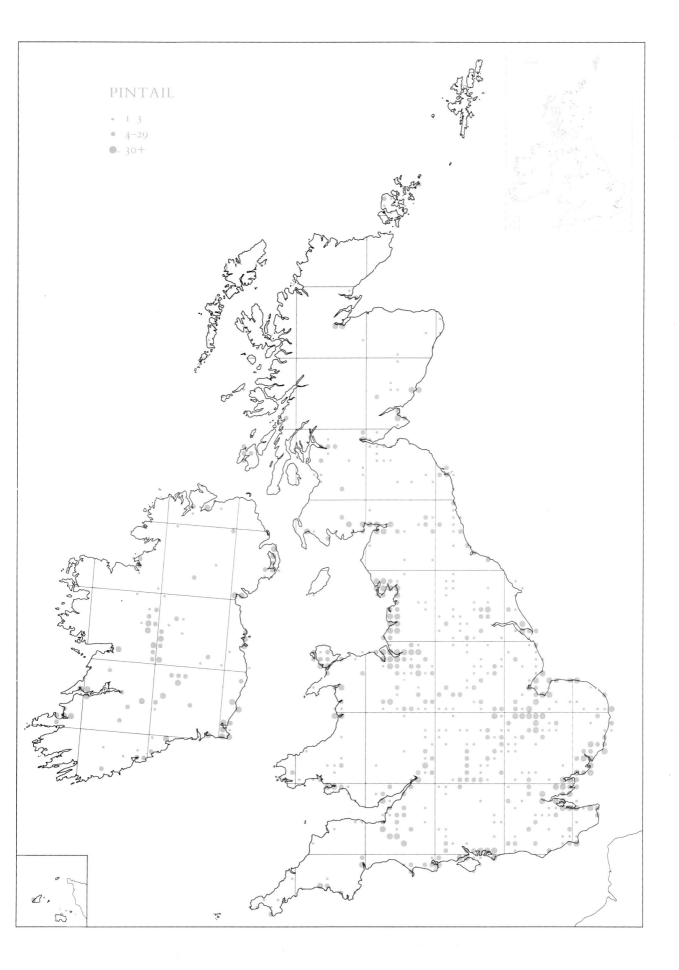

PINTAIL

- · 1–3
- ● 4–29
- ● 30+

Shoveler

Anas clypeata

Whilst a female Shoveler may briefly escape detection amongst female Mallards *A. platyrhynchos*, the male Shoveler is clearly distinctive. The snowy breast and chestnut flanks are diagnostic, but above all one notices the long spatulate bill. The lamellae or corrugations on the inside of the bill are more pronounced than in any other northern hemisphere duck, so that it is particularly well adapted for filter feeding.

Like most other ducks, the Shoveler is virtually absent from the East Anglian chalk and from hilly and mountainous areas. The species is particularly scarce and local in Scotland and northernmost England, where there is a paucity of low-lying standing water. The map understates the extent to which Shovelers prefer fresh water. Except in Essex, Kent and Dublin there are few estuaries which hold many more than 35. A number of apparently coastal concentrations are on enclosed waters a short distance inland.

The only studies of Shovelers' food have taken place on some coastal sites and the Ouse Washes—not entirely typical habitats. In salt water, *Hydrobia* snails are favoured, and in brackish water seeds and insects. On the Ouse Washes (Cambridgeshire/Norfolk) the Shoveler is the most carnivorous dabbling duck, preferring snails, crustaceans and insects, as well as seeds (Thomas 1978). Food is usually obtained while swimming rather than by upending. They probably feed both by day and night, at least in undisturbed areas.

In Britain and Ireland, as in NW Europe as a whole, gatherings of more than a few hundred Shovelers rarely occur. An exception is Lough Owel (Westmeath), where up to 2,000 have occurred in autumn, but fewer stay for the winter. If disturbed, these birds move to the nearby Lough Iron (Hutchinson 1979). Otherwise, only about a dozen places in Britain and Ireland regularly hold over 250 Shovelers between November and February, and none more than 400.

The movements of British and Irish Shovelers are by no means clear. The breeding population, estimated at about 1,000 pairs in the *Breeding Atlas*, apparently moves to France and Spain in the autumn, to be replaced by immigrants from as far east as western Siberia, many of which in turn move on southwards later in the winter (Ogilvie 1962, Perdeck and Clason 1980). Britain formerly held its highest numbers in February or March (Atkinson-Willes 1956), but nowadays there is a clear November peak. It is possible that the succession of mild winters from the mid 1960s to mid 1970s precluded the need for return migrants from Spain and France to stop off in Britain, and that this habit has persisted (Owen *et al* 1986). In Ireland, however, several places still carry their largest numbers in February or March, although these birds may simply have wintered elsewhere in Ireland.

At the time of the November peak there are about 9,000 Shovelers in Britain and 8,000 in Ireland. In Britain the numbers decline steadily during the winter, only 5,000–7,000 nowadays being present in February and March, compared with perhaps 8,000–10,000 in the 1960s, when the spring passage was much larger. In Ireland, there may be as few as 4,000 by January, although (as mentioned above) there is evidence of an increase in spring.

Numbers in Britain and Ireland are less significant internationally than those of most wildfowl. About 20,000 Shovelers were thought to winter in NW Europe in the early 1970s, and some 25,000 pairs to breed in the region and to winter further south. NW Europe therefore probably supported about 100,000 birds, allowing for non-breeders (Scott 1980). Recent analyses by the IWRB show a continuing increase throughout Europe.

D. G. SALMON

Total number of squares in which recorded: 909 (24%)

No. of birds seen in a day	Number (%) of squares		
	Britain	Ireland	TOTAL (incl. C.I.)
1–7	367 (50%)	75 (43%)	442 (49%)
8–34	232 (32%)	49 (28%)	281 (31%)
35+	135 (18%)	57 (29%)	186 (20%)

References

ATKINSON-WILLES, G. L. 1956. *National Wildfowl Counts 1954–55*. The Wildfowl Trust, Slimbridge.

OGILVIE, M. A. 1962. The movements of Shoveler ringed in Britain. *Wildfowl Trust Ann. Rep.* 13: 65–69.

OLNEY, P. J. S. 1965. The autumn and winter feeding biology of certain sympatric ducks. *Trans. VI Cong. Int. Union Game Biol., Bournemouth, 1963:* 309–322.

PERDECK, A. C. and C. CLASON. 1980. *Some Results of Waterfowl Ringing in Europe.* IWRB Special Publ. 1. IWRB, Slimbridge.

SCOTT, D. A. 1980. *A Preliminary Inventory of Wetlands of International Importance for Waterfowl in Western Europe and North-west Africa.* IWRB Special Publ. 2. IWRB, Slimbridge.

THOMAS, G. J. 1978. *Breeding and Feeding Ecology of Waterfowl at the Ouse Washes, England.* Ph.D. Thesis, Council for National Academic Awards.

Breeding Atlas p 70

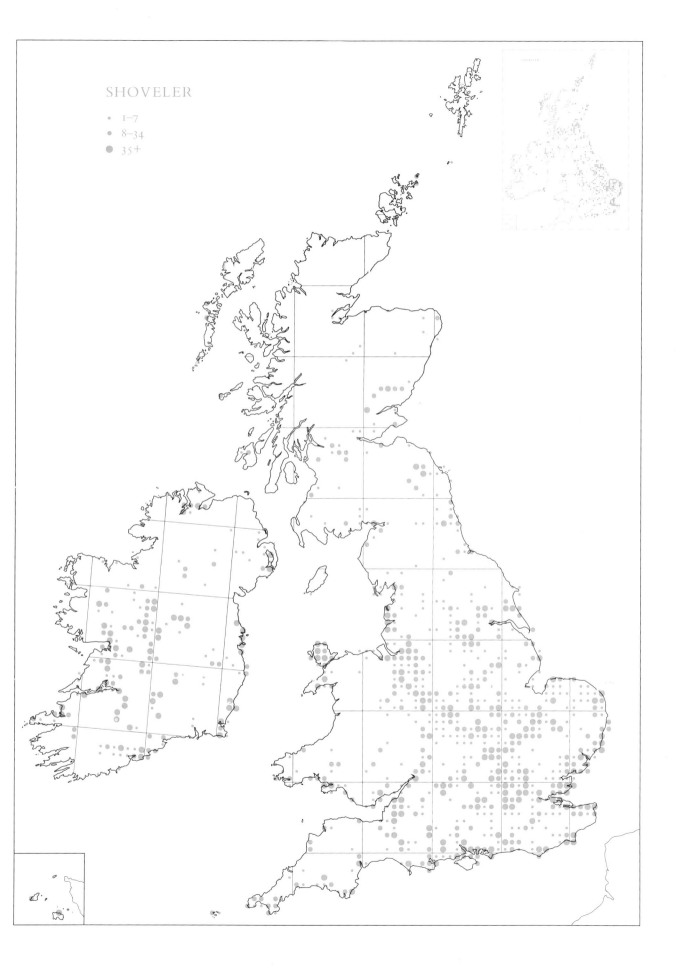

SHOVELER

- • 1–7
- • 8–34
- ● 35+

Red-crested Pochard

Netta rufina

The striking pink bill and golden head of the drake Red-crested Pochard contrast handsomely with the black, brown and white body and wings, but the initial excitement of discovering one is likely to be tempered by the thought that it might well have originated from feral stock.

There were isolated breeding records in Lincolnshire in 1937 and Essex in 1958, and since 1968 a pair or two have nested in most years at localities chiefly in the southern half of England. Such records almost certainly refer to individuals that have escaped from waterfowl collections, in which this species is frequently represented, and it is not surprising that the current winter distribution is mainly centred within a 150 km radius of London, an area that contains many waters bearing ornamental wildfowl.

Most sightings in Britain are on fresh water; in particular on reservoirs, lakes and flooded gravel pits, especially those fringed by *Phragmites* and other vegetation, although these waters may be of quite small dimension. Reports have come also from freshwater marshes, rivers and, occasionally, from tidal water whilst a few have been identified in offshore movements of other ducks.

Food consists mainly of aquatic vegetation, particularly *Chara*, and is obtained both by diving and upending. Early morning and evening are characteristically the periods of greatest feeding activity. Between times, individuals will often rest motionless on the water amongst the flotillas of Tufted Ducks *Aythya fuligula* and Pochards *A. ferina* that occur at such locations. With heads tucked down, females, and drakes not in full plumage, may easily be overlooked. In late summer, during the period of moult, this species sometimes associates with Mallards *Anas platyrhynchos* or even Coots *Fulica atra*.

Its main haunts extend eastwards from the Black Sea into Asia but there are disjunct breeding populations in western Europe including the Netherlands, West Germany and Denmark (recently declined). In southern France, and particularly Spain, numbers are substantial (*BWP*). Evidence for the arrival here of Red-crested Pochards from overseas was presented by Pyman (1959) who drew attention to the late summer moult assemblies that occur in the Netherlands and NW Germany. These birds later move SW to winter in the N Mediterranean basin. Pyman's analysis was prompted by exceptional numbers of this species in the late 1950s on the Essex reservoirs, mainly at Abberton where there were 22 in November 1956 and up to 16 (though perhaps 26 in all) in September/October 1957. There were 19 again in October 1960. Influxes of such numbers did not continue, however, and with hindsight a concurrent decline in the Danish breeding population may be relevant in this context.

The Essex birds were included in the estimate of 30–50 per year from 1951–61 (British Ornithologists' Union 1971) during which time it was described as 'particularly numerous'. The winters of 1981–84 produced records of 14 at the Cotswold Water Park (Wiltshire/Gloucestershire) where there is now a breeding colony, 14 at Audley End (Essex), and 12 at Bourton-on-the-Water (Gloucestershire) but approximately 90% of all sightings were of 1–3 birds.

The occasional occurrences in Ireland, southern Scotland and northern England suggest some winter wandering and it is of interest that a flock of 8, in each case containing 6 drakes, was reported on consecutive days in January 1982 at Hill Head (Hampshire) and Minsmere (Suffolk).

Allowing that some birds were almost certainly recorded in more than one square over the three seasons, the current winter population is probably in the range 50–100, but the small though definite increase during the last half century can be attributed more to a rise in the number of escapes and their progeny than to a genuine increase in the number of immigrants. Britain is clearly on the very fringe of the range of this species, the NW European wintering population of which was estimated by Atkinson-Willes (1972) to be 9,000.

S. COX

Total number of squares in which recorded: 82 (2%)

No. of birds seen in a day	Number (%) of squares		
	Britain	Ireland	TOTAL (incl. C.I.)
1	52 (69%)	4 (57%)	56 (68%)
2–3	15 (20%)	3 (43%)	18 (22%)
4+	8 (11%)	0 (0%)	8 (10%)

References

ATKINSON-WILLES, G. L. 1972. The international wildfowl censuses as a basis for wetland evaluation and hunting rationalization. *Proc. Int. Conf. Conserv. Wetlands and Waterfowl, Ramsar 1971*: 87–110. IWRB, Slimbridge.

BRITISH ORNITHOLOGISTS' UNION. 1971. *The Status of Birds in Britain and Ireland*. Blackwell, Oxford.

PYMAN, G. A. 1959. The Status of the Red-crested Pochard in the British Isles. *Brit. Birds* 52: 42–56.

Breeding Atlas p 446

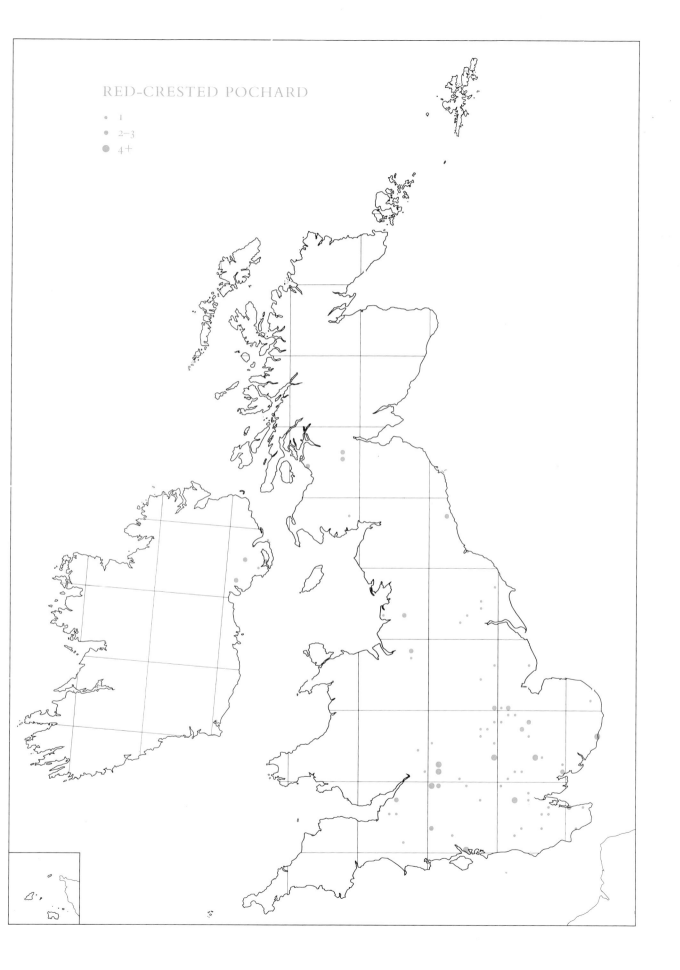

RED-CRESTED POCHARD

- 1
- 2–3
- 4+

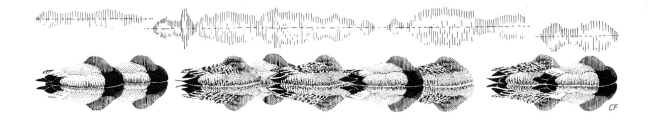

Pochard

Aythya ferina

The Pochard is a widespread wintering diving duck in Britain and Ireland, mainly confined to fresh water. It often shares waters with the Tufted Duck *A. fuligula*, but unlike the latter, is an uncommon though quite widely distributed breeding species.

Gravel pits and reservoirs, and fertile lowland lakes, are the preferred habitat of the Pochard, and this is nicely reflected in the map, with concentrations around most of the gravel pit complexes of southern and central England, and on the reservoirs and lakes around, for example, London. Concentrations of over 1,000 are not particularly common, and most of the wintering flocks are less than 500. The species is not quite so widely distributed as the Tufted Duck, as it probably prefers slightly larger waters, and it is also less frequent on lakes in towns and cities.

The breeding and winter distributions in Britain are similar, reflecting the year round habitat preference. In Ireland, the species is quite rare in summer, and confined to a relatively small number of sites in the centre and west and Lough Neagh. In winter, however, it is much more widespread, particularly in the west and north.

Pochards feed by both day and night mainly by diving in relatively shallow water. The preferred depth is as little as 1 m, but can be about 3.5 m. Dives normally take from 13–16 seconds, though up to 30 seconds has been recorded. During intensive bouts of feeding, dives are separated by pauses of no more than 5 seconds. During the dives, the bird is feeding mainly on vegetation, taken from the bottom or from submerged plants. The seeds of *Potamogeton* and the oospores of *Chara* are the commonest foods, plus the shoots, roots, and tubers of these plants. Animal food amounts to about 15% of the diet, and includes chironomid larvae and other small invertebrates. Feeding by dabbling or upending is quite frequent (*BWP*).

It is not known whether the British breeding Pochards are migratory, though it seems possible that the more northerly breeders may move some way south for the winter. The wintering population of Britain and Ireland comes from central Europe and into the USSR, mainly between about 40° and 55°N, and as far as about 80°E.

Immigration begins in September, with the peak numbers normally present in December and January. The situation is complicated, though, by the presence of a number of substantial flocks of moulting birds,

largely males, which assemble in July at, particularly, Abberton Reservoir, Essex, where 2,000–3,000 are regular, and also at Rutland Water, Leicestershire (up to 1,000). In September more than 20,000 have been found on Loughs Corrib, Derravaragh, and Cullin in Co. Galway/Co. Mayo. It is thought that these might include birds which have moulted there, as there was a single July count of about 4,000 on Lough Cullin in 1975. It is not known from how far east these moulting birds may come but most of them disperse from October onwards (Hutchinson 1979).

The largest regular flock of Pochards in Britain, of about 7,000 birds, has virtually disappeared in the last 7 years. It was on Duddingston Loch, Edinburgh. The birds fed out on the Firth of Forth on waste grain and other food from sewage outfalls. With the building of a treatment works the food source disappeared, and along with it the Pochard.

The number of Pochards wintering in Britain and Ireland has increased very considerably in recent decades. The situation in the latter country is obscured by a paucity of counts from Lough Neagh, where there was a peak count of 37,000 in winter 1965/66, though no more than 11,000 the following winter, and again 41,000 in 1979/80 and 11,000 in 1980/81. The British peak was probably around 35,000 in the late 1970s, and probably under half that in the mid 1960s (Hutchinson 1979, Owen et al 1986). The peak total in Britain is now put at around 50,000, and a further 30,000 or more in Ireland.

The NW European population of Pochards is estimated to be about 250,000, and there are some 750,000 in the Mediterranean-Black Sea region, and perhaps another 450,000 further east (Scott 1980). The largest concentrations in NW Europe are in the Netherlands, with a more dispersed distribution elsewhere.

M. A. OGILVIE

Total number of squares in which recorded: 1,800 (47%)

No. of birds seen in a day	Number (%) of squares		
	Britain	Ireland	TOTAL (incl. C.I.)
1–20	692 (50%)	206 (52%)	899 (50%)
21–94	423 (30%)	117 (29%)	541 (30%)
95+	284 (20%)	76 (19%)	360 (20%)

References

SCOTT, D. 1980. *A Preliminary Inventory of Wetlands of International Importance for Waterfowl in West Europe and Northwest Africa*. IWRB, Slimbridge.

Breeding Atlas p 80

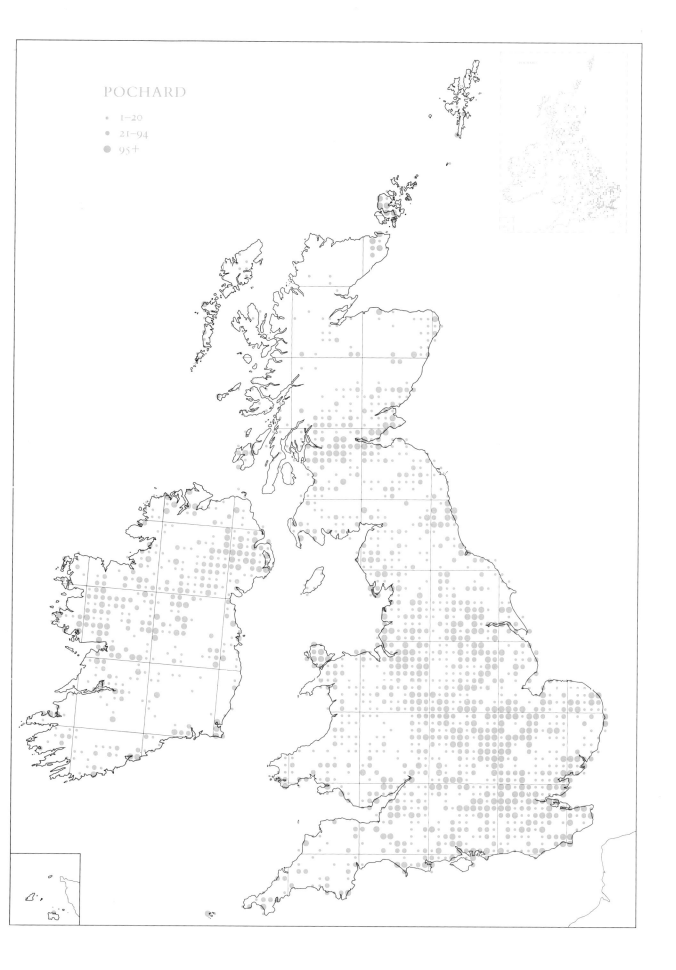

POCHARD

- • 1—20
- • 21—94
- • 95+

Ring-necked Duck

Aythya collaris

This North American diving duck has progressed in the last 30 years from being a rare vagrant to a regular visitor, if in tiny numbers, with many birds staying for prolonged periods.

The first authentic record from the British Isles, omitting a doubtful 19th century report, was in 1955. There followed a trickle of sightings through the 1960s and 1970s, with hardly a year without at least one new bird being seen. There were in addition a number of birds which were seen repeatedly at the same location, over a period of 4 or even 5 consecutive winters, though equally often absent during the summer months, when their whereabouts remained a mystery.

The appearance of scattered individuals in earlier years has been at least partly explained in terms of the increase and spread of the species into the NE of the USA and into eastern Canada. This took place during the 1940s and 1950s (Bellrose 1980).

There is no ready explanation, however, for the sudden surge in records in the late 1970s, nor for the dropping off in the last few years. This awaits necessary research into movements and weather patterns, and perhaps breeding success, in North America.

Ring-necked Ducks are nearly always found on fresh water in Britain and Ireland, usually singly, rarely 2 or 3 together where they not uncommonly consort with other diving ducks. A small number of apparent hybrids reported in recent years may be offspring of mixed pairs formed in this way.

In 1975, no new birds were seen, the first gap for several years. There followed a remarkable sequence of years, from 1976 to 1980 with, respectively, 6, 25, 13, 29, and 35 new birds. The total fell to 12 in 1981, and the same number the following year, dropping further to 7 in 1983 (*British Birds* annual rarities reports).

Ring-necked Ducks have also appeared in small numbers on the Continent in recent years, though nowhere to equal the numbers here (Brunn 1971).

M. A. OGILVIE

Total number of squares in which recorded: 16 (< 1%)

No. of birds seen in a day	Number (%) of squares		
	Britain	Ireland	TOTAL (incl. C.I.)
1	15 (100%)	1 (100%)	16 (100%)

References

BELLROSE, C. F. 1980. *Ducks, Geese and Swans of North America*. 3rd edn. Stackpole Books, Harrisburg, Pennsylvania.

BRUNN, B. 1971. North American waterfowl in Europe. *Brit. Birds* 64: 385–408.

Reports on Rare Birds in *Brit. Birds* 1957–83

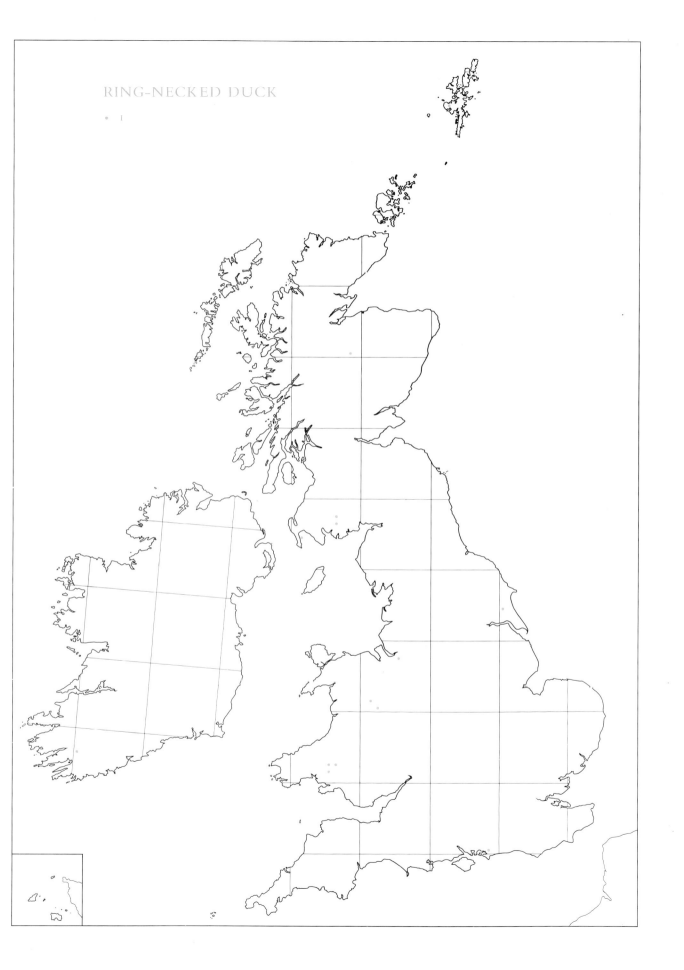

RING-NECKED DUCK

• 1

Ferruginous Duck

Aythya nyroca

The Ferruginous Duck is an extremely rare bird in Britain and Ireland. With its mahogany red plumage, white eyes and white undertail, the handsome drake is very distinctive. Finding such a splendid bird still brings a tingle of excitement to the birdwatcher's autumn. Females and immatures are less well marked and not infrequently give rise to problems of identification, owing to the close similarity of hybrids. Unless the bill tip could be seen well, Gillham *et al* (1966) regarded the Ferruginous Duck × Pochard *Aythya ferina* hybrid as inseparable from pure bred females and immatures. Full keys to hybrids and species are given in Osborne (1972).

The map probably gives a somewhat misleading view of the winter status, because for the last 30 years the pattern of records has been obscured by stray birds of captive origin. In Europe the breeding population and passage range have markedly decreased, whilst escapes from collections in Britain have considerably increased. These feral birds 'migrate', though displaced in longitude and latitude. It is against such a background that the British records must be viewed.

In the *Winter Atlas* there were 21 squares with records, evenly scattered across England and Wales, with only a single in lowland Scotland. The pattern lacks any bias towards East Anglia and the south coast that genuine migrants on autumn passage might be expected to show. The records are also evenly spread throughout the 4 winter months. It occurs on any open water much as other ducks.

Historically the species does not winter in Britain or Ireland, and it seems unlikely that many of the birds recorded in the *Winter Atlas* were truly wild. Closer investigation of one record, for instance, discloses clear evidence of a bird of captive origin. At one site a male Ferruginous Duck, which wintered from 24 September 1982 to 1 April 1983, had been reported in each of the 4 previous winters (*London Bird Reports*) and it subsequently recurred in 1983/84.

It is interesting to draw comparisons with an earlier era when fewer Ferruginous Ducks were kept in collections. Thirty-five years ago, during the 'influx' of 1950/51, 74% of the records reported to *British Birds* were in the autumn (mid September to early December). In the later period 1958–68, the autumn percentage had fallen to 46%. Already the presence of feral birds was beginning to change the pattern of records. In 1969 the *British Birds* Rarities Committee, no longer confident of separating wild birds from escapes, withdrew the species from its list.

Even in wintering areas of high population, the species tends to be solitary by nature, not forming close flocks nor closely associating with other species. No studies have been made of the seasonal variation in food preferences. It seems possible, however, that this may influence its extensive migrations to warmer climes. In captivity in western Europe, it survives well if ponds are kept ice-free and it is fed.

The species' main breeding distribution is in the USSR. It is predominantly migratory, reaching Turkey, the Middle East, Pakistan and India in winter, with smaller pockets in the Mediterranean, the Nile Valley and East Africa.

The Ferruginous Duck has never been known to breed in Britain or Ireland, either in the wild or in a feral state. But in captivity it is said by Kolbe (1979) to be easier to breed than any other diving duck. In collections it also interbreeds with other *Aythya* species, as well as *Anas*, *Netta* and Goldeneye *Bucephala clanguila*.

In Britain the species and its hybrids both occur in late autumn flocks of Pochards, suggesting that wild birds may get caught up with Pochards, or, more likely, that some escapes are of Continental origin. Date is perhaps important, for, in the wild, the Ferruginous Duck's departure from its northern breeding areas takes place in September and early October, and it usually reaches the Danube Delta and Black Sea by November. In winter, wild individuals north of 46°N (southern France) are extremely rare and the numbers in Britain are probably less than 20.

In favourable conditions, as many as 45,000 birds may winter in southern USSR, and 75,000 around the Black Sea and in parts of the Mediterranean.

K. C. OSBORNE

Total number of squares in which recorded: 21 (< 1%)

No. of birds seen in a day	Number (%) of squares		
	Britain	Ireland	TOTAL (incl. C.I.)
1	17 (81%)	0 (0%)	17 (81%)
2	4 (19%)	0 (0%)	4 (19%)

References

GILLHAM, E., J. M. HARRISON and J. G. HARRISON. 1966. A study of certain *Aythya* hybrids. *Wildfowl Trust 17th Ann. Rep.*: 49–65.

HARRISON, C. 1982. *An Atlas of the Birds of the Western Palearctic*. Collins, London.

KOLBE, H. 1979. *Ornamental Waterfowl*. English edn. Edition, Leipzig.

OSBORNE, K. C. 1972. The need for caution when identifying Scaup, Ferruginous Duck and other species in the *Aythya* genus. *London Bird Report* 36: 86–91.

VOOUS, K. 1960. *Atlas of European Birds*. Nelson, London.

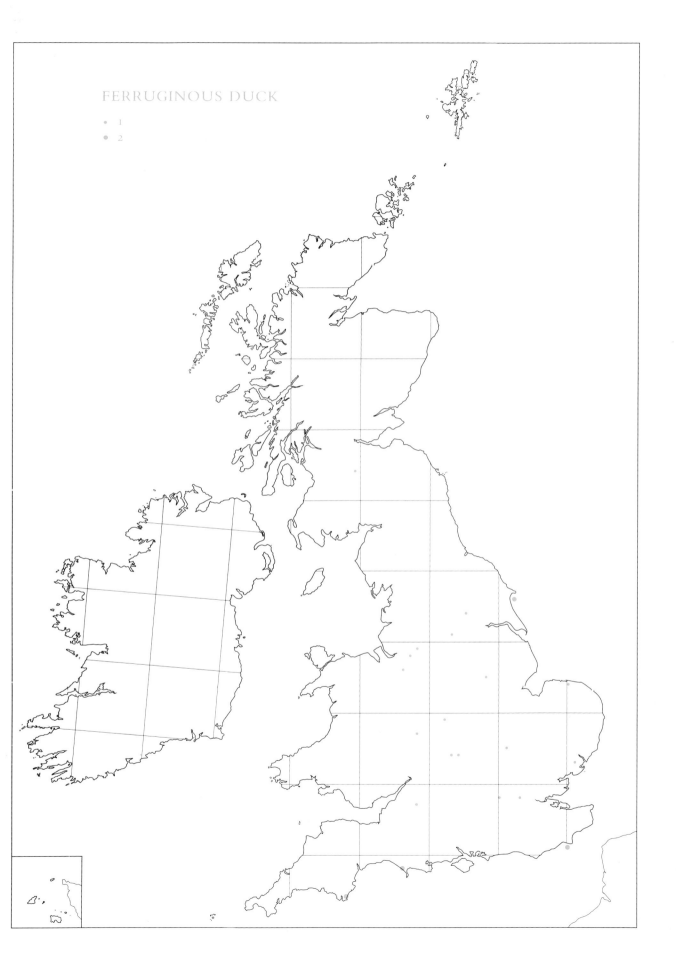

FERRUGINOUS DUCK

● 1
● 2

Tufted Duck

Aythya fuligula

The commonest diving duck in Britain and Ireland, the Tufted Duck is a widespread breeding species, while numbers in winter are greatly augmented by immigrants from northern Europe.

There are few fertile fresh waters which do not hold Tufted Ducks in winter, this being especially true of drinking water reservoirs and gravel pits in lowland areas. Acid waters, and lakes and reservoirs in upland areas, are on the whole avoided and only very small numbers, less than 5% of the total, are found on brackish or salt water habitats (Owen *et al* 1986). The map clearly shows the lowland distribution of the species, with concentrations in the Thames, Ouse and Trent valleys, on the reservoirs around London, in west central, and NW England, and on the lochs and reservoirs of central Scotland. There are important waters for Tufted Ducks in central and W Ireland, and, particularly, on Lough Neagh in Northern Ireland.

Flocks of Tufted Ducks are generally small, rarely more than 1,000. By becoming tolerant of man, Tufted Ducks have successfully moved into town and city park lakes where they supplement their natural diet with food from the public.

The breeding and winter distributions in Britain and Ireland are very similar, although the larger waters, or those without islands or thick fringing vegetation, are not used for nesting.

Tufted Ducks live mainly on animal food, which they obtain by diving with occasional upending. The preferred depth is down to about 2.5 m, but there are many records of them feeding down to at least 5 m. Dives normally last 15–20 seconds, and rarely more than 35–40. Up to 100 dives per hour are common, with 10 second pauses between dives (*BWP*).

Whilst underwater, the bill is used to pluck larger molluscs, such as the zebra mussel and the spire-shell, from the bottom or off the leaves of submerged plants. Chironomid and other larvae are taken in large quantities, and are sieved from the bottom mud while the bird maintains its body at an angle of about 45°. Plant seeds are eaten, particularly in autumn.

As males dive to greater depths and so stay down longer than females, there is some separation of the sexes in feeding flocks. Feeding is commoner during the day than during the night.

Ringing has shown that the breeding birds of Scotland move to Ireland for the winter, but those breeding in Ireland and in the rest of Britain are more or less sedentary, at least in normal winters. Immi-grants from Iceland, northern Scandinavia and Russia east to about 80°E, arrive in Britain in late September onwards and stay to early spring. In the autumn, some Tufted Ducks may move through Britain into France, and there is further onward movement in spells of hard weather. Moulting concentrations have been recorded at a few places, but the origins of the birds are unknown.

Tufted Ducks have increased enormously in Britain in the last hundred years and are still increasing. From the first breeding record in Yorkshire in 1849, the nesting population is now put at over 7,000 pairs (Owen *et al* 1986). Similarly in Ireland, where the first breeding record was in 1877 and there are now thought to be at least 2,000 pairs (Hutchinson 1979). The wintering population has similarly increased. The mid winter peak has roughly trebled since the early 1960s, and now stands at just over 60,000 (Owen *et al* 1986). Although this could be accounted for in large part by the growth of the breeding population, because many of our breeders move out of Britain for the winter, it seems more likely that there has been a genuine growth in numbers of immigrants coming to replace them. The picture in Ireland is confused by the mid winter presence on Lough Neagh of over 30,000 birds in the mid 1960s. The few complete counts since then were 29,000 in January 1978, falling to 19,000 in November 1979 and only 8,000 in the following November. It is not known whether such large numbers still occur there. Elsewhere in Ireland, a peak winter population of up to 25,000 has been estimated (Hutchinson 1979).

The NW European population of Tufted Ducks is put at over 500,000; there are a further 350,000 in the Mediterranean–Black Sea region; and at least half a million in Asia (Scott 1980).

M. A. OGILVIE

Total number of squares in which recorded: 2,042 (53%)

No. of birds seen in a day	Number (%) of squares		
	Britain	Ireland	TOTAL (incl. C.I.)
1–25	794 (49%)	216 (51%)	1,011 (50%)
26–94	493 (31%)	128 (30%)	621 (30%)
95+	327 (20%)	82 (19%)	410 (20%)

References

SCOTT, D. 1980. *A Preliminary Inventory of Wetlands of International Importance for Waterfowl in West Europe and Northwest Africa*. IWRB, Slimbridge.

Breeding Atlas p 78

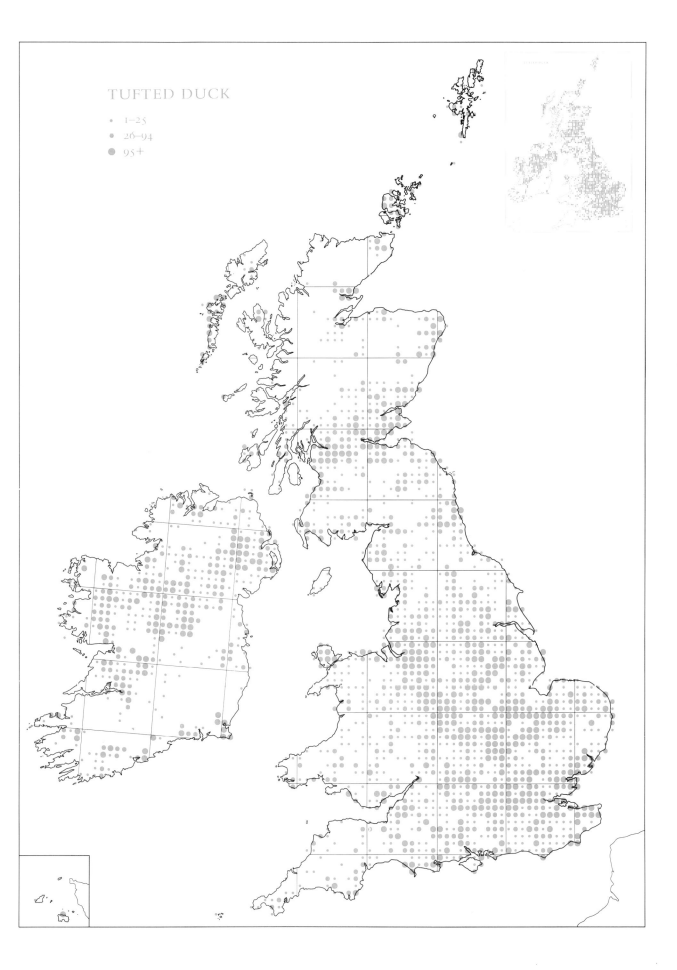

TUFTED DUCK

- 1–25
- 26–94
- 95+

Scaup

Aythya marila

Breeding in Iceland and western Siberia, the Scaup is the most exclusively marine of the diving ducks which winter in Britain and Ireland. The winter distribution pattern is coastal but small numbers occur inland on lakes and reservoirs. Although sparsely distributed it is widespread except in NW Scotland and SW England. A substantial proportion of the total winter population is found in estuaries and relatively enclosed waters at a limited number of largely traditional sites, which are highlighted on the map. In recent years, Largo Bay in the Firth of Forth, the Inner Solway, and Loch Indaal (Islay) have held more than 1,000, but flocks of several hundred are regular at Edderton Bay (Dornoch Firth), Carlingford Lough, and the Dee (Cheshire). On many other estuaries small numbers are likely to be found, frequently in close association with other diving ducks such as Goldeneyes *Bucephala clangula*. Exceptionally, for an inland site, Lough Neagh often holds at least 1,000.

Sewer outfalls have been shown to be a major factor in attracting Scaups to some Scottish sites. During the mid 1960s and in the 1970s very large flocks used to gather at Edinburgh's main sewers at Leith. Over 30,000 were recorded in some winters and for at least 15 years the annual mid winter peak exceeded 10,000 (Milne and Campbell 1973). Waste grain from breweries and distilleries was probably the main attraction although a super-abundance of small worms thriving on raw sewage was undoubtedly also important.

Reduced grain discharges and the introduction of new sewage treatment procedures resulted in the disappearance of the flocks in the late 1970s (Campbell 1984). A smaller flock at Invergordon was lost in similar circumstances. The sewer habit, which seems to be a British phenomenon, persists at other principal sites such as Largo Bay and at Loch Indaal, where distillery waste is also involved. In more natural situations Scaups are known to feed on mussels and other estuarine invertebrates.

Scaups are mainly night-feeders and typically spend the day in relatively dense flocks, when they may be particularly vulnerable to oil pollution (Campbell *et al* 1978). At Edinburgh, unless disturbed, the daytime resting flocks tended to remain near to their presumed night feeding-areas, but elsewhere (*eg* Edderton Bay) these roosts might be several kilometres away, involving regular dawn and dusk flight movements. Daytime feeding is most evident amongst Scaups feeding in more natural situations such as estuaries, and increased in frequency at Edinburgh after the introduction of sewage treatment.

Numbers at most sites start to build up in October, reaching a peak in late December or January. At most sites numbers seem to remain high for the rest of the winter but at Leith very large flocks were usually only present for a short period in mid winter, a substantial number of birds appearing to spend only a few weeks at the site, before moving to other wintering grounds presumably on the south shores of the North Sea and in the Baltic. In winter, movement in the European population is indicated by the short term occurrences of flocks of Scaups in unusual numbers or at unusual sites.

Ringing data indicate that many of the Scaups wintering in Britain and Ireland are of Icelandic origin. Eastern breeders are also present, as birds ringed in Scotland in winter have been recovered in the Baltic and Russia.

Following the changes at Leith there has been a considerable decrease in the size of the wintering population in Britain. On the basis of recent detailed studies and wildfowl counts, the peak mid winter population in Britain and Ireland is likely to be of the order of 5,000–10,000, and the wintering population in NW Europe has been estimated at around 150,000 (Atkinson-Willes 1976).

L. H. CAMPBELL

Total number of squares in which recorded: 464 (12%)

No. of birds seen in a day	Number (%) of squares		
	Britain	Ireland	TOTAL (incl. C.I.)
1–2	197 (52%)	15 (18%)	213 (46%)
3–25	130 (34%)	30 (36%)	160 (34%)
26+	53 (14%)	38 (46%)	91 (20%)

References

ATKINSON-WILLES, G. L. 1976. The numerical distribution of ducks, swans and coots as a guide to assessing the importance of wetlands in midwinter. *Proc. Int. Conf. Conserv. Wetlands and Waterfowl. Heiligenhafen, 1974*: 199–254. IWRB, Slimbridge.

CAMPBELL, L. H. 1984. The impact of changes in sewage treatment on seaducks wintering in the Firth of Forth, Scotland. *Biol. Conserv.* 28: 173–180.

CAMPBELL, L. H., K. T. STANDRING and C. J. CADBURY. 1978. Firth of Forth Oil Pollution incident, February 1978. *Marine Pollution Bulletin*: 335–339.

MILNE, H. and L. H. CAMPBELL. 1973. Wintering seaducks off the east coast of Scotland. *Bird Study* 20: 153–172.

RUTTLEDGE, R. F. 1970. Winter distribution and numbers of Scaup, Long-tailed Duck and Common Scoter in Ireland. *Bird Study* 17: 241–246.

Breeding Atlas p 76

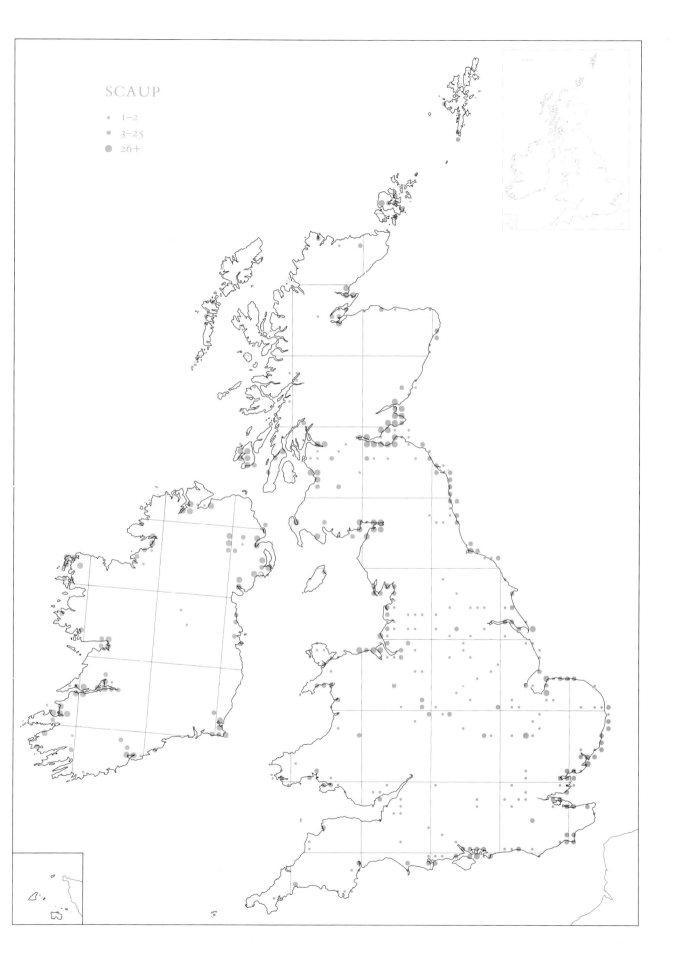

SCAUP

- 1–2
- 3–25
- 26+

Eider

Somateria mollissima

The Eider is our commonest sea duck. Within the winter flocks, the conspicuous black and white drakes frequently display to the cryptically coloured, brown females. On a calm day the evocative cooing of the males can often be heard from over a kilometre away.

Eiders have an exclusively coastal distribution, except for occasional birds blown inland during rough weather. The mainly northerly distribution closely follows that shown in the *Breeding Atlas*. However, small numbers are also recorded round the rest of the British and Irish coasts away from the breeding areas (see Table). The major concentrations occur in Shetland, SW Scotland, Cumbria and E Britain. The largest wintering flock occurs on the Tay estuary, where 14,100 Eiders were counted in November 1983.

Most of these large concentrations are found on estuaries but Eiders also occupy rocky coasts. They feed mainly on blue mussels, although a range of other molluscs, crustaceans and echinoderms are also taken (*BWP*). They obtain their prey by surface diving, by head dipping or by upending. In estuaries Eiders feed at low tide and roost over the high tide period, but time of day is also important (Campbell 1978). Thus in the Firth of Forth the dawn influx to a daytime feeding area is greatest when the last stages of the ebbing tide occur at sunrise.

Winter social behaviour and feeding have important effects on breeding performance because defence by her mate allows the female to increase her feeding rate, and hence to accumulate the body reserves necessary for breeding. At the Sands of Forvie, Grampian, the proportion of paired females increases from 10% in September to 80% in March (Spurr and Milne 1976). Females which pair after mid winter usually lay late or fail to breed.

Many breeding Eiders from Forvie, and from Northumberland, winter in the Tay and Forth estuaries (Milne 1965). Some remain at Forvie and Loch Fleet in early winter but disperse subsequently (Mudge and Allen 1980). First year birds from Forvie disperse locally, but few reach the adult wintering grounds. Eider populations in other parts of Britain probably move no further than do the Forvie birds. There are several records from the Baltic of males ringed in Britain in winter, so the Baltic is probably the main source of Eiders wintering in E England.

British Eider populations have been increasing since the end of the last century, and at Forvie winter numbers increased at an average rate of 4% per annum between 1953/54 and 1977/78. Recently, local decreases have occurred in Shetland and in the Firth of Forth. Summing the regional estimates gives a winter population of 72,000, which is probably within 10,000 birds of the true value. The Eider has a mainly Arctic distribution and the British population is at the southern edge of its range in Europe, which is thought to have a wintering population of about 2 million Eiders (Atkinson-Willes 1978). Thus only about 4% of these winter in Britain and Ireland.

S. R. BAILLIE

Regional numbers of wintering Eiders, estimated from Winter Atlas *counts, the Winter Shorebird Count and published sources.*

Northumberland	5,300
E Scotland (to Grampian)	29,000
E Scotland (N of Grampian)	3,400
N Scotland	1,000
Orkney	5,000
Shetland	8,800
W Scotland	3,200
SW Scotland	7,700
Walney	4,400
Wales and W England	1,100
S England	300
E England	1,200
Ireland	2,200
Total	72,400

Total number of squares in which recorded: 704 (18%)

No. of birds	Number (%) of squares		
seen in a day	Britain	Ireland	TOTAL (incl. C.I.)
1–19	298 (48%)	50 (66%)	349 (50%)
20–91	195 (31%)	19 (25%)	215 (31%)
92+	133 (21%)	7 (9%)	140 (20%)

References

CAMPBELL, L. H. 1978. Diurnal and tidal behaviour patterns of Eiders wintering at Leith. *Wildfowl* 29: 147–152.

MILNE, H. 1965. Seasonal movements and distribution of Eiders in northeast Scotland. *Bird Study* 12: 170–180.

MUDGE, G. P. and D. S. ALLEN. 1980. Wintering seaducks in the Moray and Dornoch Firths, Scotland. *Wildfowl* 31: 123–130.

SPURR, E. and H. MILNE. 1976. Adaptive significance of autumn pair formation in the Common Eider *Somateria mollissima* (L.). *Ornis Scand.* 7: 85–89.

Breeding Atlas p 86

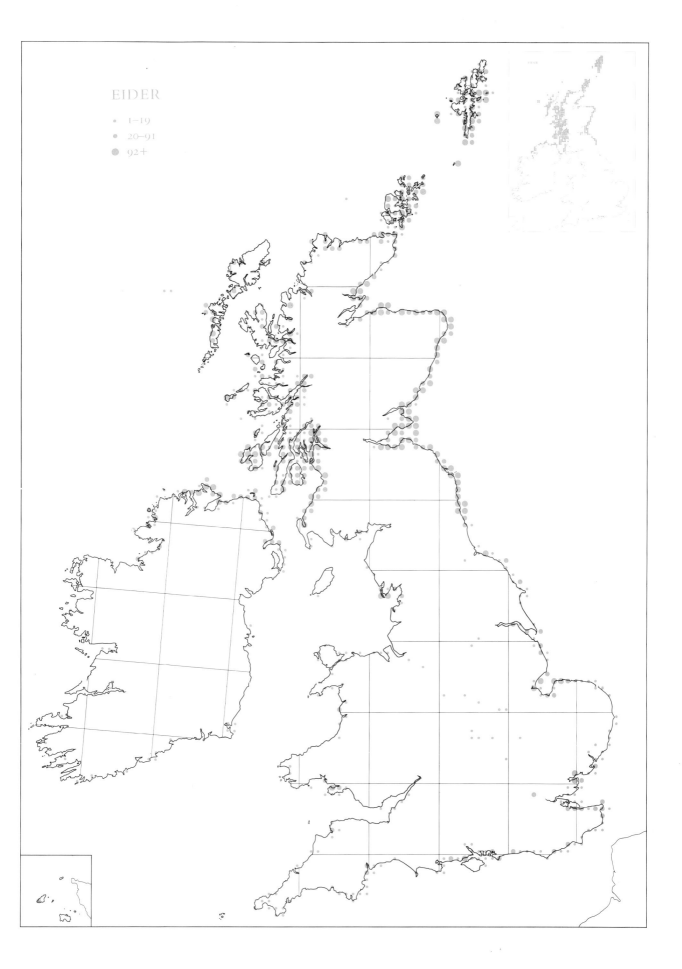

EIDER

- 1–19
- 20–91
- 92+

Long-tailed Duck

Clangula hyemalis

The Long-tailed Duck is the least known, but one of the most exciting, of the sea ducks which winter in Britain and Ireland. Its haunting calls on a calm frosty morning are amongst the more memorable of winter sounds.

The winter distribution pattern is markedly coastal, only occasional individuals or small groups occurring inland on lakes and reservoirs. Although quite widespread in small numbers, the majority occur in Scotland where the main resorts are in Shetland, Orkney, the Outer Hebrides and along the east coast, most notably the Moray Firth. In contrast with the other sea ducks, although frequently found close inshore or within estuaries, Long-tailed Ducks also occur in large numbers well offshore and for this reason are usually much under-recorded by casual ornithologists. Accordingly, the distribution map does fail to highlight the well known outstanding importance of the Moray Firth which in recent detailed surveys has been shown to hold regularly at least 10,000–15,000 each winter (Salmon 1983, J. Barrett). Orkney holds a further 6,000 or so (Hope Jones 1979) and Shetland at least another 500; elsewhere flocks are mostly very much smaller, but up to 500 do occur within the Firth of Forth.

Although occasionally occurring off most types of coastline, or in estuaries, Long-tailed Ducks are largely absent or very scarce along the indented rocky shores of NW Scotland and they generally seem to prefer areas where there are extensive shallows or shoals offshore, and where substrates are soft. Even within those areas where they are very abundant they tend to be dispersed widely in small groups of a dozen or so birds. Such groups are usually very active throughout the day, and feeding, displaying and short distance flighting take place in even the stormiest weather. Occasional glimpses of flighting groups on the horizon is often the only indication of their presence at a site.

Little is known about their preferred food in Britain and Ireland, but bivalves such as mussels, crustaceans and small fish are all likely to be important. Large scale movements at dusk to the various night roosting areas appear to be a regular feature. Hope Jones (1979) described movements of up to 12 km from inshore feeding areas to deeper water in the middle of Scapa Flow (Orkney), and regular movements of 10–12 km to at least two separate roosting areas have been recorded in the Moray Firth (Mudge and Allen 1980, J. Barrett). In these roosts the ducks are much more concentrated than by day and are potentially very vulnerable to any pollution incidents. Return movements at dawn have not been observed and must take place before it is light. Within the Moray Firth preferred day feeding areas seem to vary considerably from year to year.

The main influx of wintering birds does not take place until well into the autumn and peak numbers are not usually recorded until late December or early in the New Year. Thereafter, numbers remain high until mid February and there may be further short duration influxes during spring passage. The origins of these wintering birds are unknown but the flocks almost certainly contain both Fennoscandian and Russian breeding birds. Basing the assessment on the limited data available from the main sites it seems probable that in recent years the peak winter population of Britain and Ireland has been about 20,000. This is considerably higher than the 10,000 estimated by Prater (1981). It is unclear whether this represents a real increase, but better coverage has undoubtedly been a significant factor, particularly in the Moray Firth. The European wintering population is probably more than 500,000, mainly off N Norway and in the Baltic (Atkinson-Willes 1978) and the population in Britain and Ireland is at the southwestern limit of the winter range.

L. H. CAMPBELL

Total number of squares in which recorded: 496 (13%)

No. of birds seen in a day	Number (%) of squares		
	Britain	Ireland	TOTAL (incl. C.I.)
1–2	220 (53%)	35 (46%)	256 (52%)
3–20	108 (26%)	33 (43%)	141 (28%)
21+	90 (22%)	9 (12%)	99·(20%)

References

ATKINSON-WILLES, G. L. 1978. The numbers and distribution of sea ducks in North West Europe, January 1967–73. *Proc. Symp. Sea Ducks, Stockholm, 1975*: 28–67. Nat. Swedish Environ. Prot. Board /IWRB.

HOPE HONES, P. 1979. Roosting behaviour of Long-tailed Ducks in relation to possible oil pollution. *Wildfowl* 30: 155–158.

MUDGE, G. P. and D. S. ALLEN. 1980. Wintering sea-ducks in the Moray and Dornoch Firths, Scotland. *Wildfowl* 31: 123–130.

SALMON, D. G. 1983. *Wildfowl and Wader Counts 1982–83*. The Wildfowl Trust, Slimbridge.

Breeding Atlas p 447

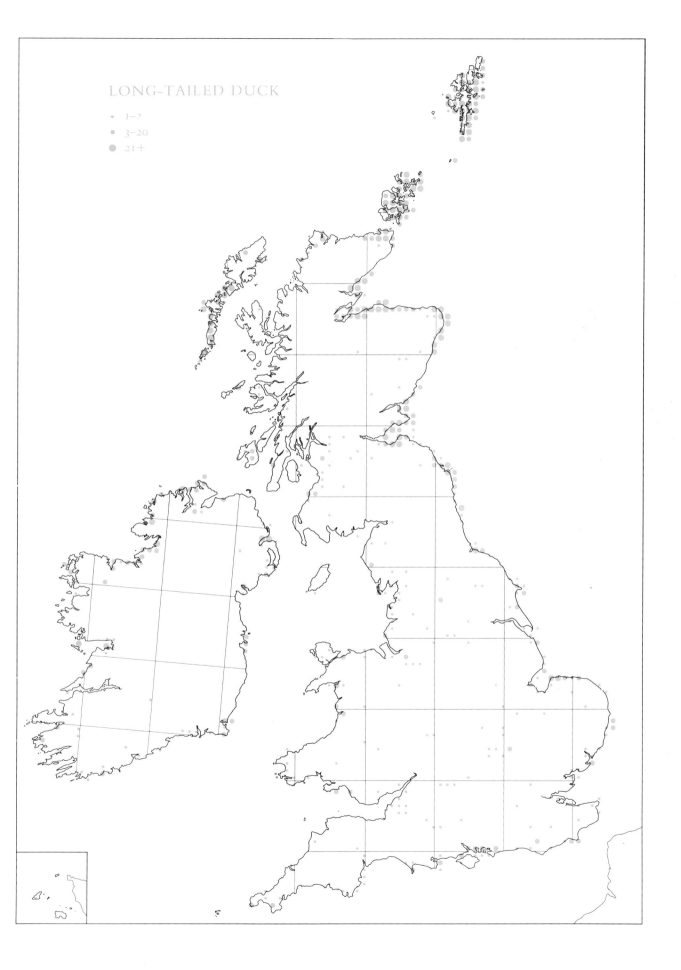

LONG-TAILED DUCK

- 1–2
- 3–20
- 21+

Common Scoter

Melanitta nigra

The Common Scoter is the least spectacular but probably one of the most familiar of the sea ducks around the coasts of Britain and Ireland. Small numbers occur in almost every month of the year and it is the most likely duck species to be seen during coastal sea watches.

Although individuals or small groups may turn up each winter on inland lakes, reservoirs and gravel pits, the winter distribution pattern is predominantly coastal, the species being widespread, and scarce only on the rockier coasts of northern and western Scotland. The bulk of the wintering population tends to be found in a relatively few large flocks off the mouths of major estuaries, or in similar situations where there are sandy substrates and shallow offshore water. Most of the known main wintering sites are pinpointed on the map, although because of the difficulties of counting this species the actual relative importance of each site is less evident. In recent years the Moray Firth, in particular off Dornoch, in Burghead Bay and Spey Bay, has been the major site, with usually at least 10,000 each winter. The relative proportion using each individual site each winter has varied considerably. The other major site is Carmarthen Bay. Prater (1981) noted a peak estimate of 25,000 in 1974 but recent counts have been much lower. Although this may partly be due to the difficulties of counting this site, it is also believed to represent a real decrease. Flocks of from a few hundred up to 1,000 are regular at several east coast sites such as St Andrews Bay, Firth of Forth, Holy Island and Flamborough, and in N Wales and NW England (*eg* Morecambe Bay), also along the south coast, especially in Sussex.

The mouth of the Thames and adjacent estuaries to the north in Essex and Suffolk are of uncertain importance but small numbers are regular, and occasional large flocks have been recorded (*eg* 7,000 at Foulness, Prater 1981). Although quite widespread around Ireland, numbers are now apparently lower than formerly (Ruttledge 1970, Hutchinson 1979).

Sandy seabeds and offshore shallows are strongly favoured by flocks of scoters. Within each site they are usually quite widely dispersed into diffuse flocks, each holding a hundred or more. They feed actively by day drifting along shore with tide, wind or current and then flying back to regain their original station. No regular dawn or dusk movements have been described and it is presumed that they remain to roost in or close to their daytime feeding areas.

Few data are available on their preferred food but mussels, sand-dwelling bivalves and sandeels are known to be eaten. In most flocks males predominate and display is frequent in calm weather in spring.

Moulting flocks are known to occur at several coastal sites, including some of those used in winter, and large numbers may be present in late summer and autumn. However, the main influx takes place in October and November, and peak numbers are usually noted from December until early February. Once they have arrived at a site, flocks seem to remain there throughout the winter and even in the Moray Firth, where 3 alternative sites are in close proximity, there has been no evidence of any regular interchange (Mudge and Allen 1980). Large-scale movements along the English Channel in autumn, and especially in spring, are often observed from vantage points such as Beachy Head and Dungeness. These movements involve flocks which winter off the French and Iberian coasts and breed in Fennoscandia and Russia; these are also the likely breeding grounds of most of the wintering population in Britain and Ireland. The wintering grounds of the small British breeding population are not known.

The wintering population was estimated by Prater (1981) to be at least 35,000 but, even allowing for poor coverage at some sites, this would now seem to be a high figure, and on the basis of recent peak counts, 25,000–30,000 for Britain and Ireland would seem to be more likely. Although numbers have been consistently high in the Moray Firth over the last 10 years, they appear to have been more variable elsewhere (*eg* Carmarthen Bay) and formerly important sites (*eg* St Andrews) are now less used.

The winter population in the western Palearctic has been variously estimated at 500,000–1,500,000.

L. H. CAMPBELL

Total number of squares in which recorded: 457 (12%)

Number (%) of squares

No. of birds seen in a day	Britain	Ireland	TOTAL (incl. C.I.)
1–9	185 (50%)	44 (51%)	229 (50%)
10–95	106 (29%)	27 (31%)	134 (29%)
96+	78 (21%)	15 (17%)	94 (21%)

References

MUDGE, G. P. and D. S. ALLEN. 1980. Wintering seaducks in the Moray and Dornoch Firths, Scotland. *Wildfowl* 31: 123–130.

RUTTLEDGE, R. F. 1970. Winter distribution and numbers of Scaup, Long-tailed Duck and Common Scoter in Ireland. *Bird Study* 17: 241–246.

Breeding Atlas p 84

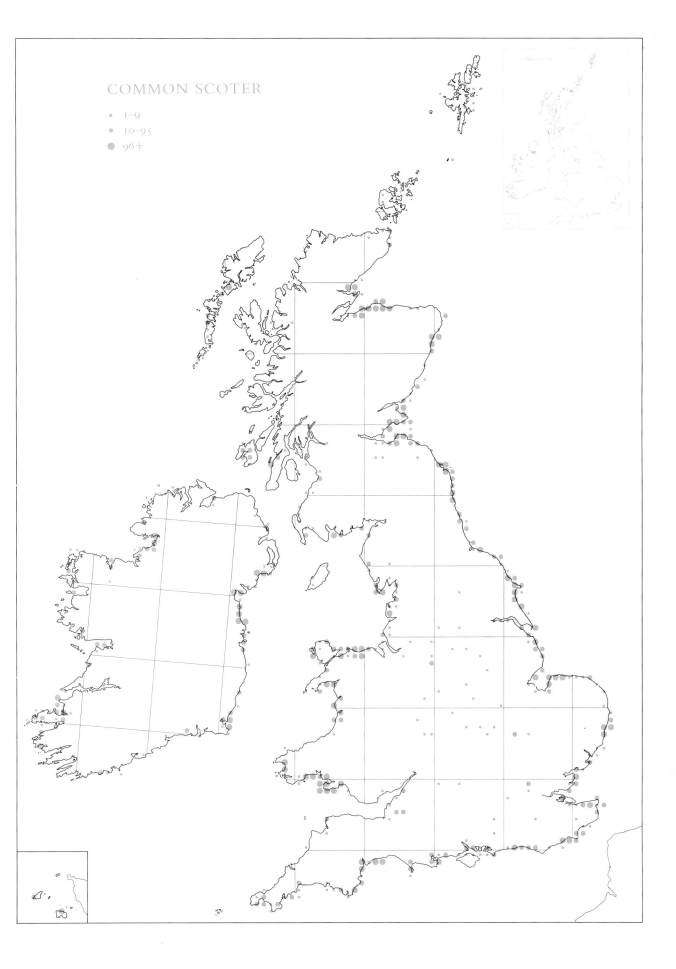

COMMON SCOTER

- · 1—9
- ● 10—95
- ● 96+

Velvet Scoter

Melanitta fusca

With its conspicuous white wing patches the Velvet Scoter is the more spectacular of the relatively common scoter species wintering in western Europe. Around much of Britain and Ireland it is a comparatively rare bird and the least abundant of the major wintering sea duck species.

Although one or two individuals turn up each winter at a few regular inland sites, the majority of records are in coastal or estuarine areas. Individuals or small groups may occasionally occur off almost all but the very exposed and rockiest coastlines, but the species is most frequent and numerous along the coasts of the North Sea. The locations of these preferred areas are clearly shown on the map.

At most sites Velvet Scoters are usually found amongst flocks of the more abundant Common Scoter *Melanitta nigra*, and in such situations it is often difficult to assess the relative abundance of the two species, except when the flocks are in flight. However Velvet Scoters rarely make up more than 10–20% of the total, and concentrations of more than 50 are unusual, except within the Moray Firth, which is currently the principal site. In recent years this area has frequently held peak numbers of several thousand, and in early 1983 a maximum count of over 8,000 was the largest number ever recorded in Britain or Ireland. Spey Bay, Burghead Bay and the outer Dornoch Firth are the main individual locations and, as with Common Scoters, the relative abundance at each varies considerably from winter to winter. Small numbers are regularly recorded in the Firth of Forth, where flocks of several hundred have also occurred, particularly in Largo Bay. In Orkney and Shetland, Velvet Scoters are probably more likely to be seen in any numbers than are Common Scoters, despite the fact that the latter breed in these islands.

Flocks of scoters are generally attracted to sandy coastal areas where there is shallow water offshore. Velvet Scoters, whilst frequently scattered throughout diffuse flocks of Common Scoters, may also occur in distinct subgroups where they feed and display on their own.

Adult males are usually predominant wherever more than a few individuals are present. Velvet Scoters are active feeders throughout the day, drifting along the shore with the tide or wind before flighting back to their feeding areas. As with Common Scoters, their preferred food is not well known but sand-dwelling invertebrates and sandeels are known to be taken. In the absence of any observations of regular dawn or dusk flighting it is presumed that they remain to roost at night close to their feeding grounds.

Small numbers of Velvet Scoters are known to moult along with more numerous Common Scoters at several coastal sites particularly in eastern Scotland (*eg* Murcar, Aberdeenshire) but total numbers are small and probably only a few hundred are present during late summer and autumn. Thereafter, numbers tend to build up during the first part of the winter and, at least in some years, this build up appears to continue until well into April. Common Scoters normally peak by early February and decline thereafter, and Velvet Scoters may at this time become the predominant species in the mixed flocks.

The peak wintering population of Britain and Ireland is believed to vary considerably from year to year, depending largely on the size of the flocks within the Moray Firth. Occasionally up to 10,000 may be present, but 2,500–5,000 is probably the more usual number. This apparent increase in the total population (Prater 1981) reflects the more intensive coverage at the principal site.

The winter population in western Europe has been estimated to be 150,000–200,000 and the main known wintering areas are in eastern Danish and southern Norwegian waters.

L. H. CAMPBELL

Total number of squares in which recorded: 179 (5%)

No. of birds seen in a day	Number (%) of squares		
	Britain	Ireland	TOTAL (incl. C.I.)
1–2	87 (54%)	13 (87%)	101 (56%)
3–10	43 (27%)	0 (0%)	44 (25%)
11+	32 (20%)	2 (13%)	34 (19%)

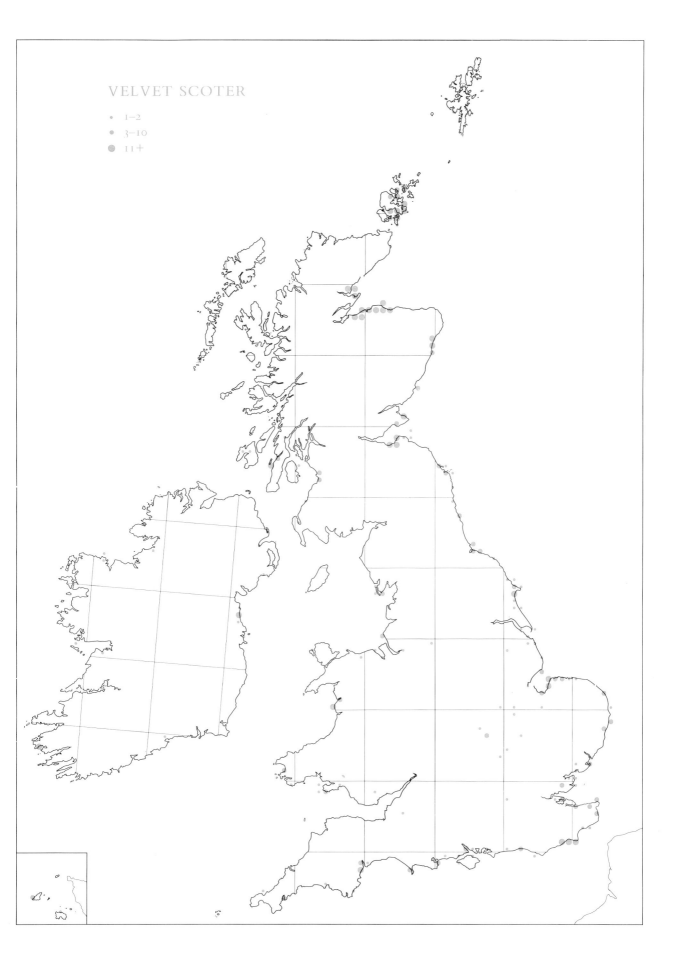

VELVET SCOTER

- • 1—2
- • 3—10
- ● 11+

Goldeneye

Bucephala clangula

The Goldeneye is one of the most attractive and best known of the diving ducks which winter in Britain and Ireland, and is now established as a regular breeding species in parts of Scotland. It is often thought of as a sea duck, but the winter distribution pattern shows that it is widespread inland as well as around most of the coastline, including the north and west. Small wintering groups, often closely associated with other diving ducks such as Pochards *Aythya ferina*, are frequent on many lochs, lakes, reservoirs, gravel pits and even rivers.

The main concentrations, on the coast or the larger inland waters, are clearly shown on the map, where reservoirs such as Abberton, Grafham and Rutland are highlighted. In recent years, although coverage has been patchy, it is clear that Lough Neagh and Lough Beg have held the largest concentrations, peak numbers occasionally exceeding 5,000 birds. The Firth of Forth is the only other area that regularly holds more than 1,000, these being found in several small and usually distinct flocks. In addition to the sites already mentioned several lochs (*eg* Strathbeg and Leven) and lakes (*eg* Windermere) regularly hold flocks of several hundred. Coastal sites with similar numbers includes the Cromarty Firth, Inverness, Firth of Tay and the Blackwater estuary in Essex.

At least in Scotland, Goldeneyes have been shown to be strongly attracted to sewers or discharges of waste from breweries and food processing plants (Pounder 1976), and one or two seem to be present at almost every active sewer on the east coast. Grain or other vegetable waste are believed to be the main attraction. Although some sewers, such as those at Inverness or Largo Bay, still hold flocks of several hundred, the largest flocks were those that used to gather along the coastline on the south side of the Forth at Edinburgh. During the mid 1960s and 1970s peak numbers in excess of 3,000 were regular, dense flocks feeding over or close to at least seven different sewer outfalls. Scaups *Aythya marila* and Pochards also gathered in large numbers, but almost all have now ceased to be present after the introduction of improved sewage treatment procedures (Campbell 1984).

Goldeneyes are day feeders but activity patterns seem to vary considerably from site to site. Tidal and diurnal patterns in feeding behaviour and distribution have been described (Campbell and Milne 1977), and dusk movements to alternative roosting sites seem to be quite regular (Campbell 1979). Away from sewers, Goldeneyes are known to feed on a range of invertebrates including crabs and small bivalves. Marked and consistent differences in the sex composition of flocks at closely adjacent sites have been described but are of unknown significance (Campbell 1977).

At most sites numbers tend to start building up in late October and are at their highest in December and January. Secondary peaks are also quite regular in spring. In hard weather numbers at many coastal sites tend to increase, as those birds wintering inland are displaced when waters ice over, and flocks may occur where they are otherwise uncommon.

Goldeneyes do not breed in Iceland but are widespread in both Scandinavia and western Russia, and the limited ringing data confirm that this is the origin of the birds wintering in Britain and Ireland. The wintering grounds of the Scottish breeding population are not known, but rivers and lochs near the breeding sites often hold wintering groups. On the basis of known peak numbers at principal sites, and their widespread occurrence inland and along the coast, it is likely that the peak population in Britain and Ireland is of the order of 10,000–15,000. The European wintering population has been estimated at around 200,000.

L. H. CAMPBELL

Total number of squares in which recorded: 1,923 (50%)

No. of birds seen in a day	Number (%) of squares		
	Britain	Ireland	TOTAL (incl. C.I.)
1–6	791 (49%)	150 (49%)	943 (49%)
7–26	507 (31%)	92 (30%)	599 (31%)
27+	316 (20%)	65 (21%)	381 (20%)

References

CAMPBELL, L. H. 1977. Local variations in the proportions of adult males in flocks of Goldeneye wintering in the Firth of Forth. *Wildfowl* 28: 77–80.

CAMPBELL, L. H. 1979. Patterns of distribution and behaviour of flocks of seaducks wintering at Leith and Musselburgh, Scotland. *Biol. Conserv.* 14: 111–124.

CAMPBELL, L. H. 1984. The impact of changes in sewage treatment on seaducks wintering in the Firth of Forth, Scotland. *Biol. Conserv.* 28: 173–180.

CAMPBELL, L. H. and H. MILNE. 1977. Goldeneye feeding close to sewer outfalls in winter. *Wildfowl* 28: 81–85.

POUNDER, B. 1976. Waterfowl at effluent discharges in Scottish coastal waters. *Scot. Birds* 9: 5–36.

Breeding Atlas p 82

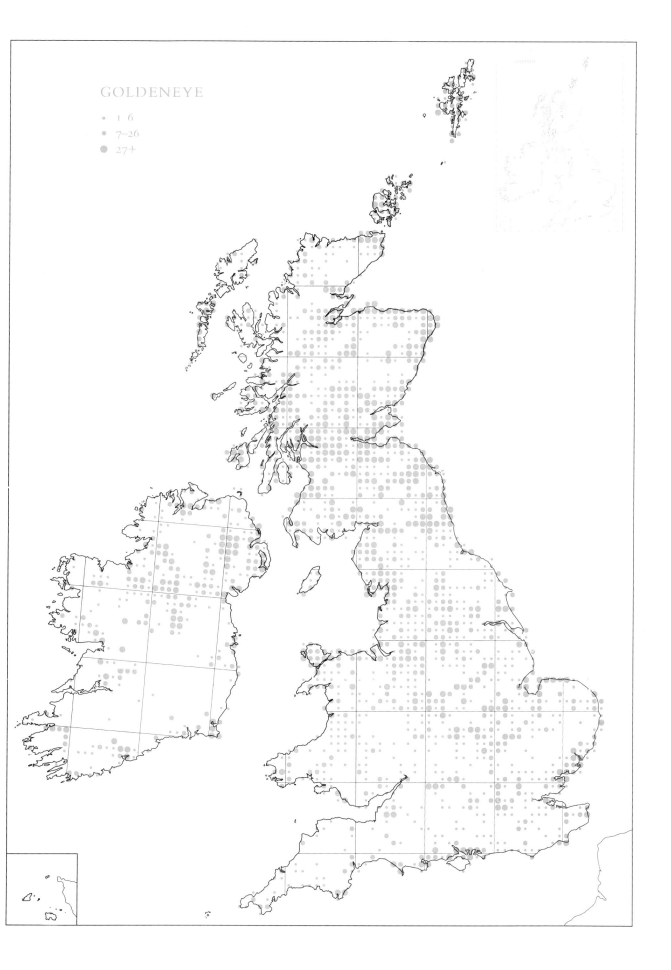

GOLDENEYE

- 1–6
- 7–26
- 27+

Smew

Mergus albellus

Smews, the smallest of the three European 'sawbills', do not nest in Britain or Ireland, and in fact they are rare in northern Scandinavia, their main breeding area being northern Russia (*BWP*).

The winter distribution map shows that Smews occur most frequently in East Anglia and SE England. Away from these areas they are uncommon, particularly so in Scotland where typical wintering numbers are only 15–20; they are very rare in Ireland.

Up to 10,000 Smews occur in winter in the Netherlands, most of them in the IJsslemeer and along the Rhine. These birds seem to be the immediate origin of many of the Smews that occur in Britain, and this view is supported by an analysis of the cold weather influx of Smews in the 1978/79 winter (Chandler 1981). This influx first became apparent in SE England in early January, following the onset of cold weather on the Continent at the end of December, and birds spread westward during the following week. Their geographical distribution was similar to that shown on the map, though the numbers in 1979 were, for recent years, exceptional, with nearly 400 birds involved.

As with many migratory bird species, immature and/or female Smews move further than the adult males, but in most winters this trend is indicated only by the predominance of 'red-headed' birds. However, in the 1979 influx, 47% of the birds in eastern England were adult males, but they became progressively fewer towards the south and west (Chandler 1984).

Smews prefer much the same habitat in winter as the Goldeneye *Bucephala clangula* and Goosander *Mergus merganser*, namely large or fairly large bodies of fresh water, where they feed by diving, mainly consuming small fish.

There has been a considerable reduction in the number of wintering Smews in Britain since the 1950s, though the reason is not immediately apparent. For example, in the 1950s the reservoirs of the London area, which were then the winter stronghold of the species, held a third to a half of the British winter population with a January/February total of about 100. Since then, numbers have declined to such an extent that during the *Winter Atlas* period the maximum London area winter counts averaged only 7. A similar trend is evident in the National Wildfowl Trust Counts. In 1963 Atkinson-Willes concluded that the British winter population was 'a few hundred birds', whilst by 1981–84 the average numbers from the January counts had fallen to only 62.

It is difficult to estimate the number of birds from the winter distribution map. Although Smews are conspicuous they are very mobile, and individuals and groups may visit a number of different waters, so that there is likely to be considerable duplication of records. From the map, totals for individual winters vary between 150 and 350. Allowing for duplication, the typical winter total nowadays in Britain and Ireland is thus likely to be no more than 100 birds.

These numbers are a small proportion of NW Europe's winter total of Smews. The total count has fluctuated considerably in recent years, but is probably more than 10,000 birds. (International Waterfowl Research Bureau, unpublished).

R. J. CHANDLER

Total number of squares in which recorded: 243 (6%)

No. of birds seen in a day	Number (%) of squares		
	Britain	Ireland	TOTAL (incl. C.I.)
1	149 (65%)	7 (58%)	156 (64%)
2	39 (17%)	3 (25%)	42 (17%)
3+	43 (19%)	2 (17%)	45 (19%)

References

ATKINSON-WILLES, G. L. 1963. *Wildfowl in Great Britain*. HMSO, London.

CHANDLER, R. J. 1981. Influxes into Britain and Ireland of Red-necked Grebes and other waterbirds during winter 1978/79. *Brit. Birds* 74: 55–81.

CHANDLER, R. J. 1984. Proportions of adult male Smews and Red-breasted Mergansers in England and Wales in 1978/79. *Brit. Birds* 77: 479–481.

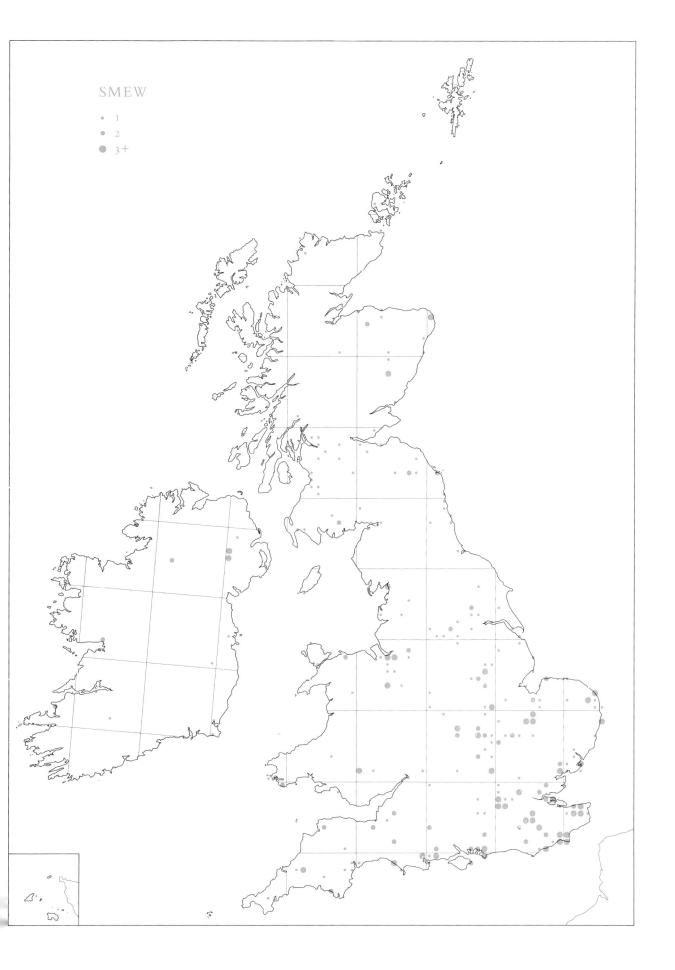

SMEW

● 1
● 2
● 3+

Red-breasted Merganser

Mergus serrator

Whether riding the choppy water of a swiftly flooding tide or displaying on a tranquil calm, a flock of Red-breasted Mergansers is a typical sight in many a northern estuary in winter.

Apart from large numbers in the Beauly Firth and the Firth of Forth, the winter flocks are usually small. More than 30 birds were reported in only about one eighth of the 10-km squares in which the birds occurred. In Ireland the corresponding proportion of 10-km squares was less than one tenth. Thus, in view of the generally small size of the flocks and the widespread nature of their distribution around sheltered parts of the more remote coastline, some under-recording is likely.

Comparison with the *Breeding Atlas*, which shows the Red-breasted Merganser to be a widespread breeding bird throughout the less mountainous areas of Scotland, suggests that the bulk of the British and Irish populations winter around the coast close to their breeding areas. In addition, however, Red-breasted Mergansers also winter along the east and south coasts of England, from the Wash southwards, and similarly, along the south and east coast of Ireland. In view of the numbers which are present near the breeding areas, it is tempting to suggest that the east and south coast birds are of Scandinavian origin. The few ringing recoveries support this suggestion, and additionally show that Icelandic birds winter off both Scottish and Irish coasts. Red-breasted Mergansers feed primarily on small fish, but at sea will also take small crustaceans (*BWP*).

In winter, the species is uncommon in inland waters, and the years 1981–84 were no exception. During hard weather, however, they appear inland, though the numbers of birds involved are small, and they rarely remain for more than a few days. Such influxes occurred in February 1956 and in February 1979, and on the latter occasion over 420 were reported inland. Analysis of this movement (Chandler 1981) suggested that the birds had come from the Baltic or adjacent North Sea coasts, and included individuals from the Russian as well as Scandinavian breeding populations.

Prater (1981) showed that the build up of the number of Red-breasted Mergansers in coastal areas commenced in July with the flocking of moulting birds, and that numbers reached their peak in December. Thereafter they declined, comparatively rapidly from March as the return to nesting areas gathered pace. The maximum number recorded during the Birds of Estuaries Enquiry was over 3,700 annually, whereas Ogilvie (1975) has suggested that 5,000–10,000 birds winter in Britain and Ireland as a whole, and Owen *et al* (1986) estimated a total of 7,000–10,000. Hutchinson (1979) quoted mid winter numbers of 2,000–3,000 in Irish coastal waters.

The actual numbers recorded during the *Winter Atlas* survey give a typical single winter total of about 9,500 birds in Britain and 1,700 in Ireland. This must be an overestimate since the totals are derived from the maximum numbers recorded in each 10-km square during each winter, but this source of error is at least in part balanced by the probably incomplete recording of the more remote coasts. This suggests that perhaps as many as 11,000 Red-breasted Mergansers winter in Britain and Ireland, a total comparable to the upper limit of previous estimates. In comparison, the NW European winter total probably exceeds 30,000 (International Waterfowl Research Bureau, unpublished).

R. J. CHANDLER

Total number of squares in which recorded: 1,087 (28%)

Number (%) of squares

No. of birds seen in a day	Britain	Ireland	TOTAL (incl. C.I.)
1–5	409 (50%)	115 (44%)	525 (48%)
6–18	257 (31%)	94 (36%)	351 (32%)
19+	159 (19%)	51 (20%)	211 (19%)

References

CHANDLER, R. J. 1981. Influxes into Britain and Ireland of Red-necked Grebes and other water-birds during winter 1978/79. *Brit. Birds* 74: 55–81.

OGILVIE, M. A. 1975. *Ducks of Britain and Europe.* Poyser, Berkhamsted.

Breeding Atlas p 90

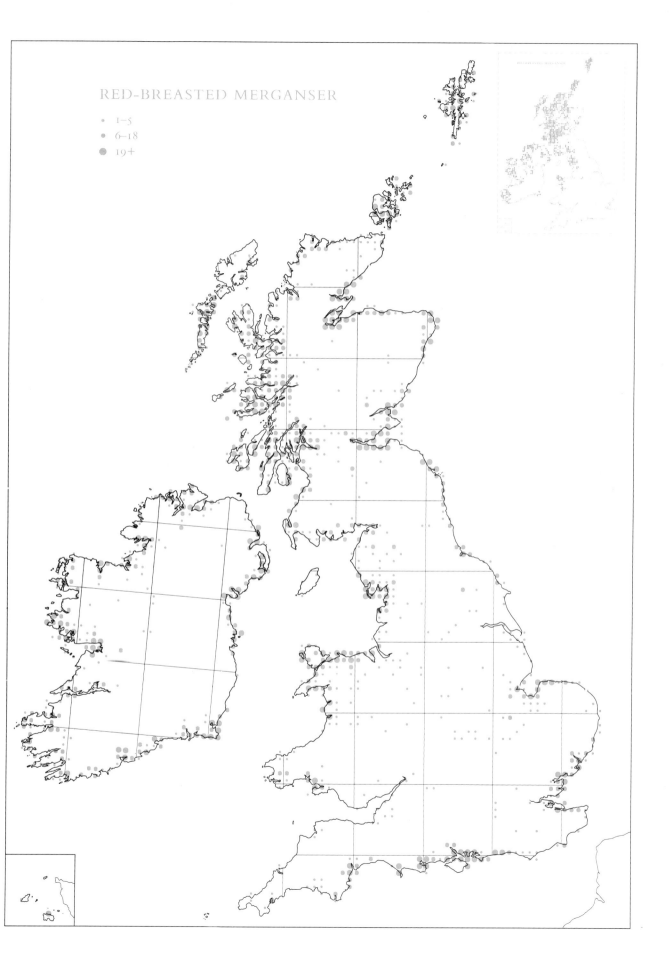

RED-BREASTED MERGANSER

- 1–5
- 6–18
- 19+

Goosander

Mergus merganser

Unlike the closely related Red-breasted Merganser *M. serrator*, the Goosander favours fresh water and is widespread inland in Britain (though not Ireland) in the winter months, occurring on many of the larger lakes and reservoirs. On the coast it occurs only locally at particularly sheltered localities.

Since first breeding in Perthshire in 1871, the Goosander has become a widespread breeding species both in Scotland and northern England, and in these areas the breeding distribution is reflected in the number of birds wintering. Considerable numbers also occur in most winters in Wales, central England and the London area. In contrast very few are seen in Ireland, where breeding commenced during the 1970s (*Breeding Atlas, Irish Bird Reports*). Only a few sites in Britain regularly hold more than 50 birds, the most notable being the Beauly Firth where up to 1,500 were recorded during the Atlas period.

In their studies in the north of England, Meek and Little (1977) have shown that Goosanders often do not move far from their natal areas in winter, and the same probably applies in Scotland. So it may be inferred that perhaps as many as three-quarters of the breeding population of Scotland and northern England, along with their surviving progeny (a total of perhaps 5,000, allowing one offspring per pair), winter in their general breeding area. Though Goosanders wintering in southern England doubtless include British birds, particularly in cold weather when inland waters further north are frozen, the few ringing recoveries suggest that many are from the Continent or Scandinavia, with recoveries in Sweden, Finland, NW Russia, the Netherlands and East Germany (Meek and Little 1977).

Goosanders will make hard weather movements when their wintering locations become frozen. The most recent of such influxes occurred in early January 1979 (Chandler 1981), when unusual numbers appeared in southern England. These would presumably have included British breeders, though the appearances of Smews *M. albellus* with the Goosanders in this influx shows that the source of many

of the birds involved was the Continental shores of the southern North Sea, particularly the Netherlands.

Goosanders feed primarily on small fish, preferring water no deeper than 4 m. At some localities, birds may leave the water on which they roost to feed by day on nearby rivers, behaviour which can lead to the number of birds being under-recorded. In contrast the species' need to move when inland waters freeze makes some duplication of records over the winter period inevitable. However, since Goosanders are a conspicuous species and make only limited use of remote coastal areas, where Atlas coverage may have been less complete, a good proportion will have been recorded. The total winter population for Britain and Ireland in each of the 3 years was close to 8,000 with 5,000 of them being in northern England and Scotland. These numbers compare with estimates of the British winter population of about 5,000 made by Owen *et al* (1986), suggesting that there is some duplication in the *Winter Atlas* records, but showing that their figure of 5,000 is certainly not an overestimate.

In comparison, the northwestern European winter total is over 100,000 (International Waterfowl Research Bureau, unpublished).

R. J. CHANDLER

Total number of squares in which recorded: 1,008 (26%)

No. of birds seen in a day	Number (%) of squares		TOTAL (incl. C.I.)
	Britain	Ireland	
1–3	499 (50%)	3 (75%)	502 (50%)
4–10	303 (30%)	1 (25%)	304 (30%)
11+	202 (20%)	0 (0%)	202 (20%)

References

CHANDLER, R. J. 1981. Influxes into Britain and Ireland of Red-necked Grebes and other waterbirds during winter 1978/79. *Brit. Birds.* 74: 55–81.

MEEK, E. R. and B. LITTLE. 1977. Ringing studies of Goosanders in Northumberland. *Brit. Birds* 70: 273–283.

Breeding Atlas p 92

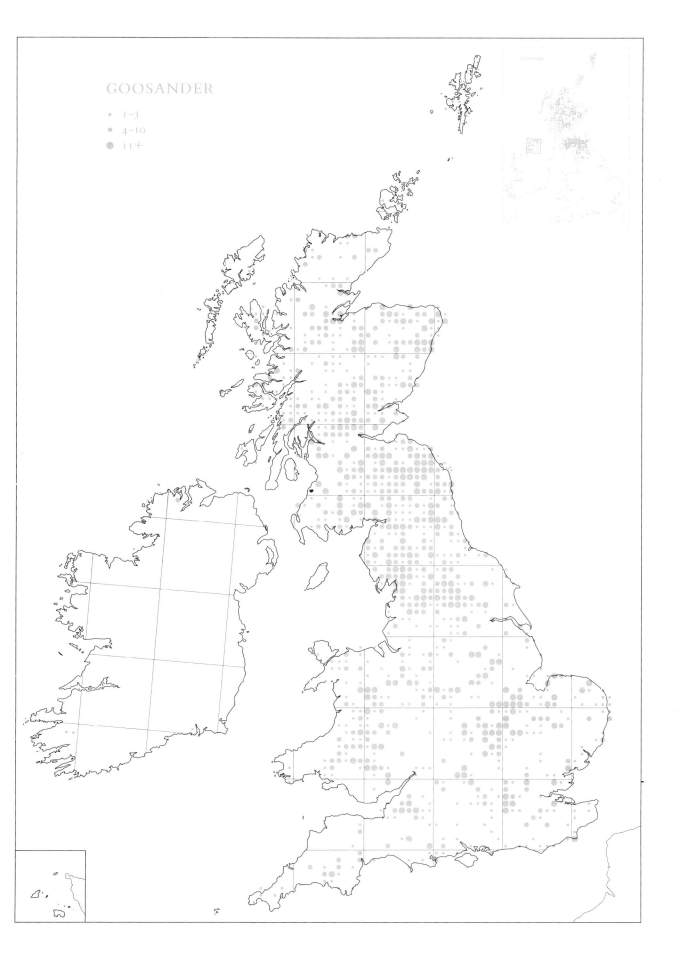

GOOSANDER

- 1–3
- 4–10
- 11+

Ruddy Duck

Oxyura jamaicensis

In 1948, the Wildfowl Trust at Slimbridge imported three pairs of Ruddy Ducks from the USA. They began breeding the following year and, in the autumn of 1957, some 20 or so unpinioned juveniles escaped. From then on, Ruddy Ducks were regularly recorded on reservoirs in Staffordshire and Somerset (now in Avon), and the first feral breeding occurred in 1960. The subsequent increase and spread is, perhaps, the most impressive since the colonisation of Britain by the Collared Dove *Streptopelia decaocto* and, by the winter of 1983/84, the population had reached 1,800 birds (Salmon and Moser 1984).

The *Breeding Atlas* revealed the presence of Ruddy Ducks in 20 10-km squares, centred on Cheshire, central England and Avon. With records from a total of 244 squares, the *Winter Atlas* clearly illustrates the remarkable spread since the early 1970s. The range has infilled and expanded (westwards into Anglesey, eastwards into Leicestershire, and north into Scotland) while to the south the map shows a wide scatter of records, relating mainly to winter 1981/82.

In winter, Ruddy Ducks are gregarious birds, gathering in large flocks on selected lakes and reservoirs. They feed mainly on animal matter by straining the ooze on lake bottoms, so shallow waters and impounded valley reservoirs are preferred to concrete reservoirs and gravel pits.

One of the most remarkable aspects of the Ruddy Duck's colonisation has been the rapid establishment of regular migration patterns. Except in severe weather, these movements are almost entirely nocturnal. Following the bird's late summer moult, peak numbers tend to occur in areas such as the Cheshire and Shropshire meres. There is then an exodus to Belvide and Blithfield Reservoirs in Staffordshire, which held up to 810 in January 1981 (A. R. Dean), and to Blagdon and Chew Valley Lakes in Avon which held up to 850 in January 1984. Good numbers now also winter within the breeding range.

The dispersal of small numbers farther afield depends upon the severity of the weather. In the hard winter of 1978/79, for example, Staffordshire was largely deserted and many birds moved south to Avon and Somerset, while over 100 dispersed more widely, reaching Ireland and Scilly in the west, and Norfolk and Kent in the east (Vinicombe and Chandler 1982). It was estimated that some 10–15% failed to survive. There was a similar widespread dispersal in 1981/82: Anglesey held over 100, Cornwall, Devon and Dorset had 161 and good numbers were in SE England, (Salmon 1982).

Unlike other British wildfowl, Ruddy Ducks have a complete pre-breeding moult, mainly in February and March, when they are again flightless. At this time, many remain on the Staffordshire and Avon reservoirs, but also a large proportion appears to return to the breeding areas to moult.

The growth of the population has been fairly accurately monitored. Hudson (1976) considered that about 70 escaped from Slimbridge between 1952 and 1973. By 1965, there were about 6 breeding pairs, increasing to some 25 pairs by 1972. By 1975, the post-breeding population was in the region of 300–350 birds and the species was increasing at around 25% a year. By 1978/79, the total had doubled to about 770 (Vinicombe and Chandler 1982) and, by 1980/81, had doubled again to 1,570. Increased mortality during the winter of 1981/82, was followed by an immediate recovery and the population in the following winter was in the region of 1,380 (Salmon 1983), rising to 1,800 a year later.

As it has no ecological rival in Britain and Ireland the remarkable increase and spread of the Ruddy Duck seems set to continue. Not only is there abundant uncolonised habitat, but the recent upsurge in Continental records indicates that its spread is unlikely to stop at the shores of the English Channel.

K. E. VINICOMBE

Total number of squares in which recorded: 244 (6%)

No. of birds seen in a day	Number (%) of squares		
	Britain	Ireland	TOTAL (incl. C.I.)
1–2	108 (45%)	5 (83%)	113 (46%)
3–10	83 (35%)	1 (17%)	84 (34%)
11+	47 (20%)	0 (0%)	47 (19%)

References

ANON. 1984. European news. *Brit. Birds* 77: 234.

HUDSON, R. 1976. Ruddy Ducks in Britain. *Brit. Birds* 69: 132–143.

SALMON, D. G. (ed.). 1982. *Wildfowl and Wader Counts, 1981–82*. Wildfowl Trust, Slimbridge.

SALMON, D. G. (ed.). 1983. *Wildfowl and Wader Counts 1982–83*. Wildfowl Trust, Slimbridge.

SALMON, D. G. and M. E. MOSER. (eds). 1984. *Wildfowl and Wader Counts 1983–84*. Wildfowl Trust, Slimbridge.

VINICOMBE, K. E. and R. J. CHANDLER. 1982. Movements of Ruddy Ducks during the hard winter of 1978/79. *Brit. Birds* 75: 1–11.

Breeding Atlas p 88

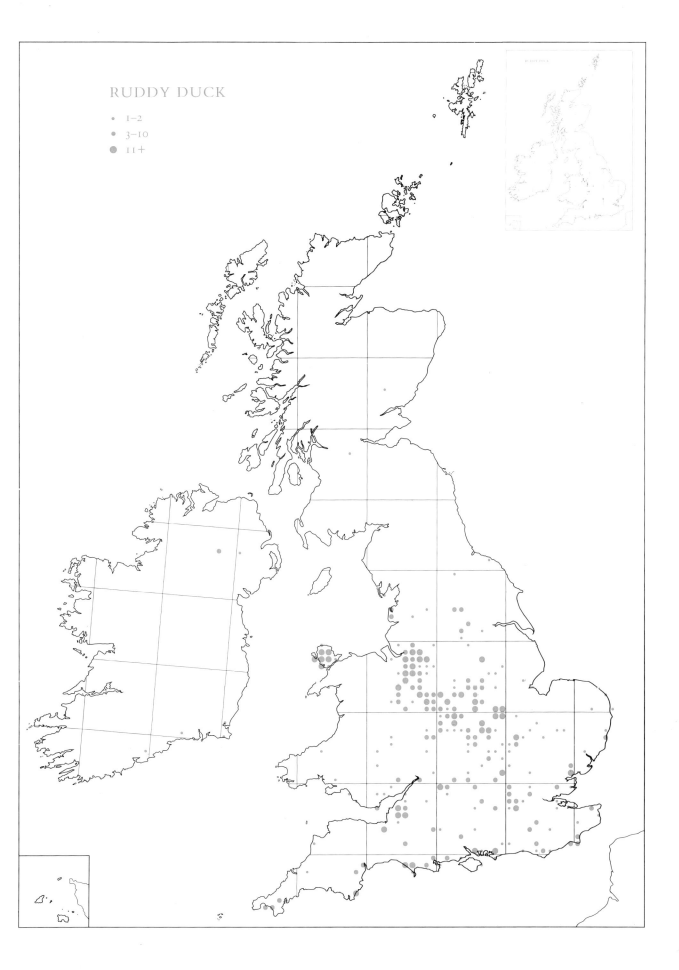

RUDDY DUCK

- • 1–2
- • 3–10
- ● 11+

Red Kite

Milvus milvus

To many birdwatchers in Britain the Red Kite is essentially a winter bird, first seen gliding majestically over some tawny bogland in central Wales, or even soaring over the open fields of eastern England, where the Red Kite was commonplace two hundred years ago. In their Welsh refuge they are much easier to see in winter than in the breeding season, when they are hidden by foliage, or hunting the high sheepwalks, far from view. There can be few British birds more spectacular, more liable to catch the breath, than a Red Kite banking overhead, touched by winter sun.

The original map of the winter distribution in the Atlas period clearly delineated the breeding area in Wales; and so for reasons of security it became necessary to present the central Wales data in a formalised way, as in the *Breeding Atlas*. The scattered records elsewhere, mostly in E England, are plotted normally. Some of these birds may be Welsh birds, but it is also likely that some are Continental immigrants, especially those in the east. There is yet no direct evidence from ringing that European birds may winter in Britain (2 German ringed birds have occurred in spring), but the absence of rings from a series of recent winter casualties in E England suggests that they are not all of Welsh origin since most Welsh birds are ringed (Davies and Davis 1973, Davis and Newton 1981).

The small remnant population of Red Kites in Wales is largely sedentary, unlike those in comparable latitudes in NW Europe, which mostly emigrate to Iberia for the winter. However, some of the young birds reared in Wales wander away from the breeding area soon after fledging, and may settle far from home for the first winter, or even longer. There are ringing recoveries of Welsh juveniles between late summer and spring in Kirkcudbrightshire, Staffordshire, Worcestershire, Herefordshire, Gloucestershire, Oxfordshire, Wiltshire, and Kent.

Adult Welsh Red Kites in winter tend to remain on or near their summer ranges, though a few shift from the less productive areas to places with more reliable food supplies. These birds tend to move back to their breeding range as early as January or February. Most Red Kites range widely during the day, often 10 km or more from the roost, and some shift around over considerable distances during the winter, especially the immatures.

Red Kites are rather gregarious at good food sources and at roosts, the record number at a recent roost being 27 birds (J. E. Davis). In winter they hunt more over the lower valleys and less over high ground than in summer, though they will still travel up to the open hills in fair weather. The main winter foods are small mammals, sheep carrion as more becomes available in late winter, animal refuse from rubbish tips and abattoirs (mostly taken by piracy), small birds, earthworms and beetles (Davis and Davis 1981).

The British population has increased very slowly under protection from its lowest ebb in the early years of the present century, when it may have numbered no more than a dozen birds (Salmon 1970, Davis and Newton 1981). The rate of increase accelerated markedly during the 1960s and 1970s, apparently due to reduced losses of full-grown birds by poisons or the gun, since the poor breeding productivity did not improve (Newton *et al* 1981). However, there has been a pause in this increase in the early 1980s, and spring numbers since 1980 have been rather static at around 110–120 birds, with autumn numbers about 130–140. The British birds probably represent about 5% of the world population, the main strongholds being in W Europe, especially in Germany and Spain.

P. E. DAVIS

Total number of squares in which recorded: 73 (2%)

No. of birds seen in a day	Number (%) of squares		
	Britain	Ireland	TOTAL (incl. C.I.)
1	50 (71%)	3 (100%)	53 (73%)
2	9 (13%)	0 (0%)	9 (12%)
3+	11 (16%)	0 (0%)	12 (15%)

The dots in the Welsh breeding area are conventionally placed in the centre of the shaded circle on the advice of the Kite Committee. The remaining dots are plotted accurately.

References

DAVIES, P. W. and P. E. DAVIS. 1973. The ecology and conservation of the Red Kite in Wales. *Brit. Birds* 66: 183–224, 241–270.

DAVIS, P. E. and J. E. DAVIS. 1981. The food of the Red Kite in Wales. *Bird Study* 28: 33–39.

DAVIS P. E. and I. NEWTON. 1981. Population and breeding of Red Kites in Wales over a 30 year period. *J. Anim. Ecol.* 50: 759–772.

NEWTON, I., P. E. DAVIS and D. MOSS. 1981. Distribution and breeding of Red Kites in relation to land use in Wales. *J. Appl. Ecol.* 18: 173–186.

SALMON, H. M. 1970. The Red Kites of Wales: the story of their preservation. In LACEY, W. (ed.) *Welsh Wildlife in Trust*. North Wales Naturalists' Trust, Bangor.

Breeding Atlas p 112

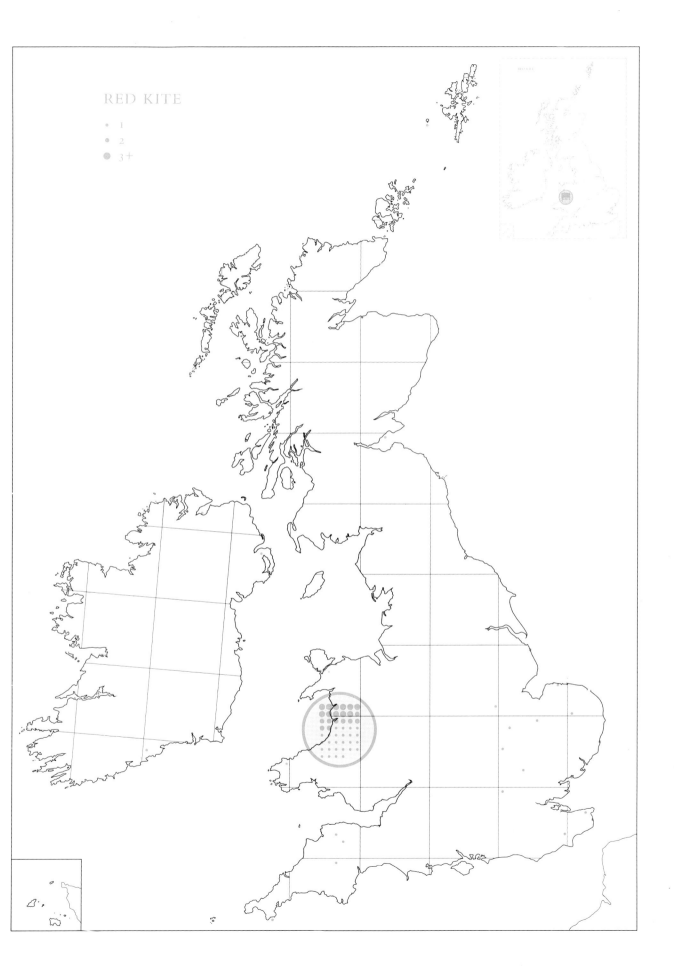

RED KITE

- 1
- 2
- 3+

Marsh Harrier

Circus aeruginosus

The characteristic V-shaped silhouette and large size combine to make the Marsh Harrier an easily recognisable bird in the fens and marshes of Britain and Europe. A male, though having about the same wing span as a Buzzard *Buteo buteo*, is nearly 40% lighter, and this low body weight, coupled with long legs, are ideal qualities in a bird which occupies open country and hunts by slowly quartering the ground.

A wintering bird was recorded for the first time in Britain just before the 1939–45 war, and even today probably no more than about 10 individuals remain to winter after the breeding season. Mostly they are females but sometimes they are accompanied by birds of the year. The bulk of the population moves south to overwinter in the Mediterranean and NW Africa. The only foreign ringing recoveries have been from NW France, Morocco and Mauritania. About half the recent overwintering records have come from the breeding areas of East Anglia, but there is a surprising number of records from S Wales, with a scattering elsewhere including SE Ireland. The winter distribution is markedly coastal.

The fluctuations in the breeding population have been documented (Underhill-Day 1984). Regular breeding began in 1927 with 1–5 pairs each year in Norfolk. In 1945 the population increased and spread. In 1958 there were 15 nests, but thereafter a decline began, probably caused by organo-chlorine pesticides, and by 1971 the population was down to a single pair.

Fortunately, this proved to be the turning point, and since then numbers have increased, probably helped initially by some immigration. In 1983, 70 young were fledged from 26 nests. Reference is made to nests rather than to pairs as Marsh Harriers can be polygynous (Hosking 1943). Simultaneously, populations have increased in Europe, particularly in Holland, where at least a fourfold increase has taken place since 1958, and there are now 800–900 nests (M. Zijlstra).

Both in summer and winter the birds hunt reed beds, salt marshes, heaths and open ground, often returning to reed beds to roost. The range of prey taken is surprisingly large, from small mammals, rats, water voles and rabbits to passerines and larger birds up to the size of Moorhens *Gallinula chloropus*, Wood-pigeons *Columba palumbus* and Grey Partridges *Perdix perdix* (Underhill-Day 1985). Most prey is captured on the ground, the hunting Marsh Harrier turning in flight and dropping with remarkable speed and agility as it stoops. Even birds as alert as Skylarks *Alauda arvensis* are taken in this way. Similar skills are shown when aerial food passes take place between male and female over the nesting area. Communal winter roosting has not become common, probably because the number of birds is still low, although it is a feature in the autumn in breeding areas before the birds migrate. Our population is still very small compared with mainland Europe, but there is nothing to prevent numbers increasing except perhaps persecution by man, which is already taking place. In recent years a few birds have been poisoned, reed beds deliberately destroyed and eggs taken by collectors, although so far this has been on a small scale. Present winter numbers cannot be accurately estimated.

J. C. DAY

Total number of squares in which recorded: 54 (1%)

No. of birds seen in a day	Number (%) of squares		TOTAL (incl. C.I.)
	Britain	Ireland	
1	47 (92%)	3 (100%)	50 (93%)
2+	4 (8%)	0 (0%)	4 (7%)

References

HOSKING, E. J. 1943. Some observations on the Marsh Harrier. *Brit. Birds* 37: 2–10.

UNDERHILL-DAY, J. C. 1984. Population and breeding biology of Marsh Harriers in Britain since 1900. *J. Appl. Ecol.* 21: 773–787.

UNDERHILL-DAY, J. C. 1985. The food of breeding Marsh Harriers *Circus aeruginosus* in East Anglia. *Bird Study* 32: 208–215.

Breeding Atlas p 116

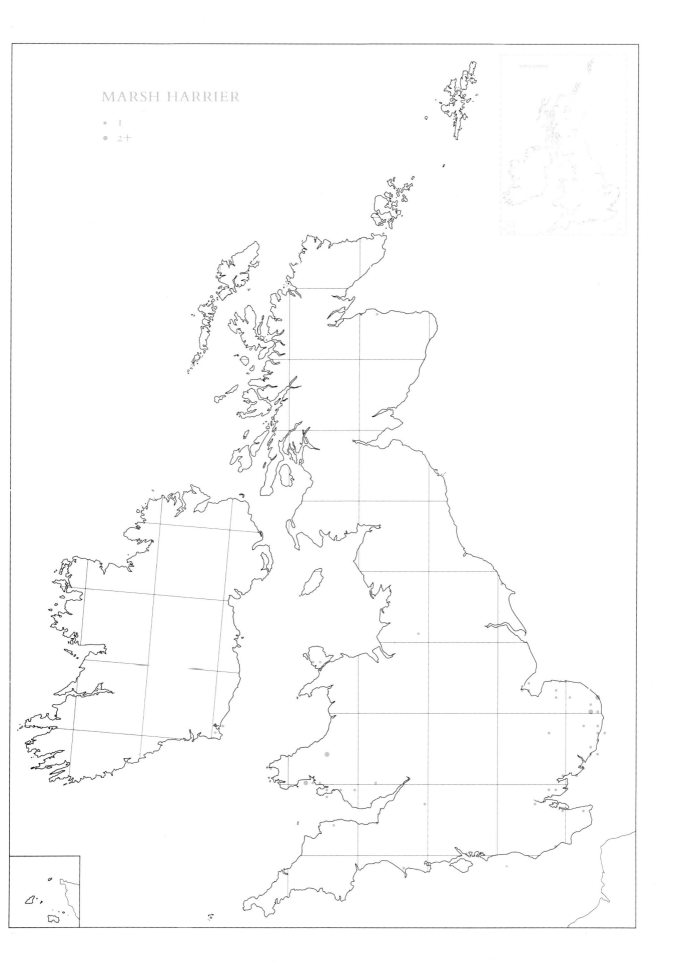

MARSH HARRIER

- 1
- 2+

Hen Harrier

Circus cyaneus

The melée of a number of Hen Harriers above their communal winter roost is an inspiring sight, recently attracting attention in places far from the raptor's traditional strongholds in Scotland, Ireland and Wales. Long known as a scarce and mainly coastal winter visitor in East Anglia and SE England, its status there suddenly improved in the mid and late 1970s and an exceptionally large influx occurred in the prolonged snow and easterly winds of early 1979.

For England, the winter map bears no resemblance to the restricted upland breeding distribution. A few uplands are regularly used in winter, but this is not typical. In the east the distribution closely follows the low land of coast, fenland and river valleys. Heathland, forestry and downland localities occupied in the south also have much suitable habitat. The English midlands are shunned.

In Scotland, the breeding distribution is loosely maintained in winter, although moorland is largely forsaken for lower farmland, marshes and conifer plantations (Watson 1977). In Wales the winter population mainly gravitates to low coastal areas.

In Ireland wide tracts of suitable habitat in the south are now greatly diminished by plantations maturing *en bloc* and by exploitation of moorland and bog for agriculture (O'Flynn 1983).

The Hen Harrier is adapted to hunt from low-level flight, using terrain and rank vegetation to mask its approach. A high ratio of wing length to body weight enables it to forage for considerable periods, gliding along between groups of wing beats. Large, open areas are therefore preferred for hunting, and are frequented in winter.

Most passerines and several waders are known as avian prey. Voles and mice make up the bulk of mammals taken. Rabbits, hares and gamebirds may be taken, mainly by the heavier female.

A survey in Britain and Ireland during the 1983/84 winter found 77 roost sites in regular use. Half were in reed beds or on marshes, the rest on rough grassland, lowland heath, heather moor and conifer plantations. At almost all sites, birds roosted communally, on the ground or on platforms of vegetation. Three sites held over 20 birds, but most much fewer.

From first light birds radiate out of the roost. The Craigheads (1956) showed that individual Hen Harriers in North America each commuted to their own limited range. This has been proved for the Hen Harrier in Orkney (Picozzi 1980) and noted in Cambridgeshire, but there is little evidence otherwise.

Of 20 mid November to February ringing recoveries of Scottish birds since the mid 1970s, 15 were reported in Scotland, 3 in England (1 NW, 1 NE, 1 E), 1 in central Ireland and 1 in Denmark. Three Dutch birds were recovered in E England. Few Orkney tagged birds have been reported on the mainland in Atlas months (6 Scotland, 1 NE England, 1 S England) (N. Picozzi). The winter increase in E England coincided with a breeding population increase in the nearby Netherlands. Cold weather movements must, however, bring birds from much further afield, long-distance movement being shown by birds from N and NE Europe (*BWP*). There is also some differential movement of the sexes, probably caused by the size difference and resulting differences in habitat and prey preferences.

Davenport (1982) estimated that England held 753 Hen Harriers during the early 1979 hard weather influx. The roost survey in January 1984 accounted for 173 at 61 sites in a mild winter. If all sites were known, complete coverage could conceivably have revealed 300 birds. On the basis of recent breeding population estimates, adjusted for mortality and partial emigration, Scotland may hold 400 wintering birds, Ireland less than 150 and Wales perhaps 50. Our winter Hen Harriers are a significant and integral part of the European population as a whole.

R. G. CLARKE

Total number of squares in which recorded: 1,192 (31%)

No. of birds seen in a day	Number (%) of squares		
	Britain	Ireland	TOTAL (incl. C.I.)
1	690 (71%)	177 (83%)	870 (73%)
2	156 (16%)	26 (12%)	183 (15%)
3+	129 (13%)	10 (5%)	139 (12%)

References
CRAIGHEAD, J. J. and F. C. CRAIGHEAD. 1956. *Hawks, Owls and Wildlife*. Stackpole Co., Pennsylvania.
DAVENPORT, D. 1982. Influxes into Britain of Hen Harriers, Long-eared Owls and Short-eared Owls in winter 1978/79. *Brit. Birds* 75: 309–316.
O'FLYNN, W. J. 1983. Population changes of the Hen Harrier in Ireland. *Irish Birds* 2: 337–343.
PICOZZI, N. 1980. Studies of the Hen Harrier. *Scot. Wild.* 16: 13–17.
WATSON, D. 1977. *The Hen Harrier*. Poyser, Berkhamsted.

Breeding Atlas p 118

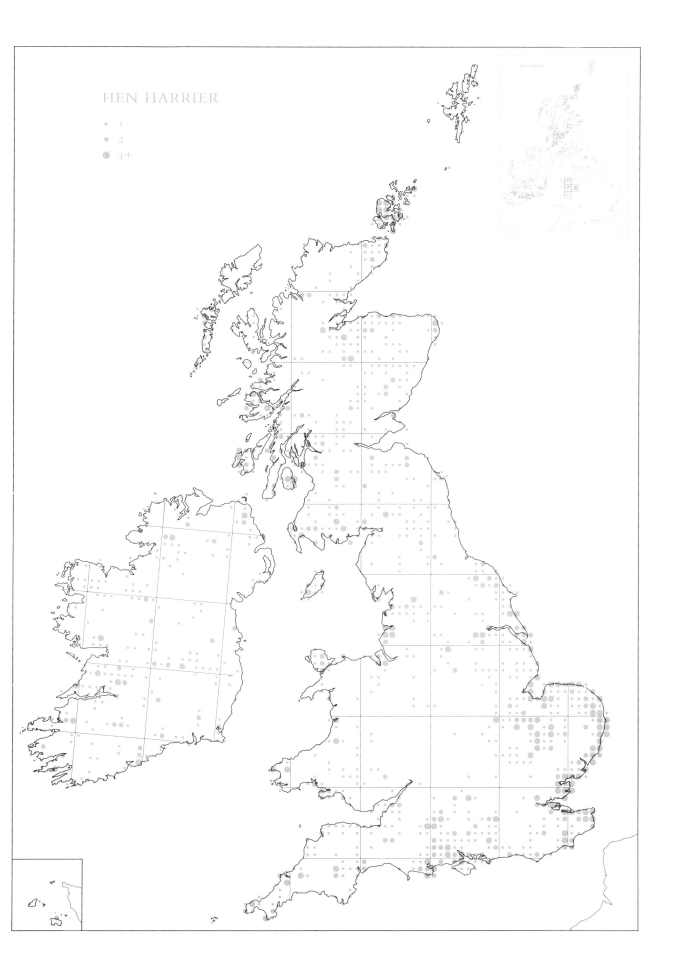

HEN HARRIER

- 1
- 2
- 3+

Goshawk

Accipiter gentilis

Goshawks are rarely seen in Britain and Ireland, even in those areas where there are established populations. In winter the most frequent view is brief as a bird crosses open country quickly returning to cover, or more prolonged if the hawk is circling low, preliminary to descent into woodland, or drifting out of sight over the horizon. By late February many British Goshawks take prolonged display flights over nesting territories and are then more obvious.

Goshawks are sedentary birds, so the distribution of winter sightings closely matches the breeding distribution, which cannot be published for fear of exposing breeding Goshawks to the attentions of some egg collectors, hawk keepers and game preservers. It is already established that such attention has dramatically lowered breeding success and has limited population increase in Britain.

Goshawks spend much of their time in woodland, killing most of their prey at, or near to, the edges. In Holland they often take Woodpigeons *Columba palumbus* at roosts or when they are feeding on beechmast in open woodland (Opdam *et al* 1977). In this study it was noted that in winter Goshawks were more prone to approach human dwellings, and often remained for weeks in small woodlots amidst cultivated land. If this applies in Britain, it would explain the distribution of winter sightings which are clustered around, but not exclusively within, the 10-km squares known to have breeding pairs. The sporadic sightings well away from known breeding areas may be escaped falconers' birds or the occasional juveniles which wander far (over 75 km) from their natal sites. Populations in western Europe have recently increased and become productive, so occasional vagrant Continental Goshawks may occur in Britain.

Even in the most severe of winter conditions, the countryside of Britain and Ireland provides an abundance of food for Goshawks compared with some of its wintering places in, for example, boreal Europe. Opdam *et al* (1977) review the winter diet showing that the predominating prey may be: Hazelhens *Bonasa bonasia* and squirrels (Finland), Woodpigeons (Holland), domestic pigeons (Germany), corvids,

Grey Partridges *Perdix perdix*, gulls and sometimes waterbirds (several places). In Sweden, Kenward *et al* (1981) showed that winter diet may be dominated by red squirrels, brown hares and Pheasants *Phasianus colchicus* (in intensive pheasant rearing areas). A winter study in Oxfordshire (Kenward 1979), using temporarily released Goshawks, listed Woodpigeons, rabbits and Moorhens *Gallinula chloropus* as the main prey. The major differences between the findings of the studies seem to indicate that Goshawks take whatever large birds or medium sized mammals are available and most easily captured.

Goshawks are still scarce in Britain and Ireland. The current population is probably derived exclusively from birds escaped or released from captivity. The exponential population increase probably slackened once fewer Goshawks were imported in the early 1980s (Marquiss 1982), and there is evidence that more young are now being taken from British nests. Nevertheless to judge from recent reports of breeding birds the population in 1983 could have been 100 pairs. Production has been low at about 1.6 young per pair but the survival of juveniles may be high, as the population is expanding. On this basis the wintering population for 1983/84 may be tentatively estimated at about 300 individuals. This population is of little international importance as the species is widespread and Goshawks are relatively abundant. They do not have stringent habitat requirements and are not as sensitive to land use change and environmental pollution as are some other predatory birds such as Marsh Harrier *Circus aeruginosus* and Peregrine *Falco peregrinus*.

M. MARQUISS

Total number of squares in which recorded: 111 (3%)

No. of birds seen in a day	Number (%) of squares		TOTAL (incl. C.I.)
	Britain	Ireland	
1	104 (95%)	1 (100%)	105 (95%)
2	6 (5%)	0 (0%)	6 (5%)

All dots are conventionally placed in the centre of the shaded circles, on the advice of the RSPB and Irish Records Panel. There is one record in Ireland.

References
KENWARD, R. E. 1979. Winter predation by Goshawks in lowland Britain. *Brit. Birds* 72: 64–73.
KENWARD, R. E., V. MARCSTROM and M. KARLBOM. 1981. Goshawk winter ecology in Swedish pheasant habitats. *J. Wild. Mgmt* 45: 397–408.
MARQUISS, M. 1982. The Goshawk in Britain: its provenance and current status. Pp 43–57. In KENWARD, R. E. and I. LINDSAY (eds). *Understanding the Goshawk*. International Association for Falconry and Conservation of Birds of Prey, Oxford.
MARQUISS, M. and I. NEWTON. 1982. The Goshawk in Britain. *Brit. Birds* 75: 243–260.
OPDAM, P., J. THISSEN, P. VERSCHUREN and G. MUSKENS. 1977. Feeding ecology of a population of Goshawks (*Accipiter gentilis*). *J. Orn.* 118: 35–51.

Breeding Atlas p 110

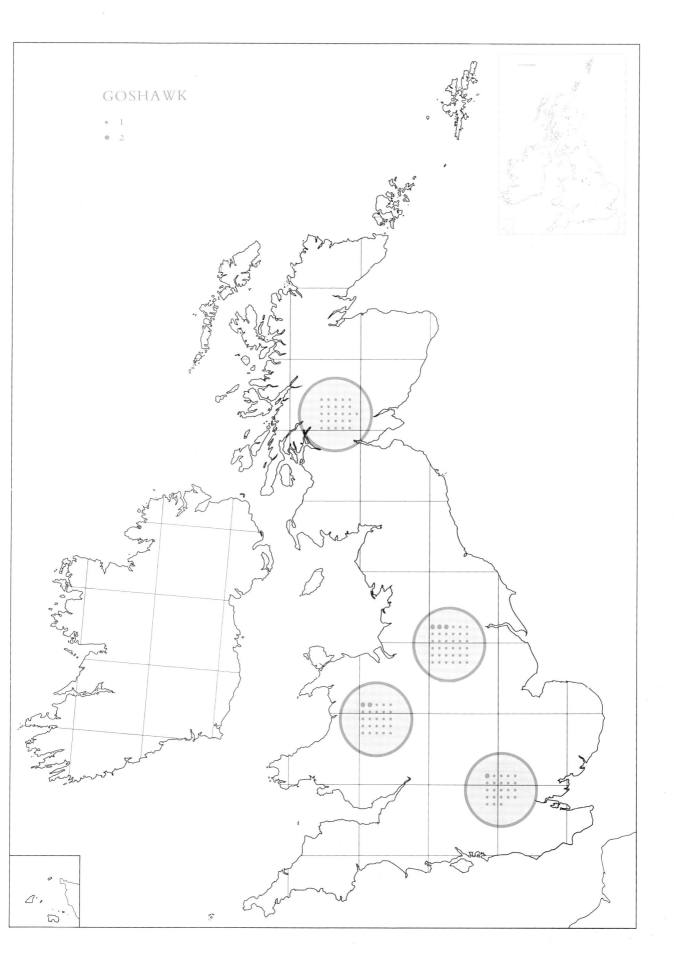

GOSHAWK

- 1
- 2

Sparrowhawk

Accipiter nisus

Wherever small birds abound in winter the Sparrowhawk is liable to appear. It is our second commonest raptor, yet it is not at all easily seen. Unobtrusive in woodland, in open country it employs the surprise of dashing low-level approach, behind hedges or along salt marsh creeks.

The map shows that the species is seen almost everywhere in Britain and Ireland, being absent only from open mountain areas which lack the woodland and small birds necessary to support the species, and from some low ground in parts of eastern England. The use of organochlorine pesticides in these agricultural areas has been particularly heavy, and these chemicals, notably aldrin and dieldrin, led to the virtual extinction of Sparrowhawks from much of Britain in the years around 1960. Since then successive restrictions in the use of such chemicals have been followed by a progressive recovery in Sparrowhawk numbers, chiefly by reducing adult mortality. The gaps in eastern England represent the remaining areas still to be recolonised (Newton and Haas 1984). A pleasing development in recent years has been the colonisation of the inner parts of several cities, such as Bristol and Edinburgh.

During winter, adult Sparrowhawks have individual home ranges, usually centred on nesting places, but overlapping widely between neighbours (Marquiss and Newton 1982). These ranges tend to be based on larger woods, but the birds hunt freely in fields and other open areas. The ranges of younger pre-breeding birds, are usually centred on smaller woods in more open country. Established birds mainly roost in woodland near their nesting places, whereas pre-breeding birds roost at various points within their range. Birds normally roost solitarily, though in small woods in extensive open areas, more than 10 birds have been counted entering the wood in the evening.

Despite extensive overlap, the sexes differ both in their preferred habitat and their preferred prey. The smaller males spend more time in woodland, taking mainly small songbirds, such as tits and finches, and occasionally larger birds, up to the size of Mistle Thrush *Turdus viscivorus* and Fieldfare *T. pilaris*. The larger females spend more time in open country, and feed mainly on Starlings *Sturnus vulgaris* or thrush species, but occasionally on larger species, up to the size of adult Woodpigeons *Columba palumbus* (Newton and Marquiss 1982). Because they hunt more in the open, females are seen more often than males, and ringed ones are recovered more frequently. The sex ratio at fledging is equal, but thereafter females are somewhat longer-lived, leading to a surplus over males.

British and Irish Sparrowhawks are resident, but soon after becoming independent the young disperse from their natal areas. Ringing in Britain and Ireland has provided no evidence for extensive movements in winter, but recoveries indicate that some birds originating from Norway, Sweden and Finland also winter in Britain, mainly in eastern districts, while others pass through in the autumn and spring. These migrants have also increased in recent years, as northern populations have recovered from the organochlorine era.

Known nesting densities suggest a breeding population in the early 1980s of around 25,000 pairs, in Britain. If the overall density is similar, Ireland will hold about another 8,000–9,000 pairs. To these at least another 40,000–45,000 non-breeders should be added, and about 66,000 young (based on a mean breeding success of 2 young per pair), giving a total resident population at the end of each summer of about 170,000 birds, reduced to about 105,000 individuals by spring. These figures exclude the small number of migrant Sparrowhawks, which winter in Britain. The Sparrowhawk occurs across the Palearctic region from Ireland to Japan, so the British stock represents a tiny fraction of the total world population.

I. NEWTON

Total number of squares in which recorded: 2,737 (71%)

No. of birds seen in a day	Number (%) of squares		TOTAL (incl. C.I.)
	Britain	Ireland	
1	1,151 (56%)	459 (70%)	1,613 (59%)
2	688 (33%)	160 (24%)	849 (31%)
3+	237 (11%)	38 (6%)	275 (10%)

References

MARQUISS, M. and I. NEWTON. 1982. A radio-tracking study of the ranging behaviour and dispersion of European Sparrowhawks *Accipiter nisus. J. Anim. Ecol.* 51: 111–133.

NEWTON, I. 1986. *The Sparrowhawk.* Poyser, Calton.

NEWTON, I. and M. B. HAAS. 1984. The return of the Sparrowhawk. *Brit. Birds* 77: 47–70.

NEWTON, I. and M. MARQUISS. 1982. Food, predation and breeding season in Sparrowhawks. *J. Zool. Lond.* 197: 221–240.

Breeding Atlas p 108

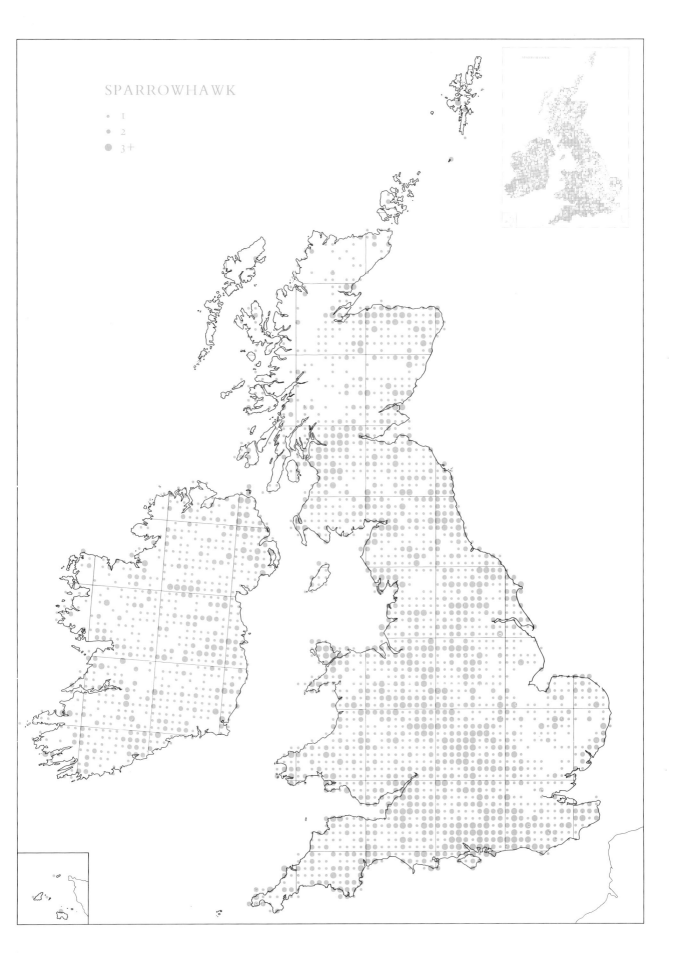

SPARROWHAWK

- · 1
- • 2
- ● 3+

Buzzard

Buteo buteo

The Buzzard, the only common large bird of prey in Britain and Ireland, is a superb flier and its loud, drawn-out, plaintive mewing is one of the most evocative upland sounds.

The winter distribution closely reflects its preferred habitat of open valleys with copses or larger woods, but in winter the species is commonest on land below 300 m when prey is less plentiful on the higher upland bogs and moors. Buzzards are common in winter through most of the western half of Britain, with strongholds in Argyll, central and W Wales, and Devon. In much of the rest of Scotland, the Lake District, N Wales, and SW Britain east to the New Forest, and in NE Ireland, they are still widespread but only patchily as common.

The winter map bears a marked similarity to that of the breeding distribution. British and Irish Buzzards are evidently rather sedentary; and this is also shown by ringing recoveries (Picozzi and Weir 1976). Adults usually remain on their territories throughout the year. Young, becoming independent during their first autumn, have to try to establish themselves between the ranges of surviving pairs, though at least during the early winter, when boundaries are not defended so vigorously, they may be tolerated within a territory.

The recent history of Buzzards in Britain and Ireland was documented by Moore (1957) and his maps for 1800, 1865, 1915 and 1954 were reproduced in the *Breeding Atlas*. The present map suggests that the population has not extended significantly since 1972 and this is confirmed by the BTO's Buzzard Survey of 1983 (K. Taylor). The British and Irish population is probably largely self contained.

The food is usually dominated by rabbits, voles and, to a lesser extent, small birds. In winter, small birds mostly leave the bleak uplands and Buzzards tend to forage more along the valleys and lower slopes, where there is also adequate shelter in severe weather. The valleys also probably contain a good deal of carrion: in Tregaron, for example, Buzzards and Ravens *Corvus corax* regularly gather at slaughterhouse offal. Nevertheless, the majority of prey is killed rather than scavenged; it may be hunted in flight or, as Dare (1957) found to be more common in winter, from a perch.

Pre-breeding territorial behaviour starts before the end of February and aerial displays are the main advertisement, which make Buzzards far more obvious than when hunting from perches. However, as the British and Irish population seems to be largely resident, the extra records do not change the general pattern of winter distribution.

Deep snow, especially if prolonged, affords small mammals some protection and Buzzards must either turn increasingly to carrion and small birds, or move elsewhere. More records are shown in eastern squares here than in the *Breeding Atlas* and this may partly reflect cold-weather movements, but the markedly coastal distribution makes it possible that some Continental birds are involved. Buzzards from N and E Europe winter in W Europe, the Mediterranean area and south into Africa, but like many other raptors that migrate on thermals, they are reluctant to undertake long sea-crossings. There is little evidence whether the scattered records in E Britain do represent immigrants from the Continent or dispersal of British stock, but there is certainly no significant influx into E Britain in winter. Also, some summer records well east of the main range suggest that such winterers may not have moved very far.

Tubbs (1974) estimated the 1970 breeding population at 8,000–10,000 pairs, and the 1983 Buzzard Survey appears likely to produce a similar figure. Newton (1979) showed an average breeding success of one young per pair (range 0.5–1.6). Thus as ringing recoveries indicate that most mortality occurs during January–May, the December population in Britain and Ireland is probably of the order of 24,000–30,000 birds. British and Irish Buzzards, which almost alone in Europe appear to be holding their own, and might even increase but for shooting and poisoning, may be considered a significant part of the W European population.

I. J. FERGUSON-LEES

Total number of squares in which recorded: 1,563 (40%)

No. of birds seen in a day	Number (%) of squares		
	Britain	Ireland	TOTAL (incl. C.I.)
1–2	649 (43%)	42 (78%)	692 (44%)
3–6	576 (38%)	10 (19%)	586 (37%)
7+	283 (19%)	2 (4%)	285 (18%)

References

DARE, P. J. 1957. The post-myxomatosis diet of the Buzzard. *Devon Birds* 10: 2–6.

MOORE, N. W. 1957. The past and present status of the Buzzard in the British Isles. *Brit. Birds* 64: 412–420.

NEWTON, I. 1979. *Population Ecology of Raptors.* Poyser, Berkhamsted.

PICOZZI, N. and D. WEIR. 1976. Dispersal and causes of death in Buzzards. *Brit. Birds* 69: 193–201.

TUBBS, C. R. 1974. *The Buzzard.* David & Charles, Newton Abbot.

Breeding Atlas p 106

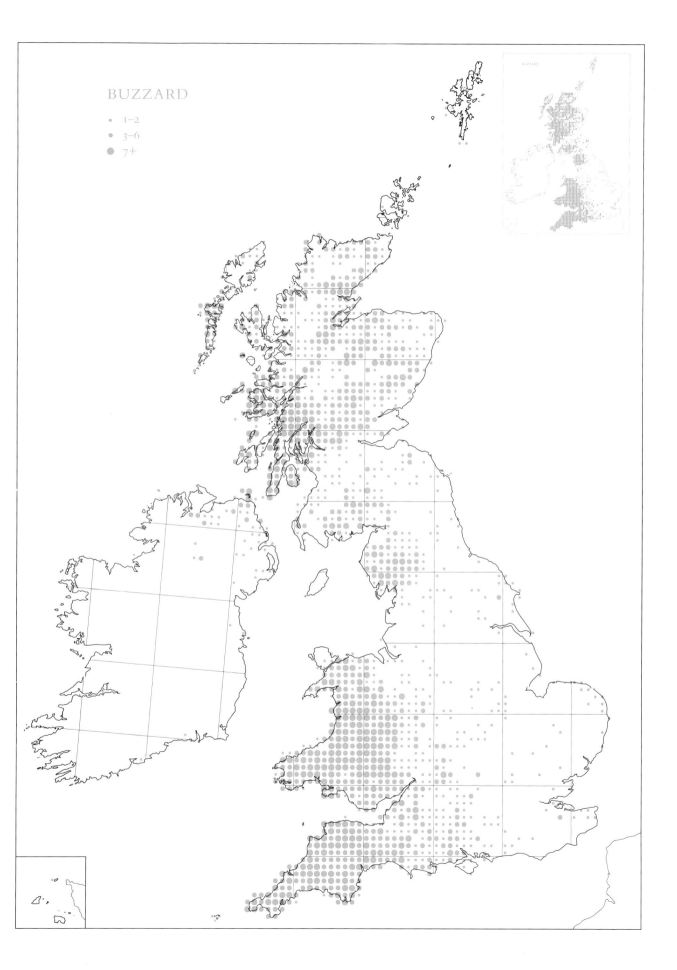

BUZZARD

- 1–2
- 3–6
- 7+

Rough-legged Buzzard

Buteo lagopus

The slow, rather ponderous hovering flight of a Rough-legged Buzzard over open country in eastern Britain could well indicate an influx winter, but numbers are not likely to be large. For a bird of its size it is often difficult to locate, as individuals cover a large hunting range.

The winter distribution has a distinct eastern bias suggesting that there is little onward movement following an autumn arrival. Indeed many individuals remain at coastal localities throughout the winter hence the concentration of dots on the East Anglian and Kent coasts. The pattern shown here is of a very typical winter distribution, unlike 1974/75 when the species was more generally spread along the south coast to Hampshire and Wiltshire (Scott 1978). The scattering of records throughout NE England and E Scotland is unusual and more characteristic of an autumn migratory arrival. In most years the main arrival, if there is to be one, takes place in late October and ends in mid to late November.

Western records in winter are exceptional, usually reflecting a marked autumn influx; although the pitfalls of identification when separating this species from a pale phase Buzzard *B. buteo* should be noted.

Wintering individuals, particularly immatures, are frequently tame, presumably a reflection of their lack of contact with human beings on their northern breeding grounds. However, each influx year results in a selection of individuals picked up weak, injured, shot or poisoned, and birds from the 1966/67 influx showed a high level of dieldrin poisoning, presumably acquired on their wintering grounds where the species is more likely to encounter an agricultural environment (Prestt *et al* 1968).

Forestry plantations, often quite small, are important winter roost sites within Britain. Usually the birds roost singly, although in peak winters small numbers may roost together.

Food is obviously a key factor controlling the numbers appearing and remaining in Britain each winter. It is known that Fennoscandian populations of Rough-legged Buzzards, the origin of British birds, fluctuate in response to population levels of Arctic rodents, and, in years of high population, marked southward migrations of the birds are recorded at many Scandinavian observation points. Should they reach Britain, most probably as a result of climatic conditions at the time of migration, their principal food appears to be rabbits, and some individuals, during the influx of 1966/67, exploited outbreaks of myxomatosis (Scott 1968).

The close association between movements and population levels in western Europe is shown by records relating to 1978 when above average numbers were reported breeding in Sweden. During the following winter, 1978/79, many wintering birds were reported from Denmark, but these disappeared around the turn of the year, at which time high numbers were reported from the Netherlands and an unusual mid winter influx took place on the British east coast in early January (Davenport 1982). In early October 1982, a marked migration occurred in SE Finland when 4,000 were recorded in a 5-day period, apparently the highest number ever noted on passage at this locality.

Except in influx years, more than 20 records in a winter is exceptional. The most recent influx, 1974/75, proved to be the largest on record, although greatly increased numbers of observers compared with those at the time of the previous century influxes will obviously affect the figures. In October 1974, as many as 250 were recorded on passage in eastern England, with a subsequent wintering population of up to 100. During the three *Winter Atlas* years the species was not particularly abundant in Britain and was absent from Ireland, and only in 1982/83 is it likely that up to 20 individuals were present throughout the winter months.

With a Fennoscandian population often in excess of 5,000 breeding pairs, Britain and Ireland never hold a significant proportion of wintering birds.

R. E. SCOTT

Total number of squares in which recorded: 93 (2%)

No. of birds seen in a day	Number (%) of squares		
	Britain	Ireland	TOTAL (incl. C.I.)
1	86 (93%)	0 (0%)	86 (93%)
2+	7 (7%)	0 (0%)	7 (7%)

References

DAVENPORT, D. L. 1982. Influxes into Britain of Hen Harriers, Long-eared Owls and Short-eared Owls in winter 1978/79. *Brit. Birds* 75: 309–316.

PORTER, R. F., I. WILLIS, S. CHRISTENSEN and B. P. NIELSEN. 1981. *Flight Identification of European Raptors*. 3rd edn. Poyser, Calton.

PRESTT, I., D. J. JEFFERIES and J. W. MACDONALD. 1968. Post-mortem examinations of four Rough-legged Buzzards. *Brit. Birds* 61: 457–465.

SCOTT, R. E. 1968. Rough-legged Buzzards in Britain in the winter of 1966/67. *Brit. Birds* 61: 449–455.

SCOTT, R. E. 1978. Rough-legged Buzzards in Britain in 1973/74 and 1974/75. *Brit. Birds* 71: 325–338.

ROUGH-LEGGED BUZZARD

- 1
- 2+

Golden Eagle

Aquila chrysaetos

The Golden Eagle is a large, though frequently elusive, raptor chiefly restricted to remote uplands in NW Britain. In the company of Ptarmigan *Lagopus mutus* and the occasional corvid it spends its winter in moorland haunts which virtually every other breeding bird forsakes.

The winter distribution map closely parallels that of the *Breeding Atlas*. This is consistent with the species' highly sedentary nature; 15 recoveries of Scottish ringed birds showed a mean dispersal distance of 55 km (*BWP*). There is a single record from Ireland of an immature bird and none from the Isle of Man. Strictly speaking, 'winter' and 'breeding' are not mutually exclusive for Golden Eagles, since nest building has been observed from November onwards (Gordon 1955, J. Watson). Adults remain on their breeding territories throughout the year. By November most juveniles have moved away from their natal territory (Gordon 1955). Of 6 juveniles wing-tagged in mid 1983, none were seen on their natal territories after December (R. Dennis, K. Brockie, J. Watson). The few sightings to the east of the main breeding range in Scotland and in Northern England, are from intensively managed grouse moors and are predominantly of immature birds.

Several studies of the food of Golden Eagles have demonstrated the importance of grouse species (*BWP*). Lockie (1964) showed that in winter in the NW Highlands, 38% of prey consisted of sheep or deer carrion. More recent studies of winter food (J. Watson, A. F. Leitch) in areas where hill sheep farming is still widespread, have shown an even greater dependence on carrion. Indeed, in much of the SW Highlands and Islands the availability of sheep and deer carrion is probably crucial to the survival of Golden Eagles during winter months.

In atrocious weather birds may remain in a sheltered place, a roost site or nesting ledge, fasting for a day or more (Gordon 1955). Each pair usually has several roost sites which are separate from, but sometimes close to, eyries. In the W Highlands birds typically choose a stunted tree such as holly or rowan on a rock ledge: in the E Highlands they will often roost in a mature Scots pine. Roosts, like eyries, are traditional and may be used for many years. Sites in use are characterised by fresh droppings, abundant downy feathers and sometimes large numbers of pellets, although the latter, if accessible, may be quickly removed by scavenging foxes (S. Rae).

On bright, windy, winter days Golden Eagles can be seen in aerial displays ranging from high circling to spectacular sky dancing with deep undulations (Brown 1976). Some of the most dramatic displays are certainly associated with advertisement and antagonistic behaviour between adjacent pairs, although similar displays may be linked with courtship (*BWP*).

In 1982 the first complete survey of the Golden Eagle breeding population in Britain was conducted (Dennis *et al* 1984). A total of 424 home ranges was occupied by pairs and another 87 by single birds. During the 1982 breeding season at least 210 young were reared to fledging, or 0.52 young per pair. This figure is within the range of 0.4–0.8 young per pair given by Newton (1979). How many of these young die by the following December and the number of 'floating' immature birds is not known. These figures give an estimate of the December population of 1,000–1,200 birds.

Dennis *et al* (1984) calculated that the British population comprised 20% of the W European breeding population. In the virtual absence of emigration and immigration in Britain, and only limited dispersive movements amongst the W European population (*BWP*), the winter figure is probably about the same.

J. WATSON

Total number of squares in which recorded: 350 (9%)

No. of birds seen in a day	Number (%) of squares		
	Britain	Ireland	TOTAL (incl. C.I.)
1	194 (56%)	1 (100%)	195 (56%)
2	104 (30%)	0 (0%)	104 (30%)
3+	51 (15%)	0 (0%)	51 (15%)

Five dots have been moved by up to 2 10-km squares on the advice of the Royal Society for the Protection of Birds.

References

BROWN, L. H. 1976. *British Birds of Prey*. Collins, London.

DENNIS, R. H., P. M. ELLIS, R. A. BROAD and D. R. LANGSLOW. 1984. The status of the Golden Eagle in Britain. *Brit. Birds* 77: 592–607.

GORDON, S. 1955. *The Golden Eagle, King of Birds*. Collins, London.

LOCKIE, J. D. 1964. The breeding density of the Golden Eagle and Fox in relation to food-supply in Wester Ross, Scotland. *Scot. Nat.* 71: 67–77.

NEWTON, I. 1979. *Population Ecology of Raptors*. Poyser, Berkhamsted.

Breeding Atlas p 104

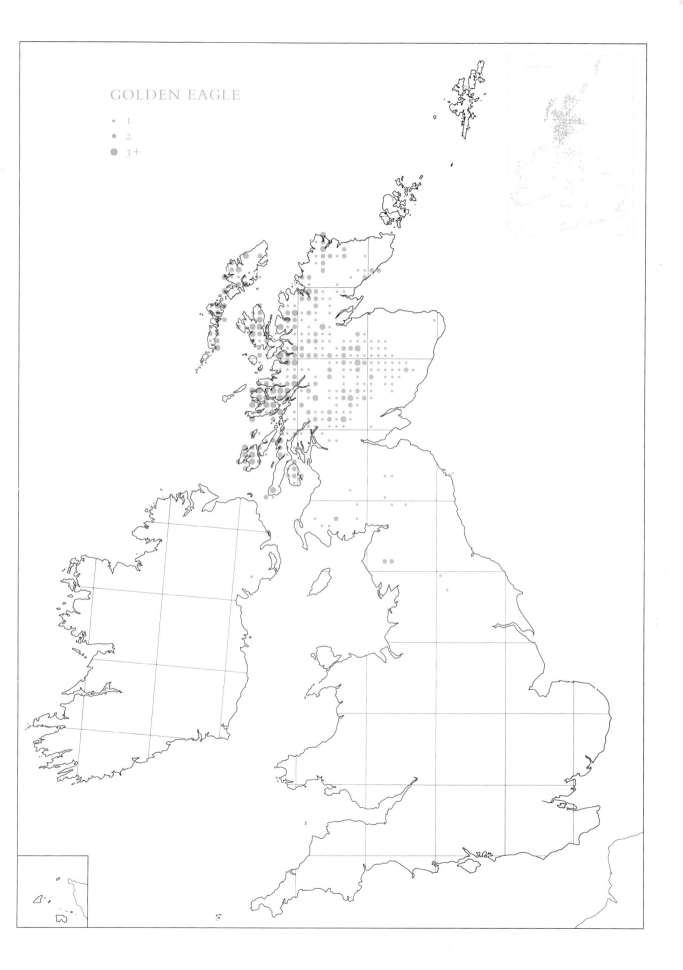

GOLDEN EAGLE

- · 1
- ● 2
- ● 3+

Kestrel

Falco tinnunculus

This delightful and common small falcon is Britain's most widespread, and probably most numerous, diurnal bird of prey at all seasons. It can be watched anywhere and few birdwatchers live far from a regular winter roost at least, if not a breeding site. The breeding population fluctuated markedly or declined in the early 1960s, particularly in the primarily arable areas of E England and the population also suffered severely in the winter of 1962/63, but had largely recovered by 1968.

The winter distribution differs from the breeding distribution, the greatest concentration being found in E England, particularly from Lincolnshire, south to Berkshire and southeast to N Kent. The counties of E England include the most obvious gap in breed-breeding distribution in England noted by the *Breeding Atlas*. Here about 57% of the total land surface is tilled, which is nearly twice the national average of 32%. In Scotland, Kestrels are most numerous in the SW quarter of the country. In Ireland, where the species is widespread, numbers are generally below those of Britain, which may only reflect the breeding position.

British Kestrels are partial migrants and Snow (1968) showed that more upland (and therefore western) birds migrated than lowland ones. Thus the greater numbers wintering in the eastern lowlands must partly reflect a higher proportion of residents. Mead (1973) showed an influx of Continental Kestrels, particularly from the northern Baltic and the Low Countries, primarily into E England between August and December. Thus many of the birds counted were presumably winter visitors from overseas, in addition to northern birds. In Scotland the reversal of the general easterly bias in winter distribution may be for climatic reasons. Manley (1952) showed that the part of W Scotland most favoured by wintering Kestrels has comparatively little snow.

The Kestrel's winter distribution suggests that cultivated land is more attractive to it than is generally realised, because the distribution shown, not only in E England but also in S England, Lancashire and on the northeast coast, shows a marked correlation with tillage. Studies of hunting behaviour in farmland (Shrubb 1980, Pettifor 1983) indicate that, even in heavily cultivated areas, Kestrels take most of their food, at least by weight, from the uncultivated habitats available, so this correlation is anomalous. However, winter populations might include many young birds because Snow (1968) showed that these are more likely to migrate than adults. Shrubb found that invertebrates, very often taken from cultivated land, formed a large percentage of the diet of first autumn birds, and earthworms, taken largely from cereal fields, were an important winter food for birds of all ages.

Wintering Kestrels also need secure roosts and these are abundant in farmland. On 1,500 ha of farmland in Sussex, 19 out of 20 winter roosts were in or on buildings giving maximum protection from the weather. Kestrels breed regularly in farm buildings there, and residents roost in the vicinity of such breeding sites throughout the year. Often, however, they have several sites in regular use within their hunting range. There is also a strong traditional element in such sites.

Estimating the wintering numbers with any accuracy is difficult and they may fluctuate, because the number of British emigrants probably varies (Snow 1968). This may also apply to winter visitors, the numbers and densities of which are, in any case, largely unknown. The British breeding population has been estimated as between 30,000 and 80,000 pairs, with presumably a very much smaller number in Ireland. Annual production was put by Brown (1976) at 2.5 young per pair that bred, and mortality at 60% in the first year by Snow. With the winter movements which take place these figures suggest a mid winter population of the order of 100,000 birds in Britain and Ireland.

M. SHRUBB

Total number of squares in which recorded: 3,142 (81%)

No. of birds seen in a day	Number (%) of squares		
	Britain	Ireland	TOTAL (incl. C.I.)
1–2	996 (41%)	637 (88%)	1,635 (52%)
3–4	910 (38%)	81 (11%)	992 (32%)
5+	509 (21%)	4 (1%)	515 (16%)

References
BROWN, L. 1976. *British Birds of Prey*. Collins, London.
MANLEY, G. 1952. *Climate and the British Scene*. Collins, London.
MEAD, C. J. 1973. Movements of British raptors. *Bird Study* 20: 259–286.
PETTIFOR, R. A. 1983. Seasonal variations and associated energetic implications in the hunting behaviour of the Kestrel. *Bird Study* 30: 201–206.
SHRUBB, M. 1980. Farming influences on the food and hunting of Kestrels. *Bird Study* 27: 109–115.
SNOW, D. W. 1968. Movements and mortality of British Kestrels. *Bird Study* 15: 65–83.

Breeding Atlas p 130

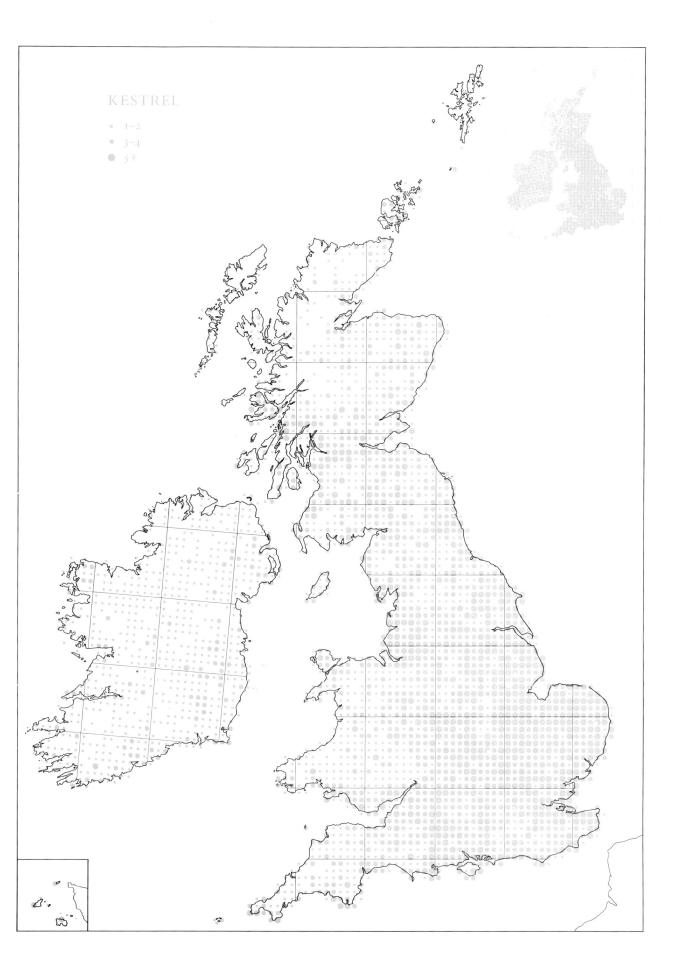

KESTREL

- 1–2
- 3–4
- 5+

Merlin

Falco columbarius

The Merlin is a small dashing falcon which may be seen in almost any open country in winter. It breeds, sparsely, in Britain's uplands. Poor weather and the absence of small birds on which it preys force it to move varying distances after breeding.

Merlins are widely believed to winter near coasts, attracted by flocks of finches and small waders. Perhaps this is partly an illusion, since coasts are popular with birdwatchers and the reactions of flocking birds draw attention to raptors which can often be seen at long ranges. The present map suggests a coastal element to the distribution, especially obvious in Scotland, including the northern and western isles, and also SE England. Inland concentrations are evident from such varied places as the New Forest to Salisbury Plain, the Fens, much of NE England and the central lowlands of Scotland, but with a wide scatter elsewhere. Merlins are clearly absent from the higher ground, especially towards the north of their breeding range. From the Lake District northward there is a descent to the lower and coastal areas in winter. In Ireland, with its milder climate and generally open but less rugged terrain, the winter and breeding distributions are more similar.

Winter foods of Merlins have not been studied but presumably consist of small open-country birds. Summer prey lists (Watson 1979, Newton *et al* 1984) refer primarily to birds caught by the smaller male. Females hunting in winter might catch more birds of the size of thrushes, Starlings *Sturnus vulgaris* and small waders. Birds are probably surprised by Merlins, approaching in short low dashes, rather than caught in aerial pursuits which, though often conspicuous, are seemingly often unsuccessful. Dense woodland is avoided, but in the lowlands of Britain and Ireland the majority of land is probably open enough for hunting Merlins, and sufficient numbers of potential prey species occur widely on farmland as well as on the coasts. Wintering Merlins are generally solitary but they sometimes appear to associate in pairs, or with another bird of prey, while hunting. Regular winter roosts of 2 or more Merlins are known, especially in E England. Heaths, reed beds, dunes and bogs are used, often near Hen Harrier *Circus cyaneus* roosts (R. Clarke *in litt*).

Patterns of movement are not fully known (review to 1972 in Mead (1973) and subsequent records from annual ringing reports). In general, the northerly populations both in Britain and Europe are more migratory. Birds from Iceland winter in Ireland and NW Britain, though some move further south into France. Passage birds ringed at Fair Isle were previously judged, on their greater size, to be Icelandic stock and are recovered on the Continent. It is now known that Shetland young also pass through Fair Isle and that they are as big as birds previously believed on size to be Icelandic. An Orkney-reared bird went to West Germany but there is as yet no certainty as to where these most northern populations winter. Otherwise, British and Irish birds probably cross the Channel rarely, though 2 from Northumberland went to France. Most however stay within 50 km of their natal sites, with young birds moving further than adults, and southerly populations probably being less mobile than northern ones. The birds wintering in SE England may be from the quite large and migratory Scandinavian populations. With no recoveries here, and 67 elsewhere in Europe (*BWP*), Britain cannot however be anything more than a minor wintering area for these birds.

The total number wintering in Britain and Ireland probably includes the great majority of the breeding population, supplemented by some Icelandic birds. Making broad estimates for the number of young per breeding pair being alive in winter plus those birds too young, or failing to breed, the native population might be 2,000–3,000 birds in mid winter. Such wide limits might be sufficient to embrace the wintering numbers here with some gains and losses from movement. This would make an average number of birds per occupied square of 2–3 which seems reasonable considering that at any one time many such squares probably held no Merlins at all, while more than 10 would be a very high density.

C. J. BIBBY

Total number of squares in which recorded: 1,217 (32%)

No. of birds seen in a day	Number (%) of squares		
	Britain	Ireland	TOTAL (incl. C.I.)
1	871 (86%)	190 (91%)	1,062 (87%)
2	109 (11%)	17 (8%)	126 (10%)
3+	28 (3%)	1 (1%)	29 (2%)

References

MEAD, C. J. 1973. Movements of British raptors. *Bird Study* 20: 259–286.

NEWTON, I., E. R. MEEK and B. LITTLE. 1984. Breeding season foods of Merlins *Falco columbarius* in Northumbria. *Bird Study* 31: 49–56.

WATSON, J. 1979. Foods of Merlins nesting in young conifer forests. *Bird Study* 26: 253–258.

Breeding Atlas p 128

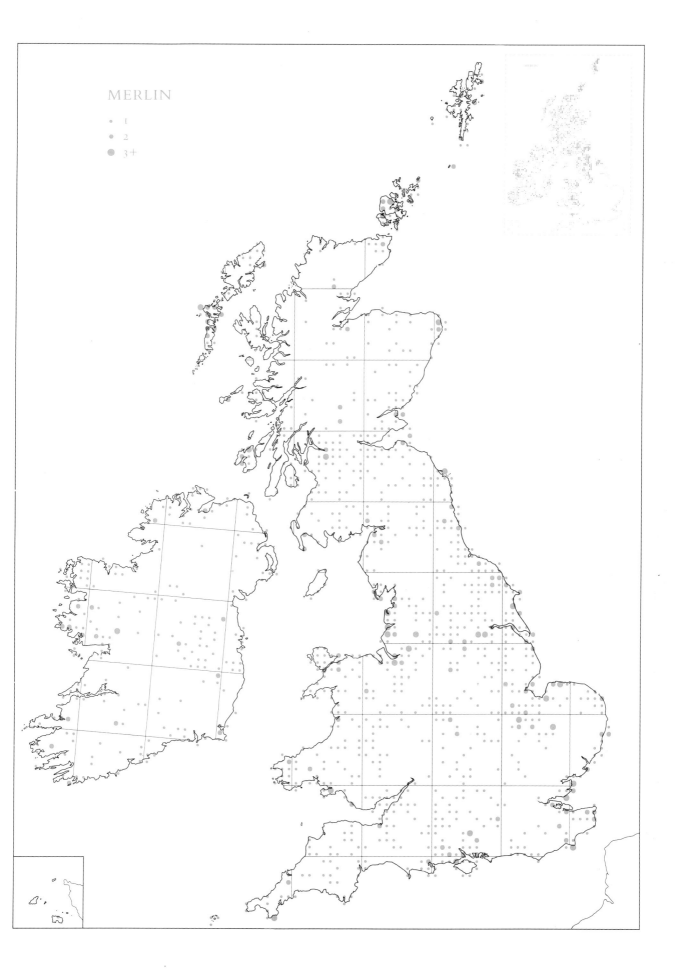

MERLIN

- • 1
- • 2
- • 3+

Peregrine

Falco peregrinus

Our most glamorous resident falcon was named during the 13th century, evidently from its habit of appearing outside the breeding season in lands where it did not nest, and so seeming to be a great wanderer.

The winter distribution shows considerable similarity to that of the breeding season, but has a more eastern spread, especially in Scotland and N England. This involves more occurrences in lowland and flat coastal districts where the bird does not breed. The young birds disperse in autumn, some taking up prospective breeding territories, and others moving to areas unsuitable for nesting where they establish winter territories and often roost on good vantage points, such as trees, tall buildings and pylons. Adult birds surplus to the breeding population, sometimes paired, may also appear in these lowland haunts.

The Peregrine survey of 1981 showed that the breeding population in Britain and Ireland had recovered from the crash of 1956–66, attributable to pesticides, to around 90% of its pre 1940 level (Ratcliffe 1984). In Ireland, by 1981, there was 83% occupation of available breeding territories (Norriss *et al* 1983). Compared with the *Breeding Atlas* the winter map shows substantial increases in Wales, SW England and many parts of Ireland.

The Peregrine is widely distributed in winter, through a considerable variety of habitats. It can turn up almost anywhere, including the middle of our largest cities, but its favourite haunts are the cliff coasts, the contrasting estuarine salt marshes and flats, the gentler moorlands and precipitous mountains, the vicinity of inland lakes and swamps, and sometimes the ordinary farmland of the lowlands. Most Peregrines winter below 400 m, but many bleak hill sites are still held, at least for roosting. The species is then mostly thinly dispersed over much of western and northern Britain, and more generally through Ireland, but its occurrences in the lowlands, especially of England, were sparse during the mapping period.

Peregrine distribution necessarily parallels food supply, and apparent winter scarcity in NW Scotland fits the supposition that the bird leaves this district as prey populations decline in autumn (Ratcliffe 1980). High mountain breeding haunts in the Highlands are also deserted during winter, because of arctic conditions and poor food supply (D. Weir). Elsewhere, established breeding pairs generally appear to occupy their nesting quarters throughout the winter, sometimes ranging far afield in search of prey, but usually returning to roost, though the sexes sometimes separate between different cliffs. The prey spectrum shifts during winter, domestic pigeons being less available, and more Woodpigeons *Columba palumbus*, wildfowl and shorebirds are taken in some areas.

Winter numbers and distribution were formerly boosted by immigration of Continental birds, which ringing data suggest came mainly from Fennoscandia (Mead 1973). Pesticidal effects have reduced this northwestern Continental population to low levels, so that this influx is at present insignificant. Ringing recoveries of first winter British Peregrines are mostly within 150 km of birthplace, and there is only one Continental recovery of a British/Irish falcon (R. Spencer). Most migrants and partial migrants evidently tend to return to the vicinity of their birthplace at the end of the winter.

The 1981 surveys gave an estimated total of at least 1,000 occupied breeding territories in Britain and Ireland, of which about 90% were held by pairs and the rest by single Peregrines. With breeding success probably averaging around 1.25 young per territorial pair, probably well over 1,000 young Peregrines fledge annually nowadays. Adult survival is generally good now that pesticide hazards are much reduced and, allowing for a non-breeding adult surplus, total population at the onset of winter is probably at least double that of the breeding population, with over 4,000 birds. The British and Irish Peregrine population is now one of the largest in Europe and is still increasing slowly.

D. A. RATCLIFFE

Total number of squares in which recorded: 1,282 (33%)

	Number (%) of squares		
No. of birds seen in a day	Britain	Ireland	TOTAL (incl. C.I.)
1	769 (76%)	223 (81%)	994 (77%)
2	208 (21%)	44 (16%)	252 (20%)
3+	29 (3%)	7 (3%)	36 (3%)

References

MEAD, C. J. 1973. Movements of British raptors. *Bird Study* 20: 259–286.

NORRISS, D. W., H. J. WILSON and D. BROWNE. 1983. Survey of the Peregrine *Falco peregrinus* breeding population in the Republic of Ireland in 1981. *Bird Study* 30: 91–101.

RATCLIFFE, D. A. 1980. *The Peregrine Falcon.* Poyser, Calton.

Breeding Atlas p 126

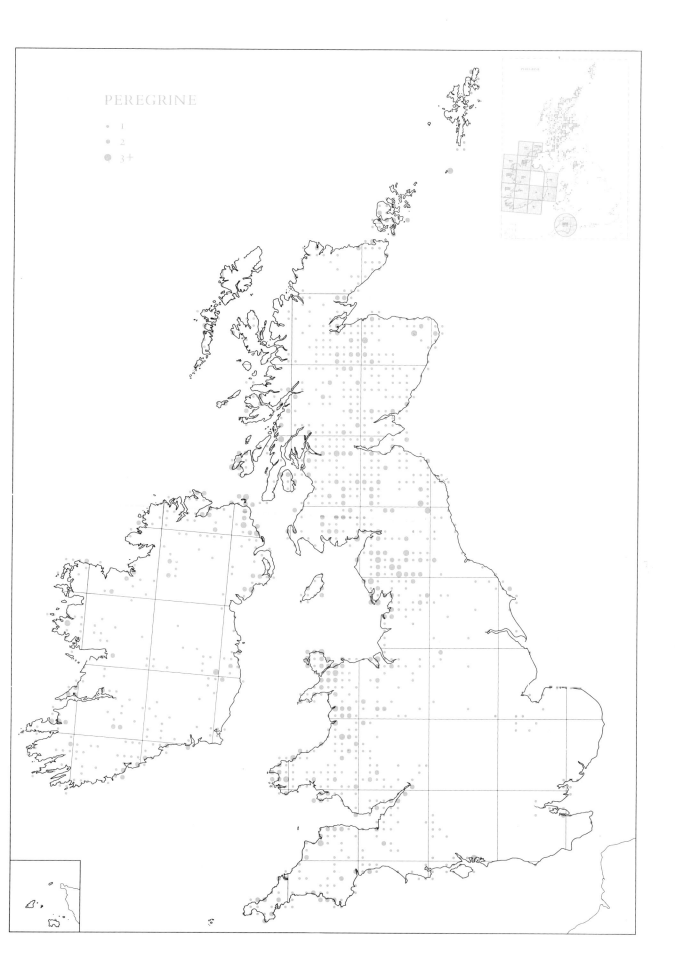

PEREGRINE

- 1
- 2
- 3+

Red Grouse

Lagopus lagopus

The Red Grouse is internationally famed as a sporting bird and well known to British and Irish birdwatchers and hill walkers as the characteristic bird of the moors, both summer and winter. The Red Grouse used to be regarded as Britain's only indigenous native bird species, but it is now considered merely a subspecies *L. l. scoticus* of the more widely distributed Willow Grouse *L. l. lagopus*. In the relatively mild winters of these islands it no longer has the Willow Grouse's white body plumage in winter, nor white primaries all the year round.

The winter and summer distributions of the Red Grouse are on the same treeless moorland where ling heather, their main food plant, is abundant (Watson and Miller 1976). They occur commonly from sea level up to 600 m, and in the central and E Scottish Highlands locally breed up to 900 m. Thus they inhabit a zone which was formerly mainly forest and scrub, but where tree growth is now prevented by burning and grazing. Indeed, grouse shooting is the main economic reason why many of the moors continue as moorland instead of reverting to forest. The map shows that the birds are most abundant in E Scotland and NE England, where heather thrives better than in the wetter west. In Ireland, they still occur in mountain regions and in low numbers on the western boglands.

Red Grouse prefer young heather, which is more nutritious as food, but they also need older heather for cover. Grouse moor management consists mainly of burning the heather in a rotation, so that the moor becomes a diverse patchwork of different-aged heather. In addition, heather is more nutritious where it grows above base-rich rocks such as limestone and epidiorite.

Grouse broods generally break up in September-October and in Britain flocks form at about the same time. The cocks take territories, and hens pair with the cocks. The loud crowing or 'becking' of the cocks, and their song flights while becking, are well known signs of their territorial behaviour, especially in early morning and at dusk, and in late winter throughout the day in fine weather with snow-free conditions.

Snowfalls make all the birds go into flocks, or packs as moorland folk know them. The birds move to feed on ridges and other places where the wind has drifted the snow off the heather. The leafless green stalks of whortleberry are another common food item. They occasionally feed in autumn and winter on grain in stubble fields, and often on berries. In heavy undrifted snow the birds may leave their home area and fly a few kilometres to snow-free vegetation on other moors, and exceptionally have been recorded feeding on hawthorn berries.

In winter they normally roost in packs on the ground, but singly or in pairs in fine weather in late winter. In deep snow each bird scratches out a hollow for roosting and on very frosty nights may dig a deep hole in powder snow.

Spring population densities vary from 2–3 pairs per km² in western Ireland and Scotland, up to about 100 pairs in peak years on good moors in the east. Spring numbers on any moor fluctuate considerably, and in some areas show a cyclic tendency with peaks approximately every 6–7 years. Breeding success also varies greatly, from virtually no young reared in the worst places in poor years, up to about 4 young reared per adult bird on good ground in the best years.

In 1911 the average annual bag in Scotland, England and Wales was estimated at about 2.5 million birds shot (Leslie 1911), so the total, including Ireland, would probably have been almost 3 million. Numbers have since declined greatly due to a variety of causes: reduced keepering, with consequent poorer moor management, overgrazing by increases in numbers of sheep and red deer, an increase of tick-borne disease, loss of moorland habitat to forestry and agriculture, and increased predation. The annual bag for Britain and Ireland now has been estimated at 260,000–660,000 (Harradine 1983). The area of heather moorland is roughly 2–2.5 million hectares, but Red Grouse occur at low numbers elsewhere, such as deer forests in the west Scottish Highlands.

A. WATSON

Total number of squares in which recorded: 903 (23%)

No. of birds seen in a day	Number (%) of squares		
	Britain	Ireland	TOTAL (incl. C.I.)
1–5	315 (42%)	126 (82%)	441 (49%)
6–22	255 (34%)	27 (17%)	282 (31%)
23+	179 (24%)	1 (1%)	180 (20%)

References

HARRADINE, J. 1983. Sport shooting in the United Kingdom: some facts and figures. Pp 63–83 in LEEUWENBERG, F. and I. HEPBURN (eds). *Proc. Int. Union of Game Biologists Working Group on Game Statistics.* Zoetermeer, Netherlands.

LESLIE, A. S. (ed.) 1911. The value of grouse shootings in Great Britain. Pp 491–502 *The Grouse in Health and in Disease.* Smith, Elder and Co., London.

WATSON, A. and G. R. MILLER. 1976. *Grouse Management.* The Game Conservancy, Fordingbridge.

Breeding Atlas p 132

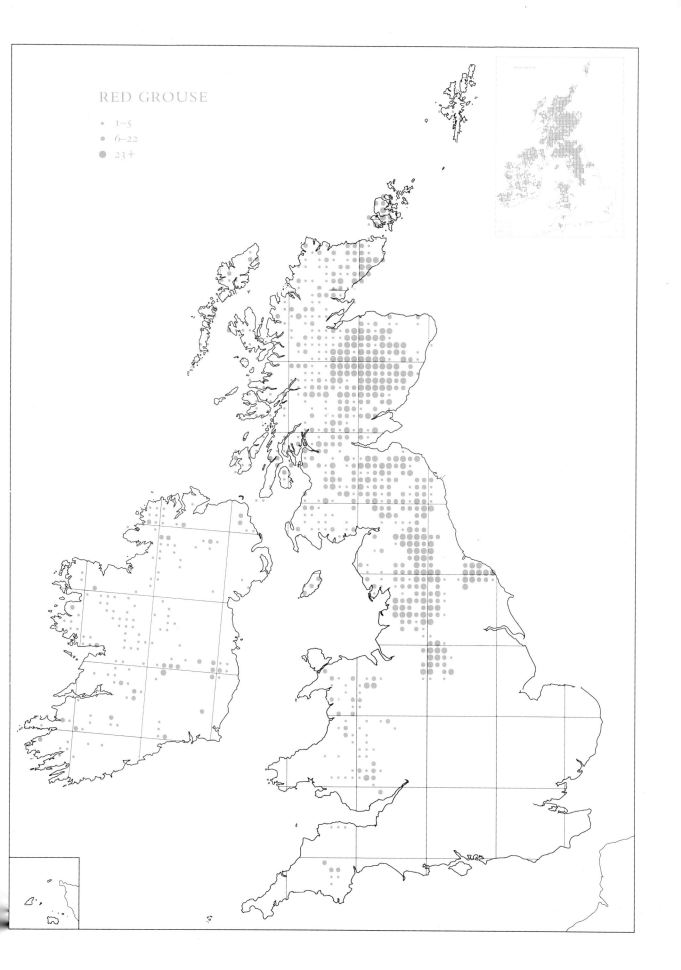

RED GROUSE

- 1–5
- 6–22
- 23+

Ptarmigan

Lagopus mutus

The Scottish race of Ptarmigan is confined to Scotland and is the hardiest British bird, living on high hills throughout the winter; it is well adapted to cope with the worst storms, and is the only British bird to turn white in winter.

The winter distribution is the same as in summer, except that in winter Ptarmigans sometimes come down to slightly lower altitudes, especially after deep snow. There they can be seen in the upper part of the moorland habitat of the Red Grouse *L. lagopus*, and indeed flocks of both often occur near each other at that time. In the Scottish Highlands and Islands they occur on stony hills, mainly from 600–1,300 m in altitude, though generally deserting ground above 1,200 m in severe winter weather. On the more exposed western and northern hills they live much lower, commonly down to 500 m and down to 200 m near Cape Wrath (Watson 1965).

Their distribution has contracted slightly since the 1800s, and they no longer live in the southern uplands. However, most of their distribution area has not changed. Their main strongholds are in the Cairngorms, the Mounth from Drumochter east to Lochnagar, and the major high tops in the central and NW Highlands. A few occur on hills in the Hebrides. Population densities are highest on mainly heathy hills with many rocks providing cover. The birds breed better and maintain higher spring stocks over base-rich rocks, such as limestone, than over the more acidic granite.

The birds feed mainly on heathy arctic-alpine plants, particularly the shoots of whortleberry, crowberry, heather, and others such as least willow. In snow the flocks move to ground swept clear by the wind. Young Ptarmigans leave the broods in August–October and frequently form flocks with old birds, occasionally even in late July. The cocks show territorial behaviour in autumn, especially on fine mornings, flying around in song flights very similar to those of Red Grouse. Their voice is very different, however, a belching, rattling, almost mechanical-like croak. Hens pair with the cocks, but both sexes live in flocks for much of the day in autumn and early winter, and during late winter in afternoon and evening, as well as when the weather is snowy.

In winter they roost in flocks but occasionally singly or in pairs in fine weather. They roost on the ground, or sometimes on big rocks, and in snowy conditions they scrape out hollows or holes in the snow. Watson (1972) gave a detailed description of the behaviour of Ptarmigans in Scotland.

Like the Red Grouse, the numbers fluctuate greatly from year to year, and Watson (1965) noticed a cyclical tendency with peaks about every ten years or so in the Cairngorms. Spring density varies from absence on some hills in trough years, up to 65 pairs per km² on the richest ground in peak years. Breeding success varies from almost nil, locally, in summers with severe snowstorms, up to 3 or more young reared per old bird. In recent years breeding success has declined drastically near the ski-lifts at Cairn Gorm, due to heavy egg predation by crows attracted by waste food dropped by tourists (Watson 1982), whilst spring stocks there have declined due to adult Ptarmigans flying into the ski-lift wires. Adult mortality, however, is usually from predation, mainly by foxes, though many are killed by Golden Eagles *Aquila chrysaetos*, some by Peregrines *Falco peregrinus* and a few by stoats. In a winter with high numbers the population of Scotland is probably 10,000–15,000 birds.

A. WATSON

Total number of squares in which recorded: 82 (2%)

No. of birds seen in a day	Number (%) of squares		
	Britain	Ireland	TOTAL (incl. C.I.)
1–4	37 (45%)	0 (0%)	37 (45%)
5–10	27 (33%)	0 (0%)	27 (33%)
11+	18 (22%)	0 (0%)	18 (22%)

References

WATSON, A. 1965. Research on Scottish Ptarmigan. *Scot. Birds* 3: 331–349.

WATSON, A. 1972. The behaviour of the Ptarmigan. *Brit. Birds* 65: 6–26, 93–117.

WATSON, A. 1982. Effects of human impact on Ptarmigan and Red Grouse near ski lifts in Scotland. *Ann. Rep. Inst. Terr. Ecol.* 1981: 51.

Breeding Atlas p 134

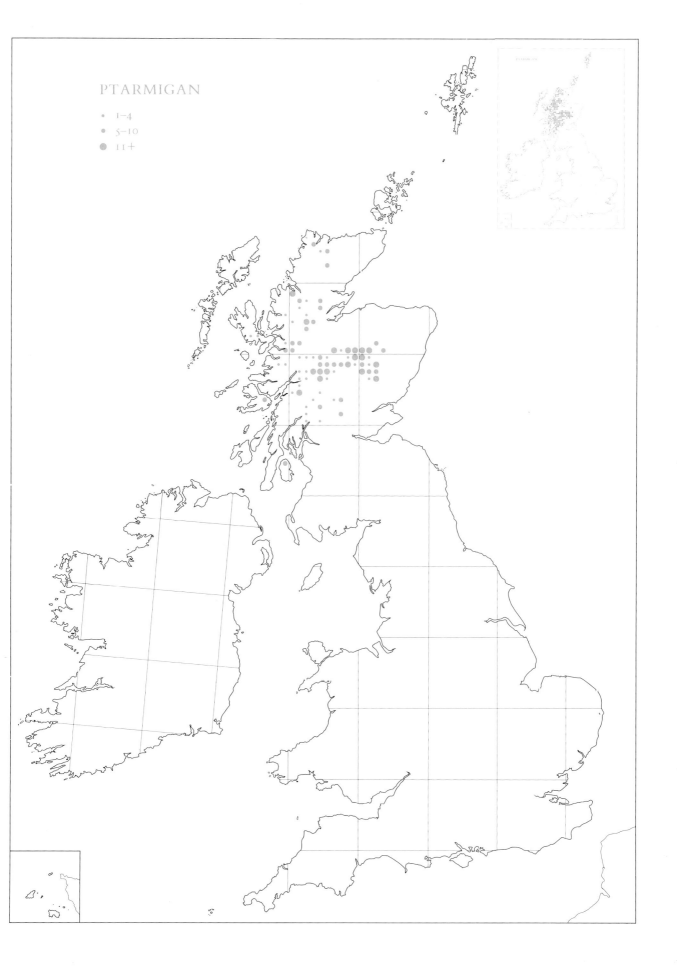

PTARMIGAN

- 1–4
- 5–10
- 11+

Black Grouse

Tetrao tetrix

The distinctive plumage of the Black Grouse male makes it one of our most striking gamebirds. Cocks are most readily seen when displaying in the early morning, and sometimes in the evenings in fields, bogs or short heather. Some may visit the lek in autumn and winter, but they leave soon after dawn.

Black Grouse are fairly sedentary, so the range shown by the map can be compared directly with that in the *Breeding Atlas*. There are no longer any Black Grouse in southern England, the last remaining birds on Exmoor having recently died out (C. Tubbs). They appear now to be less widely distributed in S and W Wales, and the decrease shown in the Peak District may be due to the effect of heavy sheep grazing which has destroyed birch scrub, blaeberry and nesting cover. According to Lovenbury *et al* (1978), the main stronghold of Black Grouse in the Peak District is in areas where there is a tight mosaic of birch woods, moorland and pasture which has not altered much since the last war. Little change in distribution seems to have taken place in Scotland except in the NW Highlands. Birds may have been overlooked there in the new forestry plantations, but it is as likely that where the canopy has closed, the dense woods are no longer a suitable habitat. There are no Black Grouse in Ireland.

A study of marked birds in NE Scotland has shown that both sexes frequented woodlands in winter. Woodland and scrub appeared to be as important for shelter and roosting as for food. The hens returned to the moor close to their nesting areas when these were snow-free. Cocks remained longer in the woodlands and were seldom regularly on the moor before March. They then roosted near the lek. However, marked Black Grouse in a nearby forest of old Caledonian pines were mainly associated with the more open parts of the forest throughout the year.

In winter, they occur singly or in small mixed or single sex flocks, but are obvious only when feeding in the open in fields, or in trees such as birch and hazel. They eat a succession of herbs, dwarf heaths, rushes, sedges, berries and shoots and buds of trees and shrubs through the year (Picozzi and Hepburn in press). In winter, the main food items are the shoots of heather and blaeberry, with birch and hazel buds and catkins, and pine buds and needles locally important. In Britain, they roost either in trees or, more usually, on the ground in long heather. Roosts in enclosed snow holes are common in Europe but in Britain, where the snow is seldom deep, this behaviour has rarely been observed.

There has been a big decline in Black Grouse numbers in many other parts of western Europe (Lovel 1979). They have been almost lost from Holland and Denmark where intensive agricultural practice has played a major part in the decline. In Britain, and elsewhere, the removal of hardwood scrub, the drainage of hills and the loss of rough pasture have destroyed essential elements of the birds' habitat. Bogs and rough pastures in particular are rich in arthropods which are an important, probably essential, feature of the diet of young chicks. In Scandinavia, where Black Grouse are still thriving, the birds occupy large clearings in mature forests soon after felling (Angelstam 1983). They may increase in Britain as forests now nearing maturity are felled.

Black Grouse may often be flushed unseen, particularly in windy weather or when perched on trees, and away from the display grounds they may be easily missed, so it is difficult to estimate numbers. Furthermore, numbers may increase or decrease by over 100% in a few years. In NE Scotland on an area of mixed moorland and woodland, there are at present one cock and 2 hens per km^2 in spring, but at least twice as many cocks were present in recent years. It would be misleading to attempt an estimate of numbers in Britain from the winter map as birds were recorded simply as present in just over half the squares, and more than 10 birds were counted in only 15% of the 10-km squares. A reasonable guess would still place them at the lower end of the 10,000–100,000 category, as in the *Breeding Atlas*.

N. PICOZZI

Total number of squares in which recorded: 316 (8%)

No. of birds seen in a day	Number (%) of squares		TOTAL (incl. C.I.)
	Britain	Ireland	
1–3	168 (53%)	0 (0%)	168 (53%)
4–8	91 (29%)	0 (0%)	91 (29%)
9+	57 (18%)	0 (0%)	57 (18%)

References

ANGELSTAM, P. 1983. *Population Dynamics of Tetraonids, especially the Black Grouse* Tetrao tetrix *L., in Boreal Forests*. Ph.D. Thesis. Uppsala University.

LOVENBURY, G. A., M. WATERHOUSE and D. W. YALDEN. 1978. The status of Black Grouse in the Peak District. *The Naturalist* 103: 3–14.

LOVEL, T. W. I. (ed.). 1979. *Woodland Grouse Symposium*. World Pheasant Association, Bures, Suffolk.

PICOZZI, N. and L. V. HEPBURN. In press. A study of Black Grouse in NE Scotland. In LOVEL, T. W. I. (ed.) *Proc. 3 Int. Woodland Grouse Symp.*

Breeding Atlas p 136

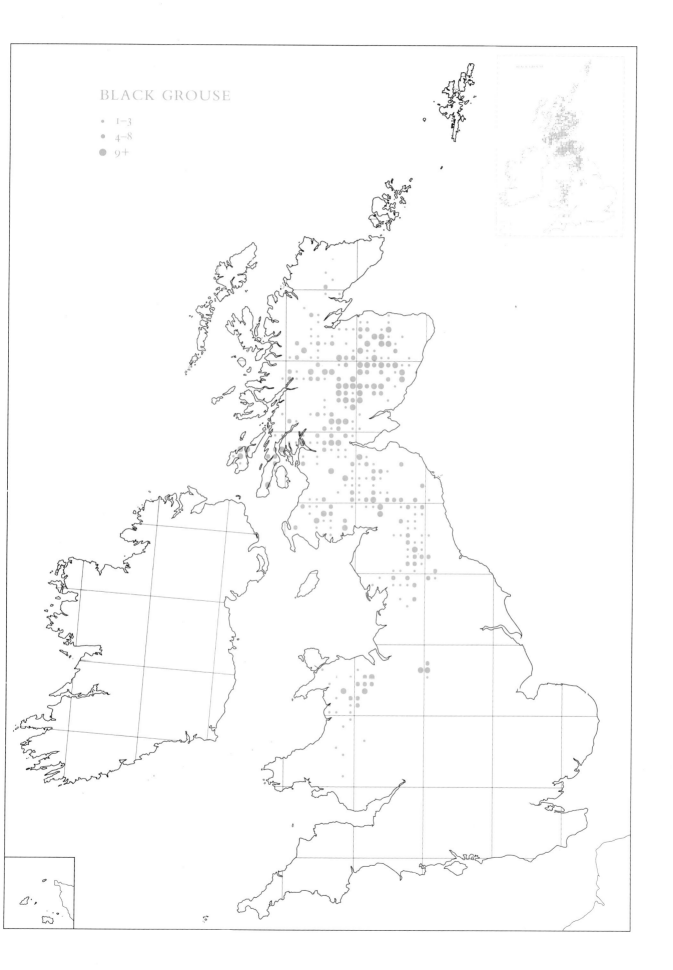

BLACK GROUSE

- 1–3
- 4–8
- 9+

Capercaillie

Tetrao urogallus

The Capercaillie is primarily a bird of Scots pine forest; its name derives from the Gaelic, possibly meaning 'Mare of the woods', the reference to a mare or horse implying its great size. The spelling Capercailzie is sometimes seen; the 'z' represents an old Scottish consonant which should be pronounced almost 'z'. Despite its large size—it is the biggest grouse in the world—the Capercaillie is silent and elusive.

The winter map shows a more restricted distribution (73 squares) than the *Breeding Atlas* (182 squares). This may be partly because, although Capercaillies are essentially resident birds, they breed in a wider range of habitats than they frequent in winter. There has, however, been a marked decline in Capercaillie densities between the preparation of the two maps (Moss *et al* 1979, and other information). This may have been accompanied by a reduction in their range, but it is also likely that birds have been missed in more 10–km squares.

Capercaillies occur most abundantly in conifer forests in E central Scotland, there being fewer in the wetter west. The highest winter densities are found in semi-natural Scots pine forests and in some mature Scots pine plantations. Another habitat widely used in summer in many parts of the bird's range is mature oak woodland, though this is now scarce in Scotland.

Needles and buds of Scots pine are the main winter food, and the birds spend most of the winter in the canopy, although they will descend to the ground on mild days and there eat some ling and blaeberry. In continental Eurasia they seem to prefer Scots pine to spruce, even when pine forms only a tiny fraction of the forest (Semenov-Tian-Shanskii 1959). However, some populations are said to subsist largely on spruce in winter (Dement'ev and Gladkov 1967), so they seem able to adapt to this food. Jones (1982) studied diet in mixed conifer plantations in Scotland and concluded that, whilst Scots pine was the main conifer eaten, larch was taken more than spruce, and Sitka spruce preferred to Norway spruce. Capercaillies made little use of lodgepole or Corsican pine but did take some ponderosa and maritime pine. Adaptability to new foods is obviously of crucial importance to the future of Capercaillies in Britain as plantations become dominated more and more by exotic trees.

Population density was unusually high in the late 1960s and early 1970s. Until then, a common view amongst foresters was that Capercaillies were vermin, and shoots were organised to keep numbers down. In the late 1960s shooting of all game became much more commercial and parties of paying guests became an important source of income to many estates. At this point, the Capercaillie changed its status from 'vermin' to a 'fine game bird'. This may have contributed to the recent decline in densities, as shooting continued on some areas where the birds had become scarce. The more responsible estates, however, regulate their shooting in relation to the numbers of birds.

Observed winter densities in different forests have varied from less than 5 to over 30 birds/km². They seem to breed best in open forest with mature trees and plenty of blaeberry on the ground (Moss *et al* 1979). Such forests are relatively scarce but may be crucial to the continued survival of our Capercaillie population. Despite their wide distribution in conifer forest of all types, most of the young may be produced in mature forests and move about to occupy the denser plantations, where breeding may not be successful enough to support a population without continued immigration.

The Scottish population, probably a few thousand birds, forms a minute fraction of the world population, whose distribution more or less coincides with that of the Scots pine. Over much of its range, Capercaillie numbers are declining in parallel with the disappearance of mature Scots pine and oak forests as these are felled by man.

R. MOSS

Total number of squares in which recorded: 73 (2%)

No. of birds seen in a day	Number (%) of squares		
	Britain	Ireland	TOTAL (incl. C.I.)
1	33 (45%)	0 (0%)	33 (45%)
2–4	28 (38%)	0 (0%)	28 (38%)
5+	12 (16%)	0 (0%)	12 (16%)

References

DEMENT'EV, G. P. and N. A. GLADKOV. 1967. *Birds of the Soviet Union*. Vol IV. Israel Program for Scientific Translations, Jerusalem (translated from 1952 original).

JONES, A. M. 1982. *Aspects of the Ecology and Behaviour of Capercaillie* Tetrao urogallus *L. in two Scottish Plantations*. Ph.D. Thesis, University of Aberdeen.

MOSS, R., D. WEIR and A. M. JONES. 1979. Capercaillie management in Scotland. Pp 140–155 in LOVEL T. W. I. (ed.) *Woodland Grouse Symposium*. World Pheasant Association, Bures, Suffolk.

SEMENOV-TIAN-SHANSKII, O. I. 1959. Ekologija teterevinyh ptits. *Trudy Laplandskogo Gosudarstvennogo Zapovednika* 5: 1–318.

Breeding Atlas p 138

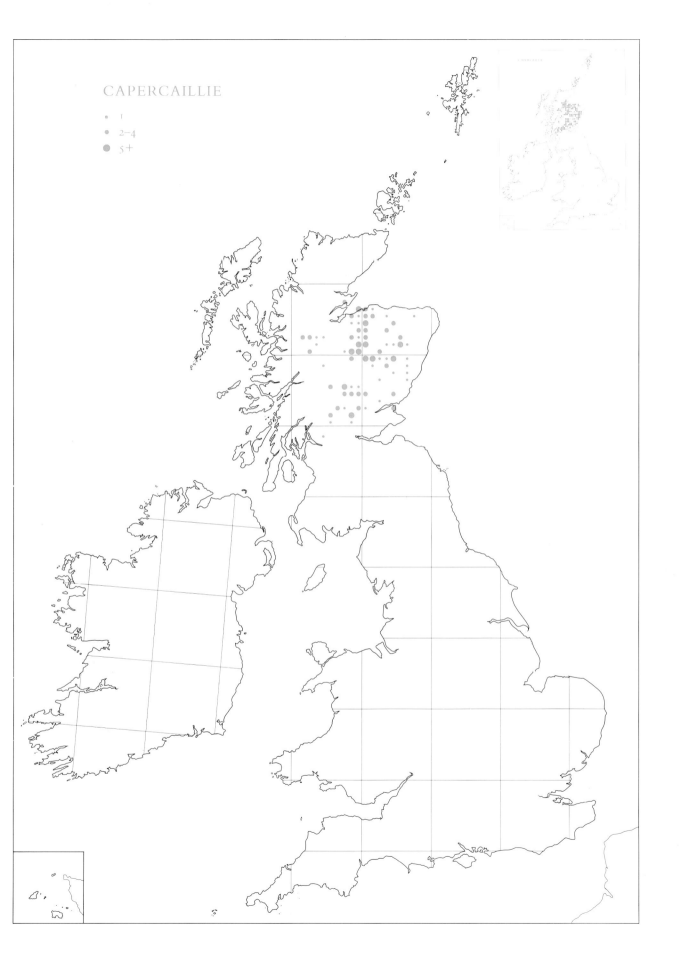

CAPERCAILLIE

· 1
· 2–4
● 5+

Red-legged Partridge

Alectoris rufa

Rather dumpy, rounded shapes, suddenly altering in outline as the alarmed birds stand almost on tiptoe with necks craned, and then a swift run across the field: such is a typical encounter with a winter covey of Red-legged Partridges.

The Red-legged Partridge is not a native to Britain, or to the neighbouring mainland Europe, but was introduced here from France. It occurs naturally in much warmer climates than ours but it seems not to be adversely affected during our winters, even severe ones. The distribution of the species was well established in the 1930s (A. D. Middleton) and, 50 years on, the pattern is very similar. However, in contrast to the Grey Partridge *Perdix perdix*, many releases have been made, usually on an annual basis and in many cases outside the area occupied in the 1930s, for example in S Scotland, in E Devon and in S Somerset. In these areas and also in Ireland, where there have been a number of releases of pure *A. rufa*, there is clear evidence of successful breeding, but whether it is sufficient to maintain stocks in the absence of further rearing is very doubtful.

Even within the main range very substantial declines have been documented amongst wild stocks since the mid 1970s. However, about 800,000 are released annually and the status of the species is confused by the fact that most releases are now of various admixtures and hybrids of *A. rufa* and the Chukar *A. chukar*. Many of these hybrids interbreed and because some progeny revert to type, it is not possible on visual evidence alone to determine whether a bird seen is pure *A. rufa* stock or whether there is an admixture of *A. chukar*. Pure *A. chukar* were released in Sussex in 1971 but their nesting success was much lower than recorded for *A. rufa* (Potts 1980).

The Red-legged Partridge is far more restricted in its distribution to the east and south, than is the Grey Partridge. Howells (1962) noted a close relationship between the range of the Red-legged Partridge in Britain and areas with less than 87 cm of rainfall per annum. In winter the habitats and food are very much like those of the Grey Partridge, except that the species favours less open habitats.

The coveys behave in much the same way as those of Grey Partridge, except that pairing up and dispersal of the pairs takes place a week or two later in the season, and heathland, even sparse woodland, are more often frequented. Male Red-legged Partridges defend individual home ranges and it is young females that leave their natal coveys to pair and settle (Green 1983). This spring movement, and the eventual density of birds remaining, is determined largely by the quantity and quality of hedgerows and other nesting cover. In two areas studied by Green, spring emigration was significantly higher in the one with least nesting cover. However, for most of the year the species is sedentary with few if any movements greater than 1 km.

In Britain, prior to the decline of the Grey Partridge, the Red-legged was often kept low in numbers by shooting. Birds in coveys of this species usually separate on being driven over guns, thus offering much easier targets. Both species are also limited by predation, so where they were helped most by predator control the Red-legged was most reduced by shooting. The net effect was that Grey Partridges often outnumbered Red-legged by 20:1 (Potts 1980).

However, shooting pressure on both partridge species relaxed considerably during the decline of the Grey Partridge, even where gamekeepers and predation control persisted, and this enabled a rapid increase in the Red-legged in the late 1950s to equal the numbers of Grey Partridges. In parts of the eastern counties densities of up to 20 pairs per km² were common. Shooting of Red-legged Partridges was organised in its own right, especially since about 1974, when releases of this species began to increase in popularity and now about 400,000 are shot annually. Later, wild stocks stabilised or even, as on the South Downs, declined. Most areas of arable land now have less than 5 pairs per km².

G. R. POTTS

Total number of squares in which recorded: 885 (23%)

No. of birds seen in a day	Number (%) of squares		
	Britain	Ireland	TOTAL (incl. C.I.)
1–15	442 (50%)	3 (100%)	445 (50%)
16–35	265 (30%)	0 (0%)	265 (30%)
36+	175 (20%)	0 (0%)	175 (20%)

References

GREEN, R. E. 1983. Spring dispersal and agonistic behaviour of the Red-legged Partridge (*Alectoris rufa*). *J. Zool.* 201: 541–555.

HOWELLS, G. 1962. The status of the Red-legged Partridge in Britain. *Game Research Association Annual Report* 2: 46–51.

POTTS, G. R. 1980. The effects of modern agriculture, nest predation and game management on the population ecology of partridges *Perdix perdix* and *Alectoris rufa*. *Advances in Ecological Research* 11: 1–82.

Breeding Atlas p 140

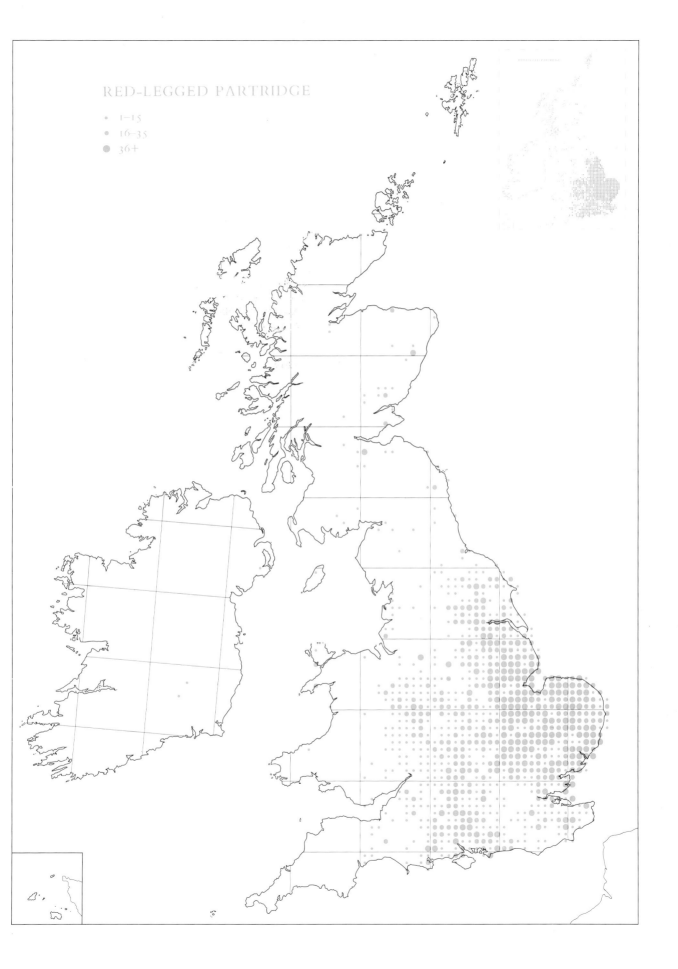

RED-LEGGED PARTRIDGE

- • 1–15
- • 16–35
- • 36+

Grey Partridge

Perdix perdix

Because they may spend their entire lives in two or three fields, Grey Partridges are amongst the most sedentary of birds. Moreover, they are so easy to see, especially around sunrise and sunset, that a complete census is often possible, providing the observer is in a vehicle and the weather is calm and dry. By contrast, most ornithologists on foot will be surprisingly unaware of their presence.

The distribution map clearly reflects the importance of the cereal growing areas to this species. In England and Wales the distribution seems to have changed little since 1969 (*Breeding Atlas*), but the range in Cornwall is far more restricted than in 1969. In almost all areas, Game Conservancy National Game Census data show a clear reduction in numbers since the *Breeding Atlas*, and the species is no longer found on some estates in Essex where farming is particularly intensive. In Scotland the distribution, as opposed to numbers, is also little changed, apart from an apparent thinning out in the southwest coastal districts.

It is in Ireland that the most dramatic reduction has occurred, a change which started in the late 19th century for reasons which are not clear. In the north there are now very few Grey Partridge and it is feared that the species may soon disappear entirely.

Partridges of both species begin the winter in family parties, or coveys, which usually consist of 2–5 or more old birds together with their young. On average there will be about 2 young with the old birds in poor years, about 8 in good ones. In Grey Partridges there is usually a surplus of cocks amongst the old birds because a quarter of hens is killed each year during incubation, most typically by foxes. Coveys roost well out into fields, by preference on plough land. In soft snow, roost holes are often made. Food is mainly grain and weed seeds (especially those of *Polygonum* spp.). As these become scarce through the winter, green food predominates, especially winter wheat or barley and chickweed.

Pairing begins amongst old birds in the covey, usually in mid winter, unless the weather is especially severe. Later the young cocks leave the covey to pair with non-siblings. Pairing and the spring dispersal are usually completed by the end of February.

Winter weather is not often a problem for partridges. Even in prolonged blizzards the daily mortality rates are lower than those during incubation. Nevertheless there is evidence from North America and eastern Europe that food shortages occur during prolonged, deep or ice covered snow.

From being the most numerous species of bird on farmland in parts of eastern England, with densities up to 350 per km^2 in the best localities at the start of winter, it is now unusual to find more than 70 birds per km^2, the average being around 20. Spring stocks average about 5 pairs per km^2 for the arable areas, fewer in predominantly grass areas. In especially favoured areas up to 25 pairs per km^2 can still be found. The average early autumn stock in Britain and Ireland is put at less than one million, though formerly there was at least twice that number shot.

In cereal growing areas numbers of partridges are determined, and limited, by the amount and quality of nesting cover, the predation rate on the nests, and an abundance of the right kind of insects, such as plant bugs, sawfly larvae, weevils, leaf beetles, diurnal ground beetles etc, to provide food for the young chicks. Modern farming methods, especially the use of herbicides, have reduced the numbers of these insects, causing a considerable decline in chick survival rate since the 1930s. Recent research at the Game Conservancy has shown that chick survival rate can be increased where cereal headlands are left unsprayed with pesticides.

Meanwhile the Grey Partridge has the doubtful distinction of having declined in 29 countries.

G. R. POTTS

Total number of squares in which recorded: 1,542 (40%)

No. of birds seen in a day	Number (%) of squares		
	Britain	Ireland	TOTAL (incl. C.I.)
1–11	770 (51%)	26 (93%)	796 (52%)
12–21	443 (29%)	2 (7%)	446 (29%)
22+	300 (20%)	0 (0%)	300 (19%)

References

POTTS, G. R. 1980. The effect of modern agriculture, nest predation and game management on the population ecology of partridges *Perdix perdix* and *Alectoris rufa*. *Advances in Ecological Research* 11: 1–82.

POTTS, G. R. 1984. Monitoring changes in the cereal ecosystem. Pp 128–134 in JENKINS, D. (ed.) *Proceedings of the NERC/ITE Symposium No. 13 'Agriculture and the Environment'*. Monks Wood Experimental Station, Huntingdon.

RANDS, M. R. W. 1985. Pesticides use on cereals and the survival of grey partridge chicks: a field experiment. *J. Appl. Ecol.* 22: 49–54.

Breeding Atlas p 142

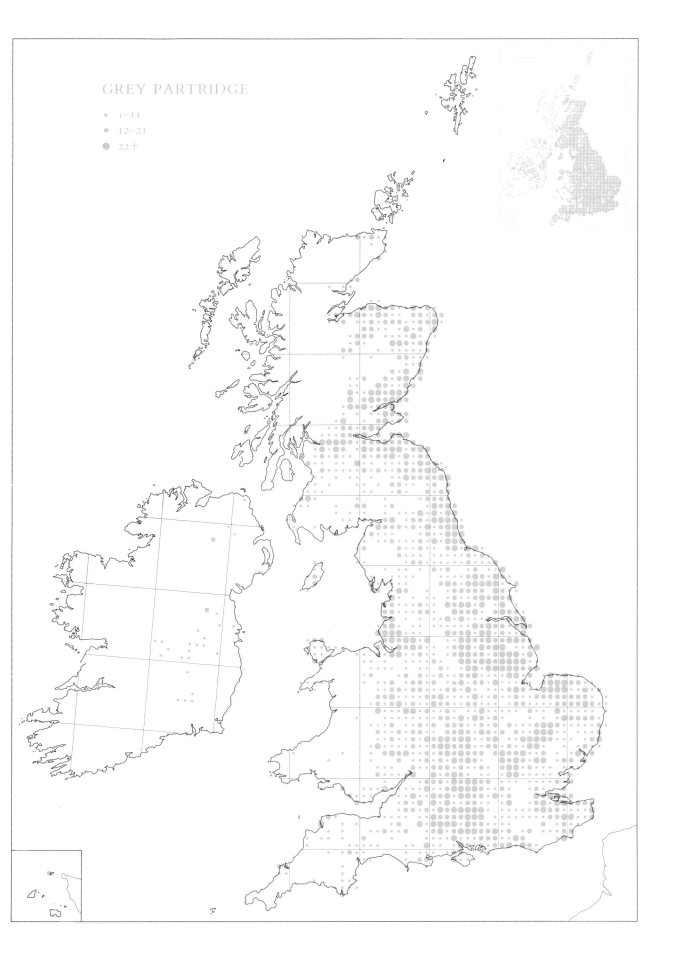

GREY PARTRIDGE

- · 1–11
- ● 12–21
- ● 22+

Pheasant

Phasianus colchicus

The Pheasant is the commonest gamebird in Britain and Ireland, preferring wooded agricultural lowland. During the winter it is often seen feeding at the field edge in the early morning and dusk, retiring to woodland during the day.

The Normans most likely introduced the Pheasant into Britain in the late 11th century. It occurred in Ireland late in the 16th century. It was domesticated by the Romans who used it for the table. With the arrival of shotguns in the 17th and 18th century, driven Pheasants became a sport of the landed gentry. By the 19th century artificially reared birds were released and looked after by gamekeepers who also began to control predators of game. The opportunistic habits of the Pheasant probably enabled it to spread throughout most of Britain at this time. It is present in most 10-km squares with the exception of the W Highlands of Scotland and parts of the uplands of the north of England and Wales. It occurs over most of Ireland although its distribution is less complete in the southwest, particularly near the coast.

Pheasants are sedentary birds, so the winter and breeding distributions are similar. In a wing tagging programme organised by the Game Conservancy, 61% were shot within 400 m of their point of release, and less than 1% dispersed further than 2 km.

In winter, highest numbers occur in East Anglia, Lincolnshire, Hampshire, Wiltshire and parts of Kent, and on some estates in central and N England and parts of Scotland. The Pheasant is much less abundant in Ireland and numbers vary between counties. Those counties in the west and north with smaller fields and large areas of bog, hold fewer birds than those in the east and south with a greater amount of tillage, and the latter areas are where more have been released for shooting.

During early winter, Pheasants form feeding flocks and eat primarily spilt grain, blackberries, grass seeds and acorns (Lachlan and Bray 1973). Later they feed on roots and tubers of Solanaceae and Compositae, weed seeds such as those of fat hen, and maize where available. On many shooting estates maize is grown as a game-crop or fed to the birds to decrease the likelihood of birds wandering on to neighbouring estates. In spring more animal food is eaten, mainly in the form of carabid and staphylinid beetles, spiders and flies.

In winter, females have their own hierarchy within the winter group, although birds are known to enter and leave the group regularly. Group size varies between 2 and 4 birds, but sometimes groups contain more than 20 individuals. Males generally associate in groups of 2, or more rarely 3, and remain so until they begin to set up territories in late March or early April. Winter groups of Pheasants comprising only one sex are significantly more prevalent than would be expected. Females are more gregarious than males but with the onset of spring the proportion of female groups accompanied by males increases (Ridley 1983).

Predation by foxes is often very high in winter. During the last two decades the numbers of Pheasants reared and released per 100 ha has more than doubled in some regions. According to the National Game Census the number of foxes on farmland in Britain may also have increased (Tapper 1980), and predation of poults immediately after release is often very high (Bray 1967). The wild population in winter in Britain is probably about 8 million and the Game Conservancy estimates that 15 million Pheasants are released annually. Of these about 45% are shot annually and, of the remainder, about half are lost through unknown causes, such as predation, during late winter. The Common Birds Census index suggests that the breeding population is steadily increasing but the numbers of wild birds shot, according to the National Game Census, may not have changed during the last two decades (Tapper 1982). In Ireland the situation is unclear.

D. A. HILL

Total number of squares in which recorded: 2,829 (73%)

No. of birds seen in a day	Number (%) of squares		
	Britain	Ireland	TOTAL (incl. C.I.)
1–8	808 (39%)	579 (79%)	1,390 (49%)
9–33	733 (35%)	132 (18%)	866 (31%)
34+	555 (26%)	18 (3%)	573 (20%)

References

BRAY, R. P. 1967. Mortality rates of released Pheasants. *Game Conserv. Ann. Rev. for 1967*: 14–33.

LACHLAN, C. and R. P. BRAY. 1973. A study of an unmanaged Pheasant population at Brownsea Island, Dorset, England. *Trans. X Int. Union. Game Biol. Congr. Paris 1971*: 609–617.

RIDLEY, M. W. 1983. *The Mating System of the Pheasant* Phasianus colchicus. D.Phil. Thesis, University of Oxford.

TAPPER, S. C. 1980. The status of some predatory mammals. *Game Conserv. Ann. Rev. No. 11*: 48–54.

TAPPER, S. C. 1982. National Game Census: the 1981/1982 season. *Game Conserv. Ann. Rev. No. 13*: 117–121.

Breeding Atlas p 146

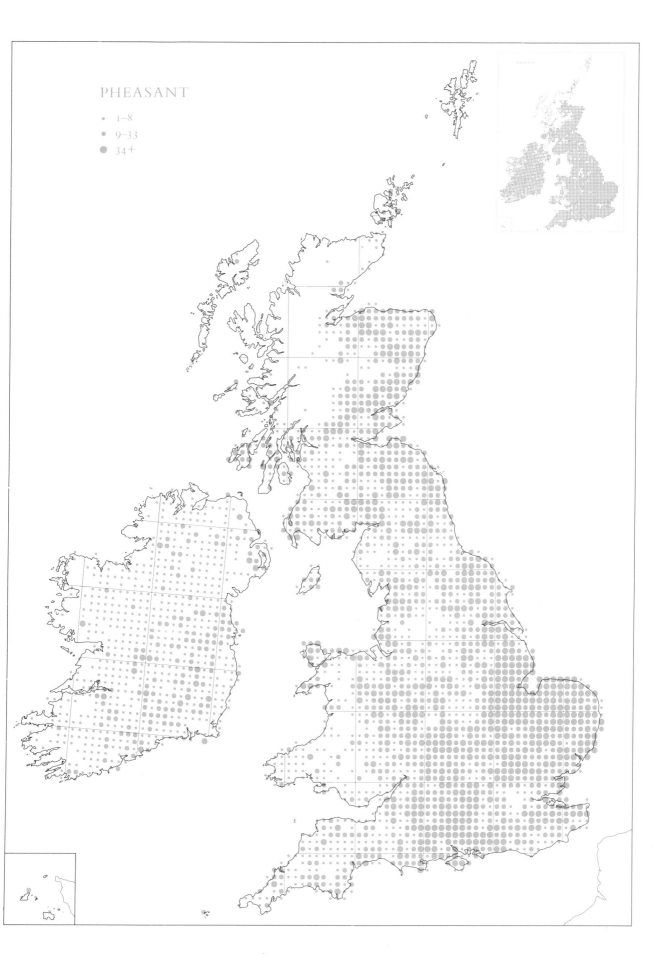

PHEASANT

- 1–8
- 9–33
- 34+

Golden Pheasant

Chrysolophus pictus

The Golden Pheasant was introduced to Britain from the hills of central China and has not spread far from the few spots where it was first released. Despite the gaudy colours of the male, the species is rarely seen at any time of year, because it skulks in thick cover. There are four main centres of population: the Brecklands in Norfolk and Suffolk, the South Downs in Hampshire and West Sussex, part of Gloucestershire and part of Galloway in SW Scotland. Elsewhere, there are small isolated groups of Golden Pheasants in plantations and woods.

There is no evidence of any migratory movement either in the wild or the feral state, and Golden Pheasants stick to their half-grown conifer thickets throughout the year.

Very little is known of their biology. Indeed Beebe's (1931) statement that 'probably no other bird in the world is so well known in captivity and so easy to breed, and yet, at the same time, with haunts, habits, and general life in the wild state so absolutely unknown', is still true today. Except for Beebe's own work, there have been no studies of their wild or feral habits.

Part of the reason for this ignorance is that Golden Pheasants are shy, ground-living birds with a preference in Britain for almost impenetrably dense stands of coniferous trees. They are much more fussy than Pheasants *Phasianus colchicus* about habitat and are found almost exclusively in plantations of about 10–30 years old. Such woods have no undergrowth at all and the trees grow so close together as to exclude nearly all the light. So long as it stays on the ground, the Golden Pheasant can easily move about; flying is virtually impossible and, even in the open, the species is a weak and reluctant flyer.

This preferred habitat is probably similar in structure to the bamboo scrub inhabited in the wild. An interesting exception, though, is a feral population of Golden Pheasants living near Petersfield in Hampshire, where some birds are found in mature yew forest. Underneath the close growing trees it is dark and bare, enclosed above and on all sides but, like the conifer plantations, the floor is open.

For most of the year Golden Pheasants are solitary. In winter, though, they seem to gather into small groups of up to 10 birds, segregated by sex, although this may merely reflect congregation at feeding sites. Although rarely leaving their thickets, they are occasionally seen in open fields or clearings in the early morning or late evening. Their diet probably consists partly of vegetable matter (shoots, seeds and the like), and in places they may depend on grain put out by gamekeepers for Pheasants. There is also circumstantial evidence that they are insectivorous; in captivity they need a high protein diet and take animal food readily. Droppings, thought to be from this species and full of the remains of ants, have been found in their haunts. Certainly, among the leaf litter on the bare forest floors there is little to eat except insects.

The commonest sign of their presence is the call of the male in spring. Though mostly heard between March and May, this can be given as early as October, and on warm evenings males are sometimes in full cry in late January. The call consists of two loud harsh, grating squawks, the second generally louder and higher-pitched than the first: 'ker-cheek'. In bad weather the male may crow from his perch in a roosting tree.

Generally the feral Golden Pheasants seem to be holding their own, with perhaps 1,000–2,000 birds. The species is never likely to spread far from its present centres because of its very sedentary habits and the fragmented nature of coniferous woodland in lowland England. None the less, as a colourful and harmless rarity, the species is a welcome addition to the fauna.

M. RIDLEY

Total number of squares in which recorded: 47 (1%)

No. of birds seen in a day	Number (%) of squares		
	Britain	Ireland	TOTAL (incl. C.I.)
1	25 (53%)	0 (0%)	25 (53%)
2	13 (28%)	0 (0%)	13 (28%)
3+	9 (19%)	0 (0%)	9 (19%)

References

BEEBE, W. 1931. *Pheasants, their Lives and Homes*. Henry Doubleday, New York.

DELACOUR, J. 1977. *Pheasants of the World*. 2nd edn. Spur Press, London.

LEVER, C. 1977. *The Naturalised Animals of the British Isles*. Hutchinson, London.

Breeding Atlas p 148

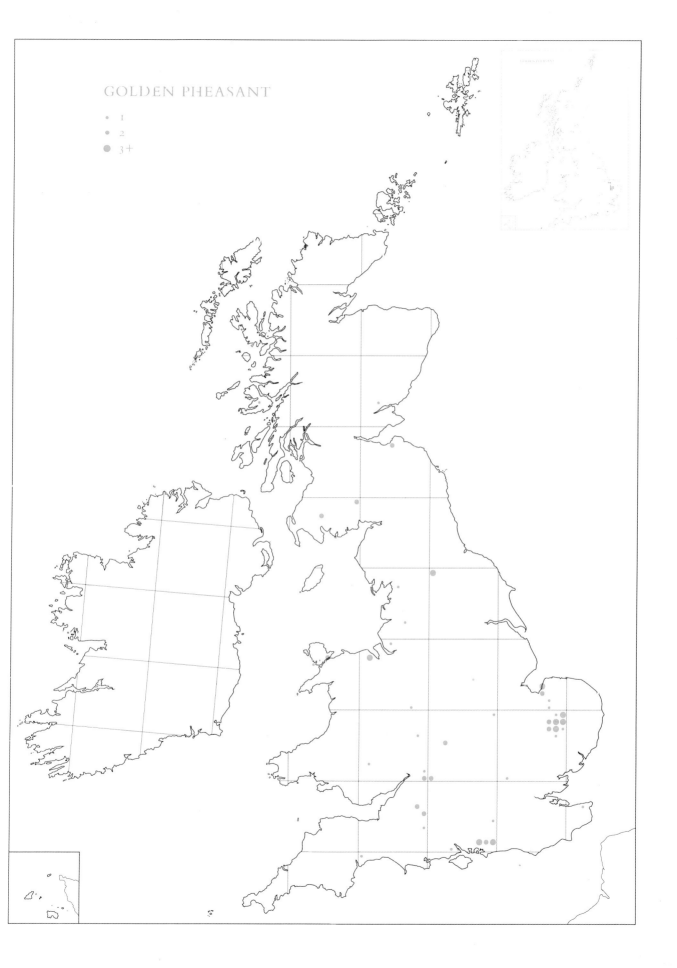

GOLDEN PHEASANT

- • 1
- • 2
- ● 3+

Lady Amherst's Pheasant

Chrysolophus amherstiae

Lady Amherst's Pheasant is one of the most elegant and colourful of all birds. It also produces one of the harshest and least pleasing squawks. In China, the name translates as 'flower pheasant', which well describes the male's rather unusual mixture of colours: whites, greens and reds. Like the closely related Golden Pheasant *Chrysolophus pictus*, it is a feral bird introduced from China to a few localities, where it hides itself in dense coniferous thickets.

Lady Amherst's Pheasants were first sent to Britain in 1828 and have been living ferally in Bedfordshire for most of the 20th century. Unfortunately, much of the captive stock and some feral birds have a small amount of Golden Pheasant blood in them, many hybrids having been produced in captivity. Since the two species also hybridise in the feral state it is important that they continue to occupy separate feral ranges in Britain. In the wild their ranges do not seem to overlap, or, where they do, Lady Amherst's Pheasant lives at a higher altitude.

There is one main population in Britain, in Hertfordshire, Bedfordshire and Buckinghamshire. It stems from introductions from Woburn and Whipsnade and occupies a patchwork of coniferous plantations all the year round. In exactly the same way as the Golden Pheasant, the species is found only in immature woods of a certain age, when the undergrowth has been killed off by the closing of the canopy and before the trees thin out enough to let ground vegetation emerge again. This is especially noticeable near Little Brickhill, where there is a mosaic of plantations of different ages, and only the half-grown thickets with dense stands of trees contain Lady Amherst's Pheasants.

Apart from this, very little is known of the species' habits. There is some tentative indication that it is more solitary in winter than the Golden Pheasant. It emerges from cover as rarely as that species, and likewise only at dawn and dusk. Males are much more

easily seen than females, because of their brighter colours. Of its diet, virtually nothing is known.

Nor has Lady Amherst's Pheasant ever been studied in the wild state. In SW China and NE Burma it inhabits isolated mountain ridges covered with stunted vegetation, consisting of tangled bamboo and rhododendron thickets. It lives farther south than the Golden Pheasant but it is found at higher altitudes (up to about 3,000 m) and so experiences much the same climate of harsh winters and wet summers. Britain's weather therefore presents it with no difficulties. In the wild, and in Britain, an occasional feather, usually one of the male's long barred white tail feathers, is the commonest sign of its presence. Males are still sold in China for their plumage.

As with Golden Pheasants, males begin to crow in early spring and continue to call at dawn and dusk until summer. The call is easily distinguished however, because it has three syllables rather than two, with the emphasis on the first 'cheek ker-chek'. Males move steadily around their own small patches of forest, giving these calls, so they are probably territorial. Bailey (1945) found that in one part of Sichuan, in spring, males were easily heard in the scrub and, although difficult to flush, could be seen by careful stalking. Much the same is true of feral Lady Amherst's Pheasants in Britain.

Britain is probably the only place in the world where perhaps 200–500 of these fabulous birds live in a feral state. Their wild range in China, Tibet and Burma is small, inaccessible and their status there is perhaps precarious. So every effort to encourage and study Lady Amherst's Pheasants in Britain is to be welcomed.

M. RIDLEY

Total number of squares in which recorded: 7 (<1%)

No. of birds seen in a day	Number (%) of squares		
	Britain	Ireland	TOTAL (incl. C.I.)
1–2	3 (43%)	0 (0%)	3 (43%)
3–5	1 (14%)	0 (0%)	1 (14%)
6+	3 (43%)	0 (0%)	3 (43%)

References
BAILEY, F. M. 1945. *China-Tibet-Assam*. Jonathan Cape, London.

Breeding Atlas p 150

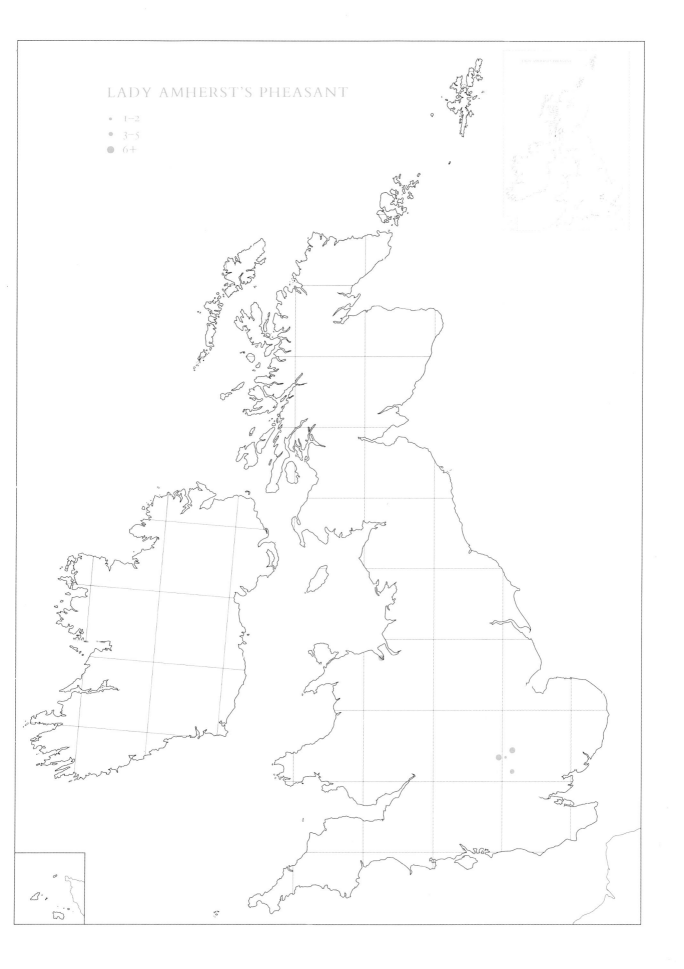

LADY AMHERST'S PHEASANT

- 1—2
- 3—5
- 6+

Water Rail

Rallus aquaticus

The Water Rail is one of the most elusive birds, winter and summer alike. It is the prime skulker in dense wetland vegetation, its body as well adapted in its lateral compression to slipping between the reed stems as are its long-toed feet to supporting it on soft mud or floating leaves. Its plumage, a mixture of browns, greys and buffs, camouflages it well, and every movement it makes seems to be considered beforehand, executed slowly and carried out with stealth. In summer, breeding Water Rails draw attention to themselves by horrific pig-like squealing cries, but such advertisement of their presence is rare in winter. Only when conditions are really hard, when frozen mud and water force the Water Rails to seek food outside the shelter of their protective vegetation, or when the observer is particularly stalwart and prepared for a long quiet wait, are they likely to be seen well.

Against this background, it is interesting to see that the winter distribution of Water Rails is at least as wide as that of summer birds portrayed in the *Breeding Atlas*. Clearly the distribution of suitable swamps, and their chances of remaining unfrozen through the winter, play a major role in determining this distribution, and if the bird was more conspicuous there is little doubt that it would be reported even more widely.

In Scotland, the winter pattern resembles that of the breeding season, but with more positive squares in winter in Orkney and Shetland. In England and Wales the pattern is roughly the same between seasons, though occupied squares are denser overall in winter and there are appreciably more records from Devon, Cornwall and along the Welsh coast. Only in Ireland does there seem to be little change in distribution, coupled with fewer squares with records in winter than in summer, but perhaps this is a reflection of recording difficulties where ornithologists are fewer and potentially suitable habitats more numerous.

Under normal conditions, Water Rails have a very varied diet, including a wide range of wetland invertebrates, ranging in size from insects and their larvae to shrimps and molluscs; to which can be added many vertebrates they may encounter, such as frogs and newts, and an unknown proportion of vegetable matter. This includes energy-rich tuberous roots and rhizomes, seeds and berries (including grain), and (less profitably) grasses.

When weather conditions become severe, Water Rails are forced by hunger to tackle carrion and also larger live prey, often including birds, of which 9 species have been recorded. These attacks are characterised by an initial stealthy stalking approach, ending in a rush to seize prey, which is then battered to death on the ground. The Water Rails themselves may be at risk too, as there are records of several Grey Herons *Ardea cinerea* catching, drowning and eating Water Rails flushed from hiding on the Dee Marshes in Cheshire (Flegg 1981). Normally, Water Rails are solitary or only loosely gregarious during the winter months, but there are places, for example the Dee Marshes, where concentrations, sometimes of hundreds of birds, occur.

Ringing recoveries provide little evidence of movement of British and Irish breeding birds. There are recoveries of birds moving into Britain and Ireland from the Continent for the winter. Most arrivals were in October and November, and came on westerly or southwesterly bearings. Returning in spring (March and April), the heading of most recovered birds was, interestingly, SE rather than E or NE as might be expected. Recoveries come from most countries of northern Europe, and from as far afield as Sweden, Poland and Czechoslovakia. Despite its terrestrial habits, ineffectual looking wings and apparently feeble flight, the Water Rail is clearly a competent long-haul migrant.

Attaching numbers to such a secretive and enigmatic species is a difficult task. The *Breeding Atlas* suggested a summer population in Britain and Ireland of 2,000–4,000 pairs: it seems most probable that these remain during the winter, and that their numbers are considerably augmented by incoming migrants. There is little factual evidence on population changes, though land drainage may have some adverse impact.

J. J. M. FLEGG

Total number of squares in which recorded: 981 (25%)

No. of birds seen in a day	Number (%) of squares		
	Britain	Ireland	TOTAL (incl. C.I.)
1	447 (55%)	97 (57%)	545 (56%)
2	183 (23%)	33 (19%)	216 (22%)
3+	178 (22%)	40 (24%)	220 (22%)

References

FLEGG, J. J. M. 1981. *A Notebook of Birds*. Macmillan, London.

FLEGG, J. J. M. and D. E. GLUE. 1973. A Water Rail Study. *Bird Study* 20: 69–79.

Breeding Atlas p 152

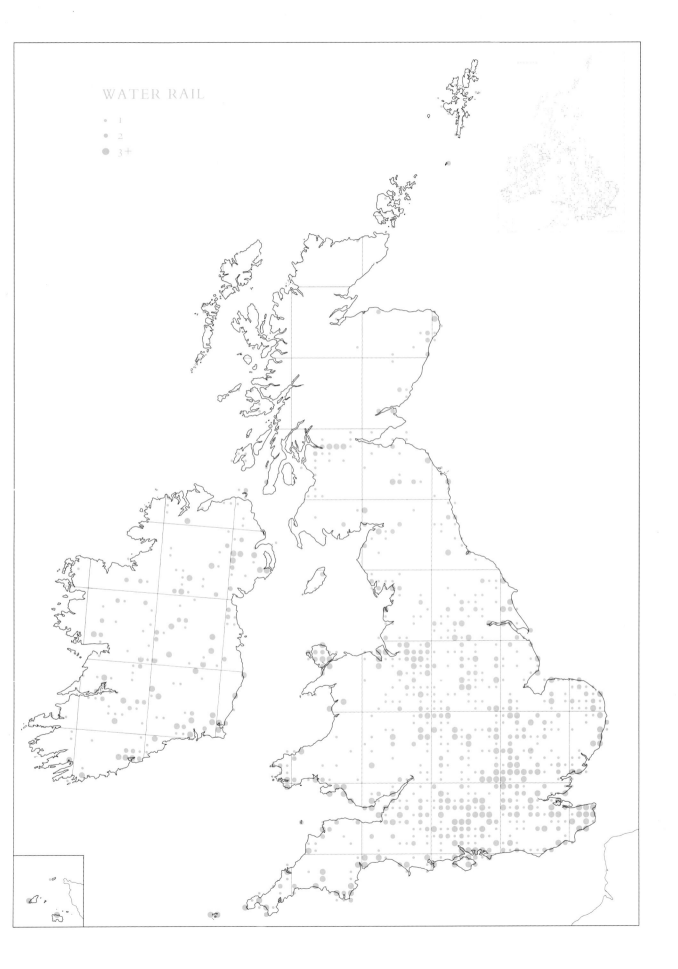

WATER RAIL

- 1
- 2
- 3+

Moorhen

Gallinula chloropus

Equally at home on a town canal or a secluded rural pool, the Moorhen is the commonest riparian bird in Britain and Ireland. It is particularly easy to see in the lowlands in winter, when our residents are joined by migrants from colder parts of Europe and flocks form to feed beside areas of fresh water.

A striking feature of the Moorhen's winter distribution is the absence of birds on high ground. The principal upland areas of Britain and Ireland all show clearly as expanses of white on the map; for example, the Pennines, central Wales and the Wicklow Mountains. The clearest demarcation between unpopulated high ground and occupied lowlands is in Scotland. Here, a band of Moorhen records abuts the mountains, running northeast along the Highland Boundary Fault through Strathmore to the coastal plains of the Grampian region, with only a smattering of birds in a few of the glens. Moorhens are scarce throughout the year in much of the Highlands and western islands of Scotland, but elsewhere they do penetrate the uplands in spring and summer (*Breeding Atlas*).

In winter, Moorhens are most numerous in central England, East Anglia and SE England, where manmade features such as canals, drainage channels, reservoirs and flooded pits provide a diversity of habitat. The numbers along canals and other lowland waterways can be drastically reduced by removal of channel and bankside vegetation in watercourse management works. Even the occasional overhanging bush or tree and patch of channel weed left intact during more sympathetic management can provide habitat for a pair of Moorhens throughout the year.

Moorhens eat a variety of plant and insect food which they collect from or near water. Some birds, mainly young and adults wintering away from their breeding areas, form small feeding flocks in autumn and winter. These flock birds sometimes roost together on open meadows, or use reed beds if threatened by predators. Other Moorhen pairs stay in their territories in winter, defending a small 'core' of the former territory as a feeding area. If core areas freeze, territorial Moorhens join the winter flocks on neutral ground but move back when milder weather returns.

In prolonged periods of icy weather many Moorhens die. The BTO's Waterways Birds Survey index for Moorhens fell following the harsh winters of 1978/79 and 1981/82, and cold winters cause marked fluctuations in populations elsewhere in Europe (*BWP*). Moorhens are usually double or triple brooded, so population recovery following such declines is often rapid.

The Moorhens which breed in Britain and Ireland are resident, in contrast to birds in northern Europe which are partially or wholly migratory; Moorhens are absent in winter from their breeding areas in northern Scandinavia, for example. Our resident birds, which seldom move more than 20 km, are joined in autumn and winter by migrants from a large part of NW Europe, especially Sweden and Denmark. These migrants return to their breeding areas when the winter flocks break up in February.

The *Breeding Atlas* suggested a British and Irish Moorhen population of 300,000 pairs, based on a conservative estimate of 100 pairs per occupied 10-km square. On this basis, even without allowing for the influx of migrants, the winter population would be over a million birds. Britain and Ireland are thus important for the Moorhen in a European context, both because of the large resident population and because the area is used as a wintering ground by birds from other countries.

K. TAYLOR

Total number of squares in which recorded: 2,693 (70%)

No. of birds seen in a day	Number (%) of squares		
	Britain	Ireland	TOTAL (incl. C.I.)
1–10	750 (39%)	569 (74%)	1,319 (49%)
11–37	664 (35%)	177 (23%)	842 (31%)
38+	507 (27%)	23 (3%)	532 (20%)

References

MARCHANT, J. H. and P. A. HYDE. 1980. Aspects of the distribution of riparian birds on waterways in Britain and Ireland. *Bird Study* 27: 183–202.

TAYLOR, K. 1984. The influence of watercourse management on Moorhen breeding biology. *Brit. Birds* 77: 141–148.

TAYLOR, K. and J. H. MARCHANT. 1983. Population changes for waterways birds, 1981–1982. *Bird Study* 30: 121–126.

WOOD, N. A. 1974. The breeding behaviour and biology of the Moorhen. *Brit. Birds* 67: 104–115.

Breeding Atlas p 158

MOORHEN

- · 1–10
- ● 11–37
- ● 38+

Coot

Fulica atra

NB

The Coot, our largest species of rail, is most in evidence during summer, when its vociferous territorial squabbling draws it to the attention of even casual waterside strollers. In winter it maintains a lower profile, aggregating in large, but comparatively peaceful, flocks on large lakes and rivers or even, during a prolonged freeze, on salt water.

The winter distribution shows a close similarity to that of summer. Small-scale movements, which take the birds from breeding waters to the larger (ice-free) lakes and reservoirs or salt water, are not disclosed by census techniques. Little is known about such local movement, although one pilot study (J. Horsfall) found that several colour-marked individuals wandered over several counties during the course of one winter. Because Coots tend to move during darkness these movements pass unnoticed and reinforce the impression of a low population turnover among winter flocks.

This suggestive evidence for frequent local movement in winter is rather at odds with the species' reputed persistence in the face of hard weather. Whereas ducks will desert a lake as icing progresses, at least some Coots will remain until icing is complete and the birds are left standing in a despondent huddle. In extreme cases this persistence can be suicidal. During the winter of 1963, at an Oxfordshire lake, some Coots remained on thick ice until they no longer had the strength to fly—when they were picked off by local foxes (pers. comm.). These persistent individuals might be the resident birds, which had bred the previous year and were unwilling to forsake an established territory since, in milder years, the males will attempt to defend a territory year-round. They may well pay a high price for their tenacity (Visser and Cave 1982). However, harsh winters do not seem to affect the total numbers of breeding birds in the following year, probably because there are always non breeders waiting to fill vacant sites (Visser 1979).

The large scale movements of the Coot are rather better known. European ringing has shown a general movement S and W in autumn, especially to coasts with equable climates, such as those of Britain, Ireland and France (Fog 1969), and some of our visiting birds come from as far away as Russia (Brown 1955).

During winter, as always, the Coot is opportunistic in diet, sometimes grazing in fields. Although their mainstay in most of Britain and Ireland appears to be pondweed (especially Canadian waterweed), they may concomitantly ingest many of the invertebrates present in the foliage. At some sites in Britain the zebra mussel might be as important a food as it is in Europe (Suter 1982). Unlike the diving ducks, Coots always bring their food to the surface before consumption, a characteristic which has one interesting consequence—it makes food stealing a possibility. This behaviour can be very common, with some (older? larger?) individuals consistently stealing the majority of their food, and thereby avoiding the costs incurred by frequent diving to a depth of 4–5 m (pers. obs.). This social hierarchy might possibly be responsible for lowered fat levels and disproportionate mortality of juvenile females in winter (Visser 1979).

The recent expansion of possible habitats through gravel extraction in southern Britain may have boosted breeding populations locally (Parslow 1973), but their effect on the wintering population is less certain. With some winter influx from the Continent we might expect that the population would exceed 10,000–100,000 pairs present in summer and, indeed, the *Winter Atlas* estimates would suggest a total of 200,000 birds as not at all unreasonable.

J. A. HORSFALL

Total number of squares in which recorded: 2,063 (53%)

No. of birds	Number (%) of squares		
seen in a day	Britain	Ireland	TOTAL (incl. C.I.)
1–20	749 (47%)	281 (62%)	1,031 (50%)
21–118	496 (31%)	123 (27%)	620 (30%)
119+	360 (22%)	51 (11%)	412 (20%)

References

BROWN, R. G. B. 1955. The migration of the Coot in relation to Britain. *Bird Study* 2: 135–142.

FOG, J. 1969. (Studies on the Coot (*Fulica atra*) in the marshland Vejlerne, North Jutland, and on the migration of Danish breeding populations.) *Dansk Orn. Foren. Tidsskr.* 63: 1–18. (English summary)

PARSLOW, J. 1973. *Breeding Birds of Britain and Ireland.* Poyser, Berkhamsted.

SUTER, W. 1982. (Feeding ecology of diving ducks and Coots wintering on the upper Rhine near Lake Constance.) *Orn. Beob.* 79: 225–254 (English summary).

VISSER, J. 1979. Selective mortality in the Coot during the severe winter of 1978/79. *Institute for Ecological Research (Arnhem, Holland), Progress Report 1979:* 7–11.

VISSER, J. and A. J. CAVE. 1982. Local survival of the breeding birds in a Coot population. *Institute for Ecological Research (Arnhem, Holland), Progress Report 1982:* 12–18.

Breeding Atlas p 160

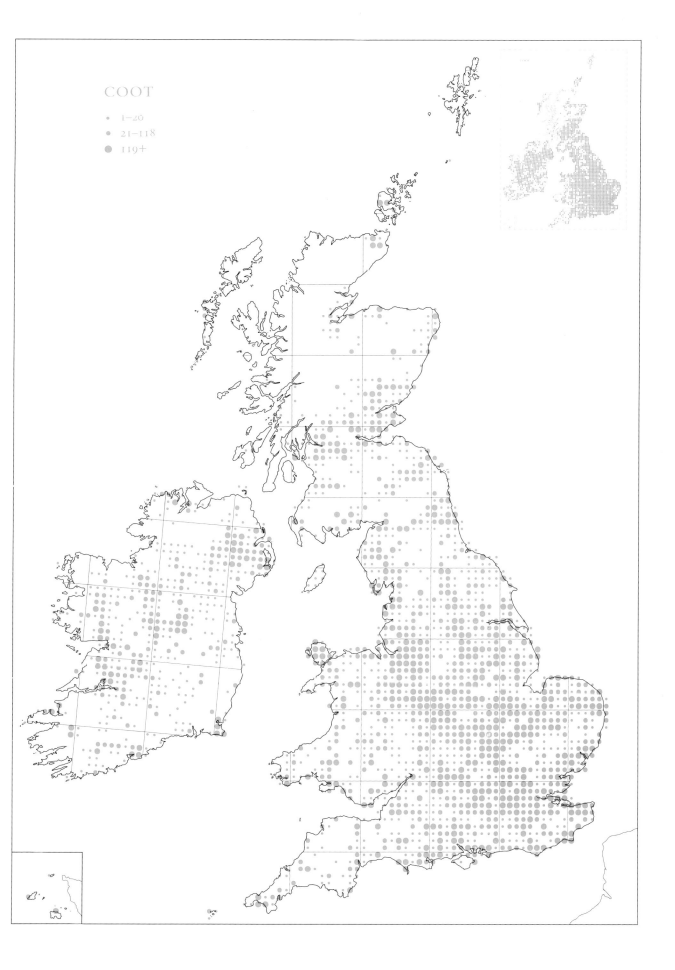

COOT

- 1–20
- 21–118
- 119+

Oystercatcher

Haematopus ostralegus

The Oystercatcher is a familiar and unmistakable coastal species which has caused much controversy over its supposed competition with man.

Most of our breeding birds winter on the coasts of Britain and Ireland, where they are joined by immigrants. Adults leave the estuaries in February and March and start returning in late July. The origins of these birds differ between coasts. Birds wintering on the west coast of Britain and in Ireland breed in Scotland, the Faeroes and Iceland whilst those wintering on the east coast of Britain are almost exclusively of Norwegian origin (Dare 1970).

The biology of Oystercatchers is closely dependent upon that of shellfish. Cockles and mussels are lucrative, thick-shelled prey that other waders are incapable of opening. With their powerful beaks and strong musculatures Oystercatchers are well adapted to open these bivalves, and the abundance of these prey species (plus the other bivalves *Macoma balthica* and *Scrobicularia plana*) largely determines the distribution of the largest winter gatherings. Six estuaries hold over 50% of Britain's Oystercatcher population, but as they also take polychaete worms, crabs and limpets Oystercatchers are found around practically the entire coast.

In parallel with the increase in inland nesting recorded in the *Breeding Atlas*, there has also been an increase in feeding in fields up to 7 km inland especially around the Irish Sea and the Solway. Seeking for earthworms appears to be a recent habit which Dare (1966) suggested originated in the 1962/63 winter after much of the estuarine prey had been killed by the harsh weather.

As Oystercatchers are usually faithful to their wintering grounds, populations appear fairly constant from year to year. This situation can alter markedly if there are dramatic changes in the prey population. Between the winters of 1960/61 and 1963/64 the vast cockle stocks of Morecambe Bay practically disappeared and the number of birds plummeted from about 120,000 to 11,000 (Dare 1966). The fate of the missing birds is unknown although Dare suggested they may have moved to the Wadden Sea. A similar, though reverse, phenomenon occurred on the Ribble Estuary (Lancashire) in which a 2,000-fold increase in the number of cockles resulted in a four-fold increase in the number of Oystercatchers (Sutherland 1982). There was evidence that juveniles and immatures were disproportionately abundant during the year of population increase; in the subsequent years the declining population consisted predominantly of adults. Thus it seems that juveniles and immatures

move to estuaries with unexploited food whilst adults return to previous haunts.

The Oystercatchers' skill at opening cockles and mussels has made them unpopular with fishermen with whom they may compete for food. During the winter of 1963/64 there was a massive spatfall of cockles on the Burry Inlet which led to excellent yields in subsequent years. By the time the cockle population had returned to its usual level, Oystercatcher numbers had increased from 8,000 to 15,000. The fishermen demanded a cull of Oystercatchers to return the population to earlier levels, and a total of 10,000 was shot in the autumns of 1973 and 1974. Ironically, after this cull had been carried out, the cockle population plummeted for unknown reasons. Horwood and Goss-Custard (1977) reanalysed the data and suggested the impact of Oystercatchers had been exaggerated. The public outrage, the shifting of opinion towards conservation and the subsequent re-analysis of the Burry Inlet data make it unlikely that such a cull will be repeated.

The Birds of Estuaries Enquiry estimates the British and Irish wintering population as 300,000 birds, which probably accounts for more than 45% of Europe's Oystercatchers.

W. J. SUTHERLAND

Total number of squares in which recorded: 1,535 (40%)

No. of birds seen in a day	Number (%) of squares		
	Britain	Ireland	TOTAL (incl. C.I.)
1–44	621 (53%)	146 (41%)	768 (50%)
45–225	321 (27%)	138 (39%)	460 (30%)
226+	234 (20%)	70 (20%)	307 (20%)

References

DARE, P. J. 1966. The breeding and wintering populations of the Oystercatcher (*Haematopus ostralegus* Linnaeus) in the British Isles. *Fishery Invest. Lond. Ser.* ii 25 (5): 1–69.

DARE, P. J. 1970. The movements of Oystercatchers *Haematopus ostralegus* L., visiting or breeding in the British Isles. *Fishery Invest. Lond. Ser.* II 25(9): 1–137.

HORWOOD, J. W. and J. D. GOSS-CUSTARD. 1977. Predation by the oystercatcher *Haematopus ostralegus* in relation to the cockle *Cerastoderma edule* (L.) fishery in the Burry Inlet, South Wales, *J. Appl. Ecol.* 14: 139–158.

SUTHERLAND, W. J. 1982. Food supply and dispersal in the determination of wintering population levels of oystercatchers *Haematopus ostralegus. Est. Coast and Shelf Science* 14: 223–229.

Breeding Atlas p 162

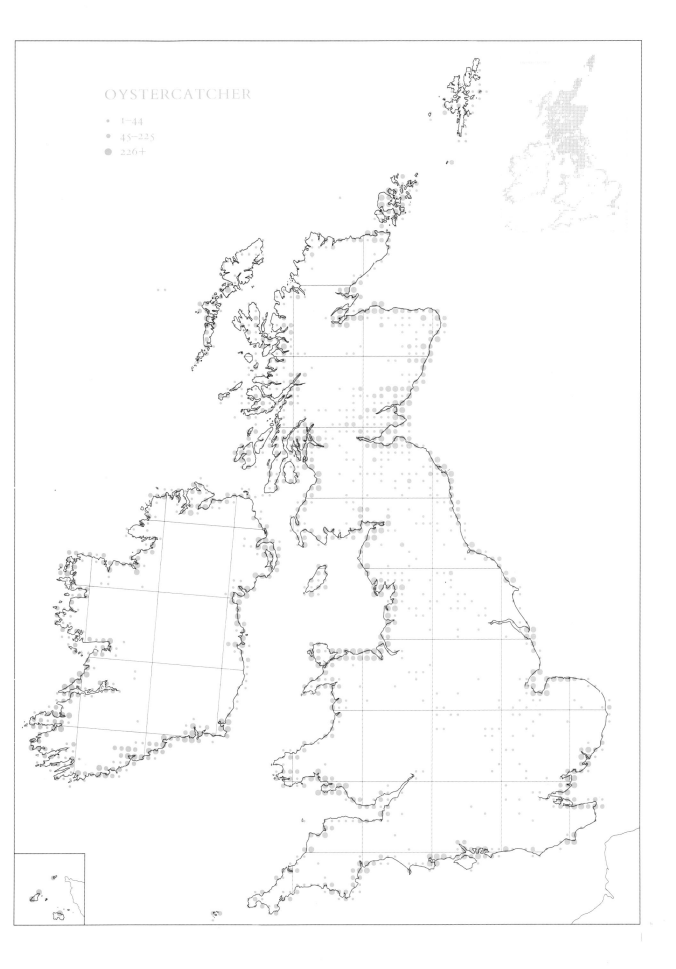

OYSTERCATCHER

- • 1–44
- • 45–225
- ● 226+

Avocet

Recurvirostra avosetta

The Avocet, whose elegant shape and distinctive pied plumage have become nationally familiar as the emblem of the RSPB, first started regular wintering in England in 1947, the year in which it also recolonised Britain as a regular breeder.

The winter distribution is largely on estuaries along the Channel and southern North Sea coasts of England; with concentrations in Devon/Cornwall and Suffolk. There are a few winter records elsewhere around the coast, including Ireland.

Wintering Avocets tend to frequent those estuaries in which the substrate is largely fine silt. The birds often feed communally in shallow water on a rising tide, sweeping the bill from side to side. Such behaviour is probably associated with feeding on opossum shrimps which congregate in large numbers to form a band at the edge of the rising water. Ragworms, too, are probably frequently taken, as they are on the Continent (Tjallingii 1971). In Suffolk, wintering Avocets roost gregariously on salt marshes or, with higher tides, they frequent islets of sparsely vegetated mud in shallow lagoons. On the Tamar the birds may remain swimming in a flock for much of the high tide period.

Until the mid 1970s most Suffolk birds had departed by the end of October, leaving only a few to overwinter. Subsequently an increasing number of what is apparently the local breeding population has overwintered. Ringing indicates that some British Avocets join autumn moulting concentrations in the Netherlands before moving to winter on coastal marshes in Spain and Portugal, if not N and W Africa (Cadbury and Olney 1978).

In Devon, Avocets do not arrive until late October, well after the main departure from Suffolk, and most usually leave by the end of February. One Avocet, colour-ringed in Suffolk, was seen on the Tamar in 4 successive winters 1971–75 and again in 1979/80 but it is probable that the majority of birds are from other NW European breeding populations. On 2 December 1981 at least 94 Avocets were seen off the Sussex coast, where a spring passage has also been observed.

The Figure below shows that except for a slight decline in the mid 1960s there was a fairly steady increase in the total numbers of Avocets wintering in Britain and Ireland until 1980/81. The sharp increase in 1981/82 is largely attributable to the increased Suffolk population. Since 1980/81 the Bri-

tish wintering population has represented over 50% of the total of adults and juveniles at the end of the previous breeding season. In the mid winter period of 1983/84 there were about 385 birds in Britain.

Over the period 1978–83 an average of about 34,400 Avocets has been counted in January on the Atlantic coasts of Europe, mainly in France and Portugal, though 600 or so have been wintering on the North Sea coast of the Netherlands and Germany (IWRB data). Britain is at the northwest extremity of the wintering range of the Avocet.

C. J. CADBURY

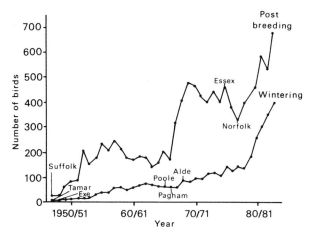

Post-breeding numbers (pairs and fledged young) in East Anglia, and maximum numbers of wintering Avocets in Britain and Ireland 1947–84. The start of regular breeding and wintering in particular areas is indicated.

Total number of squares in which recorded: 55 (1%)

No. of birds seen in a day	Number (%) of squares		
	Britain	Ireland	TOTAL (incl. C.I.)
1–2	27 (53%)	4 (100%)	31 (56%)
3–7	13 (26%)	0 (0%)	13 (24%)
8+	11 (22%)	0 (0%)	11 (20%)

References

CADBURY, C. J. and P. J. S. OLNEY. 1978. Avocet population dynamics in England. *Brit. Birds* 71: 102–121.

TJALLINGII, S. T. 1971. De Kluten van de Dollard. *Waddenbulletin* 6: 5–9.

Breeding Atlas p 198.

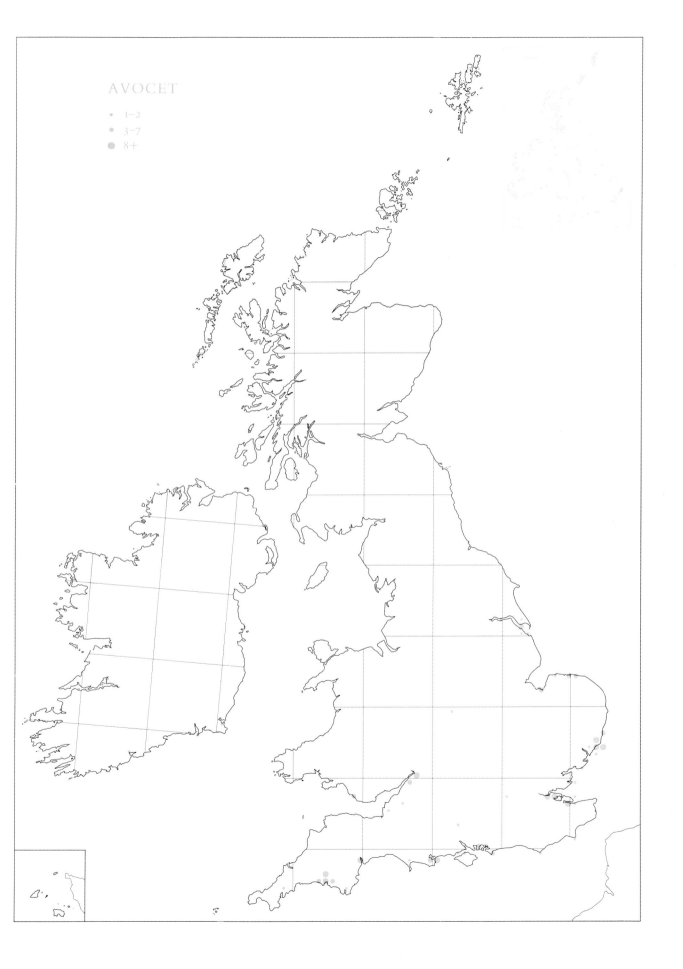

AVOCET

• 1—2
• 3—7
● 8+

Ringed Plover

Charadrius hiaticula

.NB

Found around almost all our coasts in winter, Ringed Plovers can be remarkably inconspicuous until they call or dart to catch a prey animal. This is because their disruptive head and breast markings can cause them to merge with the background, until they move.

The winter distribution is largely coastal, with small numbers at some inland wetland sites. These inland occurrences are mainly in lowland eastern England and do not generally coincide with the inland sites recorded in the *Breeding Atlas*, which were mainly upland areas and river systems in northern Britain and Ireland, and some East Anglian heaths. The rocky coasts, cliffs and other narrow, exposed shores, mainly in NW Scotland and SW Britain, are avoided in winter. Most other coastal areas are used, though not all by breeding birds in summer, probably because of human disturbance. The main winter concentrations are on areas of broad sandy beaches and muddy sand in estuaries, where the birds feed on a wide variety of small invertebrates, especially worms and crustaceans (Pienkowski 1982, *BWP*). Plovers hunt visually, standing still, scanning an area for signs of movement which indicate the presence of prey at or near the sand surface.

Some Ringed Plovers remain near their breeding areas in winter (Pienkowski 1984, N. E. Buxton), giving rise to the concentrations in the Thames estuary, NE England/SE Scotland, Orkney and the Outer Hebrides. Many others move westwards, as feeding conditions become more severe in the colder east, where low temperatures increase food demand but make prey inactive and therefore difficult to detect (Pienkowski 1982). Thus there are high numbers on Irish Sea estuaries and at suitable sites around Ireland. Because some British birds return to their breeding areas as early as February, this concentration in the west in winter may be even more marked than recorded on the map.

In addition to British breeding birds, some Continental birds, mainly from the Wadden Sea and Baltic coasts, winter in Britain and Ireland. In the south, colour-ringed birds from East Germany have been seen (A. Siefke). Some British breeding birds move south to the Continent. Birds from the larger arctic breeding populations occur only on spring and autumn passage.

The *Breeding Atlas* estimated the number of pairs in Britain and Ireland as 8,000, but the 1983 Wader Study Group/Nature Conservancy Council Survey of the Uists doubled the previous estimate for the area to 2,100 (Green 1983), making the total about 9,000 pairs. This is perhaps equivalent to a winter population of about 30,000 birds, after allowing for young produced and surviving. Prater (1981) estimated the mid winter population of Ringed Plovers in Britain and Ireland to be 10,000–15,000. However, the map suggests that the real total may be more than 20,000. This difference from Prater (1981) is not surprising as the Birds of Estuaries Enquiry (and the Wetlands Enquiry in Ireland) did not attempt to cover all non-estuarine coasts, some of which are very important to this species. In fact as a result of the BTO/WSG Winter Shorebird Count, the wintering population is now known to be 25,000–30,000 birds. In addition, Hutchinson (1979) estimated 5,000–10,000 birds in Ireland, making a total of about 35,000. Allowing for the emigration of some birds and immigration of others, the breeding and wintering estimates are now of the same order of magnitude.

Many more Ringed Plovers winter in SW Europe and Africa, where this species forms a much higher proportion of the shorebird community (Pienkowski 1981). Britain and Ireland are on the northern edge of the species wintering range, but the coasts are obviously of great importance to the locally breeding birds and short distance migrants.

M. W. PIENKOWSKI

Total number of squares in which recorded: 1,031 (27%)

No. of birds seen in a day	Number (%) of squares		
	Britain	Ireland	TOTAL (incl. C.I.)
1–18	414 (54%)	102 (40%)	517 (50%)
19–60	221 (29%)	84 (33%)	307 (30%)
61+	137 (18%)	69 (27%)	207 (20%)

References

GREEN, G. H. 1983. WSG/NCC survey of waders breeding on the Hebridean machair and adjacent land, 1983. *Wader Study Group Bull.* 39: 5–8.

PIENKOWSKI, M. W. 1981. Differences in habitat requirements and distribution patterns of plovers and sandpipers as investigated by studies of feeding behaviour. Proc. IWRB Feeding Ecology Symp., Gwatt, Switzerland, September 1977. *Verh. Orn. Ges. Bayern* 23: 105–124.

PIENKOWSKI, M. W. 1982. Diet and energy intake of Grey and Ringed Plovers, *Pluvialis squatarola* and *Charadrius hiaticula*, in the non-breeding season. *J. Zool. Lond.* 197: 511–547.

PIENKOWSKI, M. W. 1984. Behaviour of young Ringed Plovers *Charadrius hiaticula* and its relation to growth and survival to reproductive age. *Ibis* 126: 133–155.

Breeding Atlas p 166

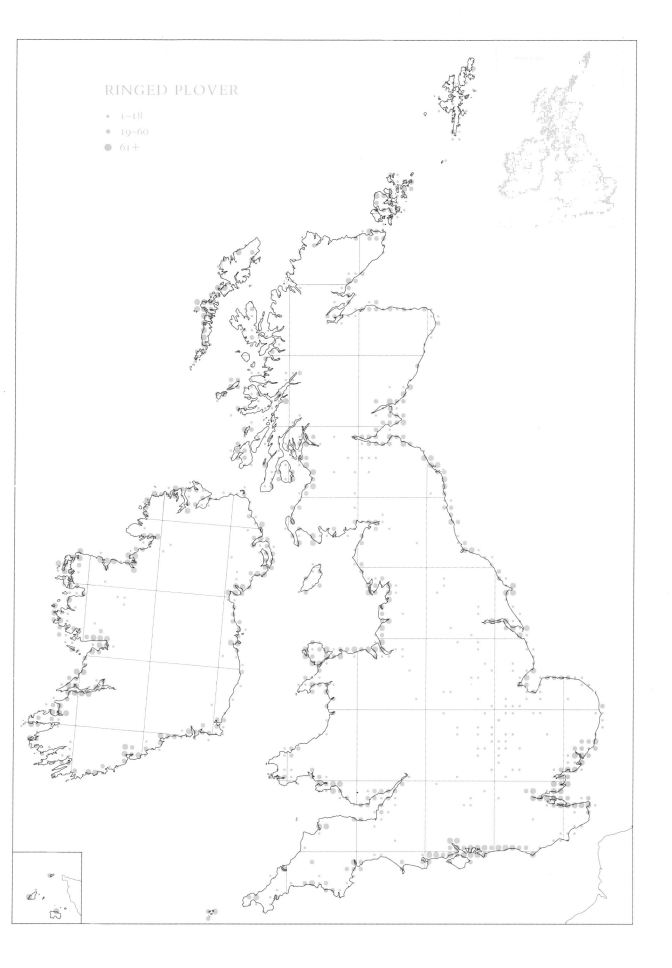

RINGED PLOVER

- • 1–18
- • 19–60
- ● 61+

Golden Plover

Pluvialis apricaria

Wintering flocks of Golden Plovers are found throughout much of lowland Britain and Ireland. Often accompanied by Lapwings *Vanellus vanellus*, and sharing similar habitats and behaviour, these two species are sometimes termed the 'grassland plovers'.

The winter distribution contrasts with that of the breeding season, when Golden Plovers are confined to the British uplands and the NW fringe of Ireland. Wintering Golden Plovers avoid land above 200 m, although some reappear close to their moorland breeding grounds in late February (Parr 1980).

The map shows a marked concentration of wintering Golden Plovers in northern England, roughly between Morecambe Bay, the Dee Estuary, and along the Humber. Other regions of Britain supporting large numbers include the Firth of Forth south to Tyneside, E Kent and the SW England peninsula. Most large flocks in Britain winter close to, or on, the coast and few occur in central England or in East Anglia (see also Fuller and Lloyd 1981). In Ireland there are major wintering grounds in the NE and along the south coasts but vast concourses of Golden Plovers also occur well inland, particularly in the Shannon lowlands (Hutchinson 1979).

Wintering Golden Plovers depend for food on various types of agricultural land (Fuller and Youngman 1979, Fuller and Lloyd 1981). In most parts of Britain, grassland is the preferred feeding habitat. Permanent pastures are preferred both to leys and arable land, probably because larger densities of soil invertebrates occur in old grassland. In Scotland, Ireland and northern England, birds regularly feed in the intertidal zone. In southern Britain Golden Plovers feed most frequently on arable land in early and late winter. Arable land, especially plough, is strongly preferred for roosting, but in inland Ireland damp grassland is chosen, and in N Britain, Wales and Northern Ireland roosts are frequently on inter tidal flats.

The species is well known for its use of traditional wintering grounds. Flocks in southern England regularly return to 'flock ranges' outside which they rarely occur (Fuller and Youngman 1979). Within flock ranges, certain favoured feeding fields are typically shared with Lapwings and Black-headed Gulls *Larus ridibundus*, and an extremely complex association has evolved between these three species (Barnard and Thompson 1985). Lapwings congregate in fields with high densities of earthworms and are used by Golden Plovers as indicators of good feeding areas. The gulls steal worms from both Golden Plovers and Lapwings. The relationship is not entirely one sided, however, because the plovers appear to benefit from the early warning of predators given by the gulls.

Maritime France, Britain and Ireland are the main European wintering grounds of Golden Plovers (*BWP*), and many of those wintering in Ireland and in western Britain are of Icelandic origin. The British and Irish breeding populations are probably mainly resident, but Britain also draws birds from Scandinavia and from further east. Major influxes of Golden Plovers come into Britain between October and December although in parts of northern Britain, such as SW Scotland, numbers have usually declined by the end of December. If the weather is mild the birds stay in England but in cold winters they undertake hard weather movements, mostly southerly or southwesterly, similar to those described for Lapwings.

An approximate total of 695,000 Golden Plovers was recorded in the *Winter Atlas* with more than 300,000 each for Britain and Ireland. This total was derived by summing the peak counts in each square. Previous estimates of numbers have been of the order of 200,000 in each country (Hutchinson 1979, Fuller and Lloyd 1981). The *Winter Atlas* estimates are probably high because they may include double counts of flocks which moved from one locality to another in response to hard weather. Nevertheless, flocks can be difficult to find and it is likely that many were overlooked during Atlas fieldwork. The wintering populations of Britain and Ireland may each be in the range of 200,000–300,000.

R. J. FULLER

Total number of squares in which recorded: 1,971 (57%)

No. of birds seen in a day	Number (%) of squares		
	Britain	Ireland	TOTAL (incl. C.I.)
1–120	780 (52%)	211 (46%)	995 (50%)
121–495	459 (30%)	115 (25%)	575 (29%)
496+	270 (18%)	131 (29%)	401 (20%)

References

BARNARD, C. J. and D. B. A. THOMPSON. 1985. *Gulls and Plovers: the Ecology and Behaviour of Mixed-species Feeding Groups*. Croom Helm, London.

FULLER, R. J. and D. LLOYD. 1981. The distribution and habitats of wintering Golden Plovers in Britain, 1977–1978. *Bird Study* 28: 169–185.

FULLER, R. J. and R. E. YOUNGMAN. 1979. The utilisation of farmland by Golden Plovers wintering in southern England. *Bird Study* 26: 37–46.

PARR, R. 1980. Population study of Golden Plover *Pluvialis apricaria*, using marked birds. *Ornis Scand.* 11: 179–189.

Breeding Atlas p 170

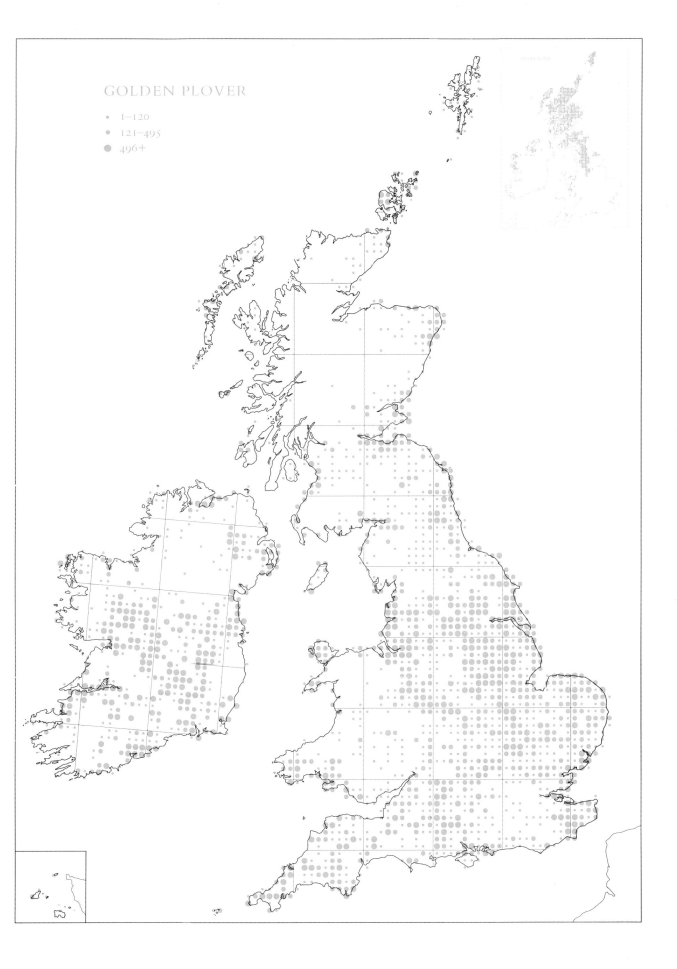

GOLDEN PLOVER

- 1–120
- 121–495
- 496+

Grey Plover

Pluvialis squatarola

Although Grey Plovers are often seen roosting at high water within dense flocks of Knots *Calidris canutus* and Dunlins *C. alpina*, they avoid such flocks while feeding. Instead, Grey Plovers characteristically space out across the higher mudflats, away from the concentrations of other waders at the tide edge.

The winter distribution is almost entirely coastal, the few records inland probably being of juveniles on migration. Grey Plovers are concentrated on the larger and muddier estuaries, particularly in SE England from the Wash to the Solent and in NW England. They are widespread but less abundant elsewhere in Britain and Ireland, but absent from large areas of N and W Scotland, Orkney and Shetland.

Grey Plovers eat a variety of burrowing intertidal invertebrates, their diet changing between sites in parallel with the prey species available (Pienkowski 1982). Their feeding method relies upon not disturbing prey temporarily present at the surface of the mud, so Grey Plovers never feed in tight flocks. On some, but not all, intertidal areas they defend feeding territories. A fixed area of mud may be defended by the same individual each low water period, by day and night, throughout several successive winters. However, within an estuary, Grey Plovers do not defend feeding sites on all mudflats and territoriality is more likely under certain conditions of prey availability, bird density and habitat type (Townshend *et al* 1984). Night feeding may provide at least as much of their food requirements as daytime feeding.

Grey Plovers visiting Britain and Ireland come to us from the W Siberian breeding grounds. Their migrations are complex and occur throughout the non-breeding period. In August the Wash is the most important area in Britain and Ireland for Grey Plovers, with up to 2,000 moulting and 2,000 passage birds (Branson and Minton 1976). Juveniles arrive in September and October; and in November, after moulting, some adults and juveniles migrate south to SW Europe and W Africa; others remain all winter, and more birds arrive from mainland Europe. The same pattern is seen at Teesmouth, where further influxes occur in December of birds that left the European coast due to low temperatures there, followed by an arrival in late winter of Grey Plovers moving north after spending the mid winter period further south in Europe. A gradual emigration, probably to the Wadden Sea, occurs during February and March, and spring passage during April and May. This pattern of movements is probably typical for east and south coast estuaries. In W Britain and Ireland there is a smaller autumn passage; also some westerly movement from the Wash (*eg* to the Severn) may occur in November.

The pattern of intertidal territorial behaviour and timing of seasonal movements of each individual are determined during the first autumn of life, following competition especially with adults (Townshend 1985). Larger juveniles are more likely to acquire territories and more likely to stay at Teesmouth all winter.

The number of Grey Plovers recorded by the Birds of Estuaries Enquiry increased steadily during the 1970s, perhaps due to a reduction in shooting pressure and a series of good breeding seasons. Certainly, year to year variation in the number arriving in Britain and Ireland each autumn is due mainly to differences in the number of juveniles. Because of their complex pattern of seasonal movements it is difficult to estimate the total number of Grey Plovers visiting Britain and Ireland during the whole non-breeding period.

Recent counts from the Birds of Estuaries Enquiry and Hutchinson's (1979) estimate for Ireland support a total of nearly 20,000 birds in January. This constitutes more than one third of the European winter population (about 50,000, *BWP*). Britain and Ireland are at the northern edge of the range of the Grey Plover in mid winter. Large numbers of Grey Plovers also occur on the Wadden Sea in autumn and spring and in W France, Iberia and W Africa in mid winter, with mainly males in the north of the range and females in the south.

D. J. TOWNSHEND

Total number of squares in which recorded: 621 (16%)

No. of birds seen in a day	Number (%) of squares		
	Britain	Ireland	TOTAL (incl. C.I.)
1–6	231 (49%)	78 (52%)	311 (50%)
7–65	132 (29%)	51 (34%)	186 (30%)
66+	101 (22%)	21 (14%)	124 (20%)

References

BRANSON, N. J. B. A. and C. D. T. MINTON. 1976. Moult, measurements and migrations of the Grey Plover. *Bird Study* 23: 257–266.

PIENKOWSKI, M. W. 1982. Diet and energy intake of Grey and Ringed Plovers, *Pluvialis squatarola* and *Charadrius hiaticula*, in the non-breeding season. *J. Zool. Lond.* 197: 511–549.

TOWNSHEND, D. J. 1985. Decisions for a lifetime: establishment of spatial defence and movement patterns by juvenile Grey Plovers (*Pluvialis squatarola*). *J. Anim. Ecol.* 54: 267–274.

TOWNSHEND, D. J., P. J. DUGAN and M. W. PIENKOWSKI. 1984. The unsociable plover—use of intertidal areas by Grey Plovers. Pp 140–159 in EVANS, P. R., J. D. GOSS-CUSTARD and W. G. HALE (eds), *Coastal Waders and Wildfowl in Winter*. University Press, Cambridge.

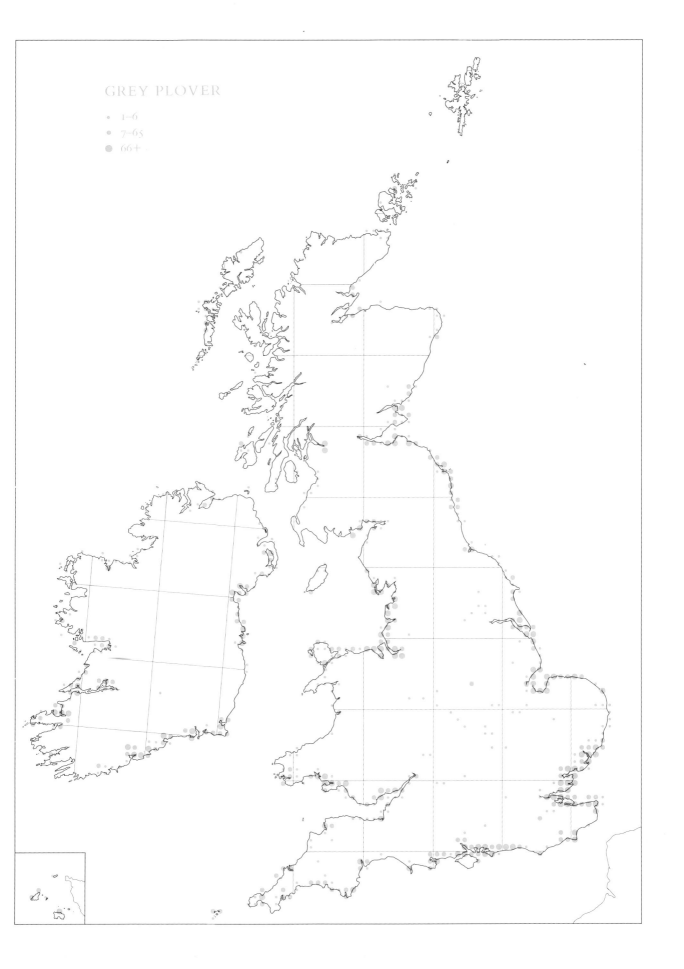

GREY PLOVER

- 1–6
- 7–65
- 66+

NB.

Lapwing

Vanellus vanellus

The Lapwing is the most widespread wintering wader in Britain and Ireland. It is highly gregarious and large flocks can be encountered at any time of the year between June and March.

Wintering Lapwings avoid the higher ground of N and W Britain. The winter map shows that although Lapwings are widely distributed throughout all lowland regions, numbers are greatest in southern and central Britain and Ireland. Central England holds an exceptionally large concentration of wintering Lapwings which extends north from the Vale of Aylesbury as far as Nottinghamshire. The main northern strongholds are west of the Pennines.

From November to February the density of Lapwings in many regions is higher on grassland than on arable land (Lister 1964, Fuller and Youngman 1979). This may explain why the species occurs in lower numbers in the intensively arable regions of East Anglia than in the mixed farming land of the midlands. Roosts are mainly on cultivated land, especially plough.

Lapwings feed in particular fields year after year. Such traditional feeding sites probably offer reliable sources of invertebrate food but the species is also opportunistic, exploiting temporary food sources such as freshly ploughed fields and the edge of floodwater. Lapwings suffer heavily from piracy by Black-headed Gulls *Larus ridibundus* (see Golden Plover) but the birds feed commonly at night when food stealing by gulls is not a problem. Nocturnal activity seems to be most frequent around the full moon period when the birds spend much of the day roosting (Milsom 1984).

A high proportion of Lapwings wintering in Britain is of Scandinavian, Danish, Dutch and N German origin (Imboden 1974). Many British bred Lapwings also winter in Britain, but some move to the Continent and many birds reared in northern Britain over-winter in Ireland. Although movements into Britain from the Continent start in June, the main immigrations are in November and December. Spring emigrations may commence in February, but the main departure from central England can be quite sudden, with all birds leaving for their breeding grounds by mid March.

Together with western France and Iberia, Britain and Ireland form the major European wintering grounds of Lapwings. The distribution of birds within these countries can, however, be strongly modified by cold weather. Severe frost and snow deprive Lapwings of their food and consequently they move rapidly away from badly affected areas. Most hard weather movements are in a southerly or southwesterly direction, or towards nearby coasts where Lapwings can feed on the unfrozen shores. After short spells of hard weather plovers may return within a few days of the thaw. In central England such local movements of birds occur in most winters. Prolonged freeze-ups, such as the 1962/63 winter, force most plovers to leave Britain and the birds may not return to their winter feeding grounds for the remainder of the winter. In really hard winters Ireland can become a major refuge for Lapwings but there was no evidence that this happened in 1981/82.

It is difficult to estimate numbers of Lapwings wintering in Britain and Ireland because the species is so widespread and mobile. The sums of the peak counts made in each square during the *Winter Atlas* were approximately 2,050,000 for Britain and 550,000 for Ireland. These totals must not be treated as population estimates because there may have been much double counting of birds which moved in response to hard weather, particularly in the 1981/82 winter. On the other hand Atlas fieldworkers undoubtedly missed many flocks. Even if the *Winter Atlas* counts overestimated numbers by 50% the combined British and Irish population would well exceed 1,000,000 birds.

R. J. FULLER

Total number of squares in which recorded: 3,065 (79%)

No. of birds seen in a day	Number (%) of squares		
	Britain	Ireland	TOTAL (incl. C.I.)
1–435	1,032 (46%)	491 (60%)	1,525 (50%)
436–1,500	719 (32%)	208 (26%)	927 (30%)
1,501+	497 (22%)	114 (14%)	613 (20%)

References

FULLER, R. J. and R. E. YOUNGMAN. 1979. The utilisation of farmland by Golden Plovers wintering in southern England. *Bird Study* 26: 37–46.

IMBODEN, C. 1974. Zug, Fremdansiedlung und Brutperiode des Kiebitz *Vanellus vanellus* in Europa. *Orn. Beob.* 71: 5–134.

LISTER, M. D. 1964. The Lapwing habitat enquiry, 1960–61. *Bird Study* 11: 128–147.

MILSOM, T. P. 1984. Diurnal behaviour of Lapwings in relation to moon phase during winter. *Bird Study* 31: 117–120.

Breeding Atlas p 164

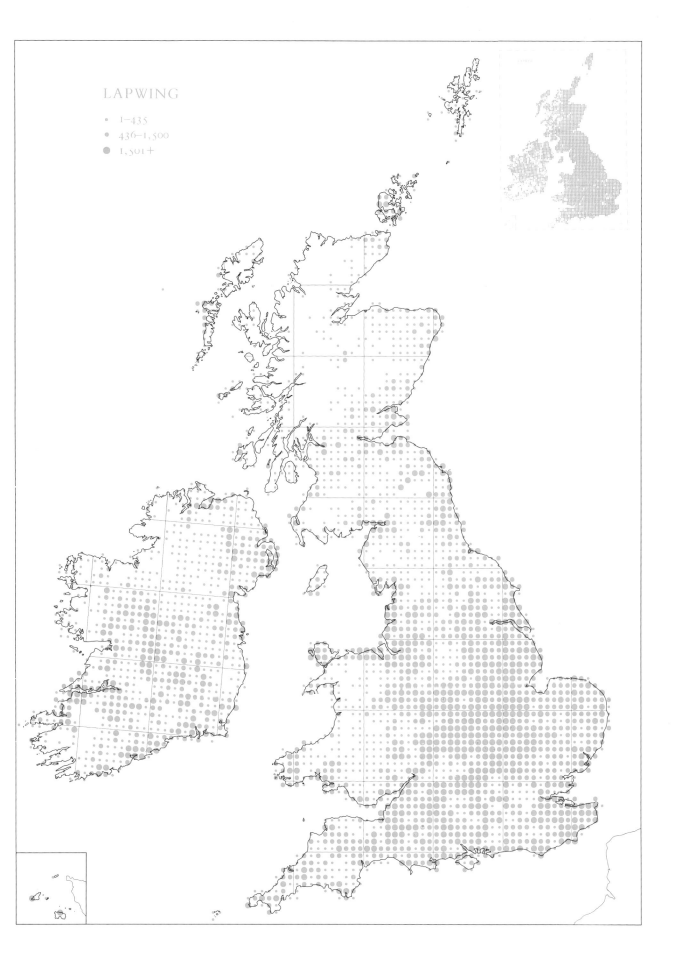

LAPWING

- 1–435
- 436–1,500
- 1,501+

Knot

Calidris canutus

Knots are high-Arctic breeding waders concentrating in large assemblies on Britain's and Ireland's main estuaries during the winter. At high tide they form massive and tightly packed roosting flocks. Their close formation in aerial flights are a characteristic spectacle as they circle and land to roost on beaches, salt marshes, or sometimes on inland fields.

The winter map reflects a concentration of numbers on certain key estuaries of Britain and Ireland. Recent Birds of Estuaries Enquiry and Irish counts have shown that there are 8 sites which support more than 10,000 Knots in winter (Salmon and Moser 1985). These sites alone hold over half of the winter population. During mid winter, Knots are at their most dispersed and flocks are found also on the smaller estuaries. Ringing recoveries have shown the species to be very mobile during the winter, both within and between estuaries.

Knots remain gregarious whilst feeding on mud-flats, where they take a variety of bivalve molluscs such as *Macoma*, also worms and crustaceans. As with other species of wader, their specialised habitat requirements make them particularly vulnerable to reclamation and pollution of estuaries.

Recent research has confirmed the location of the winter quarters of the two populations occurring in the European area, and has shown the species' dependence during different seasons on certain key estuaries. The population of Knots wintering in Europe, south to France, is from breeding areas in Greenland and eastern Canada. During the late 1960s and early 1970s, as a result of major efforts by European Wader Ringing Groups, the migrations of this population became clearer. In autumn, large moulting flocks build up in the Dutch Wadden Sea following arrival from the breeding grounds. From November to February, there is a movement of these birds into British east and west coast estuaries, where they join with existing flocks, which have moulted in Britain, to give the high mid winter numbers. Towards spring, most of the birds move to the Irish Sea estuaries, where fat is laid down prior to departure in mid May for Iceland and the Arctic breeding grounds. Large numbers also migrate northwards via the German Wadden Sea.

More recently, populations of Knots breeding in Siberia have been shown to winter in Africa (Dick *et al* 1976). These populations do not reach Britain in significant numbers, although on migration they are found on the same European estuaries (notably in Germany) which are also used by the Greenland and Canadian populations.

The Estuaries Enquiry has shown that since the late 1960s, there has been a decline in the total numbers of Knots of Greenland and Canadian origin. Peak numbers in Britain and Ireland of 400,000 in 1971/72, declined to 230,000 in 1973/74. Annual monitoring by the Estuaries Enquiry since then has revealed no evidence of a recovery to the former levels. A series of poor breeding seasons in the Arctic, paralleling those of other species in the same areas such as the Pale-bellied Brent Goose *Branta bernicla* (Prater 1981), is thought to be responsible for the decline of the numbers of Greenland and Canadian birds and could warrant careful monitoring, especially considering the sensitivity of the species to changes or reclamation at a limited number of key estuaries.

W. J. A. DICK

Total number of squares in which recorded: 444 (12%)

No. of birds seen in a day	Number (%) of squares		
	Britain	Ireland	TOTAL (incl. C.I.)
1–32	187 (51%)	34 (45%)	223 (50%)
33–600	97 (27%)	34 (45%)	131 (30%)
601+	82 (22%)	8 (10%)	90 (20%)

References

DICK, W. J. A., M. W. PIENKOWSKI, M. WALTNER and C. D. T. MINTON. 1976. Distribution and geographical origins of Knot *Calidris canutus* wintering in Europe and Africa. *Ardea* 64: 22–47.

MARCHANT, J. H. 1981. (ed.) *Birds of Estuaries Enquiry 1976–77 to 1978–79*. B.T.O., Tring.

SALMON, D. G. 1982. (ed.) *Wildfowl and Wader Counts 1981–82*. Wildfowl Trust, Slimbridge.

SALMON, D. G. and M. E. MOSER (eds). 1985. *Wildfowl and Wader Counts 1984–85*. Wildfowl Trust, Slimbridge.

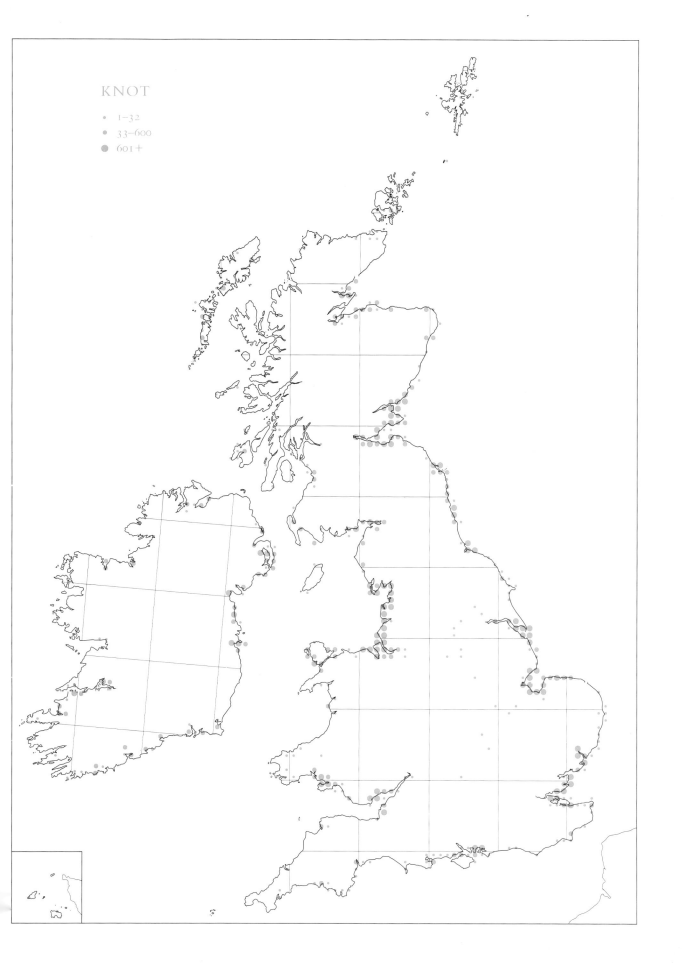

KNOT

- 1–32
- 33–600
- 601+

Sanderling

Calidris alba

Sanderlings are strikingly white, small waders characteristic of open sandy sea beaches. They rush along the wrack line or tidal edge, and for a bird of their size must surely hold the speed record for running. In their search for food they often pursue the retreating waves and attempt to pick small items from the water, then scamper back as the next wave approaches.

Their winter distribution in Britain and Ireland emphasises their dependence on long sandy shores, very few of which occur along the cliff-bound SW of England, western Wales and western Scotland. The largest numbers of birds, often about 2,000, concentrate each winter on the Ribble estuary and southwards towards Liverpool, around the R. Alt. Another notable area, holding over 1,500 birds, whose importance was discovered only very recently, includes the shores of the Uists and Benbecula in the Outer Hebrides, and those in Orkney.

On the open sea beaches, where the sand is relatively coarse-grained by comparison with intertidal sediments in many estuaries, the foods available to Sanderlings are rather restricted. At Teesmouth, the main prey is a fairly small polychaete worm *Nerine cirratulus*, which the birds take by probing when the sand is wet. This explains in part why birds often feed near the tide edge. Because *Nerine* occurs in a relatively narrow band around the high water of neap tides, Sanderlings have to forage on smaller prey at other stages of the tidal cycle, notably small shrimp-like crustaceans *Bathyporeia* spp. and *Eurydice pulchra*. These are hunted visually and often taken whilst they are swimming in the backwash from the waves—hence the frequent behaviour of the Sanderlings, running up and down the beach as each wave breaks and recedes. At low water the birds may move to mussel scars to feed on recently settled spat (tiny mussels); at high water, Sanderlings often work their way along the strand line to hunt wrack-flies and sandhoppers. They feed usually in flocks, particularly when they are searching for worms, for these tend to occur in patches of high (and low) density. The composition of these flocks, however, changes from day to day. In some wintering areas, some, but not all, birds defend territories. In California, wintering Sanderlings abandon territories if birds of prey, particularly Merlins *Falco columbarius*, are present. In autumn and spring they may roost communally both at low and high waters, but in winter, the diurnal roosting times are shortened and may be omitted altogether. Night roosts are often in different sites from daytime roosts and, when the tide is suitable, birds continue to feed at night, though on what is not known.

The Sanderlings wintering in Britain and Ireland are believed to consist primarily of birds that have bred in Siberia, but an unknown (though probably small) proportion are from the population breeding in Greenland. They arrive in Britain in July and August, congregating on a few major sites to moult, *eg* the Wash, Dee and other open estuaries in NW England. Many birds also pass through Britain and Ireland at this time, to destinations in W Africa and beyond. After moulting, most birds leave the Wash, some moving north to Teesmouth where they join the flock that had moulted there. As the winter proceeds, birds spread out from the main autumn centres. Some individuals 'patrol' considerable distances of coast while others remain faithful to a very restricted length of beach.

According to Prater and Davies (1978), about 10,000 Sanderlings winter in Britain and another 2,000 in Ireland. The index of Sanderling numbers, derived from the Birds of Estuaries Enquiry, is highly variable from year to year but shows no long-term trend. The winter total represents about 50% of the numbers estimated to winter in the whole of western Europe, but less than 10% of the whole western Palearctic migration flyway population, most of which winters on the coasts of Mauritania, Namibia and South Africa.

P. R. EVANS

Total number of squares in which recorded: 400 (10%)

No. of birds seen in a day	Number (%) of squares		
	Britain	Ireland	TOTAL (incl. C.I.)
1–19	141 (49%)	54 (49%)	197 (49%)
20–94	80 (28%)	43 (39%)	123 (31%)
95+	66 (23%)	13 (12%)	80 (20%)

References

MYERS, J. P., P. G. CONNORS and F. A. PITELKA. 1979. Territory size in wintering Sanderlings. *Auk* 96: 551–561.

PRATER, A. J. and M. DAVIES. 1978. Wintering Sanderlings in Britain. *Bird Study* 25: 33–38.

WADER STUDY GROUP. 1980. Sanderling studies. *Wader Study Group Bull.* 30: 18–31. (Papers by P. R. EVANS, D. M. BREAREY and L. R. GOODYER (pp 18–20), N. C. DAVIDSON (pp 20–21), P. N. FERNS (pp 22–25), J. P. MYERS (pp 26–31).)

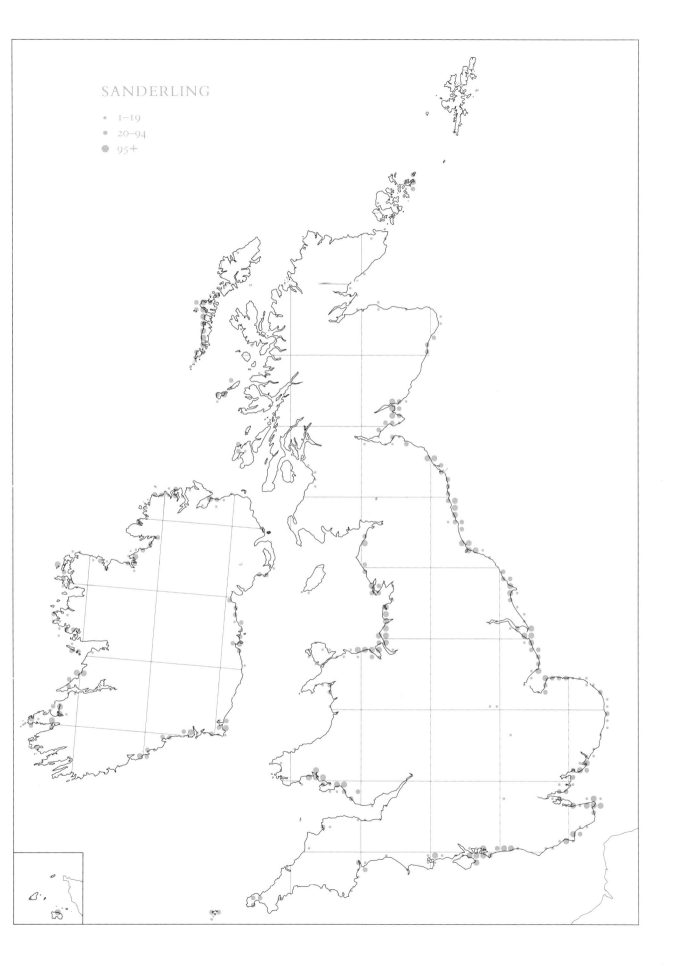

SANDERLING

- · 1–19
- · 20–94
- · 95+

Little Stint

Calidris minuta

Little Stints are the smallest of the common passage waders, often occurring in small groups with Dunlin *C. alpina*, from which they are immediately distinguishable by their dainty build and short straight bills. Even in darkness Little Stints can be picked out by their shrill peeps amongst the more raucous calls of the Dunlin.

Much larger numbers occur in autumn than in spring, and numbers vary between years. Each year a few remain and overwinter in Britain and Ireland.

The map reflects remarkably accurately the pattern of occurrence as indicated by published records in the Scottish, Irish and county bird reports. Genuine overwintering in Britain has occurred as far north as the Ribble on the west coast, and Teesmouth on the east, but the records since the 1950s show that most Little Stints occur in the southern coastal counties of England. The Dee and Mersey estuaries form a separate northern stronghold. In Scotland there have been several records after 15 November, but these could all be regarded as probable autumn stragglers. In Ireland, where the frequency of passage is much lower than in Britain (Prater 1981), there have been relatively few birds overwintering.

In November and December, many records are for inland localities such as reservoirs and old style sewage farms. About a quarter of these birds will stay until December, then move on. The great majority of the January and February records are from estuaries and coastal locations; often those with industrialised shorelines where reclamation schemes have left clear sand, mud and pools which are available for feeding during the high tide period, the birds picking insects and crustaceans off the surface.

The Little Stint breeds on the Palearctic tundras, and it is the population breeding to about 45°E which migrates down the Atlantic seaboard and through Europe on its way to wintering quarters, which are mainly in Africa south of the Sahara. Some remain north of the Sahara to winter in Mauritania, Morocco and along the Mediterranean coast of Africa, as well as up the Atlantic coast of S Europe (*BWP*). Up to

1982, 1,068 Little Stints had been ringed in Britain and Ireland, producing only 18 recoveries (Mead and Hudson 1983). Although only a tiny proportion of those handled were caught in winter, 2 were recovered. One ringed during December in Cheshire was recovered the following April in the Netherlands, presumably on its way back to its breeding area. Another ringed in its first autumn on Southampton Water was controlled there in January two winters later.

The Handbook listed only 22 records of Little Stints wintering in Britain and Ireland between 1831 and 1937. Four other records appear to have been overlooked. Since 1940 at least 560 individuals have overwintered in Britain and Ireland. An increase in the number of some overwintering waders was noted as early as 1954 (Barnes 1956). The change for Little Stints seems to have started in the 1930s. The increases are shown in the Figure. The records so far published for the period since 1980 indicate that the rate of occurrence is still on the increase.

Although increasing in numbers, there are fewer than 30 Little Stints wintering in Britain and Ireland, where they are on the extreme northern edge of the winter range. In Iberia, where a considerable increase in overwintering birds has been recorded during the past 20 years, approximately 600 remain each winter, mainly in Portugal (*BWP*).

H. INSLEY

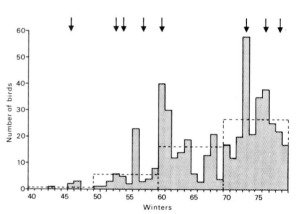

The number of Little Stints recorded in each winter. Dotted lines indicate ten year averages; arrows indicate the peak autumns. Data are taken from county bird reports.

Total number of squares in which recorded: 45 (1%)

No. of birds seen in a day	Number (%) of squares		
	Britain	Ireland	TOTAL (incl. C.I.)
I	33 (81%)	2 (50%)	35 (78%)
2	3 (7%)	0 (0%)	3 (7%)
3+	5 (12%)	2 (50%)	7 (16%)

References

BARNES, J. A. G. 1956. Delayed emigration of certain birds in Autumn 1954. *Brit. Birds* 49: 167–171.

MEAD, C. J. and R. HUDSON. 1983. Report on Bird-Ringing for 1982. *Ringing and Migration* 4: 281–320.

LITTLE STINT

- 1
- 2
- 3+

Purple Sandpiper

Calidris maritima

The Purple Sandpiper is a small wader whose habit of feeding along the tide edge of rocky shores, plus its cryptic plumage and reluctance to flush, mean that it is easily overlooked. However, its confiding nature allows one to approach closely, and it is only then that one can see the purple sheen on the back feathers of the winter plumage.

The winter distribution reflects the pattern previously described by Atkinson *et al* (1978), who found that Purple Sandpipers were concentrated in NE Britain. They are common on all rocky shores down the east coast of Scotland and NE England, and become scarce south of Yorkshire where the coast is predominantly of sand or shingle. Although rocky shores occur again in SW England, Wales and southern Ireland, Purple Sandpipers remain relatively scarce there. The mainland coast of western Scotland and Inner Hebrides also have few Purple Sandpipers, but the reason for those absences is not known.

Purple Sandpipers start arriving on the east coast in July and immediately begin moulting. In October and November birds arrive on northern and western coasts of Scotland from different breeding areas (see below), having already moulted. Numbers are at a maximum during mid winter and may begin to fall by March, though departure of the east coast birds does not start until April/May. First-year birds leave as well as the adults (Atkinson *et al* 1981). A few pairs have recently remained to breed in the mountains of Scotland (Dennis 1983).

Purple Sandpipers are virtually restricted to the rocky shore, where small flocks or single birds forage. They feed on a large variety of marine invertebrates but mainly mussels, winkles, and dog whelks (Feare 1966). In some localities they may forage on banks of rotting sea-weed on the high water mark where they eat the larvae, pupae and adults of the kelp fly. The size of food items is usually in the range of 1–5 mm, and female Purple Sandpipers, which are larger than males, tend to take larger items. At high tide they gather to roost on off-shore skerries, the mainland shore or on piers.

Purple Sandpipers show a strong site tenacity through the winter; movements of more than 5 km are rare and the longest recorded was 30 km. They also return each year to the same stretch of shore (Atkinson *et al* 1981). One bird was retrapped on the Isle of May 14 years after ringing and it is likely to have spent each winter in this area.

The origins of the Purple Sandpipers in Britain are only partially known. From ringing recoveries, sightings of birds colour-ringed in Norway, and an analysis of bill lengths, it was concluded that the majority of the population in eastern Scotland came from Norway (Atkinson *et al* 1981). The Norwegian population is characterised by short-billed birds. Further north in Scotland and on the Outer Hebrides, there are few short-billed birds, and more of a long-billed population, which may originate from either Iceland or Canada (Tay and Orkney Ringing Groups 1984). In addition to the ringing recoveries in Scandinavia, there have been 2 from Greenland; one was ringed on the west coast of Britain and the other on the east. One was recovered in October and so might have been a migrant from Canada travelling via Greenland.

Atkinson *et al* (1978) have estimated the British (not including Ireland) winter population at between 14,500 and 23,000. The value of 14,500 was based largely on casual records and may be an underestimate of the actual population. Thus the upper, modified figure of 23,000 is probably a better estimate. No surveys of this species have yet been done in Ireland, but summing the maximum counts gives just over 2,000 birds.

Purple Sandpipers winter further north than any other arctic-breeding wader and can be found within the Arctic Circle of Norway, in Iceland and SW Greenland. Thus, Britain and Ireland are in the southern part of the winter range. The populations to the south of Britain are relatively small. About 2,000 winter in France, and the species also occurs regularly in small numbers in northern Spain and Portugal.

R. W. SUMMERS

Total number of squares in which recorded: 519 (13%)

No. of birds seen in a day	Number (%) of squares		
	Britain	Ireland	TOTAL (incl. C.I.)
1–10	191 (47%)	75 (65%)	266 (51%)
11–49	113 (28%)	33 (28%)	147 (28%)
50+	97 (24%)	8 (7%)	106 (20%)

References

ATKINSON, N. K., M. DAVIES and A. J. PRATER. 1978. The winter distribution of Purple Sandpipers in Britain. *Bird Study* 25: 223–228.

ATKINSON, N. K., R. W. SUMMERS, M. NICOLL and J. J. D. GREENWOOD. 1981. Population, movements and biometrics of the Purple Sandpiper *Calidris maritima* in eastern Scotland. *Ornis Scand.* 12: 18–27.

DENNIS, R. H. 1983. Purple Sandpipers breeding in Scotland. *Brit. Birds* 76: 563–566.

FEARE, C. J. 1966. The winter feeding of the Purple Sandpiper. *Brit. Birds* 59: 165–179.

TAY AND ORKNEY RINGING GROUPS. 1984. *The Shorebirds of the Orkney Islands.* Tay Ringing Group, Perth.

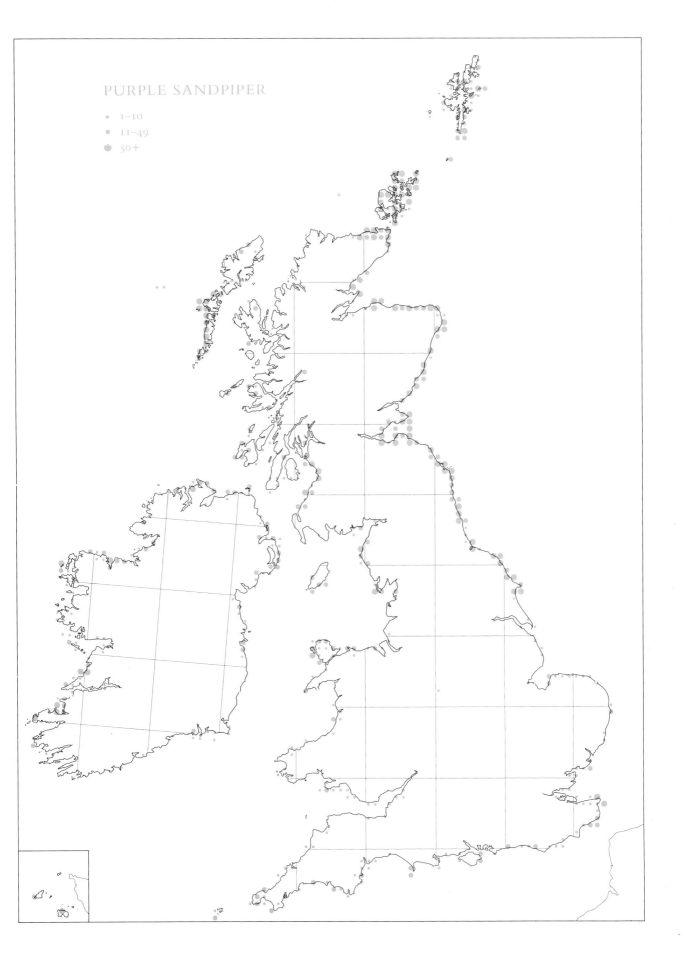

PURPLE SANDPIPER

- 1–10
- 11–49
- 50+

Dunlin

Calidris alpina

The Dunlin is the most abundant of our shore waders in winter, occurring almost anywhere on the coast where mud is present. The tightly packed, concerted aerobatics of large flocks moving to high-water roosts are one of the major attractions of large estuaries.

In winter, Dunlins are predominantly coastal, with large concentrations at estuaries and other large tidal flats. They commonly occur also on most other parts of the coast, except cliffs and very exposed situations, particularly in the northwest. Smaller numbers occur at inland sites, especially at migration times, and mainly from Yorkshire southwards in Britain and in Ireland. At such sites, they require exposed mud or shallow water, for example at sewage farms or on the banks of reservoirs.

In winter, Dunlins feed mainly on small invertebrates living in mud. These are often detected tactually by the bill, and small prey may even be swallowed while the bill is still in the mud. The birds generally feed in flocks, staying close to the tide edge, where the prey animals tend to be nearer the surface than are those on drying mud. The birds may form large roosting flocks at high water but, particularly in mid winter, feeding may continue in nearby fields and at night. The probability of very severe weather, when food is most needed and most difficult to find, is greatest in the east of Britain. Accordingly, birds wintering in the northeast carry the largest mid winter fat reserves to aid survival over such periods, whereas those in the southwest accumulate little fat (Pienkowski *et al* 1979).

The winter distribution differs totally from the breeding one, which features moorland, machair and some salt marshes, mainly in the north (*Breeding Atlas*). Different birds are involved in the two seasons: British and Irish breeding birds winter further south, probably in W Africa, whilst the birds wintering in Britain and Ireland arrive from northern Scandinavia and USSR. Birds from Iceland and Greenland pass through Britain in spring and autumn (Hardy and Minton 1980, *BWP*).

In autumn and early winter, the Wash and the Wadden Sea, extending from Denmark along the German and Netherlands coasts, are particularly important moulting sites, possibly because their vast areas give greater safety from land-based predators while the birds' flying abilities are impaired. In October–November, after moulting, many birds move westwards to areas of milder winter climate. In the Wadden Sea, in addition to colder weather, there is more chance than further west of tides being held over the feeding grounds by high winds (Pienkowski and Evans 1984). Some areas, (*eg* east coast of England, Irish Sea estuaries of Britain, SW Netherlands) both lose and gain Dunlin populations at this time; whilst others receive their main influx for the mid winter period (*eg* E Scotland, Ireland, S and SW England and Wales, France and Iberia) (Pienkowski and Pienkowski 1983). In February to April many birds return eastwards again, before the migration to the breeding grounds. Within each seasonally used area, individual birds tend to be faithful to particular sites, both within and between years (Symonds *et al* 1984). (Symonds *et al* 1984).

Winter counts indicate the population size of the nominate race (from N Scandinavia and USSR) to be about 1.5 million, while that of the other E Atlantic populations (Greenland, Iceland, Britain, Ireland and Baltic basin) to be about 1 million (*BWP*). About half a million of the former spend the winter in Britain and Ireland. Population numbers have fluctuated over the period of census in the last 15 years, particularly further south in Europe. This may reflect variable breeding success in different years in Arctic areas.

Britain and Ireland are extremely important areas for Dunlins, holding about half of the W European mid winter population and probably many other individuals of E Atlantic populations during migrations.

M. W. PIENKOWSKI

Total number of squares in which recorded: 1,065 (28%)

No. of birds seen in a day	Number (%) of squares		
	Britain	Ireland	TOTAL (incl. C.I.)
1–90	425 (52%)	108 (44%)	535 (50%)
91–900	221 (27%)	97 (39%)	319 (30%)
901+	169 (21%)	41 (17%)	211 (20%)

References

HARDY, A. R. and C. D. T. MINTON. 1980. Dunlin migration in Britain and Ireland. *Bird Study* 27: 81–92.

PIENKOWSKI, M. W. and P. R. EVANS. 1984. Migratory behavior of shorebirds in the western Palearctic. Pp 73–123 in BURGER, J. and B. L. OLLA (eds). *Shorebirds: Migration and Foraging Behavior*. Plenum, New York and London.

PIENKOWSKI, M. W., C. S. LLOYD and C. D. T. MINTON. 1979. Seasonal and migrational weight changes in Dunlins *Calidris alpina*. *Bird Study* 26: 134–148.

PIENKOWSKI, M. W. and A. E. PIENKOWSKI. 1983. WSG project on the movement of wader populations in western Europe: eighth progress report. *Wader Study Group Bull.* 38: 13–22.

SYMONDS, F. L., D. R. LANGSLOW and M. W. PIENKOWSKI. 1984. Movements of wintering shorebirds within the Firth of Forth: species differences in usage of an intertidal complex. *Biol. Conserv.* 28: 187–215.

Breeding Atlas p 194

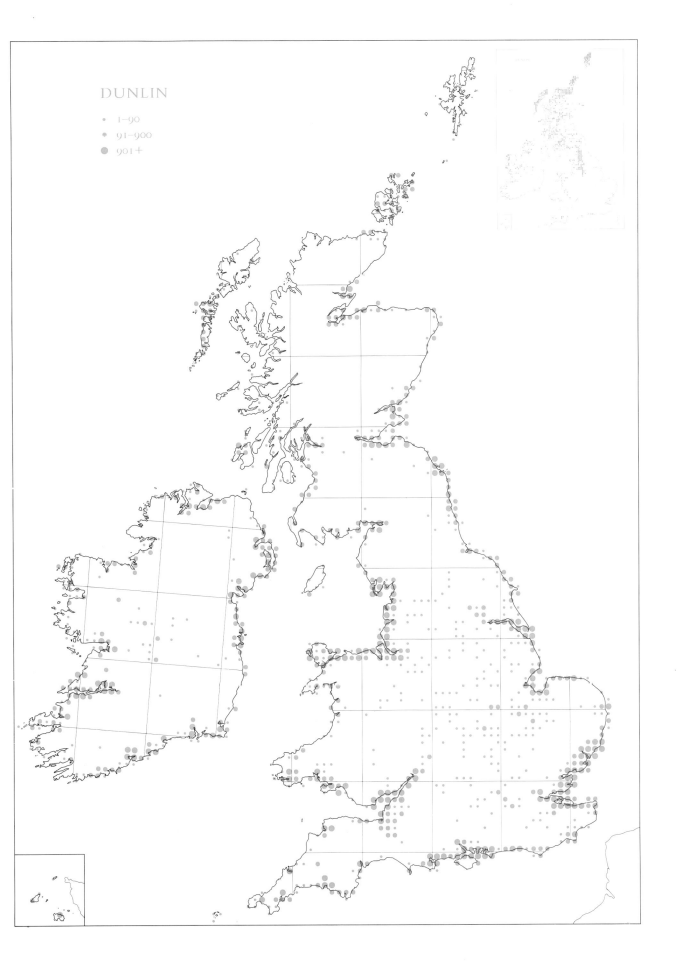

DUNLIN

- · 1–90
- · 91–900
- ● 901+

Ruff

Philomachus pugnax

The Ruff is a rare breeding bird in Britain and only small numbers winter in Britain and Ireland. The majority of Ruffs wintering here are males and the sexes tend to keep apart. They are difficult to find or count because of their frequent habit of feeding on flooded fields during the day, returning to their main haunts at dusk. They can easily be overlooked altogether, because some individuals can suggest characteristics of other wader species of similar size, with which they tend to associate.

The winter distribution is very thinly spread over most of Britain and Ireland. Though the Ruff is not really an estuary bird, the majority of the birds are found on or near the coast. The main concentrations are along the south coast and the eastern side of England. Except for a small concentration in Lancashire and Cheshire the distribution is sparse along the west coast of England and Wales. The E Midlands of Britain seems to support the majority of inland birds. Other than the Ouse Washes there are only three important inland sites. The Firth of Forth is the only regular site in Scotland, but Ruffs occur infrequently along the north and west coasts of Scotland, and in Orkney, but are absent from Shetland. There is a very thin spread throughout Ireland, with almost half on or near the south coast, particularly the Shannon Estuary and Cork Harbour.

The Ruffs wintering in Britain and Ireland are usually found singly or in small groups, in contrast with vast flocks in the main wintering areas in Africa. Ruffs are both nocturnal and daytime feeders and are often found feeding in or near the muddy margins of lakes or pools. They may be seen probing with their relatively short bills into the mud of mining subsidence flashes or the soft soil of flooded meadows. They pick items from the surface of the ground, or from clumps of grassy vegetation in fields where their favoured insect larvae foods can be found most easily. On the coast they often feed on the wetland areas behind sea walls, but also occur regularly on the seashores and tidal mudflats. At times of freezing temperatures they can be forced on to these estuarine areas to feed on crustaceans and molluscs, etc.

Ruffs in Britain and Ireland are probably part of a small wintering population that lies within western and southwestern Europe (Prater 1973). Some birds stay here throughout the winter. However, severe weather conditions can cause large scale movements to areas where food can still be obtained. Birds staying within a given locality can be very mobile, moving upwards of 30 km during the course of the day. An overwintering Ruff has been recovered during the breeding season near Yakutsk, USSR, which indicates that some of the birds can come from as far as eastern Siberia.

Because Britain and Ireland lie on the northern edge of the wintering grounds large fluctuations in numbers can be expected from year to year, or from month to month, depending on weather conditions. The Ruff was first recorded wintering in Britain as recently as 1934/35 and since then the numbers have shown a steady increase.

Prater (1973) estimated that the population was about 1,200 in 1966–1971. Comparing his map of England and Wales with the *Winter Atlas*, shows that this increase may be continuing, especially in central and NE England. A comparison of the Birds of Estuaries Enquiry results of 670 Ruffs for the winter of 1982/83 (Salmon 1983), with the *Winter Atlas* map, shows that just over half the dots coincide. From these sources it is estimated that there was a maximum of about 1,400 Ruffs in Britain and Ireland during the Atlas years.

J. SORENSEN

Total number of squares in which recorded: 247 (6%)

No. of birds seen in a day	Number (%) of squares		
	Britain	Ireland	TOTAL (incl. C.I.)
1–2	109 (49%)	9 (36%)	118 (48%)
3–16	66 (30%)	13 (52%)	79 (32%)
17+	47 (21%)	3 (12%)	50 (20%)

References
PRATER, A. J. 1973. The wintering population of Ruffs in Britain and Ireland. *Bird Study* 21: 245–250.
SALMON, D. G. 1983. *Wildfowl and Wader Counts 1982–1983*. Wildfowl Trust, Slimbridge.

Breeding Atlas p 196

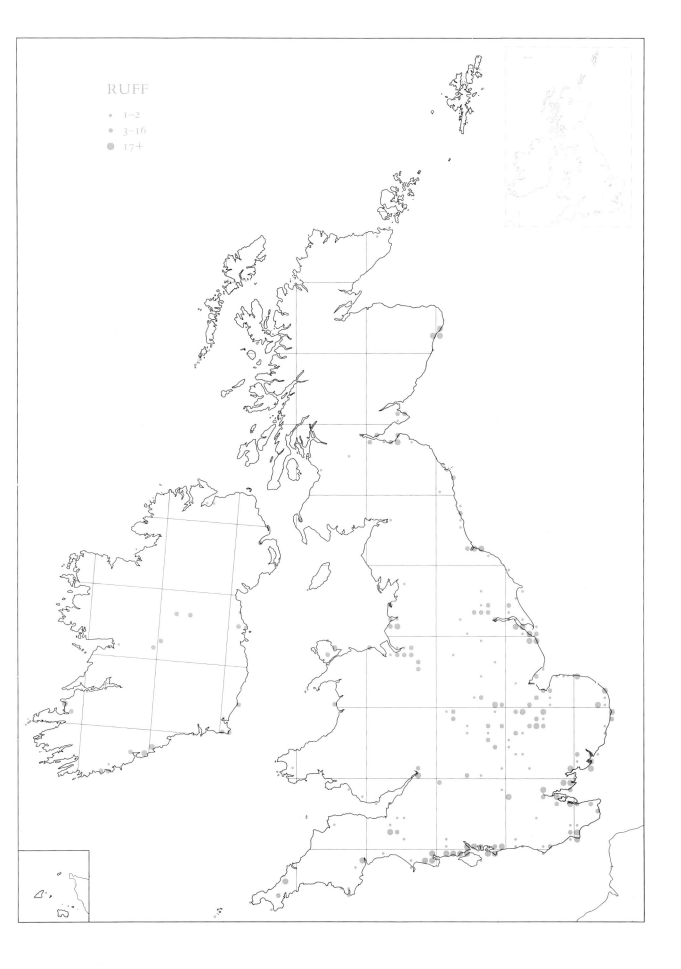

RUFF

- 1–2
- 3–16
- 17+

Jack Snipe

Lymnocryptes minimus

The Jack Snipe is a smaller relative of the Common Snipe *Gallinago gallinago*, and one of its vernacular names is the delightful 'Half Snipe'. The two species are similar in some aspects of their habitat preferences, feeding behaviour, morphology and plumage, but distinctly different in others. It is probably more common than is generally realised, for it is unobtrusive. It remains more or less silent in winter. Before the moment of flushing, the bird will lie prone, relying on its effectively cryptic plumage to escape detection. If directly disturbed, as when almost trodden on, one of its particular characteristics is to erupt suddenly from the ground. The typically short, direct escape flight, somewhat hesitating in nature, ends with a sudden return to the ground with wings closed.

South of 55°N the Jack Snipe is a visitor or passage bird, and on migration and during the winter is less gregarious than the Common Snipe, usually occurring singly or in twos and threes. The winter distribution map shows that it occurs at many widely scattered sites, but this is not a complete record since inevitably the species has been under-recorded. Direct disturbance is almost essential to reveal presence, and the species may be locally abundant. Although the map shows that it is largely absent from the moorland and mountainous regions of Britain and Ireland, many of the gaps on lower ground cannot be taken as indicating total absence of the species.

Outside the breeding season the Jack Snipe frequents shallow, wet and muddy habitats, preferring rather more cover than its relative. It is, nevertheless, a ground bird and avoids open, deep or saline water.

The Jack Snipe feeds in dense grass and low cover, taking a diet of larvae and adults of many insects, molluscs, worms and plant material, particularly seeds. As with other snipe it feeds by probing in soft ground, sometimes bobbing up and down. In addition Jack Snipe may feed from the surface. The fact that it feeds more on the surface and takes a greater proportion of plant material than the Common Snipe may be related to its relatively shorter bill. Again, its greater use of plant material may help it to manage better than the Common Snipe in severe weather, for several observers have noted it retains better condition during harsh weather than its larger relative (Vesey-FitzGerald 1946). The Jack Snipe has also been observed tapping the ground with its bill, apparently to bring springtails to the surface (Johnsgard 1981).

The species appears to be mainly nocturnal or crepuscular. It roosts solitarily, usually in its area feeding unless the weather is frosty. Commonly, it lands a few metres away from its roost and then approaches along a habitual winding path.

The Jack Snipe winters mainly in western and southern Europe and northern Africa. Throughout this area it is somewhat thinly distributed, but the largest numbers are probably in the western maritime countries, including Britain, Ireland and the Iberian peninsula. All recoveries have been of birds ringed in the winter or on passage, and this has resulted in there being rather limited information on its movements in relation to its breeding areas. The general pattern, however, is for a broad southwesterly movement across Europe in autumn, starting in the second half of August, reaching the northern and eastern coasts of Britain in mid September, peaking in October and lasting through November. The return passage occurs mainly in April.

Inevitably there is rather little information on the Jack Snipe's population size and status. Few countries have produced any estimates of breeding pairs, and for the winter non-breeding population there are few reliable data, largely because the species is so readily overlooked. Some indications are available from sportsmens' bags, however, since the proportion of Jack Snipe in the total snipe bag gives some indication of its relative abundance. The British Association for Shooting and Conservation has estimated that some 10,000 Jack Snipe were being shot annually by its members in the early 1980s, based on a sample of 1,541 birds from throughout the country, in which there was one Jack Snipe for every 8 Common Snipe. With a probable wintering population of Common Snipe in Britain and Ireland totalling many hundreds of thousands, it is thus possible that the corresponding winter population of Jack Snipe is as many as 100,000. However, the counts recorded in the *Winter Atlas* fieldwork suggested a much smaller number. There is no information on whether the population of this elusive species has changed but its numbers must relate to the availability of suitable marshy habitats.

J. HARRADINE

Total number of squares in which recorded: 788 (20%)

No. of birds seen in a day	Number (%) of squares		
	Britain	Ireland	TOTAL (incl. C.I.)
1	352 (55%)	91 (61%)	444 (56%)
2–3	183 (29%)	40 (27%)	223 (28%)
4+	101 (16%)	18 (12%)	121 (15%)

References

JOHNSGARD, P. A. 1981. *The Plovers, Sandpipers and Snipes of the World*. University of Nebraska Press, Lincoln and London.

VESEY-FITZGERALD, B. 1946. *British Game*. Collins, London.

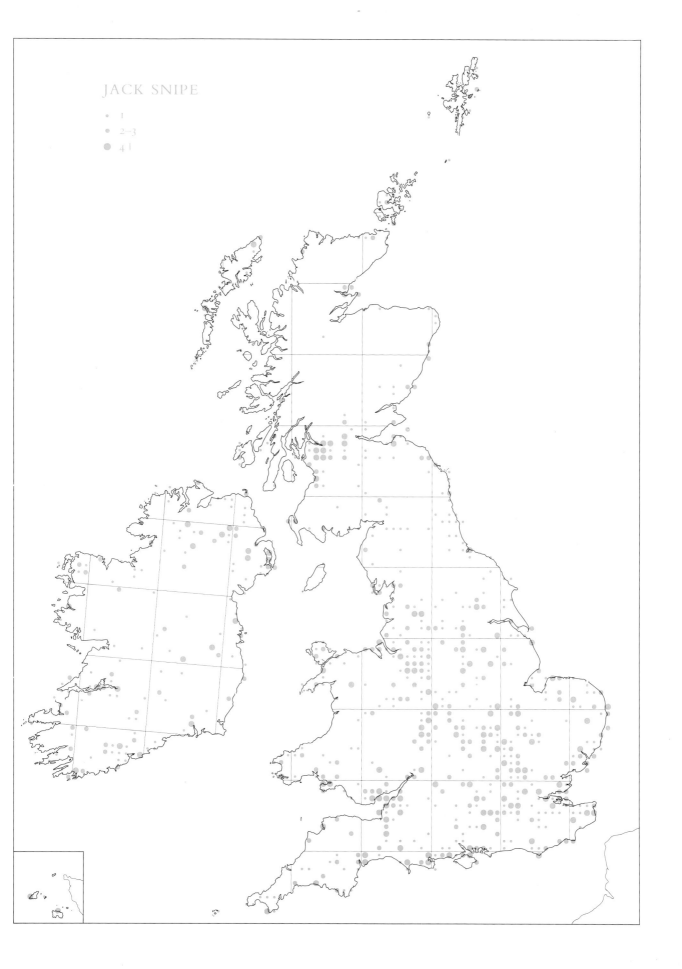

JACK SNIPE

- 1
- 2–3
- 4

Snipe

Gallinago gallinago

Common Snipe visit inland and coastal marshes, bogs and stream sides during the winter. Their long bill, erratic flight and rasping 'scaap' call single them out and give them a special place in the countryside. Their distribution in winter is determined by suitable habitats, as well as migration routes and weather. The habitats where Snipe breed in these islands almost invariably attract larger numbers during the winter. Outside the breeding season, Snipe can also be found on temporary small, wet areas.

The winter map reflects a widespread distribution, resulting from both the southward movement of birds fledged in northern parts of Britain and Ireland, and the arrival of overseas migrants. Their association with lowland areas in southern Britain and the bogs of southern Ireland is clear.

A large proportion of the Snipe which winter in Britain originate from countries around the Baltic Sea. In late summer, autumn and early winter such birds move southwest through Denmark. Some cross the North Sea into southern Britain whilst the remainder follow the European coast, through the Low Countries into France, Iberia and even North Africa. Those which arrive in Britain either winter here, continue to Ireland or cross the Channel into France. Recoveries of ringed Snipe show a strong loyalty by individuals to particular migration routes and winter quarters. Severe weather encourages birds to move south and west. Ireland and W and N Scotland receive birds from Iceland and the Faeroes.

Feeding occurs mainly during the first half of the night and at dawn. During the day most Snipe rest and preen on the water's edge if undisturbed or in cover. At dusk, Snipe gather at traditional sites which can, typically, be a wet *Juncus* bog. Here they will feed actively again, but before dawn most will have dispersed to day-time feeding or roosting areas.

Snipe are catholic in their winter diet. A considerable amount of vegetable matter and seeds may be ingested, but whether this is incidental to eating earthworms and tipulid larvae is not clear. Certainly, Snipe will take a wide range of soil invertebrate fauna, including beetles and flies and their respective larvae. The effect, however, is that as winter progresses, Snipe increase their body weight by as much as 20–25% by laying down a thick layer of fat. This not only helps to keep them warm but serves as a food reserve when the ground is frozen.

When cold weather strikes, Snipe can be quick to respond. Most birds move rapidly south and west to escape the adverse conditions. A small number, however, try to stick it out. They take to feeding on the margins of streams and rivers where the ground has yet to freeze. The extra fat that they have laid down will last them about a week. When the thaw arrives and they are able to return to their normal feeding areas, they are quick to put that weight back on again—perhaps within a fortnight.

In February and March, birds which have moved into the south and west start returning to the east and north, re-occupying their normal breeding grounds by mid May.

Estimates of the autumn and winter population in northwestern Europe are difficult to make, but it has been estimated that 20–30 million birds pass through northwestern Europe in the late summer (Hepburn 1984). For Britain and Ireland an indication is given by the size of the sportsmen's annual bag. Since at least 85,000 are estimated to be shot each year (Harradine 1983), the wintering population must be many hundreds of thousands. Their behaviour makes them easily overlooked until disturbed.

With respect to population changes, a decline was noted in Britain and Ireland in the early 19th century but there was a subsequent increase and range expansion in the first part of the 20th century. Some local declines and range extensions occurred between the 1940s and 1960s. Since then there has been no evidence of any significant change in the main centres of breeding population located in the north and west of Britain and in Ireland (*Breeding Atlas*). In southern Britain, however, breeding populations have probably been affected by loss of suitable habitats due to drainage and land improvements for agriculture (Smith 1983).

J. SWIFT

Total number of squares in which recorded: 2,929 (76%)

No. of birds seen in a day	Number (%) of squares		
	Britain	Ireland	TOTAL (incl. C.I.)
1–8	1,025 (49%)	478 (57%)	1,505 (51%)
9–36	593 (28%)	244 (29%)	837 (29%)
37+	466 (22%)	121 (14%)	589 (20%)

References

HARRADINE, J. 1983. Sport shooting in the United Kingdom: some facts and figures. Pp 63–83 in LEEUWENBERG, F. J. and I. R. HEPBURN, (eds). *Proc. 2nd Mtg. Working Group on Game Statistics, Zoetermeer, 1982.*

HEPBURN, I. R. 1984. *Migratory Bird Hunting in European Community Countries.* FACE Commission on Migratory Birds. Unpub. report.

SMITH, K. W. 1983. The status and distribution of waders breeding on wet lowland grasslands in England and Wales. *Bird Study* 30: 177–192.

Breeding Atlas p 174

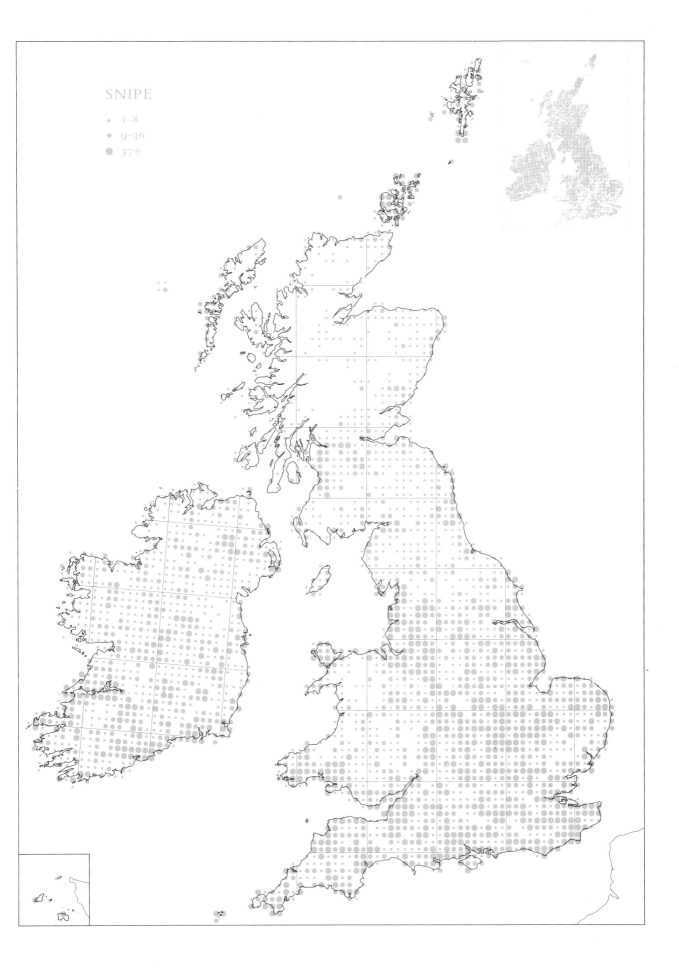

SNIPE

- 1–8
- 9–36
- 37+

Woodcock

Scolopax rusticola

The Woodcock, although related to the waders, is physically and behaviourally adapted to a woodland existence. Its cryptic colouration blends perfectly with the leaf or needle litter of the woodland floor. Large eyes, set well back in the head, confer all round vision. Short, strong legs allow it to spring rapidly into the air, whereafter large, rounded wings permit a fast escape, either directly up through the canopy, or by weaving acrobatically between the tree trunks.

It is a secretive species, usually solitary in its habits and visibly active only at dawn and dusk. These attributes combine to make Woodcocks hard to locate and have therefore contributed to an under-recording of its distribution and an underestimate of numbers. Nevertheless, the map shows the species to be generally distributed over much of Britain and Ireland, with the notable exception of high ground in Scotland and N England. During severe winters birds may move away to Ireland or SW Europe.

The species' wider distribution in winter by comparison with the *Breeding Atlas* is consistent with its use of a wider range of woodland types and age classes. This includes the vast areas of new forest plantation in Scotland, Wales and Ireland, scrub (*eg* the Burren in Co. Clare) and even relatively open areas such as bracken or heather covered hillsides, moorlands and hedgerows, particularly in W Ireland.

The reasons for the abundance of Woodcocks on the east and west coasts of Britain are not clear, but there may be several causes. A mild autumn gives rise to a protracted period of autumn migration, with Woodcocks still arriving in the west of Ireland in mid December (Wilson 1982a). Cold weather in Europe moves Woodcocks normally wintering further north and east, into Britain first, and then to Ireland if the severe weather is prolonged, and more birds are then found on the coast, especially the saltings.

Hirons (1982) and Wilson (1982a and b) with ringing and radio-telemetry studies have shown that Woodcocks are faithful to their wintering areas. They roost in small areas (0.6–8.1 ha) of cover within woodland by day, and at dusk fly to nearby fields (5.5–40.0 ha in area) where they alternate between

bouts of feeding, principally on earthworms, and roosting. Throughout the winter period, Woodcocks regularly leave the woodland 8–63 minutes after sunset and return 72–19 minutes before sunrise. Adult Woodcocks tend to fly furthest and usually at lower light intensities than first year birds. Their behaviour only alters markedly during periods of severe weather. In woodland cover during the day they become more active, presumably feeding. At night they are unsettled and restless, moving from field to field for up to 3–4 hours until they find an unfrozen feeding area, usually a spring or ditch where they spend the rest of the night.

The wintering population comprises migrants from Norway, Sweden and Finland principally (Alexander 1946), but with a suggestion that significant numbers of Russian Woodcocks may winter also.

Reliable censusing techniques have not been developed for Woodcocks, hence an estimate of the overwintering population of both islands is not possible. It is undoubtedly large, because the Game Conservancy's National Game Census gave an average 0.88–7.25 Woodcocks bagged annually per km², and the annual estimated bag for Britain is around 200,000 birds (Tapper and Hirons 1983). The mild oceanic climate of Britain and Ireland, particularly of the western extremities, provides the ideal overwintering conditions for migratory Woodcocks from NW Europe, with Ireland of particular strategic importance during severe winters.

H. J. WILSON

Total number of squares in which recorded: 2,237 (58%)

No. of birds seen in a day	Number (%) of squares		
	Britain	Ireland	TOTAL (incl. C.I.)
1	891 (51%)	258 (55%)	1,149 (51%)
2–3	556 (31%)	126 (27%)	682 (30%)
4+	315 (18%)	87 (19%)	406 (18%)

References

ALEXANDER, W. B. 1946. The woodcock in the British Isles. *Ibis* 88: 271–286, 427–444.

HIRONS, G. J. M. 1982. The diet and behaviour of the Woodcock *Scolopax rusticola* in winter. *Proc. 14 Int. Congr. of Game Biologists.* Dublin: 233–238.

TAPPER, S. C. and G. J. M. HIRONS. 1983. Recent trends in woodcock bags in Britain. Pp 132–137 in KALCHREUTER, H. (ed.). *Second European Woodcock and Snipe Workshop.* IWRB, England.

WILSON, H. J. 1982a. Wintering site fidelity of Woodcock *Scolopax rusticola* in Ireland. *Proc. 14 Int. Congr. of Game Biologists.* Dublin: 219–231.

WILSON, H. J. 1982b. Movements, home-ranges and habitat use of wintering woodcock in Ireland. Pp 168–178 in DWYER, T. J. and G. L. STORM. (eds). *Woodcock Ecology and Management.* Wildlife Research Report 14, United States Department of the Interior, Washington D.C.

Breeding Atlas p 176

WOODCOCK

- · 1
- ● 2–3
- ● 4+

Black-tailed Godwit

Limosa limosa

Tall, elegant and gregarious, Black-tailed Godwits have a much more limited distribution in Britain and Ireland than the more widespread but decidedly drabber Bar-tailed Godwits *L. lapponica*.

The Black-tailed Godwits which winter in Britain and Ireland are of the Icelandic breeding race *L. l. islandica*. Some birds may nest in northern Scotland, and there is a noticeable passage from the end of June onwards as birds move south to winter in Britain, Ireland, France and probably Iberia. Most of Europe's breeding birds are of the nominate race *L. l. limosa* which winter mainly in West Africa north of the equator; a small number breed in England, mainly in East Anglia, and there may be a small passage, but few if any winter.

The main concentrations in winter, as in autumn, are on the estuaries of the south coasts of Ireland and England, inland in the Shannon valley, on the Stour and Hamford Water in eastern England and on the Ribble and Dee in NW England. The preferred estuaries are muddy, and where Black-tailed Godwits occur at the same sites as Bar-tailed Godwits they are usually found feeding on the inner estuary where the sediments are finer, while the Bar-tailed Godwits prefer sandier banks on the outer estuary. Black-tailed Godwits form relatively tight flocks while feeding, normally separate from other waders, though sometimes with Redshanks *Tringa totanus*. Although there have not been many studies of winter diet, Black-tailed Godwits appear to feed largely on worms at this season. Lugworms and ragworms are favourites on the Ribble (Hale 1980) and earthworms inland in France (*BWP*), though a current Irish study indicates that *Hydrobia* and small bivalves are important at Clonakilty estuary. When high tide covers the coastal feeding zone they fly to roosts, normally on damp pasture but often on reclaimed land and only rarely on stony shores. Frequently they fly several kilometres inland to suitable pasture. In western Ireland, flocks of several hundred birds winter on flooded pastures at sites in the River Shannon valley and on the edge of a few lakes; these show up well on the map. Here they occur close to large numbers of Icelandic Golden Plovers *Pluvialis apricaria*, though mixed flocks are unusual.

Black-tailed Godwits occur in peak numbers in the period from mid August to mid September. In Britain there is a fall in numbers in October, but this is far less marked in Ireland where numbers at most sites are not much lower in December than in autumn.

There is an increase in S and SW England after low numbers in November, but the reason is unknown (Prater 1981). From January onwards, Black-tailed Godwits decrease on the Irish south coast and assemble on the Shannon estuary (where over 16,000 have been counted in April) and on the Little Brosna in the Shannon valley (up to 4,600 in February). Except for the cold winter of 1962/63, when Black-tailed Godwits were scarce in S and SW England, there was a steady and sustained increase in numbers in Britain from the early 1930s, when less than 100 wintered, to the mid 1970s (Prater 1975), and a considerable increase was also noted in Ireland (Ruttledge 1966). This increase in wintering numbers was attributed to higher breeding numbers in Iceland and followed climatic amelioration. From the mid 1960s, a cooling of the spring climate was noted and a decline in wintering numbers was predicted (Prater 1975). This followed, and after the early 1970s the decline was rapid, the population reaching its nadir in 1977/78 in Britain when only 20% of the numbers wintering in 1972/73 were counted (Marchant 1981). Since then, there has been a steady recovery in Britain and numbers in Ireland appear to be holding up well.

The winter population in Ireland was estimated at about 8,000–10,000 birds in the years 1971–75 (Hutchinson 1979); in Britain there are presently perhaps another 4,000–5,000 (Birds of Estuaries Enquiry reports). There are no more recent estimates of numbers in Ireland.

C. D. HUTCHINSON

Total number of squares in which recorded: 246 (6%)

No. of birds seen in a day	Number (%) of squares		
	Britain	Ireland	TOTAL (incl. C.I.)
1–4	90 (60%)	31 (33%)	122 (50%)
5–120	38 (25%)	37 (39%)	75 (30%)
121+	23 (15%)	26 (28%)	49 (20%)

References

HALE, W. G. 1980. *Waders*. Collins, London.

MARCHANT, J. H. (ed.). 1981. *Birds of Estuaries Enquiry 1976–77 to 1978–79*. BTO, Tring.

PRATER, A. J. 1975. The wintering population of the Black-tailed Godwit. *Bird Study* 22: 169–176.

RUTTLEDGE, R. F. 1966. *Ireland's Birds*. Witherby, London.

Breeding Atlas p 182

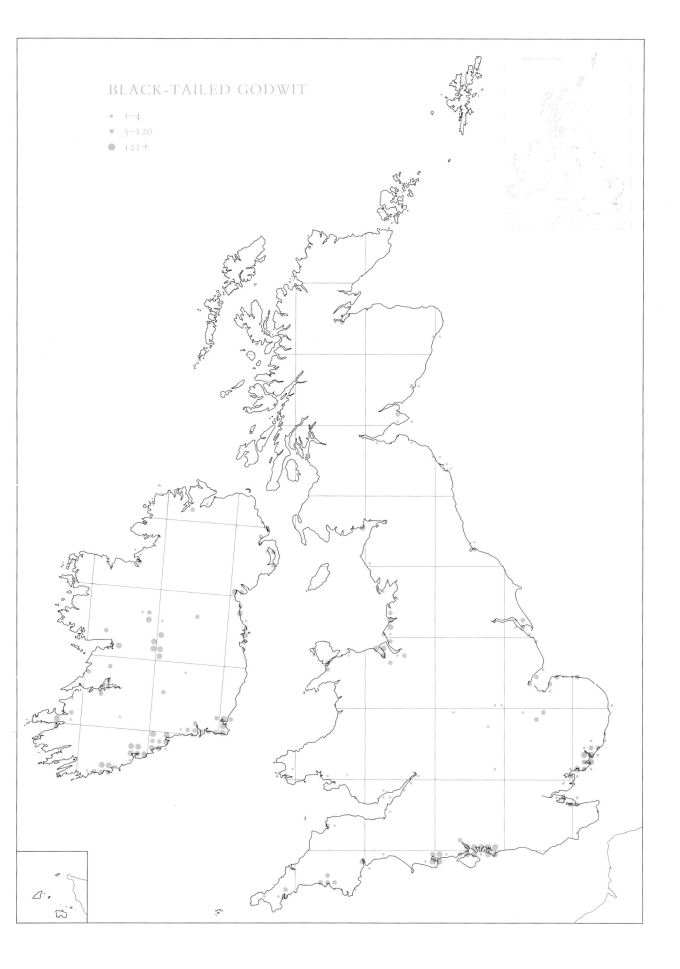

BLACK-TAILED GODWIT

· 1–4
· 5–120
● 121+

Bar-tailed Godwit

Limosa lapponica

There can be few finer sights at the coast on a clear winter's day than the arrival of a flock of Bar-tailed Godwits (or 'speethes' as the old Northumbrian wildfowlers used to call them) at their high water roost. They often fly many kilometres from their feeding grounds to a safe and isolated sandbar or shingle spit, which they may approach from a great height, gliding gently downwards until they arrive over the roost, when they plummet erratically earthwards, as though shot, before braking and landing so gently, one after another, that one marvels at their co-ordination.

The winter distribution of this species is almost entirely coastal; indeed, it is rare to find birds feeding even just inland of coastal sea defences. Unlike other waders which are restricted entirely to intertidal feeding areas (*eg* Sanderling *Calidris alba*), Bar-tailed Godwits may be found both on sandy and muddy shores, so they are more generally distributed along the North Sea coasts of Britain, as well as in NW England, the Outer Hebrides and Ireland. Fewer occur along the coasts of southern England and the Bristol Channel than might have been expected, though their absence from the largely cliff-bound coasts of SW England, W Wales and western Scotland is not surprising.

In more sandy areas, godwits feed preferentially on the largest worms they can find, notably the lugworm. These they hunt visually, waiting until a worm backs up its L-shaped burrow to defaecate at the sand surface, then running forward to probe into the newly formed worm cast. Because the horizontal gallery of the lugworm's burrow usually lies too deep for even the long bill of the godwits to reach, the birds must react quickly to the sign that a worm is near the surface. Often they are slightly late and break the worm as they try to extract it. On muddier estuaries, from which lugworms may be absent, Bar-tailed Godwits take other polychaetes, such as the ragworm, as well as the bivalve *Macoma balthica*. At the lowest levels of the intertidal zone, the sand-mason worm may be an important prey.

Bar-tailed Godwits normally feed in flocks at the tide edge, the larger females (with their longer bills and legs) feeding in deeper water than the smaller males. By following the retreating and advancing tides, they track the zones in which their prey are most active and therefore conspicuous. In cold conditions, when lugworms and ragworms become less active, the godwits feed more by touch, probing for the smaller worms which lie just below the surface, within reach of their long bills.

The breeding areas from which Bar-tailed Godwits migrate to winter in Britain and Ireland include arctic Russia and western and central Siberia. Large flocks gather in August to moult on the Wash and the Ribble, but once they have grown new flight feathers (by late October), many leave these estuaries, some from the Wash moving northwards along the east coast of England. Others continue to arrive in eastern England throughout late autumn and early winter, many from the Dutch Wadden Sea, and numbers increase in NW England and Ireland in the same period. Peak numbers are reached in some northern estuaries (*eg* Firth of Forth) as late as February in most years, just before the large exodus of birds from Britain to the Wadden Sea, where they moult into breeding plumage before departing for the Arctic in May.

The number wintering in Britain and Ireland was estimated at nearly 60,000 in the mid 1970s, but has fluctuated considerably since then, partly (it is supposed) in response to fluctuations in breeding success in the Arctic, but certainly in relation to the severity of the winter conditions in the Wadden Sea. The total western European wintering numbers have been estimated at over 100,000, but another 600,000 winter along the coast of NW Africa, chiefly on the Banc d'Arguin in Mauritania. (The eastern Siberian race *Limosa lapponica baueri* winters in SE Asia and Australasia).

P. R. EVANS

Total number of squares in which recorded: 560 (15%)

No. of birds seen in a day	Number (%) of squares		
	Britain	Ireland	TOTAL (incl. C.I.)
1–18	201 (52%)	82 (47%)	284 (51%)
19–175	102 (26%)	62 (36%)	164 (29%)
176+	81 (21%)	30 (17%)	112 (20%)

References

EVANS, P. R. 1979. Adaptations shown by foraging shorebirds to their intertidal invertebrate prey. Pp 357–366 in NAYLOR, E. and R G. HARTNOLL (eds). *Cyclic Phenomena in Marine Plants and Animals*. Pergamon Press, Oxford.

SMITH, P. C. 1975. *The Winter Feeding Ecology and Behaviour of the Bar-tailed Godwit*. Ph.D. Thesis, University of Durham.

SMITH, P. C. and P. R. EVANS. 1973. Feeding ecology and behaviour of the Bar-tailed Godwit. *Wildfowl* 24: 135–139.

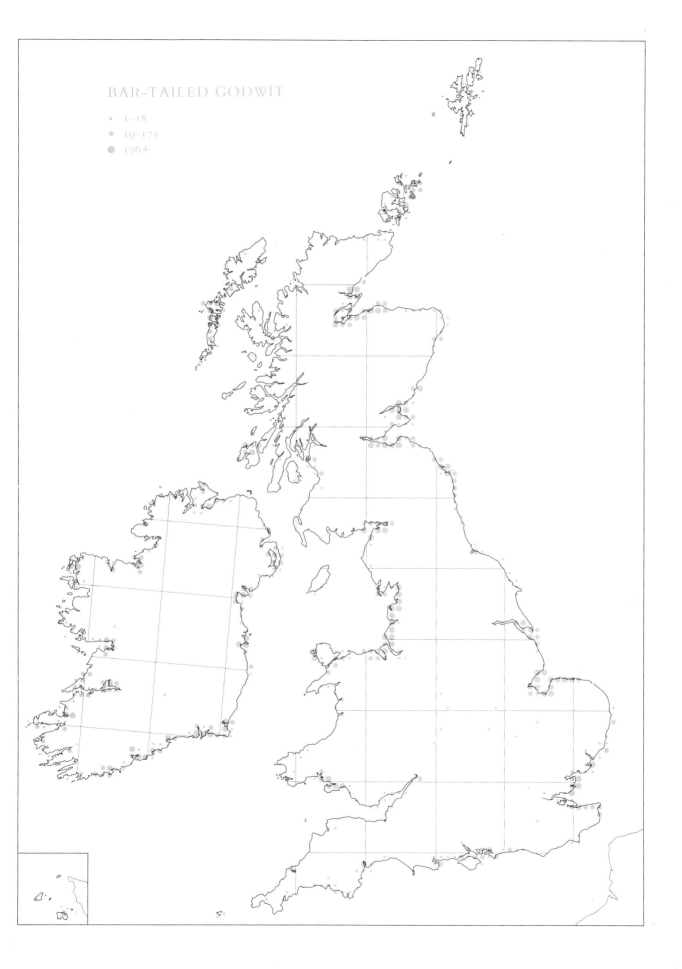

BAR-TAILED GODWIT

- 1–18
- 19–175
- 176+

Whimbrel

Numenius phaeopus

The Whimbrel is a familiar coastal bird in spring and autumn, identifiable from afar by its rippling call. Although superficially very similar to the Curlew *N. arquata*, the smaller size and shorter, more sharply curved bill are distinctive features when the two species are seen together.

The main wintering area of the nominate race which breeds in Europe is Africa south of the Sahara, and very few are known to winter in Europe (*BWP*). The number of squares in which they were recorded is, therefore, surprising. Not so surprising is their concentration in the milder south and southwest, broadly delineated by the 6°C January isotherm. Whimbrels were considered to be rare in winter in Ireland up to 1965, with only about 10 records (Ruttledge 1966), but from the mid 1960s it became clear that a few wintered every year in Cork Harbour and occasionally elsewhere in Co. Cork. There is no evidence that there was any change in status: the increase in records coincided with, and almost certainly resulted from, an increase in interest in waders in Ireland. Similarly, the rather widespread series of records on the map cannot be considered to represent an increase in wintering: in the past, no serious attempt was made to visit all the likely wintering areas.

Whimbrels occur in estuaries, on salt marshes at coastal lagoons and on rocky shores. In winter they tend to be solitary. As would be expected for such a scarce wintering bird there have been no studies of feeding behaviour in Europe at this season. In spring and autumn a wide variety of prey has been recorded including molluscs, crustaceans and polychaete worms (*BWP*). Temperature, and not a scarcity of these prey items, appears to be the factor limiting numbers occurring in winter.

The *Breeding Atlas* showed a small population of under 200 pairs centred on Shetland and the Outer Hebrides, but there are about 300 pairs on Shetland now (Berry and Johnston 1980). These birds have shown sensitivity to climatic change, declining in numbers with climatic amelioration and increasing with the cold springs and early summers since the early 1950s. Two birds ringed in Shetland in summer have been recovered in Ghana, so it is known that some, if not all, of the British breeding population winters in Africa. Birds ringed in Britain on passage in autumn have been recovered on their breeding grounds in Finland and the USSR. The origin of our wintering birds is at least as likely to be passage birds from the Continent remaining, as to be Scottish bred birds.

Spring passage of Whimbrels is concentrated on the south coast from mid April and reaches a peak in late April and early May. Up to 3,300 have been counted moving north over Cork Harbour (Pierce and Wilson 1980), and a roost of 1,500–2,000 is recorded at Steart Island in Somerset (Prater 1981). These numbers are much below the roosts of up to 30,000 which have been recorded in spring in the Netherlands, West Germany and Belgium. The birds have almost all moved on by the end of May. Autumn passage begins in July, reaching a peak in August and declining through September. Numbers on the North Sea coast and in southern England are higher in autumn than in spring, the reverse of the situation in western Britain and Ireland, where the spring passage is so marked (Prater 1981).

As a wintering bird in Britain and Ireland the Whimbrel is scarce, the total probably being less than 30 in any one year. There is no evidence of any change in winter status.

C. D. HUTCHINSON

Total number of squares in which recorded: 41 (1%)

No. of birds seen in a day	Number (%) of squares		
	Britain	Ireland	TOTAL (incl. C.I.)
1	17 (81%)	12 (67%)	31 (76%)
2	3 (14%)	5 (28%)	8 (20%)
3+	1 (5%)	1 (6%)	2 (5%)

References

BERRY, R. J. and J. L. JOHNSTON. 1980. *The Natural History of Shetland*. Collins, London.

PIERCE, S. and J. WILSON. 1980. Spring migration of Whimbrels in Cork Harbour. *Irish Birds* 1: 514–516.

RUTTLEDGE, R. F. 1966. *Ireland's Birds*. Witherby, London.

Breeding Atlas p 180.

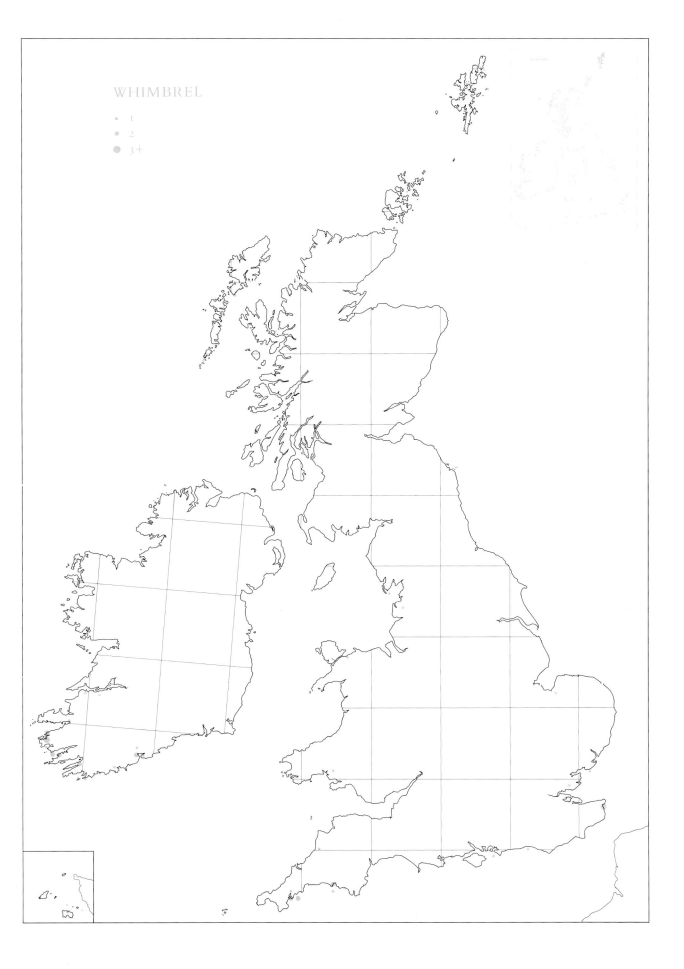

WHIMBREL

- 1
- 2
- 3+

Curlew

Numenius arquata

Curlews are perhaps the best known of our wintering waders; their haunting calls as they fly to high-tide roosts epitomise the wildness of our coasts in winter.

In Britain the map shows an essentially coastal distribution with the species present in a high proportion of the coastal squares. There are the expected concentrations on large muddy estuaries like Morecambe Bay and the Wash (which recorded the highest counts in the Birds of Estuaries Enquiry — Prater 1981), but the *Winter Atlas* has also revealed the importance of some of the Scottish islands for Curlews: for example, 18,000 birds were found in Orkney in 1983 (Tay and Orkney Ringing Group 1984), mostly on rocky shores, a habitat not covered by the Estuaries Enquiry.

In England and Wales, there are some areas inland which traditionally hold wintering flocks of Curlews. Concentrations of up to 1,000 birds are present in Cheshire and Shropshire, where they roost on industrial settling beds, and in much of the country small flocks can be found feeding in permanent pastures and roosting on wetlands or even moorland. In contrast the distribution in Ireland is far from coastal, with large numbers of Curlews wintering throughout the country, especially in the west. The Shannon Valley is particularly favoured with concentrations at the major inland loughs, and birds are widespread throughout Connacht as a whole. Elsewhere birds are found up to 50 km inland.

In Britain the Curlews' preferred winter habitat is the large estuarine mudflats, where they feed on worms such as ragworm, and crabs and molluscs. In early autumn, numbers at high tide roosts are at a peak, but they drop markedly as winter progresses. Bainbridge and Minton (1978) suggested that this decline coincided with the start of the shooting season, causing flocks to disperse inland. The removal of Curlews from the list of quarry species in the Wildlife and Countryside Act 1981 may therefore bring some changes in this winter behaviour. An alternative theory is that more birds feed inland in winter, when ragworms burrow deeper into estuarine mudflats. In particular, the short-billed male birds would be disadvantaged by this, and Elphick (1979) and Townshend (1981) found a high proportion of males wintering and feeding inland.

Curlews are faithful to their winter sites and it appears that most birds stay in one area from the start of the autumn moult through to the spring migration. Winter recoveries of 81% of birds ringed in winter were within 30 km of the ringing site (Bainbridge and Minton 1978), and only in the last five years have recoveries shown any indication of migration 'stopovers'. It is uncertain whether birds wintering inland are of local breeding stock; certainly many British birds migrate in a southwesterly direction, onto the west coast estuaries or into Ireland, with some southern breeders moving south into France or Iberia. Britain and Ireland also receive many Curlews in winter. Birds from the discrete coastal Norwegian population winter largely in Scotland, most Swedish and Finnish birds spread over the whole of Britain and Ireland, and Continental birds from Belgium to Russia occur in southern Britain, though their main wintering grounds are France and Iberia.

Prater (1981) estimated that 90,000 Curlews winter on the British and Irish estuaries and suggested a total wintering population of 125,000. However, the *Winter Atlas* counts suggest that perhaps 50,000 birds winter inland in Ireland and 5,000–7,000 inland in Britain. With the addition of a further 45,000 on the non-estuarine coasts of Britain (preliminary results of BTO/Wader Study Group Winter Shorebird count), a better estimate would be 200,000 birds. This represents well over half of the Curlews wintering on the European-African Atlantic flyway, and shows the exceptional importance of Britain and Ireland to Curlews in winter.

I. P. BAINBRIDGE

Total number of squares in which recorded: 2,198 (57%)

No. of birds seen in a day	Number (%) of squares		
	Britain	Ireland	TOTAL (incl. C.I.)
1–40	811 (57%)	293 (38%)	1,105 (50%)
41–209	351 (25%)	298 (39%)	652 (30%)
210 +	268 (19%)	172 (23%)	441 (20%)

References

BAINBRIDGE, I. P. and C. D. T. MINTON. 1978. The migration and mortality of the Curlew in Britain and Ireland. *Bird Study* 25 : 39–50.

ELPHICK, D. 1979. An inland flock of Curlews *Numenius arquata* in mid Cheshire, England. *Wader Study Group Bull.* 26 : 31–35.

TAY AND ORKNEY RINGING GROUPS. 1984. *The Shorebirds of the Orkney Islands.* Tay Ringing Group, Perth.

TOWNSHEND, D. J. 1981. The importance of field feeding to the survival of wintering male and female Curlews *Numenius arquata* on the Tees Estuary. Pp 261–273 in JONES, N. V. and W. J. WOLFF (eds). *Feeding and Survival Strategies in Estuarine Organisms.* Plenum Press, New York.

Breeding Atlas p 178

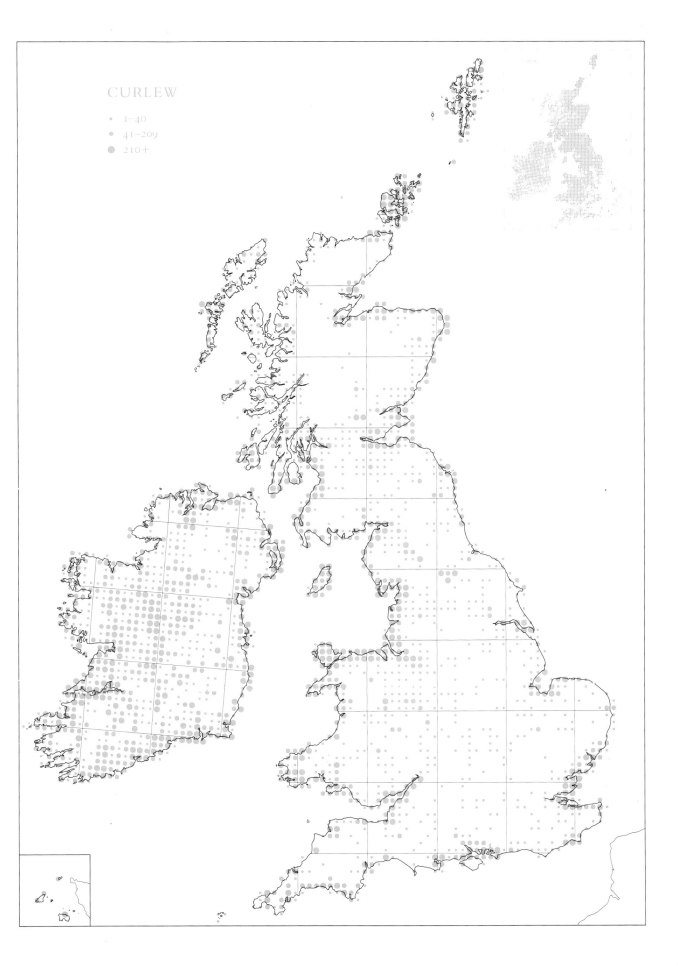

CURLEW

· 1–40
· 41–209
● 210+

Spotted Redshank

Tringa erythropus

The Spotted Redshank often first draws attention by its piercingly loud disyllabic call note, a rising 'chu-wit'. In winter its pale grey upperparts and white underparts distinguish it readily from its close relatives, even at a distance. It is a relatively scarce wader in Britain and Ireland in winter, much less numerous and widespread than at passage times.

Autumn passage birds occur fairly frequently at inland waters in Britain and Ireland, but in winter the Spotted Redshank is almost exclusively a coastal bird. During the *Winter Atlas* period, there were only 12 inland records in England and Wales of which 10 were of single birds. Coastal records are well-scattered around the coasts of England and Wales, although the scarcity in NW England is striking. In Scotland there were none in the west except for a single record from North Uist, and most wintering birds were on the outer Firth of Forth. Some sites held only a single bird, but there is a clear tendency for this species to winter in small groups. Particular concentrations occur on the N Kent and Essex estuaries, the Hampshire coast and SW Wales. Largest counts from the Birds of Estuaries Enquiry in most winters are from the Medway, where the peak was 25 birds in 1983/84, the Swale, the Beaulieu River and Milford Haven. Numbers in Ireland are smaller than in England and Wales but there are small concentrations around the Wexford Slobs, Cork Harbour and Galway Bay.

Winter habitat of Spotted Redshanks in Britain and Ireland is chiefly at estuaries which offer plenty of soft, silty mud. Sandy estuaries and open coasts are usually avoided. In some localities, as for example at Cley and Minsmere, the main habitat is shallow brackish coastal lagoons, but some individuals wintering in such places may commute to nearby estuarine mud at times.

The food of this species has been studied for passage birds in the Netherlands (Holthuijzen 1979). Main items in September were ragworms, shore-crabs, the goby *Potamochistus,* and *Corophium.* It is likely that the diet is similar in winter. Individual birds may be well scattered along creeks at low tide, but tend to assemble along the line of the incoming tide. The extraordinary behaviour of feeding flocks has been described by Taverner (1982). Scattered individuals may suddenly gather at a single spot and begin feeding frenziedly in a dense flock. Such behaviour always occurs in at least belly-deep water and flocks are often seen swimming and upending. Quiet quacking calls are given constantly. After perhaps 20 minutes or so, the concentration breaks up, sometimes re-forming, after an interval, at a new location. Feeding sites and prey rarely overlap with those of the Redshank *T. totanus.* Food species are largely similar to those of Greenshank *T. nebularia,* but the Spotted Redshank tends to select smaller items and feeds mostly in finer-grained mud.

Scandinavia is the nearest part of the breeding range and is the presumed origin of most of our passage and wintering birds, but there are as yet no ringing recoveries linking us with any part of the breeding range. It would seem that most wintering individuals arrive during the main period of autumn passage. Little is known of any movements within the winter period. There is a record of a single bird visiting Galway for 9 consecutive years, believed to be the same individual on each occasion.

The *Winter Atlas* map and counts for the Estuaries Enquiry suggest that, in most winters, between 80 and 200 Spotted Redshanks winter in Britain and Ireland. Probably fewer than 500 winter on the Atlantic coast of Europe as a whole. Numbers vary quite widely between years but there is no evidence of any recent trend in population size.

Spotted Redshanks nest in a broad band across Eurasia from Sweden to NE USSR, and winter mostly in Africa (but are scarce south of the equator), the Mediterranean basin, India and SE Asia. Those wintering in Britain and Ireland are the most northerly of all.

W. G. HALE and J. H. MARCHANT

Total number of squares in which recorded: 161 (4%)

No. of birds seen in a day	Number (%) of squares		TOTAL (incl. C.I.)
	Britain	Ireland	
1	82 (66%)	27 (73%)	109 (67%)
2	17 (14%)	5 (14%)	23 (14%)
3+	24 (20%)	5 (14%)	29 (19%)

References

HOLTHUIJZEN, Y. A. 1979. The food of the Spotted Redshank *Tringa erythropus* in the Dollard. *Limosa* 52: 22–33.
TAVERNER, J. H. 1982. Feeding behaviour of Spotted Redshank flocks. *Brit. Birds* 75: 333–334.

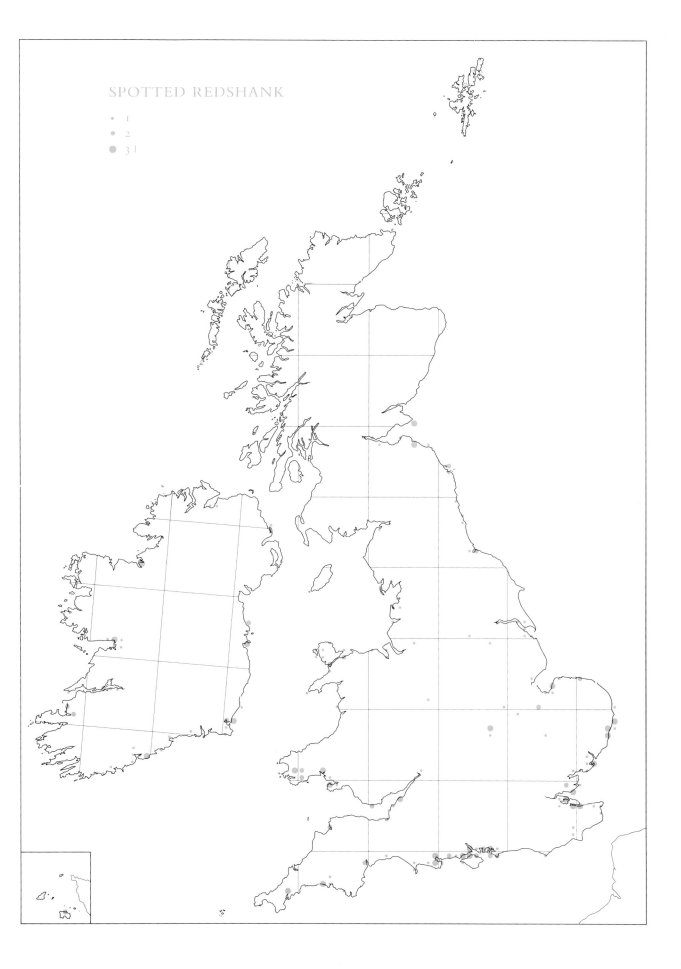

SPOTTED REDSHANK

- • 1
- • 2
- ● 3

Redshank

Tringa totanus

Throughout the year the Redshank's frequent calling attracts attention to its presence. A medium sized wader, it is immediately recognised in flight by the broad, white trailing edge to its wings, its white back and rump and usually bright red legs.

In comparison with the breeding season, the Redshank's winter distribution is more coastal, and it occurs along all the coasts of Britain and Ireland where there is suitable feeding habitat. Some Redshanks winter inland, this habit being commoner the further south one goes, but Redshanks remain inland in winter only so long as prolonged frosts do not affect the ground. When they can no longer feed they move to coastal areas.

During the winter, Redshanks occupy areas from which they are absent during the breeding season, such as the S coasts of Ireland, W Wales, Devon and Cornwall where they are common winter visitors.

Their winter food consists mainly of marine invertebrates collected on the mudflats, *Hydrobia*, *Corophium* and nereid worms being the chief food items, though away from the shore fresh water invertebrates and insects are taken. Their habit of feeding on the upper areas of the shore, which freeze more easily, means that Redshanks are more vulnerable than many other waders to spells of cold weather, and are amongst the commonest fatalities in such conditions.

Redshanks usually feed singly or in small groups. On smaller estuaries, particularly in the south of England, some individuals take up winter feeding territories which are defended against other Redshanks; on larger estuaries and in N Britain this is rare.

Ringing recoveries and observations on colour-marked Redshanks, show that the British and Irish breeding population is less migratory than any other, and many winter on the coastal areas on which they breed. In addition to hard weather movements there is probably considerable movement between estuaries. Colour marking has shown movements away from small estuaries in winter, probably in search of better food supplies, but usually other birds move in. Thus, the population of Redshanks on many smaller wintering areas appears stable but is probably

transitory. However, some birds visit the same wintering areas year after year, as shown by individual, wing-tagged Ribble breeding birds, which are known to winter regularly in Jersey, Devon and W Wales. In general juvenile birds tend to make longer migratory journeys than adults, and there is evidence to suggest that movement of the British breeding population is a slow drift south until January, with a more direct return journey north.

Hale (1984) suggested that hybridisation between previously separated populations has resulted in larger individuals which are better able to winter further north, and they constitute the British and Icelandic populations. Many Icelandic birds move into Britain and Ireland in winter and it is likely that the majority of our wintering birds are of Icelandic origin. There is also evidence of movement of Continental birds into Britain and Ireland, particularly during hard weather on the Continent. These are birds of the western European hybrid zone which have bred in Denmark, Holland and Belgium.

The wintering population of Ireland probably consists of Icelandic birds, of residents and many Scottish breeders, and some birds from the north of England.

The wintering population of Redshanks in Britain and Ireland has been estimated at approximately 95,000 (Prater 1981). The difficulties of counting wintering Redshanks probably leads to underestimates so our wintering population probably well exceeds 100,000 birds. Figures from the 15 years of the Birds of Estuaries Enquiry have shown a steady decline in the January population levels in Britain (BOEE reports). Declines have been particularly marked on some estuaries such as the Clyde.

As wintering areas Britain and Ireland are by far the most important in Europe, harbouring some 75% of the total. This is probably of the order of 15–20% of the world population of the species which almost certainly exceeds 500,000 birds and may well top the **million** mark.

W. G. HALE

Total number of squares in which recorded: 1,607 (42%)

No. of birds seen in a day	Number (%) of squares		
	Britain	Ireland	TOTAL (incl. C.I.)
1–14	611 (51%)	192 (49%)	805 (50%)
15–120	356 (29%)	123 (31%)	480 (30%)
121 +	243 (20%)	78 (20%)	322 (20%)

References

HALE, W. G. 1971. A revision of the taxonomy of the Redshank, *Tringa totanus*. *Zool. J. Linn. Soc.* 50 : 199–268.

HALE, W. G. 1973. The distribution of the Redshank in the winter range. *Zool. J. Linn. Soc.* 53 : 177–236.

HALE, W. G. 1980. *Waders*. Collins, London.

HALE, W. G. 1984. The changing face of European wintering areas. In EVANS, P. R., J. D. GOSS-CUSTARD and W. G. HALE. (eds). *Coastal Waders and Wildfowl in Winter*. University Press, Cambridge.

Breeding Atlas p 188

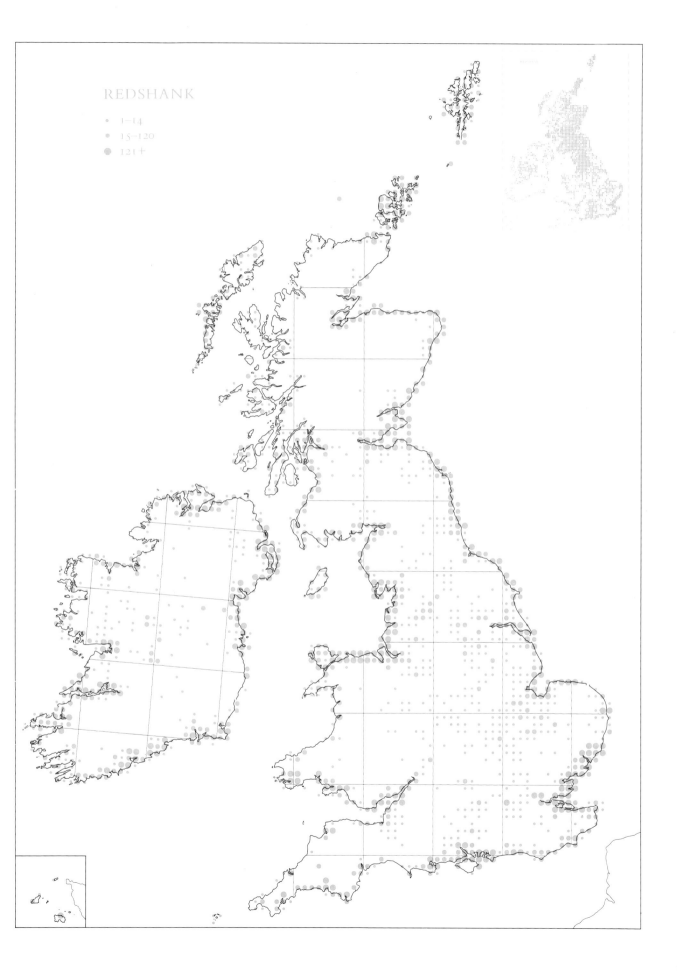

REDSHANK

- 1–14
- 15–120
- 121+

Greenshank

Tringa nebularia

The shrill 'tew-tew-tew' call of the Greenshank is the most obvious indication of its presence on estuaries or small creeks in winter. The birds themselves in their grey and white plumage are inconspicuous against the mud, but they take flight readily, flashing white rump and dark wings, and calling repeatedly.

The winter distribution in Britain and Ireland is predominantly westerly, with perhaps three-quarters in Ireland. One of the most striking features of the map is the extent of the distribution. Very few Greenshanks winter in eastern Britain, but in SW England, Wales and western Scotland Greenshanks are found in small numbers on many estuaries. In Ireland they are found almost anywhere there is a stretch of mud, except on the east coast south of Dublin and on the northeast coast. The principal winter Greenshank localities in Britain and Ireland in 1969–75 were mapped by Prater (1981) and concentrations of over 25 were recorded for 6 estuaries, 5 of which were in Ireland.

The Greenshank's summer distribution is quite different. The species nests across most of northern Scotland and one pair bred in western Ireland in 1972 and 1974. The breeding population has been estimated at 805–905 pairs (Nethersole-Thompson and Nethersole-Thompson 1979). There have been only two recoveries of Scottish ringed birds: one was recorded in Co. Cork in October and one in France in September. The Cork bird may have been wintering, but the French bird was clearly moving south. However, the timing of spring migration provides a strong indication that our wintering birds are drawn from the Scottish breeders. Scottish Greenshanks are back on their territories in early April, about a month earlier than Scandinavian breeders, and in approximately the same period that birds leave the Irish and W British estuaries. In SE Britain relatively few winter, but passage is noticeable in April and May, presumably involving Scandinavian birds. It was thought that the wintering population in Britain and Ireland was less than the Scottish breeding population, after taking account of recruitment, and that the remainder

of the Scottish birds winter farther south, in France or on the Mediterranean or NW African coasts. However, it now appears that a much larger proportion of Scottish breeders may spend the winter in these islands than was previously suspected.

Greenshanks feed extremely actively. They probe in the mud and in vegetation but also pursue prey in shallow water by dashing forward with head and bill outstretched. The diet includes more fish than any other European wader (Burton 1979). Even on the shore, Greenshanks feed on shrimps, small fish, *Nereis* worms and crabs, rather than on the small *Hydrobia* and *Corophium* which Redshanks *T. totanus* prefer. These prey items are widely dispersed in a variety of habitats and help to account for the wide distribution of the species in Ireland.

Prater (1981) estimated a total winter population of about 600 for both islands. From the number of squares in which birds were recorded during 1981/82 to 1983/84 it can be seen that this is a substantial underestimate and one might guess at a total winter population of over 1,000, but probably less than 1,500.

The Greenshank is an abundant breeding bird in Scandinavia and the USSR, but almost all these birds are believed to winter south of the Sahara (*BWP*). Our birds are important because they appear to represent the bulk of the Scottish breeding population and because this population is the most westerly in Europe. Annual indices for the Birds of Estuaries Enquiry indicate that the species is maintaining its numbers but the sample is small and excludes most of the Irish winterers.

C. D. HUTCHINSON

Total number of squares in which recorded: 480 (12%)

No. of birds seen in a day	Number (%) of squares		
	Britain	Ireland	TOTAL (incl. C.I.)
1–2	171 (69%)	107 (46%)	278 (58%)
3–5	49 (20%)	69 (30%)	118 (25%)
6+	27 (11%)	56 (24%)	84 (18%)

References

BURTON, P. J. K. 1979. The Greenshank's food. Pp 174–177 in NETHERSOLE-THOMPSON, D. and M. NETHERSOLE-THOMPSON. *Greenshanks*. Poyser, Berkhamsted.

NETHERSOLE-THOMPSON, D. and M. NETHERSOLE-THOMPSON. 1979. *Greenshanks*. Poyser, Berkhamsted.

Breeding Atlas p 190

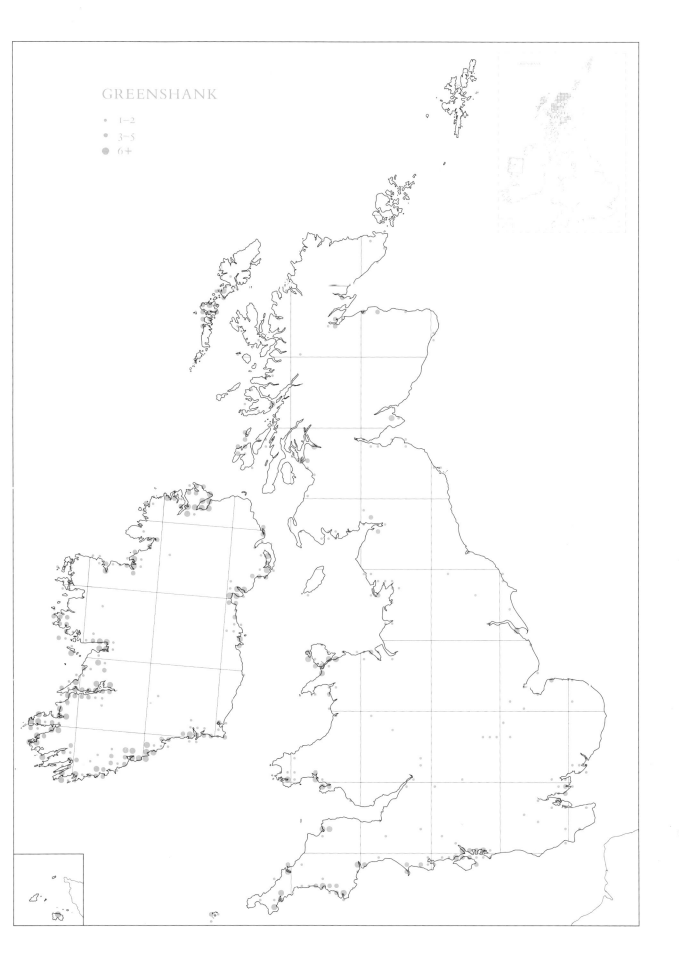

GREENSHANK

- · 1–2
- ● 3–5
- ● 6+

Green Sandpiper

Tringa ochropus

Green Sandpipers are most elusive birds in winter and for most fieldworkers their only contact would be a single wader, with white rump and black wings, flushed from a ditch or pool, flying off high with a liquid 'klu-eet-weet' call. Green Sandpipers are passage migrants and winter visitors to Britain and Ireland and generally occur in ones and twos at scattered inland localities, with very few records from estuaries and coastal sites. They are nowhere numerous and even on passage are seldom found in large numbers. The distribution map shows that there were most records in SE England. Those in the rest of England, Wales and southern Ireland were mostly of single birds, and there were very few records from Scotland.

Green Sandpipers breed in the sub-boreal zone from Fennoscandia eastwards and are one of the earliest waders to return on autumn passage. They are regularly recorded in late June, although the peak does not occur until August. During passage they can occur in concentrations of up to 20 or so birds at inland wetland areas, such as gravel pits and sewage works. However Britain and Ireland are on the northern limits of the species' wintering range and only a few birds remain after October. There are also a few wintering areas elsewhere in NW Europe, but the majority of the population apparently spends the winter in the Mediterranean basin and in Africa south of the Sahara.

In winter, Green Sandpipers can be found on the margins of streams, ditches, farm ponds, gravel pits and sewage works. They often occur near chalk streams and at watercress beds where the shallow water is particularly suitable for them. There are also occasional records of birds using wet farm gateways and small floods in cultivated fields. Their food is largely aquatic invertebrates (*BWP*) although there are observations of them occasionally taking small fish. In specially suitable feeding sites numbers can build up. For instance up to 15 have been observed in mid winter on a small disused watercress bed in southern England. In that situation individual birds were intensely territorial, but such behaviour has not been reported elsewhere (Smith *et al* 1984). Birds apparently roost away from the feeding areas but no information is available on the sites used.

There is considerable evidence that individual birds may return to the same wintering areas for a number of years. However, there can also be much movement between sites during the course of the winter, particularly during periods of severe weather when some sites become untenable and birds may be forced to change, move south or leave these islands altogether. In much of N England and Scotland the weather is probably too severe to allow Green Sandpipers to remain on shallow fresh waters through the winter. There are as yet no ringing recoveries to indicate the origins of our wintering birds, although a pullus ringed in Finland was recovered in Morocco in December.

With such a secretive and mobile species it is difficult to arrive at an estimate of the wintering population. An analysis of county bird reports for the 5 winters preceding the *Winter Atlas* period (Smith in prep) indicates a maximum of around 600 birds in Britain and Ireland. This figure must however be treated with some caution. Movements between sites during the course of the winter would lead to an overestimate, whilst an unknown number of birds may not have been located or reported to the county bird recorders. A realistic figure for the wintering population is therefore probably in the range 500–1,000 birds. This represents a very small proportion of the western Palearctic breeding population of some 450,000 pairs (T. Piersma).

K. W. SMITH

Total number of squares in which recorded: 593 (15%)

No. of birds seen in a day	Number (%) of squares		
	Britain	Ireland	TOTAL (incl. C.I.)
1	338 (62%)	31 (67%)	371 (63%)
2	104 (19%)	8 (17%)	112 (19%)
3+	103 (19%)	7 (15%)	110 (19%)

References

SMITH, K. W., J. M. REED and B. E. TREVIS. 1984. Studies of Green Sandpipers wintering in southern England. *Wader Study Group Bull.* 42 : 15.

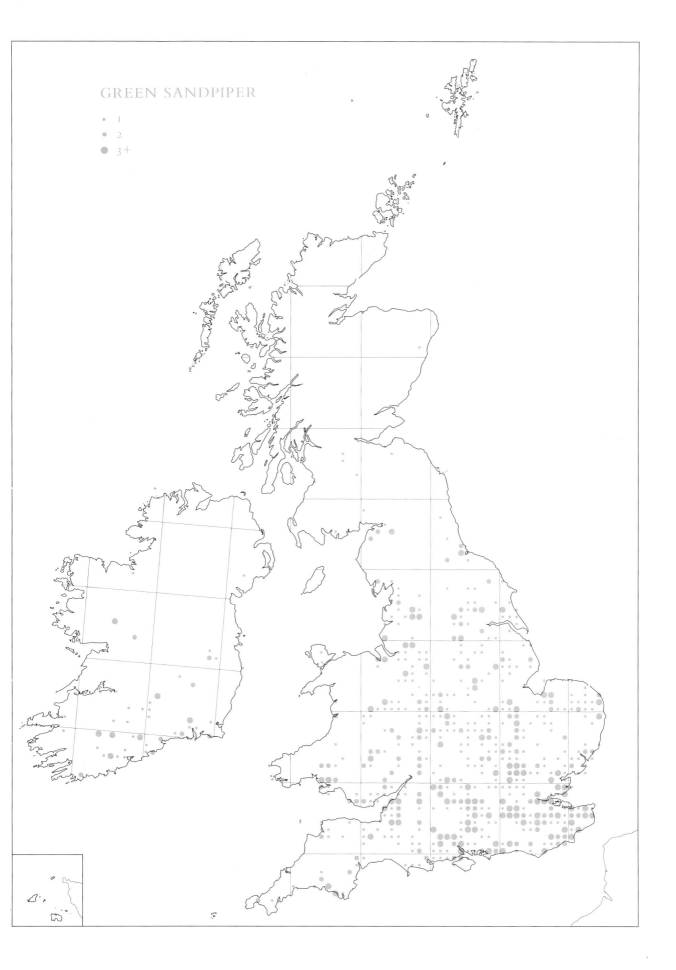

GREEN SANDPIPER

- • 1
- • 2
- ● 3+

Common Sandpiper

Actitis hypoleucos

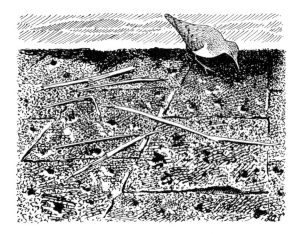

The Common Sandpiper's habit of bobbing prominently at the water's edge, or uttering its arresting call as it skims low over the surface on diagnostically bowed wings, make it a relatively conspicuous species. Despite this however, birds may remain contentedly within very restricted areas for long periods during the winter, and many which are not casually flushed must pass undetected.

As one would expect of a species at the extreme northern fringe of its world wintering range, it is very scarce with a patchy distribution. The records display a coastal bias and a concentration towards the southwest, with very few occurring elsewhere. Analysing the records from estuarine sites for the period 1969–1975, Prater (1981) found that about 65% of the total wintering population was in SW England. The present survey confirms this concentration of records and the results suggest that, taking inland records in addition to the coastal ones, the region holds about 50% of the entire population of Britain and Ireland. Although the species is almost certainly under-recorded in SW Ireland, where squares received minimal coverage, the paucity of records from the east coast is notable.

The distribution of winter records is almost an exact reversal of the breeding situation, with virtually no overlap in the ranges. That an entirely different type of habitat is utilised in winter is hardly surprising, for the fast flowing streams frequented in summer are now often raging torrents and upland lakes inhospitably barren and windswept. There is no evidence to show whether or not it is birds of the breeding population which remain to winter. These may well move south to be replaced by birds which nest at higher latitudes. A strong autumn passage is recorded from mid July to September, when large numbers occur on the east coast of England, with fewer in Ireland. Very few are seen after September.

In winter, Common Sandpipers resort to a fairly wide variety of habitats, varying from inland lakes, both natural and artificial at lower altitudes, to coastal estuaries and harbours. It is normally the inner reaches of estuaries which are favoured, especially areas having expanses of exposed stone or gravel, though birds are not infrequently found at estuary mouths, particularly where sea-walls and embankments are present. Heavily industrialised areas are occasionally inhabited when they are found adjacent to waterways, and sites such as settling ponds are frequented. Loyalty to favoured sites can be strong, some being occupied year after year and they may occasionally be defended against invaders. The effect of severe weather on the species is unknown, but birds at inland localities are more likely to be disadvantaged through freezing of lakes and waterways, and there may be a movement to the coast in hard winters. Common Sandpipers are normally found singly and seldom associate with other species, though during several winters birds at a site in Cork Harbour foraged with Starlings *Sturnus vulgaris* at a dump of animal feedstuff. Normally, though, the food is small invertebrates collected from the water's edge.

The normal winter range is south of the Sahara, but small numbers are recorded in the Mediterranean basin and in the maritime areas of western Europe, north as far as these islands. Wintering in Britain and Ireland has been known for many years, but appears to have increased in the past three decades. Prater (1981) estimated that the total number present in estuaries in winter did not exceed 50 birds, with as many again at other sites. The results of the present survey suggest that this is an accurate assessment, but with the possibility that the Irish population is underestimated.

Due to their scarcity during the winter months, it is likely that most Common Sandpipers will attract more than the casual glance; they certainly deserve more now that there have been several instances of overwintering in Britain by the very similar Spotted Sandpiper *A. macularia*.

K. PRESTON

Total number of squares in which recorded: 236 (6%)

No. of birds seen in a day	Number (%) of squares		
	Britain	Ireland	TOTAL (incl. C.I.)
1	141 (74%)	22 (55%)	166 (70%)
2	37 (19%)	9 (22%)	46 (19%)
3+	15 (8%)	9 (22%)	24 (10%)

Breeding Atlas p 186

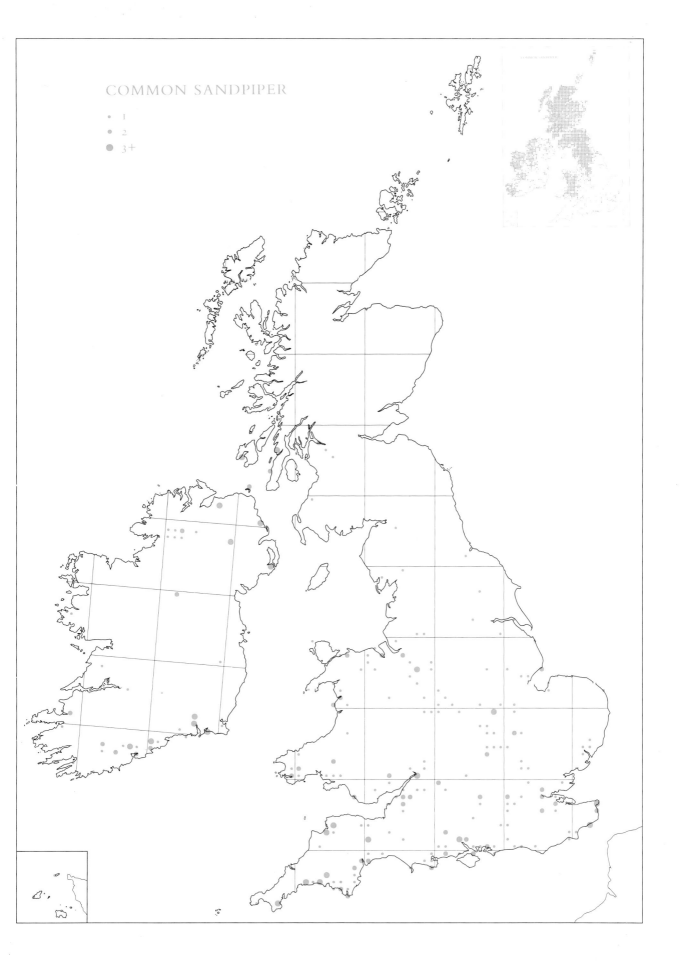

COMMON SANDPIPER

- 1
- 2
- 3+

Turnstone

Arenaria interpres

The Turnstone is a common coastal wader frequenting estuaries, sandy beaches and, particularly, rocky shores. Its chittering call and striking wing pattern in flight make it one of the easiest of waders to recognise.

In winter, Turnstones are found along the entire coast line of Britain and Ireland, but are relatively scarce along the northwest coast of mainland Scotland and the Inner Hebrides.

As the name suggests, Turnstones are adept at turning over small stones to obtain hidden food items, though they also push aside fronds of wrack, and lift the trailing leaves of eel grass, probe sand and hammer barnacles when feeding. Turnstones have an extremely varied diet, but the main food items in Britain are shrimps, winkles and barnacles (Harris 1979). Small winkles are eaten whole and the shell is crushed in the gizzard, but with large winkles the foot, only, is torn from the shell.

Turnstones generally forage in small flocks with a more or less stable membership, and males usually dominate females when feeding. When the tide rises, larger numbers congregate to roost, often with other wader species, on exposed rocks, salt marshes and sand spits. Some continue to forage at high tide, either on banks of washed up kelp, or inland on grass fields.

The breeding range encompasses much of the high Arctic and also extends southward into Scandinavia. Autumn migration to Britain starts in July and includes Scandinavian and Canadian/Greenland birds. The latter population remains to moult and spends the winter whilst the former puts on fat for further migration to W Africa, where they moult and winter (Branson *et al* 1979).

The birds that stay for the winter show site tenacity from autumn to spring, and movements of over 10 km are rare. They also tend to return to the same stretch of shore each winter (Metcalfe and Furness 1985).

There are usually about 15% of first-year birds in the winter flocks but fewer after a poor breeding season. This happened in 1972, resulting in only 5% first-year birds in the winter flocks. The minimum annual survival of adults is 86% (Metcalfe and Furness 1985).

Turnstones put on a moderate amount of fat in winter in order to guard against food shortages, but it is lost by March. In April and May, fat for migration back to the breeding grounds is accumu-lated. The return to Greenland and Canada in early May, when they have only moderate amounts of fat, involves a stop-over in Iceland where birds can refuel. Birds that leave Britain in late May with a full load of fat could migrate to Greenland without stopping in Iceland (Clapham 1979). A few first-year birds migrate with the adults but most remain to summer on our coasts. The Scandinavian Turnstones which winter in Africa do not return through Britain on spring migration.

The winter population of Turnstones on British estuaries may be about 11,000, and Prater (1981) estimated that the overall winter population was in the order of 25,000, excluding Ireland which probably has well over 5,000 on the rocky shores. However, detailed surveys on the open shores of eastern Scotland (between Berwickshire and Orkney) has revealed a total of 15,000 (Summers *et al* 1975, Tay and Orkney Ringing Groups 1984), so the total population in Britain and Ireland is probably closer to 50,000.

The Turnstone has a cosmopolitan distribution during the non-breeding season, and Britain lies in the northern part of this range. They can be found on the rocky shores of New Zealand and South Africa, and coral islands and mangrove swamps of the tropics as well as the temperate shores of the Atlantic and Pacific Oceans.

R. W. SUMMERS

Total number of squares in which recorded: 933 (24%)

No. of birds seen in a day	Number (%) of squares		
	Britain	Ireland	TOTAL (incl. C.I.)
1–32	317 (47%)	147 (57%)	464 (50%)
33–100	198 (30%)	84 (33%)	284 (30%)
101 +	156 (23%)	27 (10%)	185 (20%)

References

BRANSON, N. J. B. A., E. D. PONTING and C. D. T. MINTON, 1979. Turnstone populations on the Wash. *Bird Study* 26: 47–54.

CLAPHAM, C. 1979. The Turnstone populations of Morecambe Bay. *Ringing and Migration* 2: 144–150.

HARRIS, P. R. 1979. The winter feeding of the Turnstone in North Wales. *Bird Study* 26: 259–266.

METCALFE, N. B. and R. W. FURNESS 1985. Survival, winter population stability and site fidelity in the Turnstone *Arenaria interpres*. *Bird Study* 32: 207–214.

SUMMERS, R. W., N. K. ATKINSON, and M. NICOLL. 1975. Wintering wader populations on the rocky shores of eastern Scotland. *Scot. Birds* 8: 299–308.

TAY AND ORKNEY RINGING GROUPS. 1984. *The Shore Birds of the Orkney Islands*. Tay Ringing Group, Perth.

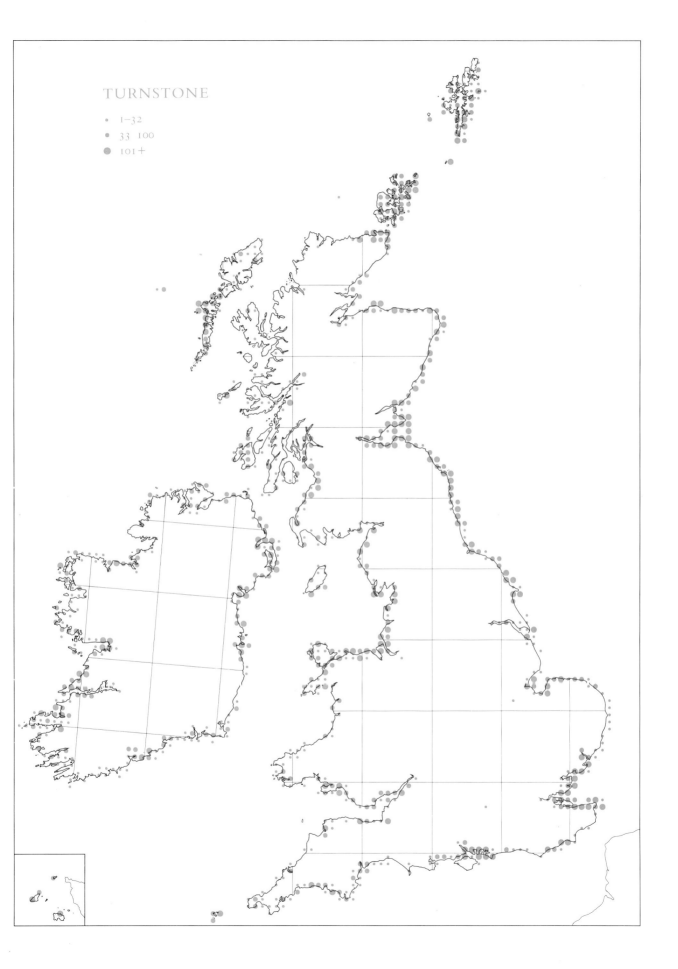

TURNSTONE

- 1–32
- 33–100
- 101+

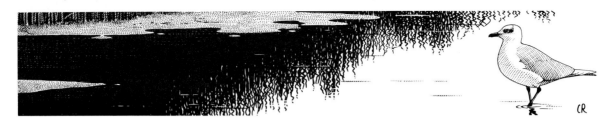

Mediterranean Gull

Larus melanocephalus

The Mediterranean Gull is most often found by the dedicated gull watcher who patiently enjoys, or endures, scanning through large flocks of Black-headed Gulls *L. ridibundus*. The species may indeed be partly responsible for the recent upsurge in interest in gulls, being not only uncommon but also one of our most attractive gulls. Its discovery is a prize to be relished.

The winter distribution in England and Wales is partly a reflection of the abundance of its close congener the Black-headed Gull. In S Scotland it is rare but increasing. In Ireland, it is scarce and largely confined to the east coast. In England and Wales there are few stretches of coastline greater than 50 km without Mediterranean Gulls in winter, but it is most common on the south coast of England, from Cornwall to Kent, these counties containing all but four of the squares of highest abundance. Nearly half (69) of the occupied squares in Britain are south of London. The species presence in 31 well distributed inland squares in England is notable and refutes the statement in *BWP* that it 'does not normally winter inland, except in Netherlands'. The coastal winterers may travel some distance inland to take a fresh water bathe.

In winter, many Mediterranean Gulls favour particular sites. Some individuals have returned during many successive winters, for example at Hartlepool, Cleveland, from 1956/57 to 1970/71. They usually associate with Black-headed Gulls, the only species with which successful hybridisation has been recorded, but in some areas where Kittiwakes *Rissa tridactyla* are common, persistent association occurs with this more distant relative. The behaviour of Mediterranean Gulls closely matches that of Black-headed Gulls and, as with almost all gulls, they largely prosper from human activities, exploiting fish quays, trawlers during fish gutting operations, power station cooling system outlets, rubbish dumps, sewer outlets, etc. Their natural food in winter is mainly marine fish and snails, supplemented by earthworms and a wide variety of insects.

There is a protracted autumn arrival during July to November and another peak of records during March and early April (Sharrock 1974). Detailed studies at Weymouth, Dorset (D. J. Fisher), and at Blackpill, West Glamorgan (Hume 1976), revealed a regular turnover of birds during February–May. Fisher (*in litt*) analysed all English south coast records up to 1976 and found that adults and second-year birds move east much earlier than do first-year birds, commencing in February or even in late January. This is not surprising as many adults return to their breeding grounds by March. Small numbers of our wintering birds may breed undetected in Britain but the origin of the majority is not clear. The only foreign recovery is of a chick, ringed on Riems Island on the Baltic coast of East Germany in 1966, which bred in Hampshire in 1968 (Taverner 1970).

There had been only 4 records prior to 1940, but by 1960 between 10 and 20 were recorded annually (Sharrock 1974), and by 1963 it had become too common to remain on the list of species considered by the British Birds Rarities Committee. This increase did not immediately affect northern England. Yorkshire had its second record in 1958 and averaged under 2 per year from then till 1972, but by 1975 was enjoying over 25 annually (Appleby and Britton 1979). The number of birds present is confused by wandering individuals but, with over 200 recorded, the December population is probably between 100 and 150 birds in Britain and Ireland.

The world population is increasing and may now exceed 170,000 pairs, the vast majority in the Black Sea colonies. Most of these winter in the Mediterranean (*BWP*). So, in the wider context, the British population is not significant. Why this tiny proportion should wish to winter in our relatively hostile climate, often alongside Glaucous Gulls *L. hyperboreus* from the high Arctic, remains a mystery.

D. J. BRITTON

Total number of squares in which recorded: 159 (4%)

No. of birds seen in a day	Number (%) of squares		TOTAL (incl. C.I.)
	Britain	Ireland	
1	109 (77%)	9 (56%)	119 (75%)
2	23 (16%)	4 (25%)	27 (17%)
3 +	10 (7%)	3 (18%)	13 (8%)

References

APPLEBY, R. H. and D. J. BRITTON. 1979. Mediterranean Gulls in Yorkshire. *The Naturalist* 104: 135–143.

HUME, R. A. 1976. The pattern of Mediterranean Gull records at Blackpill, West Glamorgan. *Brit. Birds* 69: 503–505.

SHARROCK, J. T. R. 1974. *Scarce Migrant Birds in Britain and Ireland*. Poyser, Berkhamsted.

SHARROCK, J. T. R. 1983. Rare breeding birds in the United Kingdom in 1981. *Brit. Birds* 76: 1–25.

TAVERNER, J. H. 1970. Mediterranean Gulls nesting in Hampshire. *Brit. Birds* 63: 67–79.

Breeding Atlas p 448

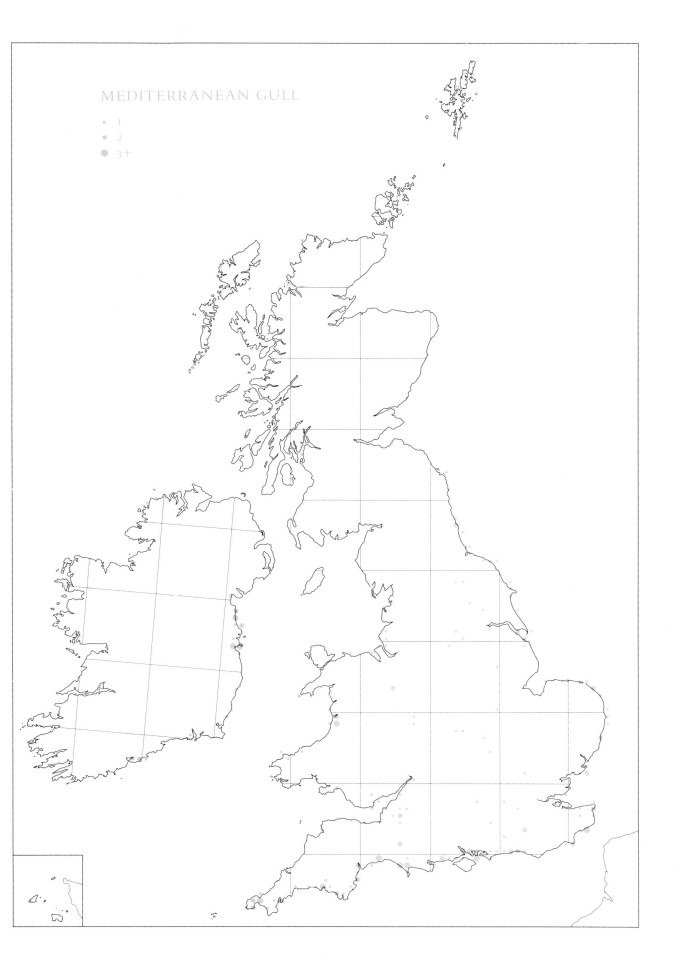

MEDITERRANEAN GULL

- 1
- 2
- 3+

Little Gull

Larus minutus

CR.

Little Gulls are small, fragile-looking gulls, typically found in winter flying over the sea on lee shores after gales. Their delicate feeding action, dipping to the surface of the water to snatch food items, makes them conspicuous at a season when the terns have left our shores, and few other gulls feed in this manner.

They can be seen in winter in very small numbers along much of the east coast of southern Scotland, England and Ireland, and scattered along the south and west coast of England and Ireland, with local concentrations. The numbers of birds at these sites vary from winter to winter and within winters, apparently in response to weather conditions, but flocks of over 50 are extremely rare and appear mainly in the Irish Sea, though even there not every year.

Interpretation of the map is complicated by our lack of knowledge of the winter distribution of Little Gulls throughout their range. They appear to winter offshore, but not to be truly pelagic, for after strong winter gales small flocks occur close to land along much of the western seaboard of Europe from the North Sea south to the coast of W Africa and in the Mediterranean, Black and Caspian Seas (Hutchinson and Neath 1978). Very large numbers pass the French and Dutch coasts in late autumn, totalling about 10,000 in the latter case, but their ultimate destination is unknown. By far the largest number ever recorded on the west coast of Europe was a count of 5,000–10,000 in St Brieuc's Bay, Brittany, on 24 December 1974 (*Brit. Birds* 68 : 347, 1975). First-year birds are thought to move farther south and this is borne out by the British and Irish records, in which adults and second year birds predominate in winter. A further problem in interpreting the map is that the food preference in winter has never been studied, so it is impossible to relate the distribution of the birds to the distribution of their prey. The winter food is described in *BWP* as probably chiefly fish and marine invertebrates, but this appears to be a deduction drawn from feeding behaviour rather than the result of examination of food items taken. Certainly, Little Gulls in winter appear to feed far less over inland lakes and coastal lagoons than over the sea, and there

are few inland records on the map. It seems likely, from their appearance after onshore wind, that small numbers winter out of sight of land in the North Sea and Irish Sea and a very few west of Ireland, and that these come close to land during onshore gales.

Little Gulls breed over a wide area of N central Europe from Denmark eastwards and move W and S in winter. Ringing has been concentrated at relatively few sites around the Baltic, and birds have been recovered in Britain from these areas, but it is not known whether some of our birds originate from farther east. Substantial numbers of birds now occur around our coast in autumn as juveniles disperse and adults move, first to sheltered bays to moult, and then W and S in late September and October (Hutchinson and Neath 1978). There has been a remarkable increase in numbers on passage since the mid 1950s, and this increase is reflected to a lesser extent in the winter numbers. The increase has been so remarkable that it must represent an increase in breeding numbers and probably also breeding range. Little Gulls have attempted to nest in Norway and in England (on 3 occasions) since the early 1970s and have bred successfully at a number of locations in North America since 1962.

The size of the wintering population is difficult to gauge but there are probably 150–350 in the Irish Sea and about the same number in the North Sea close to the east coast of Britain. The number scattered off the south and west coasts and coasts of Ireland is probably less than 100 in total. These numbers increase substantially from March onwards as birds begin to return towards their breeding colonies from wintering areas to the south.

C. D. HUTCHINSON

Total number of squares in which recorded: 235 (6%)

No. of birds seen in a day	Number (%) of squares		
	Britain	Ireland	TOTAL (incl. C.I.)
1	103 (55%)	24 (52%)	128 (54%)
2–4	47 (25%)	14 (30%)	61 (26%)
5+	38 (20%)	8 (17%)	46 (20%)

References
HUTCHINSON, C. D. and B. NEATH. 1978. Little Gulls in Britain and Ireland. *Brit. Birds* 71: 563–581.

Breeding Atlas p 448

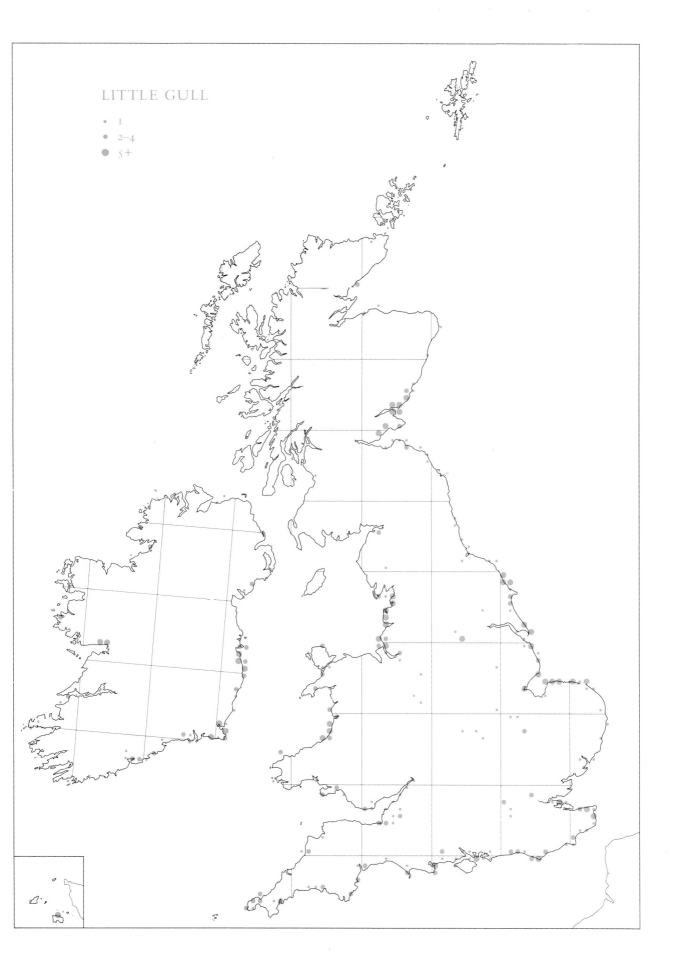

LITTLE GULL

- 1
- 2–4
- 5+

Black-headed Gull

Larus ridibundus

Never *black*-headed (plain chocolate would be nearer the mark), the white head and dark smudge of this species at the start of each winter seem calculated to confuse the tyro birdwatcher. On the other hand by late February, many Black-headed Gulls have their dark hoods, whilst all year round the buoyant, rather tern-like flight, and prominent white leading edge to the wing distinguish it from most other gulls.

Only at the start of this century did Black-headed Gulls begin to become regular winter visitors to inland areas, venturing there in search of food rather than occurring as storm-driven oddities.

The *Breeding Atlas* shows the Black-headed Gull to be widespread, both inland and coastally, to the north and west of central England, with a few large colonies in the south and southeast. In winter, the picture shows a striking change, as in both England and Ireland the vast majority of those 10-km squares uninhabited in summer have wintering records. The Black-headed Gull is lacking only in the uplands of northern England, central Wales and the Scottish Highlands.

During winter, Black-headed Gulls frequent a wide range of habitats, ranging from estuaries and coastal marshes, through grazing land and plough to inland wetlands, refuse tips, even urban parks, playing fields and, quite frequently, gardens. Clearly their choice of diet is wide, the basic 'worms and other soil invertebrates' obtained from ploughed fields and pastures being augmented by garden bird feeding scraps and by refuse from rubbish tips. As in the summer, wintering Black-headed Gulls tend to be gregarious, feeding in dense flocks behind a working plough or in more widely dispersed gatherings on the less rich feeding afforded by grassland. Inland feeding and roosting localities are abandoned only during periods of severe winter weather, when the ground is hard-frozen or snow covered, and when fresh water roosting sites are frozen over. In such circumstances, most Black-headed Gulls seek the nearest sheltered coastal waters, where food and safe roosting are available.

In the evening, flocks will move to open water to roost. Sometimes these roosts are on sheltered estuaries, but most Black-headed Gulls in Britain and Ireland roost on fresh water, ranging from natural lakes to reservoirs and ballast or mineral extraction pits. The increase of man-made waters in Britain and Ireland, must be an important factor in accounting for the Black-headed Gulls wide winter distribution.

Ringing recoveries showed that the majority of Black-headed Gulls breeding in Britain and Ireland tended to disperse for the winter, and that the proportion of overseas recoveries was small, suggesting that most of the population remained through the winter (Flegg and Cox 1972). Additionally, large numbers of immigrants from northern Europe, as far afield as Scandinavia, Finland, the Baltic SSRs and Poland, can be expected to augment the resident population (Horton *et al* 1984).

Gribble (1976) showed that the resident population of Black-headed Gulls has increased greatly during this century, and the *Breeding Atlas* suggested a population of between 150,000 and 300,000 pairs. Gull roost counts, in January 1983, gave a total of 1,877,000 Black-headed Gulls, over 1,000,000 of which were at inland sites (Bowes *et al* 1984). This figure must be regarded as conservative because of the problems of coverage in remote areas and it did not include Ireland. The current winter Black-headed Gull population may be of the order of 3,000,000 birds in Britain and Ireland, of which perhaps about two thirds are of Continental origin.

The Black-headed Gull is widely distributed across temperate Europe and Asia as far as the Pacific Ocean, though little is known of its numbers and movements in the eastern (and geographically major) part of its range. It seems probable, however, that a significant proportion of the breeding birds from the western part, westwards from Russia, winter here.

J. J. M. FLEGG

Total number of squares in which recorded: 3,137 (81%)

	Number (%) of squares		
No. of birds seen in a day	Britain	Ireland	TOTAL (incl. C.I.)
1–380	957 (42%)	599 (70%)	1,558 (50%)
381–1,490	748 (33%)	197 (23%)	946 (30%)
1,491 +	569 (25%)	63 (7%)	633 (20%)

References

BOWES, A., P. C. LACK and M. R. FLETCHER. 1984. Wintering gulls in Britain, January 1983. *Bird Study* 31: 161–170.

FLEGG, J. J. M. and C. J. COX. 1972. Movement of Black-headed Gulls from colonies in England and Wales. *Bird Study* 19: 228–240.

GRIBBLE, F. C. 1976. Census of Black-headed Gull colonies in England and Wales in 1973. *Bird Study* 23: 139–149.

HORTON, N., T. BROUGH, M. R. FLETCHER, J. B. A. ROCHARD and P. I. STANLEY. 1984. The winter distribution of foreign Black-headed Gulls in the British Isles. *Bird Study* 31: 171–186.

Breeding Atlas p 216

BLACK-HEADED GULL

- 1–380
- 381–1,490
- 1,491+

Ring-billed Gull

Larus delawarensis

The Ring-billed Gull was first recorded in Britain in March 1973, when an adult was discovered at Blackpill, Swansea, West Glamorgan (Hume 1973). During the following three years, this locality gathered 11 records and it was not until 1976 that the Welsh monopoly was finally broken. The first Irish records were in 1979 and, by the end of 1980, the British and Irish total had risen to 44. There can be little doubt that the Ring-billed Gull was occurring here before 1973 but its similarity to the closely related Common Gull *L. canus* hindered its earlier discovery. In 1981, however, there was a remarkable upsurge in records, with some 55 recorded, followed by 76 in 1982, 89 in 1983 and 84 in 1984 (Vinicombe 1985, Rogers *et al* 1985) making it now our most numerous North American visitor.

The winter distribution fits that expected for a trans-Atlantic vagrant, with most records being in the west, particularly in Ireland, SW England and S Wales. Most have come from coastal towns and cities (particularly Belfast, Dublin, Cork, Swansea, Penzance, Plymouth and Weymouth) which not only attract gulls, but also provide experienced birdwatchers who check their local gull flocks. In eastern Britain Ring-billed Gulls are still extremely rare with no records at all from the well-watched east coast counties, from Lincolnshire to E Sussex.

Like most gulls, they are catholic in their choice of habitat and food. In North America the Ring-billed Gull breeds in the western interior and in NE Canada and the Great Lakes. The eastern populations winter mainly down the American eastern seaboard to the Gulf of Mexico. Numbers in North America are currently increasing rapidly. Although most British records have been coastal, Ring-billed Gulls also occur inland in some areas, such as Avon, where they associate with Common Gull flocks which feed mainly on upland pasture.

The patterns of Ring-billed Gull occurrences in Britain and Ireland are rather complicated. The large 1981 influx involved mainly first year birds which, it is thought, were trans-Atlantic refugees from an exceptionally severe North American winter. The high totals in the succeeding 2 years were undoubtedly due mainly to leftovers from the 1981 influx. This theory is supported by the fact that 65% of those recorded in 1981 were first year birds, while in 1982 44% were second year and by 1983 66% were adult. Although some first winter Ring-billed Gulls are swept across the Atlantic during their autumn migrations, most seem to arrive from December to February. The bulk of the American east coast population winters on a latitude equivalent to that of Spain and NW Africa, so it seems likely that many birds cross the Atlantic much farther south. This is borne out by a number of records in France, Spain, Morocco and the Azores (where there were as many as 50 in 1980). This phenomenon undoubtedly accounts for the fact that there is a pronounced spring passage in western Britain and Ireland, with a peak in late March, as birds head north up the European coast. Adults are distinctly rare after the end of April, while second year birds have generally moved through by the end of May, both presumably having headed north with Common Gulls. Non-breeding first year birds tend to move through rather later in spring, and some summer on our coasts amongst the residual flocks of Common and Black-headed Gulls *L. ridibundus*. Records of adults gradually increase from late July onwards when, presumably, a southward return begins (Vinicombe 1985).

Some 21 Ring-billed Gulls were reported in the 1981/82 winter, 35 in 1982/83 and 39 in 1983/84. Owing to identification difficulties, these totals must inevitably represent the tip of an iceberg and it seems highly probable that, in the *Winter Atlas* years at least, the annual British and Irish total must have reached three figures.

Viewed against the current population growth in North America, it seems unlikely that the Ring-billed Gull will ever regain its former status as a rarity. The 1981 influx was probably exceptional and, although such influxes may recur, it seems likely that numbers will eventually stabilise at something below their present level. At the same time there would seem to be no reason why the Ring-billed Gull should not eventually breed on this side of the Atlantic.

K. E. VINICOMBE

Total number of squares in which recorded: 49 (1%)

No. of birds seen in a day	Number (%) of squares		
	Britain	Ireland	TOTAL (incl. C.I.)
1	26 (90%)	14 (70%)	40 (82%)
2	3 (10%)	4 (20%)	7 (14%)
3+	0 (0%)	2 (10%)	2 (4%)

References

HUME, R. A. 1973. Ring-billed Gull in Glamorgan: a species new to Britain and Ireland. *Brit. Birds* 66: 509–512.

ROGERS, M. and the RARITIES COMMITTEE. 1985. Report on rare birds in Great Britain in 1984. *Brit. Birds* 78: 556.

VINICOMBE, K. E. 1985. Ring-billed Gulls in Britain and Ireland. *Brit. Birds* 78: 327–337.

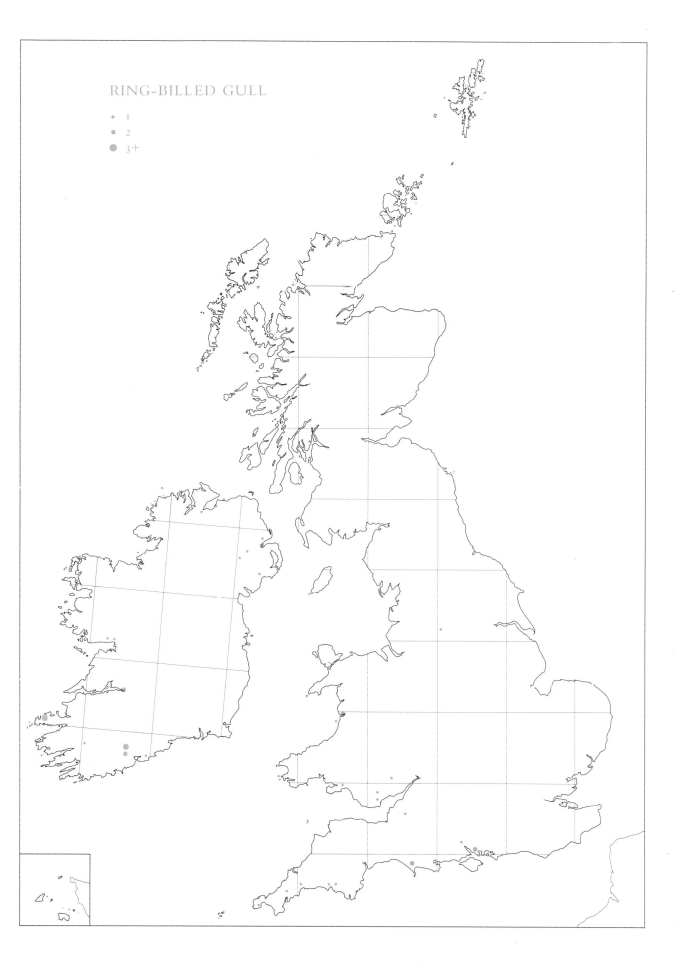

RING-BILLED GULL

- • 1
- • 2
- • 3+

Common Gull

Larus canus

To birdwatchers in England and Wales it is only in winter that the epithet 'common' seems appropriate for this gull, for only then does it become numerous and widespread. In summer it is largely confined to Scotland and Ireland, but in winter it is far more common throughout Britain and Ireland mostly on inland farmland or on sandy beaches on the coast (Vernon 1970). It often feeds far inland returning at dusk to roost on estuaries or lakes and reservoirs.

The winter map shows a wide distribution but with an absence from much of the higher mountainous areas above 300 m and tracts of peat moorland. The preferred feeding areas on farmland are near the suitable roosting sites. The Common Gull shows a marked preference for feeding on well-grazed grassland, particularly on well-drained limestone soils, and often above 100 m in altitude (Vernon 1970). The short kept turf on airfields and playing fields are also exploited. For instance there are high numbers (above 500 per 10-km square) on the Cotswolds linked with the large gull roost at Frampton on the Severn estuary. The high numbers for the London area are presumably based on counts of the species roosting on the London reservoirs. There are many feeding flocks in several parts of N and NW England, again feeding on grazed pastures inland with important roost sites, inland and coastal, several of which contained over 10,000 Common Gulls in recent counts (Hickling 1977, Prater 1981). In Scotland and Wales, roosting is primarily along the coast, especially at estuaries, plus a few important inland roosts on reservoirs. In Ireland, the winter distribution is fairly widespread, except for the peat moorlands, but in smaller numbers. Highest concentrations occur on the coast with sandy shores for roosting sites, and near grazed pastures.

Earthworms provide the bulk of food obtained in winter, except in times of severe weather (Vernon 1972). The loam soils of limestone pastures are known to harbour higher populations of worms than clay soils. Fields being ploughed (mainly in autumn or early spring) are also exploited for earthworms. After heavy rain, low land subject to flooding is also visited for earthworms, often in mixed flocks with Black-headed Gulls *L. ridibundus*. In severe winters, when grassland is frosted or snow bound, earthworms become unavailable. Common Gulls then resort to scavenging for food or feeding more on the coast, on sandy shores where molluscs (cockles for example) are the main source of food. In extreme winter condi-

tions there may be movements further south, to Ireland, or to the Continent. The majority of wintering birds come from breeding colonies in Scandinavia, Denmark and Germany, with smaller numbers from Holland, the USSR and Iceland (Vernon 1969). The first migrants reach this country in July and continue until late October. Return movements occur during the first half of April. The winter quarters of Common Gulls from British and Irish breeding colonies is less clear. Ringing results indicate that some Scottish first year birds winter in Ireland. In Ireland, counts suggest that many first year birds move south, possibly to the Continent. Counts done for the 1983/84 winter Gull roost survey gave totals of 332,253 in England and Wales (183,816 inland), and 128,849 (55,115 inland) for Scotland (Bowes *et al* 1984). Several large coastal roosts were not counted, so coastal figures are certainly an underestimate. Estimates derived from the *Winter Atlas* data give 423,000 Common Gulls for England and Wales, 211,500 for Scotland and 67,500 for Ireland, giving an estimated total of some 702,000 wintering birds. Britain and Ireland, with their comparatively milder climate, clearly form an important wintering area for N European breeding populations.

J. D. R. VERNON

Total number of squares in which recorded: 2,741 (71%)

No. of birds seen in a day	Number (%) of squares		
	Britain	Ireland	TOTAL (incl. C.I.)
1–78	998 (45%)	369 (71%)	1,370 (50%)
79–400	701 (32%)	120 (23%)	821 (30%)
401+	518 (23%)	32 (6%)	550 (20%)

References

BOWES, A., P. C. LACK and M. R. FLETCHER. 1984. Wintering gulls in Britain, January 1983. *Bird Study* 31; 161–170.

HICKLING, R. A. O. 1977. Inland wintering of gulls in England and Wales, 1973. *Bird Study* 24: 79–88.

VERNON, J. D. R. 1969. Spring migration of the Common Gull in Britain and Ireland. *Bird Study* 16: 101–107.

VERNON, J. D. R. 1970. Feeding habitats and food of the Black-headed and Common Gulls. Part I. Feeding habitats. *Bird Study* 17: 287–296.

VERNON, J. D. R. 1972. Feeding habitats and food of the Black-headed and Common Gulls. Part II. Food. *Bird Study* 19: 173–186.

Breeding Atlas p 214

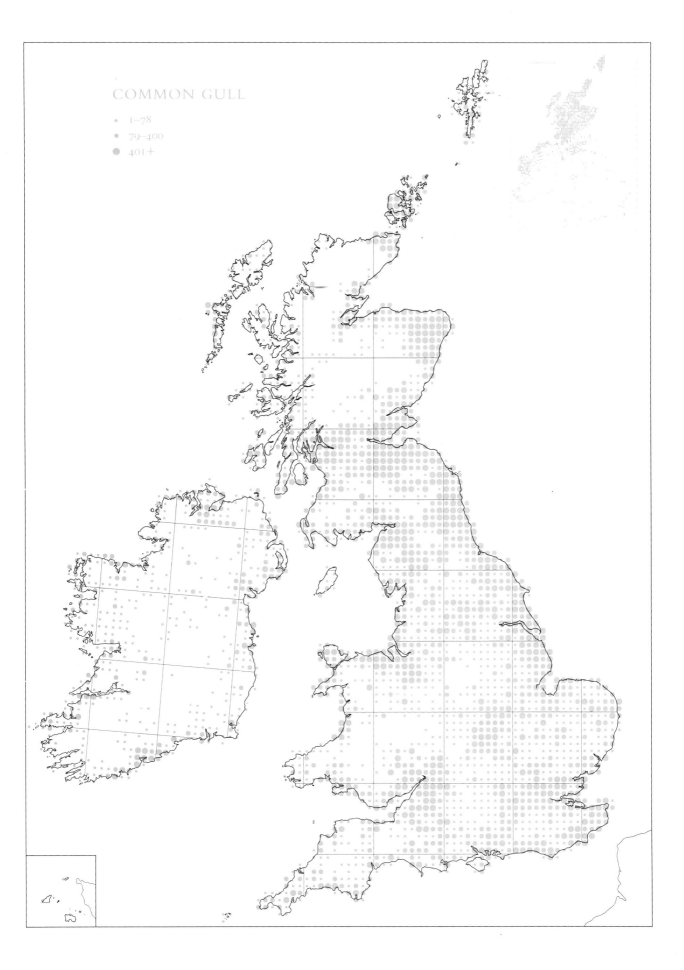

COMMON GULL

- 1–78
- 79–400
- 401+

Lesser Black-backed Gull

Larus fuscus

The Lesser Black-backed Gull is a migrant whose migratory pattern has changed during the past 40 years. It was formerly a complete migrant, with only occasional birds remaining here in winter. Now large numbers are seen in Britain in winter, mainly in the southern half of the country. The flight, to the safe water-borne roosts, of large gulls in formation makes an impressive sight on a winter evening.

The southern distribution shown by the map suggests a fairly even spread of this gull over England. Other investigations however have disclosed that the main concentration is along a broad band stretching from Lancashire and Yorkshire, southeastwards across the industrial midlands, to the London area. This part of Britain has the densest human population, whose needs have created reservoirs adjacent to abundant sources of food.

Lesser Black-backed Gulls are more common inland than on the coast, except for Merseyside. There the BTO enquiry of January 1983 recorded 10,190 birds roosting on the coast, out of a total coast count for the whole of Great Britain of 13,726. These birds have an obvious connection with the great breeding colonies on Walney Island in Cumbria and at Tarnbrook on the Lancashire Pennines.

The breeding distribution is in strong contrast to the wintering pattern, for breeding is at its densest on the coasts of W and NW England and on the central Scottish coast (*Breeding Atlas*). The wintering pattern also contrasts with that of the Herring Gull *L. argentatus*, which has a much larger coastal component. Irish birds breed mainly on the western and southwestern coasts, and the scarcity of birds in Ireland in winter suggests that those birds may migrate to Iberia.

In winter all our gulls share a common routine, with the roost as the key. Although gulls have few predators they seem to need a large area of water for safe roosting. From this secure base they can forage over arable land and rubbish tips, sewage works and similar plentiful sources of food. The importance of the roost is clearly shown when a new reservoir—

for instance, Draycote Water in Warwickshire, and Rutland Water in Leicestershire—enables gulls to exploit new feeding grounds. The Lesser Black-backed Gull is found much more on arable ground than the Herring Gull, especially on its late-autumn passage, when flocks may loaf by the day on ploughed land.

Migrants of the British and the three Scandinavian races reach Britain in October. There is a continuing passage for another three months, but a survey in 1979/80 showed that numbers continue to fall until March (Hickling 1984). Baker (1980) related changes in wintering numbers to changes in the migratory pattern: third year and older birds no longer migrate as far south in autumn as formerly, and by September are already beginning to move northwards again. He concluded that by December most are back in Britain. This interpretation is difficult to reconcile with the continuous reduction noted in wintering birds in Britain. In this connection it is of interest that Hosey and Goodridge (1980) found that in the colony at Walney Island only half of breeding Lesser Black-backed Gulls had returned by March, although by then Herring Gulls were all back in occupation.

Since 1953, when 165 individuals were found wintering inland in England and Wales, there has been regular monitoring of numbers. These have risen steadily: 6,960 in 1963, 25,057 in 1973, to 44,564 in 1983. In January 1983 the number of Lesser Black-backed Gulls counted at all sites in Britain, excluding Ireland, was 58,144 (Bowes *et al* 1984), and there were unknown but probably small numbers at coastal sites not covered. With a rough estimate of 5,000–10,000 in Ireland, the total number wintering must be of the order of 70,000 birds.

R. A. O. HICKLING

Total number of squares in which recorded: 1,682 (44%)

No. of birds seen in a day	Number (%) of squares		
	Britain	Ireland	TOTAL (incl. C.I.)
1–6	715 (49%)	150 (65%)	865 (51%)
7–45	417 (29%)	59 (25%)	479 (28%)
46+	315 (22%)	23 (10%)	338 (20%)

References

BAKER, R. R. 1980. The significance of the Lesser Black-backed Gull to models of bird migration. *Bird Study* 27: 41–50.

BARNES, J. A. G. 1961. The winter status of the Lesser Black-backed Gull. *Bird Study* 8: 127–147.

BOWES, A., P. C. LACK and M. R. FLETCHER. 1984. Wintering gulls in Britain, January 1983. *Bird Study* 31: 161–170.

HICKLING, R. A. O. 1977. Wintering of gulls in England and Wales, 1973. *Bird Study* 24: 79–88.

HICKLING, R. A. O. 1984. Lesser Black-backed Gull numbers at British inland roosts in 1979/80. *Bird Study* 31: 157–160.

HOSEY, G. R. and F. GOODRIDGE. 1980. Establishment of territories in two species of gull on Walney Island, Cumbria. *Bird Study* 27: 73–80.

Breeding Atlas p 210

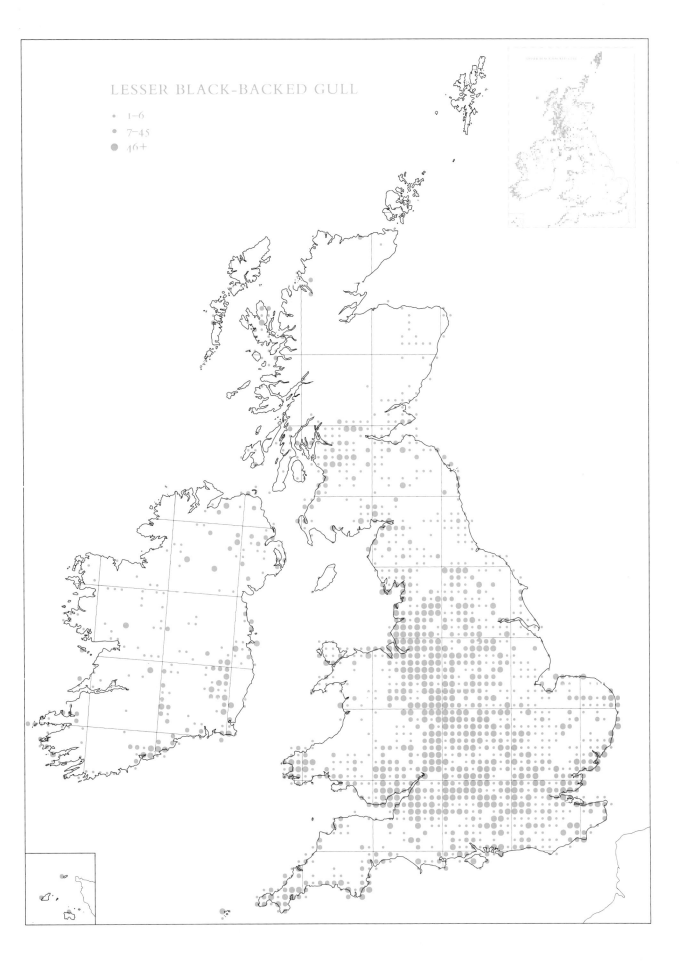

LESSER BLACK-BACKED GULL

• 1–6
• 7–45
● 46+

Herring Gull

Larus argentatus

The Herring Gull is a noisy and aggressive bird, dominating other species (except the Great Black-backed Gull *L. marinus*) at any wintering gathering of gulls. It favours coastal and inland centres of human population, where it can exploit edible wastes to be found within a short flight of a suitable roost.

The map shows the Herring Gull to be ubiquitous in winter. The few squares without birds are mainly in the highland areas of Britain and in the centre of Ireland. Not one coastal square is without its attendant Herring Gulls, and the greatest numbers are along all east coasts, along the south coast of England, and N Wales. Inland wintering birds are concentrated in the densely populated area between the firths of the Forth and the Clyde, and in a broad southeasterly band across England from Lancashire, through central England to the London area. Relatively few birds were found in Ireland away from the east coast. There is ringing evidence to show that some Irish birds move northeastwards into the Clyde area, and also eastwards to the west midlands of England.

Even in winter the Herring Gull is primarily a coastal bird, with its greatest concentrations at our larger ports. It scavenges at city refuse tips, sewage works, docks, fish quays and food processing plants. It will also feed on the natural foods to be obtained along the tide line or estuarine mud flats. It is less likely than some gull species to feed on farmland invertebrates. The communal roost sites include mud flats and the sea close inshore. Inland it shares reservoirs and gravel pits with the closely related Lesser Black-backed Gull *L. fuscus* and the smaller gulls.

Ringing studies in northern England and southern Scotland (Coulson *et al* 1984) have revealed that a large proportion of the gulls in the northeast belong to the N European race *L. a. argentatus*. Stanley *et al* (1981) reported that the range of measurements of London wintering gulls suggests that this wintering population, also, is probably composed mainly of birds from northern Europe. This race is separable with certainty only in the hand; and it is only recent

techniques of catching gulls in large numbers, that has revealed their presence. On the other hand, birds of the Mediterranean race *L. a. michahellis* (the Yellow-legged Herring Gull), which have for some years been pressing northwards along the Channel coast of France, are now being increasingly identified in SE England.

After breeding, there is a general shift of the population towards those places favoured in winter. Thereafter there is little movement, except that some of the dense coastal populations of E Scotland and NE England gradually drift south. Thus, in the London area, the greatest numbers occur in January, though they do not stay long. Hosey and Goodridge (1980) record that most of the breeding population of the large Walney Island colony has returned by March.

A series of BTO enquiries based on roosts has established the numbers of this and other species of gull in winter. The last count was in January 1983, when the Herring Gull roost-counts in Britain, excluding Ireland, were:

Inland	70,721	England and Wales	159,497
Coastal	204,911	Scotland	116,135
TOTAL	275,632	TOTAL	275,632

These totals are minimum figures. There were certainly several other large roosts along coasts, and Scotland was rather thinly covered by this survey. Allowing for this, and for those in Ireland, the total is perhaps in the region of half a million birds.

Inland gulls in England and Wales increased from 56,000 in 1963 to 103,000 in 1973. In the 1983 survey, numbers had declined to 47,000, a decrease of 54%, and further investigation is clearly needed.

R. A. O. HICKLING

Total number of squares in which recorded: 3,032 (79%)

No. of birds	Number (%) of squares		
seen in a day	Britain	Ireland	TOTAL (incl. C.I.)
1–70	1,128 (49%)	400 (54%)	1,529 (50%)
71–400	703 (31%)	199 (27%)	903 (30%)
401+	462 (20%)	135 (18%)	600 (20%)

References

COULSON, J. C., P. MONAGHAN, J. E. L. BUTTERFIELD, N. DUNCAN, K. ENSOR, C. SHEDDEN and C. THOMAS. 1984. Scandinavian Herring Gulls wintering in Britain. *Ornis Scand.* 15: 79–88.

HICKLING, R. A. O. 1977. Inland wintering of gulls in England and Wales, 1973. *Bird Study* 24: 73–80.

HOSEY, G. R. and F. GOODRIDGE. 1980. Establishment of territories in two species of gull on Walney Island, Cumbria. *Bird Study* 27: 73–80.

STANLEY, P. I., T. BROUGH, M. R. FLETCHER, N. HORTON and J. B. A. ROCHARD. 1981. The origins of Herring Gulls wintering inland in southeast England. *Bird Study* 28: 123–132.

Breeding Atlas p 212

HERRING GULL

- 1–70
- 71–400
- 401+

Iceland Gull

Larus glaucoides

CR

Iceland Gulls are uncommon birds from the Arctic—which makes them exciting birds to see. As they turn up at places where large numbers of commoner gulls gather (and some have returned to the same site year after year) they are, perhaps, not so hard to find as some other species of similar status. Glaucous Gulls *L. hyperboreus* are more likely to be misidentified as Iceland by inexperienced observers than *vice versa*, but identification problems have been clarified and interest in gulls has much increased in recent years (Grant 1982).

The winter distribution is more markedly western than the Glaucous Gull's, and this has been further increased in the years during the survey period when numbers were higher than usual. Their distribution inland is more restricted, and more in the north and west midlands area of England, than that of the Glaucous Gull. Apart from a few refuse tips and reservoir roosts where they have been regular for years, many of these inland reports are of casual passage or wandering birds, which must exaggerate the total numbers involved.

Iceland Gulls are found in much the same kind of places as Glaucous Gulls in winter, including fish quays, refuse tips and sewage outflows. They eat fish and waste food of all kinds, and they can also be found feeding actively (as opposed to loafing) on fields, with smaller gulls, presumably looking for earthworms and perhaps also grain. Inland, they roost on large reservoirs with other gulls.

Iceland Gulls breed on the west and east coasts of Greenland. The W Greenland birds mostly disperse very locally after breeding. Of 557 ringing recoveries, 550 were in the breeding area, and the smaller eastern population has yielded no recoveries (*BWP*).

It must be these migratory eastern birds, however, which visit Iceland from September or October to April or May. They can be quite common, especially in the north, and some move on to the Faeroes and Britain and Ireland. They arrive here from October or November, but mostly as late as Christmas time

or January in the south. They are regular in Scotland with 50–60 birds in most winters, but some exceptional years may involve 200 or more, as in 1980/81 and 1982/83. The distribution is considerably influenced by the latter winter, when Iceland Gulls were more numerous and widespread than usual.

In 1979, numbers were about average, with 60 birds in Scotland including Shetland. Early in 1981, 200 birds were present, including 50 in Shetland, and there was a more westerly bias, with 30 in Lewis (Western Isles). There were 180 recorded in 1982, and the first three months of 1983 produced many more still. In Grampian and other parts of the east coast, numbers were low. Early 1984 repeated the influx to the north and west, particularly in harbours, and many islands had record numbers. Why recent influxes should have occurred is difficult to explain. Exceptionally severe winter weather on the east coast of North America may be one reason. The continuing decline of fishing industries in Iceland and elsewhere may also force birds to move further south in winter.

Ireland also had exceptional numbers in this period. The average had been about 12 a year but in 1981 there were 58. In February 1983 and January 1984 (when 75 were reported from the north coast alone) all previous Irish records were eclipsed and the westerly bias to the distribution reinforced.

In NE England, 6–10 may usually be present, but in Norfolk it is a rare bird (1983, with 8 records involving 4 or 5 birds, was an exception). Before 1981, Cornwall had few birds, but records increased to over 20 in 1983. The west midland (especially Staffordshire) reservoirs have often had more birds, with 70 between 1969 and 1979 and generally greater numbers since, with as many as 5 together—an exceptional number so far inland.

In a normal year, Britain and Ireland may have as few as 70–80 Iceland Gulls but recent influxes have resulted in well over 250, even over 300 in 1983 and 1984. Reports in widely separated areas may often refer to the same individuals, however, somewhat reducing the overall total away from the major recent concentrations, so the higher figures could be slight overestimates.

R. A. HUME

Total number of squares in which recorded: 380 (10%)

No. of birds seen in a day	Number (%) of squares		
	Britain	Ireland	TOTAL (incl. C.I.)
1	206 (72%)	49 (53%)	255 (67%)
2	37 (13%)	12 (13%)	49 (13%)
3+	45 (16%)	31 (34%)	76 (20%)

References
GRANT, P. J. 1982. *Gulls: a Guide to Identification*. Poyser, Calton.

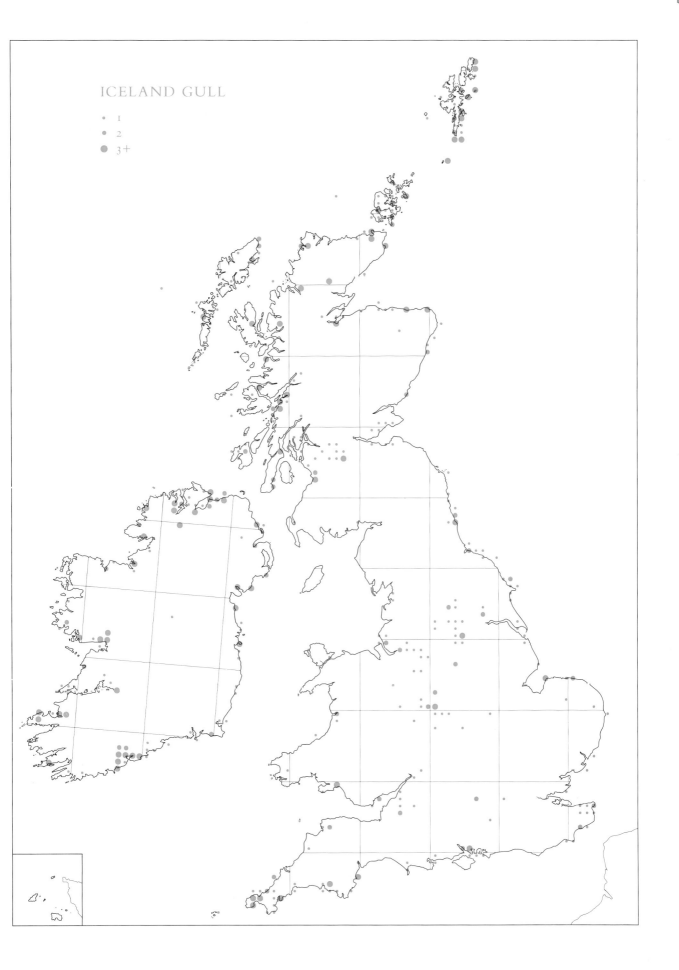

ICELAND GULL

• 1
• 2
● 3+

Glaucous Gull

Larus hyperboreus

The Glaucous Gull is a large, aggressive gull which may be surprisingly easy to spot amongst commoner species. Like the Iceland Gull *L. glaucoides*, its habit of frequenting places such as harbours, refuse tips and reservoir roosts inland makes it easier to locate than its small numbers would imply. Earlier assertions that adults are rare, and that only wandering immatures visit Britain and Ireland, are now thought mistaken. Adults are seen regularly and there seems to be a tendency for individuals to return to the same wintering sites over a series of years.

The map reflects a chiefly coastal distribution with a northerly bias. Concentrations occur at British and Irish harbours but the wide coastal spread, especially in Orkney and Shetland and along the east coast, indicates the variety of shoreline sites which may be visited. Inland, records are concentrated near the tips and reservoirs of urban hinterlands, notably, close to Greater Manchester and central England.

Inland, they feed with Herring Gulls *L. argentatus* and Lesser Black-backed Gulls *L. fuscus*, particularly at refuse tips but probably also on fields, taking earthworms and other invertebrates. They spend much time loafing on fields and return each evening to roost on undisturbed waters, though individuals may change their venue from night to night. Local fluctuations, daily and from year to year, can often be related to the availability of food at tips.

On the coast, fish quays, sewage outflows and strandline refuse also provide food. Quiet beaches, sand bars, rocky islets, rooftops and piers are used as loafing and roosting places.

The Glaucous Gull breeds from the high-Arctic to sub-Arctic coasts and has retreated northwards somewhat. Little is known about the origin of our wintering birds. Those breeding in the Canadian Arctic and W Greenland are resident or move south into eastern America. The E Greenland population is more migratory and largely winters in Iceland, though some may penetrate as far as Britain and Ireland. The Icelandic breeding population is mostly resident, and a large proportion is of hybrid Glaucous × Herring Gull

stock. Not many hybrids are seen, so it is probable that few Iceland-bred birds visit us. Eurasian breeders winter as far north as weather conditions allow, but influxes into Britain after gales and cold spells may involve this population. Some Svalbard birds clearly move southwest to Norway, Faeroes, Iceland and Greenland (*BWP*) and may drift further south (Dean 1984). A few birds arrive in Britain in September, but most come much later and some not until early January. Even areas where they are regular have casual records of passage or wandering individuals, seen once or just for a few days. Elsewhere, especially inland, most records are of this nature, which may indicate a high degree of duplication in reports but could imply that many go undiscovered for most of the winter.

Many of the birds wintering in Britain occur in Shetland and Orkney. Shetland may have 30–40 most winters, occasionally well over 100 or even 250. In Britain as a whole, they probably range from under 200 to 450–500, or sometimes rather more, each winter. In Ireland, they are also subject to much fluctuation but the average is about 70 per year.

Large influxes to isolated areas (especially Shetland, Fair Isle and, in the past, the Firth of Forth) have long been known, and are often associated with northerly and easterly gales. In 1980/81 a more general increase brought exceptional numbers, from Shetland (270) to Cornwall (15), with 80 at Galway (more than half the Irish total that year) and perhaps 500–600 in Britain and Ireland all told. The influxes coincided with increased numbers of Iceland Gulls. This and the more westerly distribution of the Glaucous Gull during the influxes suggest that these individuals are from Greenland, perhaps coming directly across the Atlantic following fishing fleets. Recent winters have seen a more regular pattern of occurrences in the southwest and Kent, and a consolidation elsewhere, but this may prove to be a temporary phenomenon, partly due to increased awareness of and interest in gulls.

R. A. HUME

Total number of squares in which recorded: 527 (14%)

	Number (%) of squares		
No. of birds seen in a day	Britain	Ireland	TOTAL (incl. C.I.)
1	278 (70%)	78 (61%)	356 (68%)
2	61 (16%)	20 (16%)	82 (16%)
3+	59 (15%)	30 (23%)	89 (17%)

References

DEAN, A. R. 1984. Origins and distribution of British Glaucous Gulls. *Brit. Birds* 77: 165.

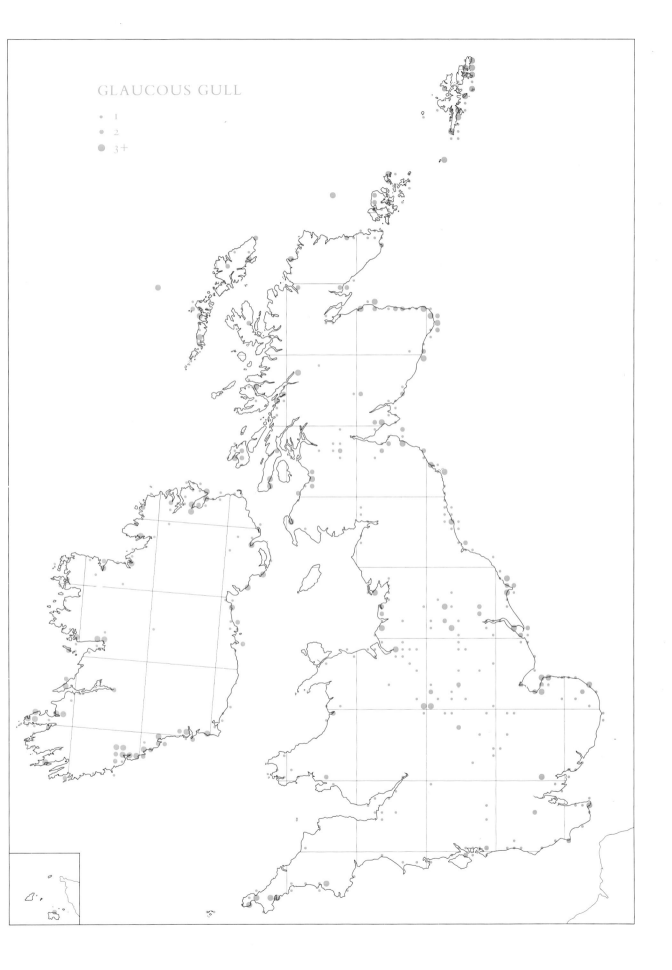

GLAUCOUS GULL

- 1
- 2
- 3+

Great Black-backed Gull

Larus marinus

The Great Black-backed Gull is the largest, and most maritime of our *Larus* gulls. Unfortunately, its predatory and piratical feeding habits have earned it the further distinction of being the most notorious. For this reason it is often persecuted by farmers, in defence of their livestock, and by conservationists in defence of more vulnerable bird species, the adults, eggs and young of which may fall prey to these formidable birds. During summer, the Great Black-backed Gull is comparatively solitary, and the large, dense breeding colonies, so characteristic of other gulls, are rare. In contrast, during winter, large concentrations of several thousand birds occur on certain coasts in Britain, especially Shetland and Fair Isle.

Though the Great Black-backed Gull is a coastal nester, the map clearly demonstrates that, in winter, it occurs in comparatively large numbers inland throughout much of England, and to a lesser extent in Scotland. It retains a predominantly coastal distribution in Wales and Ireland. During winter it takes advantage of the abundant food supplies available at refuse tips near urban areas. Thus its inland distribution is to some extent tied to centres of human population. Studies with marked birds have shown that, inland, outside of the breeding season, females are seen twice as often as males, particularly in autumn (Coulson *et al* 1984). None-the-less, most Great Black-backed Gulls still appear to forage mainly on natural marine foods in winter, although they do make some use of waste fish obtained around fishing vessels (Watson 1981). At most winter feeding sites they tend to dominate other gulls.

The *Breeding Atlas* shows that the Great Black-backed Gull is almost completely absent, as a breeding bird, from the east coast of Britain south of the Firth of Forth. During winter however, large numbers are found in these areas, several thousand birds having been counted, for example, on the Northumberland and Durham coasts on the same day (Coulson *et al* 1984). These are predominantly adult birds, and ring-ing recoveries have shown that they originate from breeding colonies along the entire coast of Norway. This is in marked contrast to the Norwegian Herring Gulls *L. argentatus* overwintering in Britain, which come mainly from the extreme north of Norway. These Norwegian adult Great Black-backed Gulls show a marked tendency to return to the same wintering areas from year to year, whereas ringing studies suggest that the immatures wander over large areas. The Great Black-backed Gulls leave Norway as early as July, most having arrived in Britain by the end of September. These birds rarely penetrate to the west coast of Britain, but winter along most of the east coast, like the Norwegian Herring Gulls. However, unlike Herring Gulls, there is no appreciable colour or size variation between the British and Norwegian breeding populations of Great Black-backed Gulls.

The Great Black-backed Gulls wintering on the west coast of Britain, and presumably those also in Ireland, are predominantly local breeding birds. Analysis of ringing recoveries has shown that the British breeding population is resident and, although there is a general southward movement in winter, movements over 300 km are rare (Harris 1962).

The British population of Great Black-backed Gulls has increased since around 1880, and Operation Seafarer in 1969–70 estimated the breeding birds in Britain and Ireland at over 25,000 pairs. It is difficult to judge the extent to which the native population in winter is augmented by the Scandinavian visitors, since many of the latter feed almost entirely at sea, and the numbers present on our coasts fluctuate greatly from day to day, presumably in response to changing sea conditions. However, Britain, Ireland and Norway together hold over 50% of the estimated 155,000 breeding pairs of Great Black-backed Gulls in the western Palearctic (*BWP*). Therefore, even allowing for the fact that only a proportion of the Norwegian birds overwinters in Britain, our wintering population is of some international importance.

P. MONAGHAN

Total number of squares in which recorded: 2,542 (66%)

No. of birds seen in a day	Number (%) of squares		
	Britain	Ireland	TOTAL (incl. C.I.)
1–10	1,006 (50%)	241 (45%)	1,248 (49%)
11–59	599 (30%)	183 (35%)	783 (31%)
60+	401 (20%)	107 (20%)	511 (20%)

References

COULSON, J. C., J. BUTTERFIELD, N. DUNCAN, S. KEARSEY, P. MONAGHAN and C. THOMAS. 1984. Origin and behaviour of Great Black-backed Gulls wintering in northeast England. *Brit. Birds* 77: 1–11.

HARRIS, M. P. 1962. Recoveries of ringed Great Black-backed Gulls. *Bird Study* 9: 192–197.

WATSON, P. S. 1981. Seabird observations from commercial trawlers in the Irish Sea. *Brit. Birds* 71: 82–90.

Breeding Atlas p 208

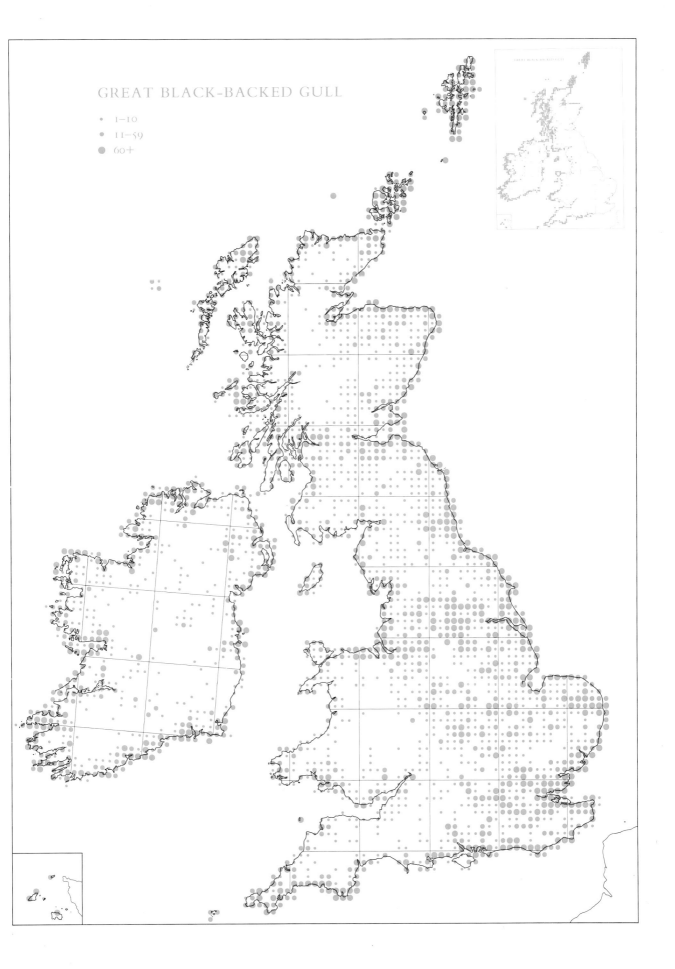

GREAT BLACK-BACKED GULL

- 1–10
- 11–59
- 60+

Kittiwake

Rissa tridactyla

The Kittiwake is best known for its call, from which it derives its common name, and for the large, crowded and noisy colonies which occur on steep sea cliffs around most of Britain and Ireland and in more northern coastal areas on both sides of the Atlantic.

The Kittiwake is the most oceanic of our breeding gulls and, north of 40°N, is commonly found in winter in flocks across the whole of the North Atlantic, often hundreds of kilometres from land. The birds roost on the sea. These extensive winter movements are confirmed by a long series of recoveries in Newfoundland, Labrador and Greenland of chicks ringed in Britain and Ireland. This oceanic distribution also involves Kittiwakes from more northern colonies in Norway and arctic USSR, and throughout the North Atlantic there is considerable mixing of birds from all breeding areas. As recently as 20 years ago it was rare to find Kittiwakes on the coast of Britain in late November and December, apart from groups of birds passing along the coast some distance off-shore. More recently, small numbers occur throughout the winter around harbours and fish docks, and this new habit accounts for part of the distribution shown on the map. In particular, this habit explains the records in Kent, Lancashire and Cheshire, areas without large breeding colonies. However, it is not known whether these Kittiwakes are from British colonies or are birds which are far from their nesting areas. The date of return of adults to the colonies varies considerably from area to area and from colony to colony. In a few colonies, Kittiwakes start to re-occupy the nesting sites in January, but elsewhere it is February or even early March before birds arrive. At a colony at North Shields, Kittiwakes re-occupied the colony progressively earlier between 1954 and 1970, with a few birds being seen on nesting ledges by Christmas Day in 1969. Since then, however, the return date has become steadily later again, and in the last few years the first birds did not return until the latter part of February, some two months later. In general, the older breeding birds return to the colony first and

young birds (those about to breed for the first time) do not arrive until April. Thus the winter distribution map consists of two components: some old Kittiwakes which have recently returned to the vicinity of their breeding colony and others which have found new winter feeding areas.

The number of inland records is surprising and difficult to explain. These inland records are concentrated in England, with only 3 in Wales, about 7 in Scotland and 2 in Ireland. Kittiwakes do not readily move inland and it is likely that many of these records are of storm-driven birds, which are 'wrecked' in an unfamiliar habitat. Many of the inland birds are later found dead and it is likely that they are already weak or ill when driven inland. In general, Kittiwakes do not seem to be able to feed adequately on inland waters although they have been seen taking young salmonids in the upper tidal reaches of the River Tyne.

During the breeding season the main food of the Kittiwake is fish but, in the Arctic, crustaceans also form an important component of their food. Little is known of the food obtained in the Atlantic during the winter but it is unlikely that fish remains the main food. The few pieces of information available suggest that planktonic marine invertebrates (crustaceans, molluscs and marine worms) become the main source of food.

The winter records consist of less than 1% of the birds that would have been reported in the summer. In winter the great majority of Kittiwakes are still at sea, and, perhaps, only 1,000 birds are within easy view around the coast (and inland). In the new year the numbers increase but will, even so, vary from day to day.

J. C. COULSON

Total number of squares in which recorded: 876 (23%)

No. of birds	Number (%) of squares		
seen in a day	Britain	Ireland	TOTAL (incl. C.I.)
1–6	373 (55%)	74 (38%)	447 (51%)
7–42	182 (27%)	69 (36%)	253 (29%)
43+	124 (18%)	50 (26%)	176 (20%)

References

COULSON, J. C. and C. S. THOMAS. 1985. Changes in the biology of the Kittiwake *Rissa tridactyla*: a 31 year study of a breeding colony. *J. Anim. Ecol.* 54: 9–26.

Breeding Atlas p 218

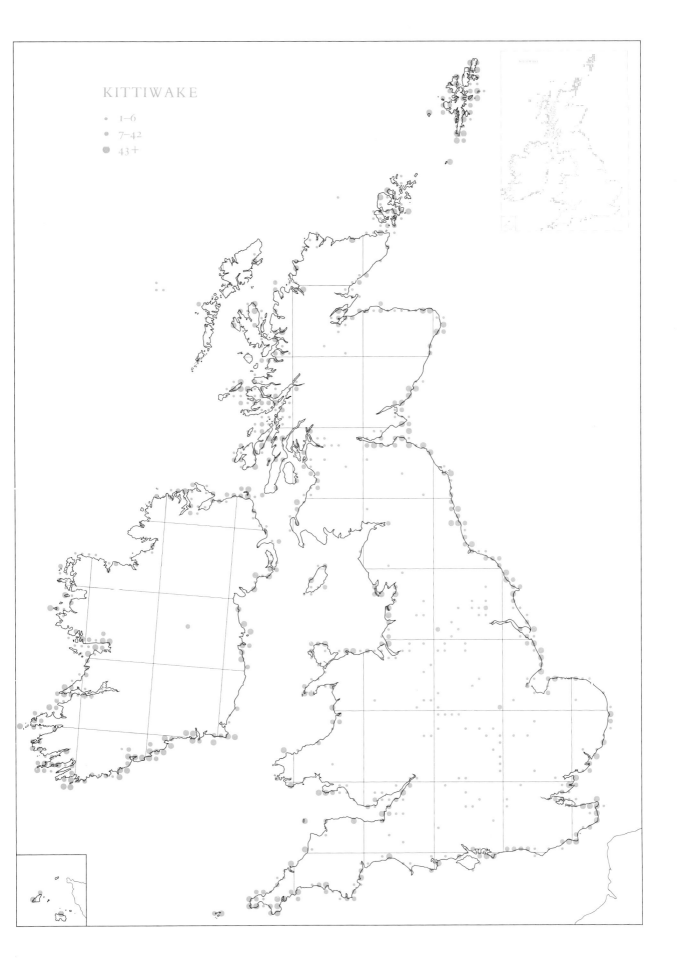

KITTIWAKE

- 1–6
- 7–42
- 43+

Guillemot

Uria aalge

The Guillemot is not uncommonly seen in winter, for it often fishes close to land and numbers of dead or moribund individuals are regularly drifted ashore. Its rather elongated form, pointed bill, dark upperparts and contrasting white underparts (in winter plumage, including the neck and throat) and characteristic habit of suddenly ducking under the water with partly spread wings, soon identify it.

This species is far more widespread in winter than in summer; Guillemots occur, for example, off SE England although none nest between Flamborough Head and the Isle of Wight. It is commonest just offshore, and can be seen anywhere around the coasts, especially in the north and west, and is sometimes abundant (as in Shetland), occurring well up firths and tidal lochs. Guillemots visit breeding colonies during the winter. Several surprising gaps in the winter distribution (*eg* none were recorded at the large colonies at Clo Mor, North Rona and Skomer) are surely artefacts as birds will have been ashore at some time. The auk wreck in February 1983 (see under Razorbill *Alca torda*) resulted in at least 10,000 Guillemots washed ashore, and strong winds blew dying birds inland. However, the overall effect on winter distribution was far less than in Razorbill, Puffin *Fratercula arctica* and Little Auk *Alle alle*.

Guillemots leave the colonies between June and August, and the adults then undergo the main moult of the year, during which they are flightless for 6–7 weeks (Birkhead and Taylor 1977), and attain the white-necked winter plumage. Birds start to make short, early morning visits to some colonies from October and these individuals immediately begin to moult back into breeding plumage. Harris and Wanless (1984) have shown that these are breeding males and females returning to their nest sites. These late autumn returns have become earlier in recent decades (Taylor and Reid 1981). West coast birds generally return later (*eg* in December in Wales and Bristol Channel) but October visiting has been reported in S England and Ireland. Visits continue throughout the winter with perhaps a hiatus in mid winter.

Feeding birds often gather in small flocks and dive for a wide variety of fish, squid, pelagic worms and crustaceans.

Guillemots disperse widely during the winter, with first year birds (which become independent a couple of months after they have left the colony) migrating farthest. However, most ringed birds found dead in Britain and Ireland during the winter come from British and Irish colonies. These are augmented on North Sea coasts by a few birds from the Faeroes, Norway and Heligoland.

Stowe and Harris (1984) put the breeding population of Britain and Ireland at 1.1 million birds, which compared with an estimated 600,000 in 1969/70, and suggested that the population had increased by 5% per annum. Most recent census data suggest this rate may be slowing down in some areas. No winter population estimate is available.

M. P. HARRIS

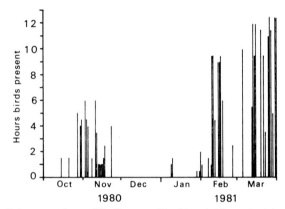

Colony attendance of Guillemots at Fowlsheugh (Grampian) during the 1980/81 winter as shown by time lapse photography every 30 minutes.

Total number of squares in which recorded: 750 (19%)

No. of birds seen in a day	Number (%) of squares		
	Britain	Ireland	TOTAL (incl. C.I.)
1–4	306 (51%)	75 (50%)	383 (51%)
5–20	175 (29%)	41 (27%)	217 (29%)
21+	115 (19%)	34 (23%)	150 (20%)

References

BIRKHEAD, T. R. and A. M. TAYLOR. 1977. Moult of the Guillemot *Uria aalge. Ibis* 119: 80–85.

HARRIS, M. P. and S. WANLESS. 1984. The effect of the wreck of seabirds in February 1983 on auk populations on the Isle of May (Fife). *Bird Study* 31: 103–110.

STOWE, T. J. and M. P. HARRIS. 1984. Status of Guillemots and Razorbills in Britain and Ireland. *Seabird* 7: 5–18.

TAYLOR, K. and J. B. REID. 1981. Earlier colony attendance by Guillemots and Razorbills. *Scot. Birds* 11: 173–180.

Breeding Atlas p 232

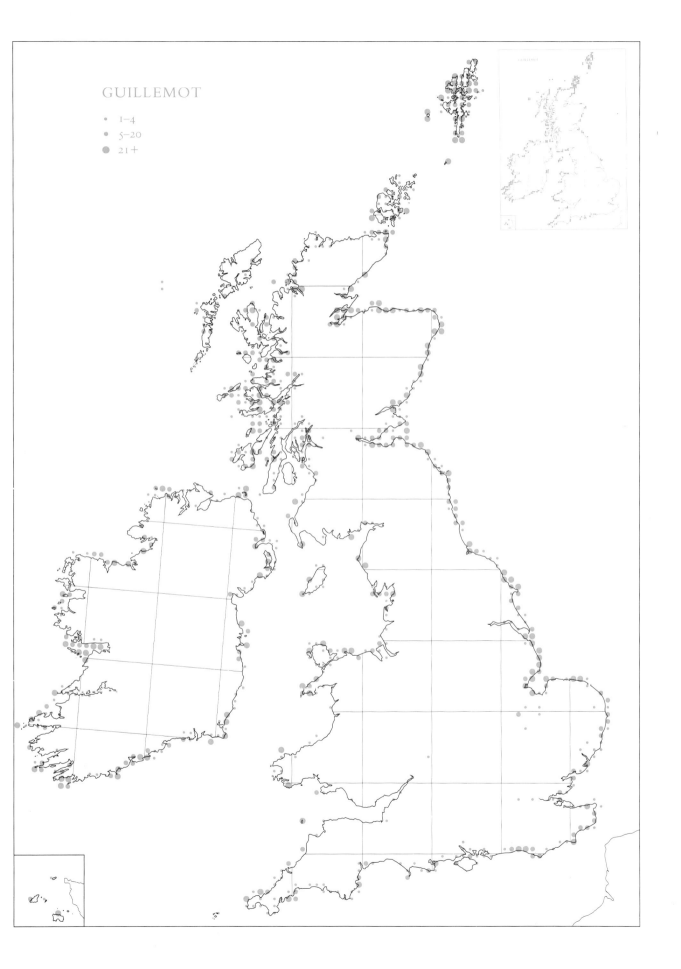

GUILLEMOT

- 1–4
- 5–20
- 21+

Razorbill

Alca torda

The Razorbill is restricted to the North Atlantic, and Britain is one of the strongholds of this strikingly handsome auk. The distribution is approximately the same as that of the Guillemot *Uria aalge*, both in winter and summer, but Razorbills are usually far less common. In winter plumage they are difficult to separate from Guillemots at a distance and many records are lost within the 'unidentified auk' category.

The species is more widespread in winter than in summer, occurring for example in SE England where none breed. The main map of all records includes those during a major wreck of seabirds which occurred in E Britain in February 1983. The small map on p. 424 shows details of records in 1981/82 and 1983/84 and is probably the normal winter pattern in Britain and Ireland.

Such wrecks occur fairly frequently but this was more spectacular and better documented than most (4 papers in *Bird Study* 31: 79–110). Corpses collected included 17,986 Razorbills, 10,170 Guillemots, 1,642 Puffins *Fratercula arctica*, 1,207 Little Auks *Alle alle*, and 7 Black Guillemots *Cepphus grylle*, on coasts from Orkney to Kent, the highest density being between Lothian and Suffolk. Some auks were also blown inland. The first signs of anything untoward were large numbers of auks inshore in Shetland in January, although this is now almost an annual occurrence, and in the Beauly and Moray Firths in February. Razorbills and Guillemots stopped visiting Scottish colonies about 25 January and did not return until 19 February. Dead and dying auks came ashore in February after the wind became easterly. These birds were emaciated and only 4 out of a thousand examined had any food in their stomachs. Blake (1984) concluded that the wreck was due to a combination of adverse weather and changing patterns of abundance of sprats. Ringing and morphological studies showed that most of the birds were British.

Razorbills vacate the colonies by mid August and adults moult into winter plumage. During the moult they are flightless and most birds then shun land until February or March. However, at some colonies in

E Scotland, breeding adults visit their ledges in October or November. Such visits are sporadic and, as they occur just after dawn, are frequently overlooked, but are probably becoming more widespread. The map underestimates the winter numbers of Razorbills at some north and east breeding areas.

The limited data on food, derived from hard remains in stomachs of dead birds, show that winter food is mainly fish such as sandeel, sprat, herring, whiting and other Gadidae. Pelagic worms and crustaceans are also taken. Razorbills probably take more sandeels than do Guillemots (Blake 1983). Migration patterns are complicated but, generally, first year birds move further than adults (Mead 1974). Young from Irish Sea colonies winter off France and Iberia and in the Mediterranean. Adults rarely move further than France. Many N British Razorbills visit Norway but many others are recovered much further south. Ringing also shows that some Russian, Norwegian and probably many Icelandic Razorbills winter around Britain.

Lloyd (1976) speculated that the British and Irish breeding population was roughly 150,000 pairs, or 70% of the world population as it was then known. However, it is now realised that the Icelandic population is much larger than previously thought; but many of these birds winter in our area, hence we still have responsibility for the majority of Razorbills. No winter population estimate is available.

M. P. HARRIS

Total number of squares in which recorded: 618 (16%)

No. of birds seen in a day	Number (%) of squares Britain	Ireland	TOTAL (incl. C.I.)
1–3	220 (48%)	87 (54%)	307 (50%)
4–16	144 (32%)	43 (27%)	189 (31%)
17+	89 (20%)	32 (20%)	122 (20%)

References

BLAKE, B. F. 1983. A comparative study of the diet of auks killed during an oil incident in the Skagerrak in January 1981. *J. Zool. Lond.* 201: 1–12.

BLAKE, B. F. 1984. Diet and fish stock availability as possible factors in the mass death of auks in the North Sea. *J. Exp. Mar. Biol. Ecol.* 76: 89–103.

LLOYD, C. S. 1976. An estimate of the world breeding population of the Razorbill. *Brit. Birds* 69: 298–304.

MEAD, C. J. 1974. The results of ringing auks in Britain and Ireland. *Bird Study* 21: 45–86.

Breeding Atlas p 230

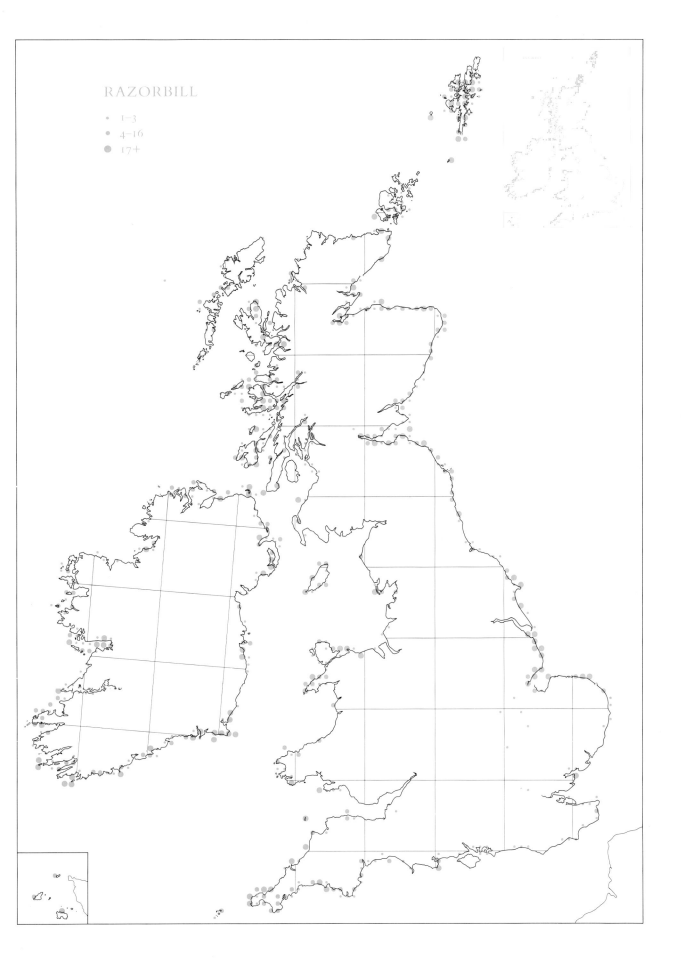

RAZORBILL

- • 1–3
- • 4–16
- • 17+

Black Guillemot

Cepphus grylle

The name Black Guillemot is somewhat misleading in winter, for this dynamic little seabird moults the spectacular black summer dress and adopts a whitish-grey plumage, making it very difficult to spot in the grey winter light and the rough seas. From the strongholds in the north comes the Shetland name 'Tystie', which is widely used today and is similar to most Scandinavian names for the species.

The winter map indicates a fairly even distribution around the rocky northern and western coasts of Scotland and Ireland, with the island groups of Shetland, Orkney, and the Hebrides of particular importance as they offer a large number of suitable sheltered feeding areas. The long stretches of Welsh and English coastline, dominated by pebbles, sand and mud, are clearly not favoured by Tysties. Although Shetland appears to hold more Tysties in winter than other areas, this result is almost certainly biased by recent intensive studies there, in which Tysties were only counted when the seas were calm, making the birds far more obvious. Winter distribution closely matches that in summer (see the *Breeding Atlas*), confirming the relatively sedentary life style at this southern fringe of the Black Guillemot's range, and the broadly similar niche in the different seasons.

Little is known of Tystie ecology outside the breeding season. The general pattern in winter appears to be a regular daily dispersal from roost aggregations (in sheltered waters if available), to the foraging areas around all available rocky coasts. Tysties have been observed roosting on cliff ledges on rough winter nights (R. A. Broad), and in some instances large numbers have perished during winter storms (Formosov, in Petersen 1981). Tysties forage largely amongst weed on the sea bed, avoiding areas with sandy bottoms lacking seaweed cover, and are mostly found in water depths of 1–40 m (P. J. Ewins, Nilsson 1982). The scanty information on winter diet suggests that in addition to inshore fish species, significant quantities of Crustacea and a wide variety of other invertebrates are taken, possibly due to fish scarcity at this time of year.

In N Scotland the first adults moult back into summer plumage in January, and on fine mornings engage in dawn displays on the sea at breeding localities.

Tysties have a holarctic distribution, and as a breeding species are most numerous within the Arctic Circle (Croxall *et al* 1984). In such regions many may be forced to move south in winter, depending on the prevailing ice conditions. At present the only evidence of any winter immigration is provided by 2 Swedish birds recovered in their first winter on the east coast of England. There are no recoveries of British or Irish ringed Tysties in other countries. ing results suggest some limited movement, particularly of immatures (the longest being 869 km—a chick ringed on Fair Isle and shot in its first winter in Essex). When sexually mature, at 3–4 years, adults are less likely to move far from the breeding regions: of all winter recoveries, 78% were within 100 km of the ringing site, emphasising the relatively sedentary life-style when compared with our other breeding auks.

The *Breeding Atlas* gives the total population as 8,340 pairs, based on the 1969/70 Operation Seafarer results. Recent surveys indicate that the real figure may be 2–3 times this value (Ewins and Tasker 1985), *ie* 33,000–50,000 breeding birds. In Shetland an average of 1.2 young fledged per breeding attempt (Ewins and Perrins unpubl.), which when combined with population parameters given by Petersen (1981), gives an estimated 25,000–30,000 immature and sub-adult birds in December. As there is no evidence of emigration, and probably little immigration, the December Tystie population is estimated to be 58,000–80,000 birds around Britain and Ireland.

Although lack of meaningful counts prevents any assessment of status changes, most suitable areas appear to support a healthy population.

P. J. EWINS

Total number of squares in which recorded: 512 (13%)

No. of birds seen in a day	Number (%) of squares		
	Britain	Ireland	TOTAL (incl. C.I.)
1–3	192 (56%)	86 (51%)	278 (54%)
4–10	80 (23%)	54 (32%)	134 (26%)
11 +	72 (21%)	28 (17%)	100 (20%)

References

CROXALL, J. P., P. G. H. EVANS and R. W. SCHREIBER. 1984. *Status and Conservation of the World's Seabirds.* ICBP Technical Publication No. 2. Cambridge.

EWINS, P. J. and M. L. TASKER. 1985. The breeding distribution of Black Guillemots *Cepphus grylle* in Orkney and Shetland, 1982–84. *Bird Study* 32: 186–193.

NILSSON, L. 1982. (Winter distribution of the Black Guillemot *Cepphus grylle* along the Baltic coast of Sweden) (Engl. summary). *Anser* 21: 89–92.

PETERSEN, A. 1981. *Breeding Biology and Feeding Ecology of Black Guillemots.* D.Phil. Thesis, University of Oxford.

Breeding Atlas p 234

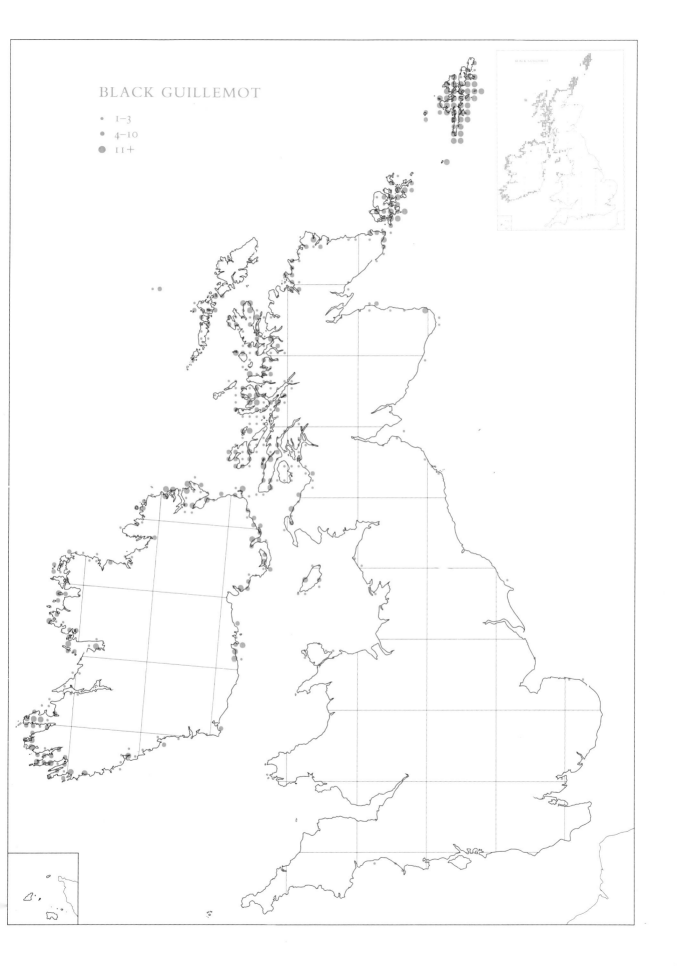

BLACK GUILLEMOT

- · 1–3
- ● 4–10
- ● 11+

Little Auk

Alle alle

RG

The Little Auk is a pelagic species in winter, spending its time some distance offshore, and rarely visible from the coast except when strong winds drive it onshore. Flocks or 'flights' of Little Auks are fairly regular near Shetland and, with onshore winds, not uncommon along the east coast of Britain in late October and early November. In particularly stormy conditions wrecks may occur with birds being blown well inland.

The distribution and number of records on the map clearly show the effects of the unusual weather conditions that caused a major wreck of auk species in February 1983 (see also map p. 424). During strong northeasterly winds, flights of up to 3,500 Little Auks were observed moving north up the east coast of Britain. Over 1,200 Little Auk corpses were picked up on beaches from N Scotland to Kent, with the highest densities between East Lothian and Suffolk (Underwood and Stowe 1984). The RSPB's Beached Birds Surveys for the period 1972–1982 shows that most records of dead birds come from E Scotland, NE England and East Anglia, in January and February.

Most of the 100 inland records relate to this incident and were southwest of the highest concentrations of coastally wrecked birds. Razorbills *Alca torda*, Guillemots *Uria aalge* and Puffins *Fratercula arctica* were also wrecked in unusually high numbers on the coast and many were reported inland.

In the wreck in February 1950, many hundreds of birds were blown onshore and inland in SW England and Ireland, indicating that a large number of birds was wintering off the southwest coast of Ireland.

The Little Auk breeds in the high Arctic. It begins to leave its colonies in August and as the sea starts to freeze it moves further south into the Norwegian Sea. Studies at sea (Blake *et al* 1984) have shown that it is distributed widely throughout the northern North Sea during the winter, moving back north in March. Concentrations have been observed off northern Denmark in October and January, and north of the Dogger Bank in February (Joiris 1983). All of the populations are of the race *A. a. alle* except for the Franz Josef Land birds *A. a. polaris,* which are larger. The birds seen in the North Sea probably originate from colonies in Spitzbergen and further east, and some large specimens have been attributed to *A. a. polaris.* Greenland birds which winter off the east coast of North America may reach our seas and could have been responsible for the wreck in 1950 (Sergeant 1952).

The Little Auk is highly gregarious, forming large breeding colonies. This gregarious nature is also reflected in its numbers at sea. Although sightings at sea are rare, flights off the coast often number hundreds and sometimes thousands. Little Auks feed on zooplankton, small crustacea and small fish which presumably are difficult to catch in bad weather. Post mortem examinations of individuals wrecked during February 1983 showed that they were short of food (Hope Jones *et al* 1984) and their weakened condition, combined with adverse weather, was probably responsible for the wreck.

The world population of Little Auks has been estimated at 30 million, and it may be the most numerous sea bird in the world. The numbers occurring around the coast of Britain and Ireland are not known. Britain and Ireland are at the southern edge of the wintering range of the Little Auk, but individuals have been recorded much further south in Portugal, Spain, Italy, Malta, Madeira and the Azores. During the February 1983 wreck there were unusually high numbers in the Netherlands, France and the Channel Islands.

C. HARBARD

Total number of squares in which recorded: 248 (6%)

No. of birds seen in a day	Number (%) of squares		
	Britain	Ireland	TOTAL (incl. C.I.)
1	138 (61%)	15 (88%)	155 (63%)
2–3	39 (17%)	0 (0%)	40 (16%)
4+	51 (22%)	2 (12%)	53 (21%)

References

BLAKE, B. E., M. L. TASKER, P. HOPE JONES, T. J. DIXON, R. MITCHELL and D. R. LANGSLOW. 1984. *Seabird Distribution in the North Sea.* NCC, Huntingdon.

HOPE JONES, P., C. F. BARRETT, G. P. MUDGE and M. P. HARRIS. 1984. Physical conditions of auks beached in eastern Britain during the wreck of February 1983. *Bird Study* 31: 95–98.

JOIRIS, C. 1983. Winter distribution of seabirds in the North Sea: an oceanological interpretation. *Le Gerfaut* 73: 107–123.

SERGEANT, D. E. 1952. Little Auks in Britain, 1948 to 1951. *Brit. Birds* 45: 122–133.

UNDERWOOD, L. A. and T. J. STOWE. 1984. Massive wreck of seabirds in eastern Britain, 1983. *Bird Study* 31: 79–88.

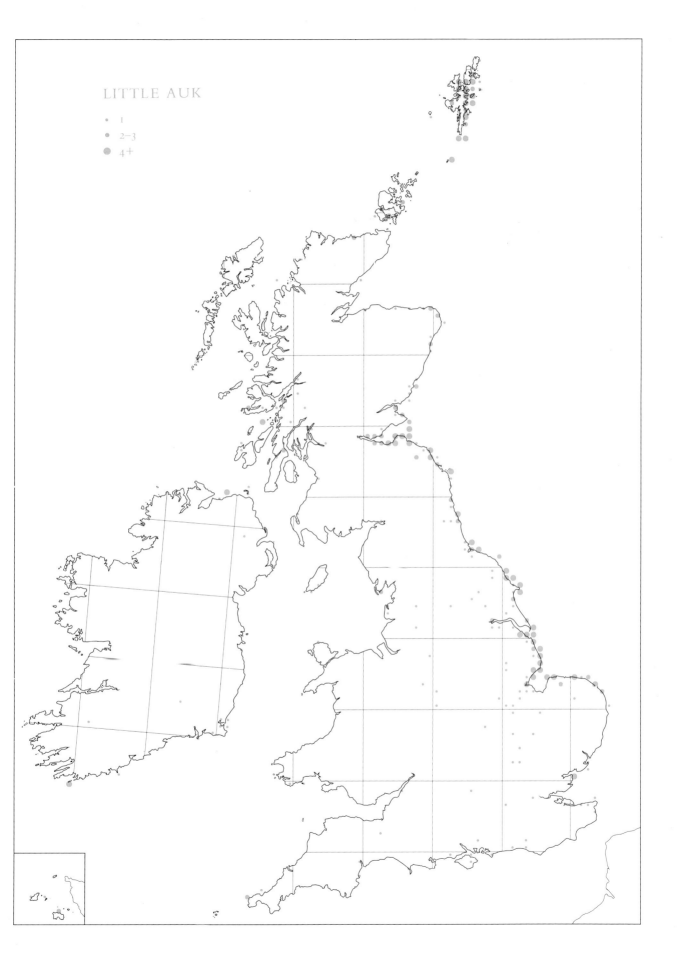

LITTLE AUK

- 1
- 2–3
- 4+

Puffin

Fratercula arctica

The Puffin in its breeding plumage is familiar to us all. It nests in large numbers on isolated islands and steep, inaccessible mainland cliffs where it can be seen standing about on grassy tops, or gathered in rafts on the nearby sea. The situation in winter is very different, for the beak loses its colour, the face becomes dark and the birds all but disappear into the vastness of the oceans.

Normally the Puffin is pelagic in winter and, apart from the occasional bird migrating rapidly north or south just within sight of the most exposed headland, records probably refer to oiled or sick individuals. The picture for 1981/82 and 1983/84 from around Ireland and W Britain is typical of a normal winter, *ie* virtually no records, and is shown on the smaller map on this page. The 1982/83 winter was atypical: most of the Puffins along the east coast of England and Scotland, and all the inland records, were victims of an auk wreck in February 1983 (see Razorbill).

Puffins leave British colonies in August. The young fledge and depart alone but are soon followed by the adults and immatures, which by then are shedding the horny plates at the base of the beak, the cere and the eye-ornaments. A healthy Puffin does not approach land again until the spring. Reports of flocks or even small groups of Puffins are rare in the winter, so presumably the species is solitary at this season. As in the summer, fish is the staple food. In Britain, sandeels, sprats, herrings and some gadoid fish (*eg* whiting and haddock) predominate. Further north capelin and arctic cod are eaten. Quantities of pelagic worms, small squid and planktonic crustaceans are also taken.

The main moult occurs just before the breeding season, unlike the other Atlantic auks which moult after breeding. The Puffin is then flightless although the wings are still adequate enough to be used for swimming underwater. The timing of the moult varies, being earlier in birds from east coast colonies and later on the west. The variation in the moult allows a few birds from NE Scotland to return to the colonies by the end of February, whereas west coast popula-

tions do not return until late March or early April.

Puffins nesting in W Britain and Ireland disperse very widely in winter. Ringed birds have been recovered from Newfoundland to Italy, and from Greenland to the Canary Islands. A guess puts the winter density of Puffins in the N Atlantic as one every 1–2 km² of sea and certainly very few are seen by ocean-crossing ornithologists. East coast birds mostly remain in the North Sea (where they are joined by some Norwegian birds), but increasing numbers now go through the English Channel to the Bay of Biscay. None appear to winter in the Irish Sea.

M. P. HARRIS

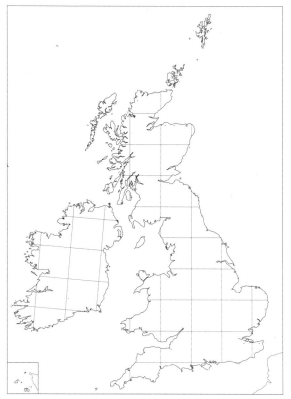

The distribution of the Puffin in the 1981/82 and 1983/84 winters combined. The scale of abundance is as for the main map.

Total number of squares in which recorded: 126 (3%)

No. of birds seen in a day	Number (%) of squares		
	Britain	Ireland	TOTAL (incl. C.I.)
1	62 (54%)	5 (46%)	67 (53%)
2–4	31 (28%)	4 (36%)	36 (29%)
5 +	21 (18%)	2 (18%)	23 (18%)

References

HARRIS, M. P. 1984. *The Puffin*. Poyser, Calton.

HARRIS, M. P. and J. R. G. HISLOP. 1978. The food of young Puffins *Fratercula arctica*. *J. Zool. Lond.* 185: 213–236.

HARRIS, M. P. and R. F. YULE. 1977. The moult of the Puffin *Fratercula arctica*. *Ibis* 119: 535–541.

Breeding Atlas p 236

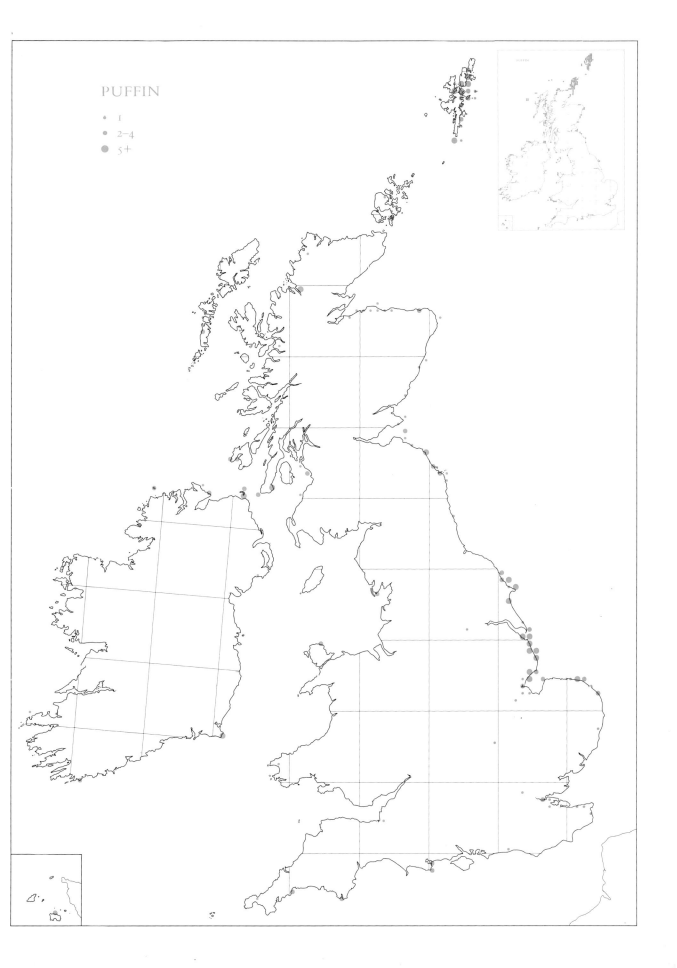

PUFFIN

- · 1
- ● 2–4
- ● 5+

Rock Dove and Feral Pigeon

Columba livia

The Rock Dove is the sole ancestor of all forms of the domestic pigeon. Feral pigeons have derived from domestic pigeons that strayed, were lost or were abandoned by their owners. For the most part they originate from the Rock Dove-like old time dovecote pigeons, racing homers and nondescript domestic pigeons. In some places Rock Doves appear to interbreed very little with domestic or Feral Pigeons, but in others there seems to have been considerable interbreeding. Separation of Rock Doves from Feral Pigeons is not always easy, and where individual birds are concerned may be impossible. In Britain many hundreds, possibly thousands, of lost young racing homers are yearly added to the feral populations in some areas.

The map shows that Feral Pigeons are now widespread and they do occur in what are regarded as the last strongholds of wild Rock Doves in N and W Scotland, the Hebrides, Shetland and the W Irish coast. Rock Doves and Feral Pigeons are normally resident but with dispersal of some juveniles. On Fair Isle, however, the Rock Dove is said to be a regular passage migrant. Seasonal migration of Rock Doves has also been claimed for some Saharan areas. Changes of roosting and/or feeding sites by Feral Pigeons, commonly in response to human activities, usually involve movements of at most a few kilometres. Differences between the winter map and that in the *Breeding Atlas* are more likely to represent movements of the recorders rather than of the birds.

Rock Doves, and many coastal populations of Feral Pigeons, roost in caves or on sheltered ledges of sea cliffs. They feed mostly in nearby arable land or grass pasture (in the western Scottish islands particularly on the machair), principally on weed seeds, cultivated grains and pulses and small snails. Elsewhere, Feral Pigeons are sometimes based on inland cliffs but more often on buildings or on ledges under bridges. Especially in the suburbs, suitable buildings may be in short supply and many birds roost perforce on roofs where they have no overhead protection and are soaked in really heavy rain.

Rural populations of Feral Pigeons, like Rock Doves, feed mainly on farmland. Those living in towns and some suburbs rely largely on bread or other food given to them, or on food scavenged from wharves or warehouses where grain is handled and spilled. In winter, competition from other birds,

especially gulls, is often intense.

Where Feral or Rock Pigeons feed on farmland, they tend to aggregate in large numbers on fields which are still productive. When disturbed on the feeding site, a large feeding flock may behave as a unit, rising to fly a little way or circle and then alight again; but usually the birds come and go in small groups and, though less often than in spring or summer, in pairs or singly. They often feed in company with Stock Doves *Columba oenas* and/or Woodpigeons *C. palumbus*. Commonly, the species separate at once when they rise but sometimes mixed groups of Feral Pigeons and Stock Doves will fly together for a short distance. When the three species are together on cabbage fields in winter, the Woodpigeons usually feed mainly on the leaves of the crop, whereas Feral Pigeons and Stock Doves take weed seeds.

In farmland it is unlikely that food competition with Stock Doves is an important factor, as although Rock Doves are found mainly where Stock Doves are absent, Feral Pigeons and Stock Doves are widely sympatric.

The Rock Dove in Britain is at the northwestern edge of its range. Feral Pigeons are now almost worldwide in distribution, occurring well to the north of the species' natural range and in the far south of South America. Estimates of numbers of birds occurring in Britain and Ireland are very difficult to make because of the problem of deciding which are feral and which are domestic.

D. GOODWIN

Total number of squares in which recorded: 2,249 (58%)

No. of birds seen in a day	Number (%) of squares		
	Britain	Ireland	TOTAL (incl. C.I.)
1–30	872 (46%)	274 (78%)	1,146 (51%)
31–114	593 (31%)	58 (17%)	652 (29%)
115+	431 (23%)	18 (5%)	451 (20%)

References

DAVIS, P. 1963. The Birds of Fair Isle. *Fair Isle Observatory Bull.* 5: 3–11, 34–45, 70–90, 114–134.

GOODWIN, D. 1981. Some personal notes on Rock Pigeons. *Avic. Mag.* 87: 19–33.

GOODWIN, D. 1983. *Pigeons and Doves of the World.* 3rd edn. Brit. Mus. Nat. Hist., London.

HEWSON, R. 1967. The Rock Dove in Scotland in 1965. *Scot. Birds* 4: 359–371.

Breeding Atlas p 240

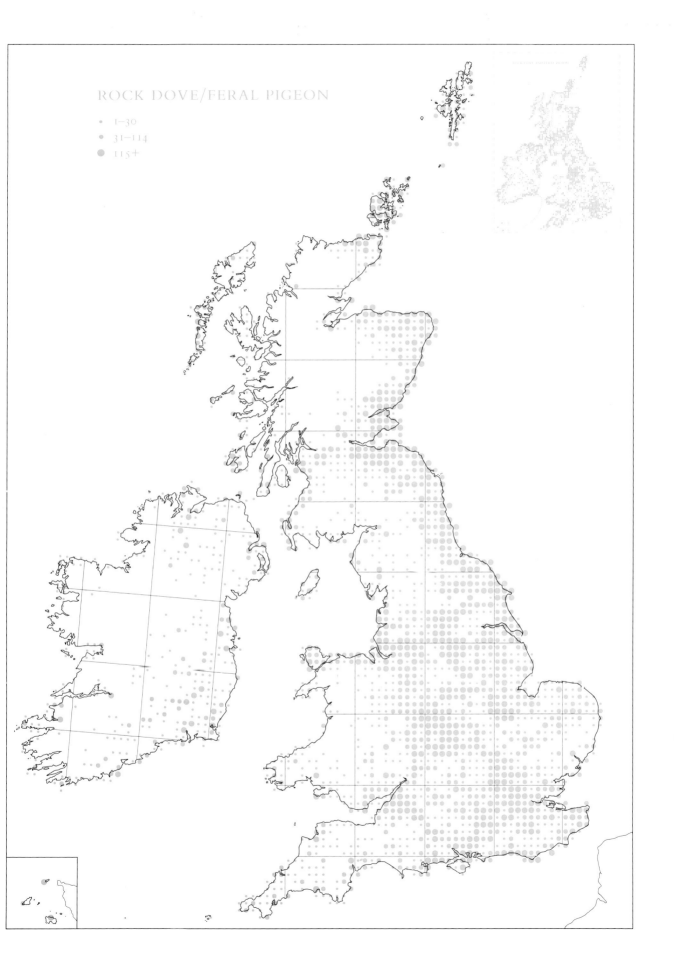

ROCK DOVE/FERAL PIGEON

- 1–30
- 31–114
- 115+

Stock Dove

Columba oenas

The Stock Dove is amongst the scarcer winter species, most frequently seen as groups of 10–50 birds erupting from cereal stubbles and weedy arable fields.

The winter distribution is rather similar to that of the *Breeding Atlas*. Most of the population lies within England and Wales, and in Scotland the species is concentrated in the principal agricultural areas in the south and along the east coast. In Ireland the majority of sightings came from the wheat and barley areas of the southeastern half of the island and from the more localized cereal areas of Ulster. Outside these areas records were scarce, particularly in the *Breeding Atlas* areas west of the river Shannon and on the mountains of Kerry and of Wicklow. Such a contraction in range is less apparent within Britain, though Common Birds Census densities of this species decrease with altitude.

The winter biology of the Stock Dove has received little attention beyond the year-round study of its diet by Murton *et al* (1964). Throughout the year Stock Doves mainly feed on weed seeds, though grain is taken from cereal stubbles when available, mostly from October to December. Even then weed seeds (principally of *Sinapsis* and *Brassica* species such as charlock and rape, but also including chickweed, fathen and various species of *Polygonum*) constitute a significant fraction of the diet. Fallow or ploughed land, and areas where there is still some stubble, are the main feeding habitats from January through to March. The massive increase since the *Breeding Atlas* in the winter barley acreage in Britain must have influenced this species but this effect has not been investigated (Robertson 1984).

Ringing recoveries reflect the sedentary nature of the species in Britain. They show that 74% of birds were found within 8 km of the ringing site, and only 11% moved more than 40 km (Murton 1966). However, some Continental birds winter in Britain.

Stock Doves spread northwards during the latter half of the 19th century, largely in response to the expansion of arable farming. The British population fell sharply between 1950 and 1961 with the introduction of toxic seed-dressings, to which the Stock Dove was especially vulnerable because of its habit of taking seeds from the spring sowings. In the areas of intensive arable production Stock Doves were largely wiped out at this time. With subsequent restrictions on organo-chlorine chemicals, the species has recovered and regained much of its former numbers and range. The most intensively arable areas may no longer be favoured as much as formerly, partly because of loss of nesting holes through the removal of old farm buildings and of copses and hedges with big old trees, and partly because regular herbicide applications reduce the abundance of weed seeds (O'Connor and Shrubb in press). The winter distribution in Britain in fact shows greatest densities in the areas of mixed farming, with numbers decreasing as either arable farming or pastoral farming dominates. In Ireland the intensification of cereal farming has not progressed to the same degree and the correlation with cereal growing continues.

The *Breeding Atlas* estimated a breeding population of just over 100,000 pairs in Britain and Ireland, but with continued increase in the Common Birds Census index this might now be the size of the British population alone. However, the *Winter Atlas* data correspond to only 30,000–63,000+ birds. Within Britain, CBC densities decrease sharply westwards, so that in the *Breeding Atlas* the halving of average densities, before extrapolating to all squares with Stock Doves, was probably not conservative enough as a downwards adjustment. Nevertheless, there is probably also a degree of under-recording of Stock Doves in the course of the *Winter Atlas*.

R. J. O'CONNOR

Total number of squares in which recorded: 1,925 (50%)

No. of birds seen in a day	Number (%) of squares		
	Britain	Ireland	TOTAL (incl. C.I.)
1–14	750 (45%)	203 (79%)	954 (50%)
15–59	546 (33%)	40 (15%)	588 (31%)
60+	367 (22%)	15 (6%)	383 (20%)

References

MURTON, R. K. 1966. A statistical investigation of the effects of Woodpigeon shooting as evidenced by the recoveries of ringed birds. *Statistician* 16: 183–202.

MURTON, R. K., N. J. WESTWOOD and A. J. ISAACSON. 1964. The feeding habits of the Woodpigeon *Columba palumbus*, Stock Dove *C. oenas* and Turtle Dove *Streptopelia turtur*. *Ibis* 106: 174–188.

O'CONNOR, R. J. and C. J. MEAD. 1984. The Stock Dove in Britain, 1930–1980. *Brit. Birds* 77: 181–201.

O'CONNOR, R. J. and M. SHRUBB. In press. *Farming and Birds*. University Press, Cambridge.

ROBERTSON, H. A. 1984. *Ecology of the Collared Dove* Streptopelia decaocto *in relation to other British Columbidae*. D. Phil. Thesis, University of Oxford.

Breeding Atlas p 238

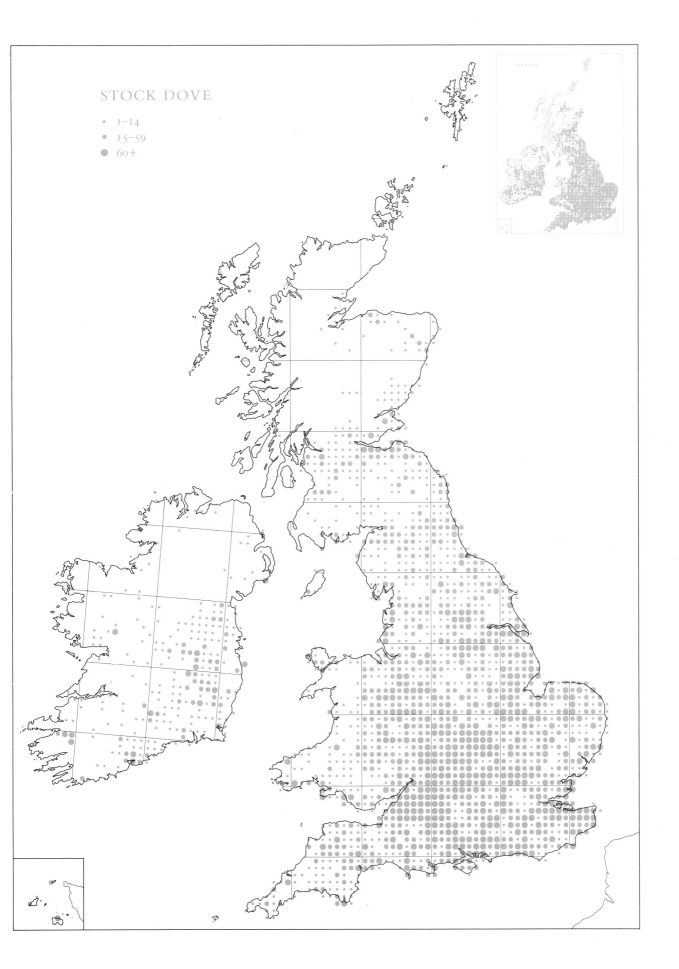

STOCK DOVE

- · 1–14
- ● 15–59
- ● 60+

Woodpigeon

Columba palumbus

In hard winters after falls of snow, large flocks of Woodpigeons can be seen resembling grey carpets around the few crops still visible, for although initially a woodland species they have coped very well with the changes wrought in our countryside by intensive farming and are now the major avian pest in Britain.

Woodpigeons breed almost everywhere in Britain and Ireland except on the higher hills and mountains. Whilst this widespread distribution is reflected in the winter map it is also clear that the largest winter concentrations occur in the major arable farming areas, namely central, southern and eastern England and the central lowlands of Scotland. Woodpigeons do feed on natural foods, such as acorns, beech nuts and a wide range of berries, throughout the winter, but these are insufficient to maintain the large population. The acreage of certain crops is the major limiting factor on population size.

In late autumn, Woodpigeons gather in large flocks on cereal stubbles, and when these are exhausted move to feed on winter cereal sowings. However, it is the food supply between January and March which provides the major check on population growth (Murton 1965). In the 1950s attempts to reduce Woodpigeon numbers through large scale shoots in autumn and early winter failed, since this did little more than reduce winter levels of natural mortality by creating less competition for food.

In the 1950s and 1960s, Woodpigeons survived the lean winter period by feeding mainly on clover and weeds present on pastures and leys. However, in the late 1960s and early 1970s the areas of grass and clover declined as more land was put to cereal growing. In addition, the increased use of herbicides and a switch from spring-sown to winter-sown cereals meant less fallow land containing weeds. These agricultural changes reduced the Woodpigeon population in arable areas in the early 1970s (I. R. Inglis and A. J. Isaacson). Nowadays oilseed rape, which is available throughout the winter months, largely fills the gap previously occupied by clover. A recent survey of oilseed rape growers (Lane 1983) indicates that Woodpigeon damage is their major problem and it is more severe than damage caused by insects and disease.

Evidence, both from direct observations and from the recovery of marked birds, indicates that British Woodpigeons move little in winter. Nevertheless there is a change of behaviour in November, particularly in young birds, towards an increasing tendency for southerly flights. The birds living in poor feeding areas such as the Lake District show this shift more markedly than do individuals in the more favourable areas like the southeast (Murton and Ridpath 1962). There is little evidence that British birds migrate to the Continent although some do migrate from the southwest to Ireland, and immigration from the Continent occurs on a small scale.

It is impossible to provide an accurate figure for the number of Woodpigeons in Britain and Ireland. The species is not often counted during Common Birds Census work as the Woodpigeon's breeding period extends well beyond the normal peak of census activity. Murton (1965) estimated that there were approximately 5.8 million birds in July in Britain, rising to well over 10 million at the end of the breeding season. He based this estimate on data derived from regular population scans of a 1,050 ha study site in Cambridgeshire. Monitoring of Woodpigeon numbers on this site is still continuing (I. R. Inglis and A. J. Isaacson) and recent data can be used to provide a more up to date estimate. Assuming that the changes in Woodpigeon numbers on this site are representative, which may not be true, a rough estimate can be derived for 1983 of 4.8 million birds at the lowest point of the cycle, rising to just under 10 million at the end of the breeding season. There is no information on the numbers in Ireland but the map indicates that numbers are likely to be lower than in Britain.

I. R. INGLIS

Total number of squares in which recorded: 3,305 (86%)

No. of birds seen in a day	Number (%) of squares		
	Britain	Ireland	TOTAL (incl. C.I.)
1–245	899 (38%)	745 (80%)	1,647 (50%)
246–1,135	828 (35%)	169 (18%)	999 (30%)
1,136+	642 (27%)	17 (2%)	659 (20%)

References

LANE, A.B. 1983. Benefits and hazards of new crops: oilseed rape in the UK. *Agric. Ecosystems and Envir.* 10: 299–309.

MURTON, R. K. 1965. *The Woodpigeon*. Collins, London.

MURTON, R. K. and M. G. RIDPATH. 1962. The autumn movements of the woodpigeon. *Bird Study* 9: 7–41.

Breeding Atlas p 242

WOODPIGEON

- 1–245
- 246–1,135
- 1,136+

Collared Dove

Streptopelia decaocto

Our only small, resident dove, this bird is a familiar winter sight in gardens and on telephone wires, especially in lowland areas. Yet those who have taken up birdwatching only within the last 20 years may find it hard to appreciate that the widely distributed and locally common Collared Dove did not occur here before the 1950s.

Formerly restricted in Europe to the extreme southeast (Turkey and the Balkans), a major expansion to the west and northwest began about 1930; the Netherlands and Scandinavia were reached in 1949, and Britain and Ireland were colonised from the mid 1950s (Hudson 1972).

In its original homeland in southern Asia, the Collared Dove inhabits dry, open and cultivated country where scattered trees, bushes and hedgerows provide cover. In colonising Europe the species has had to adapt to cooler and wetter climates, and success seems to have been based on selecting sites where food (especially grain) is readily available through human agency. Hence Collared Doves in Europe are more closely tied to human habitations. They occur commonly in villages, towns and city suburbs, and even city centres in some places, but are generally scarce in open countryside except in the vicinity of farm buildings. The present distribution map reflects this dependence on man, with the birds being thinly spread or absent in areas where human density is low—mainly the major upland areas such as the Scottish Highlands, the Pennines and Cheviots, and mid Wales, but noticeable also in the southwestern peninsula and even along the East Anglian Heights. The patchy distribution in Ireland likewise follows broadly the pattern of human density.

The *Winter Atlas* map is broadly similar to that in the *Breeding Atlas*, both because colonisation of suitable areas was almost completed by 1972, subsequent changes being in terms of density, and because Collared Doves are basically resident birds. The second point needs some comment, however. The past range expansion was accomplished by long movements, often of 200–500 km, undertaken mainly by immature birds. Ringing recoveries and bird observatory records showed that immigration into Britain continued during post-colonisation years, as did westerly movements within Britain and from Britain to Ireland. More recently there have been signs that this form of dispersal is being reduced as population size levels off (see below). In the 1960s and early 1970s, about 40% of ringing recoveries involved movement of more than 20 km, but now such recoveries are only about 20%, and fewer foreign-ringed Collared Doves are being found in Britain.

Collared Doves are gregarious outside the breeding season. Substantial flocks will gather in prime feeding areas where grain is stored or spilled, such as around flour mills, maltings, docks and chicken farms, and thereby may become something of a pest locally. Cereals are a major food all year, though the birds also take a variety of seeds and berries from wild and garden plants. Collared Doves also roost socially, and in districts where the species is common there can be several hundred together. Winter roost sites are chosen which provide protection from predators as well as shelter from inclement weather: conifers, holly and thick ivy are especially favoured.

The British and Irish population was assessed in the *Breeding Atlas* as 30,000–40,000 pairs. The Common Birds Census index indicated continued increase to 1976, flattening out thereafter until virtual stability was reached from about 1982; but the CBC does not measure prime Collared Dove habitat, only the overspill into rural areas (Hudson and Marchant 1984). The breeding population must now exceed 50,000 pairs but there is no way of assessing reliably the upper limit. The breeding season is protracted, each pair being able to produce 4–6 broods per year. With juvenile mortality at 69% and annual adult mortality at 39% (Coombs *et al* 1981), there should be a minimum winter population of 150,000 birds.

R. W. HUDSON

Total number of squares in which recorded: 2,332 (60%)

No. of birds seen in a day	Number (%) of squares		
	Britain	Ireland	TOTAL (incl. C.I.)
1–13	845 (45%)	335 (75%)	1,182 (51%)
14–49	600 (32%)	87 (19%)	688 (30%)
50 +	435 (23%)	25 (6%)	462 (20%)

References

COOMBS, C. F. B., A. J. ISAACSON, R. K. MURTON, R. J. P. THEARLE and N. J. WESTWOOD. 1981. Collared Doves (*Streptopelia decaocto*) in urban habitats. *J. Appl. Ecol.* 18: 41–62.

HUDSON, R. 1972. Collared Doves in Britain and Ireland during 1965–1970. *Brit. Birds* 65: 139–155.

HUDSON, R. and J. H. MARCHANT. 1984. Population estimates for British breeding birds. *Commissioned Research Rept. to CST, Nature Conservancy Council.* BTO, Tring.

Breeding Atlas p 246

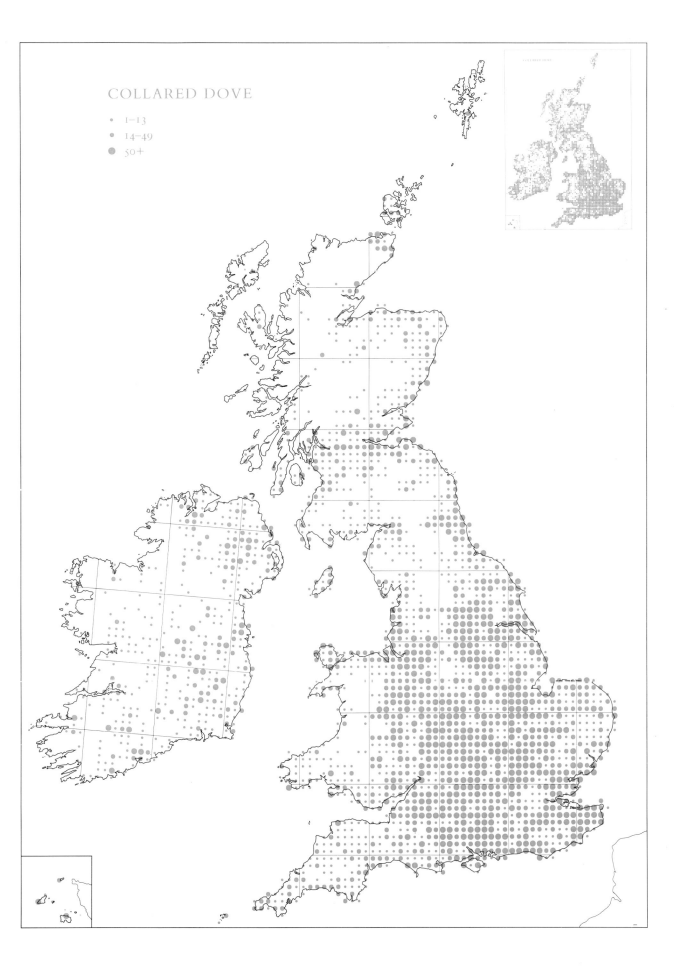

COLLARED DOVE

- · 1–13
- · 14–49
- ● 50+

Ring-necked Parakeet
(Rose-ringed Parakeet)

Psittacula krameri

This fast-flying green parrot, which frequently screeches both in flight and at rest, especially on sunny days, is now a familiar sight in certain areas for it has become established in Britain after introduced and escaped birds formed local breeding populations. These are mainly in suburban areas, indicating its dependence on man for survival in this northern environment, and the colonisation is essentially a feature of the last 20 years. The Ring-necked Parakeet was added to the British List in 1983 as a category C species (an established feral bird which is self-maintaining).

Because the birds are sedentary, the winter map shows a distribution similar to that of summer, with populations in Greater London, Greater Manchester, Merseyside, Surrey, Sussex and Kent. So far, it has been recorded in 50 counties in Britain, but it is rare in Wales and Scotland. There are no records from Ireland or the Isle of Man.

The favoured feeding habitats for Ring-necked Parakeets are gardens, parks and orchards, where they are normally seen singly or in pairs. In Britain they are omnivorous which accounts for their success here. There are no records of deaths, even in the hardest winters. They feed at all times of the day, but with an emphasis on early morning and late afternoon. The most popular early winter food is apples on trees but they are rarely completely consumed: the birds take one to three pecks from a fruit and then move on to the next. This wasteful foraging can cause damage to crops, and so gives the species a bad name. Throughout the winter, especially where apples are scarce, Ring-necked Parakeets are seen at birdtables and nut feeders, where they are top of the peck order. There are few records of the species feeding on the ground in Britain.

During the winter period the Ring-necked Parakeet is highly gregarious, roosting in tall trees, broadleaved and conifers both being chosen. Roosts are usually in suburban parks or in countryside not far from human dwellings and gardens. Roosts break up soon after daybreak as birds move to the feeding localities. In the evening the roost is occupied before darkness, and both arrival and departure in the roosting area may be accompanied by considerable noise, especially in good weather.

During the winter some local feeding movements take place. After the early winter habit of frequenting farmland and parks they move mainly into suburban gardens, especially in periods of snow or hard frost. There are no records of Ring-necked Parakeets migrating into or out of Britain, although individuals have been seen in observatory areas along the south coast of England, especially at Dungeness.

By late winter most adults are at their breeding sites; the Ring-necked Parakeet being one of the few species in Britain that start breeding in winter. Communal roosts break up after Christmas as birds pair up for breeding. Eggs may be laid from January onwards in old nest cavities of Green Woodpecker *Picus viridis* and Great Spotted Woodpecker *Dendrocopos major*, but other holes in trees, and sometimes buildings, may be used.

The current population in Britain is about 1,000 individuals, although it should be made clear that the species is under-recorded, probably because it is a feral bird and was not on the British List until 1983. Since the publication of the *Breeding Atlas* the Ring-necked Parakeet has increased its numbers considerably. Should the numbers ever match those in parts of Africa or India it could become a serious pest to gardeners, horticulturalists and farmers. Apart from man this species seems to have no natural predators.

The Ring-necked Parakeet is a resident in the Afrotropical and Oriental Regions, where it is collected and exported through the pet trade to many European countries, including Britain.

Introduced populations of this species are now well established in Belgium, the Netherlands and West Germany. In other areas of the Western Palearctic, colonies are found in Israel and Egypt.

BRIAN HAWKES

Total number of squares in which recorded: 68 (2%)

No. of birds seen in a day	Number (%) of squares		TOTAL (incl. C.I.)
	Britain	Ireland	
1	41 (61%)	0 (0%)	41 (61%)
2–3	12 (17%)	0 (0%)	12 (17%)
4 +	15 (21%)	0 (0%)	15 (21%)

References
FORSHAW, J. M. and W. T. COOPER. 1978. *Parrots of the World.* David & Charles, Newton Abbot.

Breeding Atlas p 452

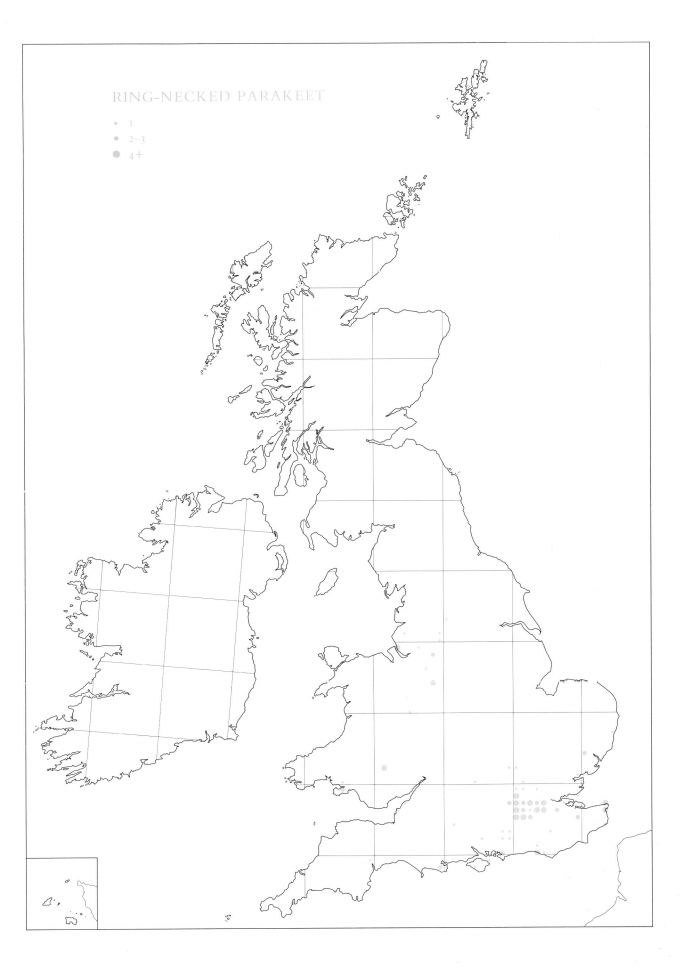

RING-NECKED PARAKEET

- 1
- 2–3
- 4+

Barn Owl

Tyto alba

The sighting in late afternoon sun of a Barn Owl's moth-like form quartering silently along snow bound field margins, over young plantations or frozen marshes, provided a fitting climax to many *Winter Atlas* field trips.

The winter map indicates a widespread but patchy distribution throughout much of England, Wales, S Scotland and Ireland. As in the breeding season, farmland below 300 m, where winters are not too severe, provides the main habitat with its open fields and hedgerows providing ideal hunting grounds; whilst old buildings and hollow trees offer safe winter roosts as well as nesting places.

Cold winter weather influences the feeding behaviour, choice of roosting site and overall distribution of the Barn Owl. During the coldest months when mortality of adult birds is highest, Barn Owls may move to the most protected recesses of trees and buildings, hunt closer to farmsteads, switch to lower altitudes in hilly areas, or move on to coastal marsh and arable farmland.

Snow cover, high winds and heavy rain all inhibit hunting and this inability to tolerate prolonged spells of extreme weather explains the Barn Owl's absence from many upland areas of Britain. Those birds in Sutherland, along the south side of the Moray Firth, and coastal strip of Aberdeenshire are among the most northerly wintering Barn Owls in the world. Elsewhere in Scotland most birds inhabit the milder SW region, the Borders and certain outlying islands.

The absence or scarcity of Barn Owls in many of the intensely arable, built-up, or highly residential areas and industrial places in central and southern England can often be attributed to excessive disturbance by man at roosts, and to lack of ground supporting sufficiently high densities of the small rodents which provide the main component of their diet.

The winter and summer distributions show considerable overlap as most adult Barn Owls remain paired throughout the winter, often roosting side by side, and are largely sedentary. Young disperse by late September, though few travel far. Of 995 recoveries of all age groups, 76% were within 20 km of the ringing place, only 3% of ringed birds being found more than 100 km distant.

The relatively high frequency of Barn Owls located in counties bordering the North Sea may, in part, reflect an apparently small but variable autumn arrival of birds of the darker Continental subspecies *T. a. guttata*. Field observations are supported by the recovery in Essex, Somerset and Kent of one pullus ringed in Belgium and two pulli ringed in the Netherlands.

The Barn Owl is very easily overlooked, especially in winter, and the results shown on the map may well represent a considerable underestimate of the true picture. Nocturnal hunting activities, and a very limited vocabulary outside the breeding season, make detection difficult. During spells of sharp frosts and heavy snowfall Barn Owls are forced to hunt for longer periods and may be seen at any time of the day, as was the case especially in the 1981/82 winter.

The *Breeding Atlas* found 2–4 pairs per occupied 10–km square. Barn Owls are sexually mature in their first full summer (evidence from ringing), and produce 1–6 young (average brood size 3.1), with breeding not attempted in some seasons—cold spring weather, death of a mate and shortage of microtine rodents may prevent nesting. Allowing that three quarters of fledged young die before their first February, and that small numbers of Continental immigrants arrive in some years, one may place the mid winter population of Britain and Ireland in the order of 12,500–25,000 birds.

This upper limit tallies with Blaker's (1934) population estimate for England and Wales alone, giving some indication of the long term decline in Barn Owl numbers that has taken place both in Britain and Ireland this century (reviewed in the *Breeding Atlas*). For one of the most widely distributed birds in the world, our population represents a small fraction on the northern extremity of its range.

D. E. GLUE

Total number of squares in which recorded: 1,278 (33%)

No. of birds seen in a day	Number (%) of squares		
	Britain	Ireland	TOTAL (incl. C.I.)
1	926 (81%)	119 (88%)	1,047 (82%)
2	191 (17%)	16 (12%)	208 (16%)
3+	23 (2%)	0 (0%)	23 (2%)

References

BLAKER, G. B. 1934. *The Barn Owl in England and Wales.* RSPB, London.

BUNN, D. S., A. B. WARBURTON and R. D. S. WILSON. 1982. *The Barn Owl.* Poyser, Calton.

GLUE, D. E. 1973. Seasonal mortality in four small birds of prey. *Ornis Scand.* 4:97–102.

GLUE, D. E. 1974. Food of the Barn Owl in Britain and Ireland. *Bird Study* 21:200–210.

MIKKOLA, H. 1983. *Owls of Europe.* Poyser, Calton.

Breeding Atlas p 250

BARN OWL

· 1
· 2
· 3+

Little Owl

Athene noctua

The Little Owl's plump upright posture and flat-headed appearance with striking broad white 'eye-brows' and frowning facial expression are a familiar sight during the winter in much of lowland Britain.

The Little Owl is an introduced species that has established itself from a series of releases. By the end of the 19th century Little Owls were breeding regularly in Kent, Bedfordshire, Northamptonshire and Rutland, and further releases led to a rapid expansion over the following 25 years northwards to the Scottish border. Subsequently the range extended more slowly with periodic decreases attributed to persecution by man, pesticide contamination, and losses during severe winters like those of 1946/47 and 1962/63 (reviewed in the *Breeding Atlas*). Breeding was first proved in Scotland, in Berwickshire, in 1958 and wintering is now possible in the maritime zone of Dumfries and Galloway in SW Scotland, and there are sporadic records as far north as East Lothian and Dumbarton, though not in the *Winter Atlas* years for the latter area. Further expansion may well be limited by low winter temperatures preventing access to the major invertebrate and small mammal elements of the Little Owl's winter diet. There have been four confirmed sightings of Little Owls in Ireland (the one during the *Winter Atlas* period is mapped) and there has been no attempt at nesting.

The winter distribution embraces the majority of well-timbered low-lying agricultural areas in S, central and N England and also the border regions into central and S Wales. As in summer, farmland is the preferred habitat, especially where there are well established hedgerows, copses, tree fringed streams and wood clumps, while orchards and tree dotted parkland are also strongly favoured.

The great majority of Little Owls rely on trees for winter shelter as well as for nesting places, less often occupying isolated buildings, rock clefts or cavities like rabbit burrows. This accounts in part for their scarcity and absence in winter from many areas of heath, down, saltings and dunes in S and E England.

A lack of tree cover and inability to tolerate prolonged periods of ice and snow cover exclude Little Owls from many upland areas in mid Devon, Cornwall, the Cambrian Mountains, much of N and W Wales, the N Pennines, the Lake District and North Yorkshire Moors. A more equable maritime climate and suitable roost sites allow the occupation of bare coastal headlands, cliffs, and quarries in parts of SW England and Wales.

The winter distribution is similar to that shown by the *Breeding Atlas*. This is to be expected since Little Owls are largely sedentary, a fact demonstrated by ringing—of 322 recoveries (all age groups) 71% were within 10 km of the ringing place. The pair bond appears strong and many adult birds roost at or close to the nesting place in winter. Some individuals do wander, outside the breeding season, 2% of ringed birds are found over 100 km from the ringing place.

The Little Owl is more easily located in winter than the other British owls. Its extensive vocabulary includes an often repeated and far carrying plaintive 'kiew, kiew' and a loud yelping 'wherrow, wherrow' which are delivered by day, especially from February when territory proclamation begins in earnest. Individuals often emerge in daylight to sun from a vantage place such as a tree branch, post, or a building.

Taking the *Breeding Atlas* estimated population of 7,000–14,000 pairs based on a conservative 5–10 pairs per occupied 10–km square, an average brood size of 2.4, that breeding is attempted in three out of every four years (cold springs and food shortage inhibit them in some seasons), and that about 60% of nestlings die within four months of fledging, the mid winter British population is probably in the order of 19,000–38,000 individuals. In just over a century since the first successful breeding attempt, the British population of Little Owls has increased substantially throughout most of England and Wales and represents an established element on the northwest fringe of its range, though the species is common throughout much of central and southern Europe.

D. E. GLUE

Total number of squares in which recorded: 1,022 (26%)

No. of birds seen in a day	Number (%) of squares		
	Britain	Ireland	TOTAL (incl. C.I.)
1	566 (55%)	1 (100%)	567 (55%)
2	327 (32%)	0 (0%)	327 (32%)
3+	128 (13%)	0 (0%)	128 (13%)

References

FITTER, R. S. R. 1959. *The Ark in our Midst*. Collins, London.

GLUE, D. E. 1973. Seasonal mortality in four small birds of prey. *Ornis Scand.* 4: 97–102.

GLUE, D. E. and D. SCOTT. 1980. Breeding biology of the Little Owl. *Brit. Birds* 73: 167–180.

HIBBERT-WARE, A. 1937–38. Report of the Little Owl food inquiry, 1936–37. *Brit. Birds* 31: 162–187, 205–229, 249–264.

MIKKOLA, H. 1983. *Owls of Europe*. Poyser, Calton.

Breeding Atlas p 254

LITTLE OWL

- 1
- 2
- 3+

Tawny Owl

Strix aluco

The squat, round-headed and short-tailed form silhouetted at dusk on a branch, post or television aerial heralds the emergence of a Tawny Owl from its daytime roost, but many more are first detected in winter by the familiar wavering hoot.

The winter map indicates that Britain's most numerous and successful owl winters widely over most of the mainland. It occurs occasionally in Ireland. Though often roosting in the tree cavities of broad-leaved woods and forests, in winter the Tawny Owl also occurs in parks, farmland, and coniferous forests. Its scarcity in low-lying parts of E England, along rocky coastlines and in some upland regions may be attributed to a paucity of mature timber.

On relatively bare open tracts of farmland, coastline and industrial waste ground, disused buildings and rock cavities provide suitable winter shelter. In this century the Tawny Owl has penetrated much of suburbia, even some of large cities.

Sea presents a barrier for the Tawny Owl. They winter on Skye, Anglesey and a few on the Isle of Wight but were not located on most other islands.

The winter and summer ranges overlap considerably as the Tawny Owl is strongly territorial and highly sedentary relying on excellent vision and hearing and a good memory of its territory's structural components, for winter survival (Southern 1970). Few birds travel far—84% of 824 recoveries were found within 10 km of the ringing place and less than 1% over 100 km. Established pairs may be seen in the same tree throughout the year. The extreme winter climate on the Continent causes more birds to wander.

In winter, Tawny Owls tend to roost high by day and their mottled brown plumage blends effectively with the adjacent tree trunk or foliage, but once disturbed their position is revealed by the persistent alarm cries from smaller birds that repeatedly mob them. There is an extraordinary variety of calls during the non-breeding season. Inexperienced young compete with established birds for territories, with wails and screams during disputes, in addition to the long drawn out courtship hooting of the male, the less clearly phrased hoot of the female, and the 'kewick' contact calls (Southern 1970). From December through to February courtship feeding and calling is progressively centred around the future nest site.

A general decline in the numbers of Tawny Owls in Britain during much of the 19th century was attributed to regular persecution (Parslow 1973). Four of the five Tawny Owls released near Belfast in 1900 were known to have been shot. Persecution, especially by keepers, is a hazard, and ringed birds are still recovered after being illegally trapped and shot (Glue 1973), while many more are killed on roads, railways or in collision with overhead structure.

The first 30 years of this century saw a widespread increase in numbers and expansion of range, especially northwards, up to 1950. This increase coincided with a period of climatic amelioration, and the success of the Tawny Owl may also be attributed to the birds' ability to survive well in severe winter weather, its physical dominance over the other British owls (Mikkola 1983) and its catholic diet. When small rodents become scarce the Tawny Owl switches to alternative prey, notably shrews, birds, moles, frogs, insects and earthworms (Southern 1954). Similarly, the Tawny Owl's occupation of suburban and industrial areas is due in part to its exploitation of food items such as the house mouse, an ability to tackle large prey such as the brown rat and to snatch birds at communal roosts (Mikkola 1983), even raiding bird tables.

The *Breeding Atlas* gives the population as 10,000–100,000 pairs, though probably in the upper half of this range. Tawny Owls are single-brooded but fail to lay in some years of food shortage (Southern 1970). On average a pair will raise 2.3 young, and less than one half of these young will survive, so the mid winter population will be between 35,000 and 350,000 individuals. Thus the British population represents a relatively small but discrete fragment on the NW fringe of the Tawny Owl's world range.

D. E. GLUE

Total number of squares in which recorded: 1,683 (44%)

No. of birds seen in a day	Number (%) of squares		TOTAL (incl. C.I.)
	Britain	Ireland	
1	801 (48%)	0 (0%)	801 (48%)
2	551 (33%)	0 (0%)	551 (33%)
3+	331 (20%)	0 (0%)	331 (20%)

References

GLUE, D. E. 1973. Seasonal mortality in four small birds of prey. *Ornis Scand.* 4: 97–102.

MIKKOLA, H. 1983. *Owls of Europe.* Poyser, Calton.

PARSLOW, J. 1973. *Breeding Birds of Britain and Ireland: a historical survey.* Poyser, Berkhamsted.

SOUTHERN, H. N. 1954. Tawny Owls and their prey. *Ibis* 96: 384–410.

SOUTHERN, H. N. 1970. The natural control of a population of Tawny Owls *Strix aluco. J. Zool. Lond.* 162: 197–285.

Breeding Atlas p 256

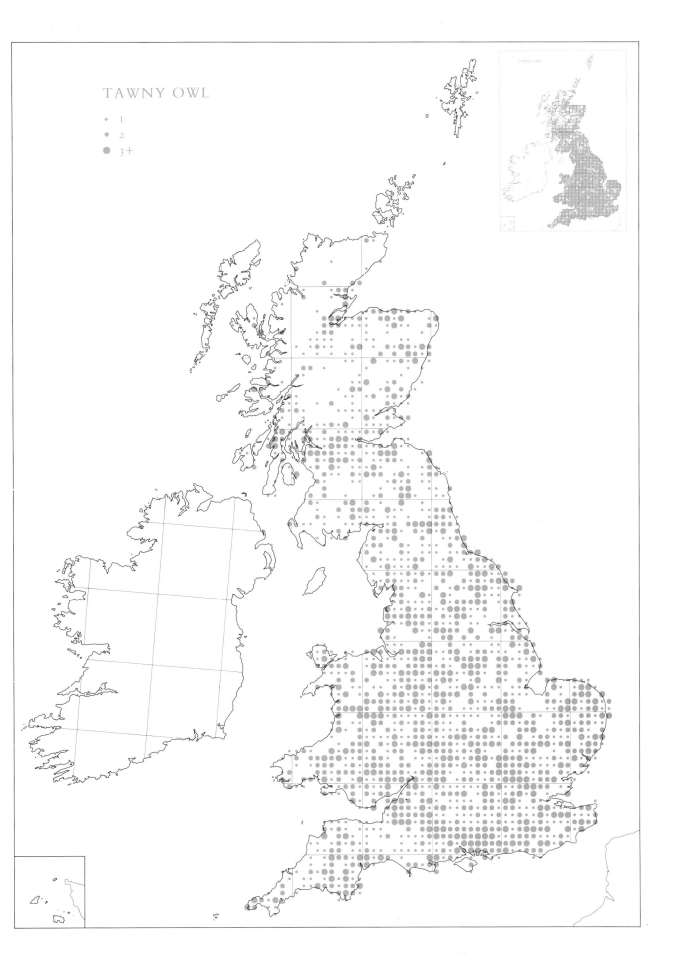

TAWNY OWL

- · 1
- · 2
- · 3+

Long-eared Owl

Asio otus

Perched silent and motionless by day beside a conifer trunk or amongst the dense foliage of thorn scrub, and aided by its very effective cryptic plumage, the Long-eared Owl represents one of our most elusive and least studied over wintering birds.

The winter distribution map should be interpreted with caution. Many birds will have escaped detection, including those in many favoured haunts such as woods of spruce and pine, thickets and overgrown hedges on farm, down and moorland.

Nevertheless the winter range is clearly a very patchy one. The bulk of Long-eared Owls winter in the eastern half of Britain and the bird is notably scarce throughout most of SW England, Wales and in W Scotland north of the Firth of Clyde. Even in eastern England and Scotland it is often local, with concentrations in many coastal areas where most sightings are of birds wintering in thorn and elder scrub, in shingle or sand dune slacks, and on marsh and farmland. Most observations in daylight are of passage parties, and individuals are seen arriving off the sea in the Scottish islands and northeast coast.

Inland, many concentrations indicate roosts on impoverished and sparsely timbered areas on sedimentary rocks. The downland of calcareous soils in the south, heathland of glacial drifts in the east, and moorland and hill pasture on sandstones and grits in the western midlands and N England, support most wintering owls.

The Long-eared and Tawny Owl *Strix aluco* have overlapping ecological needs including food, nest and roosting requirements, and so physical competition occurs. In Ireland, where the larger species is absent, the Long-eared Owl is widely distributed throughout much of the northeast, central and southern parts, from coastal marsh to inland bog and farmland, even penetrating some residential areas.

There is a considerable overlap of the winter and the breeding ranges. Young Long-eared Owls disperse randomly in their first winter, but adults are largely sedentary, often returning annually to the same wood or group of trees. This is supported by ringing results—of 148 recoveries of all ages, 35% were found within 10 km, but 26% travelled further than 100 km.

In contrast the northernmost European population migrates to temperate climes in most winters. The evidence of 26 foreign-ringed owls recovered, mostly in eastern Britain, indicates that we recruit birds from much of N Europe with some coming from as far afield as 26°E and 61°N. A few of these birds were recovered at inland roosts ranging as far west as Co. Mayo.

The Long-eared Owl's strongly nocturnal and arboreal habits, and the fact that it is largely silent in mid winter, make detection very difficult. The territorial song of the male, its display flight, and the principal calls of the female begin in late January prior to nest selection and some clutches are laid in late February. Occasionally, owls hunt at dawn and dusk, quartering for their chief prey items, the field vole in Britain and the wood mouse in Ireland, or exploiting evening roosts of sparrows, finches and Starlings *Sturnus vulgaris* which form an important element of the diet in winter.

The patchy distribution of the Long-eared Owl has developed principally during this century and, coinciding with the successful expansion of the Tawny Owl's range in Britain, may well be due in part to competition. The overall winter population is very difficult to assess, due to the difficulties of detection and the variable influx of immigrants. Invasions involving several thousands of owls occur in some winters, as in 1975/76, and can be attributed to crashes in the numbers of microtine rodents on the Continental breeding grounds. The *Breeding Atlas* estimated 3,000–10,000 pairs in Britain and Ireland, with 1–5 young per pair (average brood size 2.4) produced most summers. With an influx from the Continent each late autumn, the mid winter population is likely to be in the range of 10,000–35,000 individuals.

D. E. GLUE

Total number of squares in which recorded: 350 (9%)

No. of birds	Number (%) of squares		
seen in a day	Britain	Ireland	TOTAL (incl. C.I.)
1	154 (59%)	76 (87%)	230 (66%)
2	46 (18%)	9 (10%)	55 (16%)
3+	63 (24%)	2 (3%)	65 (19%)

References

GLUE, D. E. 1977. Breeding biology of Long-eared Owls. *Brit. Birds* 70: 318–331.

GLUE, D. E. and G. J. HAMMOND. 1974. Feeding ecology of the Long-eared Owl in Britain and Ireland. *Brit. Birds* 67: 361–369.

HAWLEY, R. G. 1966. Observations on the Long-eared Owl. *Sorby Record, Sheffield.* 2: 95–114.

MIKKOLA, H. 1976. Owls killing and killed by other owls and raptors in Europe. *Brit. Birds* 69: 144–154.

MIKKOLA, H. 1983. *Owls of Europe*. Poyser, Calton.

Breeding Atlas p 258

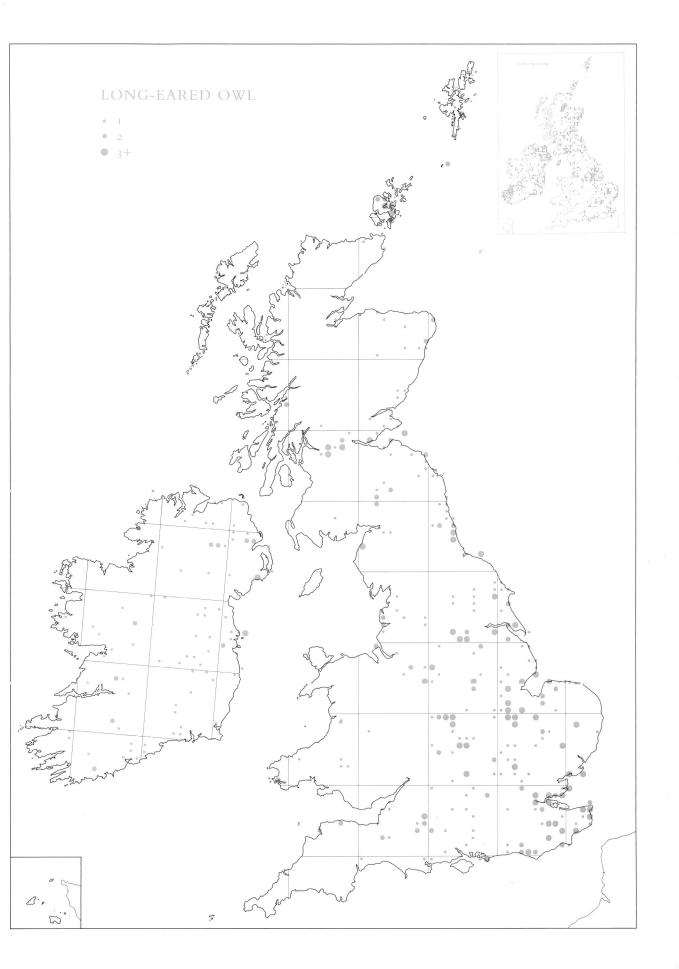

LONG-EARED OWL

- • 1
- • 2
- • 3+

Short-eared Owl

Asio flammeus

Floating low down with a wavering and rolling flight, punctuated by occasional glides before banking and wheeling high on stiff long narrow wings, the Short-eared Owl provides a welcome winter encounter over many tracts of remote open country.

The winter map shows how the Short-eared Owl is fairly generally distributed over most of Britain and parts of Ireland. In Britain many concentrations occur each winter in east coast counties and near estuaries. These will include transient late immigrants as well as feeding and roosting birds. Inland, many high counts are in wetland habitats such as the Ouse Washes, and on many of the chalk downlands in S Britain. In Ireland, also, the highest numbers of Short-eared Owls are to be encountered on coastal salt marsh and farmland. In winter many Short-eared Owls travel far and wide in search of food. Individuals may well traverse several 10-km squares during the course of one winter and occupy another in a later year. This highly mobile and nomadic behaviour is illustrated by ringing results. Of 77 recoveries of British-ringed Short-eared Owls of all age groups, only 28% were found within 10 km, and 52% travelled further than 100 km. Young birds disperse randomly, and often travel far, mostly in the southern sector. Ten owls ringed in Britain were later found in Spain (5), France (2), Belgium (1), USSR (1) and Malta (1).

From late August to November, when some home-bred birds depart, a variable but large number of Short-eared Owls arrive from the Continent. Ten owls ringed in Finland (4), Sweden (2), Belgium (1), Iceland (1), Norway (1) and West Germany (1), have been recovered in Britain, mostly in east coast counties, though one travelled as far west as Cheshire.

There is some overlap between the winter and breeding ranges, but the strong correlation of breeding Short-eared Owls with tracts of moorland is not so pronounced in winter and many nesting sites are left vacant. This represents in part a movement of owls to coastal and inland marshes in winter, an area popular with birdwatchers, and some owls may have been overlooked on upland moors and fells.

Most Short-eared Owls are relatively easy to observe in winter. Though rather silent during the non-breeding season and hunting chiefly at or approaching dusk, they are often abroad in full daylight. Wandering individuals roost in casual settling places, but communal roosts, on the ground amidst tall coarse grasses, heather, sedges or scrub, are used over many years.

Short-eared Owls are opportunist feeders and will take whatever prey they come across and can catch most easily (Clark 1975). In Britain, in grassy places during winter, the chief food item is the field vole. When numbers of these reach plague proportions owls gather to exploit their temporary abundance. Elsewhere, rats, shrews, mice and rabbits dominate the diet. In Ireland the brown rat and wood mouse are the chief prey, but small flock-feeding birds form a significant section of the diet.

The erratic but significant local increases in the number of Short-eared Owls, in Britain this century, have been attributed to greater afforestation (with high densities of microtine rodents during the early stages of tree growth) and a reduction in the amount of persecution by man (summarised in the *Breeding Atlas*).

Taking the *Breeding Atlas* minimum of 1,000 pairs which may apply in poor vole years, and the optimistic possibility of 10,000 pairs in peak years, and that from 1–7 young (average brood size 3.8) are produced in most summers (BTO nest records), plus the fact that a sizeable number of owls arrive each autumn from the Continent, the mid winter population of Short-eared Owls is likely to be in the range of 5,000–50,000 individuals for Britain and Ireland. This represents a small fraction of the Short-eared Owl's circumpolar holarctic and discontinuous South American world population.

D. E. GLUE

Total number of squares in which recorded: 1,023 (26%)

No. of birds seen in a day	Number (%) of squares		
	Britain	Ireland	TOTAL (incl. C.I.)
1	517 (53%)	33 (70%)	550 (54%)
2–3	307 (32%)	10 (21%)	319 (31%)
4+	149 (15%)	4 (9%)	154 (15%)

References

CLARK, R. J. 1975. A field study of the Short-eared Owl *Asio flammeus* (Pontoppidan) in North America. *Wildlife Monogr.* No. 47.

GLUE, D. E. 1977. Feeding ecology of the Short-eared Owl in Britain and Ireland. *Bird Study* 24: 70–78.

LOCKIE, J. D. 1955. The breeding habits of Short-eared Owls after a vole plague. *Bird Study* 2: 53–69.

MIKKOLA, H. 1983. *Owls of Europe.* Poyser, Calton.

PICOZZI, N. and R. HEWSON. 1970. Kestrels, Short-eared Owls and Field Voles in Eskdalemuir in 1970. *Scot. Birds* 6: 185–190.

Breeding Atlas p 260

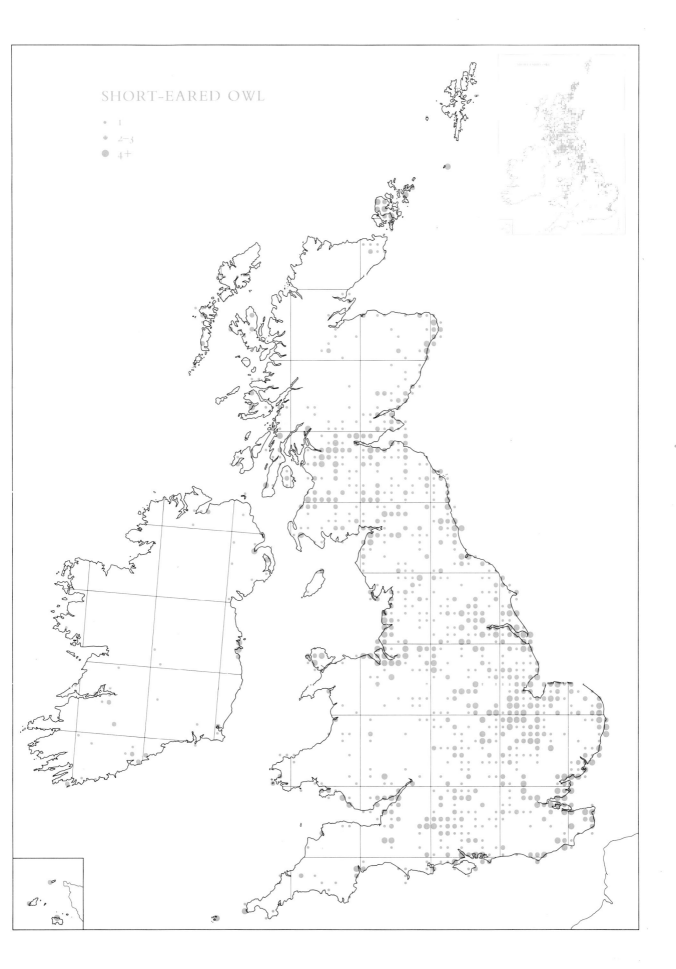

SHORT-EARED OWL

- 1
- 2–3
- 4+

Kingfisher

Alcedo atthis

The electric-blue dazzle of a Kingfisher speeding over open water is like a bolt of summer lightning in the winter scene; beautiful yet out of place. This contrast is strangely appropriate, for the Kingfisher suffers more than most birds during harsh winter weather.

The Kingfisher needs access to relatively still water to catch its staple food of sticklebacks and other small fish. Its feeding method of plunge-diving after sighting prey from a perch or after hovering is unsuited to the upland torrents. Consequently, the highest densities of Kingfishers throughout the year are on the slow-flowing rivers in the lowlands of England, Wales and Ireland. The concentration of Kingfishers in these lowland areas shows clearly on the winter distribution map. The stronghold of the species is in central and southern counties of England where rivers, canals, lakes and other areas of inland fresh water provide a variety of suitable habitats. This variety is lacking in many parts of Scotland, where the Kingfisher's inland range is mainly confined to the low ground of the Borders and the central lowlands. A belt of winter sightings between and in the valleys of the rivers Forth and Clyde neatly picks out the central lowlands on the map.

Although the maps of Kingfisher distribution in winter and in the breeding season are similar in the inland strongholds, there are contrasts in other areas. Some Kingfishers breed on upland waters where the stream gradient is less than 25 m/km and many of these higher reaches are deserted in the winter. This is particularly apparent when comparing the winter and breeding season maps for Wales and Ireland. Another contrast with the breeding season is in the large number of winter records from coastal areas. There are winter sightings along coasts near all parts of the Kingfisher's breeding range, with notable clusters around the Irish coast. The two main components of the Kingfisher's winter distribution, the retreat from higher ground and the winter movement to the coast, are a response to its greatest winter enemy—ice.

Ice locks the Kingfisher's larder, and in hard winters where ice cover is widespread, the species suffers heavy mortality. Coastal areas provide ice-free havens in some cold spells, but in very harsh winters, such as the winter of 1962/63, even coastal waters freeze. The Kingfisher was the species hardest hit by the 1962/63 cold winter, with reports of total extermination in some areas. Welsh breeding numbers fell by around 85% at this time, but there was no drastic reduction in Ireland, where some coastal waters had remained open during the winter. Kingfishers are prolific breeders, rearing 2 or sometimes 3 broods each year, and local populations can thus quickly recover from the effects of a harsh winter.

British and Irish Kingfishers are rather sedentary, the majority of recoveries being less than 9 km from the ringing site. Longer-distance movements are mainly recorded in autumn, when there is general dispersal of young birds moving away from parental territories. Adults remain in their territories throughout the year unless ice forces them to move away, but each member of a pair tends to avoid the other in winter until courtship activity begins again in January or February. There is no evidence that any Kingfishers from the Continent visit Britain or Ireland in winter.

The *Breeding Atlas* suggests a British and Irish Kingfisher population of 5,000–9,000 pairs in summer, based on an estimated 3–5 pairs per occupied 10-km square. On this basis, the winter population would be in the range of 9,000–15,000 birds. These include the westernmost part of a world population which is spread from warmer areas of Eurasia to the Oriental region.

K. TAYLOR

Total number of squares in which recorded: 1,294 (34%)

No. of birds seen in a day	Number (%) of squares		
	Britain	Ireland	TOTAL (incl. C.I.)
1	674 (65%)	201 (79%)	876 (68%)
2	256 (25%)	41 (16%)	299 (23%)
3+	107 (10%)	12 (5%)	119 (9%)

References

DOBINSON, H. M. and A. J. RICHARDS. 1964. The effects of the severe winter of 1962/63 on birds in Britain. *Brit. Birds* 57: 373–434.

MARCHANT, J. H. and P. A. HYDE. 1980. Aspects of the distribution of riparian birds on waterways in Britain and Ireland. *Bird Study* 27: 183–202.

MORGAN, R.A. and D.E. GLUE. 1977. Breeding, mortality and movements of Kingfishers. *Bird Study* 24: 15–24.

SMITH, M. E. 1969. The Kingfisher in Wales: effects of severe weather. *Nature in Wales* 11: 109–115.

TAYLOR, K. and J. H. MARCHANT. 1983. Population changes for waterways birds, 1981–82. *Bird Study* 30: 121–126.

Breeding Atlas p 266

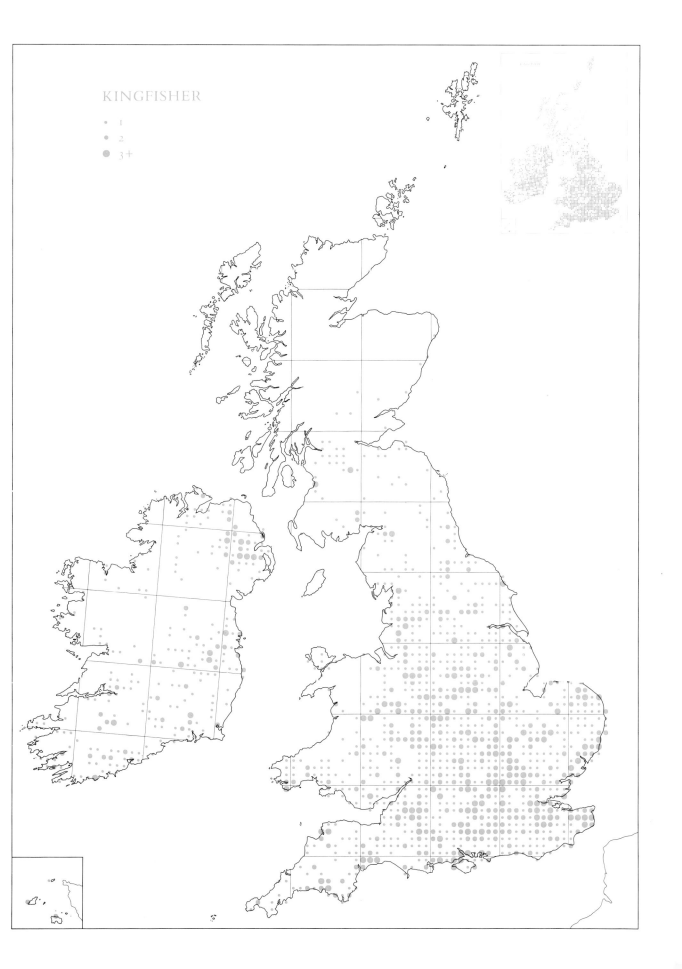

KINGFISHER

- 1
- 2
- 3+

Green Woodpecker

Picus viridis

In winter, Green Woodpeckers are solitary birds and are often detected only when they are disturbed from their favourite grassland feeding area, whereupon they quickly fly up into the surrounding trees, usually calling as they go. There they often remain motionless on the trunk concealed by a limb, occasionally looking round. The birds seem to have regular feeding sites, which was a great help to *Winter Atlas* field workers.

The distribution map shows that they are widespread in S England and Wales although their scarcity is indicated by the high number of blank squares. Together with many other woodland species the Green Woodpecker is absent from a band of E England running from Lincolnshire to Essex. This is probably the result of the lack of mature woodland and the fact that most of the woods are surrounded by arable farmland which does not provide suitable feeding areas. In N England and Scotland, both recolonised only since about 1940, the distribution is very patchy indeed, the birds being restricted to some parts of the lowlands, and a few in the highlands. They are absent from the Scottish islands, the whole of Ireland and the Isle of Man. Green Woodpeckers are most abundant in S England and particularly so in the Home Counties, West Sussex and Hampshire. There is also a concentration of records in the Brecklands of East Anglia. The birds are very sedentary and there is a close similarity between the winter and breeding distributions. There is an increase in range in NE Scotland however, which may indicate a continuing northward spread. In SW Scotland the number of winter records was far lower than in the breeding season. The lack of records in SW England may be due to poor coverage rather than any change of range. They are the most shy of our three woodpecker species, so it is probable that some will have been missed.

Green Woodpeckers favour open mature woodland, parkland, heaths and commons. They require mature trees as nest sites but do much of their feeding outside the woodlands on pasture, where they regularly attack the nests of ants, taking eggs, grubs and adults. Old pastures appear to be particularly important. They also attack decaying timber, seeking the adults and larvae of beetles and other invertebrates (*BWP*).

Because they collect much of their food from the ground they can suffer badly in prolonged periods of cold weather. The 1962/63 winter was thought to have resulted in some local reductions of numbers, particularly in Lancashire, NE England and central England. Some of these populations have apparently still not recovered. In cold conditions, hard-pressed Green Woodpeckers have been recorded attacking beehives but it is not clear what food items they are taking. They do not habitually take artificially provided food in gardens but will feed happily on secluded lawns.

The ringing recoveries of Green Woodpeckers do not indicate any large scale movements, either within this country or from the Continent.

There are few data on which to base an estimate of the total population of Green Woodpeckers although the *Breeding Atlas* concluded that there were between 15,000 and 30,000 breeding pairs. On this basis there could be 40,000–70,000 individuals present in mid winter. However, in the absence of large-scale survey data this estimate must be treated with some caution.

K. W. SMITH

Total number of squares in which recorded: 1,342 (35%)

No. of birds	Number (%) of squares		
seen in a day	Britain	Ireland	TOTAL (incl. C.I.)
1	769 (57%)	0 (0%)	769 (57%)
2	312 (23%)	0 (0%)	312 (23%)
3+	261 (19%)	0 (0%)	261 (19%)

Breeding Atlas p 270

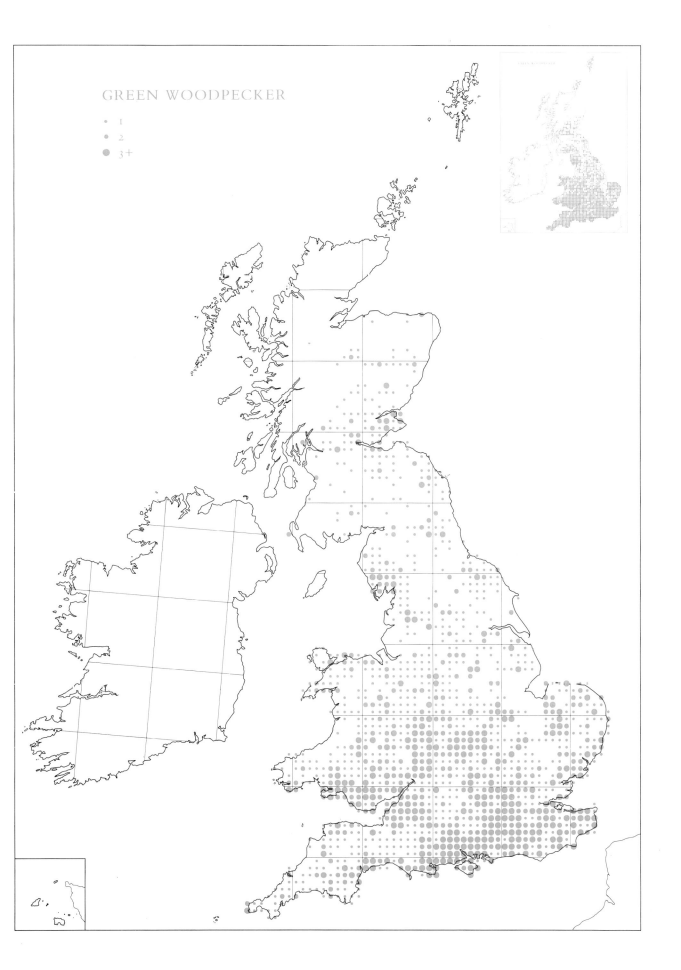

GREEN WOODPECKER

- 1
- 2
- 3+

Great Spotted Woodpecker

Dendrocopos major

In winter, Great Spotted Woodpeckers occur in most woodlands, well wooded gardens, copses and even hedgerows. They can be very secretive but usually betray their presence by occasional loud 'tchick' calls. On warm days in late winter they may indulge in noisy territorial displays and drumming.

The distribution map shows them to be most abundant in southern England, particularly in the Home Counties, Sussex and Hampshire, but with good numbers through central England to the northwest. In common with a number of woodland species, Great Spotted Woodpeckers are absent from the fenlands of East Anglia. In much of SW England, Wales and Scotland the distribution is very patchy and they are absent from the higher ground. There are only scattered records from northern Scotland and, in common with all woodpeckers, Great Spotted are not present in the Isle of Man or in Ireland, except in years of exceptional movements out of Scandinavia.

The overall distribution is very similar to that of the *Breeding Atlas* but there are far fewer winter records in Scotland and SW England. There is no evidence of large-scale movements from these areas in the winter so that it is probable that these low numbers reflect the difficulty of locating the birds with limited fieldwork in winter. In the present century the Great Spotted Woodpecker has spread back into Scotland, and it is thought that widespread afforestation will have increased the area of suitable habitat, so aiding this spread. Comparison of the winter distribution with that in the *Breeding Atlas* indicates that there has not been a substantial spread over the last decade.

Great Spotted Woodpeckers are found both in deciduous and coniferous woodland. In winter they eat a variety of seeds, depending on availability, including those of beech, hazel, hornbeam, oak and conifers. 'Anvils' fashioned in the bark of the trees are regularly used to assist in the extraction of kernels. They also take invertebrates gleaned from the bark of trees, excavated from rotting timber and found behind decaying bark. These include a wide range of over-wintering species such as insects, their larvae, wood-lice and spiders. In the coniferous woods especially in Scandinavia, where, in winter, Great Spotted Woodpeckers feed almost exclusively on conifer seeds, anvils are often betrayed by heaps of discarded cones littering the forest floor.

Studies in central and eastern Europe have shown that Great Spotted Woodpeckers are territorial there in winter, feeding and roosting within their exclusive area. It is probable that similar behaviour occurs in this country, but it is clear that some birds can be found outside the normal breeding areas during the winter.

Although Great Spotted Woodpeckers are essentially sedentary in this country they do wander more widely than other woodpecker species. The majority of ringing recoveries are less than 10 km from the place of ringing, but there is a single record of a British ringed bird recovered in Belgium. The northern subspecies, which is somewhat larger than our own, is reported at east coast ringing sites in autumn, particularly in irruption years. One ringed in autumn at Spurn Bird Observatory was recovered in mid winter in Cambridgeshire.

Great Spotted Woodpecker populations have been increasing in this country during this century. However, since the late 1960s, there has been a rapid rise, with the Common Birds Census index increasing from approximately 100 in 1966 to 250 in 1983. In England this is apparently the result of Dutch elm disease (Osborne 1983) which has provided an abundant food supply on and beneath the bark of dead and dying timber. The dead elms are not widely used as nest sites, and once the bark has fallen off there is little food available for the woodpeckers. It is therefore probable that populations will stabilise or fall in the near future.

The *Breeding Atlas* estimated the Great Spotted Woodpecker population as 30,000–40,000 pairs. Allowing for the increased population over the last decade it is probable that the mid winter population is now between 150,000 and 200,000 birds.

K. W. SMITH

Total number of squares in which recorded: 1,732 (45%)

No. of birds seen in a day	Number (%) of squares		
	Britain	Ireland	TOTAL (incl. C.I.)
1	771 (44%)	0 (0%)	771 (44%)
2–3	669 (39%)	0 (0%)	670 (39%)
4+	291 (17%)	0 (0%)	291 (17%)

References

OSBORNE, P. 1983. The influence of Dutch elm disease on bird population trends. *Bird Study* 30: 27–38.

Breeding Atlas p 272

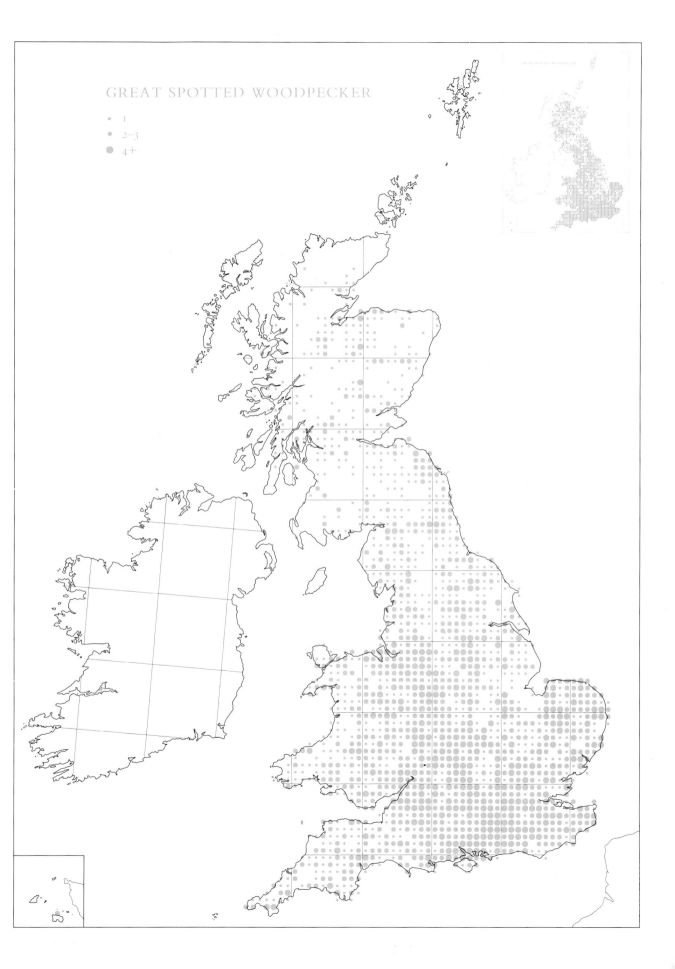

GREAT SPOTTED WOODPECKER

- · 1
- · 2–3
- · 4+

Lesser Spotted Woodpecker

Dendrocopos minor

Lesser Spotted Woodpeckers are rather elusive birds which in winter can be particularly difficult to locate. Their habit of feeding high in the trees and of uttering few calls, outside the breeding season, makes them a challenge to the birdwatcher. They are often only found after a careful, neck-straining search of all the birds in a foraging tit flock. On warm days in February their display flights, 'pew pew pew pew' calls and soft drumming may make them far more conspicuous and less difficult to locate. However, there is little doubt that this species will have been much under recorded in the *Winter Atlas*.

The distribution map shows the Lesser Spotted Woodpecker to be most abundant in SE and central England and East Anglia, with very few records in Wales and in southwestern and northern England. They are absent from Ireland and the Isle of Man and do not occur further north than Northumberland, except for an occasional record in Scotland in summer. As with the two other woodpecker species, the winter distribution is remarkably similar to that of the breeding season. However, in SW and NW England and parts of Kent and E Sussex, the winter records are relatively low. This may be the result of changes in the species' distribution over the last decade but is more likely to be due to the difficulty of detecting the birds in winter.

Lesser Spotted Woodpeckers occur largely in deciduous woodland but are not limited to extensive woods. They can be found in the smallest farmland copse, hedgerow trees, and lines of willows and alders along river banks. They usually forage high in the trees, moving rapidly through the topmost branches. There is little information on their diet in winter, but birds collected on the Continent were found to have been eating the adults and larvae of wood-boring beetles, Lepidoptera larvae and spiders (Glue 1982). The Lesser Spotted Woodpecker is only a rare visitor to garden feeding stations. The recent devastating outbreak of Dutch elm disease has been to the temporary benefit of these woodpeckers (Osborne 1983) in providing an abundance of invertebrate food, in and under the bark of dead and dying elm trees. In a 52 ha wood in Kent the breeding population rose from one or two pairs to about 15 pairs whilst the elms were dying (Flegg and Bennett 1974). However, dead elms do not provide nest sites for Lesser Spotted Woodpeckers and, once they have lost their bark, support low numbers of invertebrates. Therefore, in the long term, woodpecker numbers are likely to fall.

Lesser Spotted Woodpeckers are ringed only in small numbers but all recoveries to date indicate that they are essentially sedentary. There are no data to suggest any movements to or from the Continent.

In the *Breeding Atlas* the British breeding population was very tentatively estimated as between 5,000 and 10,000 pairs. If this estimate is accepted, then in winter there may be approximately 20,000–40,000 individuals in this country. This estimate must be treated with some caution as our current knowledge of this bird is so limited that the population levels are little more than a guess.

K. W. SMITH

Total number of squares in which recorded: 749 (19%)

No. of birds seen in a day	Number (%) of squares		
	Britain	Ireland	TOTAL (incl. C.I.)
1	502 (67%)	0 (0%)	503 (67%)
2	186 (25%)	0 (0%)	186 (25%)
3+	60 (8%)	0 (0%)	60 (8%)

References

FLEGG, J. J. M. and T. J. BENNETT. 1974. The birds of oak woodlands. Pp 324–340 in MORRIS, M. G. and F. H. PERRING (eds). *The British Oak*. Classey, Faringdon.

GLUE, D. 1982. *The Garden Bird Book*. Macmillan, London.

OSBORNE, P. 1983. The influence of dutch elm disease on bird population trends. *Bird Study* 30: 27–38.

Breeding Atlas p 274

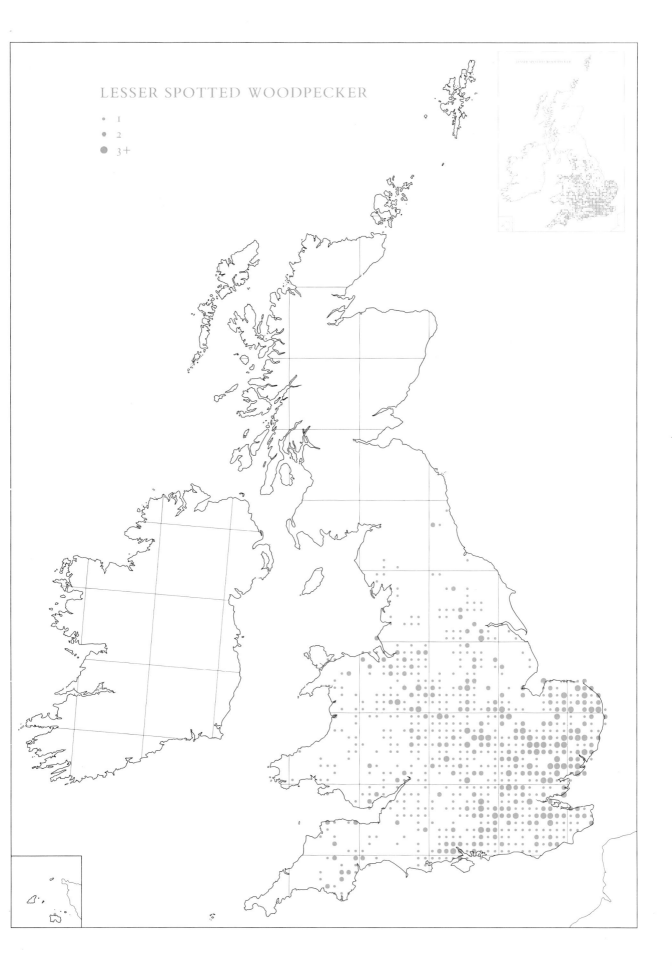

LESSER SPOTTED WOODPECKER

- 1
- 2
- 3+

Woodlark

Lullula arborea

"Tho' earth look dark and cold, that voice
Will still be sweetly singing,
And make the chilly heart rejoice
With notes of comfort ringing"

So wrote an early Hereford ornithologist in describing the Woodlark's winter song. Though the song is beautiful and distinctive, it is irregular in winter. Without song the species can be difficult to locate. Rarely are more than a few birds found together and they are often mixed with other species, especially Skylarks *Alauda arvensis*.

The map shows that in winter Woodlarks are mostly confined to Hampshire and W Surrey with some in Devon and a few elsewhere. There were no records in Ireland where it is a rarity, although it has bred on 3 occasions (Ruttledge 1966).

The Handbook describes the British Woodlark population as resident, but there is now considerable evidence that at least part of it is migratory, as the *Winter Atlas* shows a much reduced population compared with the breeding season, and there is evidence of passage in autumn (Sitters 1986).

Although there are a few records of birds apparently breeding and wintering in the same place, most breeding areas are deserted in winter suggesting that there is a distinction between summer and winter habitat requirements. When breeding, Woodlarks are found in open, often marginal, country with scattered trees and bushes, including heathland as in the New Forest, recently felled and restocked forestry plantations as in Breckland, and places where scrub has been cleared by fire as on the Hampshire/Surrey border. During the winter, Woodlarks spend much of the time in fields feeding on seeds and insects, sometimes in association with Skylarks.

Birds leave the main breeding areas during the early autumn and there is a small but distinct passage during October when low numbers are recorded at a wide variety of locations, especially on the south coast. There is no direct evidence of cross-Channel movement, though this no doubt occurs. Little movement takes place during November, December and January, although small numbers occasionally appear during severe winter weather, usually in company with Skylarks. The origin of these birds is uncertain but they are probably from the Continent, appearing as a result of weather movements. Birds return to the breeding areas in late February and early March, and it is possible that the *Winter Atlas* records cover the early part of the return movement.

The fact that severe winter weather depletes the breeding population, as it did in 1962/63 and in 1981/82, implies that although there is movement away from the breeding grounds most birds do not go very far; perhaps no further than N France.

At the time of the *Breeding Atlas*, Woodlarks were recorded in 195 10-km squares in Britain and the population was estimated at between 200 and 450 pairs. After that time the range contracted, with the population reduced to its lowest in the mid 1970s. Since then there has been a remarkable increase in numbers in the Hampshire/Surrey border area and to a lesser extent in the New Forest and the Breckland forests. The severe winter of 1981/82, however, reduced the population in Hampshire and Surrey. Total numbers now are probably much the same as they were in 1968–1972, but the distribution is more restricted.

County bird reports give the breeding population during 1981–83 as 210–430 pairs, with the majority in Hampshire and Surrey. The Woodlark is normally double-brooded and the average brood is 3–4. Thus, if the population were entirely resident, potential winter numbers would be well over 1,000 birds. Even allowing for the difficulty of locating the species, it is clear that a substantial part of the population leaves the country in winter, and the data suggest a population of 150–200 birds in winter.

The Woodlark populations of Scandinavia and central and eastern Europe are migratory. This means that Britain is on the northern edge of the winter range. No doubt climatic changes have been responsible for some of the fluctuations that have occurred in the population, as has severe winter weather. Availability of breeding habitat is also an important factor.

H. P. SITTERS

Total number of squares in which recorded: 56 (1%)

	Number (%) of squares		
No. of birds seen in a day	Britain	Ireland	TOTAL (incl. C.I.)
1–2	31 (55%)	0 (0%)	31 (55%)
3–6	16 (29%)	0 (0%)	16 (29%)
7+	9 (16%)	0 (0%)	9 (16%)

References
RUTTLEDGE, R. F. 1966. *Ireland's Birds*. Witherby, London.
SITTERS, H. P. 1986. Woodlarks in Britain, 1968–83. *Brit. Birds* 70: 105–116.

Breeding Atlas p 278

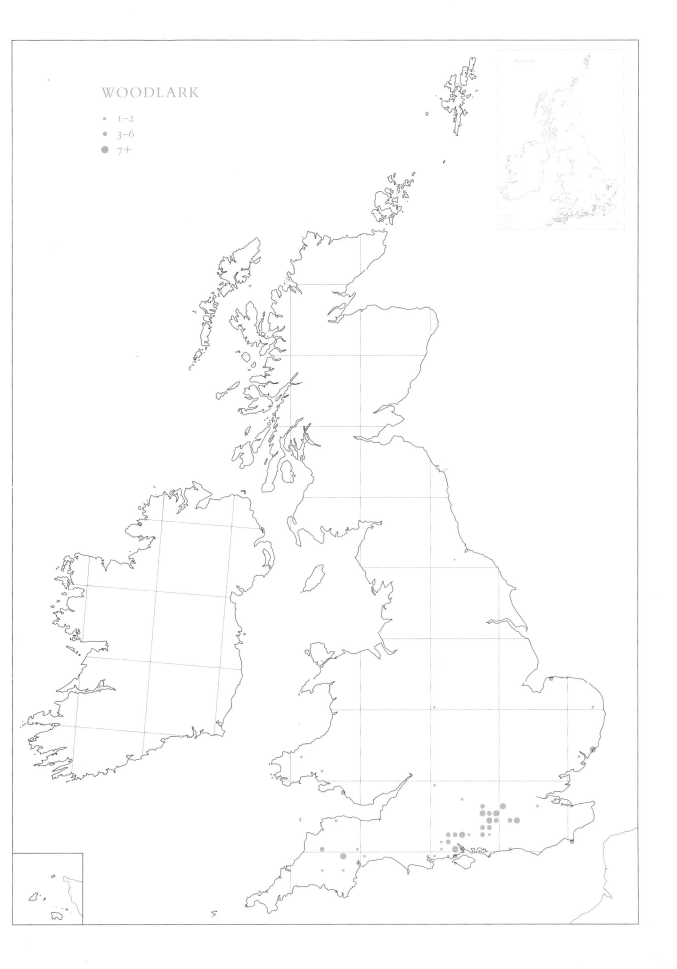

WOODLARK

- 1–2
- 3–6
- 7+

Skylark

Alauda arvensis

The Skylark is one of the most numerous and ubiquitous breeding birds of open country in Britain and Ireland, and is probably the species which has benefitted most from deforestation for cultivation and livestock. In winter, when many of its summer haunts become bleak and inhospitable, it has a more restricted distribution. In the *Breeding Atlas*, Skylarks were reported from nearly all squares, but in winter the species was absent from high ground and scarce in Ireland, Wales and NW Britain. The largest numbers were found on lowland mixed and arable farming areas, in southern and eastern England, and southeastern Scotland, and also near coasts, particularly those with extensive dunes, beaches, salt marshes or machair.

The high numbers of Skylarks recorded on arable farmland are in accord with an analysis of Common Birds Census results by Williamson (1967), who showed that breeding density was highest where a large proportion of the farm was sown to cereals rather than grass. Since cereals provide much of the Skylarks' winter food, this relationship is not surprising. Skylarks are presumably attracted to coastal marshes and dunes by the supplies of seeds there, which also attract many finches and buntings.

On arable farmland in winter, Skylarks feed on cereal grain, weed seeds, leaves and frost damaged vegetables. In autumn, cereal grain is abundant on stubbles and sowings, and weed seeds are exposed by cultivation and harvesting. During this time of plenty, Skylarks may only spend about half of their time feeding and there is a resurgence of singing, chasing and 'skylarking', after a quiet period during the moult in August and September. Food is less easily obtained after fields have been ploughed and cultivated and new crops have germinated. In mid winter the birds spend over 96% of their time looking for food, and graze autumn-sown cereals, oilseed rape, clover, kale and weeds. Weed seeds are gleaned from ploughed land but are often too scarce for this to be profitable (Green 1978). The first sowings of spring barley, in February or March, bring this period of food shortage to an end.

Many Skylarks feed solitarily but some form flocks, usually consisting of tens or hundreds of birds, which feed and fly in close association. Roosting birds are dispersed on the ground in rough grass or, if on bare arable land, often in a wheel rut of a tractor to gain some shelter from the wind.

British Skylarks are joined by visitors from NE Europe in winter; large numbers are seen arriving from the Continent in October and November at coastal bird observatories. Birds have also been seen leaving Britain in autumn, but whether these are British birds or the immigrants moving on is unknown. Within Britain in winter there are movements of tens of kilometres (Flegg 1980). High ground is abandoned and birds move away from snow-covered areas.

Winter counts on three arable farms in East Anglia in three winters gave a mean October–February density of 200 Skylarks per km² (range 130–280). The map shows this to be an area of comparatively high density, so if it is assumed that the average numbers of Skylarks per occupied 10-km square was 10,000, then the total population for Britain and Ireland would be about 25 million birds. This estimate is broadly in line with the *Breeding Atlas* figure of 2–4 million pairs, allowing for young of the year and winter visitors.

R. E. GREEN

Total number of squares in which recorded: 2,695 (70%)

No. of birds seen in a day	Number (%) of squares		
	Britain	Ireland	TOTAL (incl. C.I.)
1–30	909 (43%)	447 (75%)	1,359 (50%)
31–140	687 (33%)	111 (19%)	798 (30%)
141+	498 (24%)	38 (6%)	538 (20%)

References

FLEGG, J. J. M. 1980. Biological factors affecting control strategy. Pp 7–19 in WRIGHT, E. N., I. R. INGLIS and C. J. FEARE. (eds). *Bird Problems in Agriculture.* British Crop Protection Council, Croydon.

GREEN, R. E. 1978. Factors affecting the diet of farmland Skylarks. *J. Anim. Ecol.* 47: 913–928.

WILLIAMSON, K. 1967. The bird community of farmland. *Bird Study* 14: 210–226.

Breeding Atlas p 280

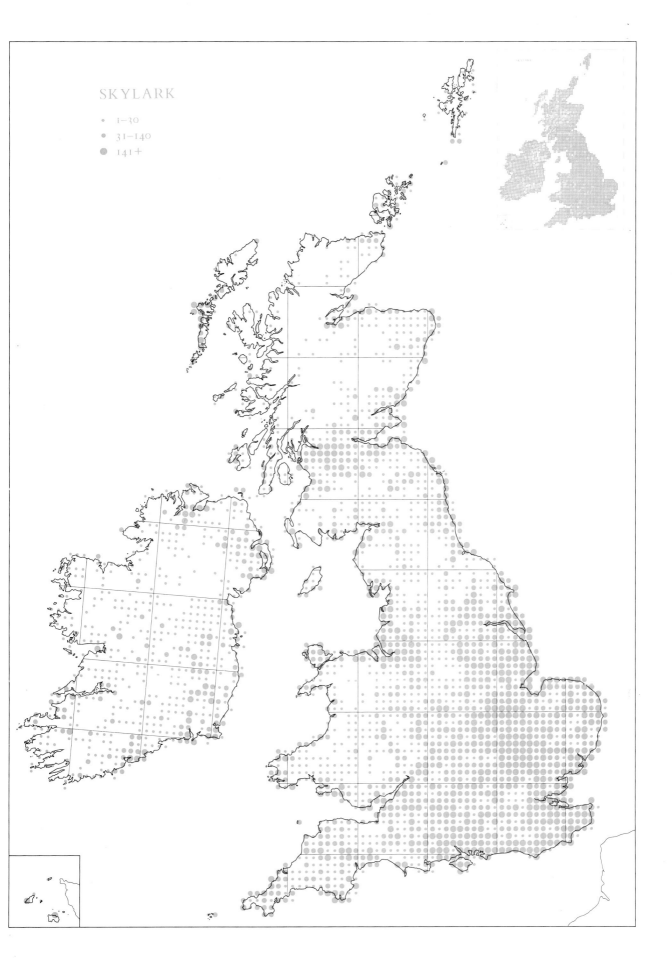

SKYLARK

- 1–30
- 31–140
- 141+

Shorelark

Eremophila alpestris

The Shorelark is typically a passage migrant and winter visitor to coastal sites, where it feeds, along with other larks, finches and buntings, among salt marsh and sand dune vegetation. Its low crouching progress while feeding and the clear 'tsee-it' call are characteristic of the species, though it can be a very difficult bird to locate, especially when present in small numbers.

Peak counts are recorded in late autumn, and there is a subsequent decrease to mid winter, indicating an onward movement to Continental areas. The birds remaining in Britain are distributed along the east coast, with the main concentrations from the Humber to the Thames estuaries. The group of records from the Dee/Mersey area indicates a recent extension in the wintering range to the west coast. Shannon (1974) documented the spread along the south coast and into the Irish Sea during the period between 1969 and 1973, at a time when counts in excess of a hundred birds were being made at many east coast sites. Despite a marked decline in the last decade, with counts now rarely rising into double figures, the use of the west coast sites has continued, but there are no records from Ireland during the survey period.

The distribution is governed by the availability of a specialised habitat consisting of extensive, developing salt marsh with an adjacent dune system. This is typical of the traditionally used sites at Spurn (Yorkshire), Donna Nook and Gibraltar Point (Lincolnshire), and Cley (Norfolk). The birds feed on the exposed salt marsh at low tide, mainly on the seeds of *Salicornia*, and retreat at high tide to the shingle areas among the dunes where many of the dune annuals provide an abundance of wind- and waterborne seeds. Occasionally they may move further inshore, especially when disturbed, onto rough pasture and arable land. A flock is very mobile within these habitats and may forage along several kilometres of suitable coastline, but often has one or more preferred areas where food is most abundant, and here the birds are most easily located. In early winter they are often quite confiding, allowing observation at close quarters, but become increasingly wary as winter advances. Fewer records in the later part of the winter may be due in part to this behaviour, though some continuing movement southwards, increased by severe weather, accounts for most of the decrease.

Shorelarks wintering in Britain belong to a population which breeds in northern Eurasia, from southern Norway, through Fennoscandia, north of the Arctic Circle, as far east as the Kolyma river. Southern Scandinavia was colonised only two centuries ago and it is thought that it is from here that British birds originate, although there are no ringing recoveries to substantiate this. A southward extension of the breeding range in recent decades, and a report of possible breeding in Scotland in 1972/73 (Watson 1973), coincided with the increase in birds visiting Britain. The proportion of the population which crosses the North Sea is very small. Departure from Fennoscandia takes place in a southeasterly direction and most of the birds winter in NE and Central Europe. Favourable weather conditions may carry more birds westwards in some winters but this does not significantly affect the long-term fluctuations which are such a feature of this species' occurrence in Britain.

The map clearly indicates the very low numbers of Shorelarks currently wintering here. Allowing for birds overlooked during the survey, it is still unlikely that total numbers in any of the three winters exceeded 300 birds, though this number may show a five-fold increase in years when the species is most numerous.

R. LAMBERT

Total number of squares in which recorded: 53 (1%)

Number (%) of squares

No. of birds seen in a day	Britain	Ireland	TOTAL (incl. C.I.)
1–2	24 (45%)	0 (0%)	24 (45%)
3–6	19 (36%)	0 (0%)	19 (36%)
7+	10 (19%)	0 (0%)	10 (19%)

References

SHANNON, G. R. 1974. Studies of less familiar birds. 174. Shore Lark and Temminck's Horned Lark. *Brit. Birds* 67: 502–511.

WATSON, A. 1973. Shore Larks summering and possibly breeding in Scotland. *Brit. Birds* 66: 505–508.

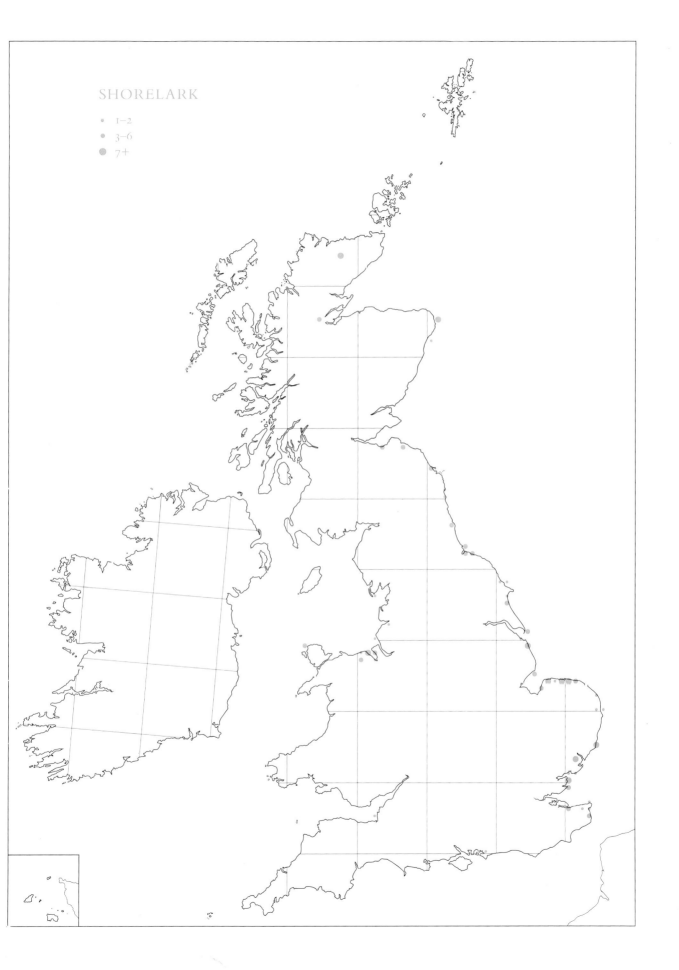

SHORELARK

- 1–2
- 3–6
- 7+

Meadow Pipit

Anthus pratensis

Wintering Meadow Pipits are gregarious birds. Squatting low in the wind, they feed industriously and, but for the distinctive thin call when they rise briefly into the air, are unobtrusive. Indeed, with no song-flight to help winter identification, the Meadow Pipit has a good claim to be for the tyro birdwatcher the classical, indeterminate 'small brown bird'.

Comparison with the *Breeding Atlas* shows that both in summer and winter the Meadow Pipits in Britain and Ireland cover almost the same geographical range. Although the *Breeding Atlas* maps were not quantified, the breeding densities quoted are often high, whereas the winter map shows many fewer birds north of, about, Lancashire. Thus there can be no doubt that there is a substantial movement southward, and perhaps southwestward in autumn. Even in the milder climate of Ireland, about two thirds of the squares with more than 43 individuals lie in the southwestern half of the country.

At the same time there are marked altitudinal changes in distribution, for the uplands, which have some of the high breeding densities, are inhospitable in winter and largely deserted. It should be remembered that any map showing the highest single count in three winters tends to exaggerate the species' true status. For example, in one Lake District square, Meadow Pipits were found only once in five winters and then, atypically, in a flock of 20 above the snow-line. Most of the gaps in winter distribution apparently relate to high ground, and perhaps also to extensive forest cover. Urban 'oases' are often quite well populated, especially in cold weather. Everywhere, the largest numbers chiefly occur on low ground.

Winter flocks of Meadow Pipits are straggly, and usually comprise fewer than 100 birds. According to *The Handbook*, their diet throughout the year is mainly of arthropods, supplemented by small worms and seeds. Specially favoured inland habitats include sewage works, shores of lakes and rivers, recently ploughed land, pasture land and root crops on which farm animals are fenced. Coastal birds often join Rock Pipits *Anthus (s.) petrosus* searching the high-tide wrack.

The origins of our wintering Meadow Pipits are not known. From August to late October there is a vast southward emigration, and very few ringed birds of proven British or Irish origin have been recovered here in December and January. From September there is also a considerable influx of birds from the north, many of which may winter with us, for in normal winters those ringed after late October seldom produce recoveries south of Britain. Recaptures have shown that some ringed individuals return to the same prescribed area in successive winters. Being ground feeders, Meadow Pipits find snow cover inimical and there is ringing evidence that severe cold weather may drive some wintering birds to Brittany, and even as far south as northern Spain.

As, year by year, more uplands are afforested and more marginal land is brought into cultivation (Body (1983) reported the loss of rough grazing to be 2.25 million ha in 20 years) the Meadow Pipit population seems likely to fall. The high average Common Birds Census Index for the years 1973–84 could mean that although the total numbers may be decreasing in areas with habitat loss, the density may have increased in the remaining areas, which are those covered by the CBC. The *Breeding Atlas* estimated the population at probably over 3 million pairs. Allowing two surviving young per pair, and guessing that emigration removes 80% of adults and young, the population in December could be 2–2.5 million, to which should be added an unknown number of winter visitors. The mid winter population of Britain and Ireland may thus lie in the range of 1–2.5 million, although the upper figure would require an *average* of nearly 800 birds per occupied square. Such numbers would obviously be much too high for many northern squares.

Zink (1975) has shown that most European Meadow Pipits winter in Iberia, a few passing on into North Africa. The population wintering in Britain and Ireland is certainly a small proportion of the whole. On the other hand it includes, in Scotland, the most northerly wintering of all Meadow Pipits.

R. SPENCER

Total number of squares in which recorded: 3,246 (84%)

No. of birds seen in a day	Number (%) of squares		TOTAL (incl. C.I.)
	Britain	Ireland	
1–16	1,135 (49%)	505 (55%)	1,640 (51%)
17–43	657 (28%)	310 (33%)	969 (30%)
44+	522 (23%)	112 (12%)	637 (20%)

References

BODY, R. 1983. *Agriculture: The Triumph and the Shame.* Temple Smith, London.

COULSON, J. C. 1956. Mortality and egg production of the Meadow Pipit, with special reference to altitude. *Bird Study* 3: 119–132.

ZINK, G. 1975. *Der Zug europäischer Singvögel. Ein Atlas der Wiederfunde beringter Vögel.* Lieferung 2. Vogelwarte Radolfzell-Möggingen.

Breeding Atlas p 394

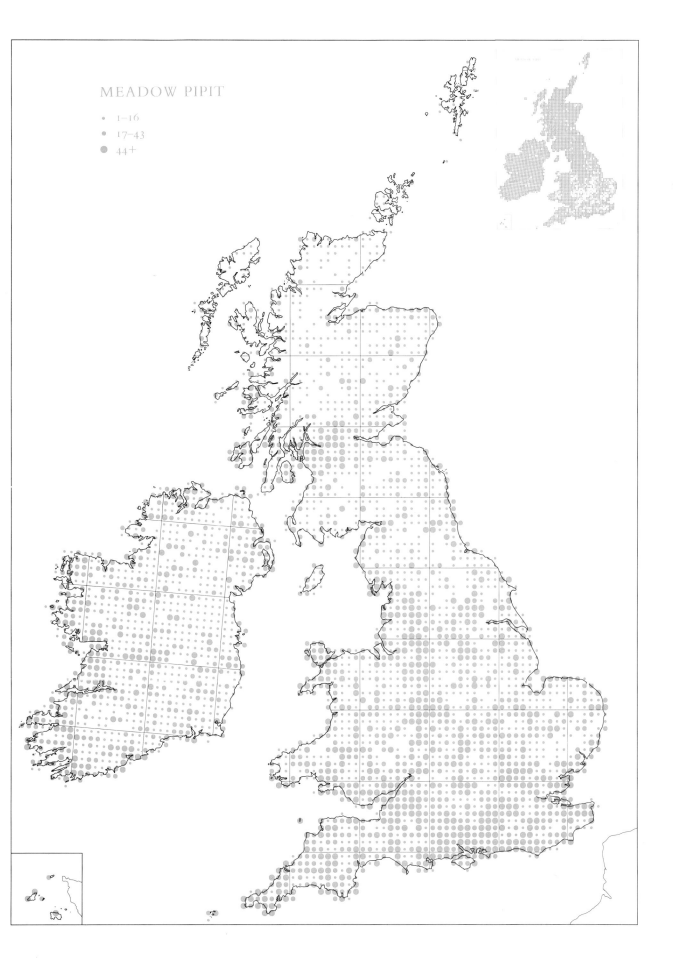

MEADOW PIPIT

- · 1–16
- · 17–43
- ● 44+

Rock Pipit and Water Pipit

Anthus (s.) petrosus and A. (s.) spinoletta

Small grey birds on the shore, hopping about among rocks and seaweed, is the traditional view of the Rock Pipit *Anthus (s.) petrosus*. But in the winter they also occur in other habitats and the local residents are supplemented by immigrants from Scandinavia, and by Water Pipits *Anthus (s.) spinoletta*.

This species complex has a Holarctic distribution. Recently, some forms have been considered to be full species (BOU Records Committee, A. G. Knox in prep.), although the present author disagrees with this decision. The Rock Pipit breeds and winters in Britain and Ireland, with separate subspecies distinguished by some authors in the Outer Hebrides, and on the Northern Isles of Scotland and the Faeroe Islands. The Scandinavian Rock Pipit *A. (s.) littoralis*, Water Pipit, and American Water Pipit *A. (s.) rubescens* has been recorded rarely in winter. On the Atlas cards the Water Pipit was not distinguished separately but, where appropriate, observers often specifically noted that Water Pipits were involved and subsequent appeals in *BTO News* and to Regional Organisers clarified a few other cases.

The birds of the species complex are difficult to distinguish in the field and the information available on their separate distributions in Britain and Ireland is sparse. The first map gives the winter distribution of the whole complex, without discrimination of species and subspecies, and shows that the birds winter all along the coastlines of Britain and Ireland. Birds are present in all places where the British Rock Pipits breed (cf *Breeding Atlas*), and also occur on stretches of coast which lack suitable rocky shores for breeding, and even regularly on sandy beaches (Gibbs 1956). There are about 65 records of birds found inland at distances of more than 20 km from the coast. These birds have apparently followed large rivers upstream. Most of these inland sites lie south of 54°N, where January mean temperatures are above 3°C, and only 4 are in Ireland.

Except from Shetland, there are only a few records of pipits identified as Rock Pipits spending the whole winter inland. Rock Pipits are, however, seen regularly at several inland sites in southern England during the autumn and spring (Johnson 1970), but it is not known whether these birds are migrants from northern breeding sites or if they are vagrants from the closest breeding populations.

Of the many reports of migrating pipits which can be found in the literature, only a few are definite Rock Pipit observations. Between 1955 and 1982, 16 birds, which had been ringed on Fair Isle during the breeding season (before end of August), were recovered at distances of 100–850 km, and one bird was recovered at Den Helder, Netherlands (BTO Ringing Reports). This agrees with Williamson's (1965) statement that, in autumn, the birds leaving Fair Isle are probably all young ones. Also a bird ringed on Lundy (Bristol Channel) in autumn was recovered in Ireland, near Wicklow, during the following breeding season. Evans (1966) reported no long-distance recovery from 2,000 Rock Pipits ringed at Skokholm (W Wales), and there are none from birds ringed elsewhere in Britain.

The Rock Pipit feeds most of the year on the shore, mainly in the intertidal zone. The grassland above the shore is used for foraging only during the breeding season, when young are fed exclusively on prey collected in the vegetation. Gibb (1956) found that birds wintering in Cornwall fed mainly on small periwinkles, chironomid larvae and amphipods. Birds seen inland in England feed on river banks, by reservoirs, sewage farms and gravel pits. In Shetland they also feed on arable land and in gardens (Venables and Venables 1955).

The Scandinavian Rock Pipit breeds along the whole of the Scandinavian coast and in Denmark (Pethon 1967). Some birds winter in or close to their breeding sites, but many migrate southwards and winter as far south as Portugal, Sicily and Malta (*The Handbook*, Zink 1975). They appear regularly on the east and south coasts of England, mainly on spring passage, from mid March till April, but the increase in numbers reported at this time might be because their breeding plumage makes distinction from the Rock Pipit easier. In spring the Scandinavian Rock Pipit is a frequent migrant in S Scotland and on Fair Isle (MacMillan 1970), and a good many of the 'Rock-type' pipits passing through the Isle of May are probably this race (Eggeling 1974). There seems to be only one record in Ireland (Tory Island, Co. Donegal) and one from the west coast of Britain (Pembrokeshire) (Johnson 1970).

As in its other wintering areas, the Scandinavian Rock Pipit is rarely found inland in Britain, but some inland birds may have been confused with Water or Rock Pipits. Johnson (1970) mentions inland records in the London area, in Surrey, in Cambridgeshire and in Middlesex.

In Britain, Scandinavian Rock Pipits feed in the same habitat as the native birds, including sewage farms and along rivers (Johnson 1970).

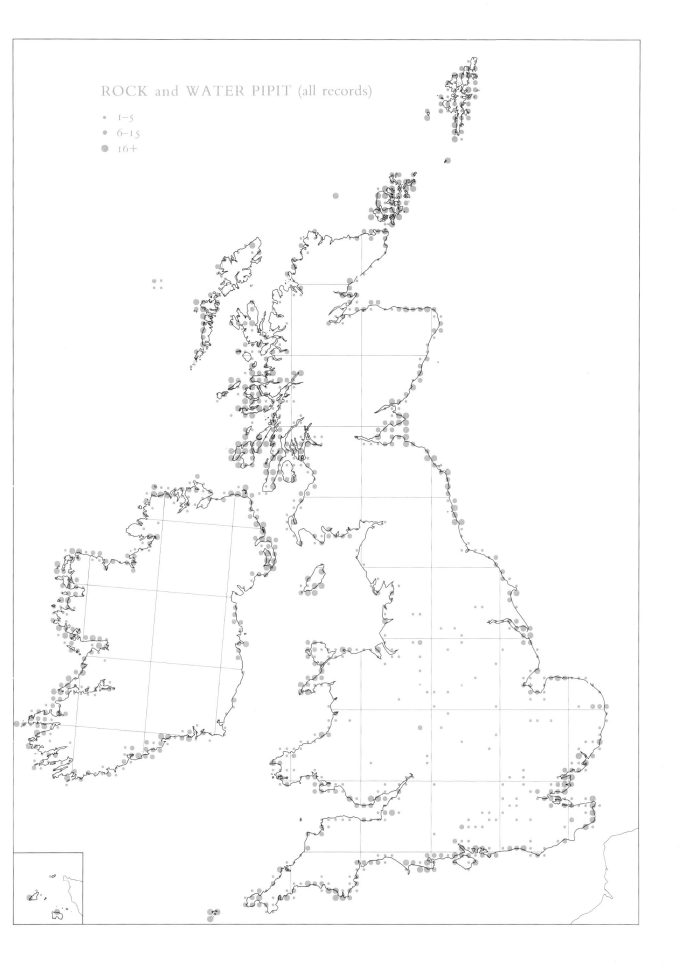

ROCK and WATER PIPIT (all records)

· 1–5
· 6–15
● 16+

able that the records were of vagrants rather than of regular migrants.

The *Breeding Atlas* suggested a population for British and Irish Rock Pipits of over 50,000 pairs. This suggests a wintering population of the order of 100,000–150,000 birds, and there are certainly some migrants of the Scandinavian race to be added to this figure. The number of Water Pipits in any one winter is unlikely to exceed 100 or so.

J. P. BIBER

Water Pipits can be considered partly as vagrant, partly as migratory. They breed in the European mountains south of 51°N, most commonly at altitudes of 1,300–2,500 m, where they inhabit meadows, pastures and rocky grassland slopes. The birds leave their breeding grounds between August and November. Many of them winter in the lowlands, relatively close to breeding areas, but some migrate several hundreds of kilometres in directions between NNW and ESE. As far as can be seen from ringing recoveries there is no preferred direction, and wintering areas lie in Belgium, along the Channel and Atlantic coast of France, Portugal and the Mediterranean coasts from Spain to Italy (Zink 1975). Water Pipits are also seen regularly on the coasts of N Africa, from Morocco to Tunisia, in Crete and Cyprus and in small numbers in northern Germany and the Netherlands. They have been recorded as winter visitors in Britain since 1859.

The second map gives the distribution of those individuals specifically identified as Water Pipits. Most of the records are in the southern part of England, and many are close to large towns, which suggests that the distribution could partly reflect the observer availability rather than the true distribution of the birds. There are a few accepted records from Scotland and from Ireland, though none of the latter during the winters of the *Winter Atlas*. Most Water Pipits are seen between October and early April, although birds determined as such have been observed as early as mid August (4–6 weeks after the juveniles become independent in Switzerland) and as late as the beginning of May.

The preferred feeding habitats of Water Pipits in Britain are (in order of decreasing importance) watercress beds, coastal fresh water or brackish pools or marshes, inland fresh water marshes, or rivers and sewage farms (Johnson 1970). They use salt water habitats very little, which are the preferred feeding grounds of Rock Pipits. Both forms may meet on river banks, reservoirs, sewage farms and in gravel pits. Unlike the Rock Pipit, Water Pipits roost communally in Britain.

The so-called American Water Pipit breeds in NE Siberia, North America and W Greenland, and winters south to Russian Turkestan and eastern China, and from northern California to the Gulf of Mexico. It has occurred in Britain and Ireland but it is prob-

ROCK PIPIT COMPLEX
Total number of squares in which recorded: 1,148 (30%)
(map on previous page)

Number (%) of squares

No. of birds seen in a day	Britain	Ireland	TOTAL (incl. C.I.)
1–5	419 (48%)	127 (46%)	548 (48%)
6–15	272 (31%)	102 (37%)	374 (33%)
16+	175 (20%)	49 (18%)	226 (20%)

WATER PIPIT
Total number of squares in which recorded: 93 (2%)

Number (%) of squares

No. of birds seen in a day	Britain	Ireland	TOTAL (incl. C.I.)
1	45 (48%)	0 (0%)	45 (48%)
2–4	32 (35%)	0 (0%)	33 (35%)
5+	16 (17%)	0 (0%)	16 (17%)

References

EGGELING, W. J. 1974. The birds of the Isle of May—a revised status. *Scot. Birds* 8 (Spec. Suppl.): 93–148.

EVANS, P. R. 1966. Some results from the ringing of Rock Pipits on Skokholm 1952–1965. *Rep. Skokholm Bird Observatory 1966*: 22–27.

GIBB, J. 1956. Food, feeding habits and territory of the Rock Pipit *Anthus spinoletta*. *Ibis* 98: 506–530.

JOHNSON, I. G. 1970. The Water Pipit as a winter visitor to the British Isles. *Bird Study* 17: 297–319.

MACMILLAN, A. T. 1970. Scottish bird report 1969. *Scot. Birds* 6: 62–128.

PETHON, P. 1967. Systematic note on the Norwegian Rock Pipit. *Nutt. Mag. Zool.* L5: 44–49.

VENABLES, L. S. V. and U. M. VENABLES. 1955. *Birds and Mammals of Shetland*. Oliver and Boyd, London & Edinburgh.

WILLIAMSON, K. 1965. *Fair Isle and its Birds*. Oliver & Boyd, London and Edinburgh.

ZINK, G. 1975. *Der Zug europäischer Singvögel. Ein Atlas der Wiederfunde beringter Vögel*. Lieferung 2. Vogelwarte Radolfzell-Möggingen.

Breeding Atlas p 398

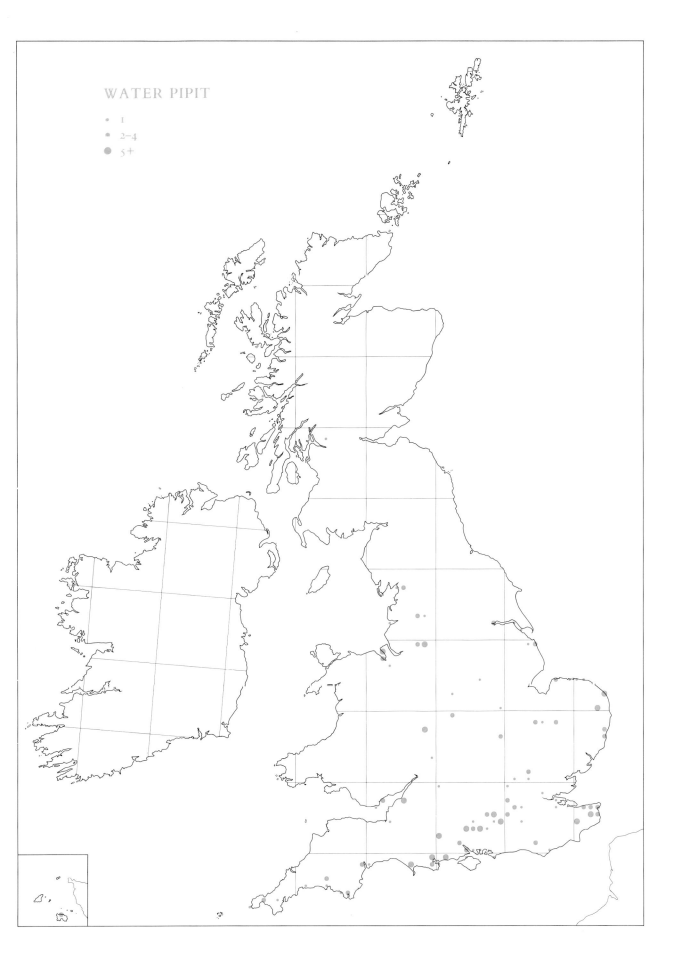

WATER PIPIT

- 1
- 2–4
- 5+

Grey Wagtail

Motacilla cinerea

The Grey Wagtail, with its long tail and graceful aerial manoeuvres, is one of the most attractive birds of fast flowing streams and rivers.

In the winter, Grey Wagtails are widespread in Ireland and southern Britain, although in eastern England they are largely confined to the coastal areas. In the north of England and Scotland, Grey Wagtails occur mainly in lowland and coastal areas, and in these regions they are much more sparsely distributed than in the breeding season. In Britain, the southwest is clearly the winter stronghold for this species.

Observations at coastal observatories have shown a passage of Grey Wagtails during the summer and autumn (Sharrock 1969). Ringing recoveries have also shown that many Grey Wagtails from northern Britain move south to southwest in the autumn, to England and Ireland or across the Channel to France (Tyler 1979). Some birds probably reach Spain, Portugal or North Africa, to which most Scandinavian and many central European Grey Wagtails also move (Zink 1975). Those birds remaining in Scotland form the most northern wintering population other than a few Scandinavian birds.

Some of the winter records of Grey Wagtails are undoubtedly of Continental birds, because Danish, Belgian and East German birds have all been recovered or controlled in the winter months in southern Britain (Tyler 1979).

During the autumn and winter there is also an altitudinal movement of Grey Wagtails, down from the mountains and hills, especially in Scotland. Birds are then found in a wider range of habitats than during the breeding season and are to be seen at sewage works, in farmyards, especially around slurry pits or manure heaps, on lowland rivers and canals, at watercress beds, by pools and lakes, around buildings in towns, in gardens and on coastal marshes.

In the breeding season Grey Wagtails obtain much of their food from riverine habitats. In the winter some birds remain by rivers and streams, feeding on aquatic invertebrates, but those that frequent farms, towns and gardens take a wide variety of food items. These include dungflies, small worms and midge larvae from sewage filter beds, small fish such as sticklebacks from ponds, amphibian larvae available from

February in parts of Britain, and in severe weather bread and other household scraps. They have been recorded searching Feral Pigeon *Columba livia* droppings in towns for insects and taking maggots from fishing tackle shops (C. Lynch).

Some Grey Wagtails establish individual winter territories but they leave them at dusk to roost communally in reed beds, in bramble patches, in scrub, trees or buildings. Roosts rarely exceed 50 birds and are often alongside those of Pied Wagtails *M. alba*.

Grey Wagtails suffer severely in prolonged bouts of snow and frost. In the 1962/63 winter they were the most badly affected species, apart from the Kingfisher *Alcedo atthis* (Dobinson and Richards 1964). Populations soon recover however, and the *Breeding Atlas* field work was carried out at a time when the population was probably high (estimated as 25,000–50,000 pairs). The breeding range of Grey Wagtails has continued to spread in lowland areas since 1972. Palmer (1982) recorded a substantial increase in the London area between *Breeding Atlas* years and 1981. The hard winter of 1981/82 again took its toll and the Grey Wagtail population may have been considerably reduced during the *Winter Atlas* years. Although numbers of birds emigrating and immigrating are unknown, Merritt *et al* (1970) believed the numbers of Grey Wagtails in Sussex in the winter to be similar to, or possibly less than, the breeding population. Many 10-km squares in northern Britain are unoccupied in the winter, but a perhaps high estimate of 20 birds per 10-km square, in the occupied squares, gives a winter population of about 40,000 birds.

S. J. TYLER

Total number of squares in which recorded: 2,155 (56%)

No. of birds seen in a day	Number (%) of squares		
	Britain	Ireland	TOTAL (incl. C.I.)
1	659 (44%)	257 (39%)	917 (43%)
2–3	595 (40%)	275 (42%)	871 (40%)
4+	238 (16%)	127 (19%)	367 (17%)

References

DOBINSON, H. M. and A. J. RICHARDS. 1964. The effects of the severe winter of 1962/63 on birds in Britain. *Brit. Birds* 57: 373–434.

MERRITT, W., R. R. GREENHALF and P. F. BONHAM. 1970. A survey of the Grey Wagtail in Sussex. *Sussex Bird Report 1969*: 68–80.

PALMER, K. H. 1982. The breeding season status of the Grey Wagtail in the London Area, 1979–81. *London Bird Report* 47: 106–122.

SHARROCK, J. T. R. 1969. Grey Wagtail passage and population fluctuations in 1956–67. *Bird Study* 16: 17–34.

TYLER, S. J. 1979. Mortality and movements of Grey Wagtails. *Ringing and Migration* 2: 122–131.

ZINK, G. 1975. *Der Zug europäischer Singvögel. Ein Atlas der Wiederfunde beringter Vögel.* Lieferung 2. Vogelwarte Radolfzell-Möggingen.

Breeding Atlas p 402

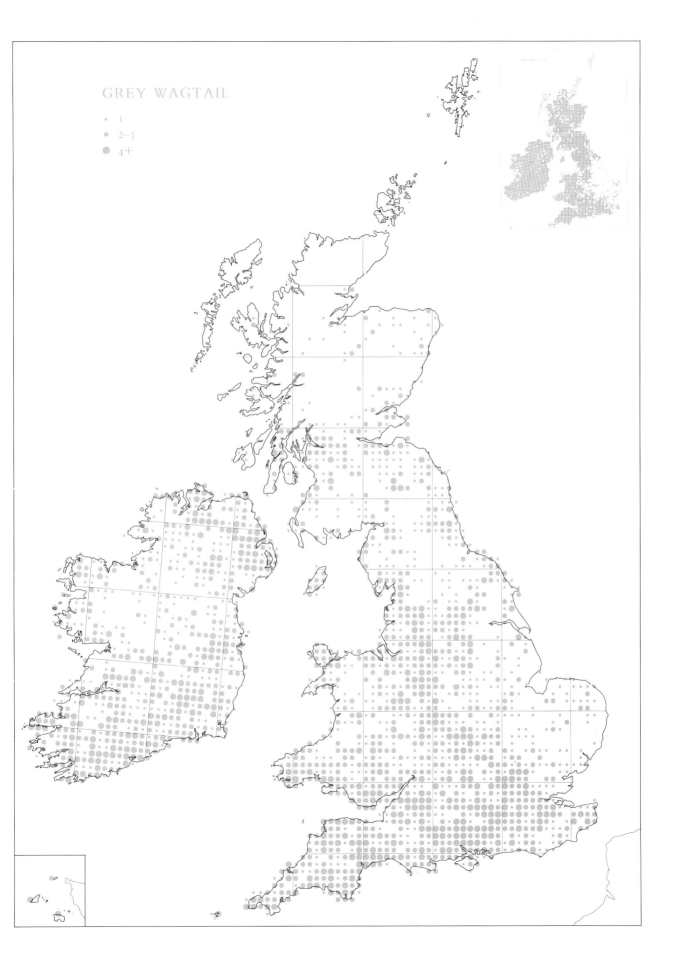

GREY WAGTAIL

- 1
- 2–3
- 4+

Pied Wagtail

Motacilla alba

HB.

With its loud 'chis-ick' flight call and distinctive plumage, the Pied Wagtail is one of the most conspicuous small birds inhabiting open country in winter.

The winter distribution in Britain is not as widespread as it is in summer. Pied Wagtails are absent from high ground and are scarce in Scotland except for the coastal areas. The species is commonest in Ireland and southern Britain, especially in lowland meadows and along river systems. It also occurs around reservoirs, sewage farms and in towns where, even in winter, it can be seen picking small insects from roads and sometimes the roofs of buildings.

Ringing recoveries show that birds in southern Britain are largely sedentary, with movements usually being less than 50 km. Some first year birds may emigrate to western Europe, especially in cold weather, and in very cold winters many adults may emigrate too. By contrast, the population in northern Britain, both adult and juvenile, is largely migratory. Southerly movements begin in August and continue to November, with the main passage at coastal observatories occurring in September and October. There is a return movement north in late March and early April. Most of the birds winter in central and southern England but many go to the west coasts of France, Portugal and Spain, and some even reach Morocco (Davis 1966). In southern England, winter numbers reach a peak in December and early January.

Many birds roost communally in warm and sheltered sites, particularly low bushes, reed beds and sewage works, where several thousand may congregate each night. Individuals may join roosts to decrease predation and perhaps also to gain information about the location of good feeding areas, by following others from the roost the next morning. Most birds feed within 12 km of the roost, and the catchment areas of neighbouring roosts may overlap. In January, densities of Pied Wagtails in the Thames Valley may be, on average, 8 per km² (Broom *et al* 1976).

The main diet in winter is small invertebrates, particularly beetles, spiders, adults and larvae of flies, earthworms and small molluscs. Small seeds are also eaten and, in cold weather particularly, flocks may congregate on rubbish dumps to feed on artificial food supplies. Winter mortality can be high, and the breeding population decreased by 55% on farmland after the cold winter in 1962/63, and by 12% after the 1978/79 winter (Cawthorne and Marchant 1980).

Many birds feed in flocks, particularly where food is abundant. Some, however, defend feeding territories throughout the winter. In mid winter, individuals may feed for over 90% of the daytime and collect one small prey item every 3–4 seconds throughout the day. Even with this high feeding rate the birds only just manage to balance their energy expenditure (Davies 1982). Territory owners not only defend their territories against conspecifics but also against other species which compete for the same food, including Meadow Pipits *Anthus pratensis* and Grey Wagtails *M. cinerea*. Territory ownership is announced by a distinctive territorial call, 'chee-wee'.

When food is scarce in territories, owners may join flocks to feed, though they still return periodically to defend their territories. If food becomes abundant, owners (which are often males) sometimes share their territories with 'satellites' (usually females or first-winter juveniles). When food becomes very abundant, territory defence ceases and all intruders are tolerated. The flexible social behaviour enables the Pied Wagtail to respond appropriately to temporal and spatial changes in their winter food supply (Davies and Houston 1981).

The *Breeding Atlas* estimated the breeding population to be 500,000 pairs in Britain and Ireland. Because of mortality and emigration, both of which will depend on the severity of the winter, it is very difficult to estimate the numbers in Britain in December, but the population is probably in the region of 0.75 to 2 million birds.

N. B. DAVIES

Total number of squares in which recorded: 3,027 (78%)

No. of birds seen in a day	Number (%) of squares		TOTAL (incl. C.I.)
	Britain	Ireland	
1–7	1,090 (53%)	481 (50%)	1,572 (52%)
8–18	462 (22%)	391 (41%)	853 (28%)
19+	513 (25%)	87 (9%)	602 (20%)

References

BROOM, D. M., W. J. A. DICK, C. E. JOHNSON, D. I. SALES and A. ZAHAVI. 1976. Pied Wagtail roosting and feeding behaviour. *Bird Study* 23: 267–279.

CAWTHORNE, R. A. and J. H. MARCHANT. 1980. The effects of the 1978/79 winter on British bird populations. *Bird Study* 27: 163–172.

DAVIES, N. B. 1982. Territorial behaviour of Pied Wagtails in winter. *Brit. Birds* 75: 261–267.

DAVIES, N. B. and A. I. HOUSTON. 1981. Owners and satellites: the economics of territory defence in the Pied Wagtail, *Motacilla alba*. *J. Anim. Ecol.* 50: 157–180.

DAVIS, P. 1966. The movement of Pied Wagtails as shown by ringing. *Bird Study* 13: 147–162.

Breeding Atlas p 400

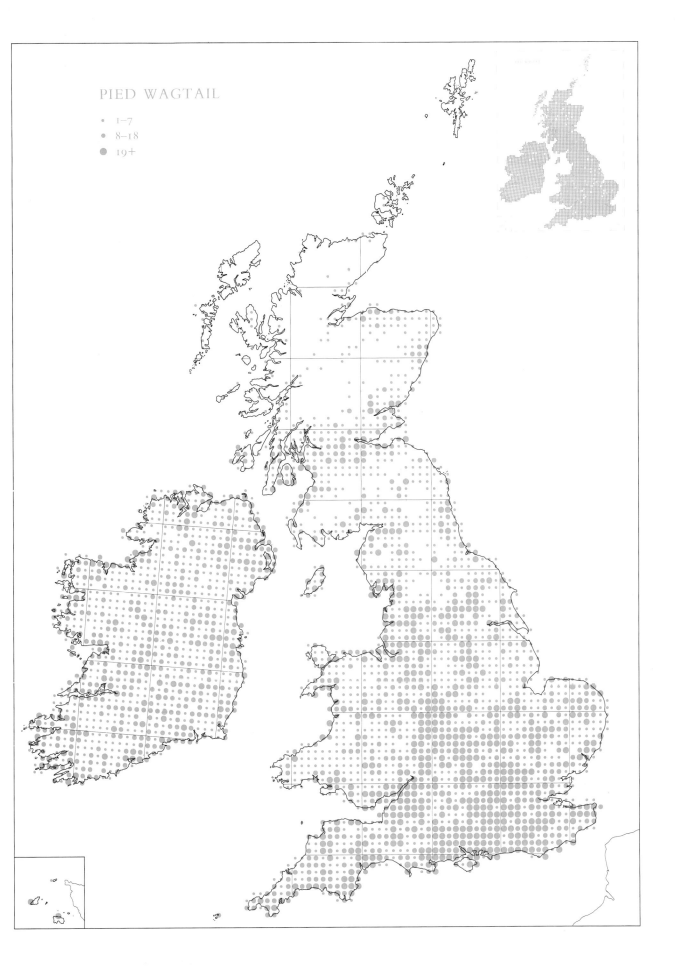

PIED WAGTAIL

· 1–7
· 8–18
· 19+

Waxwing

Bombycilla garrulus

There can be few more exciting winter visitors than the Waxwing. Its attractive plumage is unusually colourful in a season dominated by monotones. A feeding flock, acrobatically reaching for berries and presenting a variety of memorable poses, makes a charming sight.

It is popularly supposed that Waxwing irruptions occur approximately every ten years, but none of the three winters surveyed here coincided with a 'Waxwing year' although in 1981/82 there were many more than in either subsequent winter (p. 32). Yet the distribution map shows a scatter which is largely consistent with most maps of Waxwings in Britain—namely, a predominantly eastern bias in Scotland and England (notably the industrial northeast) with a subsidiary concentration in the well watched suburban parks and gardens of the western midlands of England. The urban connection is inevitable, as Waxwings arrive when berries in the countryside have already been stripped by earlier migrants such as Fieldfares *Turdus pilaris* and the other thrushes. In the period under review, flocks of 10 or more occurred in Scotland and NE England with two in East Anglia. In irruption years, flocks in the two former areas are numbered in three or even four figures. In the invasion of 1965/66 unprecedented numbers occurred. The figure of 11,300 quoted by Cornwallis and Townsend (1968) for the first half of November, is an accumulation of numbers recorded each day, a flock of 100 remaining for a week and counted daily scoring 700. Even so, thousands of birds were involved. Waxwings are scarce in Ireland, except in irruption years.

In Britain, Waxwings are as inextricably associated, in art and in reality, with red berries as Crossbills *Loxia curvirostra* with pine cones or Goldfinches *Carduelis carduelis* with thistles. Yet individuals have been observed for lengthy periods flycatching from telephone wires—which is not really surprising considering their summer diet is exclusively mosquitoes. Even so, their chief winter food is the berries of the rowan and when these are not available the berries of other trees and shrubs.

It is the rowan berry which provides the key to their irruptive behaviour. Waxwings of the nominate race breed in the remote taiga, from Fennoscandia into western Siberia. In most years they breed in fairly low densities and are rarely seen—the first nest was only found in 1856. But occasionally the population peaks. Warm weather is conducive to a high survival rate among young Waxwings and also produces a heavy crop of rowan berries. This ensures above-average survival the following winter and the birds may not arrive in central Europe and Britain until February, if at all. But in the following year, when the Waxwing population is at its highest, 'tired' trees almost invariably produce poor berry crops. This peak pressure on food supply results in an early and large scale irruption. Lack (1954) suggested the earliness of the movement is caused by the psychological stresses resulting from high numbers and has survival value in stimulating the birds to fly in advance of the failure of food before starvation weakens them. Some ringing returns suggest that dispersal may be random (for instance a Waxwing ringed in Poland in February 1937 was recovered 5,000 km to the east the following winter). But there are many biological and meteorological advantages favouring a fixed southwesterly preferred direction: the position of the Scandinavian high pressure area in autumn, the line of least resistance in light northeasterly winds, the guiding lines of the Baltic coast, and the ameliorating influence of the Gulf Stream producing the best berry crops. Small numbers (up to 100 or so) of Waxwings probably arrive every year and field observations suggest that some areas in Scotland and NE England are regular wintering sites. Only in invasion years do the birds occur here in significant numbers. Britain is, after all, on the extreme western edge of the bird's range and is only invaded when pressure on the food supply in continental Europe is very great. However, Britain can continue to look forward to periodic invasions of this most delightful visitor.

B. BLAND

Total number of squares in which recorded: 156 (4%)

No. of birds seen in a day	Number (%) of squares		
	Britain	Ireland	TOTAL (incl. C.I.)
1	67 (45%)	4 (57%)	71 (46%)
2–4	48 (32%)	3 (43%)	51 (33%)
5+	34 (23%)	0 (0%)	34 (22%)

References

CORNWALLIS, R. K. 1961. Four invasions of Waxwings during 1956–60. *Brit. Birds* 54: 1–30.

CORNWALLIS, R. K. and A. D. TOWNSEND. 1968. Waxwings in Britain and Europe during 1965/66. *Brit. Birds* 61: 97–118.

LACK, D. 1954. *The Natural Regulation of Animal Numbers*. Clarendon Press, Oxford.

SVARDSON, G. 1957. The 'invasion' type of bird migration. *Brit. Birds* 50: 314–343.

Breeding Atlas p 450

WAXWING

- • 1
- • 2–4
- ● 5+

Dipper

Cinclus cinclus

The Dipper, a passerine remarkable for its aquatic habits, is commonest on the fast-flowing hill streams in the north and west of Britain, in the mountainous rim of Ireland and on some rocky lowland rivers. The wintering and breeding ranges coincide closely; wintering Dippers are frequent throughout Wales and much of northern Britain, excluding Orkney, Shetland and some western isles. They are patchily distributed in SW England and apparently absent from much of central Ireland.

Records in winter of isolated individuals on the east coast and in southern England are probably immigrants from the Continent, either of the nominate race *cinclus* from Scandinavia or possibly of the central and W European race *aquaticus*. (Several were identified as being 'Black-bellied' Dippers.) By contrast, the British and Irish races, *gularis* and *hibernicus*, are very sedentary (Galbraith and Tyler 1982). Some local movements from the high moorland streams to more lowland reaches may accompany the onset of winter conditions and, in severe weather, Dippers may even move to feed along estuaries and coastal areas.

Dippers begin breeding early, some having laid before the end of February. Many winter records may therefore refer to birds on breeding territories.

In winter Dippers take a wide range of prey. From an analysis of 368 faecal pellets containing 4,850 prey-items, Ormerod and Tyler (1986) estimated that the aquatic stages of mayflies (3%), stoneflies (1%), caddis flies (20%), true flies (3%) and molluscs (6%) provided 33% by weight of the diet of Dippers wintering in the catchment of the River Wye in 1984/85. Fish, predominantly bullheads but also small salmonids, comprised over 60% of the diet by weight and were more frequently taken than during the breeding season (Ormerod 1985). Numerically, small items such as blackflies, baetid mayflies and fresh water limpets provided 50% of the dietary items recorded and clearly represent readily used sources of food.

Dippers roost during the winter in crevices in cliffs, in or on the old nest, in stonework, in drainpipes or on ledges and girders below bridges. Some roost singly or in pairs at any particular site, but eight or more birds may be present at certain favoured bridges or tunnels.

The major peak in Dipper mortality occurs following the breeding season and, by December, the population of Britain and Ireland would be similar to the breeding population of 60,000 birds (*Breeding Atlas*). This number exceeds that produced from the winter records, almost two thirds of which refer to, at most, 2 birds per 10-km square. However, personal observations in Wales and the Welsh borders indicate that more realistic values are 10–40 birds per 10-km square, giving a winter estimate of 15,000–60,000.

The Waterways Bird Survey has indicated that Dipper populations are remarkably stable between years and, unlike Kingfishers *Alcedo atthis* and Grey Wagtails *Motacilla cinerea*, they do not decline following severe winters. However, Ormerod *et al* (1985) noted a decrease between the 1950s and 1982 amongst a population of Dippers breeding on a Welsh river which had become progressively more acidic following the afforestation of part of its catchment. Throughout Wales, Dippers are scarce on acidic streams which have high concentrations of dissolved aluminium and which drain conifer afforested areas (Ormerod *et al* in press). The studies indicate that Dipper populations may be affected by human activities which increase stream acidity.

s. j. tyler and s. j. ormerod

Total number of squares in which recorded: 1,508 (39%)

No. of birds seen in a day	Number (%) of squares		
	Britain	Ireland	TOTAL (incl. C.I.)
1	416 (36%)	156 (44%)	572 (38%)
2–3	474 (41%)	159 (45%)	633 (42%)
4+	262 (23%)	41 (12%)	303 (20%)

References

GALBRAITH, H. and S. J. TYLER. 1982. Movements and mortality of the Dipper as shown by ringing recoveries. *Ringing and Migration* 4: 9–14.

ORMEROD, S. J. 1985. The diets of breeding Dippers and their nestlings in the catchment of the River Wye, mid-Wales: a preliminary study by faecal analysis. *Ibis* 127: 316–332.

ORMEROD, S. J., N. ALLISON, D. HUDSON and S. J. TYLER. 1986. The distribution of breeding Dippers (*Cinclus cinclus*; Aves) in relation to stream acidity in upland Wales. *Freshwater Biology* in press.

ORMEROD, S. J. and S. J. TYLER. 1986. The diet of Dippers wintering in the catchment of the River Wye, Wales. *Bird Study* 33: 36–45.

ORMEROD, S. J., S. J. TYLER and J. M. S. LEWIS. 1985. Is the breeding distribution of Dippers influenced by stream acidity? *Bird Study* 32: 33–39.

SHAW, G. 1979. Functions of Dipper roosts. *Bird Study* 26: 171–178.

Breeding Atlas p 326

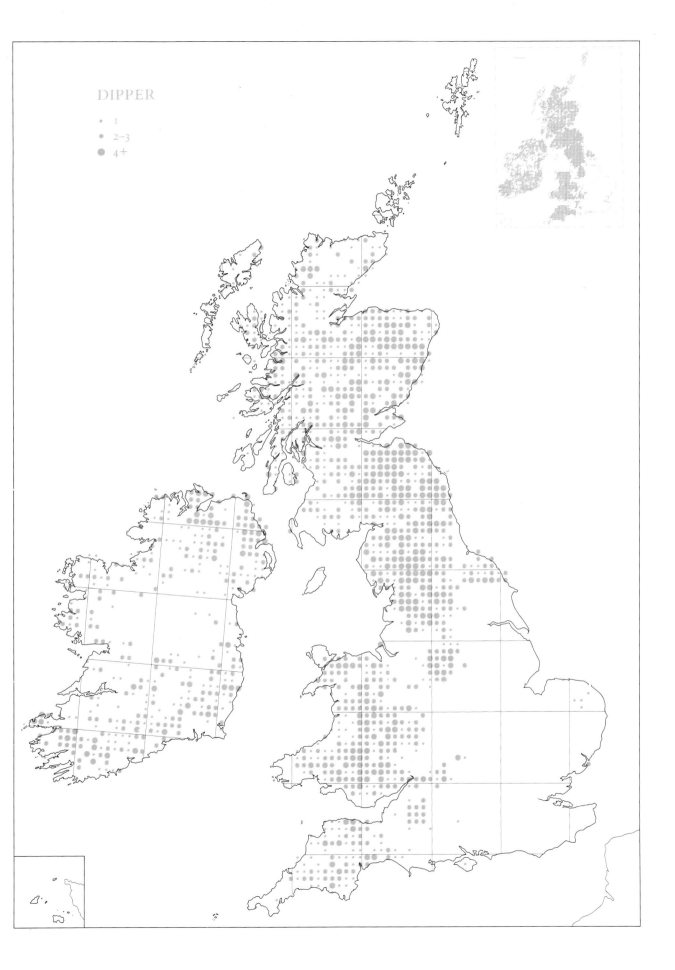

DIPPER

- 1
- 2–3
- 4+

Wren

Troglodytes troglodytes

By its ability to feed beneath snow cover in winter, this species, to a degree, lives up to its scientific name and becomes at least partly 'subterranean'. It is generally inconspicuous outside the breeding season but draws attention by its loud calls and song which can be heard all the year round.

In winter, the Wren is almost ubiquitous, found even on remote islands such as Foula and St Kilda. The only notable difference from the map in the *Breeding Atlas* is absences from some mountainous squares in N and W Wales, N England, the Southern Uplands and Highlands of Scotland, and the moorland flows of Lewis and northernmost Highland Region. Wintering densities decrease generally from south to north, but in Scotland there are more in the central lowlands than elsewhere. Irish densities are comparable to those at similar latitudes in Britain.

Many Wrens are individually territorial in winter and defend their feeding area with vigorous alarm calls and song. Habitat preferences differ from those in summer, however. Most breeding sites support many fewer wintering birds, and some exposed breeding habitats, such as remote uplands and moorlands, are completely deserted. Hedgerows on farmland, a secondary habitat (Williamson 1969), also are commonly empty in winter. In contrast, territories are often established in habitats not used for nesting, notably reed beds. This behaviour gives way, sometimes by February, to spring territoriality, with re-invasion of more exposed sites and more frequent song.

Competition for winter territories may begin in July. Winter survival is likely to be better among territory holders because of their knowledge of a particular patch and their claim, only infrequently disputed, to its various feeding and roosting sites. If the winter territory is suitable for nesting, the owner is able, unless evicted, to make an early start to breeding. The losers in territorial disputes probably formed the majority of Wrens wintering in loose flocks in a Berkshire reed bed (Hawthorn 1975).

Wrens feed on insects and spiders, occasionally seeds, mostly low in dense vegetation or on the ground. Owing to their size and agility, and especially to their readiness to enter holes and crevices, they are able to forage in sites inaccessible to other birds. Many such sites are still available during snowy weather, when snow rarely penetrates to the centres of bushes or to the base of dense ground vegetation: in those circumstances, Wrens may feed and roost under a blanket of snow. For short periods during especially severe weather, territory holders and others may gather from a wide area to roost communally, often in a nestbox. In 1962/63, a record 50 Wrens was counted in a single box.

Ringing recoveries show that most Wrens move only short distances between summer and winter, with no preference for direction, but that a few move further, mainly southwards (Hawthorn and Mead 1975). Cold weather may stimulate onward southerly movements. A few British birds reach France, and recoveries also link Britain with Sweden, Belgium and the Netherlands. There is apparently a small arrival and passage of Continental birds, mainly evident in SE England. The four separate island races—in St Kilda, the Western Isles, Fair Isle, and Shetland—are not known to move, but the Shetland race is joined by small numbers of Continental migrants in winter.

As a tiny bird the Wren chills relatively rapidly, and has little potential for storing fat, and is thus exceptionally vulnerable to extreme cold or to conditions which prevent feeding. Owing to this vulnerability and to its high breeding potential, its numbers vary more between years than those of any other species monitored by the Common Birds Census. In a typical year, however, the estimated 4–5 million pairs in Britain and Ireland might produce a mid winter population in the range 12–20 million. The scale of immigration is too small to affect this estimate.

Wrens breed right across the Palearctic from Iceland and Morocco to Kamchatka and Japan; some upland and northern parts of the range are completely deserted in winter. In North America, the 'Winter Wren' is resident north to Alaska on the Pacific slope but is only a winter visitor to southern USA.

J. H. MARCHANT

Total number of squares in which recorded: 3,573 (93%)

No. of birds	Number (%) of squares		
seen in a day	Britain	Ireland	TOTAL (incl. C.I.)
1–12	1,299 (50%)	525 (53%)	1,824 (51%)
13–24	755 (29%)	295 (30%)	1,051 (29%)
25+	528 (21%)	166 (17%)	698 (20%)

References

HAWTHORN, I. 1975. Wrens wintering in a reed-bed. *Bird Study* 22: 19–23.

HAWTHORN, I. and C. J. MEAD. 1975. Wren movements and survival. *Brit. Birds* 68: 349–358.

WILLIAMSON, K. 1969. Habitat preferences of the Wren on English farmland. *Bird Study* 16: 53–59.

Breeding Atlas p 324

WREN

- · 1–12
- ● 13–24
- ● 25+

Dunnock

Prunella modularis

The archetypal small brown bird, solitary, shy and retiring, often in dense undergrowth, the Dunnock (= Hedge Sparrow) is one of the most common and widespread birds in Britain and Ireland, and from January onwards its song is one of the characteristic winter sounds of scrubland, woodland and gardens.

Ringing recoveries show that Dunnocks in Britain are very sedentary; most individuals probably spend their whole lives within a radius of 0.1–1 km. This is in contrast to the population in northern continental Europe, which migrates south for the winter. Some of these Continental migrants appear on passage in eastern Britain in autumn but there is no evidence of a large influx of winter visitors. Some British Dunnocks, especially coastal ones, get excited around September as if they are going to migrate, but as far as we know they never do. The winter map is, therefore, very similar to the distribution map of the breeding season. The Dunnock is absent from the high mountain areas of Britain and Ireland (typical habitat of other species of accentor) but is otherwise widely distributed.

It favours habitats with dense undergrowth and is one of the eleven most common woodland birds, but it is also common in farmland hedgerows, downland and marshland scrub, dune and coastal scrub and surburban parks and gardens (Fuller 1982).

The Dunnock is mainly solitary in winter, though up to six individuals may have overlapping ranges and may aggregate temporarily at rich food sources. In these aggregations, females are subordinate to the larger males and when food is scarce the females are forced to wander more widely in search of food. In harsh winters, females may suffer higher mortality (Birkhead 1981, Snow and Snow 1982, Davies and Lundberg 1984). Most of the Dunnock's food is obtained on the ground by gleaning or turning over small leaves. The diet consists of a mixture of small seeds (*eg*, grasses, nettle, dock) and invertebrates (*eg*, beetles, spiders, earthworms, flies and springtails). The BTO's Garden Bird Feeding Survey shows that the Dunnock is abundant in winter at rural garden feeding stations, and takes food widely in most suburban and many inner city gardens (Glue 1984). Dunnocks are most often to be watched shuffling unobtrusively on the lawn beneath hedges or the bird-table, only occasionally venturing up on to vacant raised surfaces and rarely feeding from hanging containers. They take a wide variety of small seeds, picking and probing for fragments of peanuts and all types of farinaceous foods, less often berries and small pieces of fat, meat and fruit. In mid winter, individuals feed for over 90% of the daylight hours, dropping to 60–70% in March (Bishton 1986, Davies and Lundberg 1985).

Males begin to sing from mid January to early February. It is common for 2 or 3 males to have overlapping song territories and the mating combinations, which begin to form in late February and March, are very variable, including simple pairs (monogamy), a male with 2 females (polygyny), a female with 2 or 3 males (polyandry) or 2 or 3 males sharing 2, 3 or 4 females (polygynandry) (Birkhead 1981, Snow and Snow 1982, Davies and Lundberg 1984). The species is therefore very difficult to census unless all the individuals are colour ringed.

The breeding population is estimated to be 5 million 'pairs' (*Breeding Atlas*). Assuming a pair of Dunnocks produces 6 fledged young per breeding season, that half of these die before December, and that half of the 35% annual adult mortality occurs by mid winter, the December population can be estimated as roughly 20 million birds for Britain and Ireland.

N. B. DAVIES

Total number of squares in which recorded: 3,359 (87%)

No. of birds seen in a day	Number (%) of squares		
	Britain	Ireland	TOTAL (incl. C.I.)
1–11	1,066 (44%)	610 (65%)	1,676 (50%)
12–23	801 (33%)	231 (25%)	1,032 (31%)
24+	551 (23%)	95 (10%)	651 (19%)

References

BIRKHEAD, M. E. 1981. The social behaviour of the dunnock, *Prunella modularis*. *Ibis* 123: 75–84.

BISHTON, G. 1986. The diet and foraging behaviour of the dunnock *Prunella modularis* in a hedgerow habitat. *Ibis* 128: (in press)

DAVIES, N. B. and A. LUNDBERG. 1984. Food distribution and a variable mating system in the dunnock, *Prunella modularis*. *J. Anim. Ecol.* 53: 895–912.

DAVIES, N. B. and A. LUNDBERG. 1985. The influence of food on time budgets and the timing of breeding in dunnocks, *Prunella modularis*. *Ibis* 127: 100–110.

FULLER, R. J. 1982. *Bird Habitats in Britain*. Poyser, Calton.

GLUE, D. (ed.) 1984. *The Garden Bird Book*. Papermac, London.

SNOW, B. and D. SNOW. 1982. Territory and social organisation in a population of dunnocks, *Prunella modularis*. *J. Yamashina Inst. Ornithol.* 14: 291–292.

Breeding Atlas p 392

DUNNOCK

- · 1–11
- ● 12–23
- ● 24+

Robin

Erithacus rubecula

The Robin is one of our best loved birds and was chosen by vote as the British national bird. This popularity is partly a reflection of its confiding nature, which is especially evident during the winter. In addition, the Robin's distinctive warble is one of the few songs which can be heard in mid winter. These characteristics mean that it is unlikely that this species was overlooked in many 10-km squares.

The winter distribution is very similar to that shown in the *Breeding Atlas*, with two important exceptions. First, Robins are not found in some upland areas in which they breed. At least part of this retreat is the result of altitudinal migration, although some individuals may move much further (see below). Secondly, Robins winter at sites in the Hebrides, Orkney and Shetland where they rarely breed. In the first two cases, many of the birds involved have moved short distances from nearby breeding sites. However, most of the birds wintering in Shetland are probably Scandinavian.

The widespread distribution of wintering Robins reflects their catholic choice of habitats. Most territories contain at least some mature trees and the map shows that Robin densities tend to be low in poorly wooded areas (*eg*, upland areas in north, fens of East Anglia). However, some treeless habitats (*eg*, reed beds, sand dunes, scrub) can contain large numbers of Robins. Analysis of wintering densities in different habitats around Oxford suggests that the presence of abundant cover within 2 m of the ground is an important feature of most occupied sites.

Although Robins have been recorded feeding on a great variety of food items (Lack 1943, Mead 1984), most of their diet consists of invertebrates captured on the ground and of fruit. Vegetable food is more important during the winter than at other times, although it rarely accounts for more than 10% of energy intake. The importance of ground-living prey to wintering Robins means that periods of snowfall can result in heavy mortality, as in the winter of 1981/82.

During the winter, Robins of both sexes defend individual territories although communal roosting has been observed (Swann 1975). Detailed studies (*eg* Burkitt 1924–27, Lack 1943) have demonstrated that in lowland Britain and Ireland, males typically defend the same territories throughout their lives. By contrast, most females do not winter at their breeding sites. Some habitats, especially in upland areas, are totally abandoned by both sexes. Breeding sites are vacated between late June and late November, with great variation between habitats; females leave earlier on average than do males. Ringing recoveries (Mead 1984) suggest that most of these movements between breeding and wintering sites involve distances of less than 5 km, perhaps more in the north. Seasonal changes in Robin density suggest that many birds move into habitats which are unsuitable for breeding (*eg*, reed beds, suburban areas without mature vegetation). Birds move back to breeding sites between late December and early May. A few British and Irish Robins winter abroad (probably less than 5% of females and very few males). Most foreign ringing recoveries (Mead 1984) have occurred along the western seaboard of Europe from the Netherlands south to Iberia, although one bird from Surrey was found in Switzerland. Continental Robins (from at least as far northeast as Finland) regularly pass through Britain between mid August and November, to their wintering grounds in SW Europe and N Africa.

Since the *Breeding Atlas* estimate, of about 5 million breeding pairs, the Common Birds Census index for farmland has declined by about 20%. Taking account of this and other recent data, a more reasonable estimate of the breeding population during the *Winter Atlas* period would be 3.5 million pairs (Mead 1984). Population studies in a variety of habitats suggest that the average pair rears about 2 chicks to independence each year. Assuming that the net movement of Robins in and out of these islands probably is small, the December population during the *Winter Atlas* fieldwork may have exceeded 10 million birds for Britain and Ireland. This probably represented between 5 and 10% of the European population.

D. HARPER

Total number of squares in which recorded: 3,557 (92%)

	Number (%) of squares		
No. of birds seen in a day	Britain	Ireland	TOTAL (incl. C.I.)
1–19	1,275 (50%)	498 (50%)	1,775 (50%)
20–35	769 (30%)	301 (30%)	1,071 (30%)
36+	519 (20%)	190 (20%)	711 (20%)

References

BURKITT, J. P. 1924–27. A study of the Robin by means of marked birds. *Brit. Birds* 17: 294–303; 18: 205–207; 19: 120–124; 20: 91–101.

LACK, D. 1943. *The Life of the Robin*. Witherby, London.

MEAD, C. J. 1984. *Robins*. Whittet Books, London.

SWANN, R. L. 1975. Communal roosting by Robins in Aberdeenshire. *Bird Study* 22: 93–98.

Breeding Atlas p 354

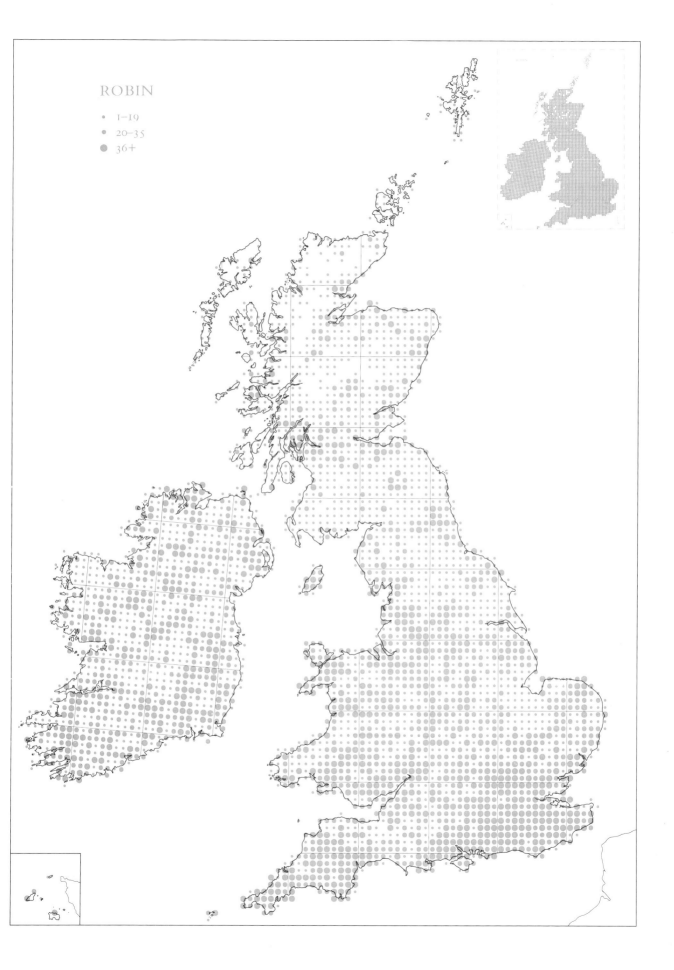

ROBIN

- · 1–19
- · 20–35
- ● 36+

Black Redstart

Phoenicurus ochruros

In Britain the Black Redstart is best known for its recent colonisation and spread as a breeding species, particularly associated with the London bomb-sites during the second world war. However, as long ago as the mid 19th century it was known as a passage migrant and scarce winter visitor.

The winter map shows that it still occurs only in small numbers in any one locality and that it is largely coastal in distribution. The main areas of concentration are along the west and south coasts of Wales from Anglesey to the Gower peninsula; from the southwest peninsula (probably the main winter stronghold) and stretching along the coast to Kent; and the east coast of Ireland. Smaller numbers are scattered elsewhere around the coasts of W Ireland and in Britain north to Cumbria and Yorkshire. The species is regular in SW and SE Scotland but very sporadic elsewhere. There are very few inland records except in S England and an occasional record from central England.

This is a very different distribution pattern from that in the *Breeding Atlas* which shows the main concentrations of records coming from the London area, the coastal towns of the southeast and a few industrial sites in central England. Since the publication of the *Breeding Atlas,* nesting Black Redstarts have spread further westwards and northward. The majority of breeding sites are in inner urban areas such as industrial complexes, power stations, gas works and docks and warehouses (Morgan and Glue 1981).

In winter, Black Redstarts are still to be found in some of their breeding haunts in urban industrial areas but are also much more widely distributed in small towns and gardens, and particularly around the coasts on cliffs and beaches.

There is virtually nothing recorded on the winter diet of these birds in Britain. In general the food is described as mainly insects and other small invertebrates, as well as berries in autumn and winter. In Scotland the birds appear to feed on invertebrates on the tidal wrack. The main prey items of birds wintering in evergreen oak woodland in S Spain were found to be ants and small beetles (Herrera 1978).

Most Black Redstarts leave the breeding areas of northern and central Europe to winter around the Mediterranean, and there are records of birds ringed in Britain recovered in Spain and Portugal in January (Langslow 1977). In spring the arrival of migrants on the south coast begins in early March, and in autumn the peak passage is during late October/early November (Riddiford and Findley 1981). This very extended migration season makes it difficult to interpret the origins and destinations of the birds involved and, as yet, there are no clear indications of movements involving the British wintering population. A Black Redstart ringed in winter in Britain (Gloucestershire) was recovered in October in Suffolk. Continental movements to and from Britain have been recorded from as far east as Czechoslovakia, and it may be speculated that at least some of our wintering birds are escaping the harsh Continental conditions by travelling west instead of to the more traditional southerly wintering areas. The fact that Black Redstarts may be found in winter at sites occupied during the breeding season also suggests that some British breeders overwinter.

The Black Redstart has become an addition to Britain's breeding avifauna this century, and since the first regular breeding in 1923 the population has risen to 100 pairs (Morgan and Glue 1981). No such data exist for the winter numbers but counting the symbols on the map the winter population in Britain and Ireland is probably about 500 birds.

R. A. MORGAN

Total number of squares in which recorded: 406 (11%)

No. of birds seen in a day	Number (%) of squares		
	Britain	Ireland	TOTAL (incl. C.I.)
1	226 (70%)	54 (64%)	280 (69%)
2	49 (15%)	21 (25%)	71 (17%)
3+	43 (14%)	10 (12%)	55 (14%)

References

HERRERA, C. M. 1978. Datos sobre la dieta invernal del colirrojo tizon *Phoenicurus ochruros* en encinares de Andalucia occidental. *Donana Acta Vertebrata* 5:61–71.

LANGSLOW, D. R. 1977. Movements of Black Redstarts between Britain and Europe as related to occurrences at observatories. *Bird Study* 24:169–178.

MORGAN, R. A. and D. E. GLUE. 1981. Breeding survey of Black Redstarts in Britain, 1977. *Bird Study* 28:163–168.

RIDDIFORD, N. and P. FINDLEY. 1981. Seasonal movements of Summer Migrants. *BTO Guide 18.*

Breeding Atlas p 350

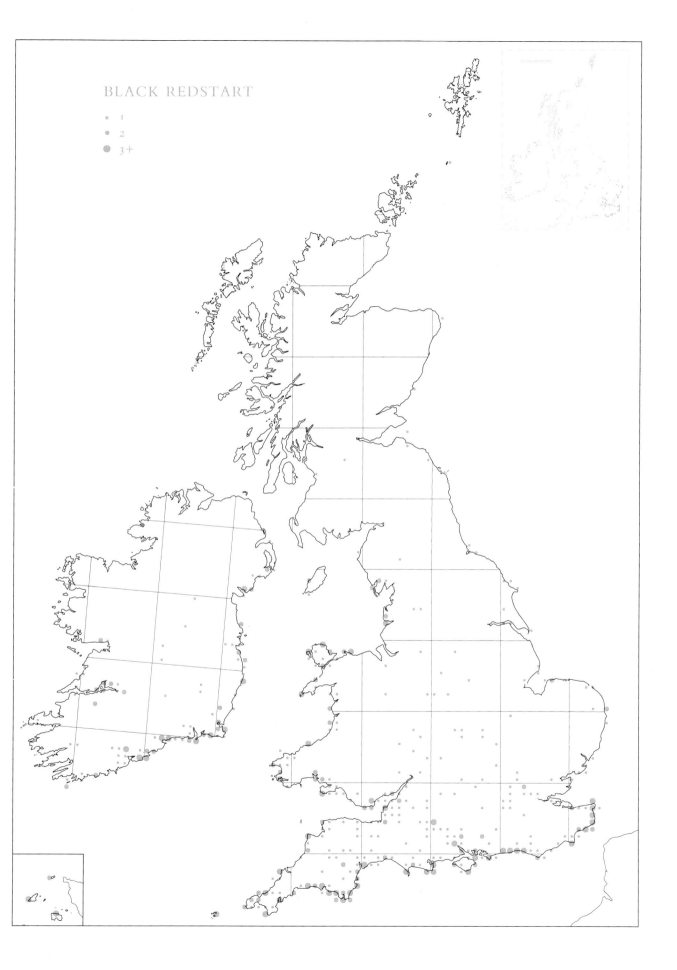

BLACK REDSTART

- • 1
- • 2
- ● 3+

Stonechat

Saxicola torquata

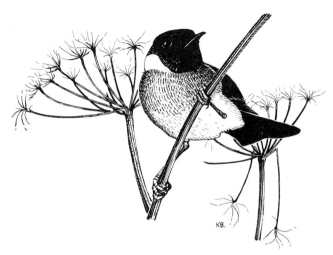

Basically a sedentary species in Britain and Ireland, the Stonechat is in general loyal to well defined territories throughout the year. It needs a comparatively mild winter climate, and reasonable freedom from human disturbance. A Stonechat territory must contain certain permanent features, such as a number of perches up to 1.5 m high from which it can seek its insect prey, ground cover of heather and coarse grasses which is not too dense to permit access to the bare soil, and one or two observation or song posts up to 6 m high. Uncultivated open land with small shrubs and scattered perennials (gorse, various Umbelliferae, etc) is most favoured, as this remains largely unchanged in structure throughout the seasons (Agatho 1960–61, Johnson 1971a).

In Britain, the Stonechat's winter range is broadly similar to its breeding distribution (*Breeding Atlas*) and is bounded roughly by the 4°C January mean isotherm. It tends to desert the higher breeding places in the Scottish Highlands and the English Lake District, with a corresponding build up of numbers in the southern and central counties of England. A few birds migrate south. In Ireland, where the breeding distribution is much more uniform, there is simply a tendency to move to the coast.

The formation of winter pairs begins in September, when adult Stonechats have emerged from moult and the young of the year have assumed their first winter plumage. The pair bond is then relaxed and wandering young, as well as adults which have left less hospitable breeding territories, compete for mates within established and favourably placed territories.

There may be a marked preference for some sites in winter and others during the breeding season, a few remaining in constant occupation throughout the year (Phillips and Greig-Smith 1980).

By some time in October, all pairs occupy the territories in which they will remain for the winter. At first, boundaries are defended vigorously but, once they are confirmed and established, both sexes spend their time feeding, usually in close company, on the ground. The male's duller winter plumage may well cause the pair to be completely overlooked at this time, when they may even join flocks of finches foraging through their territory (Johnson 1961). Except when competition is fierce, winter territories may be much larger than the area used for breeding but, at all times, close contact is maintained between the pair.

In late January, territorial activity increases, greater initiative is shown by the male and more rigid boundaries are established. The male sings regularly by mid February, and courtship begins in early March.

On the continent of Europe, Stonechats move south to winter on the Atlantic seaboard, throughout the Iberian Peninsula, in the northern Mediterranean zone, the Mediterranean islands and NW Africa. In the habitats which British and Irish emigrant birds share with locally resident Stonechats in winter, their familiar gorse, heather and Umbelliferae may be replaced by the vines and maquis of southern Europe or the *Palmetto* scrub and *Ziziphus* thorn of littoral and Saharan N Africa.

In view of its sedentary, ground feeding and largely insectivorous habits and the fact that its main dispersal to winter territories is during the fine weather of early autumn, the Stonechat is extremely vulnerable to the severe cold weather. On the other hand, being triple brooded it can recover rapidly from hard winters. Few reliable data exist on which to base an accurate estimate of the winter population of Stonechats in Britain and Ireland. The *Breeding Atlas* suggested 30,000–60,000 pairs breeding in 1972. Field experience shows that the winter population overall is unlikely to differ widely from that of the breeding season.

E. D. H. JOHNSON

Total number of squares in which recorded: 1,385 (36%)

No. of birds seen in a day	Number (%) of squares		
	Britain	Ireland	TOTAL (incl. C.I.)
1–2	576 (63%)	234 (50%)	810 (58%)
3–4	174 (19%)	92 (19%)	268 (19%)
5 +	158 (17%)	146 (31%)	307 (22%)

References

AGATHO, BR. 1960–61. De Roodborsttapuit (*Saxicola torquata rubicola* L.) een onderzoek naar zijn leef wijze en broed biologie. *Publikaties van het Natuurhistorisch Genootschap in Limburg, Reeks* 12 : 166–175.

JOHNSON, E. D. H. 1961. The pair relationship and polygyny in the Stonechat. *Brit. Birds* 54 : 213–225.

JOHNSON, E. D. H. 1971a. Observations on a resident population of Stonechats in Jersey. *Brit. Birds* 64 : 201–213, 267–278.

JOHNSON, E. D. H. 1971b. Wintering of *Saxicola torquata* in the Algerian Sahara. *Bull. Brit. Orn. Club* 91 : 103–107.

PHILLIPS, J. S. and P. GREIG-SMITH. 1980. Breeding and wintering sites of Stonechats. *Bird Study* 27 : 255–256.

Breeding Atlas p 344

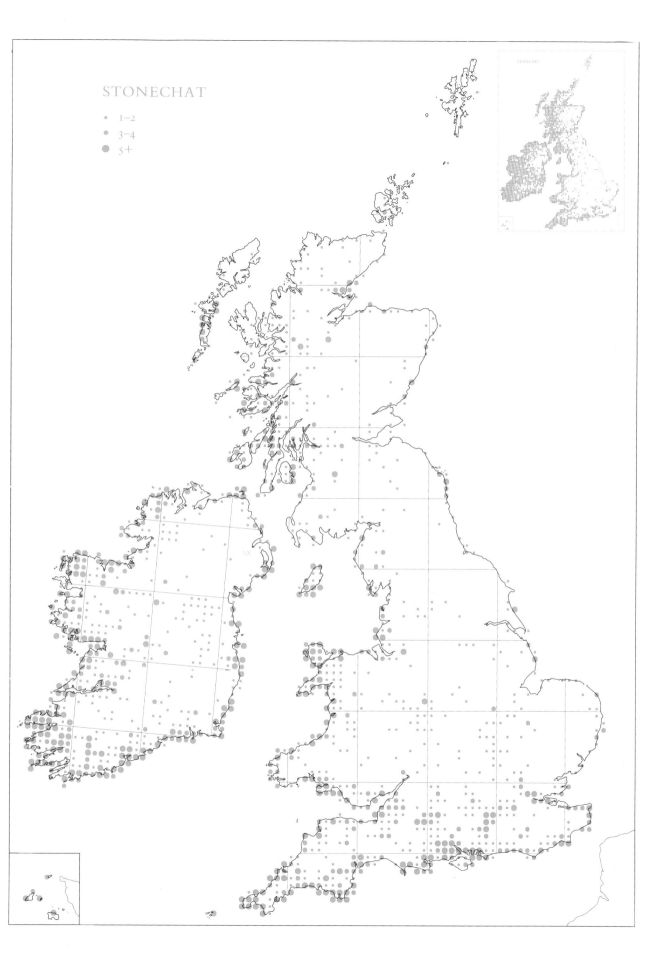

STONECHAT

- 1–2
- 3–4
- 5+

Blackbird

Turdus merula

In winter, in Britain and Ireland, the Blackbird is as familiar and as nearly ubiquitous as it is in the breeding season. The map shows that it occurs in winter in the vast majority of the 10-km squares, most of the gaps being in the Scottish Highlands where conditions may be too severe for even this most adaptable of the thrushes.

The more or less uniform distribution shown on the map conceals the fact that the composition of the Blackbird population wintering in Britain and Ireland is extremely complex. British breeding birds are partial migrants, with marked regional differences in the tendency to migrate and in the directions taken (Snow 1966). Birds breeding in Scotland and northern England are most migratory, those from central England less so, and those from southern England least so. In their first autumn most of the migratory individuals from Scotland and northern England move southwest or westsouthwest into Ireland; a smaller number migrates less far in a northwest direction without leaving the British mainland. Birds born in southern England tend to move either westwards or south into France. The tendency to migrate is apparently independent of age and sex, but urban and suburban birds may be less migratory than rural birds.

Superimposed on the British and Irish breeding stock, is a huge influx of winter visitors. These Blackbirds are from the populations breeding in Scandinavia, Germany and the Low Countries and, increasingly in recent years, from the Baltic States, Finland and adjacent parts of Russia (Spencer 1975); a change that may reflect the increasing 'urbanization' (and hence the likelihood of ringing) of Blackbirds in northeastern Europe.

Blackbirds seem little prone to hard weather movements compared with the other thrushes. Even in the exceptional winter of 1962/63 there was no positive, ringing evidence of such movements, though some areas were apparently evacuated in the most severe cold spell (Simms 1965). In the less extreme winters covered by the field work for the *Winter Atlas*, it is thus not surprising that the picture is much the same for each of the winters, and for the early winter and late winter periods. Nevertheless, there is some regular movement in the course of a winter. The Blackbirds which move from N Britain to winter in Ireland tend to move gradually towards the south-west of Ireland and then, at the end of winter, to move gradually northeast (Snow 1978).

In spite of the fact that, overall, many British Blackbirds migrate, some local populations are highly sedentary. Even in the extreme north, in Shetland, the local breeding population is almost completely sedentary (Venables and Venables 1952). An Oxford garden population studied over 4 years was also sedentary: no bird was recovered more than 2 miles (3 km) from where it was ringed, and all established territory-holders remained through the winter. Such birds actively defend their territories except in the most severe weather, when territory boundaries break down and the birds forage wherever they can find food. The winter visitors, by contrast, apparently live in loose flocks and forage socially.

In winter, Blackbirds may roost singly in their territories, in small groups, or in large groups of up to many hundreds, the larger roosts occurring especially where a clump of suitable cover is surrounded by more sparsely vegetated areas suitable only for feeding. A very large communal roost studied by L. A. Batten, beside Brent Reservoir in N London, consisted mainly of birds drawn from neighbouring gardens.

It has been estimated that there may be over 7 million pairs of Blackbirds breeding in Britain and Ireland. With the breeding population increased by their progeny, and with a huge influx of Blackbirds from an extensive area of northern Europe, against which must be set the comparatively small fraction of the British breeding population which migrates south to France, it seems certain that the total wintering population must easily exceed 14 million, and could well exceed 20 million individuals.

D. W. SNOW

Total number of squares in which recorded: 3,627 (94%)

No. of birds	Number (%) of squares		
seen in a day	Britain	Ireland	TOTAL (incl. C.I.)
1–54	1,138 (43%)	666 (67%)	1,804 (50%)
55–114	842 (32%)	255 (26%)	1,098 (30%)
115 +	654 (25%)	67 (7%)	725 (20%)

References

SIMMS, E. 1965. Effects of the cold weather of 1962/63 on the Blackbird population of Dollis Hill, London. *Brit. Birds* 58 : 33–43.

SIMMS, E. 1978. *British Thrushes*. Collins, London.

SNOW, D. W. 1966. The migration and dispersal of British Blackbirds. *Bird Study* 13 : 237–255.

SNOW, D. W. 1978. Long-distance movements of British Blackbirds. *Ringing and Migration* 2 : 52–54.

SPENCER, R. 1975. Changes in the distribution of recoveries of ringed Blackbirds. *Bird Study* 22 : 177–190.

VENABLES, L. S. V. and U. M. VENABLES. 1952. The Blackbird in Shetland. *Ibis* 94 : 636–653.

Breeding Atlas p 340

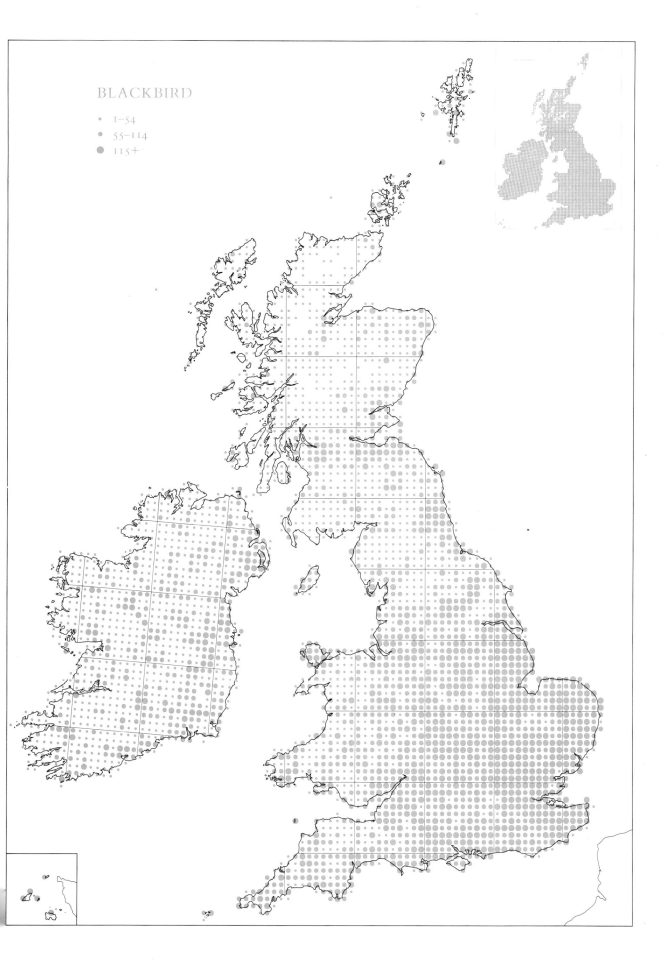

BLACKBIRD

- • 1–54
- • 55–114
- ● 115+

Fieldfare

Turdus pilaris

The 'chacking' of Fieldfares flying overhead in their characteristically loose flocks is, for the ornithologist, one of the signs of approaching winter. In Scotland the first arrivals take place in September, while in central and southern England not many Fieldfares are in evidence until mid October; but in all areas the dates are variable. Studies in Scandinavia, the area of origin of our wintering populations, have shown that the time of departure of the Fieldfare populations depends on the abundance, and hence the time of depletion, of the rowan fruit crop (Tyrväinen 1975); in years with a very heavy crop, large numbers of Fieldfares may remain in Scandinavia until well into the winter. In spite of this variability, Fieldfares consistently winter in large numbers throughout Britain and Ireland, except in the highlands and the bleakest coastal areas of NW Scotland.

In their winter quarters, too, the movements of Fieldfares are variable from year to year, evidently depending on the availability of wild fruit crops and of other food, the latter itself dependent on the winter weather. The maps for the three winters show that in the cold 1981/82 winter there was a noticeable shift of the Fieldfare population to the south of Britain, many northern areas being vacated, and in all three winters a comparison of the early-winter and late-winter maps shows a southward movement in the course of the winter. Such movements are part of the highly modifiable, nomadic, migratory behaviour which is characteristic of Fieldfares and Redwings *T. iliacus*. Fieldfares trapped in Britain have been recovered over a wide area of southern Europe in subsequent winters, from Portugal to the Balkans.

Fieldfares are, for the most part, strongly gregarious in winter, usually moving in flocks composed of their own species entirely, or with a small admixture of other thrushes and Starlings *Sturnus vulgaris*. They roost communally in a variety of sites such as hedges, osier beds, woodland, and even on occasion on the open ground. In their foraging, however, they act as more or less independent individuals, much less integrated than at other times. They feed on invertebrates taken from open fields, and also on fruit, normally avoiding wooded areas except when they come down to feed on fallen apples in orchards, a favourite food especially in hard weather. Individuals in possession of a defendable fruit supply, whether a single apple or a whole hawthorn bush or clump of hips, may be aggressive to others, but defence of fruit supplies, which is so important for wintering Mistle Thrushes *T. viscivorus*, is much less highly developed behaviour in the rather smaller, more gregarious Fieldfare.

Although they are larger than Blackbirds *T. merula* and might be thought from their more northern range to be more hardy, Fieldfares are apparently less well able than Blackbirds to withstand very severe winter conditions, probably because they are less versatile in their feeding ecology. Thus, in northern Scotland during a prolonged cold spell, Fieldfares lost weight and many died, while Blackbirds put on weight during the same period (Swann 1980). The Fieldfares were feeding almost exclusively on cotoneaster berries, which declined sharply in numbers, whereas the Blackbirds were also feeding on a variety of food put out by man. The depletion of wild fruit supplies almost certainly accounts for the general southward movement of Fieldfares in the course of the winter.

These movements make it almost impossible to put more than a very tentative figure, or rather range of figures, on the winter population of Fieldfares in Britain and Ireland. A realistic figure would depend on synchronised counts in a large number of areas, and would be valid only for the time of the counts. On the assumption that the numbers shown on the map for each square on the map were all present at the same time, and assessing the three grades of abundance as 25, 250 and 1,000, a calculated wintering population would be about a million birds.

D. W. SNOW

Total number of squares in which recorded: 3,351 (87%)

No. of birds seen in a day	Number (%) of squares		TOTAL (incl. C.I.)
	Britain	Ireland	
1–165	1,111 (45%)	567 (63%)	1,681 (50%)
166–500	758 (31%)	245 (27%)	1,003 (30%)
501 +	583 (24%)	82 (9%)	667 (20%)

References

SWANN, R. L. 1980. Fieldfare and Blackbird weights during the winter of 1978–79 at Drumnadrochit, Inverness-shire. *Ringing and Migration* 3 : 37–40.

TYRVÄINEN, H. 1975. The winter irruption of the Fieldfare *Turdus pilaris* and the supply of rowan-berries. *Orn. Fenn.* 52 : 23–31.

Breeding Atlas p 332

FIELDFARE

- · 1–165
- ● 166–500
- ⬤ 501+

Song Thrush

Turdus philomelos

Visually less conspicuous in winter than its commoner relative the Blackbird *T. merula*, and a more skulking feeder, the Song Thrush to some extent compensates by its voice; on many mild late autumn and winter days, when feeding conditions are easy, territory-holding males sing loudly and persistently, often until well into dusk.

British Song Thrushes are considerably more migratory than Blackbirds. The map shows that the populations breeding in the Scottish Highlands, northern Pennines and other mountain areas leave their breeding quarters. An early analysis of ringing returns (Lack 1943) indicated that some 48% of adult British Song Thrushes and 64% of first-year birds migrate, but only 5% and 24% respectively were recovered outside Britain and Ireland, all of them in France and Spain. Many Scottish and northern English Song Thrushes migrate to winter in Ireland, the Irish breeding population being, so far as is known, non-migratory. A higher proportion of individuals migrate from north Britain than from central and southern England.

Superimposed on this pattern of movement of the British breeding population is an influx of Continental birds, from Belgium and Holland, to winter mainly in the southern half of England (Goodacre 1960). These birds are racially more or less identical to British birds and their presence would not be detectable except by ringing. Also, many Song Thrushes from farther north, especially Scandinavia, pass through Britain to winter mainly in southern France and Iberia. These populations of the larger, greyer-brown nominate race should, under good field conditions, be distinguishable from the smaller, warmer-brown British race *clarkei*, especially if both are seen together. There is still little evidence from ringing that Scandinavian birds remain to winter in Britain or Ireland, but evidence from museum specimens (*The Handbook*) suggests that they regularly do so, and the small population shown on the map as wintering in Shetland, where the species does not breed, must surely be Scandinavian breeding birds.

In addition to their normal autumn migration, Song Thrushes are very prone to hard-weather movements in winter. These are best documented for the exceptionally severe 1962/63 winter, when a large number of Song Thrushes moved from northern England in a W-WSW direction into Ireland, and from southern and central England in a WSW-SW direction into Devon and Cornwall or south to France. Many of those that had first moved into SW England later made a second move to France.

Like the other thrushes, Song Thrushes feed to a large extent on earthworms in winter, when the weather is mild enough for them to be available, and on fruits. Unlike the other thrush species, they are well known to exploit another food source, large or medium-sized snails, whose shells they break open by hammering against a stone or other suitable 'anvil'. Snails are an important food resource for Song Thrushes, especially in summer droughts and in hard weather in winter, when other animal food may be scarce or unavailable. In coastal marram grass, a favourite wintering habitat in Scotland, they are probably dependent on *Cepaea* snails. Whether the local availability of snails affects the winter distribution of Song Thrushes is a question that needs study; for instance, they appear to be scarce or absent in winter from sandy (calcium-poor) woodlands, where snails are probably also scarce. The 10-km squares of the *Winter Atlas*, most of which contain a variety of habitats, including gardens, are too coarse a grid to show such an effect.

The Song Thrush's breeding population in Britain and Ireland has been estimated at some 3.5 million pairs. Since less than a quarter of the breeding population and young of the year migrate to the Continent in winter, and those that remain are increased by an influx of winter visitors from the Low Countries, it may tentatively be concluded that the wintering population in Britain and Ireland is not greatly different from the breeding population; 6–10 million birds would be reasonable estimate.

D. W. SNOW

Total number of squares in which recorded: 3,327 (86%)

No. of birds seen in a day	Number (%) of squares		TOTAL (incl. C.I.)
	Britain	Ireland	
1–11	1,196 (51%)	508 (53%)	1,704 (51%)
12–25	678 (29%)	298 (31%)	976 (29%)
26 +	483 (20%)	159 (17%)	647 (19%)

References

GOODACRE, M. J. 1960. The origin of winter visitors to the British Isles. 6. Song Thrush (*Turdus philomelos*). *Bird Study* 7 : 108–110.

LACK, D. 1943. The problem of partial migration. *Brit. Birds* 37 : 122–130.

Breeding Atlas p 334

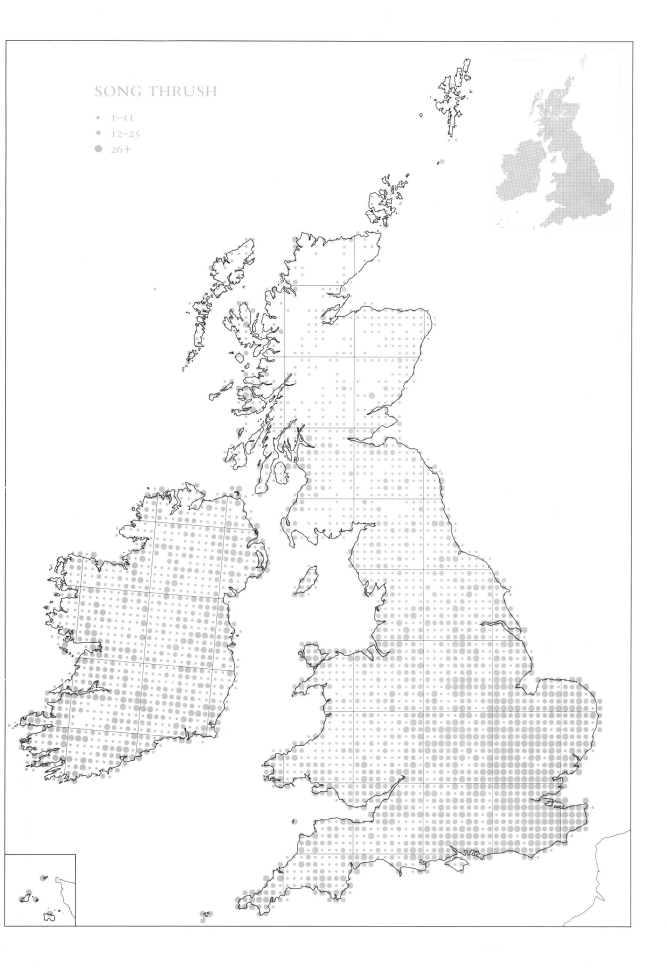

SONG THRUSH

- · 1–11
- ● 12–25
- ● 26+

Redwing

Turdus iliacus

The high-pitched, sighing flight call of this abundant, wintering thrush is as characteristic of the approach of winter as the Fieldfare's *T. pilaris* louder chacking, though much less obtrusive. Equally, the confused choruses of parties of Redwings, as they gather in tree tops before their departure, is one of the signs of spring.

The Redwings that visit Britain and Ireland in large numbers are predominantly from the Scandinavian, Finnish and Icelandic breeding populations (Goodacre 1960, Zink 1981). Fennoscandian birds have been recovered mainly in England, and Icelandic birds in Scotland and Ireland, but the migratory pattern is complex and the Continental and Icelandic populations overlap to some extent in their winter quarters. Specimens of the dark, heavily streaked Icelandic race *coburni* have been identified from southern parts of Britain (*The Handbook*). The winter quarters of the small Scottish breeding population (not racially separable from the Scandinavian) are not yet known.

Perhaps even more than Fieldfares, Redwings tend to be nomadic in winter, moving widely in response to weather conditions and the availability of food, especially wild fruits. Thus birds that winter in Britain in one year may be in SE Europe, or even the Near East, in a subsequent winter (Zink 1981). In addition, they may make long hard-weather movements in the course of a winter; for instance, large numbers moved from England to Ireland in the severe winter of 1962/63. One bird, ringed on Fair Isle in December 1965, was found in Greece in January 1966. A general southward movement of the British wintering population is evident from the maps; and it may also be noted that in the cold winter of 1981/82 the population was more concentrated in the south than in the other winters of the Atlas field work, which were comparatively mild. Systematic observations and trapping in northern Scotland (Swann 1983) show that Redwings regularly arrive in large numbers in autumn, from late September to early November, with the peak between 10–24 October, and for the most part quickly pass on, some remaining for less than 24 hours. Few remain later in the winter, for the Redwing is the smallest of our thrushes, and is well known to be vulnerable to cold weather.

In mild weather in winter, Redwings forage much on open fields for earthworms, commonly in association with Fieldfares and other thrushes and Starlings *Sturnus vulgaris*. Unlike the Fieldfares, in cold weather they regularly forage on the ground in woodland, turning over and digging among the leaf litter much like Blackbirds *T. merula*. As fruit eaters they are most conspicuous in autumn and early winter when, with Fieldfares, they feed in flocks on hedgerow haws. Less conspicuously, single birds or small groups feed unobtrusively on fruit in gardens and wooded areas.

Any attempt to estimate the size of the wintering population of Redwings in Britain and Ireland meets with the same problems as for the Fieldfare: the numbers vary from year to year, and also in the course of a single winter, and major shifts of population may take place in response to weather and feeding conditions. Synchronous counts over a large number of sample areas would enable a rough estimate to be made, but this would be a major piece of cooperative field work. On the assumption that the numbers shown on the map were all present at the same time, and that the three grades of abundance correspond to 25, 250 and 1,000 birds, it may be calculated that the wintering Redwing population is of the order of one million birds, but it could well be considerably higher.

D. W. SNOW

Total number of squares in which recorded: 3,316 (88%)

No. of birds seen in a day	Number (%) of squares		TOTAL (incl. C.I.)
	Britain	Ireland	
1–130	1,256 (53%)	404 (44%)	1,663 (50%)
131–395	696 (29%)	297 (32%)	993 (30%)
396 +	439 (18%)	219 (24%)	660 (20%)

References

GOODACRE, M. J. 1960. The origin of winter visitors to the British Isles. 5. Redwing (*Turdus musicus*). *Bird Study* 7 : 102–107.

SWANN, R. L. 1983. Redwings in a highland glen. *Scot. Birds* 12 : 260–261.

ZINK, G. 1981. *Der Zug europäischer Singvögel. Ein Atlas der Wiederfunde beringter Vögel.* Lieferung 3. Vogelwarte Radolfzell-Möggingen.

Breeding Atlas p 336

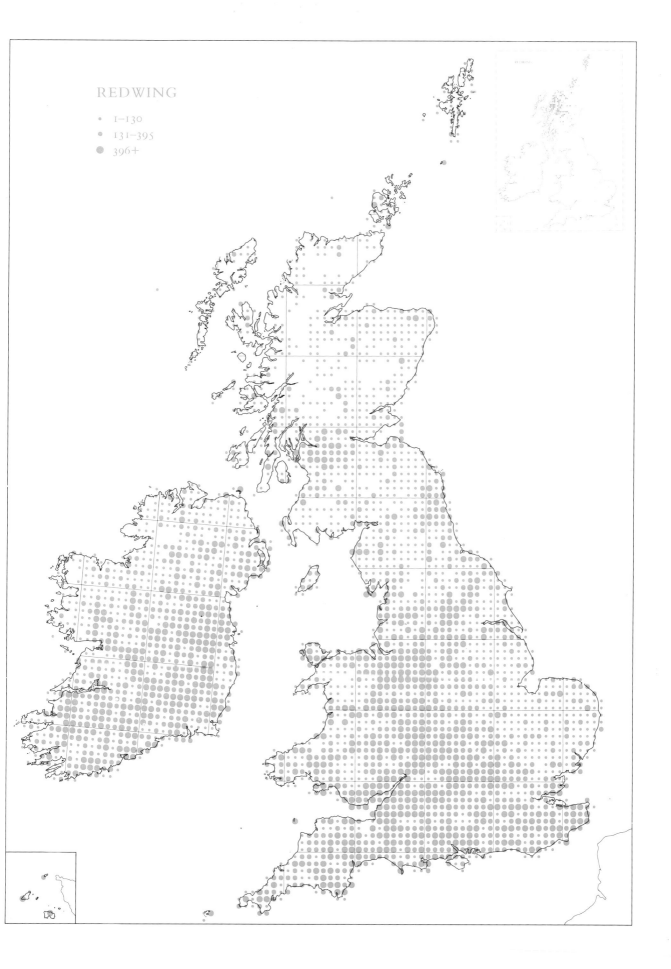

REDWING

- 1–130
- 131–395
- 396+

Mistle Thrush

Turdus viscivorus

As a breeding bird the Mistle Thrush is one of the most widely distributed species in Britain and Ireland, being absent or irregular only from parts of northern Scotland, Orkney and Shetland. Its winter distribution is very similar, but numbers are low in Scotland; in particular, the higher land is then more completely devoid of Mistle Thrushes than in the breeding season. It is apparent from the map that the winter population is densest in southeastern England, perhaps with another area of relatively high density from Lancashire and southern Yorkshire south to central England.

The lack of winter records from much of northern and upland Scotland is in accordance with ringing records, which show that Scottish-born Mistle Thrushes are highly migratory, both in their first and in later winters (Snow 1969), moving southwest to Ireland and south to France. English birds are also partially migratory, at least in their first winter (there is no evidence for long-distance movements in later winters), some moving south to France while the remainder stays within a few kilometres of its birthplace. Irish birds are apparently sedentary. There is still no evidence from ringing that the winter Mistle Thrush population of Britain and Ireland is swollen by migrants from the Continent, but observations at east coast observatories indicate that they do arrive in small numbers, though the bulk of the continental N European population winters in France and Iberia. The Irish wintering population is, however, swollen by immigrants from N Britain. It is, perhaps, most likely that the high winter population in SE and central England simply reflects a high density of the breeding population; but if Continental immigrants are numerous they may significantly swell the winter population of southern England, where they are most likely to end up. British and western European Mistle Thrushes are not racially distinguishable.

The roving bands of Mistle Thrushes which are often conspicuous in late summer and autumn do not persist into winter. These bands are apparently composed of local breeding birds and their families, and evidently break up when the adults begin to defend their winter fruit supplies and many of the young birds depart on long-distance migration. Such, at least, must be the case in central and southern England, where many (probably most) adult Mistle Thrushes are not only strictly sedentary in winter but remain for the whole November–February period close to fruit-bearing trees or shrubs which they defend, thus conserving for themselves a food supply which can last through until the following spring (Snow and Snow 1984). Active fruit-defence begins usually in October or early November, at which time—and somewhat later too, if the weather remains mild—occasional song is to be heard.

Established pairs often jointly defend a fruit supply, but single birds also do so. In southern England, hollies of moderate size, standing clear of neighbouring trees and so easily overseen and controlled, are the main trees defended; less commonly hawthorn and buckthorn. Large mistletoe clumps are regularly defended (thus giving the bird its name), and in parts of France where it is abundant, mistletoe is evidently the most important plant enabling Mistle Thrushes to remain sedentary through the winter, as holly is in southern England. To what extent young birds are able to acquire and successfully defend a fruit supply through the winter is not known; the considerable proportion of first-year birds that migrates overseas suggests that most of them cannot, and that wintering is not easy for Mistle Thrushes without the possession of an assured fruit supply, except perhaps in very mild winters. Like the other thrushes, they feed much on earthworms in mild weather.

Only the roughest guess can be made at the size of the wintering Mistle Thrush population. The departure of the adult population from N Britain and of many, perhaps most, of the birds of the year from the whole of Britain (but not Ireland), compensated by the arrival of an unknown, but probably not large, number of Continental immigrants, suggests that the winter population for Britain and Ireland must be appreciably smaller than the breeding population, perhaps in the range of 400,000 to 800,000 individuals.

D. W. SNOW

Total number of squares in which recorded: 3,175 (82%)

No. of birds seen in a day	Number (%) of squares		TOTAL (incl. C.I.)
	Britain	Ireland	
1–6	1,015 (45%)	508 (57%)	1,525 (48%)
7–14	774 (34%)	254 (28%)	1,028 (32%)
15 +	488 (21%)	132 (15%)	622 (20%)

References

SNOW, B. K. and D. W. SNOW. 1984. Long-term defence of fruit by Mistle Thrushes *Turdus viscivorus*. *Ibis* 126: 39–49.

SNOW, D. W. 1969. Some vital statistics of British Mistle Thrushes. *Bird Study* 16: 34–44.

Breeding Atlas p 330

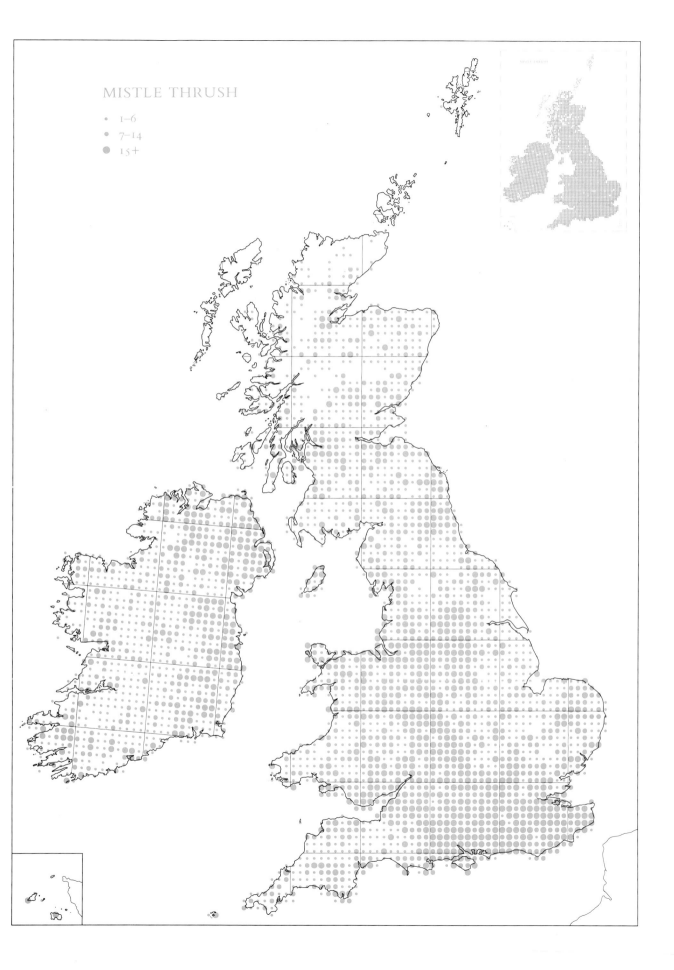

MISTLE THRUSH

· 1–6
· 7–14
· 15+

Cetti's Warbler

Cettia cetti

In scarcely more than a decade the Cetti's Warbler has become established as a resident breeding species in several lowland valleys in Britain. Its abrupt, rich song phrases are one of the most striking winter sounds in the handful of marshes where it is common. On bright, frosty mornings in mid winter it can be more readily observed than at most other times of the year, feeding among the reed litter of a *Phragmites* bed or creeping through waterside brambles.

The winter distribution corresponds to the breeding distribution extrapolated from 1977–1982 records. The population is largely restricted to Kent, the chalk river valleys of Hampshire, and the coastal marshes of East Anglia and the south west. There are none in Scotland or Ireland. Apparently suitable habitat exists in most of the river valleys of lowland England and Wales, and yet the map shows a distinct loyalty to the few original areas of colonisation.

Cetti's Warblers are usually sedentary. In winter, the males sing strongly in their breeding territories on fine days and feed with their females in low waterside vegetation, particularly brambles, willow scrub and *Phragmites*. Wet gravel pits with well grown vegetation are favoured, and the use of dry sites, recorded during the first years of colonisation (Harvey 1977), was less obvious by the 1980s. In winter, more birds are seen in reed beds, even feeding on floating reed litter, and sometimes moving out onto open marsh. As in summer, the feeding niche is on, or within 2 m of, the ground with only singing males regularly ascending higher. Cetti's Warblers tend to be solitary feeders, although sometimes two will feed together and, especially in hard frosts, they may feed close to other winter reed bed passerines. The only winter food noted is invertebrates and their eggs on leaves and twigs and in bark crevices and plant stems.

Post breeding dispersal may produce records from unusual habitats, such as gorse heath, chestnut coppice and orchards, but there is no evidence of over wintering there. By the 1980s the winter wandering which featured in the 1970s, with records well to the north and west of the mapped range, had apparently ceased. Most extralimital records now occur in October-November.

Cetti's Warblers have spread slowly north from their Mediterranean strongholds since the 1920s (Bonham and Robertson 1975). The English population increased substantially in 1975–77, but then remained relatively stable in total numbers and distribution until 1981 (see Figure). In 1981/82, sustained hard frosts caused a drop in numbers in Kent, while elsewhere the population may have doubled, presumably because the winter was less harsh. In the previous hard winter of 1978/79, the British population had dropped by 7% compared with a 40% drop in Wrens, suggesting that Cetti's Warblers are able to survive low temperatures reasonably well. However, long periods of below freezing temperatures and prolonged snow cover are damaging. In early 1985 there were 75% reductions in Kent and Suffolk.

Assuming that the polygyny found in Dorset (Bibby 1982) is general and that at least 2 young per breeding male survive to December, the total early winter population was probably less than 50 in 1973, over 300 in 1975 and between 500 and 1,000 in 1982. In spite of this impressive increase, the Cetti's Warbler's dependence on a small number of main sites makes it vulnerable to local extremes of weather.

W. G. HARVEY

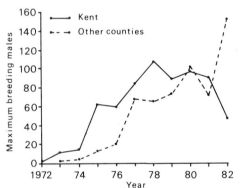

The maximum number of breeding male Cetti's Warblers in Kent and other counties.

Total number of squares in which recorded: 64 (2%)

No. of birds	Number (%) of squares		
seen in a day	Britain	Ireland	TOTAL (incl. C.I.)
1	37 (58%)	0 (0%)	37 (58%)
2–3	16 (25%)	0 (0%)	16 (25%)
4+	11 (17%)	0 (0%)	11 (17%)

References

BIBBY, C. J. 1982. Polygyny and breeding ecology of the Cetti's Warbler. *Ibis* 124 : 288–301.

BONHAM, P. F. and J. C. M. ROBERTSON. 1975. The spread of Cetti's Warblers in northwest Europe. *Brit. Birds* 68 : 393–408.

HARVEY, W. G. 1977. Cetti's Warblers in East Kent in 1975. *Brit. Birds* 70 : 89–96.

Breeding Atlas p 356

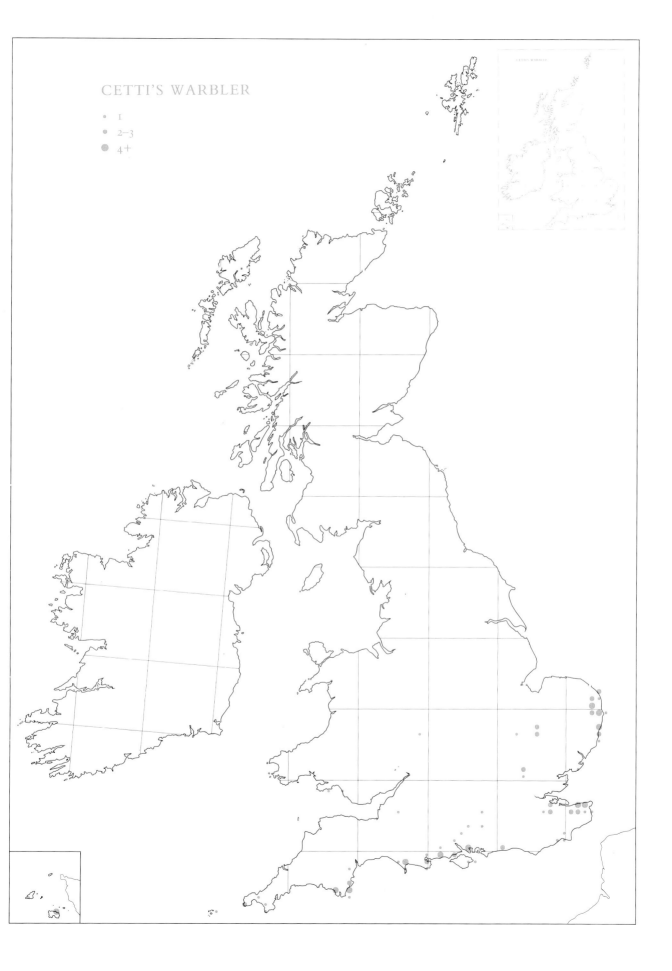

CETTI'S WARBLER

- • 1
- • 2–3
- ● 4+

Dartford Warbler

Sylvia undata

The elusive Dartford Warbler is nowhere more at home than in the maquis of the Mediterranean lands, and the small population of southern England is ever vulnerable to cold at the northern limit of the species' range. It is sedentary, with perhaps some short distance partial migration, and most birds winter in heather and gorse on the lowland heaths where they breed.

The winter map is very similar to the breeding distribution in 1984. Salient developments since the *Breeding Atlas* and the 1974 survey, have been the loss of the never large Sussex and Isle of Wight breeding populations; development of the best numbers since 1961 in Surrey and NE Hampshire; and colonisation of Cornwall for the first time in 40 years. Numbers are poorly indicated, as the bird can be very secretive, especially in winter. Observer coverage in the centre of the range was possibly less good than in Surrey, which in fact held about 20% of the breeding birds in 1984.

Numbers in Britain can fall sharply in a severe winter, which tends to restrict the distribution to the main concentration of suitable habitat in Dorset and the New Forest. Smaller outlying populations may be eliminated from Cornwall, Devon, Surrey and Sussex. Recolonisation of these areas depends much on the chance of colonists from the small nucleus reaching isolated patches of surviving heathland. Reports on surveys in 1974 (Bibby and Tubbs 1975) and 1984 (Robins and Bibby 1985) document shifts in range and numbers over the last 25 years.

Dartford Warblers feed on small invertebrates gathered in or under dense vegetation (Bibby 1979a). Gorse provides a richer food supply than heather and is the major determinant of local distribution of Dartford Warblers at all seasons. Especially during heavy snowfalls or glazing frosts, dense vegetation provides places in which birds can still move and feed. Prior to autumn dispersal, Dartford Warblers may be seen in flocks. At other seasons, they occupy territories solitarily or in pairs but are usually too widely spaced for much interaction between neighbours to be obvious. Surviving territory holders generally breed in their wintering areas. In spite of this dispersion, small communal roosts of up to ten birds have been found in winter, but nothing is known of the frequency or function of this habit (personal observation).

Movements of Dartford Warblers, representing post juvenile dispersal, but perhaps also some partial migration, mainly occur in October. Enough records have accumulated to suggest that a substantial proportion, perhaps up to 50%, is involved, irrespective of their overall abundance. Since few birds winter in Britain away from heaths, and there is also a small spring movement, it seems likely that some winter abroad, but there is no direct evidence to support this suggestion. Occasional Continental birds may reach Britain and Ireland, but the records away from breeding places may be due to native birds alone. Movements of Dartford Warblers are discussed further by Bibby (1979b).

British breeding numbers were 560 pairs in 1974 and 420 in 1984. The former number is unlikely ever to be reached again, because of habitat loss. At minimum, numbers have been as low as 11 pairs recorded in 1963. Using approximate breeding and mortality data, mid winter numbers during this survey were probably 1,500–1,800 birds. In the last 25 years the number may have varied between 25 and 2,500. If 10–50% of the British population was abroad for the winter, recent wintering numbers in Britain would be in the range 800–1,500 birds.

Numerically, this small population is a tiny outpost of a bird with a western Mediterranean distribution, where it is very abundant in scrub habitats. It is however much valued in Britain because of its characteristic association with the lowland heaths which have many additional features of interest. This habitat is very scarce and vulnerable to fire, vegetation succession and direct damage or loss from human actions.

C. J. BIBBY

Total number of squares in which recorded: 35 (1%)

No. of birds seen in a day	Number (%) of squares		
	Britain	Ireland	TOTAL (incl. C.I.)
1–2	18 (51%)	0 (0%)	18 (51%)
3–5	9 (26%)	0 (0%)	9 (26%)
6 +	8 (23%)	0 (0%)	8 (23%)

References

BIBBY, C. J. 1979a. Foods of the Dartford Warbler *Sylvia undata* on southern English heathland (Aves: Sylviidae). *J. Zool., Lond.* 188: 557–576.

BIBBY, C. J. 1979b. Mortality and movements of Dartford Warblers in England. *Brit. Birds* 72: 10–22.

BIBBY, C. J. and C. R. TUBBS. 1975. Status and conservation of the Dartford Warbler in England. *Brit. Birds* 68: 177–195.

ROBINS, M. and C. J. BIBBY. 1985. Dartford Warblers in 1984 Britain. *Brit. Birds* 78: 269–280.

Breeding Atlas p 376

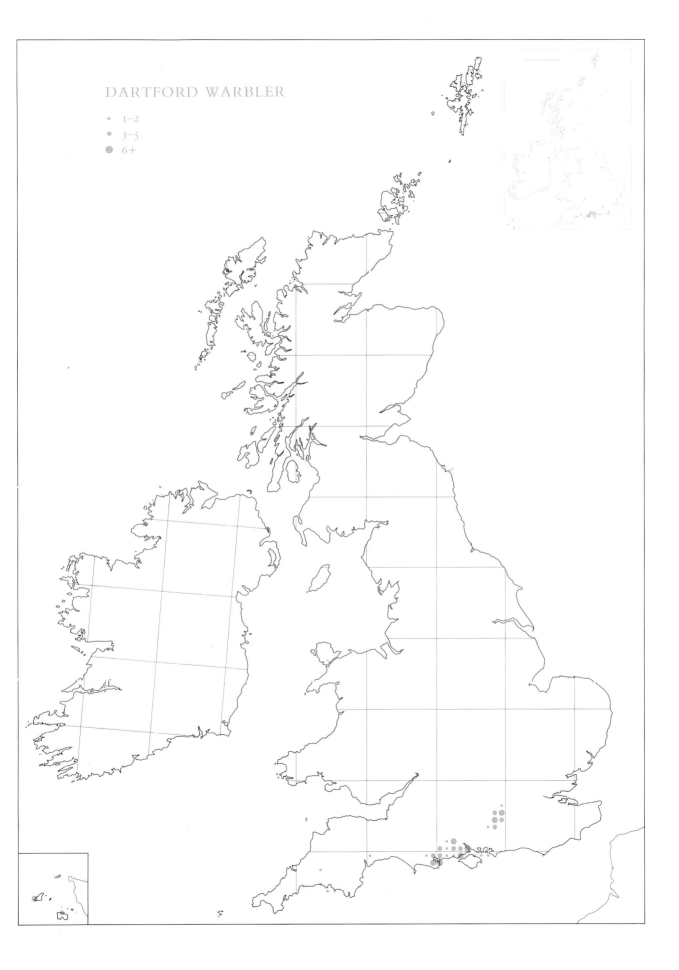

DARTFORD WARBLER

· 1–2
· 3–5
● 6+

Blackcap

Sylvia atricapilla

The Blackcap is a rather inconspicuous bird lurking in thick bushes. In spring it draws attention to itself by its powerful song but it can easily be overlooked in winter, except when it appears at a bird table. In the last 15 years it has become an increasingly frequent winter visitor to gardens. Originally, overwintering was confined to the south and west of England, but the practice is now more widespread.

The map shows a surprisingly wide distribution both in Britain and Ireland, and this is not solely the result of combining the records for the three winters, for all three showed similar features. There is a southwestern dominance, but there are many records from the east coast and from Ireland and Scotland, and quite large concentrations in central England. Wintering birds have been recorded from Orkney and Shetland, where they were not found in the *Breeding Atlas*.

A BTO survey of wintering Blackcaps, held in 1978/79, showed a similar pattern of distribution, although a third of the totals counted were in 6 southwestern counties of Britain. Ireland was not fully covered but there were many in Co. Dublin. The survey also noted the preference for suburbs. It is noticeable that many of the 92 more-populated squares are associated with large towns and their suburbs, and some of these areas may have substantial total populations. How much of this is due to a real preference for suburban gardens and how much is due to the distribution of observers is uncertain.

Wintering Blackcaps are apparently immigrants from northern and eastern Europe, arriving on the east coast in late autumn after the breeding birds have left (Langslow 1979). In early winter they appear to exist on natural food in woodland and scrub countryside and then, usually from late December, they move increasingly into gardens. Their ability to survive cold spells may be partly due to the food available on bird-tables. They seem to prefer berries and other natural food while they last, only subsequently turning to bird table food. Blackcaps are omnivorous, taking bird-seed, fat, bread, cheese, and a wide variety of other foodstuffs. Retraps of birds ringed in gardens

in winter show that on such a diet they are able to maintain, or even increase, their weight through severe weather (Leach 1981, Bland 1979). At bird-tables they are often very aggressive towards other species and sometimes towards other Blackcaps. There appears to be a fairly constant sex imbalance, with around 40% of the records being females.

The numbers recorded tend to fluctuate with the severity of the weather, both between and within winters. 1981/82 was the coldest of the Atlas winters and produced the largest total yet recorded in most areas. A cold spell in a normal winter also tends to produce more records than usual. This suggests either large-scale cold weather movements, or that a proportion of the countryside population comes into gardens only in extreme conditions. There is evidence from ringing that some birds often frequent the same gardens from mid December to late March, though there also appears to be a large transient population.

It is unfortunately not possible to make any direct comparison of numbers between the 1978/79 survey and the *Winter Atlas*, as the former was based on old counties and the latter has not attempted to count the total number of birds present. However, the growth in the overwintering habit is clear. Between 1945 and 1954 an average of some 22 records a year appeared in county reports; between 1970 and 1977 the average was 380 records a year, and the 1978/79 enquiry counted a minimum of 1,714 Blackcaps (Leach 1981). Since then the numbers have probably remained more or less the same, although slightly higher in more severe winters (Bland 1982).

A total winter population in Britain and Ireland of some 3,000 individuals seems likely. This compares with a breeding population of about 400,000. The increase in numbers wintering in Britain is correlated with the increase in numbers, and extension of range, in northern Europe (Leach 1981). Ringing has shown fidelity to wintering sites and it is likely that the Blackcap has become a permanent feature of our winter bird population.

R. L. BLAND

Total number of squares in which recorded: 976 (25%)

	Number (%) of squares		
No. of birds seen in a day	Britain	Ireland	TOTAL (incl. C.I.)
1	551 (64%)	75 (65%)	627 (64%)
2	233 (27%)	23 (20%)	257 (26%)
3+	73 (9%)	17 (15%)	92 (9%)

References

BLAND, R. L. 1979. Wintering warblers in Avon. *Bristol Ornithology* 12 : 63–66.

BLAND, R. L. 1982. Overwintering warblers 1980/81 and 1981/82. *Bristol Ornithology* 15 : 170.

LANGSLOW, D. R. 1979. Movements of Blackcaps ringed in Britain and Ireland. *Bird Study* 26 : 239–253.

LEACH, I. H. 1981. Wintering Blackcaps in Britain and Ireland. *Bird Study* 28 : 5–15.

Breeding Atlas p 368

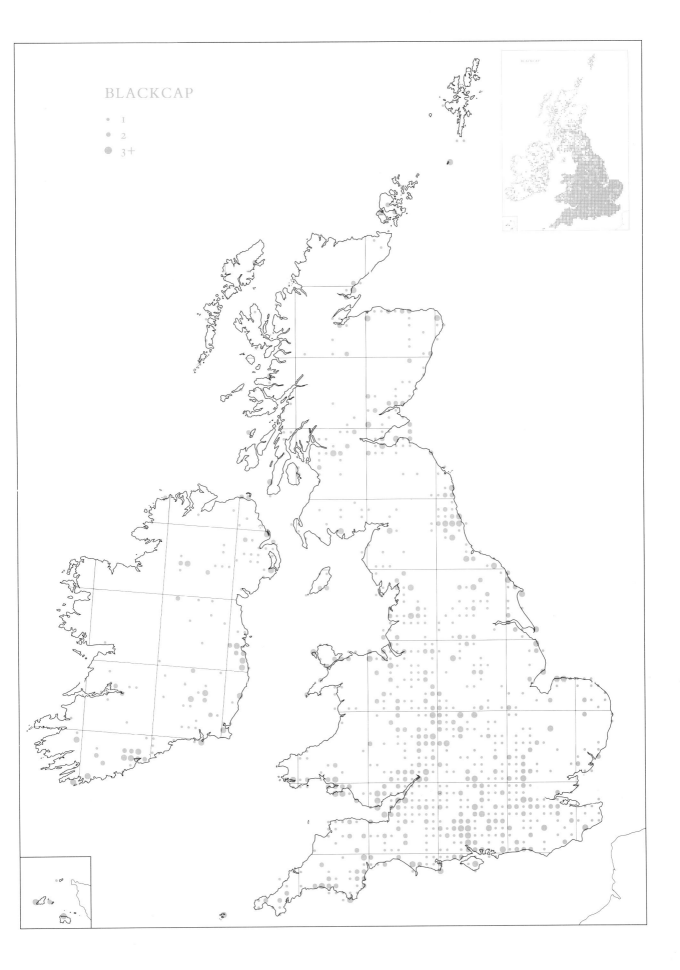

BLACKCAP

- 1
- 2
- 3+

Chiffchaff

Phylloscopus collybita

Though larger than a Goldcrest *Regulus regulus,* the wintering Chiffchaff seems so frail and so out of place that it may readily excite the observer's sympathy. 'Why?' is the word that comes to mind, and even though the Chiffchaff has, for many years, over-wintered in small numbers in the south and west of England and Ireland, we are nowhere near an answer. The general pattern of records has shown very little change over recent years.

The map shows the pattern for the three winters combined, but numbers in each year varied considerably. The concentration in the southern counties and southern Ireland is clear, with three-quarters of the squares being south of the Wash/Mersey line in England, but there are records from northern England, Scotland, and even from Orkney and the Hebrides, where it was not recorded in the *Breeding Atlas*.

Numbers in 1983/84 were about normal but in the other two winters were very abnormal. 1981/82 had markedly fewer than usual, especially after the New Year, presumably because the cold weather killed many of the wintering birds. The smaller map shows the distribution in these two winters combined and it is clear that the numbers in 1982/83 contribute many of the dots on the main map. In fact the number of squares in which Chiffchaffs were recorded in 1982/83 was more than double that for 1981/82, and the numbers in the 2 higher orders of abundance tripled.

Unlike the Blackcap, the Chiffchaff retains an entirely insectivorous diet through the winter, and it is usually seen close to waters, including industrial water, which are warm enough to sustain insect life. Ringers at Mediterranean reed bed sites are often able to catch several hundred Chiffchaffs passing through during the course of a winter but some, as evidenced by retraps, are resident. In Britain, birds are seen regularly at reed bed sites throughout the winter and are thus probably resident. In Ireland they may occur along river banks or in woods, sometimes with tits. They are not easy to find and the numbers involved could be substantial. Severe weather, such as in 1981/82, readily leads to the destruction of the population.

Many British Chiffchaffs winter in the Mediter-ranean region, in western parts of France and south of the Sahara. Ringing recoveries from Britain and Ireland to W Africa (and *vice versa*) have so far been reported for Mauritania (1), Senegal (3), Gambia (3) and Mali (1). Winter ringing recoveries at home provide evidence that some local breeding birds remain for the winter and that 2 birds overwintered in the same area in successive seasons. There is also evidence of Continental birds wintering in Britain, with 3 recent recoveries of birds, ringed between 24 October and 1 November in the Netherlands, Belgium and Jersey, found in December or January in Hertford-shire, Hampshire and Avon respectively. There is no information as to the origin of these birds, unlike the intriguing series of recoveries linking British and Irish wintering Blackcaps with Central Europe. The estimate for the breeding season was 300,000 pairs. In a normal year the maximum wintering population in Britain and Ireland may be 500 birds but in 1982/83 there must have been at least 1,000.

R. L. BLAND

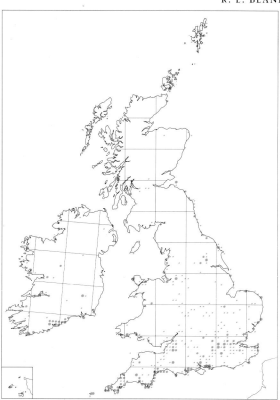

The distribution of Chiffchaffs during 1981/82 and 1983/84 com-bined. Scale of abundance as for main map.

Total number of squares in which recorded: 667 (17%)

No. of birds seen in a day	Number (%) of squares Britain	Ireland	TOTAL (incl. C.I.)
1	386 (67%)	54 (61%)	441 (66%)
2	96 (17%)	17 (19%)	113 (17%)
3 +	94 (17%)	17 (19%)	113 (17%)

Breeding Atlas p 380

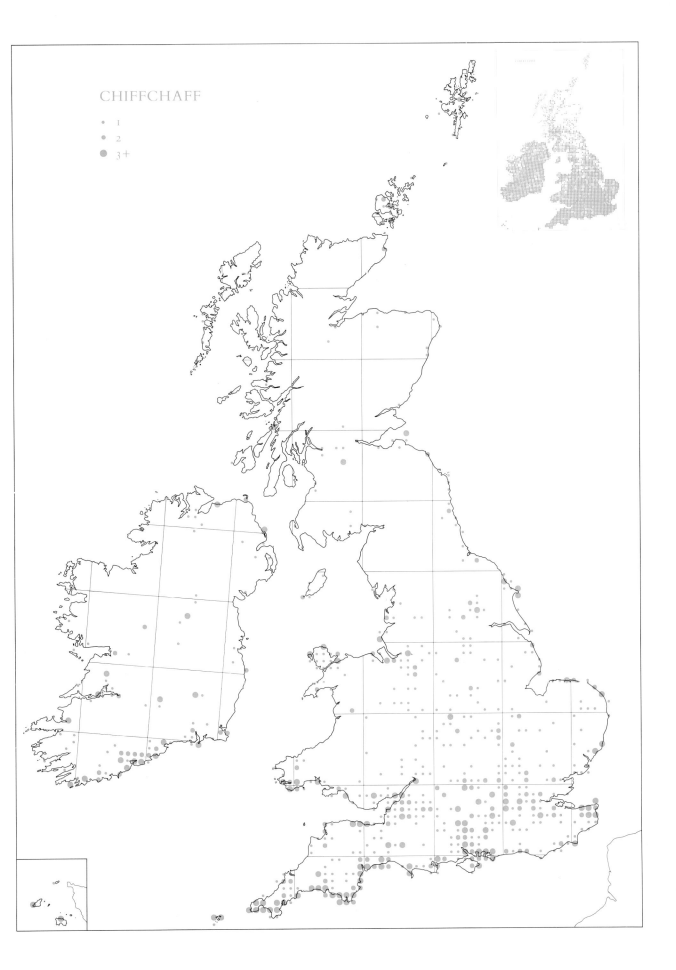

CHIFFCHAFF

· 1
· 2
● 3+

Goldcrest

Regulus regulus

Though it is the smallest British and Irish bird the tiny Goldcrest is well able to survive our winter, and its weak, thin calls are a familiar feature of woodland, gardens and scrub, even during severe weather.

Remarkably for a small bird, and in stark contrast to the other European kinglet, the Firecrest *R. ignicapillus*, even the remotest breeding site is occupied year-round, and it seems that many British and Irish Goldcrests spend most of the winter on or near the breeding territory. The winter distribution differs from that shown in the *Breeding Atlas* only in that there is evidence of some spread into eastern parts of England and Scotland where the species does not breed. In Orkney and Shetland, for example, Goldcrests are well scattered, although only a few sites are occupied in summer. As in the breeding season, however, there is a notable absence from the Western Isles, parts of the NW Highlands, and the Fens of E England, where suitable habitat is scarce. Goldcrests are found virtually throughout Ireland, and at similar densities to those in Britain; indeed, density appears to vary little, except for a decrease towards W Ireland and especially NW fringes of Scotland.

Although many Goldcrests stay close to their nesting areas for the winter, habitat choice is a little wider overall than in summer. A few are regularly found in gardens in which the species does not breed, or in scrub near fresh water or the coast, perhaps with the much scarcer Firecrest. Most birds spend the winter in loose flocks, sometimes of Goldcrests alone, but typically including Coal Tits *Parus ater*, Blue Tits *P. caeruleus* and Great Tits *P. major*, and often Long-tailed Tits *Aegithalos caudatus* and Treecreepers *Certhia familiaris*. Mild weather may spark territorial behaviour and song, even in December or January, while during severe spells Goldcrests may desert or expand their home ranges to visit nearby gardens and, on occasion, may even take food from birdtables.

Small birds chill more quickly than larger ones and are less able to store food reserves as body fat: to survive below-freezing temperatures, they need access to a relatively large amount of food, reliably,

every day. Goldcrests achieve this partly because, at least among conifers, they experience little competition for food. They are small and agile enough to search thoroughly among foliage and at the end of the smallest twigs, and the very fine bill is better adapted than that of any tit to probe between the needles of spruce and other conifers and extract small invertebrates such as springtails and insect larvae. The undersides of their toes have ridges which close together to form a good grip on tiny twigs, or even the needles of coarser conifers. Field observation and experiments have shown that Goldcrests choose small food items in preference to larger ones (Thaler and Thaler 1982). Compared with the Firecrest, the Goldcrest spends more time clinging vertically and hanging, forages more thoroughly, and moves less often from tree to tree (Leisler and Thaler 1982). Snow cover affects foraging relatively little, but heavy frosting or glazing of trunks and foliage may prevent access to the usual sources of food.

Many Goldcrests visit Britain and Ireland from N Europe and swell our winter population: ringing recoveries link us with all countries east to Finland, the Baltic States and Poland, and south to France and Switzerland. There is also considerable long-distance dispersal of locally bred birds, mainly southeasterly in autumn, often across the Irish Sea and perhaps occasionally the English Channel.

Like most small birds in temperate climates, the Goldcrest experiences wide fluctuations in population size from year to year. In an average season, however, the resident population is probably in the range 2–4 million birds in mid winter. The scale of immigration is unknown, but Continental visitors perhaps number up to a further million.

The breeding range of the Goldcrest extends from the Azores, Britain and Ireland, discontinuously across Eurasia as far as W China and the Sea of Japan. The winter range extends well to the north of us in Scandinavia, even (reportedly) north of the Arctic Circle in coastal Norway.

J. H. MARCHANT

Total number of squares in which recorded: 3,038 (79%)

No. of birds seen in a day	Number (%) of squares		
	Britain	Ireland	TOTAL (incl. C.I.)
1–8	1,040 (47%)	509 (63%)	1,551 (51%)
9–19	654 (29%)	206 (26%)	862 (28%)
20 +	536 (24%)	88 (11%)	625 (21%)

References

LEISLER, B. and E. THALER. 1982. Differences in morphology and foraging behaviour in the goldcrest *Regulus regulus* and firecrest *R. ignicapillus*. *Ann. Zool. Fenn.* 19: 277–284.

THALER, E. and K. THALER. 1982. Feeding biology of Goldcrest and Firecrest and their segregation by choice of food. *Ökol. Vögel* 4: 191–204.

Breeding Atlas p 384

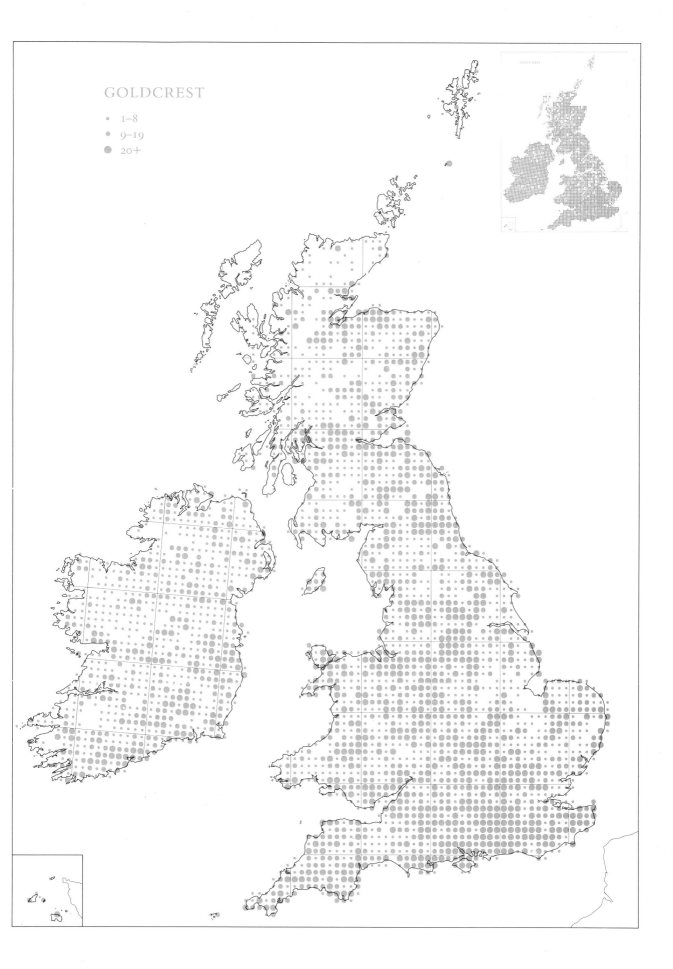

GOLDCREST

- 1–8
- 9–19
- 20+

Firecrest

Regulus ignicapillus

This green and bronze jewel of a bird can bring a touch of magic to birdwatching on a winter day by its sudden appearance among a roving party of tits or Goldcrests *R. regulus*. Encounters are sometimes so close (and often so brief) that binoculars are superfluous: the observer may even feel honoured by the confidence placed in him by the bird.

The winter distribution is largely coastal, from Cumbria in the northwest to the Borders in the northeast, the largest numbers occurring between Merseyside and Kent. Winter records anywhere north of the Lothians are exceptional. A very few are to be found in Ireland, particularly in Co. Cork. The best places to look for Firecrests in winter are in sheltered scrub or woodland edge near coasts between Devon and West Sussex, where many sites hold small parties regularly every year. Some birds winter inland, even in small groups, but it is unusual for any inland site to be occupied in successive winters. The inland records tend to be along river valleys, particularly in Northamptonshire and just north and west of London.

Winter and summer distribution correspond poorly, even allowing for the range expansion and consolidation of the breeding population which has continued since the *Breeding Atlas*. Despite the discovery of several new breeding sites since 1972, the bulk of the population is still concentrated between the New Forest and E Kent, and north to Buckinghamshire. Most British breeding sites are completely deserted in winter.

Although the two 'crests' are often seen together in winter flocks, there are interesting differences in habitat choice and behaviour between the two species. In aviary experiments with freshly-caught autumn migrants, Goldcrests preferred spruce trees to beech (independent of food availability), whereas Firecrests showed no preference. When foraging, Firecrests moved faster from tree to tree, and searched less thoroughly than Goldcrests, spending more time chasing along branches and less time climbing, hanging from twigs or gleaning foliage (Leisler and Thaler

1982). Both species feed on a variety of arthropods, but when offered food items of different sizes, Goldcrests tended to select small items and Firecrests much larger ones (Thaler and Thaler 1982). These behavioural differences are correlated with clear differences in morphology between the two species: the Firecrest has a wider gape and longer rictal bristles, enabling it to deal efficiently with larger food items, and the feet have larger toes, shorter claws and smoother soles, giving a better grip on longer branches. Firecrests are much less likely than Goldcrests to be found in spruce plantations and other habitats used for nesting. Most show some preference for coastal scrub or the vicinity of flowing fresh water. Song during mild winter weather is probably less frequent than in the Goldcrest, but has been reported in February.

In estimating the total numbers, it should be borne in mind that this is an elusive species, which may easily go undetected, and an unexpectedly mobile one which may be double-recorded in some well-watched areas. With some allowance for these factors, the average population is probably in the range 200–400 birds for Britain and Ireland. Considerable variation is known to occur between winters.

Even though the British and Irish breeding and wintering numbers are similar, most birds wintering here are probably of Continental origin. The winter distribution described in *The Handbook,* 20 years before the species was discovered breeding here, is similar to today's: the greatly increased number of reports is probably at least partly the result of more birdwatchers and sharper observation. There is as yet no clear information from ringing recoveries concerning the breeding areas of our winter visitors, or whether the British and Irish winter population includes our own breeding birds.

Unlike the Goldcrest, the Firecrest is endemic to the western Palearctic and is absent in winter from much of its breeding range. Britain and Ireland mark the most northerly point of a mainly Mediterranean and Atlantic winter distribution.

J. H. MARCHANT

Total number of squares in which recorded: 254 (7%)

No. of birds seen in a day	Number (%) of squares		
	Britain	Ireland	TOTAL (incl. C.I.)
1	141 (57%)	4 (80%)	145 (57%)
2	63 (26%)	0 (0%)	65 (26%)
3 +	40 (17%)	1 (20%)	44 (17%)

References

LEISLER, B. and E. THALER. 1982. Differences in morphology and foraging behaviour in the goldcrest *Regulus regulus* and firecrest *R. ignicapillus*. *Ann. Zool. Fenn.* 19: 277–284.

THALER, E. and K. THALER. 1982. Feeding biology of Goldcrest and Firecrest and their segregation by choice of food. *Ökol. Vögel.* 4: 191–204.

Breeding Atlas p 386

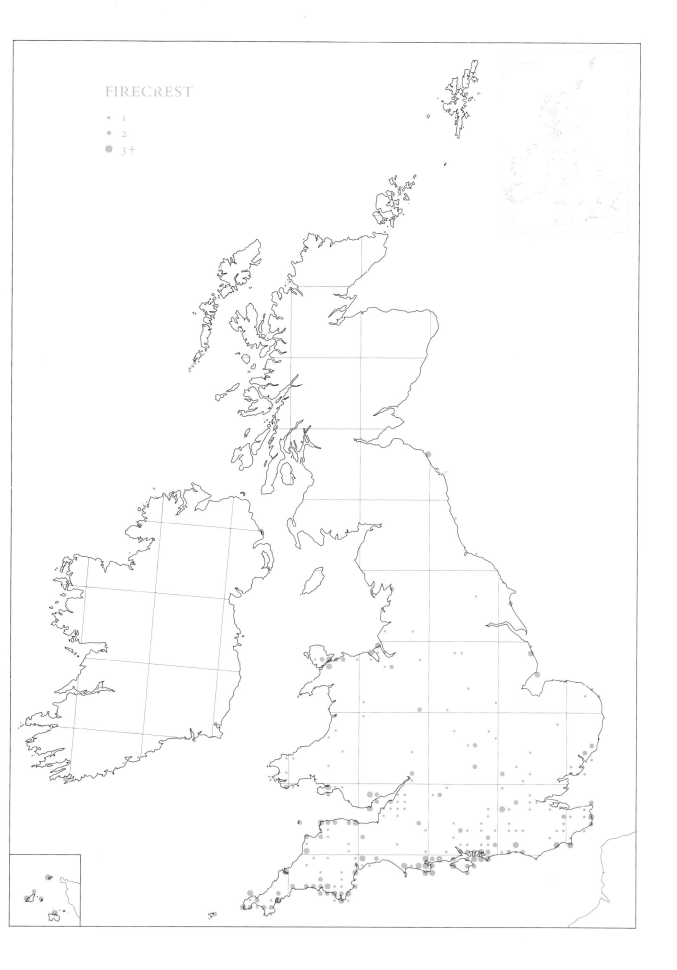

FIRECREST

- • 1
- • 2
- • 3+

Bearded Tit

Panurus biarmicus

The life of the Bearded Tit is closely tied to a single plant, the common reed. In an extensive reed bed even a large flock can disappear for hours at a time and, but for the tell-tale 'ping' call, it is easily overlooked. Rarely, except on passage, are the birds found far from marshes where reeds grow. They are generally rather sedentary but do periodically leave breeding places in large numbers.

Since the *Breeding Atlas*, the Bearded Tit has expanded its breeding range in Britain and has attempted to establish a foothold in Ireland. In 1974 the population was at least 590 pairs with breeding in 11 counties (O'Sullivan 1976). Present numbers are probably slightly higher than this. The winter distribution resembles the present breeding range but is rather more dispersed. Both follow the distribution of reed beds, which is mapped in Bibby and Lunn (1982). The main concentrations, summer and winter, are located in coastal marshes from East Anglia to Kent, with extensions along the south coast, totally determined by the occurrence of reed beds. In the present study Bearded Tits occurred at several sites in central England where breeding is infrequent but is, perhaps, becoming more regular. Some breeding sites seem to be abandoned in winter.

Bearded Tits feed largely on reed seeds in winter, extracting them with agility from the flower heads or gathering them from the ground, often along water lines (Bibby 1981). Small seeds of other plants are taken when Bearded Tits mix with flocks of other species, especially with Redpolls *Carduelis flammea*, in stands of nettle, willowherb and various sedges. These feeding habitats are usually in wet places near reeds and they cease to be important by mid winter. Bearded Tits are highly gregarious, occurring in flocks of up to 50 or more which move together and maintain close contact while feeding. On smaller sites, all the Bearded Tits in a reed bed are often found in a single flock. Ringing evidence and observation of small groups indicate that they frequently travel and winter in pairs. Numbers can be sharply reduced in prolonged periods of cold weather, but the rate of population recovery is fast. The British population is now much more widespread than previously and so is perhaps less vulnerable.

Post breeding movements occur in September and October and vary considerably in extent from year to year and site to site (Axell 1966). These are probably irruptions, due to the birds' dependence on the seeds of one plant (Bibby 1983). Conspicuous irruptions occurred between 1959 and 1973 when enormous breeding populations on the Dutch polders were involved. Long movements in various directions have been recorded within Britain and also from and to the Continent, mainly the Netherlands (Annual Ringing Reports). In the last ten years, numbers in the polders have fallen with the loss of the temporarily suitable habitat and there has not been a major irruption in this period. During the present study the winter distribution must have been due to movements of the native population, especially from East Anglia and SE England. Ireland and Scotland have always been too remote to receive more than small numbers, even in the years when large irruptions occurred.

If breeding numbers are now slightly above the 1974 estimate of 590 pairs and if allowance is made for the very considerable breeding rate of this species, recent mid winter numbers in Britain have probably been in the range 3,000–5,000 birds. Twice as many may have wintered here in the period of large irruptions from the Continent. This may not be repeated again unless further coastal engineering works in the Netherlands again produce huge if temporary areas of reed.

The Bearded Tit is very widely but patchily distributed across the Palearctic. Even in European terms, the British population is rather small because of the restricted area of habitat. A very high proportion of the large reed beds in Britain is now protected.

C. J. BIBBY

Total number of squares in which recorded: 122 (3%)

No. of birds seen in a day	Number (%) of squares		
	Britain	Ireland	TOTAL (incl. C.I.)
1–4	65 (54%)	0 (0%)	65 (54%)
5–10	36 (30%)	1 (100%)	37 (30%)
11 +	20 (16%)	0 (0%)	20 (16%)

References

AXELL, H. E. 1966. Eruptions of the Bearded Tit during 1959–65. *Brit. Birds* 59: 513–543.

BIBBY, C. J. 1981. Food supply and diet of the Bearded Tit. *Bird Study* 28: 201–210.

BIBBY, C. J. 1983. Studies of West Palearctic birds, 186: Bearded Tit. *Brit. Birds* 76: 549–563.

BIBBY, C. J. and J. LUNN. 1982. Conservation of reed beds and their avifauna in England and Wales. *Biol. Conserv.* 23: 167–186.

O'SULLIVAN, J. M. 1976. Bearded Tits in Britain and Ireland, 1966–74. *Brit. Birds* 69: 473–489.

Breeding Atlas p 328

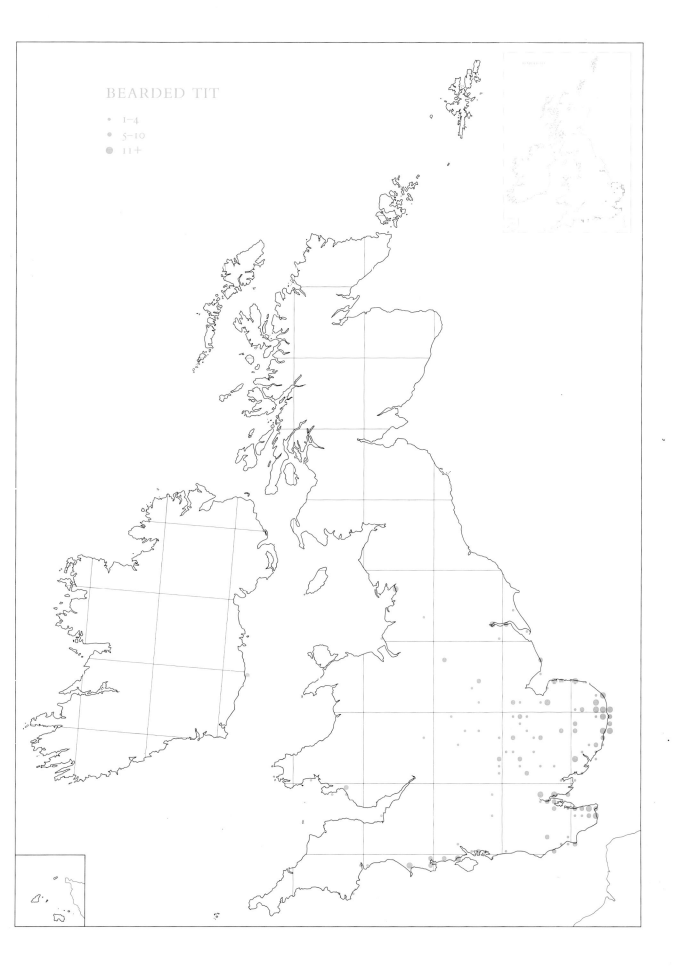

Long-tailed Tit

Aegithalos caudatus

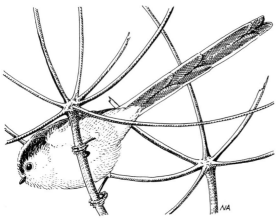

Parties of Long-tailed Tits are a common sight in woodland but tend to be less often seen in gardens. These flocks usually represent a loose family unit based upon the adults and juveniles from a single nest, often accompanied by extra adults who have helped with the nestlings. These are probably siblings of the male parent. Larger flocks may consist of several families which later split up when winter territories are established.

The distribution map shows that the Long-tailed Tit is very widespread. There are concentrations in areas with large tracts of woodland. When compared with Britain, Ireland exhibits a lower population level of birds, particularly towards the western edge of the country. This distribution reflects the lack of woodland and hedges, which are important environments for this bird. Similarly, the northernmost areas of Scotland also have fewer birds. This may be due to lack of suitable habitat or possibly to infrequent attempts to census the birds.

The winter habitat of this species is usually deciduous woodland and tall farmland hedgerows, but if conditions are very severe the birds may frequent garden bird tables, where they pick at scraps of fat, a trick that, once learnt by one bird, will be adopted by the rest of the flock. In milder weather the birds can usually be seen foraging among the twigs in the treetops, particularly those of the oak, ash and sycamore, searching for grubs, flies and other insect life. Unlike the other tits, which tend to be omnivores, Long-tailed Tits usually remain insectivorous all the year round.

The flocks divide the woodland areas into discrete territories that are aggressively defended against other Long-tailed Tit flocks. The size of each territory depends upon the relative size of the flock within the local population.

The flock roosts communally, the roost usually being located about 1 m above ground level in a dense thorn bush, such as hawthorn. The roost is formed by all of the members of the flock entering the bush, whereupon two birds huddle close together. Other birds join this arrangement by forcing their way into the middle until a compact linear roost is formed. The roost will be formed in the same bush each night unless they are disturbed, in which case the birds choose another, similar, roost site.

During February the composition of the flocks begins to alter, with the unmated females leaving the flock to join flocks occupying adjacent territories; this interchange of females probably occurs during inter-flock disputes. This phase of the life history of the Long-tailed Tit only lasts a few weeks, after which pairing of birds within the flocks is initiated. The winter flock territory is then subdivided into pair territories that may be weakly defended against other members of the winter flock. A pair will continue to roost with the winter flock until the dome of their nest is complete, when they will roost within the nest.

The British and Irish populations are usually sedentary during the winter months though there are ringing records of flocks moving over 100 km. The dispersal from the breeding areas is generally limited to a few kilometres. Winter visitors are extremely rare, northern birds being conspicuous on account of their white heads, compared with the black and white head colouration of the resident population.

Population fluctuations tend to be small except when particularly harsh conditions result in high mortality. The *Breeding Atlas* gave an estimate of 150,000 families for Britain and Ireland, which probably reflected 50,000 pairs (each nesting on average three times). A nest success rate of 16% with an average brood size of 9, survival rates of 38% for adults and 32% for juveniles, and an average of 3 adult birds per successful nest will lead to a winter population of about 96,000 birds in Britain and Ireland.

N. GLEN

Total number of squares in which recorded: 2,575 (67%)

No. of birds seen in a day	Number (%) of squares		
	Britain	Ireland	TOTAL (incl. C.I.)
1–15	909 (44%)	402 (77%)	1,312 (51%)
16–28	673 (33%)	90 (17%)	765 (30%)
29 +	468 (23%)	30 (6%)	498 (19%)

References

GLEN, N. W. 1985. *The Co-operative Breeding Behaviour of the Long-tailed Tit*. D. Phil. Thesis. Oxford University.

Breeding Atlas p 318

LONG-TAILED TIT

- · 1–15
- ● 16–28
- ● 29+

Marsh Tit

Parus palustris

The Marsh Tit and its related species, the Willow Tit *P. montanus,* present considerable identification problems to workers contributing to all atlases and similar projects. One of the most reliable field characters distinguishing these species is their respective calls and it is these that will usually alert Atlas workers to their presence. The Marsh Tit is strictly a bird of rural deciduous woodland, especially of oak and beech. It rarely occurs in coniferous woodland and despite its name, prefers rather drier open woodland than does the Willow Tit. Hence there is a tendency for the two species to be spatially separated by habitat.

The winter distribution is similar to that of the breeding season. It is rather patchy and generally corresponds with the distribution of deciduous habitat. Although the distribution of Marsh and Willow Tits may be mutually exclusive when mapped on a 2–km grid, such as has been shown for Hertfordshire, this would not be expected at a 10–km grid scale (Mead and Smith 1982). There is, however, some evidence of mutual exclusion. The low density of Marsh Tits in the London area corresponds with a high density of Willow Tits there, especially at the gravel pit complexes that surround the city. The distribution becomes gradually more patchy north of a line from the Wash to the Dee estuary. There are no records for Ireland and the Isle of Man.

The winter biology of the Marsh Tit is particularly interesting. Adults are amongst the most site faithful of all passerine species. They stay paired through the winter and remain on their large territory (which may be over 3 ha in extent, compared with 1.2 ha for Great Tit *P. major*) even in harsh weather; in milder weather both will defend it vigorously against neighbouring territory holders, with loud 'pitchou' calls.

Unpaired first-winter birds join mixed-species tit flocks in winter. Territories are not defended against these flocking individuals. Indeed territory holders frequently join such flocks whilst they are foraging within their territory, leaving the flock again when it moves into a neighbouring territory. Morse (1978) found Marsh Tits in 59% of flocks in an Oxfordshire woodland in winter, and 78% of all he saw occurred within mixed-species flocks. Marsh Tits generally feed rather low in the woodland profile and especially in the shrub layer. However, beechmast and other tree seeds form an important part of the diet in winter. Like the Coal Tit *P. ater*, this species is subordinate to Great and Blue Tits *P. caeruleus*. This may explain why Coal Tits and Marsh Tits hoard seed in winter. Marsh Tits tend to hoard seeds and insects in the morning, usually retrieving them the same day, although seeds may remain for 3 days before retrieval. Food items are stored individually in moss on or near the ground. Recent laboratory studies show that Marsh Tits have tremendous powers of recall, and usually remember where they have stored food (A. Stevens).

Marsh Tits rarely travel far from their natal wood. Only 17% of sites in the BTO's Garden Bird Feeding Survey reported this species. Of recoveries of British ringed Marsh Tits, 85% occurred within 4 km of the ringing location and less than 1% had moved more than 50 km. The distribution of recoveries shows no significant orientation and there is no recorded movement of the species to or from the Continent.

The *Breeding Atlas* estimated the British population at between 70,000 and 140,000 pairs, but since then an estimated 20% reduction has occurred. Assuming approximately 5 young fledged per pair, 60% loss of these and 25% loss of the adults by mid winter, a mean winter population of between 200,000 and 400,000 birds is estimated.

A. G. GOSLER

Total number of squares in which recorded: 1,208 (31%)

No. of birds seen in a day	Number (%) of squares		
	Britain	Ireland	TOTAL (incl. C.I.)
1–3	547 (45%)	0 (0%)	547 (45%)
4–7	407 (34%)	0 (0%)	407 (34%)
8 +	254 (21%)	0 (0%)	254 (21%)

References

GLUE, D. (ed.). 1982. *The Garden Bird Book*. Macmillan, London.

MARCHANT, J. 1983. Bird population changes for the years 1981–1982. *Bird Study* 30: 127–133.

MEAD, C., and K. SMITH. 1982. *Hertfordshire Breeding Bird Atlas*. HBBA, Tring, Herts.

MORSE, D. H. 1978. Structure and foraging patterns of flocks of tits and associated species in an English woodland during winter. *Ibis* 120: 298–312.

SELLERS, R. M. 1984. Movements of Coal, Marsh and Willow Tits in Britain. *Ringing and Migration* 5: 79–89.

Breeding Atlas p 314

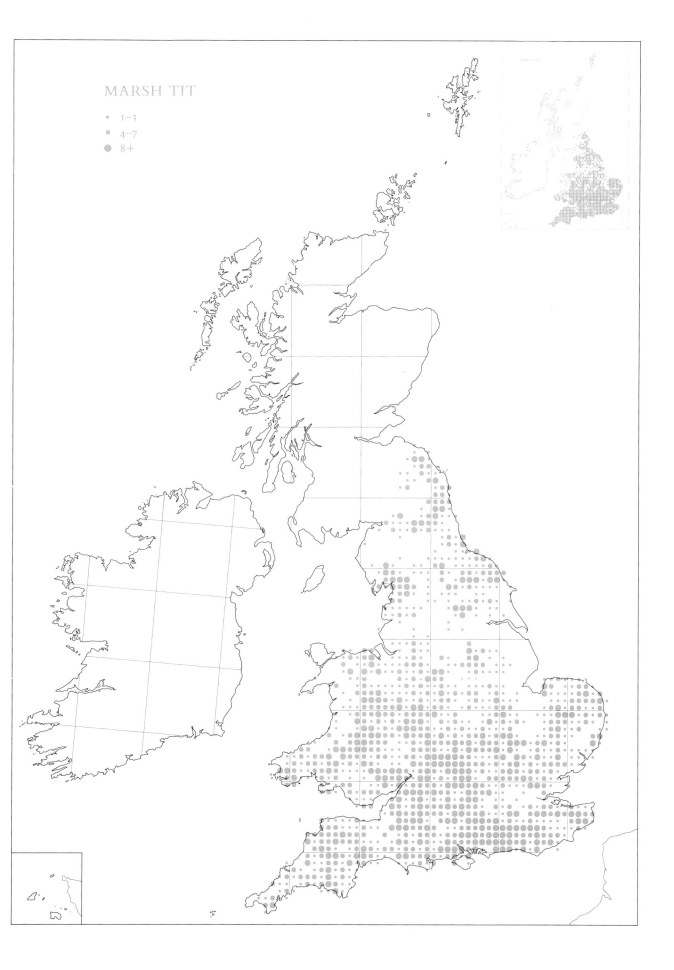

MARSH TIT

- • 1–3
- • 4–7
- • 8+

Willow Tit

Parus montanus

Although the Willow Tit was recognised as a species distinct from the Marsh Tit *P. palustris* in 1897, the problem of identification persists, and there is still a surprising lack of information on the biology of Willow Tits in Britain. Despite its distinct habitat preference, difference in appearance and characteristic nasal call—quite unlike any produced by its cousin— any atlas may contain a small degree of error.

The winter distribution is similar to that of the breeding season, and corresponds with the distribution of damp woodland habitats, carr and lowland coniferous forest. The winter distribution is therefore patchy but is rather more extensive in southern Scotland than that of the Marsh Tit, due to the predominance of coniferous forest. However, the Willow Tit is apparently less widespread in this area in winter than is shown in the *Breeding Atlas*. This may represent either a seasonal contraction of range into the most suitable habitats, or range shrinkage since the *Breeding Atlas* fieldwork. Perrins (1980) suggests that in Scotland generally, the Willow Tit is less abundant than it used to be. The greater densities of birds are found in central and southern England, the Fens and in central Wales, where it may be commoner than the Marsh Tit (Perrins 1980). It is apparently considerably rarer in SW England than its cousin.

As stated under Marsh Tit, habitat segregation is not expected to show up at the 10–km grid scale. However, a brief analysis of range overlap is worthwhile. The *Breeding Atlas* showed one or other of the species in 55% of squares. Of these, 64% contained both species, 23% contained only Marsh Tit and 13% only Willow Tit. The winter distribution shows the two species in 37.3% of squares, a decline of 17.7%. Marsh Tit only, occurs in 19.9% of squares, 16% contain only Willow Tit and, again, 64% contain both. Hence, there has been no significant change in relative distributions but an overall decline in the combined range.

Adult Willow Tits probably remain on their territories in winter. In January-February 1985, 30% of observations in an Oxfordshire woodland were of single birds, 20% were paired and 50% were in mixed species flocks (T. C. Grubb). Willow Tits join mixed-species flocks less readily than other tit species. This may reflect their distinct habitat preference.

Little is known about the winter diet of the Willow Tit except that, unlike other tits, the species makes little use of nuts such as beech mast. This may be because its bill, which is thinner than that of the Marsh Tit, is poorly adapted for hammering nuts, or because suitable tree species are not available in its preferred habitat. Willow Tits regularly store food in the same way as Marsh Tits. In Sweden, J. Eyekman found that Willow Tits frequently hoard invertebrates, and this behaviour may also be common in Britain (Gibb 1960).

In winter, Willow Tits are highly sedentary and the low density suggests that they remain on their territories. Only 10% of sites in the Garden Bird Feeding Survey reported this species, but those present were regular visitors (Glue 1982). In a small sample, 78% of ringing recoveries were within 4 km of the ringing site, but in some parts of Britain Willow Tits may be rather more mobile. All movements greater than 5 km came from E of a line between the Pennines and the Isle of Wight. This was highly significant. The Marsh Tit showed no such trend. The greatest movement recorded for a Willow Tit was 170 km (55 km for Marsh Tit). There was no significant timing or orientation of the recoveries and no Continental recoveries (Sellers 1984).

Although the Marsh Tit population has declined, there is no reason to suppose that the same has occurred in the Willow Tit, and the number ringed annually in Britain has almost doubled since 1972. The *Breeding Atlas* estimated the British population as 50,000–100,000 pairs. Assuming 5 young fledged per pair, 60% loss of chicks and 25% of adults by mid winter, a mean winter population for Britain and Ireland would be 175,000–350,000 individuals.

A. G. GOSLER

Total number of squares in which recorded: 1,152 (30%)

No. of birds seen in a day	Number (%) of squares		
	Britain	Ireland	TOTAL (incl. C.I.)
1–2	560 (49%)	0 (0%)	560 (49%)
3–5	410 (36%)	0 (0%)	410 (36%)
6 +	182 (16%)	0 (0%)	182 (16%)

References

GIBB, J. A. 1960. Populations of tits and goldcrests and their food supply in pine plantations. *Ibis* 102: 163–208.

GLUE, D. 1982. (ed.). *The Garden Bird Book*. Macmillan, London.

PERRINS, C. M. 1980. *British Tits*. Collins, London.

SELLERS, R. M. 1984. Movements of Coal, Marsh and Willow Tits in Britain. *Ringing and Migration* 5: 79–89.

Breeding Atlas p 316

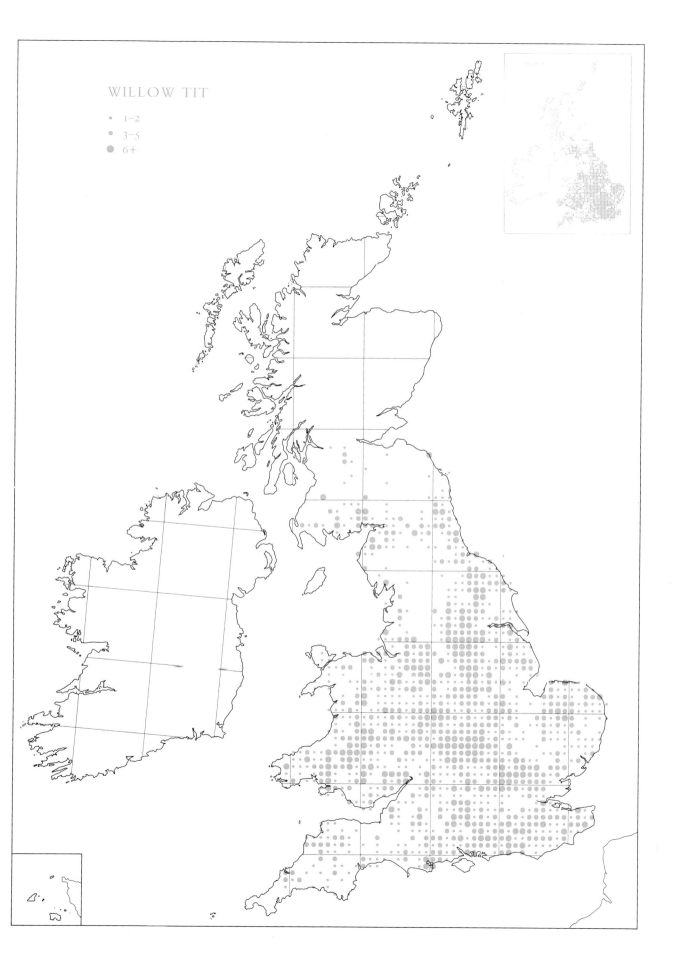

WILLOW TIT

- 1–2
- 3–5
- 6+

Crested Tit

Parus cristatus

This handsome little bird evokes, perhaps more than any other, the atmosphere of the Scottish Highland forests. Once learned, its indignant trilling is unmistakeable, and at close range the bird reveals the black and white cheeks and spiky chequered crest which are unique among British birds.

The winter distribution closely matches that of the *Breeding Atlas* and the more detailed breeding survey undertaken in 1979 and 1980 (Cook 1982). However, in the eastern part of the range, around lower Speyside, nine 10–km breeding squares have no winter records. This is possibly explained by reduced observer cover compared with the summer surveys.

Scottish Crested Tits *P. c. scoticus* are associated with Scots Pine, at all seasons, and are confined exclusively to Scotland. The traditional habitat is the extensive open pine forests of the Highland valleys. These are moist woods characterised by a dense growth of rank heather with bilberry and juniper. During this century commercial pine plantations have proliferated. This habitat of regimented trees and sparse ground cover, so different from the Caledonian Forest, has nevertheless extended the bird's range to the coasts of the Moray Firth.

Winter mortality of Crested Tits can be high in severe weather. For example, Nethersole-Thompson and Watson (1974) reported a reduction from 10 pairs to 3 pairs in part of Rothiemurchus Forest following the 1946/47 winter. However, after the cold winter 1981/82 the 19 breeding pairs at a Common Birds Census plot near Loch Garten was one more than in the previous year (Dennis 1984).

Finding food in the Highland forests in winter can be difficult. In summer, Crested Tits spend much time feeding high in the canopy, exploiting the abundant insect food. In winter they seek invertebrates in the bark crevices on branches and trunks, and pine seeds feature regularly in the diet. They descend frequently to the ground and in snowy weather often become very tame as they explore snow-free patches among the heather. Under such conditions they readily accept artificial supplies and will feed at bird-tables, peanut bags, deer skins and even dustbins. In

Norway, Haftorn (1953) found that Crested Tits supplemented their winter diet with food stored, mainly, in the previous autumn. Birds were observed wedging pine and spruce seeds, and even insects, into bark crevices.

Paired adult Crested Tits remain together throughout the winter and occupy a home range of around 15 ha, centred on the breeding territory (Deadman 1973). They will temporarily join foraging tit flocks but leave rather than stray far from the middle of their range. Their roosting habits are little known but they very seldom use nestboxes, despite regularly breeding in them.

Scottish Crested Tits are usually sedentary. In a small sample, A. Deadman, working in a Moray plantation, found a mean post-juvenile dispersal distance of 1.3 km and a maximum of 2.2 km. Longer movements must occasionally take place and the very few individuals recorded on Deeside have presumably travelled through the Cairngorms from Speyside, a distance of at least 25 km. There are few reliable Scottish records outside the usual breeding areas. About 10 have been reported in England, mostly in southern and eastern counties, at least 4 of them in winter. It is highly likely that all these individuals are of the two Continental subspecies *P. c. cristatus* from Scandinavia and *P. c. mitratus* from central Europe. Each race has been positively identified at least once.

Following a winter of average severity the breeding population is probably around 900 pairs (Cook 1982). Assuming 5 young produced by each pair, the mid June population would be 6,300 birds. Post-juvenile mortality of tits is highly variable from year to year but, assuming a figure of 50% by December, together with 25% adult mortality, the mid winter Crested Tit population is probably in the region of 3,600 birds.

M. J. H. COOK

Total number of squares in which recorded: 46 (1%)

No. of birds seen in a day	Number (%) of squares		
	Britain	Ireland	TOTAL (incl. C.I.)
1–2	24 (52%)	0 (0%)	24 (52%)
3–8	15 (33%)	0 (0%)	15 (33%)
9 +	7 (15%)	0 (0%)	7 (15%)

References

COOK, M. J. H. 1982. Breeding status of the Crested Tit. *Scot. Birds* 12: 97–106.

DEADMAN, A. J. 1973. *A Population Study of the Coal Tit* (Parus ater) *and the Crested Tit* (Parus cristatus) *in a Scottish Pine Plantation.* Ph.D. Thesis, Aberdeen University.

DENNIS, R. H. 1984. Scottish Bird Report 1982. *Scot. Birds* 12: supplement.

HAFTORN, S. 1953. Contribution to the food biology of tits, especially about storing of surplus food. Part I. The Crested Tit *Parus c. cristatus* L. K. Norske Vidensk. Selsk. Skr. 4: 9–122.

NETHERSOLE-THOMPSON, D. and A. WATSON 1974. *The Cairngorms.* Collins, London.

Breeding Atlas p 312

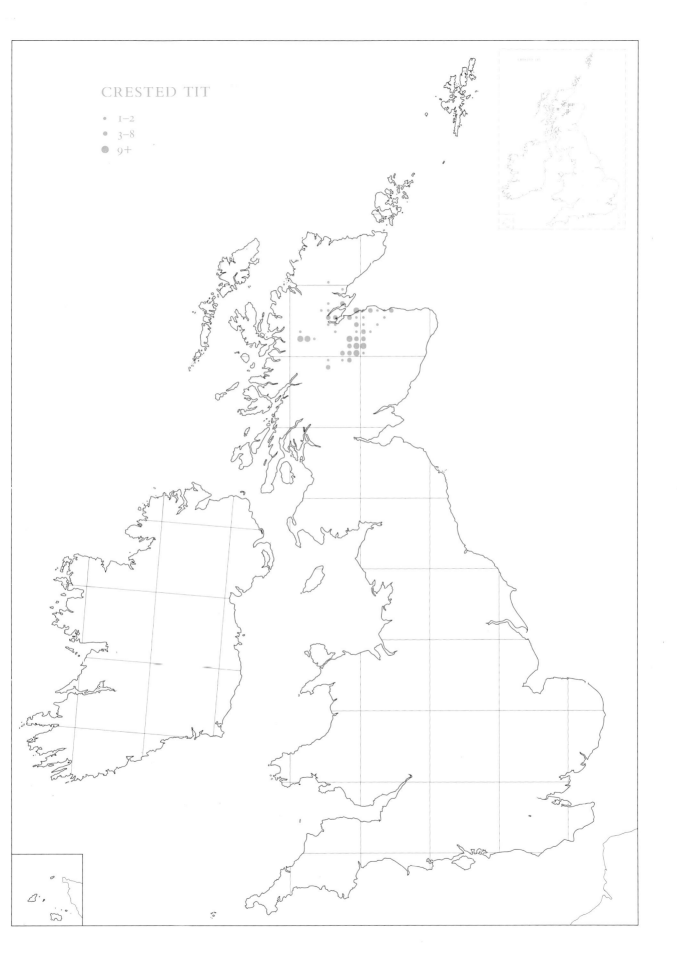

CRESTED TIT

- 1–2
- 3–8
- 9+

Coal Tit

Parus ater

The Coal Tit differs from the other common tit species in a number of ecological characteristics. Chief amongst these is its preference for coniferous forest, for which it appears to be well suited, having a narrow bill adapted for picking insects from between conifer needles. In Britain it has apparently increased in abundance in response to increased conifer afforestation. The Coal Tit appears to have a competitive advantage over Great and Blue Tits *P. major* and *P. caeruleus* only in coniferous forest. It is not rare in broad-leaved woodland, but as the smallest true tit in Britain it is subordinate to the other species in winter tit flocks.

As with many resident small passerines, the Coal Tit's distribution in winter closely parallels that of the breeding season, and the map clearly picks out those regions with little suitable habitat, such as the Fens in East Anglia. In winter the Coal Tit is not restricted to coniferous forest but may occur at a higher density there. Hence, high density squares occur more or less randomly throughout England, Wales and Ireland, corresponding with the distribution of major stands of conifers; for example, the Kielder Forest in Northumberland and Thetford Forest in East Anglia. In many Scottish forests the Coal Tit occurs at a higher density than does either the Great or Blue Tit, and its better adaptation to conifer habitat reduces the need for the altitudinal migration seen in those species.

Coal Tits are regular members of winter tit flocks in all woodland habitats. Morse (1978) found them present in 52% of flocks in a broad-leaved Oxfordshire wood. Indeed, 96% of his observations of Coal Tits were within mixed species flocks, although at very low density (mean = 0.8 birds per flock). Because of their small body volume in relation to surface area, little birds such as the Coal Tit must feed constantly in winter. Although its smaller size enables the Coal Tit to feed high in the tree canopy later in the winter than its dominant congeners, by late winter even the most insectivorous of tits must take seeds such as beechmast to survive. Hence winter movements are partly controlled by the quality of seed crops. Glue (1982) has shown that Coal Tits are more likely to visit garden birdtables in poor mast years than in good (see Figure). Coal Tits are not infrequent visitors to gardens, and 70% of participants in the BTO Garden Bird Feeding Survey reported this species. Coal Tits are, however, very sedentary. Of British ringing recoveries, 83% come from within 4 km of the place of ringing and less than 3% from more than 50 km. As might be expected, the mean recovery distance for a given year (excluding extremely local movements) correlates well with the GBFS index, and thus with the size of the mast crop (Sellers 1984). Like the Great and Blue Tits, the Coal Tit is eruptive in Europe when seed crops are poor.

The *Breeding Atlas* estimated the population in Britain and Ireland as about 1,000,000 pairs. Since then no significant change in abundance has occurred. Assuming an average productivity of 6 young fledged per pair, 60% loss of these by mid winter, and 25% for adults, the mid winter population of Coal Tits would be about 4,000,000 birds.

In Britain, the species has a slightly larger bill than on the Continent, and in SW Ireland where the Coal Tits breed largely in deciduous woodland, they have still larger bills and are differentiated as a distinct race *P. a. hibernicus*.

A. G. GOSLER

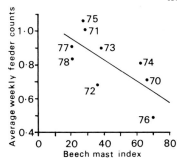

The average number of Coal Tits in gardens in relation to an index of beech mast. Redrawn from Glue (1982).

Total number of squares in which recorded: 3,032 (79%)

Number (%) of squares

No. of birds seen in a day	Britain	Ireland	TOTAL (incl. C.I.)
1–7	1,089 (48%)	490 (64%)	1,580 (52%)
8–17	625 (28%)	199 (26%)	824 (27%)
18 +	547 (24%)	81 (11%)	628 (21%)

References

GLUE, D. 1982. (ed.). *The Garden Bird Book*. Macmillan, London.

MARCHANT, J. 1983. Bird population changes for the years 1981–1982. *Bird Study* 30: 127–133.

MORSE, D. H. 1978. Structure and foraging patterns of flocks of tits and associated species in an English woodland during winter. *Ibis* 120: 298–312.

PERRINS, C. M. 1979. *British Tits*. Collins, London.

SELLERS, R. M. 1984. Movements of Coal, Marsh and Willow Tits in Britain. *Ringing and Migration* 5: 79–89.

SNOW, D. W. 1954. The habitats of Eurasian Tits (*Parus* spp.). *Ibis* 96: 565–585.

Breeding Atlas p 310

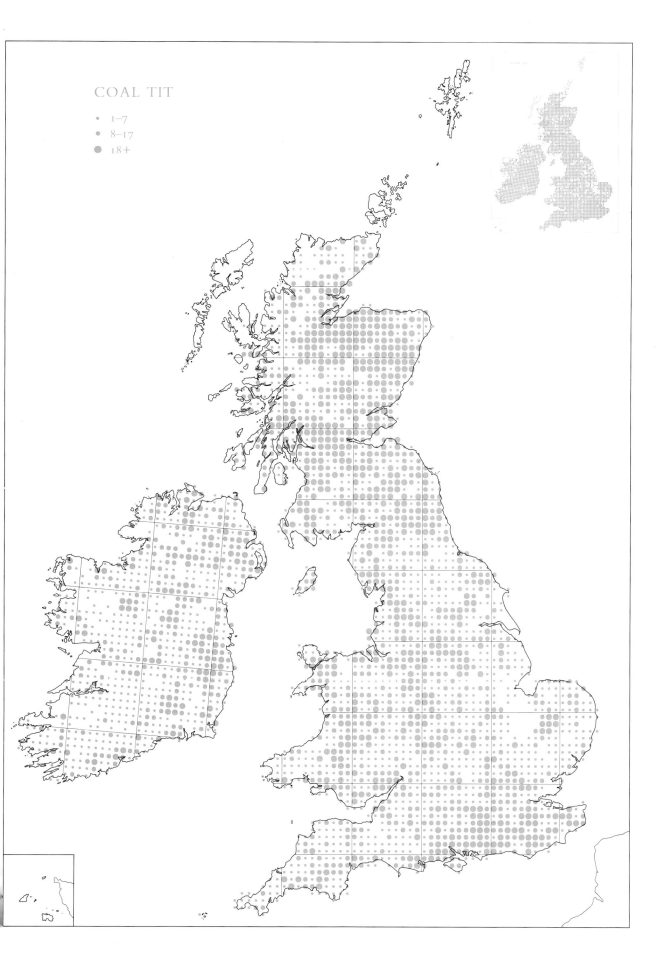

COAL TIT

- 1–7
- 8–17
- 18+

Blue Tit

Parus caeruleus

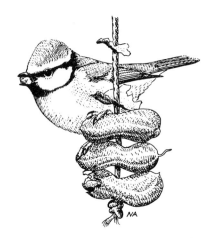

Even in a tiny city garden, where its plumage may be soiled by industrial grime, the Blue Tit is generally the first bird to discover and patronise the familiar red plastic nut bag. Indeed, its willingness to approach our houses and its engaging acrobatic feeding behaviour make it one of the best known and best loved native birds, awarded—like Jenny Wren and Robin Redbreast—the accolade of a Christian name sharing Tom with the Great Tit.

The Blue Tit breeds and winters all over Britain and Ireland except for the very highest and most remote parts of Scotland. The lack of records from the Scottish Highlands and the corresponding concentrations in valleys in winter may represent an altitudinal movement. In England, the highest densities of birds occur south and west of a line from the Thames estuary to Morecambe Bay. The distribution corresponds well with that of the human population. Edinburgh and Glasgow, Newcastle, the industrialised north, central England and London, all show high densities of Blue Tits. In southern England the areas of high densities of birds correspond with the woodlands of the Chilterns and Downs. In Ireland the distribution of Blue Tits is remarkably uniform, reflecting both the cosmopolitan nature of this species and sparse distribution of the human population.

In most places it is the commonest British tit and the species most often found flocking with others in woodland in winter. Morse (1978) found that of 220 mixed species flocks observed in deciduous woodland in winter, 207 (94%) contained Blue Tits as compared with 108 (49%) containing Great Tits *P. major*.

In autumn family flocks may be joined by Great Tits, Long-tailed Tits *Aegithalos caudatus*, Goldcrests *Regulus regulus*, Treecreepers *Certhia familiaris*, and *Phylloscopus* and *Sylvia* warblers. Later, after most of the warblers have migrated, they are joined in England by the local Nuthatches *Sitta europaea*, Marsh Tits *P. palustris*, Willow Tits *P. montanus* and Great or Lesser Spotted Woodpeckers *Dendrocopos major* or *D. minor*. After the Great Tit, Blue Tits are the dominant and most aggressive members of such flocks. Many Blue Tits in winter flocks are already paired.

As winter progresses, the diet gradually switches from invertebrates to include more seed. The tits are very inquisitive and will investigate any possible food source—leading to paper tearing and putty pecking in some years and cream stealing from milk bottles (Perrins 1980). The Blue Tits' agility means that they are able to take beech mast while it is still on the tree, after the Great Tits have been forced to feed on the ground. Blue Tit populations are less influenced by yearly fluctuations in the mast crop, though in good mast years the numbers visiting gardens may be much lower. In winter, woodland Blue Tits often leave the woods, particularly in severe weather or a year of a poor mast crop. Some return to roost in woods each evening and make daily forays into suburbia to feed at birdtables (Perrins 1980). Blue Tits keep very regular hours and probably patrol some form of 'beat' around their neighbourhood as shown by marked suburban birds coming to birdtables. 200 individuals may visit a favoured birdtable in a day, and possibly 1,000 birds in the course of a whole winter. Although winter movements may exceed 300 km, 95% of ringing recoveries come from within 10 km of the point of ringing (Perrins 1980) and in one study 94% were within 1 km (Burgess 1982). Fidelity to the breeding territory exhibited by males means that on average they tend to move less far than females. Like the Great Tit, the Blue Tit is irruptive in some years, at which time the larger, brighter Continental individuals may be found in southern and eastern England.

The *Breeding Atlas* estimated the breeding population at something over 5,000,000 pairs. Since then a 7% reduction in numbers has occurred (Marchant 1983). Assuming that on average 7 chicks fledge per pair, and 25% survive to mid winter, and 70% of adults survive, about 15,000,000 Blue Tits would be alive in Britain and Ireland in mid winter.

A. G. GOSLER

Total number of squares in which recorded: 3,395 (88%)

No. of birds seen in a day	Number (%) of squares		
	Britain	Ireland	TOTAL (incl. C.I.)
1–30	889 (36%)	824 (88%)	1,716 (51%)
31–69	897 (37%)	99 (11%)	997 (29%)
70 +	670 (27%)	11 (1%)	682 (20%)

References

BURGESS, J. P. C. 1982. Sexual differences and dispersal in the Blue Tit *Parus caeruleus*. *Ringing and Migration* 4: 25–32.

MARCHANT, J. 1983. Bird population changes for the years 1981–1982. *Bird Study* 30: 127–133.

MORSE, D. H. 1978. Structure and foraging patterns of flocks of tits and associated species in an English woodland during winter. *Ibis* 120: 298–312.

PERRINS, C. M. 1980. *British Tits*. Collins, London.

Breeding Atlas p 308

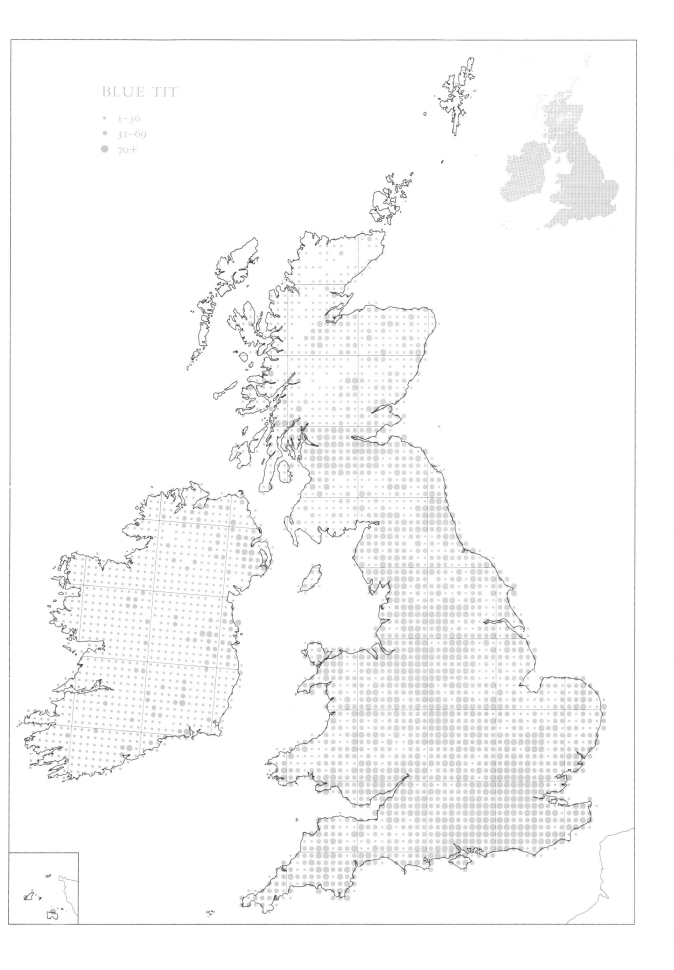

BLUE TIT

· 1–30
· 31–69
● 70+

Great Tit

Parus major

Tits are the most obvious small passerines in woodland in winter, frequently banding together in flocks containing up to 9 species (including up to 5 *Parus* species) and 40 individuals. The Great Tit is the largest British tit and a frequent member of such winter flocks. It is a particularly conspicuous species, with a wide range of calls, and occurs in woodland, farmland and suburban habitats in winter.

The winter distribution is essentially similar to that of the breeding season, with most of the country occupied. In winter however, Great Tits are absent from more 10–km squares in the far north of Scotland and the Highlands; the relatively high density of birds in the Great Glen in winter probably reflects a movement away from the higher ground and towards the more sheltered valleys. A similar movement may occur between the southern Grampians and the lower ground to the south, and between the southern uplands and the vicinity of Newcastle. In England, there are lower Great Tit densities along the cold east coast and down into the Fens. This may reflect the intensity of agriculture and fewer woodlands in the region. The species is most abundant south and west of a line joining the Thames estuary and Morecambe Bay, with an almost continuous block of high density coinciding with the chalk, and hence beech woods, of southern England. In Ireland the Great Tit occurs at lower densities than in Britain (only 10% of squares reported more than 20) with slightly higher numbers in east than west but otherwise there is no significant pattern.

The young of the year begin to form small flocks in late summer whilst the adult males remain in their breeding territories. Territorial behaviour continues into the winter, but as the days shorten and food becomes scarcer, the territory holders spend more time with the flocks. However, a resurgence of territorial behaviour may occur at any time during the winter if the temperature rises sufficiently (Perrins 1980). Morse (1978) found that over three-quarters of 108 individual Great Tits seen were in mixed species flocks, whilst the majority of the rest were alone or in single species flocks.

In autumn there is a gradual shift in diet from invertebrates (mostly gleaned from foliage) to seeds and fruit, so that by November, seeds such as beechmast and hazelnuts, form a major part of the diet. The larger size of the Great Tit means that it is less adept at the aerial gymnastics for which other tit species are well known, so that it shows a preference for ground feeding. As winter progresses, Great Tits spend an increasing proportion of their time foraging on the ground. Where beech trees are present and in years of high mast abundance, aggregations of several hundred individuals may be seen busily shuffling through leaf litter in search of beechmast.

Great Tits are largely resident in Britain and Ireland. On the Continent, however, they may be partial or full migrants and erupt westwards and southwards in years with poor beech crops (Perrins 1966). In these years, specimens of the Continental race *P. m. major* may occur in Britain (Harrison 1946). Most movements within Britain are less than 10 km, though movements of over 300 km have been recorded. Because the males are more faithful to the territory, they move less far than females. In poor mast years, or in extremely severe weather, Great Tits move out of the woods and into suburban gardens where they feed on fat and peanuts. In good mast years the movement is reversed until stocks become exhausted.

The *Breeding Atlas* estimated the British and Irish population at something over 3,000,000 pairs. Since then the population has risen by about 11% (Marchant 1983). Assuming that 5 chicks fledge per pair (Perrins 1980) some 15,000,000 first year birds might be included in the winter population (assuming no postfledging loss). First-year survival is about 20%, that of adults about 50% so that a mean winter population of about 10,000,000 birds would be appropriate.

A. G. GOSLER

Total number of squares in which recorded: 3,256 (84%)

No. of birds seen in a day	Number (%) of squares		
	Britain	Ireland	TOTAL (incl. C.I.)
1–16	947 (39%)	680 (80%)	1,629 (50%)
17–37	834 (35%)	144 (17%)	980 (30%)
38 +	623 (26%)	23 (3%)	647 (20%)

References

HARRISON, J. M. 1946. Continental Great Tit in Kent. *Brit. Birds* 39: 153.

MARCHANT, J. 1983. Bird population changes for the years 1981–1982. *Bird Study* 30: 127–133.

MORSE, D. H. 1978. Structure and foraging patterns of flocks of tits and associated species in an English woodland during winter. *Ibis* 120: 298–312.

PERRINS, C. M. 1966. The effect of beech crops on Great Tit populations and movements. *Brit. Birds* 59: 419–432.

PERRINS, C. M. 1980. *British Tits*. Collins, London.

Breeding Atlas p 306

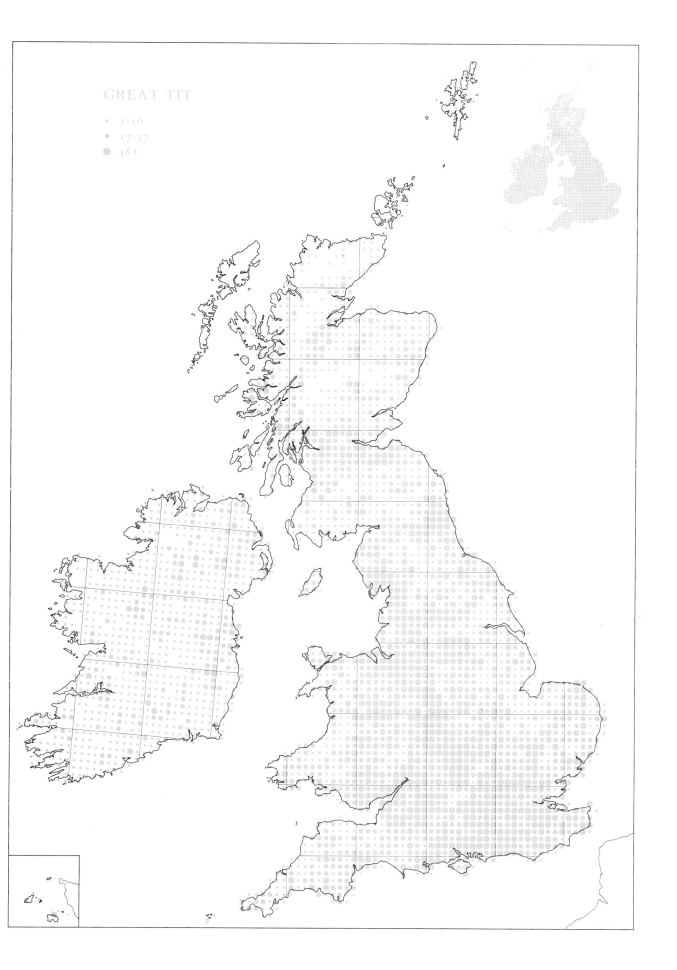

Nuthatch

Sitta europaea

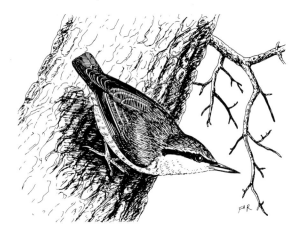

Nuthatches are not always easy to detect in winter, although on warm days their loud ringing calls may be heard from a considerable distance. From autumn onwards, they are very territorial, but will join tit flocks which pass through their territory.

The winter distribution is remarkably similar to that shown in the *Breeding Atlas*, which presumably reflects the sedentary habits of the Nuthatch. The map shows that the species is most abundant in S England, particularly in the Home Counties and in Sussex and Hampshire. The Nuthatch is absent from large areas of East Anglia, Lincolnshire and N England. In recent years, however, there has been a slight northwards extension of range and this is shown by the higher numbers of records in Durham, Northumberland, Cumbria and a few in S Scotland compared with the *Breeding Atlas*. As with the woodpeckers, there are no records in Ireland, and only one from the Isle of Man.

The Nuthatch is probably one of the most selective of our woodland species and is particularly associated with mature deciduous woods. This, together with its sedentary habits, probably accounts for its absence from many areas of East Anglia where mature woodland exists only as fragmented relics in a largely agricultural landscape.

In winter, Nuthatches feed extensively on hazel nuts, beechmast, acorns and other seeds such as hornbeam and yew, according to availability. Their habit of jamming seeds into crevices in the bark and hammering with their bill to extract the kernels is the origin of their vernacular name. In addition they also take a range of invertebrates, such as beetles and spiders, which they glean from the trunks and limbs of trees. They are able to move up or down the trunks with ease and do not use their tail as a prop in the manner of woodpeckers. Nuthatches commonly occur at garden feeding stations (Glue 1982), particularly when the garden is adjacent to mature woodland. The birds are adept at removing peanuts from feeders and taking them to the nearest tree to be eaten.

Studies of Nuthatches in Scandinavia have shown that they establish territories in the autumn which are maintained through the winter (Nilsson 1976). In the beech woods under study, the size of these territories was related to the abundance of the mast crop in autumn (Enoksson and Nilsson 1983). In years with a good mast the territories were significantly smaller than in poor years. It is probable that similar behaviour occurs in this country although, because of our warmer winters, our Nuthatches are likely to be more catholic in their diet.

The Nuthatch is extremely sedentary. In the history of the BTO ringing scheme there have been only two ringing recoveries over 5 km from the ringing site: one movement of 16 km in 1963, and one of 8 km in 1974. This sedentariness is also reflected in the similarity of the breeding and winter distributions and may account for the slowness of the species to colonize new areas, or to become established in isolated woodlands. There is no evidence from ringing recoveries of any movement from the Continent or Scandinavia. The Nuthatch occurs throughout Europe but is absent from the Low Countries and extends northwards only to southern Norway and Sweden. None of these populations make regular migrations.

Assuming a British breeding population of approximately 20,000 pairs (*Breeding Atlas*) and an annual adult mortality of 50% (Nilsson 1982) which occurs largely in the late winter and in spring, an early winter population of between 60,000 and 80,000 birds seems likely.

K. W. SMITH

Total number of squares in which recorded: 1,150 (30%)

No. of birds seen in a day	Number (%) of squares		
	Britain	Ireland	TOTAL (incl. C.I.)
1–3	550 (48%)	0 (0%)	550 (48%)
4–7	390 (34%)	0 (0%)	390 (34%)
8+	210 (18%)	0 (0%)	210 (18%)

References

ENOKSSON, B. and S. G. NILSSON. 1983. Territory size and population density in relation to food supply in the Nuthatch *Sitta europaea*. *J. Anim. Ecol.* 52: 927–935.

GLUE, D. (ed.). 1982. *The Garden Bird Book*. Macmillan, London.

NILSSON, S. G. 1976. Habitat, territory size, and reproductive success in the Nuthatch *Sitta europaea*. *Ornis Scand.* 7: 179–184.

NILSSON, S. G. 1982. Seasonal variation in the survival rate of adult Nuthatches *Sitta europaea* in Sweden. *Ibis* 124: 96–100.

Breeding Atlas p 320

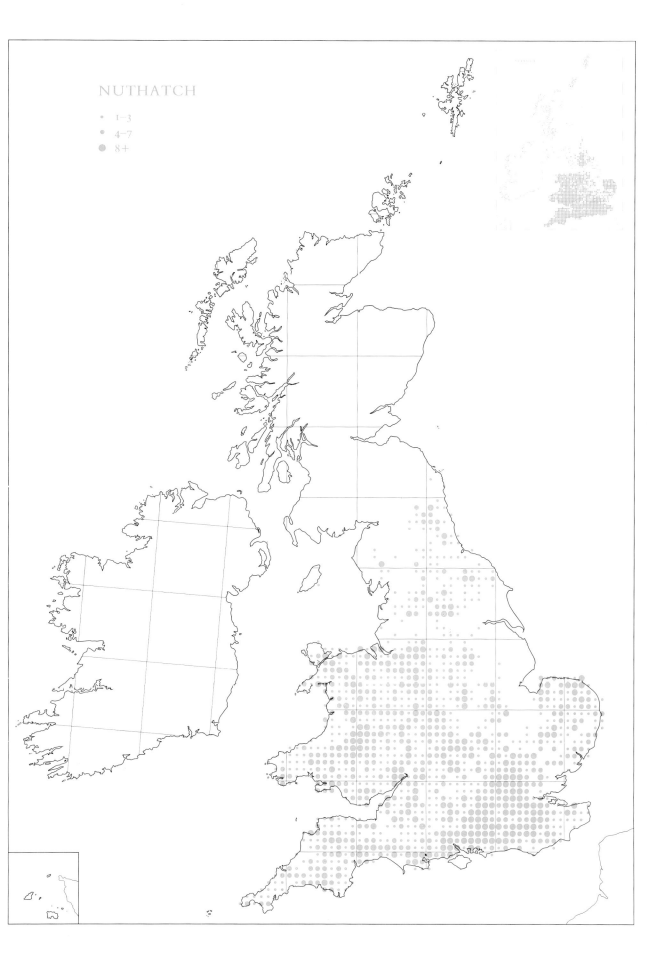

NUTHATCH

- 1–3
- 4–7
- 8+

Treecreeper

Certhia familiaris

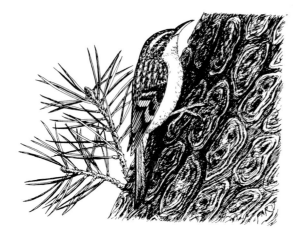

The Treecreeper is an inconspicuous bird spending much of its time climbing, mouse-like, on the trunks of trees, propped up by its relatively long, strong tail. It is effectively camouflaged by its dappled brown and black back, and its silvery-white underparts are rarely seen. Nor are the bold white wingbars, for flights tend to be brief and relatively infrequent. Thus this is an under recorded species: in summer, one prime locating feature is song, but late February would be the earliest, even in southern Britain, for this to be heard with any regularity.

The map of winter distribution falls only slightly short of that for summer in the *Breeding Atlas*. There are absences in NW Scotland, where difficulties in achieving good coverage may be a cause, and the same cause may explain the scarcity of occupied squares in the western half of Ireland. In the light of records of other species from the area, the same cannot necessarily be said of the paucity of Treecreeper records from Cornwall, which is difficult to explain as it is a mild area. Similarly interesting is the absence of evidence for any major descent from upland areas. Admittedly there are fewer occupied squares than in summer, but coverage difficulties would go a long way to explain this.

In winter, as in summer, the Treecreeper is a bird typical of deciduous or mixed woodland, found at considerably lower densities in wholly or largely coniferous stands of timber. This is in marked contrast to the situation on the Continent, where the Short-toed Treecreeper *C. brachydactyla* is primarily a bird of lowland deciduous forest, while the Treecreeper is predominantly a conifer bird. It is thought that as the ice retreated after the last Ice Age, the Treecreeper reached Britain and Ireland by accompanying the rapid northward spread of conifers. The Short-toed Treecreeper, moving north with the more slow-spreading deciduous trees, failed to reach Britain before the formation of the Channel separated England from the Continent. Subsequent climatic amelioration allowed deciduous woodland to flourish in Britain and Ireland, and the Treecreeper was able to adapt extremely well to this habitat in the absence of competition.

Though they may occasionally associate with tit flocks, in winter Treecreepers are usually to be found feeding solitarily. Their finely pointed long beaks and relatively large eyes are well adapted to seeking food—primarily small arthropods and their eggs and larvae—concealed deep in fissures in the bark. When they are feeding collectively with a range of tit species, their beaks can probe areas unreachable by the other species, thus reducing competition for scarce resources.

For roosting, most Treecreepers will seek the shelter of a crack in the timber, a natural hole, or the cavity behind a flap of bark. In areas where the American tree *Wellingtonia* is grown as a parkland ornamental, the Treecreeper has adapted fascinatingly to exploit the soft flaky bark of this alien tree, excavating in it roost cavities (shaped roughly like half a hard boiled egg), into which it retreats for the night, well camouflaged and well insulated by its fluffy flank down feathers. This habit, now apparent wherever Treecreepers and *Wellingtonias* coincide, was first noted in 1922 (Savage 1923) in Cumberland, Co. Kilkenny and Co. Down, when the comment was made that the *Wellingtonia* was introduced as recently as 1853. As it would have taken some years for these first trees to grow to a suitable size, this roosting habit evidently spread with considerable speed.

Ringing recoveries indicate that Treecreepers are among the most sedentary of birds (Flegg 1973) and there is no evidence of immigration into Britain from the Continent. Though susceptible to high mortality during cold winters, the general Treecreeper population trend in recent decades has been upwards. Allowing for under recording, the *Breeding Atlas* suggested a population of 150,000–300,000 breeding pairs: it may be that the mid winter population in Britain and Ireland now lies somewhere at or just below one million individuals.

J. J. M. FLEGG

Total number of squares in which recorded: 2,628 (68%)

No. of birds seen in a day	Number (%) of squares		
	Britain	Ireland	TOTAL (incl. C.I.)
1–2	797 (39%)	373 (65%)	1,170 (45%)
3–5	815 (40%)	148 (26%)	963 (37%)
6 +	443 (22%)	52 (9%)	495 (19%)

References

FLEGG, J. J. M. 1973. A study of Treecreepers. *Bird Study* 21: 287–302.

SAVAGE, E. V. 1923. Roosting habit of the Treecreeper. *Brit. Birds* 16: 217.

Breeding Atlas p 322

TREECREEPER

- · 1–2
- • 3–5
- ● 6+

Great Grey Shrike

Lanius excubitor

Dramatic in appearance (appropriate winter tones of grey, black, and white), attention catching in its bearing (its sentinel stance usually dominating an otherwise inanimate scene), and nowhere too familiar, the Great Grey Shrike is the highlight of many a winter day's birding.

Although Great Grey Shrikes are traditionally described as wintering in Scotland and on the east coast of England, the distribution map shows the species to be evenly distributed throughout Britain in winter. There was one record in Ireland. This is perhaps initially surprising considering the northeasterly origins of the Scandinavian breeding birds. But the species is known to be strongly territorial, both in its breeding and its winter quarters, and birds arriving together on the east coast will soon scatter, each to find its own territory from which other Great Grey Shrikes will be driven off. A wintering Great Grey Shrike demands a very large territory—in Sweden about 5–10 Red-backed Shrikes *Lanius collurio* nest within the area of one Great Grey Shrike's winter territory—and this leads to an even distribution.

A typical wintering habitat must include good hunting areas, plenty of hunting posts, and good cover in case of danger. In the days when the Red-backed Shrike was a common British breeding bird, it was noticeable how many breeding territories of this species were occupied by Great Grey Shrikes in winter. (This situation still holds true in Sweden.) It is tempting to correlate the distribution pattern for England with that for lowland heath, for which the Red-backed Shrike was selected as a particularly typical bird in the *Breeding Atlas*. It is not surprising that two related species employing similar hunting tactics should seek out the same habitat. The sit-and-wait method demands suitable and well-dispersed hunting perches. In winter, deciduous trees afford a better field of vision and consequently are preferred to conifers (even in Sweden where conifers are much more abundant). The height of perches used depends on the size of the prey hunted. Interestingly, Olsson (1984) found that although willow bushes were little used as hunting posts (6.4%), they dominated as special butchering sites (49%), a figure greatly exceeding their proportion in the territories. Junipers, however, were favoured as roosting sites.

On first arriving on their winter territories, providing the weather is still mild enough for insects to be on the wing, Great Grey Shrikes may continue to hunt flying insects as in summer. Most invertebrates, however, are spotted from a perch and caught on the ground, being seized with the bill. Rodents and shrews are also hunted by sit-and-wait tactics, Great Grey Shrikes having been observed to spot field voles at distances of 250 m. Hunting success is much higher with smaller mammals than with birds, but the more severe the winter the higher the proportion of birds in the diet, reflecting both the reduced availability of small rodents with increasing snow cover and an increased vulnerability of small passerines as feeding becomes more difficult.

With such critical territorial demands, and to maximise hunting success by thoroughly exploiting a familiar habitat, it is not surprising that individuals stay on a winter territory, even returning to the same area for several winters in succession. This, together with the fact that shrikes are frequently very obvious, even from a distance, probably means that most individuals in Britain have been logged. Allowing for the fact that the map may include some duplication of birds on the move at the beginning and end of winter, and that in the years under review Great Grey Shrikes were noticeably more scarce in many of their traditional haunts, the winter population probably exceeds 150 individuals. (The estimated winter population in Sweden is 3.7 per 100 km².)

Yearly fluctuations mainly result from annual differences in breeding performance and summer survival (related to the supply of small rodents). The Great Grey Shrike may, however, be polymorphic in its migratory tendencies (in mild winters more birds wintering further north may survive; in hard winters individuals wintering in the south may be favoured). And Britain, along with Belgium and western Germany, may provide, for the Scandinavian breeding population, a significant alternative to the harsher conditions in the more important wintering areas in south central Sweden.

B. BLAND

Total number of squares in which recorded: 239 (6%)

No. of birds seen in a day	Number (%) of squares		
	Britain	Ireland	TOTAL (incl. C.I.)
1	228 (96%)	1 (100%)	229 (96%)
2	10 (4%)	0 (0%)	10 (4%)

References

OLSSON, V. 1981. Migration and wintering area of the Great Grey Shrike *Lanius excubitor*. *Vår Fågelvärld* 40: 447–454.

OLSSON, V. 1984. [The winter habits of the Great Grey Shrike *Lanius excubitor*]. *Vår Fågelvärld* 43: 113–124, 199–210, 405–414.

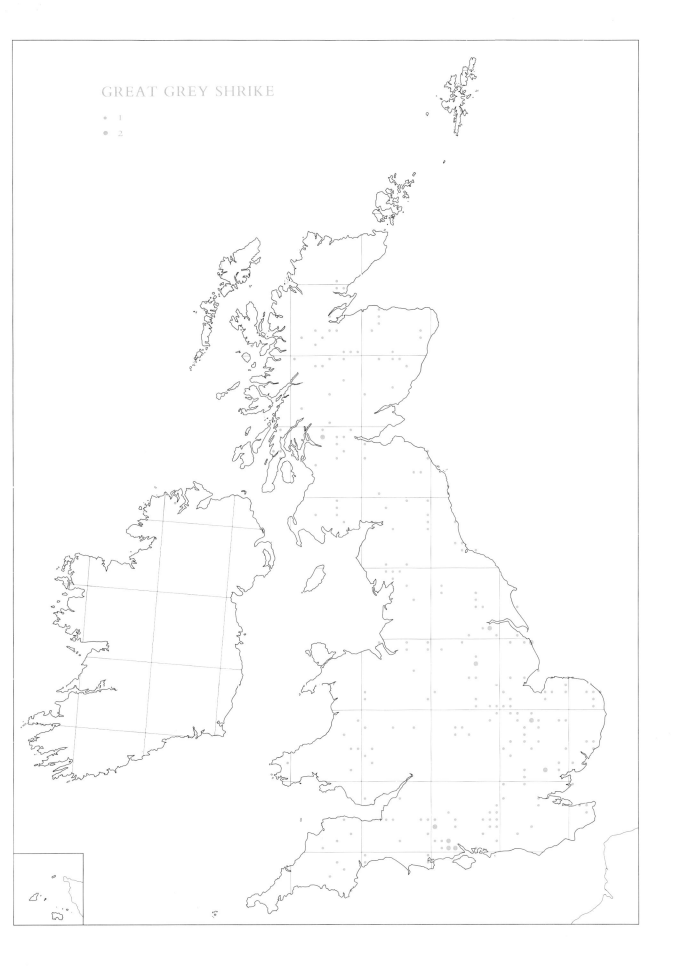

GREAT GREY SHRIKE

- 1
- 2

Jay

Garrulus glandarius

The shy and wary Jay is often located by its raucous call note or by a glimpse of its disappearing white rump. Essentially a woodland bird and the most arboreal of the Corvidae, the Jay shows a strong reluctance to forage in open habitats.

The distribution of the Jay in winter closely resembles its summer range as shown in the *Breeding Atlas*. Common throughout most of England and Wales, it is found north to Argyll and Perthshire, and in Aberdeenshire where it appears to have spread since 1972. It is scarce or absent from central Scotland, the Isle of Man, the northern Pennines, and much of the east coast from Flamborough Head to the Wash, including fenland south of the Wash. The separate race in Ireland, although widely distributed and increasing, is less numerous than in England and Wales and absent or very scarce in W and NW areas.

Throughout the year, Jays are widespread, and in places common, both in deciduous (especially oak) and coniferous woodlands. They are usually found in the more open types of woods with a thick shrub layer. They also occur in orchards, parkland and even in towns where there is adequate tree cover. Results from the Garden Bird Feeding Survey show that Jays are regularly seen in gardens, particularly rural ones, in winter, often visiting early in the morning.

Bossema (1979) showed that acorns are the staple food of Jays in winter, and described the close relationship between Jays and acorns, especially those of the pedunculate oak. During autumn, Jays store large amounts of acorns (several thousand per bird), as well as some hazel and beech nuts, by burying them in the ground. They appear to be able to relocate a high proportion of the stored food, even under the snow, probably using visual clues (*eg* saplings) noted when burying it. Bossema concluded that Jays play an important part in the dispersal of acorns and thus in the spreading of oakwoods.

The winter diet of Jays also includes cereal grains, sweet chestnuts, and invertebrates, especially beetles and earwigs. They are adaptable birds and will feed on peanuts, bread and scraps put out in gardens.

Under normal conditions British Jays are very sedentary, few moving more than 10 km. Results from ringing recoveries showed that between 1972 and 1981, 98% of Jays moved less than 50 km (Mead and Hudson 1984). However, the autumn of 1983 brought huge movements of Jays to southern and eastern England (John and Roskell 1985). For instance, over 3,000 Jays were counted passing west over Plymouth on 17 October 1983. Similar large numbers were seen elsewhere along the south and southeast coasts. Although these flocks had largely disappeared or dispersed by early November, slightly more Jays were recorded in the 1983/84 winter than in the previous two. It is believed that these movements were caused by a widespread and severe failure of the 1983 acorn crop in Britain and on the Continent. Clearly, Jays were unusually mobile in the 1983/84 winter; from October 1983 to May 1984 18% of the ringed Jays recovered had moved more than 50 km.

Numbers of Jays in Britain and Ireland have been increasing steadily during this century, especially since the 1940s. The spread has probably been assisted by a substantial decrease in the number of gamekeepers, as well as by increased afforestation. The dramatic irruption witnessed in autumn 1983 could well reflect the present high population level. Jays in northern Europe, some of which are partial migrants, may irrupt into western Europe if food is scarce. There are occasional influxes into SE England of presumed Continental birds—Jays have been seen flying in from the sea at several east coast sites.

Results from the *Breeding Atlas* suggested a population of about 100,000 pairs. Jays are single-brooded and usually raise 2–4 young (Goodwin 1976). Allowing for about half of these dying before the end of the year (many of which are shot) and taking into account the continued increase of the species, the December population for Britain and Ireland seems likely to be 350,000–400,000 birds.

A. JOHN

Total number of squares in which recorded: 2,037 (53%)

No. of birds seen in a day	Number (%) of squares		
	Britain	Ireland	TOTAL (incl. C.I.)
1–5	816 (47%)	258 (93%)	1,075 (53%)
6–10	518 (29%)	18 (6%)	536 (26%)
11 +	422 (24%)	3 (1%)	426 (21%)

References

BOSSEMA, L. 1979. Jays and oaks: an eco-ethological study of a symbiosis. *Behaviour* 70: 1–117.

GOODWIN, D. 1976. *Crows of the World.* Brit. Mus. (Nat. Hist.), London.

JOHN, A. W. G. and J. ROSKELL. 1985. Jay movements in autumn 1983. *Brit. Birds* 78: 611–637.

MEAD, C. J. and R. HUDSON. 1984. Report on bird-ringing for 1983. *Ringing and Migration* 5: 153–192.

Breeding Atlas p 302

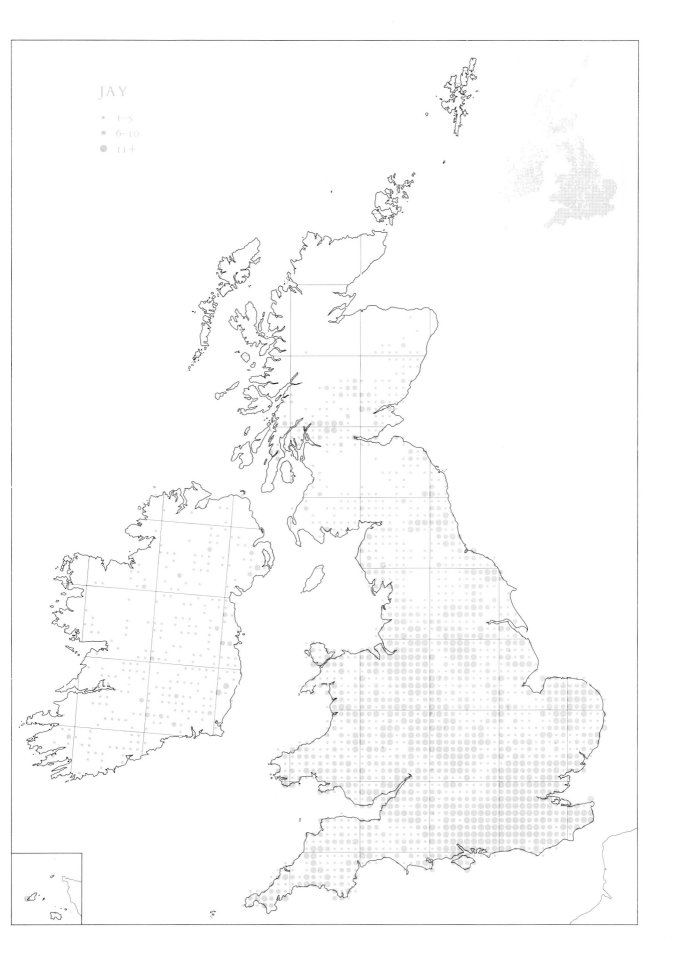

JAY

- 1—5
- 6—10
- 11+

Magpie

Pica pica

The Magpie is unmistakable: its plumage, voice and behaviour are all extrovert and during the winter months groups of up to a hundred individuals may be encountered almost anywhere, though it is patchy in Scotland and absent in the northwest.

This species is non-migratory and remarkably sedentary in Britain and Ireland, and there is no influx of Continental birds in winter. As a consequence its winter and summer distributions are almost identical. Adult Magpies tend to remain in their territories throughout the year, and if they change territory they rarely move more than 0.5 km. Immature Magpies (*ie*, up to 2 years old) spend most of their time as part of a loose flock, usually within 1 km of their natal nest. Of British Magpies ringed as chicks, 80% were recovered within 5 km of the nest. In a colour marked rural population near Sheffield the mean distance between a Magpie's natal nest and its own first breeding territory was 0.45 km, with no difference between the sexes (Clarkson 1984).

Magpies occur in a wide range of habitats, but are most abundant on grazed pasture with a few bushes and trees. Their spread into suburban and urban areas reflects their marked population increase in many parts of the country over the last 30 years (Prestt 1965, Clarkson 1984).

The Magpie is an omnivore, but with a seasonal change in diet (Tatner 1983). In summer most food consists of animal material (mainly terrestrial invertebrates). In winter the diet is vegetarian, but throughout the year small mammals are occasionally caught and eaten. An important aspect of the Magpie's winter feeding ecology is its habit of food hoarding. Caches are made in the ground; the bird carries food in a sublingual pouch, makes a small hole in the ground with its bill, regurgitates the food into the hole and then covers it up. These caches are remarkably difficult for the human eye to locate. Magpies may make 50 or so caches in a day, and items are usually recovered within 24–48 hours.

Magpies are usually monogamous and the pair remain together throughout the year. Although egg-laying does not occur until late March or April, some pairs start nest-building in mid winter, on bright sunny mornings in late December and early January.

Winter and early spring is the time when large groups of Magpies can be seen. Sometimes 20–30 birds congregate temporarily at a food source, or to mob a predator such as a fox or cat. Even larger groups occur in pre-roost assemblies and at the so-called ceremonial gatherings. Adult Magpies roost within their territories but immatures may roost either in small groups within their normal home range or, in winter, may form a large communal roost. Pre-roost assemblies typically occur with large roosts. From mid afternoon birds congregate in open areas adjacent to the roost, which may be in hawthorns or willows over water. The sight of 100 or more Magpies in a single bush is reminiscent of an over-laden Christmas tree! These birds return to their home ranges next morning with no post-roost assembly.

Ceremonial gatherings start to occur in December and reach their peak in April, just prior to the breeding season. They usually consist of 8–10 birds, although there are large spectacular gatherings of up to 50 birds. Gatherings occur on the ground or in trees—the birds noisily chasing each other. The function of these gatherings has been the cause of much speculation. Recent studies of colour marked Magpies have shown that gatherings represent different stages in territory acquisition by immature birds, including taking a territory by force. Gatherings are started by a few immature birds which are attacked and chased by territory owners. The commotion rapidly attracts other Magpies (adults and immatures), which join the gathering as spectators! (Birkhead and Clarkson 1985).

Because the Magpie is sedentary the mid winter and breeding season populations are probably very similar, *ie* 250,000–500,000 pairs in Britain and Ireland.

T. BIRKHEAD

Total number of squares in which recorded: 2,886 (75%)

No. of birds seen in a day	Number (%) of squares		
	Britain	Ireland	TOTAL (incl. C.I.)
1–20	859 (45%)	564 (58%)	1,425 (49%)
21–43	602 (32%)	285 (29%)	887 (31%)
44 +	448 (23%)	124 (13%)	574 (20%)

References

BIRKHEAD, T. R. and K. CLARKSON. 1985. Ceremonial gatherings of the Magpie *Pica pica*: territory probing and acquisition. *Behaviour* 94: 324–332.

CLARKSON, K. 1984. *The Breeding and Feeding Ecology of the Magpie* Pica pica. Ph.D. Thesis, University of Sheffield.

PRESTT, I. 1965. An enquiry into the recent breeding status of some smaller birds of prey and crows in Britain. *Bird Study* 12: 196–221.

TATNER, P. 1983. The diet of urban Magpies *Pica pica*. *Ibis* 125: 90–107.

Breeding Atlas p 300

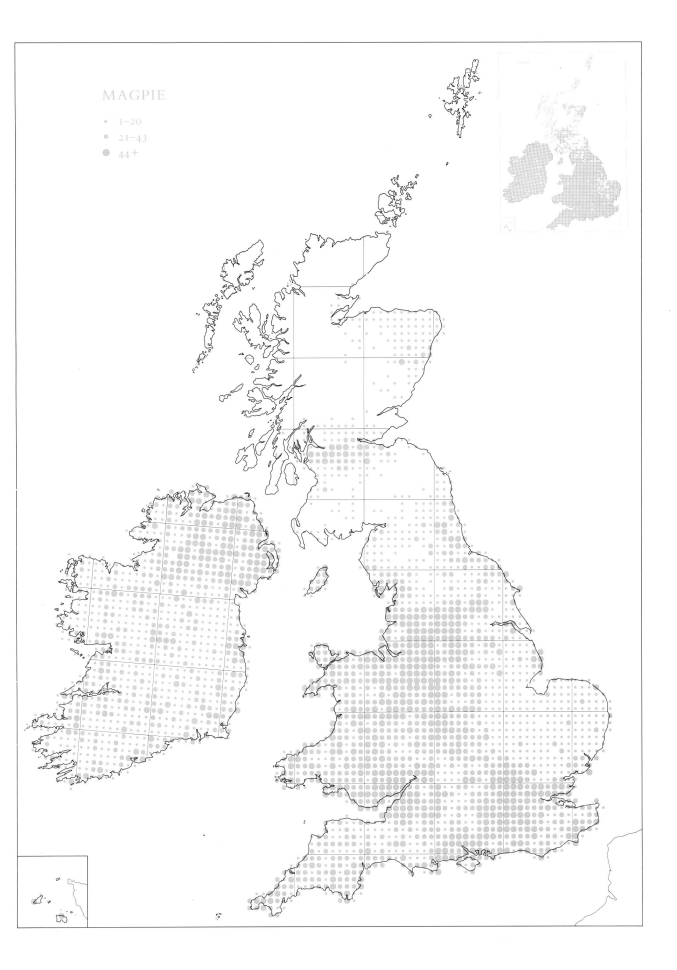

MAGPIE

- 1—20
- 21—43
- 44+

Chough

Pyrrhocorax pyrrhocorax

When the grey Atlantic rollers break against the cliffs, driving spray hundreds of metres into the air, and most birds have abandoned the western coasts, the Chough remains, tumbling above the windy headlands or feeding in busy parties on the clifftops where sheep and salt spray keep the turf short.

The *Winter Atlas* reflects the close link between the Chough and the Atlantic seaboard. It is difficult to escape the conclusion that its unique distribution reflects those areas where the winters are milder. The maritime climate is an insurance against snow and ice. Choughs must dig for their food; when the ground freezes, they starve. In Ireland many Choughs were said to have perished in the severe frosts of 1916/17 and 1962/63. In the latter winter, Choughs were seen in the suburban gardens of coastal towns, having been forced off the cliffs by snow and ice. Unlike most other native crow species, which suffer their highest mortality in the spring, most Choughs die in the hard winter months, February especially. The Choughs' range also matches the traditional livestock husbandry and pasture management of the west coast. Agricultural improvements in the 1800s may have forced it off the southern coasts of England; changing land use remains its most serious threat, destroying the soil invertebrate communities on which it relies and perhaps bringing it into more direct conflict with the Rook *Corvus frugilegus* and the Jackdaw *C. monedula*.

Choughs inhabit the narrow strip of coastal terrain, rarely wandering more than a kilometre inland. Those Choughs that breed in mountain sheep walks are the only exception to this. To what extent these few mountain pairs (confined mainly to Snowdonia and the mountain areas of Mayo, Cork and Kerry) move to the coast in winter is unknown. On the coast, Choughs are to be found either in maritime heathland or unimproved permanent pasture. Areas with short springy turf in rocky terrain seem particularly favoured, where the soils are too thin to cultivate and where sheep have grazed for centuries. In Scotland, heavily-grazed sheep and cattle pastures are the most important in all seasons (Warnes 1982).

These traditional pastures, rarely ploughed or reseeded, are rich in fly and beetle larvae on which the Chough depends. It digs for its food, probing the root mat for leatherjackets, digging bare soil and peat for beetle grubs, or hacking open cow pats for scarab larvae. Winter studies show that it avoids arable ground and improved pasture, the domain of Rook and Jackdaw. It will feed to some extent in stubbles, taking barley and oats from the surface, but this resource is mainly used in colder weather or just prior to roosting. In the extensive dune systems of Ireland and Scotland, where pasture exists, large flocks congregate, occasionally upwards of 100 birds. They feed busily on the thin sandy turf, digging for the larvae of chafer beetles. Here they also use the shoreline to feed, excavating small sand cliffs for sandhoppers or rotting seaweed for kelp fly maggots.

Apart from small scale local movements, breeding pairs rarely stray far from their breeding areas. Colour ringing of birds on Bardsey Island, N Wales, reveals a regular dispersal of young birds in August and September. The majority only move locally, returning at irregular intervals to their natal site. Occasionally there are very distant movements; the Shetland bird must have travelled at least 570 km from Islay, and sightings on the east coast of England are 210 km from the nearest breeding population on the Isle of Man (P. Roberts). The mapped record on the east coast of Ireland was almost certainly a Welsh bird blown across the Irish Sea by easterly gales.

A survey in 1982 suggested a combined British and Irish population of around 1,000 pairs (Bullock *et al* 1983). For every breeding pair there is at least one non-breeder (*ie* another 1,000 birds). Assuming 2 young per pair, of which only one may survive the first winter, we would expect an October population of 5,000 individuals and a total March population of 3,000 individuals. The British and Irish population appears to be stable, though the impression in France, Spain and Italy is that populations are declining.

I. D. BULLOCK

Total number of squares in which recorded: 243 (6%)

No. of birds seen in a day	Number (%) of squares		
	Britain	Ireland	TOTAL (incl. C.I.)
1–4	49 (56%)	86 (55%)	135 (56%)
5–11	21 (24%)	39 (25%)	60 (25%)
12 +	17 (20%)	31 (20%)	48 (20%)

References

BULLOCK, I. D., D. R. DREWETT and S. P. MICKLEBURGH. 1983. The Chough in Britain and Ireland. *Brit. Birds* 76: 377–401.

ROBERTS, P. 1985. The Choughs of Bardsey. *Brit. Birds* 78: 217–232.

ROLFE, R. 1966. The status of the Chough in the British Isles. *Bird Study* 13: 221–236.

WARNES, J. M. 1982. *The Ecology of the Chough on the Isle of Islay.* Unpub. report. Univ. Stirling/Islay Museums Trust.

Breeding Atlas p 304

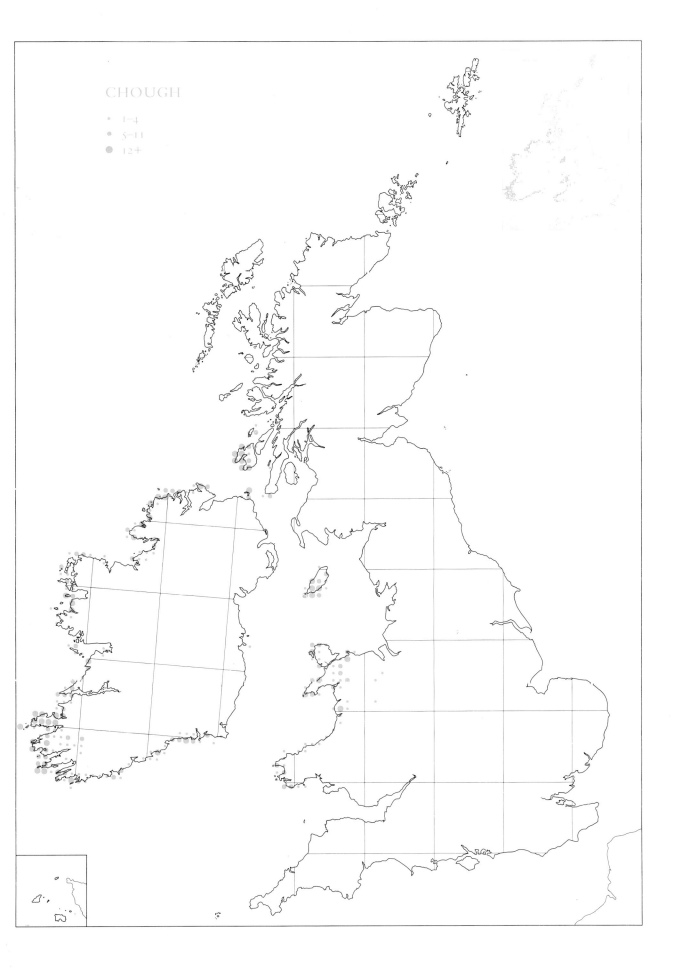

CHOUGH

- 1–4
- 5–11
- 12+

Jackdaw

Corvus monedula

These lively little crows brighten up the dullest of winter flocks with their jaunty walk and beady eyes; seen amongst a flock of Rooks *C. frugilegus* they look for all the world like high spirited schoolboys darting about among their staid schoolmasters. In the great aerial gatherings that attend their winter roosts, their sharp metallic cries sound like exploding firecrackers as they wheel and jostle in the dusk.

The winter map shows that Jackdaws occur throughout Britain and Ireland, though with some seasonal changes. There is a withdrawal from the bleaker uplands, for example the southern uplands of Scotland and the Donegal mountains in Ireland. There is a western bias in numbers, and large flocks occur in the sheepwalks of the downs and N and S Wales. Many Jackdaws cross to the milder weather and abundant pastures of Ireland.

Jackdaws feed in stubbles and freshly ploughed ground, but the great winter flocks mixed with Rooks are seen most often in pasture, particularly where grazed by sheep or cattle. The flock moves steadily over the ground, the Rooks probing deep for earthworms or leatherjackets, the Jackdaws flicking over cow pats or occasionally jumping in the air to catch dung flies. It is in winter that the food differences between the corvids become most clear-cut: Jackdaws take smaller surface prey, such as weevils and small snails, whereas Rooks dig below the ground. Jackdaws use a wider variety of grassy habitats than Rooks, searching both short and long grass for moths, spiders, beetles and flies. They will also eat weed seeds or grain (Lockie 1955). Of all the corvids they are the most likely to feed on rubbish tips; their agility and familiarity with human routine makes them the most suburban of the crows, which must stand them in good stead in severe weather. When the ground freezes, Jackdaws scavenge around farms and towns, whereas Magpies *Pica pica* and Crows *C. corone* move into the woods. This is further indication that ancestrally the Jackdaw is a bird of open grassland rather than woodland (Lockie 1955).

The pattern of roosting varies, but in general, as winter advances, more birds leave their breeding colonies to join a central roost. At this time cliff colonies tend to move inland to woodland roosts. These major roosts typically combine Jackdaws and Rooks, and occasionally also Carrion Crows, Ravens *C. corax* and Hooded Crows in Ireland (Coombs 1978). Birds wheel excitedly, chattering and cawing as dusk advances; when they finally settle there are often Jackdaws in one group of trees, Rooks in another.

There is an autumn dispersal of young birds as with other corvids; non-breeders are more likely to move away in their first and second winters (Holyoak 1971). A significant winter migration also occurs. First there is a local exodus in September and October. British birds appear to move west and south: Jackdaws ringed in Wexford in November and December have been recovered in summer in Cumbria and Wales. In October and November, Continental birds arrive on the east and south coasts. Jackdaws ringed in Norway, Sweden and Denmark are known to winter in the Low Countries and to a lesser extent in Britain. Return passage is from late March (Dungeness) to early May (Scillies).

There is some evidence that Jackdaws declined in East Anglia in the 1960s with a fall in the acreage of grass leys (Tapper 1981), whereas in parts of the west they have increased (for example colonising Irish offshore islands where they were absent in the early 1960s). The Common Birds Census index shows a net increase in the last ten years. Taking the *Breeding Atlas* estimate of 500,000 pairs, plus a probable 30% non-breeders in spring, plus 2 fledged young surviving to the winter, there may be a resident winter population in Britain and Ireland in the order of 3 million birds, swelled by an unknown number of Continental Jackdaws.

I. D. BULLOCK

Total number of squares in which recorded: 3,269 (85%)

No. of birds seen in a day	Number (%) of squares		
	Britain	Ireland	TOTAL (incl. C.I.)
1–152	1,128 (49%)	502 (53%)	1,633 (50%)
153–399	676 (29%)	305 (32%)	981 (30%)
400 +	508 (22%)	147 (15%)	655 (20%)

References

COOMBS, C. J. F. 1978. *The Crows—A Study of the Corvids of Europe*. Batsford, London.

GOODWIN, D. 1976. *Crows of the World*. Brit. Mus. (Nat. Hist.), London.

HOLYOAK, D. T. 1971. Movements and mortality of Corvidae. *Bird Study* 18: 97–106.

LOCKIE, J. D. 1955. The breeding and feeding of Jackdaws and Rooks, with notes on Carrion Crow and other Corvidae. *Ibis* 97: 341–369.

TAPPER, S. C. 1981. The effects of farming and Dutch Elm disease on Corvids. *Game Conservancy Ann. Rev.* No. 12.

Breeding Atlas p 298

JACKDAW

- · 1–152
- ● 153–399
- ● 400+

Rook

Corvus frugilegus

The Rook occurs throughout Europe and Asia and is extremely common at the northwest of its range, here in Britain and Ireland (Goodwin 1976). Its conspicuous and noisy gregarious activities make it a very familiar farmland bird throughout the year.

The map shows a widespread winter distribution that corresponds closely with the breeding distribution (*Breeding Atlas*, BTO rookeries surveys of 1975 (Sage and Vernon 1978) and 1980 (Sage and Whittington 1985)). In general, Rooks are confined to agricultural land below 300 m and, as in the breeding season, the highest densities of birds are found in Scotland, Ireland and central southern England.

In contrast to the lot of many other species, Rooks rarely suffer hardship in winter (Feare *et al* 1974). Food is plentiful and widely distributed. Flocks of Rooks are able to exploit patches of food in a highly efficient manner by feeding faster and spending less time on the lookout for predators. Rooks depend on farmland for their food, preferring mixed regimes where pasture and arable crops are almost equally distributed (A. Brenchley). They are omnivorous, and in winter feed on seeds, waste root crops and invertebrates.

Rooks generally occupy communal roosts in winter, sharing sites with Jackdaws *C. monedula*, Carrion Crows *C. corone* and other corvids where present. These roosts are usually traditional sites, often a large rookery, and birds from neighbouring rookeries travel distances of up to 20 km to roost (Patterson *et al* 1971, Coombs 1978). Roost sizes range from a few hundred to 65,000 Rooks, as recorded in NE Scotland (Patterson *et al* 1971), and these usually reflect the density of breeding Rooks within the 'catchment area' of each roost. However, the size of this 'catchment area' probably varies in relation to food abundance and/or distribution. Five large counts (over 10,000 individuals per day) were recorded in regions of low breeding density (Derbyshire, Hampshire, Lincolnshire, Perthshire and S Yorkshire) which may indicate that the distance travelled to feed or to roost may exceed 20 km. Rooks travel by well defined flight lines to reach the roost before dark, often stopping at certain pre-roost assemblies. Once the Rooks begin to congregate they no longer feed but preen or stand inactive before the final flight into the trees. The maximum number is observed at this time or as the birds leave the roost before dawn. Communal roosting behaviour breaks down in late February as the Rooks return to their own rookeries in preparation for the breeding season.

The British and Irish Rook populations are resident and for the most part sedentary. Ringing recoveries show that 72% (299 birds, mainly adults) remained in close proximity to their site of ringing. Juveniles may disperse from their natal area in their first winter but distances of over 100 km are unusual. However, Continental birds migrate south and west in winter and Rooks, mainly from the Netherlands and Germany, have been recorded in Britain.

Nearly one million pairs of Rooks were estimated to have bred in Britain and Northern Ireland in 1975 (Sage and Vernon 1978) and a population increase of 5–7% was suggested by the results of the 1980 survey (Sage and Whittington 1985). An estimated further quarter to half million pairs breed in the Republic of Ireland. Each pair rears on average a brood of two, of which only 30–40% survive to the winter and subsequently do not usually breed until their second year. When the influx of Continental Rooks is taken into account, the wintering population is likely to exceed 4 million birds.

A. BRENCHLEY

Total number of squares in which recorded: 3,220 (83%)

No. of birds seen in a day	Number (%) of squares		
	Britain	Ireland	TOTAL (incl. C.I.)
1–339	1,065 (47%)	548 (57%)	1,614 (50%)
340–888	684 (30%)	278 (30%)	962 (30%)
889 +	517 (23%)	127 (13%)	644 (20%)

References

COOMBS, F. 1978. *The Crows—A Study of the Corvids of Europe*. Batsford, London.

FEARE, C. J., G. M. DUNNET and I. J. PATTERSON. 1974. Ecological studies of the rook *Corvus frugilegus* L. in northeast Scotland. Food intake and feeding behaviour. *J. Appl. Ecol.* 11: 867–896.

GOODWIN, D. 1976. *Crows of the World*. Brit. Mus. (Nat. Hist.), London.

PATTERSON, I. J., G. M. DUNNET and R. A. FORDHAM. 1971. Ecological studies of the rook *Corvus frugilegus* L. in northeast Scotland. Dispersion. *J. Appl. Ecol.* 8: 815–833.

SAGE, B. L. and J. D. R. VERNON. 1978. The 1975 National Survey of Rookeries. *Bird Study* 25: 64–86.

SAGE, B. L. and P. A. WHITTINGTON. 1985. The 1980 sample survey of rookeries. *Bird Study* 32: 77–81.

Breeding Atlas p 296

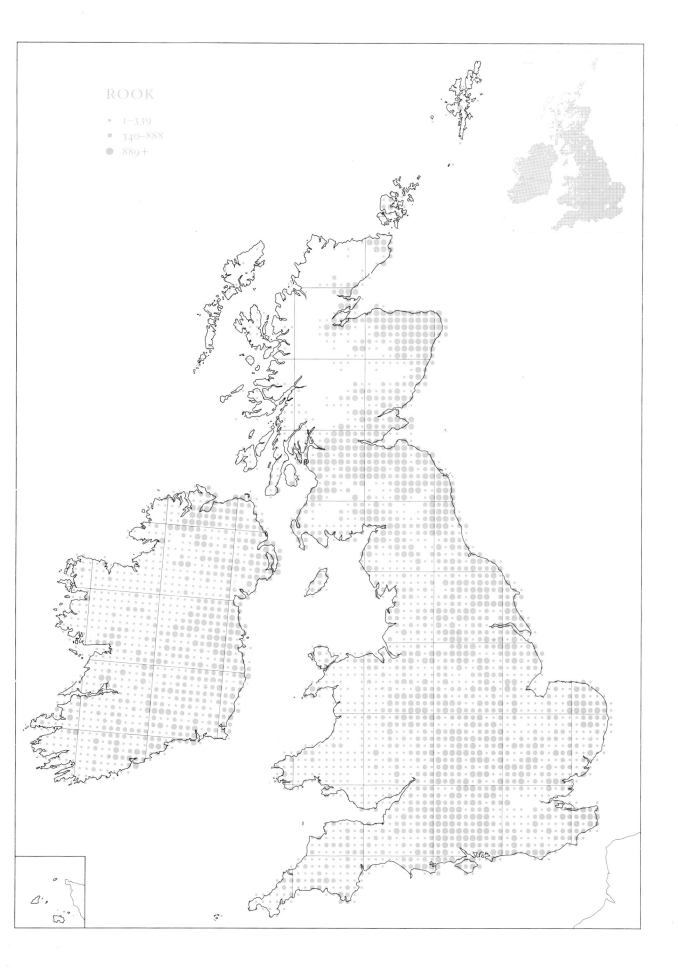

ROOK

- · 1–339
- ● 340–888
- ● 889+

Carrion Crow/ Hooded Crow

Corvus corone corone/C. c. cornix

Flocks of crows and other corvids gathering together at their evening roosts form some of the most characteristic sights and sounds of winter in the countryside.

These two crows have an extensive distribution throughout Europe and right across Asia as far as the Pacific coast. The black Carrion Crow is to be found in two quite separate parts of this range: it occurs over most of Asia in the east, and there is also a second population in far western Europe including parts of Britain. These two populations are divided by the range of the more handsome grey and black Hooded Crow, which occurs throughout northern and central Europe from the Arctic to the Mediterranean. It is generally assumed that the two colour forms of the crow evolved during the last ice age, when populations of crows became isolated for long enough to develop distinct plumages, but not for sufficient time to become reproductively isolated. They can freely interbreed, and such mixed pairs give rise to fertile offspring of intermediate colour. For this reason they are not regarded as separate species, but only as races of the same species. The hybrid zone between these populations follows an erratic course through Europe, and has changed position within historic times (see *Breeding Atlas*), but the zone is not increasing in width and so presumably the hybrids are less viable than either pure black or grey birds. Although the Carrion and Hooded Crows are so different in appearance, they are very similar in all other aspects of behaviour and general activities.

During the breeding season the distributions of Carrion and Hooded Crows in Britain are reasonably distinct, but where they meet there is a wide zone of hybridization extending approximately from Glasgow to Aberdeen. The small map on p. 374 shows the present position of this zone—see also Cook (1975) and *Breeding Atlas*. Carrion Crows are largely restricted to England and the southeastern half of Scotland. Hooded Crows are the form breeding in Ireland, the Isle of Man and the northwestern half of Scotland. The winter and summer distributions of these races show few differences. In Britain both types of crow are largely non-migratory, although

there is some short-distance dispersion of young at the end of the breeding season (Holyoak 1971) and local movements of adults. Crows from northern Europe, however, are migratory. Birds from Scandinavia, which all belong to the hooded race, are regular visitors to Britain in the winter. The maps confirm this general picture. The Carrion Crows found in Britain in winter probably almost all come from the resident British population, and their distribution is almost identical with that given in the *Breeding Atlas*. There may be some small immigration from the Carrion Crow population in Denmark and the Netherlands to account for regular sightings on Fair Isle and other Scottish islands in the north. The winter distribution of Hooded Crows, however, reflects both the resident British population and the substantial immigration of Scandinavian birds, the latter being particularly apparent down the eastern seaboard of England, although the migrants also visit Scotland in considerable numbers where they mix with flocks of the resident Hooded Crows. The hybrid crows seen in winter are mostly resident British birds and their distribution is similar to that shown in the *Breeding Atlas*. There is perhaps a higher density of these hybrids in the islands off Argyll in winter than in summer, which reflects a tendency for birds from upland areas of Scotland to move to the milder western seaboard in the winter. A small number of hybrids arrives as migrants from Europe, several dozen having been recorded from Fair Isle. The combined winter distributions of these races cover almost the entire country, making the crows one of the most widespread of all bird species in Britain in winter.

The success of the crows in achieving such a wide distribution and in occupying such a range of habitats is partly due to their catholic diet and their ability to investigate and exploit strange sources of food. Crows will eat almost any food that they can find. In winter they rely particularly on grain and other seeds in arable lowland, and in moorland areas feed largely by scavenging on carrion. They will also take a great range of vegetable foods, fruit, insects, earthworms and other invertebrates, road kills and even small birds and mammals (Coombs 1978, Holyoak 1968, Houston 1977).

Breeding birds usually remain on their territory throughout the winter, although they may regularly make short journeys further afield to good feeding sites or roosting areas. The non-breeding birds, young fledged the previous summer and migrant birds all collect together in flocks. Territory-holding birds try to prevent these flocks from invading their area, and the flocks chiefly congregate at communal feeding sites such as town rubbish dumps, sites where farm stock are being fed or along the intertidal zone on the shore. It is probably the pressure from territory-holding crows in all inland sites that causes the migrant Hooded Crows to concentrate on coastal areas. In hill farming districts Carrion and Hooded Crows are widely considered to be major pests in winter and spring, causing death or injury to trapped sheep and young lambs. Although some damage is caused it is not nearly as serious as is often suggested (Houston 1977).

In the evening the flocks collect together in com-

CARRION CROW

- · 1–48
- · 49–129
- ● 130+

References

COOK, A. 1975. Changes in the Carrion/Hooded Crow hybrid zone and the possible importance of climate. *Bird Study* 22: 165–8.

COOMBS, F. 1978. *The Crows—A Study of the Corvids of Europe*. Batsford, London.

HOLYOAK, D. 1968. A comparative study of the food of some British Corvidae. *Bird Study* 15: 147–53.

HOLYOAK, D. 1971. Movements and mortality of Corvidae. *Bird Study* 18: 97–106.

HOUSTON, D. C. 1977. The effect of Hooded Crows on hill sheep farming in Argyll, Scotland. *J. Appl. Ecol.* 14: 1–29.

Breeding Atlas p 292

munal roosts, where they are joined by many of the territory-holding birds in the neighbourhood. These winter roost sites are usually in dense woodland and, unless they are disturbed, the same sites are used every winter. Crows may roost in small groups, or collect together with the more numerous Rooks *C. frugilegus* and Jackdaws *C. monedula* (and occasionally Ravens *C. corax*) to form roosts which in some parts of the country may contain over 10,000 individuals each night.

The *Breeding Atlas* estimated about one million pairs of crows. Several breeding studies suggest that the number of young fledged varies from 1.1 to 1.7 per pair (Coombs 1978), and the heaviest mortality probably occurs in late winter. We do not know the extent to which migrant birds increase the resident population, but a figure of about 3.5 million may perhaps be reasonable for December. This must be only a small fraction of total crow numbers in Europe and Asia.

D. C. HOUSTON

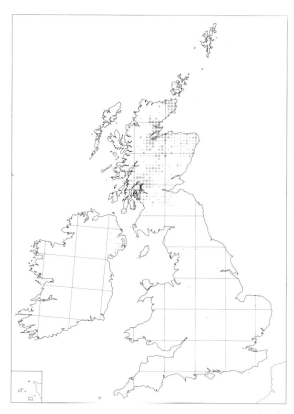

The distribution of hybrids between Carrion and Hooded races of crow. Scale of abundance as for Hooded Crow map.

CARRION CROW

Total number of squares in which recorded: 2,455 (64%)
(map on previous page)

No. of birds seen in a day	Number (%) of squares		
	Britain	Ireland	TOTAL (incl. C.I.)
1–48	1,154 (49%)	76 (94%)	1,234 (50%)
49–129	728 (31%)	2 (2%)	730 (30%)
130 +	487 (20%)	3 (4%)	491 (20%)

HOODED CROW

Total number of squares in which recorded: 1,842 (48%)

No. of birds seen in a day	Number (%) of squares		
	Britain	Ireland	TOTAL (incl. C.I.)
1–15	511 (60%)	391 (40%)	902 (49%)
16–39	178 (21%)	392 (40%)	570 (31%)
40 +	166 (19%)	204 (21%)	370 (20%)

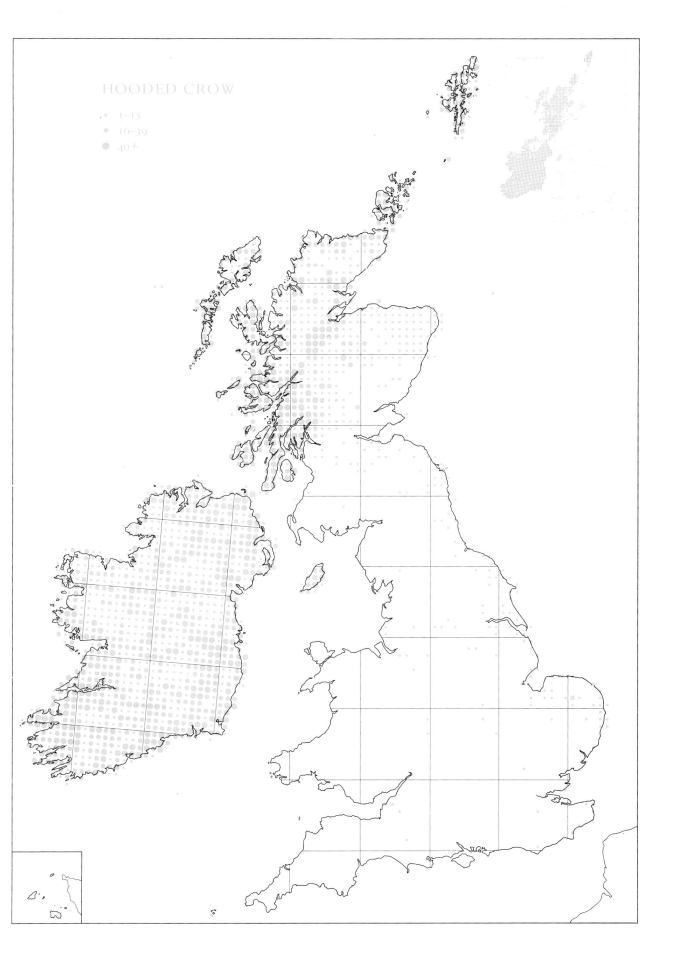

HOODED CROW

- 1–15
- 16–39
- 40+

Raven

Corvus corax

The sonorous croaks of the Raven, our largest passerine, attract attention from afar across the bleak and windswept landscapes which it favours. Yet all that can normally be seen of the species in winter, without binoculars, are some soaring and tumbling black dots against the grey clouds of otherwise empty skies.

The map shows that, in Britain, the winter distribution of the Raven is strikingly similar to the breeding range: 87% of the 10-km squares in which wintering birds were observed are also shown in the *Breeding Atlas*. The locations of the other 13% suggest a winter distribution that is no more than a marginal extension of the breeding range. With few exceptions, Ravens are confined to the west and north where they occupy upland, moorland and cliff-bound coastal habitats. They are most numerous in Devon, Wales, the Lake District, the Isle of Man and the highlands and islands of Scotland.

In Ireland, by contrast, wintering Ravens are far more widespread than the species' recorded range in the *Breeding Atlas*. This probably reflects both improved observer capacity and some expansion of range. Density, however, may be low: more than two birds were recorded in only 40% of occupied squares as compared to over 60% in Britain.

Breeding Ravens remain in or near their territories during the winter. Moreover, the breeding season starts very early, being under way in many areas by the end of February. Therefore, the winter distribution of breeding birds should be close to, if not identical to, the breeding range. The failure, in both Britain and Ireland, to observe wintering Ravens in almost a quarter of the 10-km squares where they were recorded for the *Breeding Atlas* may reflect not only an understandable observer bias against their remote habitats in winter—recoveries of ringed birds are similarly at a seasonal low in winter—but also a contraction of the breeding range. The latter is especially likely in Britain, where the total number of records on the winter map is 12% less than on the summer map, whereas in Ireland the total is 37% more.

Ravens are omnivorous, eating carrion, small live mammals, frogs, lizards, insects and even refuse, but sheep carrion forms their staple diet. In S Scotland and Northumberland a recent and substantial decline in the breeding population has been associated with the removal of sheep and the blanket afforestation of large tracts of upland sheepwalk (Marquiss *et al* 1978). Ireland's new conifer plantations are interspersed among suitable feeding habitats and, by providing nest sites, probably are contributing to an expansion of the Raven's range.

The nomadic non-breeding population comprises apparently paired birds and small flocks, but two hundred or more birds may sometimes feed and roost together. Breeding pairs normally exclude other Ravens from their territories, even in winter.

Ringing recoveries, show that, although young Ravens disperse widely through suitable habitats (Holyoak 1971), exceptionally few are reported far from established breeding areas. These recoveries also indicate that, although there is some internal movement, for instance between Scotland and N Ireland, the British and Irish population is self contained.

The *Breeding Atlas* estimated a population of some 5,000 pairs. Allin (1968) found that about 80% of nests were successful. Using this factor and an average of the mean brood sizes reported by him and Ratcliffe (1962), implies the recruitment of close to 2.3 young a year for each breeding pair, including pairs that fail. Thus 5,000 pairs give rise to a population immediately after the breeding season of 21,000. Adding non-breeding birds gives an estimated total of some 30,000. A stable population requires an annual average survival rate of about 0.6, which gives a December total of over 20,000. Taking account of a probable net decline in the number of pairs since the *Breeding Atlas*, the December total is now unlikely to exceed 20,000, or an average of almost 12 birds per occupied 10-km square for Britain and Ireland. This is a significant proportion of the European population.

G. NOONAN

Total number of squares in which recorded: 1,712 (44%)

No. of birds seen in a day	Number (%) of squares		
	Britain	Ireland	TOTAL (incl. C.I.)
1–2	440 (40%)	366 (60%)	809 (47%)
3–6	374 (34%)	186 (30%)	560 (33%)
7+	282 (26%)	60 (10%)	342 (20%)

References

ALLIN, E. K. 1968. Breeding notes on Ravens in north Wales. *Brit. Birds* 61: 541–545.

HOLYOAK, D. T. 1971. Movement and mortality of Corvidae. *Bird Study* 18: 97–106.

MARQUISS, M., I. NEWTON and D. A. RATCLIFFE. 1978. The decline of the Raven, *Corvus corax*, in relation to afforestation in southern Scotland and northern England. *J. Appl. Ecol.* 15: 129–144.

RATCLIFFE, D. A. 1962. Breeding density in the Peregrine *Falco peregrinus* and Raven *Corvus corax*. *Ibis* 104: 13–39.

Breeding Atlas p 290

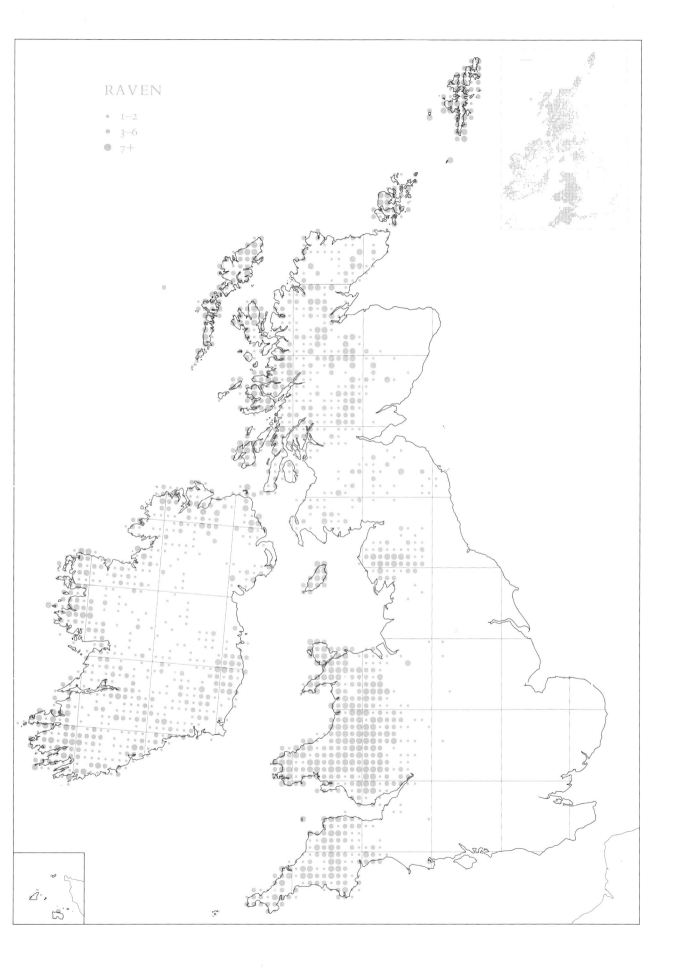

RAVEN

- 1–2
- 3–6
- 7+

Starling

Sturnus vulgaris

The Starling is one of our more familiar birds, being equally at home in rural and urban areas. One hundred and fifty years ago it was a comparatively rare bird, except in the northwest of Scotland and the Scottish islands, but since then its increase has led it to become one of our more widespread birds.

In winter, the resident British population is augmented by large numbers of immigrants from continental Europe. The winter distribution map is similar to the *Breeding Atlas* map, with Starlings occurring throughout Britain and Ireland except on higher ground in northern Scotland. There appear to be no specially favoured areas, suggesting that the immigrants disperse widely over the country. This is to be expected, since Goodacre (1959) found that birds from different European breeding areas tended to winter in different parts of Britain and Ireland.

Wintering Starlings are catholic in their selection of habitats, being found equally in the arable lands of the east and the wetter grasslands of the west. The species' winter diet is broad, encompassing grassland insects and cereal grains, and also a wide variety of other items taken from refuse tips, birdtables, sewage farms, the sea shore and elsewhere.

The sociality of Starlings is particularly apparent in winter when they feed in flocks and roost communally. During the day, most feeding flocks contain less than 50 birds but at particularly favoured sites, such as sewage farms and open air piggeries, flocks may comprise thousands of individuals. Winter food supplies for Starlings are generally plentiful, leaving birds time to spend much of the day loafing on elevated perches to rest, preen and sing (Feare 1984).

Towards dusk, Starlings begin their journey to the roost site. A roost may be used by birds that feed 20 km or more away and flocks heading for the roost are joined by others along the route. Near the roost, flocks can become very large, reaching their greatest size in the 'pre-roost assemblies' in which individuals may feed, bathe and preen before making a final flight into the roost site. This flight may be direct, with birds streaming towards and dropping into the roost, or it may involve impressive coordinated manoeuvres by enormous flocks. From a distance these aerial displays can resemble swirling clouds of smoke and they are one of the most spectacular sights of bird life.

At dawn, Starlings do not leave the roost in one mass; they depart in batches at intervals that average 3 minutes, radiating out over the surrounding feeding areas. These departures are visible on radar screens as expanding concentric rings and have been called 'ring angels' (Eastwood 1967). The adaptive significance of this behaviour, and even of communal roosting itself, is not understood (Feare 1984).

Starlings use a variety of sites for nocturnal roosting but, in winter, conifer plantations and evergreen shrubberies are the preferred sites. Reed beds are also used until the weight of birds destroys them, and roosts in deciduous trees are generally vacated when the leaves fall. Around the coasts, and especially on Scottish islands, Starlings roost on cliffs, and the trend of roosting on buildings in city centres, and on other structures, may be an extension of this habit.

The only estimate of the British and Irish winter Starling population is that of Potts (1967). His estimate of a minimum of 37 million was derived from densities of birds given by other authors and from the area of agricultural and urban land. Breeding populations in northern Scandinavia and Russia, whence many of our winter immigrants originate, have recently undergone marked declines that may have reduced our winter population (Feare 1984). In France, there are indications of a northerly shift of the wintering areas of many birds, thought to result from the attraction of readily available food at intensive animal rearing units in Normandy and Brittany (Gramet and Dubaille 1983); this agricultural development parallels recent trends in Britain.

C. J. FEARE

Total number of squares in which recorded: 3,469 (90%)

No. of birds seen in a day	Number (%) of squares		
	Britain	Ireland	TOTAL (incl. C.I.)
1–700	1,113 (45%)	621 (64%)	1,736 (50%)
701–2,060	796 (32%)	242 (25%)	1,040 (30%)
2,061+	589 (24%)	103 (11%)	693 (20%)

References

EASTWOOD, E. 1967. *Radar Ornithology*. Methuen, London.

FEARE, C. 1984. *The Starling*. University Press, Oxford.

GOODACRE, M. J. 1959. The origin of winter visitors to the British Isles. 4. Starling (*Sturnus vulgaris*). *Bird Study* 6: 180–192.

GRAMET, P. and E. DUBAILLE. 1983. Les nouvelles aires d'hivernage de l'étourneaux sansonnet *Sturnus vulgaris* sur la façade maritime ouest, étudiées en fonction de l'évolution agronomique. *Academie d'Agriculture de France; Extrait du Seance du 13 Avril*, pp 455–464.

POTTS, G. R. 1967. Urban Starling roosts in the British Isles. *Bird Study* 14: 25–42.

Breeding Atlas p 408

STARLING

· 1–700
· 701–2,060
● 2,061+

House Sparrow

Passer domesticus

The House Sparrow, that ultimate bird commensal of man, is even more obvious in winter than in summer as it gathers and feeds in town parks, gardens and farmyards, in fact in any habitat occupied by human beings.

As might be expected in such a sedentary species, most individuals in Britain and Ireland live out their lives within a compass of a kilometre or two, and the winter distribution is almost exactly that of the breeding season; both closely parallel to the human population. Some dispersion of the birds of the year occurs in the autumn and again in the spring before the start of breeding. There are also indications of a movement south along the east coast of England in autumn, although this is probably a local phenomenon. The map shows a maximum density of House Sparrows in the highly populous belt of England stretching from the industrial north to the built-up southeast, and a noticeable gap in the sparsely inhabited highlands of Scotland, as well as slightly lower numbers in Wales. The population density is lower in Ireland, but the bird is still widely distributed, occurring almost throughout.

House Sparrows are immensely social. Although they nest colonially, communal behaviour is even more evident in the winter months, when almost all activities—feeding, bathing, loafing—are carried out in groups of a few birds up to large flocks. Although members of a basically seed-eating group, they are almost omnivorous, taking all kinds of kitchen scraps, raw or cooked, seeds put out for seed-eaters, and nuts for tits. They were one of the first species to copy Blue and Great Tits *Parus caeruleus* and *P. major* taking cream from milk bottles on doorsteps, and more recently they joined the increasing group of species that now hang on to nut feeders.

Perhaps the most conspicuous winter activity of the House Sparrow is to be seen in social groups that gather in trees on duller afternoons where they carry on a conversational twittering. Birds that have bred in the previous summer usually roost in the nest hole, but the birds of the year form large communal roosts in trees and hedgerows, moving into places such as ivy-covered walls when the former sites become too exposed after the leaves have fallen.

Based on sample censuses in different types of habitat in Britain, Summers-Smith (1959) estimated a breeding population of about 9.5 million House Sparrows. Similar censuses in continental Europe and the USA, suggested a ratio of House Sparrows to man of about 0.2, which would give the current breeding population of House Sparrows as 11.8 million in Britain and Ireland. In mid winter the population is about 20% higher than at the beginning of the breeding season, giving a winter population of about 14 million House Sparrows. The population probably reached a plateau in Britain in the early 1970s and since then has shown a slight decline. On this basis it is estimated that the winter population lies between 10 and 15 million birds.

The world population of House Sparrows is probably about 500 million, making it one of the most widely distributed and numerous land species in the world.

D. SUMMERS-SMITH

Total number of squares in which recorded: 3,282 (85%)

No. of birds seen in a day	Number (%) of squares		
	Britain	Ireland	TOTAL (incl. C.I.)
1–64	962 (40%)	677 (78%)	1,640 (50%)
65–220	816 (34%)	170 (20%)	988 (30%)
221+	629 (26%)	23 (3%)	654 (20%)

References

SUMMERS-SMITH, D. 1959. The House Sparrow *Passer domesticus:* population problems. *Ibis* 101: 449–454.

Breeding Atlas p 442

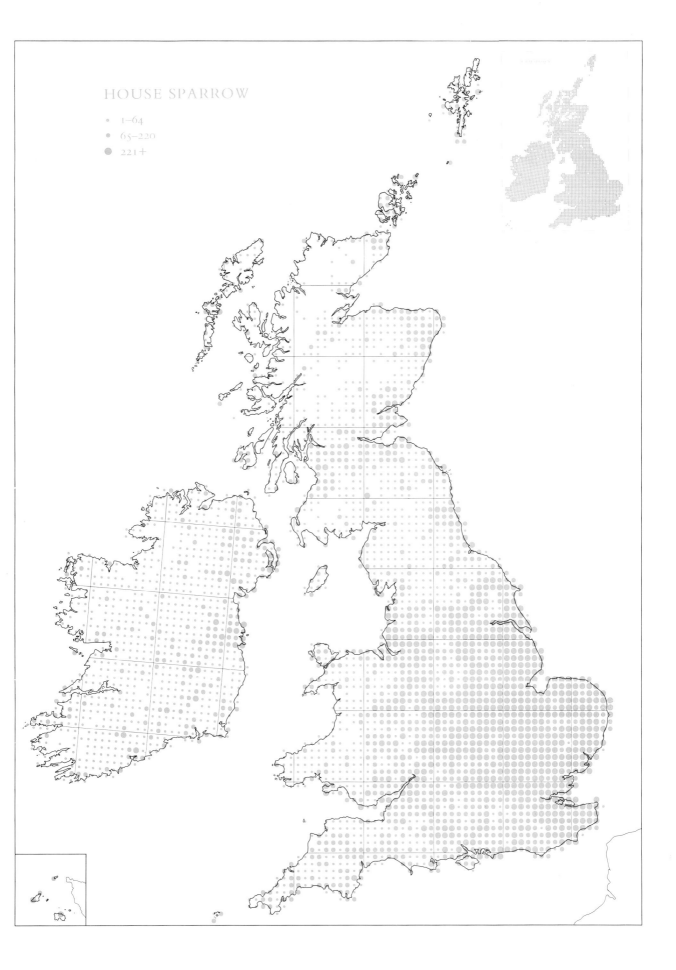

HOUSE SPARROW

- · 1–64
- ● 65–220
- ● 221+

Tree Sparrow

Passer montanus

The Tree Sparrow, that dainty relative of the much more familiar House Sparrow *P. domesticus*, is, at least in Britain and Ireland, a rather unobtrusive species. During the breeding season it is very secretive. In the winter months the bird becomes more obvious as it forms feeding flocks, often in the company of finches and buntings, in farmland and even penetrates gardens on the outskirts of towns.

The population appears to be largely sedentary. The bird, though widespread in Britain, is much less numerous than its congener and is largely lacking in the far SW of England and in W Wales. In Scotland it is mainly confined to the south and east coast lowlands. It is much less frequent in Ireland, being found mostly on the coasts, more on the east than on the west. Despite its scientific name it is generally missing from upland regions. In autumn there is a movement on the east coast. This is very variable and was more marked prior to the breeding population expansion in the 1960s, suggesting this may have been the result of immigration of birds from northern Europe. In general, however, such movement that does take place appears to be mainly of passage birds that do not boost the winter population to any significant extent.

In Britain and Ireland the history of the Tree Sparrow is a chequered one with well recorded periodic fluctuations in numbers. From a low in the 1950s, with its absence from many former haunts in England, and only sporadic breeding in Scotland apart from the southeast, a marked expansion started about 1960 so that by the time of the *Breeding Atlas* survey it was widespread in England, and had a substantial breeding range in Scotland and along the coast and around Lough Neagh in Ireland. There is some evidence, particularly from the Common Birds Census farmland results and from the ringing totals, that numbers may have decreased in the past 10 years, but this has not been detectable in a comparison of the breeding status in 1968–73 with the winter distribution in 1981–83.

The social nature of the Tree Sparrow is shown by the way flocks are formed in the winter months. These flocks, which are mostly to be found in the lower-lying agricultural land, largely reflect the size of the local breeding population, and in the regions of maximum breeding density, such as the central and south midlands of England, can contain up to several hundred birds. Although, like House Sparrows, they do feed on fallen grain, they tend rather to specialise on smaller seeds such as those of grasses and annual weeds such as goosefoot and chickweed. 'Cleaner' farming could be a factor in the reduction in numbers. At night the birds form communal roosts in thick hedgerow trees.

A breeding survey carried out by Norris (1960) in 1952, gave an estimate of 700,000 birds. The *Winter Atlas* records, combined with a mean farmland breeding density of 3.4 pairs/km², derived from the Common Birds Census results, gives a value of 820,000 birds, making 800,000 birds a likely winter population for Britain and Ireland.

In the area of overlap of range the larger, dominant House Sparrow occupies the urban role and the Tree Sparrow tends to be restricted to agricultural land, though in northern and SE Europe it shares the urban sparrow role. In Britain and Ireland the Tree Sparrow is seldom found in urban surroundings and must be regarded as a species at the limits of its range.

D. SUMMERS-SMITH

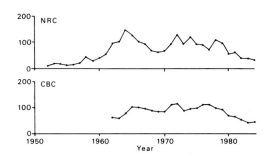

Common Birds Census and Nest Record Scheme indices of breeding numbers. 1966 = 100 in each case.

Total number of squares in which recorded: 1,537 (40%)

No. of birds seen in a day	Number (%) of squares		
	Britain	Ireland	TOTAL (incl. C.I.)
1–23	668 (48%)	101 (76%)	769 (50%)
24–70	433 (31%)	25 (19%)	458 (30%)
71+	302 (21%)	6 (5%)	308 (20%)

References

NORRIS, C. A. 1960. The breeding distribution of thirty bird species in 1952. *Bird Study* 7: 129–184.

Breeding Atlas p 444

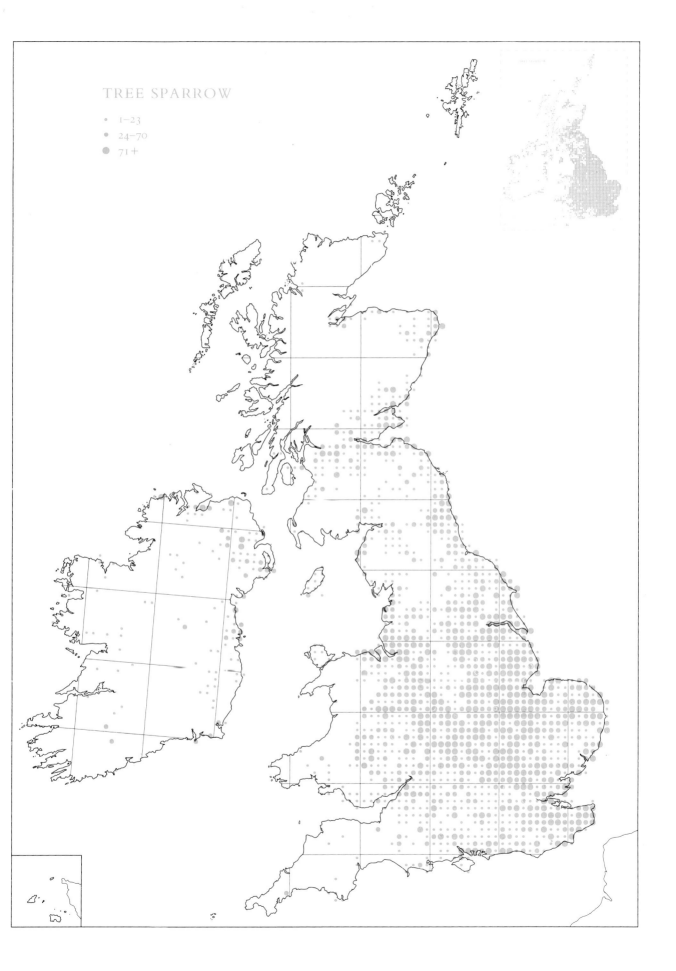

TREE SPARROW

- • 1–23
- • 24–70
- • 71+

Chaffinch

Fringilla coelebs

The Chaffinch is one of our best known British birds, becoming rather more conspicuous in winter when it often leaves its favoured woodland breeding habitat.

The distribution map shows the species to be widespread throughout most of Britain and Ireland. There are obvious gaps in some areas of high land above the tree level, mainly in the Scottish Highlands, and Chaffinches are also absent from much of the Outer Hebrides. There is a noticeably high density of wintering birds on land between about 300–800 m, covering much of Scotland and NE England, and also locally in the Welsh Marches and Dartmoor. The species is also abundant in many of the squares in central southern England which are not intensively farmed. By contrast, in Ireland there are few squares recording the highest level of abundance.

In winter the British and Irish breeding population of Chaffinches is augmented by birds from Fennoscandia and the near Continent. Resident Chaffinches are assigned to a different subspecies to the northern birds, which tend to be larger and paler. There is often a sexual difference in the migratory habits of Continental birds; indeed Linnaeus named the Chaffinch *coelebs* (bachelor) because the few birds remaining to winter in his Swedish homeland were almost all males. Ringing returns have since shown that females from Germany and Scandinavia tend to migrate further than males: in consequence there is a greater proportion of females in Chaffinch flocks in Ireland than in Britain (Newton 1972). Hard weather movements, usually to Ireland, may occur, but the Chaffinch moves much less during winter than does the Brambling *F. montifringilla*. Recovery localities of Chaffinches ringed in winter in Britain almost all lie between east and north.

Breeding Chaffinches in Britain and Ireland are normally very sedentary. Interestingly, the species is recorded in winter from many squares in Shetland, where it has rarely bred, and these are presumably Scandinavian birds, the numbers varying from one winter to another. Similarly, the species is much commoner in Orkney in winter than summer.

The British and Irish birds tend to feed in small groups in woodland or near hedgerows, whereas the Continental Chaffinches are found chiefly in large flocks in open fields (Marler 1956, Newton 1967). The immigrant birds form large communal roosts, usually in evergreens, brambles or conifer plantations, and the local birds often prefer to remain within their old territories roosting singly or in pairs.

In winter the Chaffinch's diet consists almost exclusively of small seeds which they find on the ground. They have catholic tastes, taking a wider range of seeds than any other finch, but cereal and weed seeds are the most important. They lack the specialised bill of some other finches, and cannot cope with seeds which are difficult to extract.

The Chaffinch is one of our more common breeding birds, with a population in Britain of around 5 million pairs (Hudson and Marchant 1984) and approximately 2 million in Ireland. They normally raise only one brood of 4 per year, and are one of the longer lived European passerines, with mean annual survival rates around 70% for adults and 15% for first-year birds, giving a mid winter total of some 15 million Chaffinches of British and Irish origin. The number of immigrant birds is not easily calculated, but, making reasonable assumptions about breeding density and the areas from which birds reach Britain, it seems likely that between 10 and 20 million northern Chaffinches may winter here, giving a total mid winter population for the species of around 30 million birds. This makes the Chaffinch probably the second commonest species wintering in Britain and Ireland and it is also one of the most widespread.

D. NORMAN

Total number of squares in which recorded: 3,517 (91%)

No. of birds seen in a day	Number (%) of squares		
	Britain	Ireland	TOTAL (incl. C.I.)
1–127	1,111 (44%)	648 (67%)	1,761 (50%)
128–352	818 (32%)	237 (24%)	1,056 (30%)
353+	615 (24%)	83 (9%)	700 (20%)

References

HUDSON, R. and J. H. MARCHANT. 1984. *Population Estimates for British Breeding Birds*. Unpublished report to Nature Conservancy Council, BTO, Tring.

MARLER, P. 1956. Behaviour of the Chaffinch. *Behaviour* Suppl. 5: 1–184.

NEWTON, I. 1967. The adaptive radiation and feeding ecology of some British finches. *Ibis* 109: 22–98.

NEWTON, I. 1972. *Finches*. Collins, London.

Breeding Atlas p 430

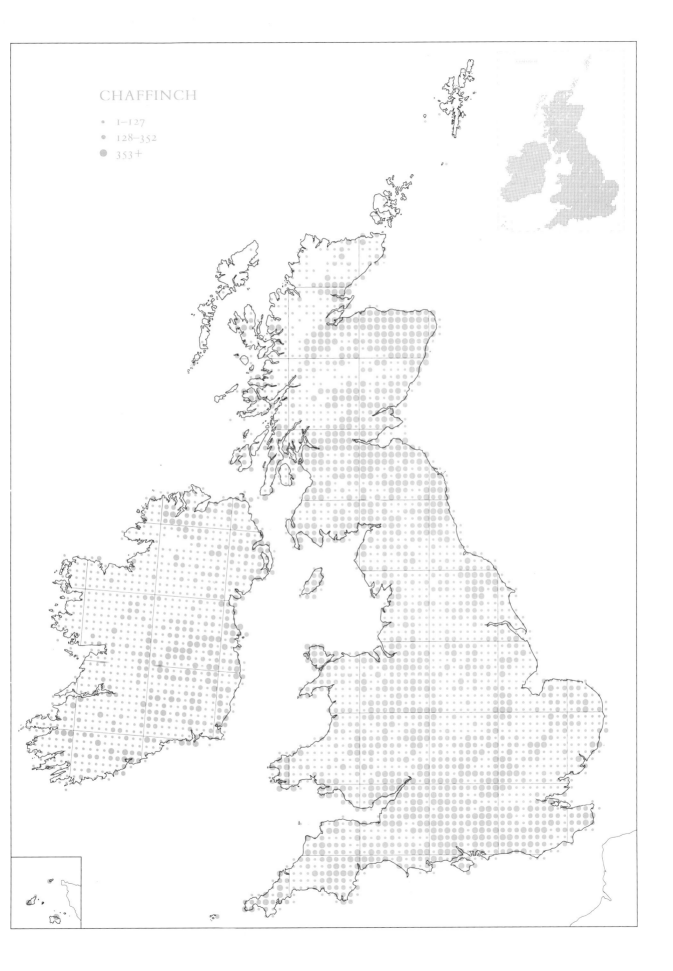

CHAFFINCH

- • 1–127
- • 128–352
- • 353+

Brambling

Fringilla montifringilla

The Brambling is a spectacularly beautiful finch, its tortoiseshell colours blending perfectly with the woodland floor where it spends much of its time.

The winter distribution of the Brambling is primarily dictated by the availability of beechmast, their favoured winter food, and they will wander all over Europe in search of an abundant supply. Since a good beech crop is irregular, the birds winter in widely differing areas from one year to another. Thus Bramblings seldom spend successive winters in the same place, and birds ringed in Britain and Ireland have been found wintering subsequently as far away as Spain, Italy and Yugoslavia.

The map shows that in winter the species is widespread but patchily distributed over most of Britain, and is distinctly scarce in Ireland. Bramblings seem to avoid the highest ground (over 800 m) but there are several local concentrations in hilly areas such as NE Scotland, parts of the Scottish Borders and N Yorkshire. It is noticeable that the species is absent from those areas where beech is not found (Perring and Walters 1962), notably the fens of E England and parts of N Scotland and W Ireland.

Outside the breeding season, when they change from their summer diet of insects, Bramblings are always found in flocks, normally ranging in size from a few birds to 500 or more. They almost invariably feed on the ground, sweeping into the tops of trees or nearby hedges when disturbed. They roost communally, often with Chaffinches *F. coelebs*. Roosts are usually in rhododendrons or young conifers, preferably with some tall trees for the pre-roost gathering. Good sites may draw birds from a large catchment area, some finches travelling several kilometres from their feeding sites. Roosts containing millions of Bramblings have been recorded on the Continent (Newton 1972) but gatherings of more than a few hundred are unusual in Britain.

Their habit of feeding on beechmast (and moving until they find it) probably enables the Brambling to reduce interspecific competition with the Chaffinch in winter, whose somewhat smaller and considerably less sharp bill cannot readily extract beech seeds. The two species are, however, often found together in winter, when they behave in all respects as if they were members of a single species. After failing to find, or exhausting supplies of beech nuts, some Bramblings occupy a wider range of habitats including, for example, sewage works (where they feed on detritus) and open fields, where they find cereal and weed seeds. They can be successful opportunistic feeders, particularly towards the end of winter, and not infrequently enter gardens, sometimes learning to hang from bags of peanuts. Large flocks have been known to feed on emergent insect larvae in early spring.

Although Bramblings have bred in Britain, they are almost exclusively winter visitors, with the majority of birds coming from Norway, Sweden and Finland, but with some individuals from as far east as the Urals. Most Bramblings vacate their breeding areas in the winter, although a good rowan crop will tempt some birds to stay in southern Finland.

Bramblings normally arrive in Britain in October or November, although they may be inconspicuous at first and may move on elsewhere in Europe. Unusually for a finch, they migrate largely at night. Food supplies can be difficult to find in periods of snow, and Bramblings readily undertake hard weather movements to the west and south.

The winter distribution maps for this species show considerable differences between the three years of the survey, as might be expected. This, and their wandering nature, makes it difficult to calculate a wintering population. British ringing totals (which include birds caught on passage as well as wintering birds) often vary by a factor of 2 or 3 in successive calendar years. In the recent well documented Brambling invasion of the Merseyside area (Norman *et al* 1981), it was estimated that 150,000 birds visited one particular roost site in a six-week period, and it is not difficult to imagine that 2,000,000 Bramblings spent part of that winter in Britain and Ireland. In some other years, by contrast, the total wintering population might be as low as 50,000 birds.

D. NORMAN

Total number of squares in which recorded: 1,811 (47%)

No. of birds seen in a day	Number (%) of squares		
	Britain	Ireland	TOTAL (incl. C.I.)
1–7	778 (48%)	126 (64%)	904 (50%)
8–40	486 (30%)	62 (31%)	548 (30%)
41+	347 (21%)	10 (5%)	359 (20%)

References

NEWTON, I. 1972. *Finches.* Collins, London.

NORMAN, D., D. CROSS and R. P. COCKBAIN. 1981. The Brambling invasion of Merseyside—1981. *BTO News* 114: 9.

PERRING, F. H. and S. M. WALTERS. 1962. *Atlas of the British Flora.* Nelson, London & Edinburgh.

Breeding Atlas p 450

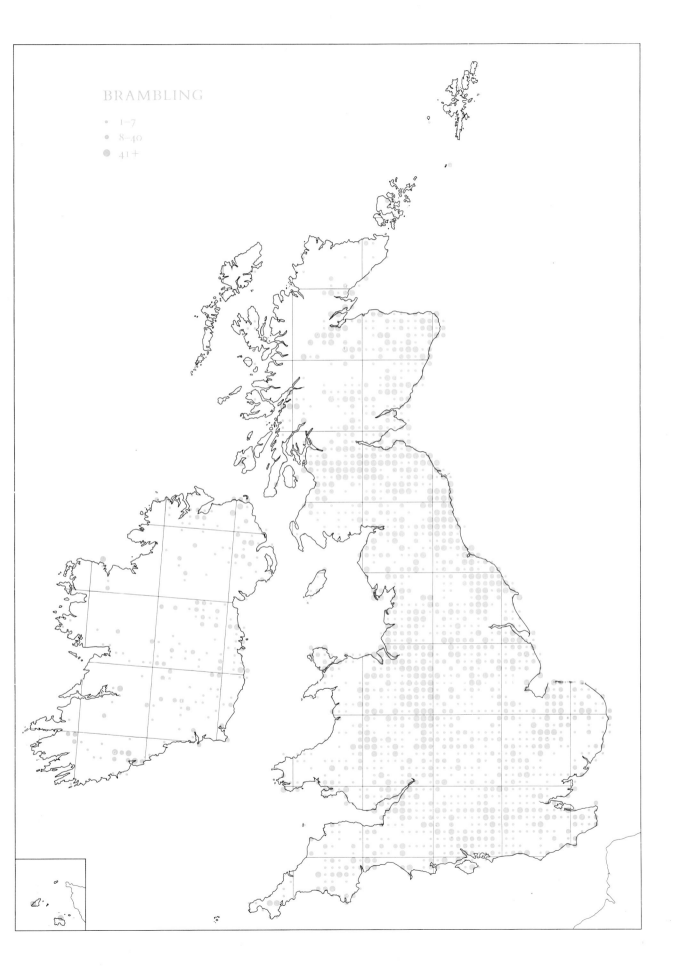

BRAMBLING

- · 1–7
- ● 8–40
- ⬤ 41+

Greenfinch

Carduelis chloris

The bulky figure of the Greenfinch is a familiar sight in winter, clinging, sometimes precariously, to the garden peanut feeder whilst driving off the smaller and more agile tits. According to the Garden Bird Feeding Survey, Greenfinches now arrive to feed at birdtables earlier each winter than they did even ten years ago (Glue 1982), either through learning and adaptation, or because of a recent annual shortfall in natural foods, perhaps due to the increased use of herbicides in agriculture.

The winter distribution of the Greenfinch, though widespread, tends to be more concentrated in lowland and coastal areas than is the breeding distribution. There is a clear association with arable farming in both Britain and Ireland, where cereal seeds and seeds of weeds which grow in brassica and sugar-beet crops (*eg* charlock, persicaria and fat-hen) provide much of their diet. Seed from unharvested or feral plants of oilseed rape is also now available in some areas. In scrub and woodland, seeds from rose-hips and brambles are commonly taken (Newton 1972); on the coast they feed on the seeds of plants growing on shingle and salt marsh (*eg*, sea rocket), or extract them from sea-buckthorn berries or rose-hips on sand dunes. Thrushes also feed on sea-buckthorn berries, ejecting the black seeds orally, or with the faeces; these may then be collected from the ground by Greenfinches (R. Spencer). Although the large bill of the Greenfinch is well adapted to take seeds of a wide size-range, there are probably too few consistently available sources of suitable seeds on most moorland and other high ground, and these areas are largely avoided.

Seed stocks are not replenished until late spring, so that Greenfinches take artificial food increasingly as the winter months pass. The number of birds in feeding flocks and communal roosts (the latter are often in rhododendron clumps) tends to increase as the food supply becomes more patchy, thus improving the chance that an isolated source of seeds will be located (Newton 1972). The Greenfinch is also a partial migrant, at least in Britain, performing southwesterly movements in the autumn and winter,

returning again the following spring (Gush 1980, Boddy and Sellers 1983).

Southward movements commence relatively late, generally in October or November, and may continue into January or even February. Many more Greenfinches breeding in eastern and central England move over 20 km, than do those from the southwestern population. The proportion of birds involved varies between areas, but may be determined by winter daylengths, mean temperatures, and long-term average food availability. High population levels, food shortages, or inclement weather, such as snow and ice which would cover most weed seeds, may alter the proportion of the population moving and the timing and extent of the movement (Boddy and Sellers 1983).

Recoveries of ringed birds have shown that only a very small proportion of British Greenfinches winter abroad, moving principally across the southern North Sea, and eastern English Channel. There is also a regular, though small, movement between Britain and Ireland in autumn, and a return in spring. A few Scandinavian, German and Dutch breeding birds may winter in, or pass through, Britain.

In 1972 the number of breeding pairs of Greenfinches in Britain and Ireland was estimated at 1–2 million pairs. In 1983 the Common Birds Census indices for farmland and woodland plots were 11% and 17%, respectively, below the levels established 11 years earlier. With an average clutch size of 5, a fledging success of about 50% (Monk 1954), probably 2 broods per year, and more than 50% of post-independence mortality possibly occurring between the New Year and mid breeding season, the population in December may be about 5–6 million birds.

The Greenfinch breeds from central Fennoscandia southwards to the European Mediterranean coast and northwestern Africa, and eastwards across Europe to the Urals and Turkey. Birds from the north of this range are completely migratory, reaching the Mediterranean countries during the winter.

M. BODDY

Total number of squares in which recorded: 2,879 (75%)

No. of birds seen in a day	Number (%) of squares		
	Britain	Ireland	TOTAL (incl. C.I.)
1–26	939 (44%)	487 (67%)	1,428 (50%)
27–93	700 (33%)	175 (24%)	876 (30%)
94+	506 (24%)	67 (9%)	575 (20%)

References

BODDY, M. and R. M. SELLERS. 1983. Orientated movements by Greenfinches in Southern Britain. *Ringing and Migration* 4: 129–138.

GLUE, D. (ed.). 1982. *The Garden Bird Book*. Macmillan, London.

GUSH, G. H. 1980. A study of Greenfinch movements in and out of Devon. *Devon Birds* 33: 75–80.

MONK, J. F. 1954. The breeding biology of the Greenfinch. *Bird Study* 1: 2–14.

NEWTON, I. 1972. *Finches*. Collins, London.

Breeding Atlas p 412

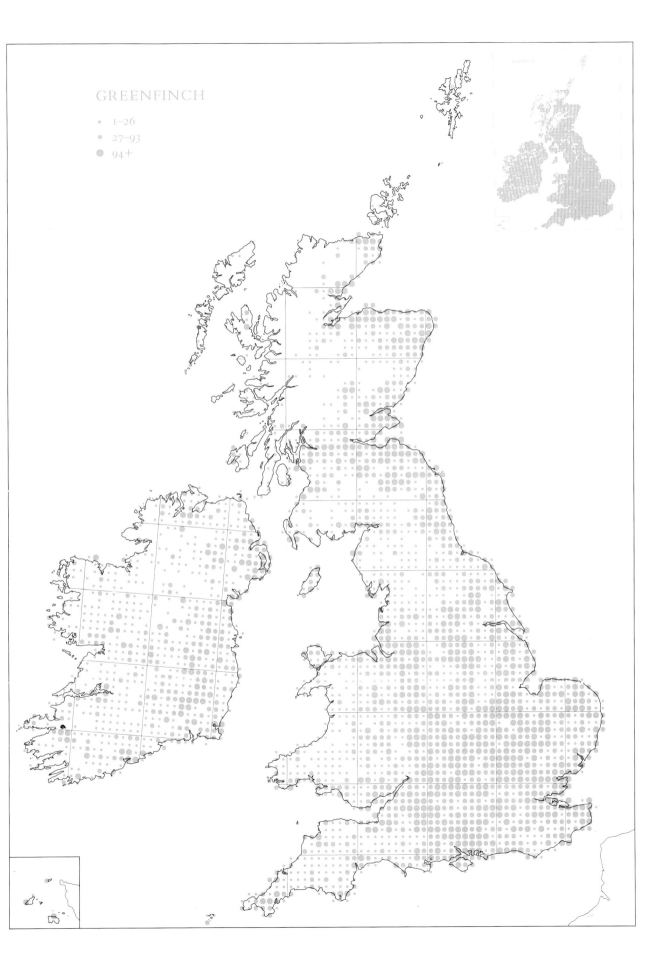

GREENFINCH

- 1–26
- 27–93
- 94+

Goldfinch

Carduelis carduelis

Parties of Goldfinches, with their liquid twittering calls and bright colours, enliven many a winter scene as they work over thistles and other weeds in search of seeds. They are somewhat elusive, however, as they range over wide areas during a day's foraging and are often present at particular sites for less than an hour at a time.

Goldfinches occur in winter over almost the whole of mainland Britain and Ireland, being absent only from extensive moorland and mountain areas, which lack their food plants. They have continued to spread northward and now breed in most of northern Britain.

Goldfinches are generally most numerous in the south, where longer growing seasons and less snow cover ensure more food. The winter distribution closely matches the breeding distribution, but locally, the birds become more widespread in open country in winter. They can then be seen on coastal flats, on waste land, overgrown rubbish dumps, neglected allotments and rough pastures, or indeed anywhere where their food plants grow. They specialise on plants in the family Compositae, especially thistles, to which the long thin bill is especially adapted (Newton 1972). A Goldfinch can cling to its food plants with ease, tear open the seedheads and probe inside with its bill. In the autumn the bird has a wide diet, preferring thistles and knapweeds, but also feeding on ragworts and groundsels, dandelions and others. As winter progresses, it becomes increasingly restricted to thistles, burdocks and teasels, but takes birch and alder seeds in some areas. It is the only finch with a beak long enough to extract teasel seeds. The females have slightly shorter beaks than the males and seldom feed from this plant.

By day Goldfinches roam the countryside from one feeding site to another, and at night they roost communally, usually in thick deciduous scrub or evergreens. The sizes of flocks vary with the food supply; in autumn when food is plentiful, groups of more than 100 individuals are not uncommon. As winter progresses, the flocks are mostly of less than 10 birds. Because of their specialised foods, they seldom mix with other finches at this season.

Most Goldfinches leave Britain in September and October each year to winter on the Continent. Ringing recoveries indicate that the British population winters in Belgium and western France and Spain (map in Newton 1972). There have been no ringing recoveries of Irish Goldfinches to suggest that they undertake the same sort of movement. The longest recorded movements span more than 2,000 km but, even in mid winter, recoveries have come from all stages of the migration route, implying that individuals vary greatly in the distances they travel. Other movements around Britain include a small westward passage to Ireland. Apparently more females than males migrate, as males predominate in resident winter flocks. In a study near Oxford during autumn, the local population dropped by four-fifths as birds left on migration, and declined further with the onset of cold weather in December–January, after which numbers remained extremely low. So little potential food remains uneaten at the end of winter that food almost certainly limits the numbers of Goldfinches which can remain here. Strangely, Goldfinches have not taken to visiting feeding trays in gardens as have some other finches.

The *Breeding Atlas* suggested an overall density of 100 pairs per 10-km square, equivalent to around 300,000 breeding pairs in Britain and Ireland. The number might increase through breeding to give a population exceeding 1.5 million individuals by the end of the summer. By late winter, numbers could well have fallen to less than 100,000 individuals, only to increase again with the return of the migrants. The population has almost certainly declined in southern regions during the last 30 years, as a result of herbicide use and various agricultural practices which have greatly reduced the numbers of thistles and other food plants.

The breeding range extends over the western two-thirds of Eurasia, but the birds are much commoner in the south of their range. In winter the most northerly areas are largely vacated and enormous numbers of Goldfinches concentrate in the Mediterranean basin, where the mild damp winters ensure the almost continuous growth and seeding of their herbaceous food plants. The British wintering population thus forms a small fraction of the total.

I. NEWTON

Total number of squares in which recorded: 2,614 (68%)

No. of birds seen in a day	Number (%) of squares		
	Britain	Ireland	TOTAL (incl. C.I.)
1–9	886 (45%)	399 (64%)	1,288 (49%)
10–25	635 (32%)	160 (26%)	795 (30%)
26+	463 (23%)	66 (11%)	531 (20%)

References

NEWTON, I. 1972. *Finches*. Collins, London.

Breeding Atlas p 414

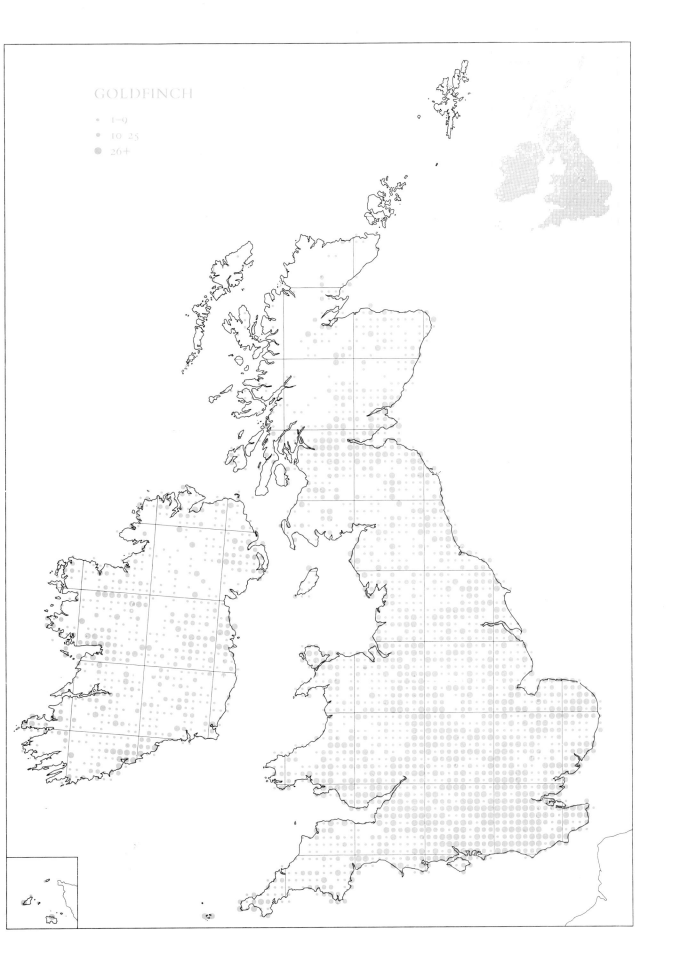

GOLDFINCH

- · 1–9
- · 10–25
- ● 26+

Siskin

Carduelis spinus

This pretty and confiding small finch is a welcome, if irregular, visitor in late winter to many gardens in S England, yet this habit is of relatively recent origin, first noticed in the 1960s (Spencer and Gush 1973). Prior to this it wintered mainly in alder woods and copses, and still does to a large extent.

Comparison of the winter and breeding distributions is complicated by the arrival of birds from the Continent. However, quite local movements clearly occur as well and may largely account for the winter distribution in Ireland and northern Scotland, where many Siskins winter near the breeding areas but at lower altitudes. Nonetheless, the most striking feature of the winter map is the extensive distribution in England and Wales, for which long-distance migrants must be mainly responsible. Concentrations from SE Wales through the west midlands, and in SE England, coincide with the Severn and Thames valleys, but also with high densities of human population.

Siskins may be seen in birches or larches in winter, sometimes with Redpolls (*C. flammea*), but the main habitat is alder, where they first obtain food from the cones and later on the ground below. Garden feeding is chiefly a feature of late winter and early spring, but the birds may come earlier to feed on cypress seeds. This food source has probably become important in recent decades with the increased planting of ornamental conifers, and may have first attracted Siskins into gardens, where they now feed readily on peanuts and fat.

During winter, Siskins form flocks of up to 50, occasionally more. Feeding on alder, a flock will work a tree from top to bottom, seeking open cones. In suburban habitats, little parties continually arrive and depart, and may range widely. It is not unusual to trap the same individual in gardens 2–3 km apart during the same day, and rapid local movements of up to 20 km are common. Nevertheless, Siskins in prime habitat may remain fairly static and isolated for many weeks. They roost in flocks of similar size to the feeding groups, in conifers, thorn scrub, alders or reed beds.

Siskins are irruptive and the extent and direction of their movements are strongly influenced by food supply. Consequently, birds wintering here one year may be of very different origin from those of the year before. Scottish bred birds certainly make up a substantial proportion of the English winter population in some years. This was probably true in the first two Atlas winters, though Scottish birds may have been more sedentary in 1983/84. Many Irish birds may be of local origin, but longer movements also occur, as for instance a bird ringed in Co. Down in January and controlled the next autumn in Estonia. Movements through Britain may be in unexpected directions: a bird ringed in Jersey in October was retrapped in Elgin on Christmas day of the same year, while spring movements may be southward or northward. Continental migrants move east–west, through the Baltic states and NW Europe. Birds ringed in Spain in winter have been controlled in Britain in subsequent winters and *vice versa*, but there is so far no evidence of Iberian breeding birds wintering in Britain. Wintering areas may differ widely from year to year: for example, a Siskin ringed at Exmouth in March was recovered near the Black Sea in the following November. Nevertheless, some individuals return over long distances to the same winter quarters. Two Siskins ringed in Surrey were later controlled in Lithuania, then retrapped in the original garden two winters later, and one of them was finally recovered in Finland.

The *Winter Atlas* period has included two years in which Siskins have been abundant in southern Britain (1981/82 and 1983/84). Their increase as a breeding species probably ensures that a reasonable number will now be present in most winters, but over a longer period more variation might be expected. If all British breeders remained here, the *Breeding Atlas* estimate suggests a minimum winter population of well over 50,000 birds. In a winter when there are many Continental immigrants, the total must be much more. Retrap and control data suggest that total numbers per 10-km square of good habitat may be of the order of 500–1,000. In some years, certainly, well over 150,000 Siskins must be wintering in Britain and Ireland, but probably less than half a million.

P. J. K. BURTON

Total number of squares in which recorded: 1,915 (50%)

No. of birds seen in a day	Number (%) of squares		
	Britain	Ireland	TOTAL (incl. C.I.)
1–18	770 (46%)	190 (77%)	962 (50%)
19–50	538 (32%)	43 (18%)	581 (30%)
51+	358 (22%)	13 (5%)	371 (19%)

References

COOPER, J. E. S. 1985. Spring migration of Siskins in north Sussex during 1984. *Ringing and Migration* 6: 61–65.

NEWTON, I. 1972. *Finches*. Collins, London.

SPENCER, R. and G. H. GUSH. 1973. Siskins feeding in gardens. *Brit. Birds* 66: 91–99.

Breeding Atlas p 416

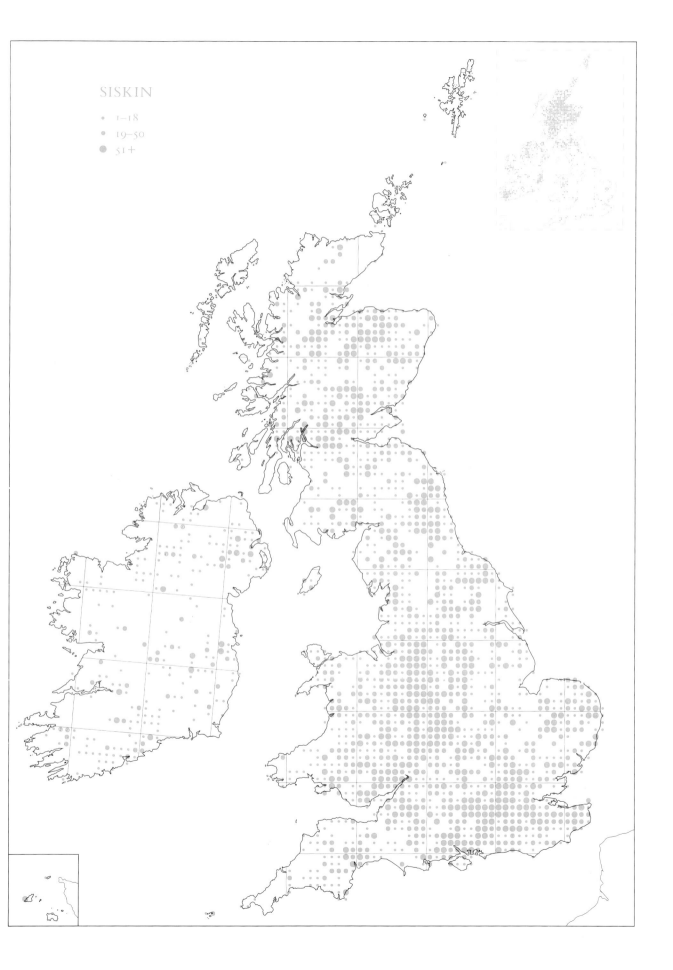

SISKIN

- 1–18
- 19–50
- 51+

Linnet

Carduelis cannabina

The Linnet is well known in farmland and scrub in summer and is often assumed to be common in winter, too. It can, however, prove rather difficult to find because the whole population of an area may congregate in one or a few flocks. This behaviour is reflected by the map, showing a widespread but rather patchy distribution with no particular concentrations.

In general, the winter distribution shows a similar pattern to that of the breeding season with the obvious exception of a marked absence from all areas of higher ground. This is particularly clear in Wales and over northern Britain. Whether this retreat is simply an altitudinal migration or whether it is these highland birds which move out preferentially (see below) is unclear. As in the breeding season, there are no Linnets in Shetland and very few on the north and west coasts of Scotland. In Ireland the average abundance appears to be lower than in Britain, and it seems to be more widespread in the southeastern half. The area of central Ulster noted in the *Breeding Atlas* as supporting few birds has very few indeed in winter.

In winter, Linnets are largely restricted to open country and they are particularly common in lowland farming areas. This is because of their near-dependence on the small seeds of the weeds taken from the ground. Such seeds become most available after the land has been cultivated. Until the 1950s there was a very large seed bank in the soil which was exposed on cultivation, and the distribution of Linnets still parallels the cultivated areas of Britain and Ireland. However, in recent years the more extensive use of herbicides has reduced the stock of seeds considerably and this is thought to be the major reason for the species' decline over most of the two countries. The species is also found on many types of waste ground, on salt marshes and even mudflats on the coast.

Linnets are usually seen in small flocks of up to about 200, or sometimes more, and often in association with other finches and buntings. Within such flocks, however, Linnets tend to remain as a sub-unit and, especially if the flock is disturbed, will fly off together and circle before landing again nearby on the ground rather than in the bushes. This habit of staying with their own kind also applies in the mixed communal roosts—again, with other finches and buntings. Roosts are most often in gorse or thorn bushes and there are regularly up to 1,500 Linnets in such a roost (Newton 1972). The sites may be used for several winters.

The British and Irish population is largely sedentary during the winter and, although there may be small movements associated with periods of hard weather, these were not enough to show any major differences between the distributions in 1981/82 and 1982/83. The main Linnet migrations occur during September and October and again in April. A proportion of the British and Irish breeding population moves south to winter in western France and parts of Iberia (map in Newton 1972), but exactly what proportion and which birds move, and the distance that individuals may fly, probably varies from year to year. In autumn, Linnets have also been seen flying west from Britain into Ireland and south out of Ireland, but unlike the main southerly migration from Britain neither movement has been substantiated by ringing recoveries. The relatively few Linnets in Ireland during the winter suggest that only a small number of British breeding birds stay in Ireland if they do fly west. In addition, some Scandinavian Linnets are thought to come to Britain for the winter, which may account for the slightly larger than average numbers in coastal NE England and SE Scotland.

Britain is on the northern edge of the winter range of the Linnet and total numbers probably vary somewhat from year to year. Since the *Breeding Atlas* estimate of between 0.8 and 1.6 million pairs, the Common Birds Census index has decreased from about 85 to 55. So, with an average brood size of four, two broods per year, about half dying before December and about half moving away from Britain for the winter, the December population seems likely to be about 3 million birds.

P. C. LACK

Total number of squares in which recorded: 2,277 (59%)

No. of birds seen in a day	Number (%) of squares		
	Britain	Ireland	TOTAL (incl. C.I.)
1–28	799 (47%)	347 (60%)	1,147 (50%)
29–98	519 (31%)	155 (27%)	676 (30%)
99 +	375 (22%)	78 (13%)	454 (20%)

Reference
NEWTON, I. 1972. *Finches*. Collins, London.

Breeding Atlas p 418

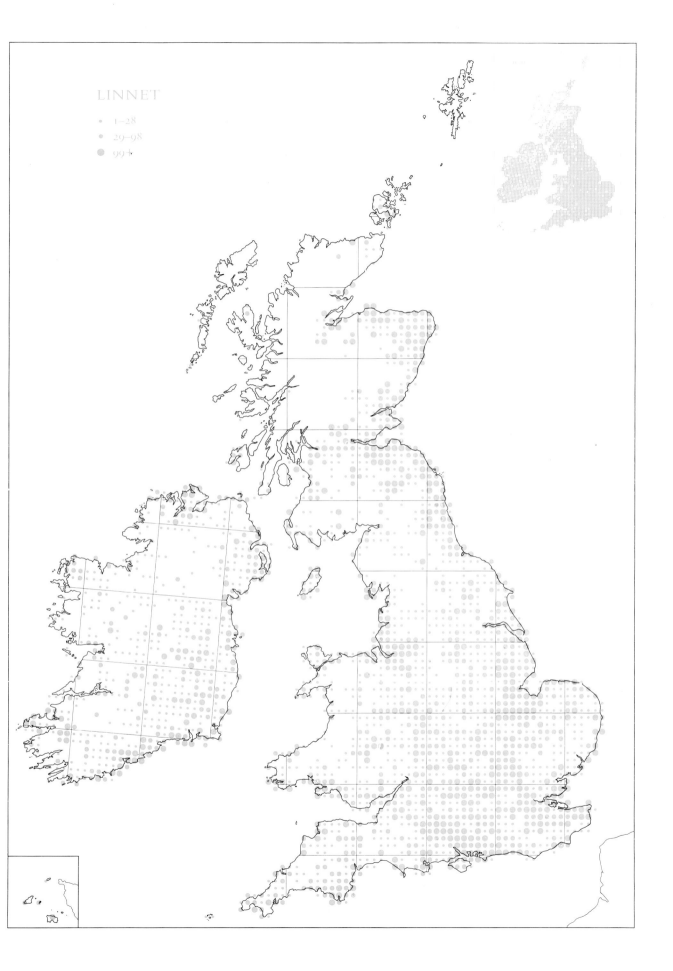

LINNET

· 1–28
· 29–98
● 99+

Twite

Carduelis flavirostris

The Twite has rather few characteristic features and field identification by sight is rarely easy. Its habit of joining flocks of other species increases the problem, but its nasal 'tsweet' call is diagnostic and often provides the first indication of its presence in such a flock. When mixed with Linnets *C. cannabina* it is difficult to gain an accurate assessment of the numbers present, though the habit of the two species, when disturbed, of forming separate flocks in flight can be helpful.

The winter distribution shows the Twite's liking for coastal sites. The upland areas shown as occupied in the *Breeding Atlas* are almost entirely vacated in winter, and those inland records which do occur are confined to areas such as the Grampian region and the southern Pennines which are *en route* from breeding to wintering areas. The thinner scatter of records in central England is less easily explained, but may again represent birds moving from the Pennines to the Essex coast. The distribution of breeding birds in coastal sites in Scotland and Ireland has similarities with the winter distribution map, indicating a more sedentary part of the population.

Twites winter mainly on salt marshes and coastal fields, and also on tide wrack. Like Linnets they are dependant on small seeds and frequent areas where these are abundant. More intensive cultivation reduces the availability of food and this may explain their absence from inland areas. Even in coastal locations they face competition from a variety of species, and large concentrations only occur where there is an abundance of food. The extensive areas of the Wash and Essex marshes traditionally form the main wintering areas on the east coast and flocks here may number over 1,000 birds in some years though up to 500 is more usual.

Utilisation of other habitats has rarely been recorded. Orford (1973) recorded a flock feeding regularly in a turnip field in the Pennines; and the unusual occurrence of birds feeding in woodland in Essex (Smart 1978) was reported in two consecutive winters. Roosting may, however, occur in wooded sites, though dense scrub, reed beds and other low herbaceous cover is preferred (Newton 1972).

It is clearly evident from ringing recoveries that the Pennine breeding birds start to move out in a southeasterly direction from late August, reaching the east coast in peak numbers from September to November, some continuing across the North Sea into the Low Countries. A decline in numbers in late November is often followed by a second peak in late December and January. This may be due to an influx of Scandinavian birds, especially in severe weather, though there is no firm evidence to support this. Orkney and the Outer Hebrides retain a high winter population, but some leave Shetland and there are two ringing recoveries which show an exchange of birds between the west coast of Scotland and Ireland. The numbers wintering in Ireland are not indicative of a large influx but the movements of Scottish birds are worthy of further investigation.

Spring migration occurs from late January and very few remain by mid March, while Fair Isle records its spring peak in April and early May. Some birds may only spend a brief period in the wintering areas.

The estimated population of 20,000–40,000 pairs in the *Breeding Atlas* would generate a net input of 50,000–100,000 birds by December. Allowing for a slight decline in the breeding population in recent years and fluctuations in the numbers wintering on the Continent, it is probable that the mid winter population in Britain and Ireland numbers between 100,000 and 150,000 birds.

R. LAMBERT

Total number of squares in which recorded: 580 (15%)

No. of birds seen in a day	Number (%) of squares		
	Britain	Ireland	TOTAL (incl. C.I.)
1–15	247 (50%)	47 (54%)	294 (51%)
16–67	138 (28%)	32 (37%)	170 (29%)
68 +	108 (22%)	8 (9%)	116 (20%)

References

NEWTON, I. 1972. *Finches*. Collins, London.
ORFORD, N. 1973. Breeding distribution of Twite. *Bird Study* 20: 51–62, 121–126.
SMART, J. H. 1978. Twites wintering in woodland. *Brit. Birds* 71: 86.

Breeding Atlas p 420

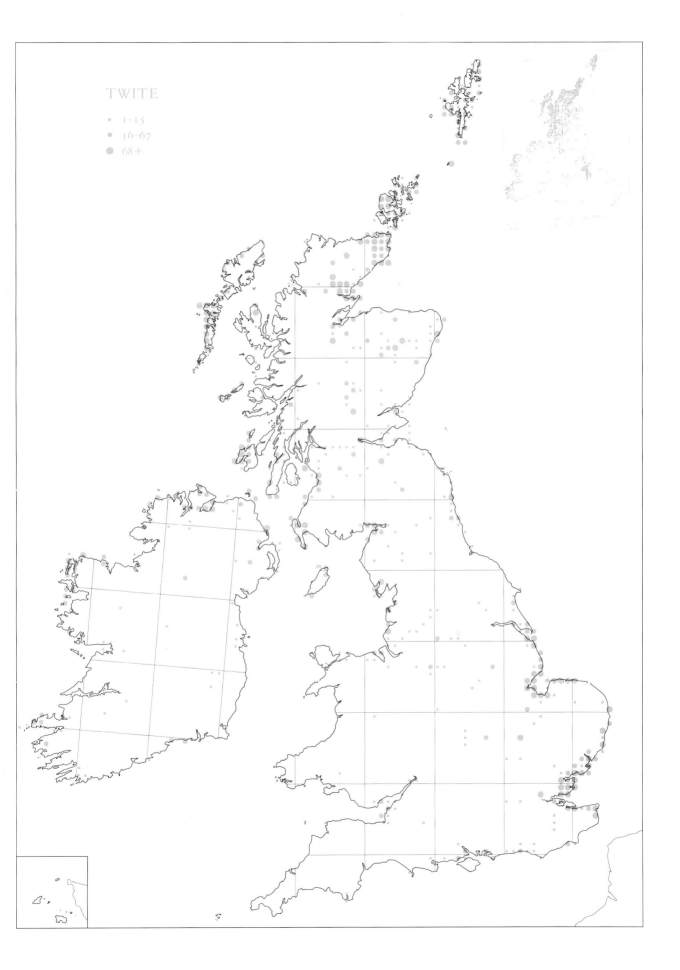

TWITE

- • 1–15
- • 16–67
- • 68+

Redpoll

Carduelis flammea

This delightful little finch is most often heard before it is seen, calling as it changes position whilst feeding at the top of a silver birch.

The winter distribution of the Redpoll throughout Britain and Ireland is determined largely by the presence or absence of birch trees and the available supply of birch seed. Comparison with the *Breeding Atlas* shows a withdrawal from northern and western Scotland, and from high ground in northern Britain. Southwest England, and the west coast of Wales support few birds, but central southern England with its birch clad lowland heaths, offers a good supply of food in some winters. Ireland has fewer records of Redpolls in winter than in summer, though there are no ringing recoveries to suggest that the birds emigrate.

In autumn, most Redpolls breeding in northern and central Britain move southwards, or southeastwards, (though recaptures of ringed birds suggest that some may be resident throughout the year). The extent, speed and timing of their migration appear to be determined by the size of the post-breeding population and by the availability of food *en route* (Evans 1969, Boddy 1984). While birch seed lasts, the birds feed on little else from July through to early spring (Newton 1967). Alder seed is also readily taken, and may support large flocks of Redpolls, together with Siskins *C. spinus*, for several months in winter. In poor years for birch and alder Redpolls either continue south to the Continent, or switch to feeding on seeds from waste ground.

The majority of our breeding birds emigrate via SE England. Formerly, large numbers were captured in Belgium during autumn and winter, to be sold as cage birds. Such trapping has now been made illegal, but the majority of overseas ringing recoveries still come from there and from southern Netherlands and northern France. If exceptionally large numbers leave Britain they may find that the food supply is little better in the Low Countries; many birds then continue their flights southwards and eastwards, for example reaching Spain in 1959 and southern France in 1964 (Erard 1966). In winter 1977/78, after an exceptionally good breeding season, ringed birds were reported in unprecedented numbers from northern Italy, Switzerland, S. France, and even Portugal.

At the time of the *Breeding Atlas* the Redpoll was increasing rapidly, but since 1977 there has been a dramatic decline in the breeding population. This seems to have been due to a high proportion (even

all) of the more distant migrants of autumn/winter 1977/78 failing to return to breed in Britain.

The *Breeding Atlas* proposed a population of 300,000 to 600,000 pairs in 1972. If we take the figure now to be 315,000 breeding pairs, averaging 1.5 broods per year, with 4–5 eggs per clutch; a fledging success of around 50%, but with significant post-fledging mortality; and a stable, or even declining breeding population, with further mortality peaking in late winter or early spring when seeds are in short supply; then the total of birds alive in mid winter may be about 1,200,000. If the proportion emigrating varies between, say, 30–70%, the number of birds in Britain and Ireland at the end of December will range between 350,000–850,000.

The Redpoll has a circumpolar distribution, with most authorities distinguishing two 'species' (Newton 1972): *C. hornemanni* (the Arctic Redpoll) a large pale form, breeding mainly on the high-arctic tundras, and recorded less than 90 times in Britain and Ireland up to 1980; and a small greyish or brownish form (*C. flammea*), breeding in more southerly, open birch and conifer forests.

The Mealy Redpoll *C. f. flammea* which breeds in northern continental Eurasia and North America, normally migrates southeastwards out of Fennoscandia, but appears in Britain in most winters, though only exceptionally in large numbers, and then usually on the east coast.

M. BODDY

Total number of squares in which recorded: 2,006 (52%)

No. of birds	Number (%) of squares		
seen in a day	Britain	Ireland	TOTAL (incl. C.I.)
1–10	720 (47%)	290 (61%)	1,011 (50%)
11–35	465 (30%)	128 (27%)	594 (30%)
36 +	346 (23%)	55 (12%)	401 (20%)

References

BODDY, M. 1984. Body weights of adult and juvenile Lesser Redpolls in central and southern England. *Ringing and Migration* 5: 91–100.

ERARD, C. 1966. Note sur les *Carduelis flammea* migrateurs en France. *Alauda* 34: 102–119.

EVANS, P. R. 1969. Ecological aspects of migration, and pre-migratory fat deposition in the Lesser Redpoll *Carduelis flammea cabaret*. *Condor* 71: 316–330.

NEWTON, I. 1967. The adaptive radiation and feeding ecology of some British finches. *Ibis* 109: 33–98.

NEWTON, I. 1972. *Finches*. Collins, London.

Breeding Atlas p 422

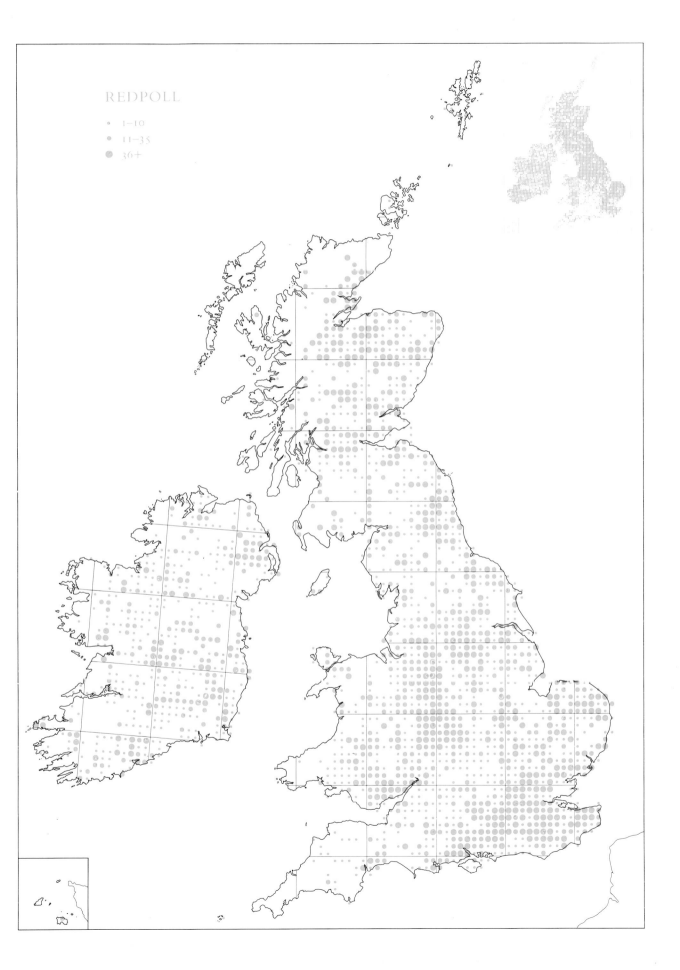

REDPOLL

- 1–10
- 11–35
- 36+

Common Crossbill

Loxia curvirostra

Scottish Crossbill

L. scotica

Crossbills eat conifer seeds and little else. Were it not for the falling cones, a party of crossbills feeding high in the trees might easily be overlooked. However, the 'chip-chip' contact calls readily draw attention to their acrobatic scramblings among the ends of the branches. Two species of crossbills regularly breed in Britain—only one in Ireland—and, because it is difficult to tell them apart in the field, they are considered together here.

The winter distribution of crossbills shows a pattern characteristic of scarce species occupying widespread, but highly fragmented, habitats. In the north of Scotland there are three main areas with good numbers of birds—one to the northwest of the Great Glen, the second in the valley of the River Spey, and the third shown clearly along the east-west valley of the River Dee. Together these form the core of the range of the Scottish Crossbill and include most of the larger relicts of the ancient Caledonian Pine Forest. The Scottish Crossbill is also found in other old conifer woods, both native and planted, in northern Scotland. The map, overleaf, showing records of the Scottish species should be considered only as a guide to its general distribution, because Common Crossbills are also present in this area (Knox in press). Many observers in the Highlands quite rightly made no attempt to distinguish between the two species. This was especially noticeable in Deeside, where most were recorded as 'crossbill sp.'. These are not shown on the Scottish Crossbill map. There are no reliable records of Scottish Crossbills south of the Highlands.

Common Crossbills, whose numbers fluctuate greatly from year to year, are found in many of the older, larger plantations of native or exotic conifers, as well as in the native pinewoods. They are seen most years in the Highlands, SW Scotland, the Kielder Forest in Northumberland, the North Yorkshire

Moors, the Peak District, the Forest of Dean, parts of Devon, the New Forest and in East Anglian woods and shelter belts. There are few crossbills in Ireland. This distribution is similar to that shown in the *Breeding Atlas*, although there have been some changes, presumably due either to the unpredictable movements of the birds, or to the selective felling of some woods and the maturation of others. There are also more records from small, isolated woods than previously. This was a result of irruptions in 1982 and 1983.

The distribution of Common Crossbills differed markedly in the three winters of the survey. During 1981/82 they were present in most or all of the 'traditional' areas, with a few birds in other woods. Numbers were generally low. In the next winter, following a small irruption of Common Crossbills from the Continent in late September and October, the number of birds in the 'traditional' areas had increased, sometimes very considerably, and they were found in many additional woods throughout Britain. A further irruption occurred in 1983, when large numbers of birds arrived, especially in Kent and Sussex. Most of the crossbills that had been present in N England during the second winter were not seen in 1983/84, and there was a substantial redistribution in the Borders and the Highlands. This unstable distribution makes the maps rather misleading since they show the composite picture over three winters, further complicated by two irruptions. In any one 'average' winter, crossbills are much scarcer than the maps suggest. A number of Parrot Crossbills *L. pytyopsittacus* also arrived in Britain during these irruptions (see next page).

Common Crossbills particularly are opportunistic colonizers, moving as their numbers or their food supply fluctuate. After each breeding season some or all of the population leaves the nesting area. Often these movements are only local, but they can involve large groups of birds travelling thousands of kilometres before settling. These irruptions can bring birds into areas where previously there were no crossbills, and, if the habitat is suitable, they may remain and breed for one or more seasons before moving on. There is evidence to suggest that some birds return to northern and eastern Europe one or more years after the irruption that brought them westwards (Newton 1970).

The local breeding populations that result from irrupting birds are often short-lived, but those in the New Forest and Brecklands are said to have been founded after the 1910 irruption. As with other Common Crossbill groups in Britain and Ireland, they appear to depend on further irruptions for their continued existence.

In winter, crossbills are usually in flocks, often feeding and calling high in the canopy. They have adapted well to many of the exotic conifer species that have been planted throughout Britain, but seem particularly to be associated with Scots pine, Norway and sitka spruces, Douglas fir and the European and Japanese larches. Occasionally they feed among deciduous trees, but usually it is not clear what they are eating. They drink frequently, often taking drops of water from the ends of conifer needles after rain, or

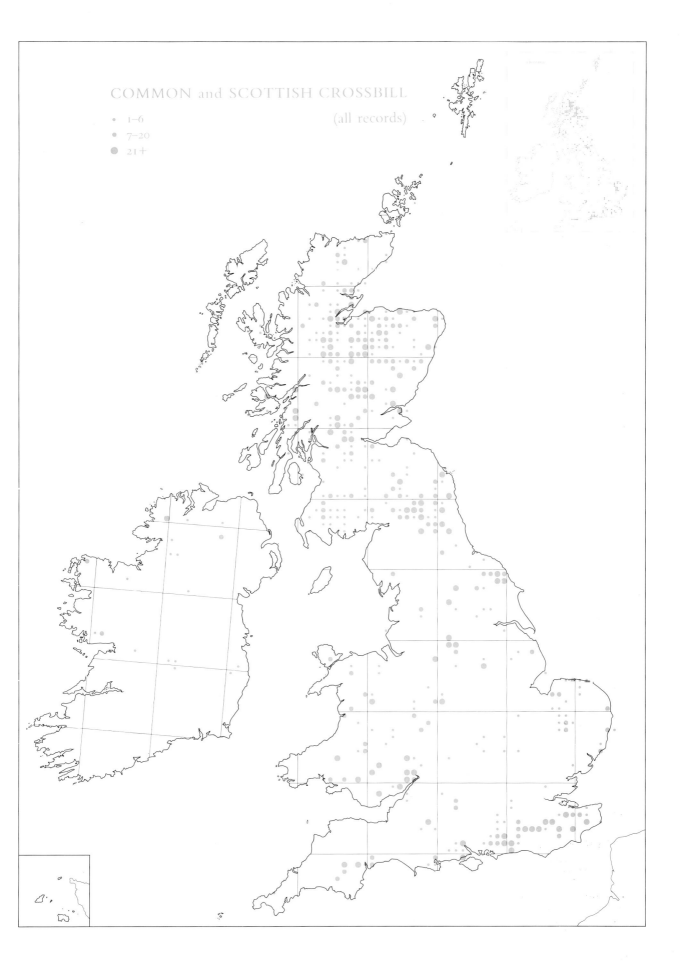

COMMON and SCOTTISH CROSSBILL

• 1–6

• 7–20

● 21+

(all records)

by eating snow. They also come to the ground to drink at streams and small puddles, and for grit or salt.

Crossbills are among the earliest of the breeding birds in Britain and as winter progresses there is a marked increase in song and display. Nesting behaviour in the Common Crossbill has been noted in every month of the year and, although they sometimes nest in late summer and autumn, the main breeding season for Common and Scottish Crossbills begins in late winter. Common Crossbills appear to nest slightly earlier than the Scottish Crossbill, but both can have nests with eggs as early as January. The maps, therefore, certainly include many breeding birds; for these species 'winter' is not the same as 'non-breeding season'. During the winter, crossbills are mainly sedentary, although some unpredictable local movements will take place as the birds wander between areas with suitable cone crops.

There are no recent estimates for the population sizes of either Scottish or Common Crossbills. In the early 1970s Nethersole-Thompson (1975) put the population of the Scottish Crossbill at about 1,500 birds. Although numbers vary from season to season in any one area, there is no reason to believe that the total has changed much since then. The *Breeding Atlas* gives the population of the Common Crossbill to be about 3,500 birds (total crossbill population of 5,000, less 1,500 for *scotica*). This is probably high for years when there has been no irruption, and at such times there could be less than 1,000 Common Crossbills in Britain and Ireland. After an irruption there is an increase in numbers, often to several times that figure, followed by a decrease over subsequent seasons until the next invasion.

The Common Crossbill is found throughout the northern conifer forests of the Old and the New Worlds, and in many isolated populations along the southern edge of the Holarctic. The subspecies found in Britain occurs from Portugal to eastern Siberia. The Scottish Crossbill is the only endemic species of bird in Britain.

The Common Crossbill has a relatively slender bill and often feeds on seeds from spruce. As the cone crops of spruce in Fennoscandia are variable and unpredictable, the Common Crossbill irrupts into Britain fairly frequently.

The Parrot Crossbill, also found in Fennoscandia, has a heavy, powerful bill and is more capable of extracting seeds from the hard cones of Scots pine. The cone crops of Scots pine fluctuate less than those of spruce (Reinikainen 1937) and, perhaps as a result of this, the Parrot Crossbill seldom comes to Britain. There have been only two Parrot Crossbill irruptions in recent years: the first in 1962 and the other in 1982, when over 120 birds arrived, mainly during October. Only a few were found through the following winter, all in the Pennines. Early in 1983 one or two pairs built nests and one pair were later seen with young. No Parrot Crossbills were seen in the summer of 1983, but a few were found again in Norfolk in October that year. A small group remained all winter at Wells, and one pair successfully bred there in February 1984 (Davidson 1985). This was the first documented nesting of Parrot Crossbill in Britain— ironically during the period of the *Winter Atlas*!

A. G. KNOX

COMMON and SCOTTISH CROSSBILLS

Total number of squares in which recorded: 457 (12%)
(map on previous page)

No. of birds seen in a day	Number (%) of squares Britain	Ireland	TOTAL (incl. C.I.)
1–6	226 (52%)	14 (78%)	240 (53%)
7–20	127 (29%)	3 (17%)	130 (28%)
21 +	86 (20%)	1 (6%)	87 (19%)

SCOTTISH CROSSBILLS

Total number of squares in which recorded: 68 (2%)

No. of birds seen in a day	Number (%) of squares Britain	Ireland	TOTAL (incl. C.I.)
1–6	34 (50%)	0 (0%)	34 (50%)
7–15	21 (31%)	0 (0%)	21 (31%)
16+	13 (19%)	0 (0%)	13 (19%)

References

DAVIDSON, C. 1985. Parrot Crossbills: a new breeding species. *Norfolk Bird Report* 1984: 98-102.

KNOX, A. G. (In press.) Crossbills: their general biology and some conservation problems. In NCC (ed.). *Glen Tanar: its Human and Natural History*. NCC, Peterborough.

NETHERSOLE-THOMPSON, D. 1975. *Pine Crossbills*. Poyser, Berkhamsted.

NEWTON, I. 1970. Irruptions of crossbills in Europe. Pp 337–357 in WATSON, A. (ed.). *Animal Populations in Relation to their Food Resources*. Blackwell, Oxford.

REINIKAINEN, A. 1937. The irregular migrations of the Crossbill, *Loxia c. curvirostra*, and their relation to the cone-crop of the conifers. *Ornis Fenn.* 14: 55–64.

Breeding Atlas p 428

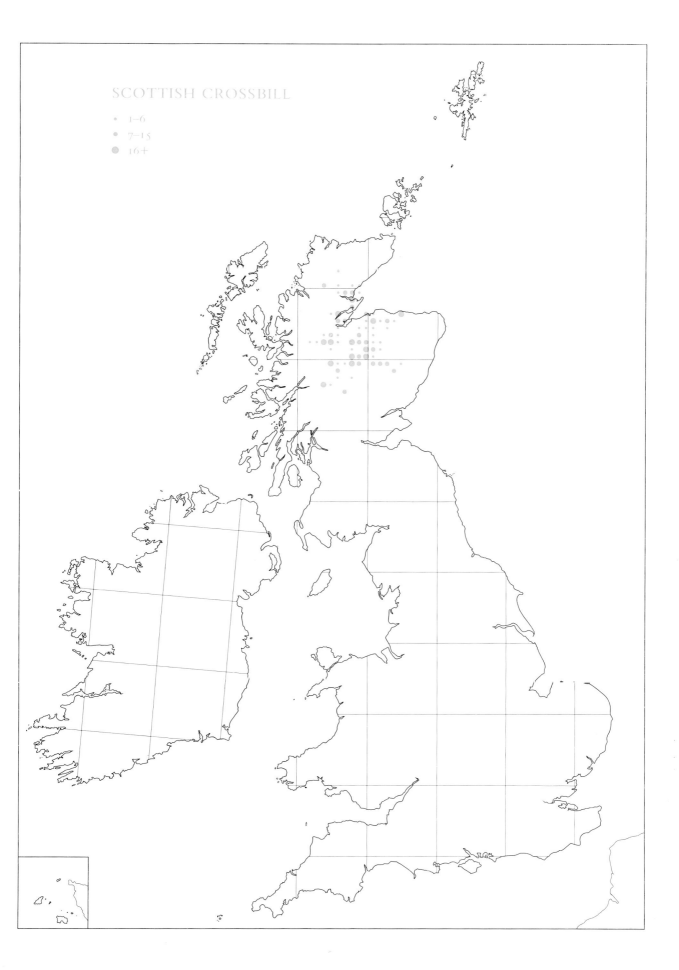

SCOTTISH CROSSBILL

- • 1–6
- • 7–15
- ● 16+

Bullfinch

Pyrrhula pyrrhula

Despite the bright plumage of the males, Bullfinches are never easy to see, and in winter usually betray their presence by the flash of white rumps as a small flock is flushed from a hedge or thicket, or by the brief contact calls that accompany their travels through woodland.

Bullfinches seem to occur almost anywhere where there is an adequate amount of woodland, or even of low scrub, over virtually the whole of Britain and Ireland, except for W and N Scotland, where records are very few. The scattered records in Orkney and Shetland, where the species does not breed, are probably migrants of the Scandinavian race. Otherwise, the pattern is almost identical with the breeding distribution, including low densities in Snowdonia and the Welsh mountains, along the Pennine chain, in the mountains of Mayo and Donegal, and in the fenland of East Anglia. There are no winter records from the Isle of Man. The avoidance of the uplands is also evident in Scotland, where there are few records in the Grampian mountains and NW Highlands.

Highest winter densities occur between east central England and the Channel coast in Kent, where the Bullfinch enjoys notoriety as a pest of commercial fruit-growing.

Insectivorous for only a brief period in summer when they are feeding young, Bullfinches subsist chiefly on the seeds of a succession of plants eaten as they become available through the year. During winter, the birds have to rely on seed stocks formed in the summer or autumn and it is the rate at which preferred foods such as bramble, ash and dock seeds are depleted that seems to determine whether or not Bullfinches turn to eating buds (Newton 1964).

Predominantly birds of woodland, Bullfinches also occupy a variety of other habitats, including hedgerows, bramble thickets, weedy arable fields, and scrub on marginal land. Their use of habitats varies seasonally with changes of diet (Greig-Smith and Wilson 1984). The concentrations of birds that gather at favoured winter feeding sites, such as a fruiting ash tree, give rise to the impression that Bullfinches regularly form substantial winter flocks. However, obser-

vation shows that most birds travel to and from such feeding places independently; and at all times of year a majority of Bullfinches are single or in pairs.

Bullfinches are largely resident, and ringing recoveries have shown that very few move more than a few kilometres (Summers 1979). Recent studies employing radio-tracking to follow the movements of individual birds (Greig-Smith 1985) have revealed that they may remain for weeks within a short distance of a good food source, before suddenly moving several kilometres to a new site. Since there is no evidence for winter territoriality, or any other social restriction on movements, this means that a single orchard or thicket may be within the range of dozens or even hundreds of Bullfinches.

In most of its range, extending from western Europe to Japan, the Bullfinch is more characteristic of coniferous forests than it is in Britain and Ireland, but no detailed studies of biology in those habitats have been made. Though northern populations are migratory, most of our Bullfinches are isolated from their Continental counterparts. The Common Birds Census has revealed a steady decline on farmland plots since the early 1970s, perhaps as a result of habitat changes such as the removal of hedgerows, whereas the index for woodland has remained high. Both habitats now have considerably lower levels than those on which the *Breeding Atlas* estimate of 600,000 pairs was based. Assuming 2–3 broods per pair, an average 0.4–1.3 young produced per nest, and using information on the relative winter mortality of adults and first-years, the mid winter population is likely to be between 1.0–1.5 million birds for Britain and Ireland.

P. W. GREIG-SMITH

Total number of squares in which recorded: 2,947 (76%)

No. of birds seen in a day	Number (%) of squares		
	Britain	Ireland	TOTAL (incl. C.I.)
1–7	1,055 (50%)	494 (60%)	1,552 (53%)
8–14	635 (30%)	218 (26%)	854 (29%)
15 +	424 (20%)	116 (14%)	541 (18%)

References

GREIG-SMITH, P. W. 1985. Winter survival, home ranges and feeding of first-year and adult Bullfinches. Pp 387–392 in SIBLY, R. M. and R. H. SMITH, (eds). *Behavioural Ecology: The Ecological Consequences of Adaptive Behaviour.* Blackwell, Oxford.

GREIG-SMITH, P. W. and G. M. WILSON. 1984. Activity and habitat use by a population of Bullfinches (*Pyrrhula pyrrhula* L.) in relation to bud-feeding in orchards. *J. Appl. Ecol.* 21: 401–422.

NEWTON, I. 1964. Bud-eating by Bullfinches in relation to the natural food-supply. *J. Appl. Ecol.* 1: 265–279.

NEWTON, I. 1972. *Finches.* Collins, London.

SUMMERS, D. D. B. 1979. Bullfinch dispersal and migration in relation to fruit bud damage. *Brit. Birds* 72: 249–263.

Breeding Atlas p 426

BULLFINCH

- 1–7
- 8–14
- 15+

Hawfinch

Coccothraustes coccothraustes

To most ornithologists, studying Hawfinches in winter is only marginally easier than in summer. They remain notoriously self-effacing and even when the woods they inhabit are leafless they easily escape notice, though their distinctive 'tzic' call-notes are identifiable from a considerable distance, and their flight-silhouette with the big, jutting head and short tail is distinctive. So little are they observed, in fact, that in several recent years their name does not appear at all in the annual index of *British Birds*. For this reason, while the Hawfinch is by no means rare in Britain, both the *Breeding Atlas* and the winter map almost certainly err in underestimating the total population. There were no records for Ireland.

Broadly speaking, the winter distribution of Hawfinches tends to correspond with the vegetation maps. They are most numerous in areas of beech, hornbeam, wych elm, yew, sycamore and wild cherry. Commercial cherry orchards are particularly favoured in autumn and flocks also congregate to pick seeds from fallen fruit in apple orchards. In hard weather, small flocks occur in parks and gardens, occasionally even in city suburbs, to strip berries from shrubs such as cotoneaster, berberis and honeysuckle, which all finches enjoy. Flocks, usually of only 10–20 birds, can often be seen crossing from one deciduous wood to another in the Chilterns, the South Downs and the New Forest heaths. They tend to return regularly to temporary feeding areas until the source is exhausted, at dusk flying to roost in adjacent patches of yew or old, ivy-clad trees.

Comparison between the maps of the *Breeding Atlas* and the winter survey show only minor differences, with the greater part of the population remaining concentrated in SE England, roughly from Hampshire to the Wash. There is an indication of some withdrawal in winter from the less hospitable coastal regions of Norfolk, Lincolnshire and eastern Yorkshire, and from southern Scotland, where few Hawfinches breed regularly. The fairly substantial populations in Lancashire and the Severn catchment area appear to be resident throughout the year.

Although apparently suitable habitat is available in many parts of Wales, Devon and Cornwall, these areas continue to be shunned by Hawfinches.

An erratic pattern of local feeding movements is characteristic of the species, but although regular migration has long been suspected in Britain, evidence is still lacking. Just over 1,000 Hawfinches have been ringed and the number of recoveries remains less than 20. The only long-distance recovery was a bird ringed in Somerset in October 1977 and recovered in Nottinghamshire in March 1980, a distance of only 293 km. A single German-ringed bird recovered in England supports the belief in an occasional influx of Continental birds, and this is borne out by the sighting of Hawfinches at light-ships and in the northern Scottish isles in winter. Vagrants have also been reported from time to time in Ireland and some in the Scillies. There are a few old records of Hawfinch flocks 'arriving' on the east coast of England.

The regular migration of Hawfinches in continental Europe is well documented. More than 5,000 have now been ringed and several hundred recovered. The northern population is strongly migratory. In France and Holland, although there is some southward movement in winter, the majority of the population, like that in Britain, remains in the breeding area. The longest distance recovery for a Continental Hawfinch was from Prague to Malaga, in southern Spain, a distance of almost 2,000 km. Winter flocks of more than 1,000 have been seen in the USSR and East Germany, up to 600 in Switzerland and 'several hundred' in Portugal, Gibraltar and the Nile Delta.

The British population appears to have increased slightly since 1957, its breeding range slowly expanding in the north and west (Mountfort 1957). The winter range shows only a marginal contraction, explainable by weather conditions. By comparison with the supposed distribution of the species in 1850, when it was believed to be rare outside the Home Counties, the Hawfinch is today relatively widespread and fairly numerous throughout the greater part of England and is beginning to penetrate Wales and Scotland. As no census has yet been carried out, the winter numbers can only be estimated; using *Breeding Atlas* figures of 10,000 breeding pairs, 20,000 Hawfinches can be assumed to winter in Britain.

G. MOUNTFORT

Total number of squares in which recorded: 252 (7%)

No. of birds seen in a day	Number (%) of squares		TOTAL (incl. C.I.)
	Britain	Ireland	
1	108 (43%)	0 (0%)	108 (43%)
2–5	100 (40%)	0 (0%)	100 (40%)
6 +	44 (18%)	0 (0%)	44 (18%)

References
MOUNTFORT, G. 1957. *The Hawfinch*. Collins, London.
NEWTON, I. 1972. *Finches*. Collins, London.

Breeding Atlas p 410

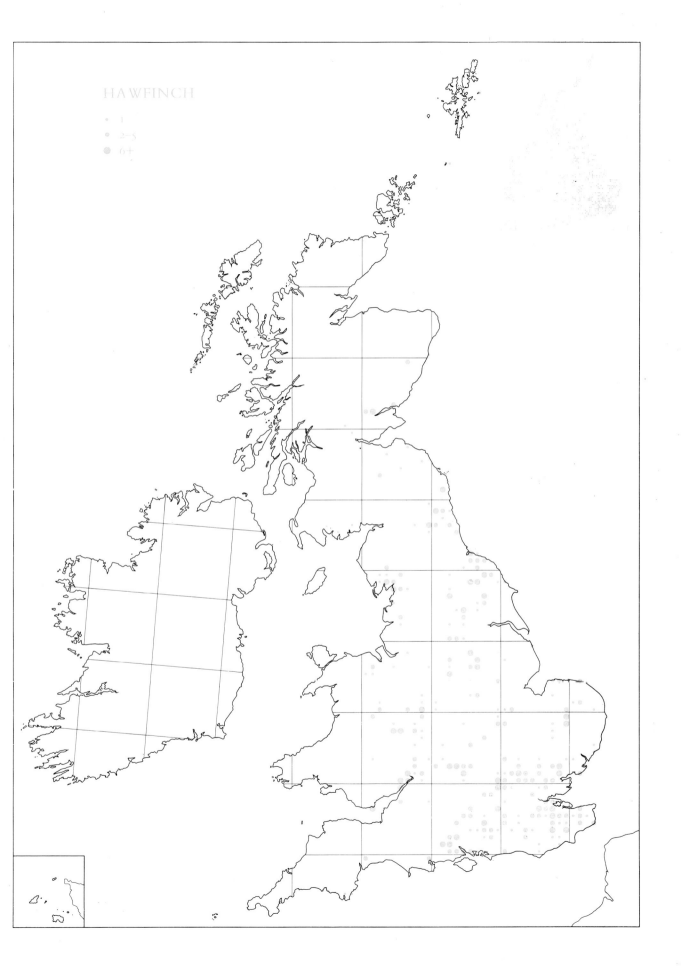

HAWFINCH

· 1
· 2–5
● 6+

Lapland Bunting

Calcarius lapponicus

Of all the species which frequent coastal habitats in winter the Lapland Bunting is the most difficult to locate and the most likely to be overlooked. Normally present only in small numbers, it is a shy, easily disturbed bird with few recognition features; familiarity with the flight note (a musical rattle) and contact call (a clear descending whistle) is the best aid in establishing its presence.

The winter distribution is confined almost entirely to the east coast of England from Northumberland to Kent. Several localities are favoured, including the main estuaries, N Northumberland and N Norfolk, all having extensive salt marshes, often grazed, and adjacent rough pastures. Away from the east coast, records are very sparse. High counts of migrants in autumn, especially in the north and west, are not sustained into winter and even in the east many birds appear to move on during the late winter.

The birds associate with Skylarks *Alauda arvensis*, finches and buntings when feeding among stubble and on rough grassland in coastal fields. These flocks are often very wary, making approach difficult. On the ground, Lapland Buntings move with a quick run which, although characteristic of the species, enables them to find rapid concealment. They feed almost entirely on seeds taken from the ground or from low-growing plants, though they have also been recorded feeding on the shore, picking through the drift-line. Roosting likewise is on the ground, either in the feeding fields or on nearby mature salt marsh.

Davis (1954) and Williamson and Davis (1956) have suggested that many of the birds visiting Britain arrive from the northwest, from Greenland via Iceland, rather than from Scandinavia. The two widely separated populations appear to migrate in directions which would not normally bring either to Britain. The Greenland birds travel southwestwards to winter in North America, whereas those from Scandinavia head southeast into south-central Asia. Arrivals of birds in Britain must therefore result from drift-migration and the numbers present be dependent upon conditions prevailing in autumn. The evidence suggests that small, regular numbers reach us from the east supplemented, in some years, by often larger influxes from Greenland. In peak years the highest counts are made in the north and west of Ireland, the west coast of Scotland and even in SW England. It is widely thought that Lapland Buntings overwinter around the southern shores of the North Sea, but this is not supported by the figures, even though some birds may be overlooked. As yet there is little information to indicate where the birds do spend the later part of the winter. As might be expected, there have been few ringed and none recovered.

A small breeding population became established, briefly, in Scotland from 1974 to 1981, a maximum of 16 pairs being involved. It is interesting to speculate whether these were Greenland birds or from the east. The former is the more likely since Scandinavian birds appear to be recorded from the southern part of the east coast and probably return to their breeding areas via the Continental coast.

The low numbers of birds present in the three winters of the survey period follow a succession of poor autumns for the species. A calculation, based on the distribution map, suggests that the current wintering population in Britain and Ireland is between 200 and 500 birds, a figure increased several-fold in peak years. There is however a possibility of duplicated counts, and the difficulty of locating groups of birds may significantly affect the accuracy of such an estimate.

R. LAMBERT

Total number of squares in which recorded: 87 (2%)

No. of birds seen in a day	Number (%) of squares Britain	Ireland	TOTAL (incl. C.I.)
1	40 (47%)	0 (0%)	40 (46%)
2–7	30 (35%)	0 (0%)	30 (34%)
8 +	16 (19%)	1 (100%)	17 (20%)

References

DAVIS, P. 1954. Reports from Observatories 1952. Lapland Bunting. *Brit. Birds* 47: 21–23.

FERGUSON-LEES, I. J. 1954. Photographic studies of some less familiar birds. 58. Lapland Bunting. *Brit. Birds* 47: 232–233.

SHARROCK, J. T. R. 1983. Rare breeding birds in the United Kindgom in 1981. *Brit. Birds* 76: 1–25.

WILLIAMSON, K. and P. DAVIS. 1956. The autumn 1953 invasion of Lapland Buntings and its source. *Brit. Birds* 49: 6–25.

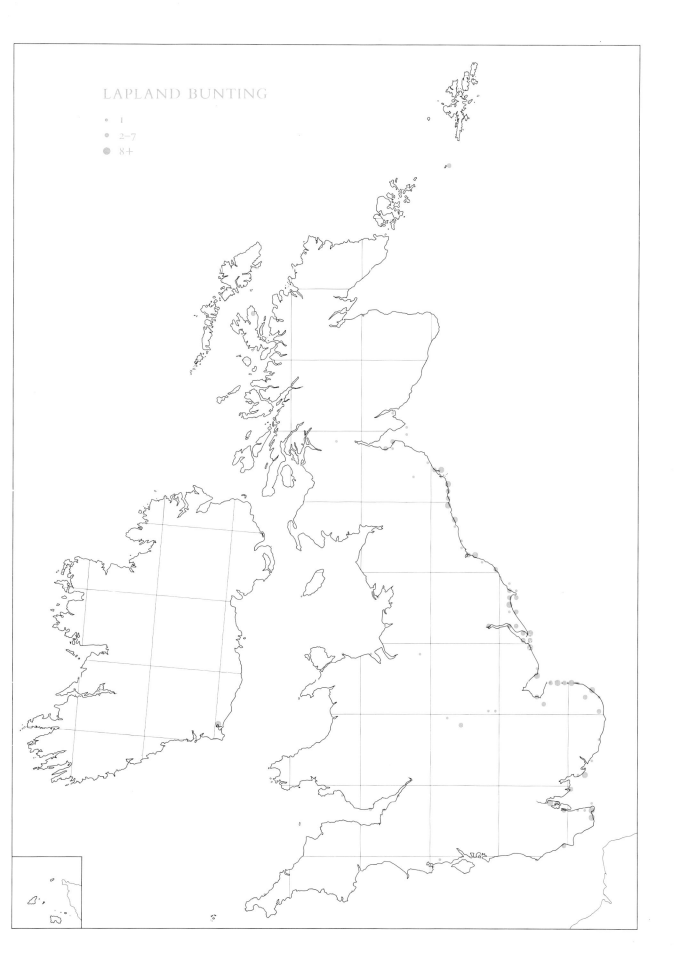

LAPLAND BUNTING

- 1
- 2–7
- 8+

Snow Bunting

Plectrophenax nivalis

One of the many attractions that coastal sites offer to casual observers and enthusiasts alike is the sight of assembled flocks of Snow Buntings busily and restlessly feeding among the tide wrack and dune fringes. The blizzard of white wing and tail markings, so characteristic of the species, draws the attention unfailingly and the birds' often confiding nature allows observation to be made at close quarters.

The coastal bias to the distribution is most evident in the southern part of Britain, but the marked preference for sandy shores is clear, throughout, from the machair of the Outer Hebrides to the many sites along the North Sea coast. Western and southern coasts hold very few birds even when suitable habitat is available. The only exception is the small concentration of records around the southern Irish Sea. In Scotland and Ireland, inland records are frequent from mainly upland sites and inland records from further south fit this pattern. The scattering of records of small numbers of birds in lowland sites in central England may well represent cold weather migration routes from the Wash and the Thames to the Severn estuaries.

The Snow Bunting is typically a bird of short, open vegetation, preferring to pick seeds from the ground or from low growing plants. Sandy shores with a carpet of dune colonising plants, or the lower levels of salt marshes, provide the most favoured sites and can support flocks several hundreds strong throughout the winter. Numbers fluctuate, no doubt with availability of food since the mobile nature of the habitat can alternately cover and uncover the seed supply. There is competition in such areas, other buntings and finches being frequent associates, but the flock remains as a unit especially in flight. The characteristic 'rolling' behaviour of the flock as it feeds, described by Henty (1979), appears to be most often seen when food is thinly scattered, the behaviour breaking down when a high density of food is found.

In upland areas the main food source is probably seeds of *Juncus* spp., though Snow Buntings have been recorded feeding from a wide range of moor grasses and heather. They also take invertebrates when available, sandhoppers forming an important element of the diet in coastal sites, and cereal grains, obtained from stubble field areas where grain has spilled. The birds generally roost on the ground or among low vegetation, though roosting in trees has been recorded.

The breeding distribution is circumpolar, with populations from North America, Iceland and north-ern Europe moving into Britain and Ireland each winter. Birds from Greenland and Iceland are the earliest arrivals in the autumn in the west and northwest. Ringing recoveries indicate a continuing passage to the southeast down the east coast and into the Low Countries. Scandinavian birds probably winter along the southern Baltic and the European coasts but there is clear evidence that this population does reach Britain, possibly on a regular basis, and it is certainly pushed southwestwards during cold winters in northern Europe. One individual ringed on Fair Isle in spring 1959 was recorded off Newfoundland in the following spring, an indication that the Greenland population may migrate either southwest or southeast under the influence of prevailing weather conditions. Nethersole-Thompson (1966) suggested that fluctuations of the small breeding population in Scotland are also a result of climatic change. Severe winters may encourage more birds to remain to take up territory, though whether these are birds which have wintered locally or further south is not known.

This tendency to be influenced by climatic factors results in large variations from winter to winter in the numbers of Snow Buntings reaching Britain and Ireland. Unusually high numbers may be present over a series of years, followed by a marked decline for a similar period. It is, therefore, difficult to assess the numbers of birds present each winter. County reports from the relevant winters indicate that numbers are currently on the low side and, in conjunction with the distribution map, a population of 10,000–15,000 birds seems likely.

R. LAMBERT

Total number of squares in which recorded: 705 (18%)

No. of birds seen in a day	Number (%) of squares		
	Britain	Ireland	TOTAL (incl. C.I.)
1–8	301 (47%)	54 (78%)	355 (50%)
9–50	205 (32%)	12 (17%)	217 (31%)
51 +	130 (20%)	3 (4%)	133 (19%)

References

HENTY, C. J. 1979. The foraging activity of Snow Buntings wintering inland in Scotland. *Bird Study* 26: 192–194.

NETHERSOLE-THOMPSON, D. 1966. *The Snow Bunting.* Oliver & Boyd, Edinburgh & London.

Breeding Atlas p 440

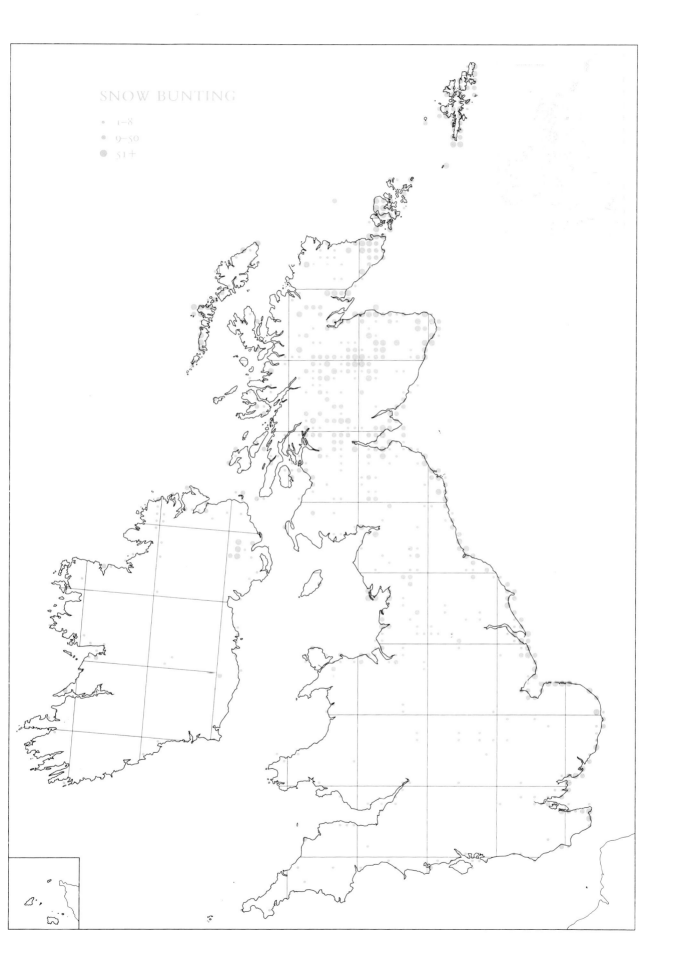

SNOW BUNTING

- 1–8
- 9–50
- 51+

Yellowhammer

Emberiza citrinella

In 1881, E. T. Booth wrote of the Yellowhammer in East Anglia that 'severe weather, though it usually drives this species from the outlying quarters to the neighbouring farms and buildings, seldom causes any general movement from one district to another'. One hundred years later, this can still be read as an acceptable summary of the response of the British Yellowhammer to winter.

The winter distribution of the species in Britain covers most of the country, with the exception of large gaps in the Highlands and Islands region of N and W Scotland, and smaller discontinuities in upland areas of S Scotland, N England and Wales. Comparison with the *Breeding Atlas* shows that the Yellowhammer is similarly scarce or absent as a breeding species over much of the Scottish Highlands and Islands, and the only distributional change in winter is a tendency towards withdrawal from upland areas generally. The difference between recorded summer and winter ranges in Ireland is more marked, with the Yellowhammer appearing to be scarce or absent over large areas of the country in winter. Given that the species is essentially sedentary in lowland areas in Britain, seasonal changes in Irish distribution are difficult to explain.

Wintering Yellowhammers are typically flocking birds of agricultural habitats, where their diet is mainly cereal grains and other large grass seeds (*eg, Festuca, Lolium*) supplemented on occasion by seeds of weeds such as dock. Almost all food is obtained from the ground although, during early autumn, birds may perch on the stout stems of cereals in order to remove ripening grain. At night Yellowhammers collect together in roosts of tens or hundreds in areas of dense scrub or marshy vegetation.

Ringing results reveal that about 70% of adult British Yellowhammers winter within 5 km of their breeding territories. Movement abroad is negligible, with the few recorded recoveries all relating to individuals caught in E England in spring or autumn. These may well have been Scandinavian breeding birds, which appear to migrate along the east coast of Britain in small numbers.

Common Birds Census results indicate that on farmland, its preferred habitat, the Yellowhammer in Britain has maintained a remarkably constant breeding population during the past 20 years, though there has been a decline in N Ireland. Fluctuations in woodland breeding numbers have been somewhat greater, but there is little indication that severe winters markedly affect overall population levels. O'Connor (1979) has provided evidence that low population levels in spring are significantly correlated with low temperatures the previous November, but this relationship is slight. Given the *Breeding Atlas* estimate of about 1,000,000 breeding pairs of Yellowhammers, and an annual adult mortality of 46%, and assuming that each pair produces two offspring surviving to mid winter, the January 1982 population level in Britain and Ireland must have been of the order of 3,500,000 individuals.

R. P. PRŶS-JONES

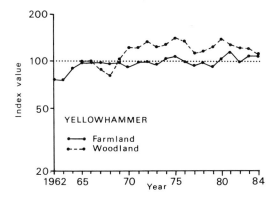

The CBC index in farmland and woodland.

Total number of squares in which recorded: 2,473 (64%)

No. of birds seen in a day	Number (%) of squares		
	Britain	Ireland	TOTAL (incl. C.I.)
1–25	843 (42%)	403 (88%)	1,248 (50%)
26–74	675 (34%)	52 (11%)	727 (29%)
75 +	493 (24%)	5 (1%)	498 (20%)

References

BOOTH, E. T. 1881/87. *Rough Notes on the Birds Observed in the British Islands*. 3 volumes. R. H. Porter and Dulau & Co., London.

EVANS, P. R. 1969. Winter fat deposition and overnight survival of Yellow Buntings (*Emberiza citrinella* L.) *J. Anim. Ecol.* 38: 415–423.

O'CONNOR, R. J. 1979. Population dynamics of some farmland species. *BTO News* 98: 9–10.

PRŶS-JONES, R. P. 1977. *Aspects of Reed Bunting Ecology, with Comparisons with the Yellowhammer*. D. Phil. Thesis, University of Oxford.

Breeding Atlas p 434

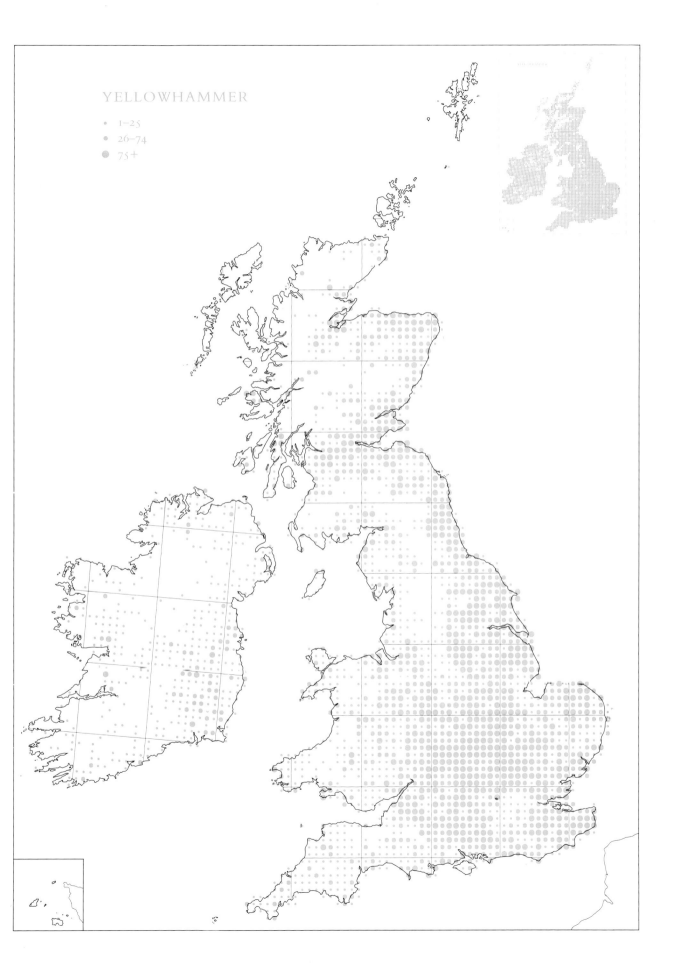

YELLOWHAMMER

- • 1–25
- • 26–74
- • 75+

Cirl Bunting

Emberiza cirlus

Male Cirl Buntings sing intermittently throughout the winter months and this can make detection easy. On the other hand, if there is no singing, the species can be difficult to find when just a few birds are mixed with flocks of finches and Yellowhammers *E. citrinella*.

Comparison of the map with that of the BTO survey in 1982 (Sitters 1985) shows that there is very little difference between the breeding and winter distributions, reflecting the fact that most of the British Cirl Bunting population is sedentary.

Cirl Buntings were recorded in only 27 10-km squares compared with 174 during the fieldwork for the *Breeding Atlas*. The British population has declined fairly steadily since the 1930s. Sitters (1982) estimated the British breeding population during the period 1968–72 as 250 to 300 pairs but the survey of 1982 showed that the numbers had fallen to a maximum of 181 pairs in 36 10-km squares (Sitters 1985). The number of squares found to be occupied during the *Winter Atlas* fieldwork is less than the number occupied during the 1982 breeding survey. In winter, however, the species is more difficult to detect. As breeding territories are fairly large, the population is more spread out than it is during the winter when birds come together to form small loose flocks.

As many birds, in winter, stay in the area of their breeding territories it is reasonable to assume that winter habitat requirements are much the same as for breeding. Typical habitat in the main range in S Devon, is predominantly agricultural country with substantial hedgerows and trees or scrub with trees on southward facing slopes. Food is chiefly corn, seeds of weeds and grasses as well as berries and some insects. During winter Cirl Buntings frequently feed on seeds in small groups in fields, sometimes amongst flocks of other finches and buntings.

There is no evidence of migration but there is a tendency for Cirl Buntings to wander in autumn and winter, occurring in small parties in localities where they do not breed. Significant movement is probably limited to a post-breeding dispersal of juveniles giving rise to occasional winter records well away from the main breeding areas. However, some of the isolated winter records are close to former breeding haunts (for example in Worcestershire and Oxfordshire) which might indicate the undetected persistence of very small breeding populations.

There have been three recoveries of British ringed Cirl Buntings; two were local but the third was a juvenile ringed at Beachy Head, Sussex, on 27 July 1975 and controlled on the Isle of May, Fife, on 11 June 1976. The species is only a vagrant to Scotland, so this movement was clearly atypical. The distance between the location of some winter records and the nearest, known breeding population would indicate that Cirl Buntings do not normally move greater distances than 100 km. Although it has been suggested that the Cirl Bunting may have colonised southern England from the Continent around the end of the 18th century, there has never been any evidence of cross Channel movement.

The 1982 breeding survey located a maximum of 181 pairs. It is therefore reasonable to suppose that, with a brood size of 3–4 and 2 broods a year the mid winter population is likely to be about 500 birds, taking into account nesting losses and mortality.

The main range of the Cirl Bunting comprises the countries bordering the northern and western Mediterranean, with an extension northwards through France to southern England. The northern edge of the distribution across Europe roughly follows January isotherms at 3°–5°C which suggests that winter temperature is a limiting factor. In England the present distribution is almost entirely south of the 5°C January isotherm, and in areas of relatively low rainfall. NW Europe has seen some climatic deterioration since the 1940s, and it is thought that this has been responsible for the decline of the Cirl Bunting population in England as well as in Belgium and NE France (Sitters 1985).

H. P. SITTERS

Total number of squares in which recorded: 26 (1%)

No. of birds seen in a day	Number (%) of squares		
	Britain	Ireland	TOTAL (incl. C.I.)
1–2	16 (62%)	0 (0%)	16 (62%)
3–5	6 (23%)	0 (0%)	6 (23%)
6+	4 (15%)	0 (0%)	4 (15%)

References
SITTERS, H. P. 1982. The decline of the Cirl Bunting in Britain, 1968–80. *Brit. Birds* 75: 105–108.
SITTERS, H. P. 1985. Cirl Buntings in Britain in 1982. *Bird Study* 31: 1–10.

Breeding Atlas p 436

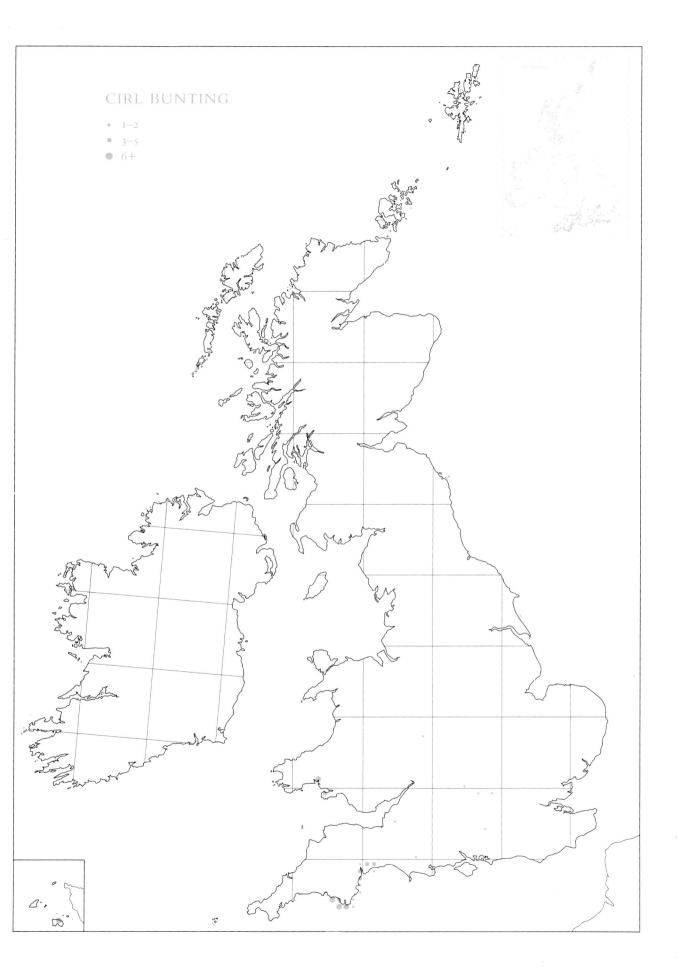

CIRL BUNTING

- • 1–2
- • 3–5
- ● 6+

Reed Bunting

Emberiza schoeniclus

In winter, Reed Buntings are considerably less obvious to the casual observer than during spring and early summer. The males' characteristic black heads and white collars are tipped with brown, there is no loud repetitive song to attract our attention, and the species is much less confined to the kind of habitat indicated by its name. As a consequence, in the past there has been confusion regarding their status in Britain and Ireland during the winter.

The *Breeding Atlas* revealed Reed Buntings as having an essentially country-wide distribution, although less common in highland regions. The winter distribution shown by the map remains widespread, but with a clear withdrawal from many upland areas of Scotland, northern England and Wales. Low numbers in the cold central parts of East Anglia may be a consequence of breeding birds moving to adjacent areas, but gaps in distribution around the mild southwest coast are surprising in view of movements into the region in winter (see below). In Ireland, winter distribution appears widespread but is patchy, perhaps because the species is easily overlooked in squares lacking repeated coverage.

British Reed Buntings are predominantly granivorous in winter, concentrating on the seeds of grasses and herbaceous plants which are taken mainly from on or near the ground (Prŷs-Jones 1977). Winter feeding flocks spread out widely over farmland and waste ground during the day (small numbers of birds sometimes enter gardens), but come together again in the evenings to form roosts in marshy areas. Trapping at such roosts in central and SE England has revealed that males generally outnumber females by about 2:1, with the imbalance tending to be greater in harsher winters.

Results from ringing indicate that less than 1% of British breeding birds move abroad in winter, and even these do little more than cross the English Channel. A somewhat greater, though still small, number of foreign breeding birds winters in Britain; these come mainly from western Scandinavia, with a few from the Low Countries and, possibly, NW Germany (Prŷs-Jones 1984). Other W Scandinavian birds migrate along the east coast of Britain to winter

further south in Europe. Within Britain itself, ringing results imply that about 40% of females and 80% of males move no more than 5 km between summer and winter. Of birds which do go further, less than 20% are recorded wintering over 100 km from their breeding areas, these travelling mainly towards the mild southwest.

Reed Buntings winter widely across western Europe, but almost entirely in regions having mean January temperatures above 0°C because prolonged or extensive snow cover cuts off access to their food resources (Prŷs-Jones 1984). Mean January temperatures in Britain are almost entirely above 0°C, but largely below 5°C, and abnormally severe weather causes Reed Buntings great hardship. Common Birds Census and Waterways Birds Survey results spanning 20 years demonstrate a large variability in summer population levels, troughs occurring immediately after the severest winters (1962/63, 1981/82) and peaks following extended series of mild ones. Since the *Breeding Atlas* estimate of more than 600,000 pairs in 1972 was made, the farmland CBC index has roughly halved. Assuming each pair produces an average of 2 offspring surviving to mid winter, and that there is an overall annual adult mortality of 43% (Prŷs-Jones 1977) and a limited winter influx of birds from abroad, a January 1982 estimate for Britain and Ireland would be about 1,200,000 birds.

R. P. PRŶS-JONES

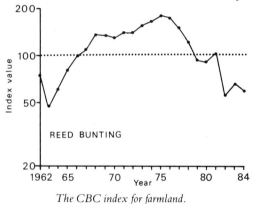

The CBC index for farmland.

Total number of squares in which recorded: 2,491 (65%)

No. of birds seen in a day	Number (%) of squares		
	Britain	Ireland	TOTAL (incl. C.I.)
1–5	780 (44%)	405 (57%)	1,185 (48%)
6–19	580 (33%)	230 (32%)	811 (32%)
20+	417 (23%)	77 (11%)	495 (20%)

References

PRŶS-JONES, R. P. 1977. *Aspects of Reed Bunting Ecology, with Comparisons with the Yellowhammer.* D. Phil. Thesis, University of Oxford.

PRŶS-JONES, R. P. 1984. Migration patterns of the Reed Bunting, *Emberiza schoeniclus schoeniclus*, and the dependence of wintering distribution on environmental conditions. *Le Gerfaut* 74: 15–37.

Breeding Atlas p 438

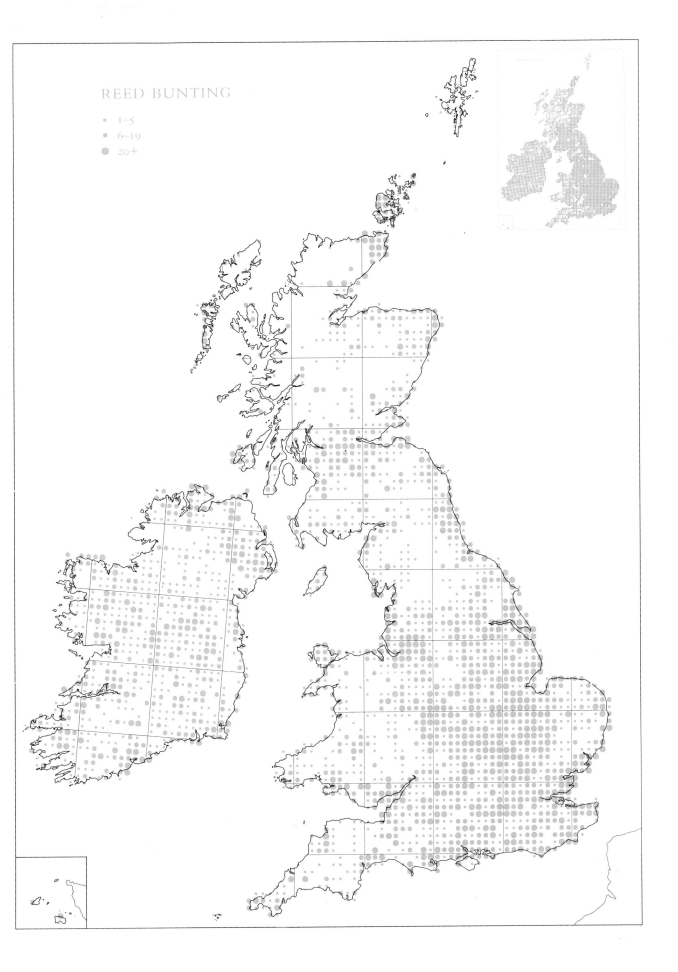

REED BUNTING

- 1–5
- 6–19
- 20+

Corn Bunting

Miliaria calandra

This is still one of the most typical birds of many areas of arable farmland in England, particularly for example on the southern chalk. But, while conspicuous through its song in summer, it is more self-effacing in winter and can be difficult to locate unless something is known of its local movements.

The winter distribution shown has two elements. Primarily the species is correlated with the main areas of cultivation in England and eastern Scotland; secondarily there is a coastal element, which is particularly evident in Scotland, the Hebrides, Ireland and East Anglia, with few birds remaining in SW England.

Comparison with Coppock (1976) shows that distribution in cultivated areas is linked most closely with cereal farming, and the figures recorded here support this, the largest numbers being found in areas where cereals dominate farming. How pleasant to have a species live up to its common name! Climatic considerations may also influence distribution, because Corn Buntings were recorded only in areas with less than 1,000 mm rainfall annually, a factor strongly influencing cereal distribution, too. Rainfall may also account for the coastal distribution outside the main range.

Comparison with the *Breeding Atlas* gives a striking picture of the steady decline described therein and also recorded in the Common Birds Census annual index. Corn Buntings are now rare in Ireland, Wales and SW England and have declined everywhere in Scotland since the early 1970s, while in the main English range there are increasing gaps in East Anglia and counties such as Lincolnshire. This decline is most probably caused by agricultural change. In western Britain the trend in the last 25 years has been from arable to grass, which may explain declines of Corn Buntings there. In the main arable districts of Britain, however, cereals have increased steadily (by 9% between 1970 and 1980), so the Corn Bunting's decline seems anomalous.

Fundamental changes in the management of cereal farms, however, have changed their character as habitats. Perhaps most significant to Corn Buntings has been the disappearance of traditional rotations. Cereals are increasingly grown continuously, rather than as part of a rotation of crops and livestock, and there is some evidence that the rotation crops once common on cereal farms, such as roots or clover, are important to Corn Buntings. A major decline in the process of cultivation, particularly in spring, changes in the timing of stubble management, in harvesting methods and, above all, the impact of herbicides on field weeds, have all restricted food supplies, and this may now be affecting all seed-eating birds in farmland (O'Connor and Shrubb 1986). Many of these changes seem likely to have most impact in winter and spring, for the Corn Bunting's summer diet includes many more insect prey.

Corn Buntings roost communally in winter, particularly in reed beds or gorse and similar low scrub, and feed in flocks. This is typical of many seed-eating birds of open country, and communal roosting helps birds find food which may be locally distributed (see Lack 1966). In parts of southern England roosts of 300–500 birds are not uncommon; such concentrations are likely to be drawn from a considerable area, suggesting that suitable roosts are scarce in good Corn Bunting terrain. The increase in cereals has been part of a rather larger increase in tilled land (10–15% in the last 20 years). Some Corn Bunting roost sites have probably been lost, which may have contributed to the decline in numbers.

Estimating winter numbers is not really possible. The *Breeding Atlas* suggested a breeding population of about 30,000 pairs and the CBC index has declined by about 10% since. But this index may be unreliable as it is usually based on rather small samples of Corn Buntings and fluctuates strongly. Distribution has also always been disjointed. The species lends itself to a winter count at roosts but few *Winter Atlas* records refer to them. In the absence of more accurate figures it is only possible to suggest that the mid winter population in Britain and Ireland is unlikely to exceed 150,000 birds, and is perhaps below 100,000.

M. SHRUBB

Total number of squares in which recorded: 747 (19%)

No. of birds seen in a day	Number (%) of squares		
	Britain	Ireland	TOTAL (incl. C.I.)
1–11	353 (48%)	10 (100%)	363 (49%)
12–50	237 (32%)	0 (0%)	237 (32%)
51+	147 (20%)	0 (0%)	147 (20%)

References

COPPOCK, J. T. 1976. *An Agricultural Atlas of England and Wales.* (Rev. edn). Faber, London.

LACK, D. 1966. *Population Studies of Birds.* University Press, Oxford.

O'CONNOR, R. J. and M. SHRUBB. 1986 (in press). *Farming and Birds.* University Press, Cambridge.

Breeding Atlas p 432

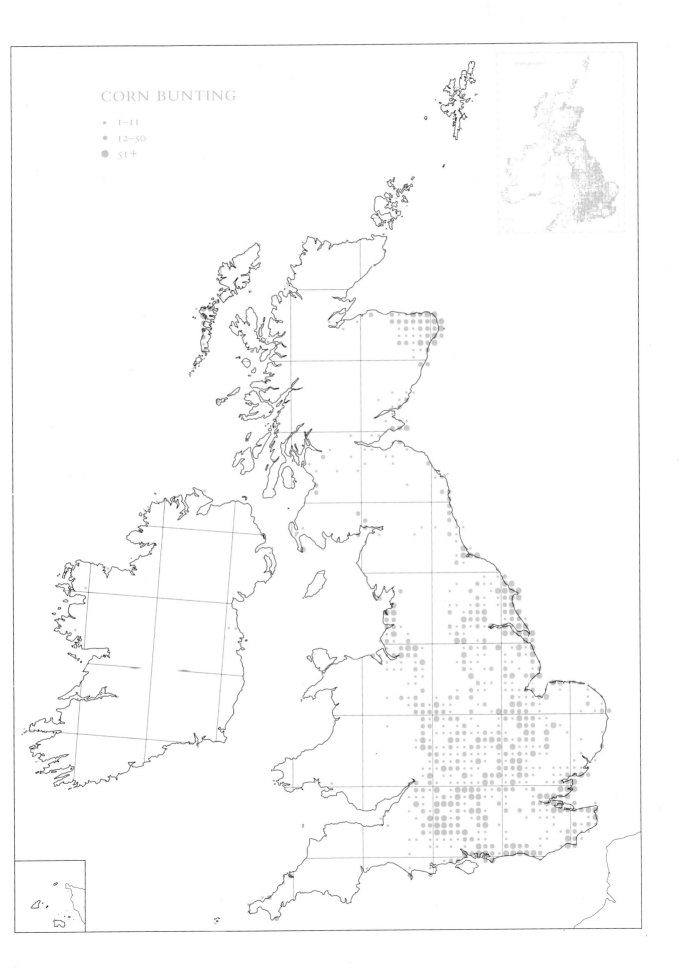

CORN BUNTING

- 1–11
- 12–50
- 51+

Grey Phalarope ·*Phalaropus fulicarius*

During the winter Grey Phalaropes flock in the open tropical and sub-tropical oceans, concentrating in areas of upwelling. The nearest major wintering area to Britain and Ireland is off the bulge of West Africa. All but two of the records shown on the map were of single birds. Some individual birds were reported several times—there was a total of 68 records sent in to the *Winter Atlas*. The monthly split was 11 in November, 18 in December, 29 in January and 10 in February. The five inland records may refer only to three individuals, one recorded during each winter of the Atlas period.

The cluster of records in NE England includes birds in each of the three winters. The scattered records in S Wales, SW England and along the south coast probably plot storm-driven birds after strong westerly winds had brought them in from the Atlantic.

C. J. MEAD

Total number of squares in which recorded: 41 (1%)

No. of birds seen in a day	Number (%) of squares		
	Britain	Ireland	TOTAL (incl. C.I.)
1	37 (95%)	2 (100%)	39 (95%)
2+	2 (5%)	0 (0%)	2 (5%)

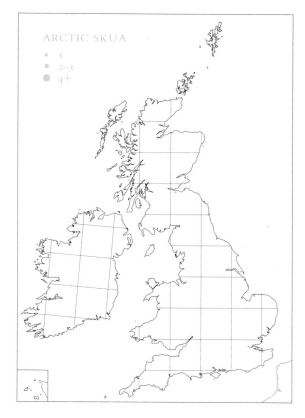

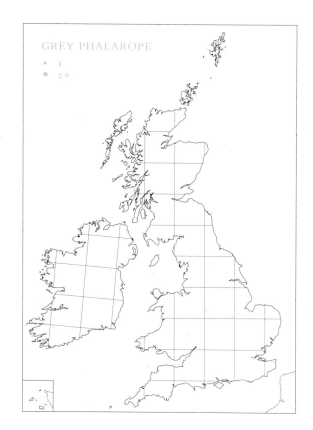

Arctic Skua *Stercorarius parasiticus*

The vast majority of Arctic Skuas which breed in or pass through Britain and Ireland winter in the South Atlantic, many of them being found off South Africa in the upwelling area of the Benguela current. However a small minority remains in the North Atlantic and the 66 records from 44 squares reported during the *Winter Atlas* work may be representative of these. In particular birds wintering in the North Sea may regularly be present along the east coast of Britain. About two thirds of the records were during the second half of November with only 11, 8 and 4 in December, January and February. Two cards showed 10 birds. Both were within three days of the start of the fieldwork period (from the Humber and the Wash) and must surely have been late migrants. No other records were of more than 4 birds.

Regular passage, in very small numbers, has been reported inland during the autumn but the only two inland records during the Atlas period, both from near Inverness, were in three days 12–14 November 1982: a period of westerly gales.

C. J. MEAD

Total number of squares in which recorded: 44 (1%)

No. of birds seen in a day	Number (%) of squares		
	Britain	Ireland	TOTAL (incl. C.I.)
1	25 (63%)	4 (100%)	29 (66%)
2–3	11 (28%)	0 (0%)	11 (25%)
4+	4 (10%)	0 (0%)	4 (9%)

Great Skua *Stercorarius skua*

Although many Great Skuas from the breeding areas in Scotland, the Faeroes and Iceland travel far to the south for the winter, some are regularly to be found in the North Atlantic during winter months. They are frequently recorded in the relatively enclosed waters of the North Sea. The rather few birds recorded during the Atlas period result from the species' pelagic habits—few come close enough to the coast to be recorded from land. Of 84 dated records submitted 26 were in November, 19 in December, 30 in January (22 of them in 1983) and 9 in February. Only one record was of more than 4 birds: 9 birds from the Norfolk coast of the Wash in November. The inland records in SE England all refer to a single bird in early January 1983.

C. J. MEAD

Total number of squares in which recorded: 58 (2%)

No. of birds seen in a day	Number (%) of squares		
	Britain	Ireland	TOTAL (incl. C.I.)
I	46 (84%)	I (33%)	47 (81%)
2–3	7 (13%)	2 (67%)	9 (16%)
4+	2 (4%)	0 (0%)	3 (3%)

Sandwich Tern *Sterna sandvicensis*

The winter records of Sandwich Terns, plotted on this map, represent a recent change in behaviour. Hudson (1973), reviewing winter records of summer migrants, listed only 9 birds in December and 2 in February (none in January). During the three Atlas winters there were 13 records in December, 24 in January and 15 in February. Many of these were from the Firth of Forth where successively one, two and three birds seem to have wintered: the first records of wintering in Scotland are commented upon by da Prato *et al* (1981).

Most Sandwich Terns move southwards to winter off the West African or South African coasts. Many hundreds of ringing recoveries show that these birds include those that breed in Britain and Ireland. Over the last 15 years or so more and more records, some of substantial flocks, show that the wintering area has extended northwards to include the Mediterranean, Portugal and the Gironde region of France. *BWP* records that 3,000, up to 700, and 50 birds, respectively, may be involved in these three areas.

C. J. MEAD

Total number of squares in which recorded: 26 (1%)

No. of birds seen in a day	Number (%) of squares		
	Britain	Ireland	TOTAL (incl. C.I.)
I	19 (79%)	I (100%)	21 (81%)
2+	5 (21%)	0 (0%)	5 (19%)

References

DA PRATO, S. R. D., J. M. DICKSON and F. L. SYMONDS. 1981. Sandwich Terns in the Firth of Forth in winter. *Scot. Birds* 11: 226–227.

HUDSON, R. 1973. Early and late dates for summer migrants. *BTO Guide* 15, Tring.

shows concentrations of sightings in coastal counties—especially those of S and SE England and SE Ireland—which would be expected of passage birds in the process of departing from these islands, and already late on their journey to African winter quarters.

R. W. HUDSON

Total number of squares in which recorded: 113 (3%)

No. of birds seen in a day	Number (%) of squares		
	Britain	Ireland	TOTAL (incl. C.I.)
1	73 (74%)	8 (62%)	81 (72%)
2–3	21 (21%)	3 (23%)	24 (21%)
4+	5 (5%)	2 (15%)	8 (7%)

House Martin *Delichon urbica*

House Martins share with Swallows *Hirundo rustica* the tendency to have an autumn migration period which is so protracted that the last few birds do not leave until winter has begun. We do not know whether such very late hirundines, which do not depart until the onset of night frosts, succeed in reaching normal winter quarters in tropical or southern Africa. Possibly the inherited (endogenous) migration programmes are defective in such individuals.

Of the total of 144 *Winter Atlas* records the majority

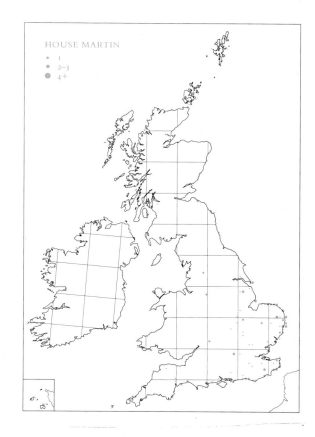

Swallow *Hirundo rustica*

The Swallow is claimed to be one of the harbingers of spring, but it is also one of the latest of the summer migrants to depart in autumn. Moreover, there are one or two out-of-season records in most winters. With *Winter Atlas* fieldwork beginning in November, it was inevitable that the tail-end of the Swallow's autumn exodus would be recorded.

There was a total of 147 *Winter Atlas* records, of which 132 were for November, but some of these may have been the same birds seen on more than one date. A further 13 records occurred in the period 1–10th December, and these clearly were very late migrants. The remaining two were noted on 4th February in Lincolnshire, and 21st February in Norfolk. Both were probably overwintering but just possibly the latter record was an exceptionally early spring arrival—it is almost impossible in late February to distinguish individuals that wintered in NW Europe from the first returning migrants. The map

(130) were for November though (as in the Swallow) it is possible that there was some duplication, with some lingering birds being seen on more than one date. A further 10 records fell within the period 1–10th December. The remaining 4 concerned attempted or actual overwintering: 22nd December in Hampshire, 24th December in Co. Louth, 10th February in Dyfed, and 12–20th February in Norfolk. The map shows the same concentration, as in the Swallow, of records in S and SE England, and presumably for the same reason; however, the sole Irish record is the Christmas Eve one mentioned above.

R. W. HUDSON

Total number of squares in which recorded: 101 (3%)

No. of birds seen in a day	Number (%) of squares		TOTAL (incl. C.I.)
	Britain	Ireland	
1	57 (58%)	1 (100%)	58 (57%)
2–3	27 (28%)	0 (0%)	28 (28%)
4+	14 (14%)	0 (0%)	15 (15%)

Wheatear *Oenanthe oenanthe*

The Wheatear shares with the two hirundines (above) a tendency for a few individuals to linger here very late into the autumn and there have been, over the years, a fair number of winter records. This is also one of the earliest of summer migrants to return in spring, with exceptionally early birds arriving in the closing days of February in mild seasons.

Winter Atlas fieldwork produced a total of 54 records, of which 47 were in November; clearly, the latter were late passage birds on their way out of Britain and Ireland. Three were found in December: 11–12th in Hampshire, 31st in Kent, and one which overwintered December–February in Sussex. The remaining 4 records were for 11th February in Cambridgeshire, 17th February in Co. Clare, 24th February in Cumbria, and 27th February in Sussex.

Late migrants and wintering birds are usually found either on the coast or, when inland, by water such as reservoirs. Presumably this reflects both the coastal emphasis of passage and a more reliable supply of insect food close to water at this difficult season of the year. The coastal concentration of the mapped registrations is very marked.

R. W. HUDSON

Total number of squares in which recorded: 51 (1%)

No. of birds seen in a day	Number (%) of squares		TOTAL (incl. C.I.)
	Britain	Ireland	
1	39 (91%)	6 (86%)	46 (90%)
2+	4 (9%)	1 (14%)	5 (10%)

Whinchat *Saxicola rubetra*

Compared with the other three passerine summer visitors dealt with here, the Whinchat is generally regarded as less prone to lingering into the late autumn and winter (Hudson 1973, Riddiford and Findley 1981). Despite this, the *Winter Atlas* produced more mid winter records for Whinchat than for Swallow *Hirundo rustica*, House Martin *Delichon urbica* or Wheatear *Oenanthe oenanthe*.

The total of 32 Atlas records included 18 for November and a further 6 for the period 1–12th December, doubtless representing a final exodus of migrants. The remaining 8 were in true winter: 31st December in Sussex, 4th January in Strathclyde, 8th January in Glamorgan, 10–27th January in Hampshire, 16th January in Isle of Man, 10th February in Sussex, 26th February in Shropshire, and 28th February in Hampshire. The mainly coastal distribution of records shown in the map is basically similar to those for the other passerine summer migrants included in this section, and presumably for the same reasons.

R. W. HUDSON

WHINCHAT
- I
- 2+

Total number of squares in which recorded: 26 (1%)

No. of birds seen in a day	Number (%) of squares		
	Britain	Ireland	TOTAL (incl. C.I.)
I	21 (88%)	1 (50%)	22 (85%)
2+	3 (12%)	1 (50%)	4 (15%)

References

HUDSON, R. 1973. Early and late dates for summer migrants. *BTO Guide* 15, Tring.

RIDDIFORD, N. and P. FINDLEY. 1981. Seasonal movements of summer migrants. *BTO Guide* 18, Tring.

The distribution of the Razorbill Alca torda *and Little Auk* Alle alle *in the winters of 1981/82 and 1983/84 combined. The scales of abundance are as for the respective species maps on p. 253 and p. 257.*

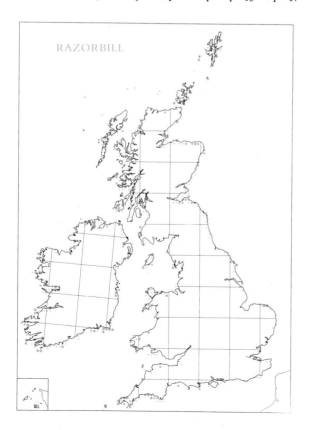

RAZORBILL

LITTLE AUK

List of other birds recorded

This list records all the other species (and some distinctive races) reported on record cards or sheets during the survey period. It includes birds which appeared to be living in a feral state although some had surely escaped from captivity. Species and races which are not on the British and Irish lists are marked with an asterisk.

The 10-km squares in which the birds were recorded are listed and the number of birds reported is shown in brackets if there was more than one.

White-billed Diver	*Gavia adamsii*	HU56 HY42 NU14 TA08
Black-browed Albatross	*Diomedea melanophris*	HP51 HP61
Cory's Shearwater	*Calonectris diomedea*	TR37
Sooty Shearwater	*Puffinus griseus*	SD16 V81
Manx Shearwater	*Puffinus puffinus*	NB03 NM54 NR15(20) NR27 NR54 NT17 NT69(2) SH58(5) SM84 TA18 D40 O30 V91
Storm Petrel	*Hydrobates pelagicus*	NG26(2) NG44 NG62 NM51 NM80 NS33 TA18 TM01 TR01 L55(3) W96
Leach's Petrel	*Oceanodroma leucorhoa*	NS31 NS33 SD33 SD45 SD57 SJ39 SM91 SN69 ST24 ST55 SY68
American Bittern	*Botaurus lentiginosus*	NS37 ST48
Little Bittern	*Ixobrychus minutus*	Jersey
Night Heron	*Nycticorax nycticorax*	NT27(20) NY16 SD46 ST56 TG03 TG31(2)
Green-backed Heron	*Butorides striatus*	TA21
Cattle Egret	*Bubulcus ibis*	SW97 SX07
Little Egret	*Egretta garzetta*	HY44
Great White Egret	*Egretta alba*	TA21 TA22
White Stork	*Ciconia ciconia*	ST17 TG50 TM47 TM48 TM55
Glossy Ibis	*Plegadis falcinellus*	TQ77 TR25(2) TR26(2) W96
*Sacred Ibis	*Threskiornis aethiopicus*	SU18 SU33 SU36 SU59 SZ68 TM46 TQ77 TR06 TR26
Spoonbill	*Platalea leucorodia*	ST35 SU10 SW53 SW84(2) SX35 SX45 SY98 SZ08 SZ09 SZ19 TF74 TG04 TM44 V72
*Flamingo species	*Phoenicopterus* spp.	NK02 NK05 NK06 NT73 NU13 NZ52 SU40(2) SY58(2) SY67(2) SZ19(2) SZ89 TG04 TM22
Whistling Swan	*Cygnus columbianus columbianus*	W96 X07
*Black Swan	*Cygnus atratus*	SD59(2) SE31 SE32(2) SH36 SH46 SH97 SJ07(2) SJ08(2) SK90 SK96 SO93 SP11 ST93 SU10 TR05 SY67 TF11 TF50 TG42 TL19 TL27 TL36(2) TL37 TL48 TM04 TM14 TM24 TQ76 TQ77 TR04
Lesser White-fronted Goose	*Anser erythropus*	SD31 SJ67 SO70(2) SP99 TF84 TG13 TG23 (Records in SJ67 and SP99 were feral birds)
*Swan Goose	*Anser cygnoides*	ST55(5)
*Bar-headed Goose	*Anser indicus*	NK04 NN17 NO55 NT83 SD95 SP73 SP84 SP85 SU43 SU53 SU66 SU67 SU75 SU92 SW72(3) SY79 SY98 TA14 TA30 TF84 TL04 TM57
Black Brant	*Branta bernicla nigricans*	SW97 TF49 TG04 TM11 TM22 TQ78 TQ89 J55
Red-breasted Goose	*Branta ruficollis*	SO70 SU10 TF84 TF94 TM01 TM13 TM22 TM33
Ruddy Shelduck	*Tadorna ferruginea*	SO70 SS87 ST55 TA21 TA30 TF49 TQ34 TQ38(8) TQ48 TQ76

Species	Scientific name	Grid references
*Wood Duck	Aix sponsa	SJ86 SK97 SP66 ST67 SU12(2) SU32 SU73(2) SU96 TA03(4) TF46(4) TL14 TL32(2) TL84 TM04(2) TQ00(5) TQ10 TQ28 TQ50(6) TQ65(3) TQ66(3) TQ74 TQ88
American Wigeon	Anas americana	NX06 NY06 SP96 SP97 SU10 SW53(3) SW62 SX64 TL08 TQ44 J18 Q30 V69
*Falcated Duck	Anas falcata	SP29
Green-winged Teal	Anas crecca carolinensis	NH64 NH66 NM73 SD31 SJ68 SJ75 SS78 SU40 SW53(2) SW73 SY98 TG04 TG42 TL48 TL59 TR01 G86 O02 O23 Q95 S40 T24 W96 X07 X08
American Black Duck	Anas rubripes	NH64 SH67 SV81
Garganey	Anas querquedula	NB56 SD46 SJ75(2) SP84 SZ68 TQ44 TQ55
Blue-winged Teal	Anas discors	ST51 SX64
*Bahama Pintail	Anas bahamensis	SJ60(3) SJ80 SJ81
*Marbled Duck	Marmaronetta angustirostris	TF57
King Eider	Somateria spectabilis	HU37 HU44 HU59 HY41 NC90 NH79 NH89(2) NJ16 NR45 NS37 G69
Steller's Eider	Polysticta stelleri	NF73
Surf Scoter	Melanitta perspicillata	NH78 NH89 NJ16 NJ26(4) NJ36 NZ62 SH37 SH67 SM84 TA18 G87 J33 J43(4) O17 T11 T12(2) W96
White-tailed Eagle	Haliaeetus albicilla	HU31(2) HU56 NC70 SE71 SP61 TM35 TM46 and several squares around Rhum where the species has been the subject of a reintroduction programme.
Gyrfalcon	Falco rusticolus	HU42 HY20 HZ27 SD26 C52
Quail	Coturnix coturnix	SH46
Spotted Crake	Porzana porzana	SD47 SK53 ST48 SU36 SU50 SY68 SZ19(2) SZ39 TF72 TG42 TL11 TQ94 TR23 TR26 TR36
Little Crake	Porzana parva	SK53
Crane	Grus grus	NS36 SJ78 SN40(2) SN65(2) SO70(3) SO90 SW86 SW96 TR26 TQ60
Great Bustard	Otis tarda	TQ77 TQ87 TQ92 TR02(3)
Stone-curlew	Burhinus oedicnemus	HU43 TG04 Guernsey
Killdeer	Charadrius vociferus	NF72 NF74 NS14 NS98 NT08 SU88 TQ26 X07
Kentish Plover	Charadrius alexandrinus	SZ79 TQ10 TQ20 TQ77
*Blacksmith Plover	Vanellus armatus	NZ91
Temminck's Stint	Calidris temminckii	SK90 SW61
Baird's Sandpiper	Calidris bairdii	TQ07
Curlew Sandpiper	Calidris ferruginea	ST28 ST36 SU31(2) SW42 SW53 SY67(2) SZ09 C42(7) Q81(5) W76 W86 Guernsey
Long-billed Dowitcher	Limnodromus scolopaceus	SW52 SW73 SW83 SZ39 W96
Hudsonian Godwit	Limosa haemastica	SX98 SX99
Upland Sandpiper	Bartramia longicauda	SJ75 SJ76
Greater Yellowlegs	Tringa melanoleuca	SJ37 Q81
Lesser Yellowlegs	Tringa flavipes	SP44 SX64 TQ60 TV69 J57 O25 W33
Wood Sandpiper	Tringa glareola	SP29 SY98 SZ19 TQ16
Spotted Sandpiper	Actitis macularia	W34 X08
Pomarine Skua	Stercorarius pomarinus	HU56 HY40 NC86(2) ND27 NH64(2) NH75(11) NJ96 SD26 SP84 TF57 TG33 TQ20 J56 M22(5)
Long-tailed Skua	Stercorarius longicaudus	SZ39

Laughing Gull	*Larus atricilla*	NS33 NZ16 NZ36 SH87 SJ06 SO70 SY29 W76 W86			SE74 SH63 SO47 SU20 SX57 SY08 SY88 SZ08 TF28 TG42 V92
Franklin's Gull	*Larus pipixcan*	SD41 SJ58 SX45			
Sabine's Gull	*Larus sabini*	NR44 NR77 SD20 SH28 SH49 SM84 SW98 SX84 SZ07(2) N45	Black-throated Thrush	*Turdus ruficollis atrogularis*	HU44
Bonaparte's Gull	*Larus philadelphia*	V55	American Robin	*Turdus migratorius*	HT93 SS14 J45 V56
Ross's Gull	*Rhodostethia rosea*	HU35 HU40 HU43 HU44 ND16 ND17 ND26 ND35 NZ52 SD31 TA09 TA18 M22 M32 S90	Sedge Warbler	*Acrocephalus schoenobaenus*	SX84
			Reed Warbler	*Acrocephalus scirpaceus*	SX84 TF55 TF74 Guernsey
			Icterine Warbler	*Hippolais icterina*	ST16
			Barred Warbler	*Sylvia nisoria*	X79
Ivory Gull	*Pagophila eburnea*	HU56 NO43	Lesser Whitethroat	*Sylvia curruca*	NU20 NZ36 SK90 SS78 SV91 TF49 TM11 TQ06 TQ23 Jersey
Common Tern	*Sterna hirundo*	NT37 SS43 TL48 TL49 TM58			
			Whitethroat	*Sylvia communis*	NT96(2) SY68 TF10 TQ50 TQ55 TR37 J06
Arctic Tern	*Sterna paradisaea*	SY68			
Forster's Tern	*Sterna forsteri*	O23	Garden Warbler	*Sylvia borin*	NC96 NJ90 NZ26 SJ28 SS64 TF55 V92
Brünnich's Guillemot	*Uria lomvia*	HY20 HY21 NC90			
Turtle Dove	*Streptopelia turtur*	NR89 SH39 TG30 TQ36	Pallas's Warbler	*Phylloscopus proregulus*	NT69 TM58(2) TV59 TR35
Great Spotted Cuckoo	*Clamator glandarius*	Alderney	Yellow-browed Warbler	*Phylloscopus inornatus*	SW62 SX59 TF49
Snowy Owl	*Nyctea scandiaca*	HU69(4) TL04	Dusky Warbler	*Phylloscopus fuscatus*	TR35
Swift	*Apus apus*	TQ77			
Hoopoe	*Upupa epops*	SH28 SJ95 SO53 SP24 SU09	Willow Warbler	*Phylloscopus trochilus*	NF72 NM25 NS36 SE31 SJ47(2) SK90 SU73 TM57 TQ65 TQ76
Wryneck	*Jynx torquilla*	SD19			
Sand Martin	*Riparia riparia*	NX15 SW43 TF74	Spotted Flycatcher	*Muscicapa striata*	SH28 SJ86 TF55
Richard's Pipit	*Anthus novaeseelandiae*	NT48 ST45 SU40 SY09 TF49 TG14(2) TG24	Red-breasted Flycatcher	*Ficedula parva*	HP60 HU56 ND49 SJ20 SJ77 SS49
			Short-toed Treecreeper	*Certhia brachydactyla*	Jersey Guernsey Herm Sark (resident in Channel Islands)
Olive-backed Pipit	*Anthus hodgsoni*	SU86			
Yellow Wagtail	*Motacilla flava*	NT96 ST76 ST85 SU60 SU70 TF20 TF49 TF52 TF71 TL21 TL29 TL37 TL91(2) TQ26	Penduline Tit	*Remiz pendulinus*	SE82(2) TR26
			Isabelline Shrike	*Lanius isabellinus*	TF55
			Rose-coloured Starling	*Sturnus roseus*	TT11 J65
Bluethroat	*Luscinia svecica*	HZ27	Serin	*Serinus serinus*	SY67 TF55 TL14 Jersey
Redstart	*Phoenicurus phoenicurus*	SC49 SJ51 SJ54 SK32 SW52 SW84 TQ57 TQ58 Jersey	Two-barred Crossbill	*Loxia leucoptera*	SK19
			Parrot Crossbill	*Loxia pytyopsittacus*	NZ13 SE20 SE27(2) SK19(20) SK28(8) SK29(7) SK38 TF84(3) TF94(4)
Pied Wheatear	*Oenanthe pleschanka*	SX86 T13			
Rock Thrush	*Monticola saxatilis*	TQ97	American Redstart	*Setophaga ruticilla*	TF55
Ring Ouzel	*Turdus torquatus*	HU67 NF74 NJ00 SD26	Little Bunting	*Emberiza pusilla*	NS14 SJ27 SJ28

Names of plants mentioned in the text

Vernacular names of plants which appear in the text are listed alphabetically. Scientific names (except algae) follow TUTIN, T. G. *et al.* 1964–1980. *Flora Europaea*. Vols 1–5. University Press, Cambridge. English names follow those in DONY, J. G., F. PERRING, and C. M. ROB. 1974. *English names of Wild Flowers*. Botanical Society of the British Isles, London.

Acorn	see Oak	Maize	*Zea mays*
Alder	*Alnus glutinosa*	Marram	*Ammophila arenaria*
Apple	*Malus domestica*	Mast	see Beech
Ash	*Fraxinus excelsior*	Mistletoe	*Viscum album*
Bamboo	*Arundinaria/Phyllostachys* spp	Mugwort	*Artemisia vulgaris*
Barberry	*Berberis vulgaris/Mahonia aquifolium*	Nettle	*Urtica dioica* (*U. urens*)
		Oak	*Quercus* spp
Barley	*Hordeum* spp	evergreen	*Q. ilex*
Beech	*Fagus sylvatica*	pedunculate	*Q. robur*
Beet	see Sugarbeet	sessile	*Q. petraea*
Berberis	see Barberry	Oat	*Avena* spp
Bilberry	*Vaccinium myrtillus*	Osier, Common	*Salix viminalis*
Birch, Downy	*Betula pubescens*	Persicaria	*Polygonum lapathifolium, P. persicaria*
Dwarf	*B. nana*		
Silver	*B. pendula*	Phragmites	see Reed, Common
Blackberry	see Bramble	Pine	*Pinus* spp
Blackthorn	*Prunus spinosa*	Corsican	*P. nigra*
Blaeberry	see Bilberry	Lodgepole	*P. contorta*
Bramble	*Rubus fruticosus* agg	Maritime	*P. pinaster*
Buckthorn	*Rhamnus catharticus*	Scots	*P. sylvestris*
Burdock	*Arctium* spp	Ponderosa	*P. ponderosa*
Buttercup	*Ranunculus* spp	Pondweed	*Potamogeton* spp
Cabbage	*Brassica oleracea*	Potato	*Solanum tuberosum*
Charlock	*Sinapis arvensis*	Pulses	Leguminosae
Cherry, Wild	*Prunus avium*	Ragwort	*Senecio jacobaea*
Chestnut, Horse	*Aesculus hippocastanum*	Rape, Oilseed	*Brassica napus* (*B. rapa*)
Sweet	*Castanea sativa*	Reed, Common	*Phragmites australis*
Chickweed	*Stellaria media*	Rhododendron	*Rhododendron ponticum*
Clover	*Trifolium* spp	Rose	*Rosa* spp
Cotoneaster	*Cotoneaster* spp (mainly *C. microphyllus* and *C. horizontalis*)	Rowan	*Sorbus aucuparia*
		Rush	*Juncus* spp
		Sea Buckthorn	*Hippophae rhamnoides*
Crowberry	*Empetrum nigrum*	Sea Lettuce	*Ulva lactuca*
Cypress	*Cupressus/Chamaecyparis* spp	Sea Rocket	*Cakile maritima*
Dandelion	*Taraxacum* spp	Sedge	*Carex* spp
Dock	*Rumex* spp	Spike-rush	*Eleocharis* spp
Eel Grass	*Zostera* spp	Spruce	*Picea* spp
Elder	*Sambucus nigra*	Norway	*P. abies*
Elm	*Ulmus* spp	Sitka	*P. sitchensis*
Wych	*U. glabra*	Sugarbeet	*Beta vulgaris*
Fat-hen	*Chenopodium album*	Swede	*Brassica napus*
Fir, Douglas	*Pseudotsuga menziesii*	Sycamore	*Acer pseudoplatanus*
Goosefoot	*Chenopodium* spp	Tansy	*Tanacetum vulgare*
Gorse	*Ulex europaeus*	Teasel	*Dipsacus fullonum*, (*D. pilosus*)
Groundsel	*Senecio vulgaris*	Thistle	*Carduus/Cirsium* spp
Haw/Hawthorn	*Crataegus monogyna*	Turnip	*Brassica rapa*
Hazel	*Corylus avellana*	Watercress	*Nasturtium officinale*
Heather (Ling)	*Calluna vulgaris*	Waterweed, Canadian	*Elodea canadensis*
Hip	see Rose	Wellingtonia	*Sequoiadendron giganteum*
Holly	*Ilex aquifolium*	Wheat	*Triticum* spp
Honeysuckle	*Lonicera* spp	Whortleberry	see Bilberry
Hornbeam	*Carpinus betulus*	Willow	*Salix* spp
Ivy	*Hedera helix*	Least (Dwarf)	*S. herbacea*
Juniper	*Juniperus communis*	Willowherb	*Epilobium* spp
Kale	*Brassica* spp	Wrack	*Fucus* spp
Kelp	*Laminaria* spp	Wrack, Knotted	*Ascophyllum nodosum*
Knapweed	*Centaurea* spp	Yew	*Taxus baccata*
Knotgrass	*Polygonum aviculare*		
Larch	*Larix* spp		
European	*L. decidua*		
Japanese	*L. kaempferi*		

Names of animals (other than birds) mentioned in the text

Vernacular names of animals which appear in the text are listed alphabetically. Scientific names follow current usage.

Ant	Hymenoptera: Formicidae
Baetid	Ephemeroptera: Baetidae
Barnacle	Crustacea: Cirripedia
Beetle	Coleoptera:
Carabid	Carabidae
Chafer	Scarabaeidae
Rove	Staphylinidae
Scarab	Scarabaeidae
Bivalve	Mollusca: Bivalvia
Blackfly	Diptera: *Simulium* spp
Bullhead	*Cotus gobio*
Caddisfly	Trichoptera
Capelin	*Mollotus villosus*
Chironomid	Diptera: Chironomidae
Cockle	Mollusca: *Cerastoderma edule*
Cod, Arctic	*Gadus morhua*
Corophium	Crustacea: *Corophium volutator*
Crab	Crustacea: Decapoda
Shore	*Carcinus maenas*
Deer, Red	*Cervus elaphus*
Dogwhelk	Mollusca: *Thais lapillus*
Dungfly	Diptera: *Scatophaga* spp
Earthworm	Annelida: Oligochaeta
Earwig	Dermaptera
Echinoderm	Echinodermata
Eel	*Anguilla anguilla*
Flatfish	*Plattichthys/Pleuronectes/Solea* spp
Fox	*Vulpes vulpes*
Frog	*Rana temporaria*
Haddock	*Melanogrammus aeglefinus*
Hare, Brown	*Lepus capensis*
Mountain	*L. timidus*
Herring	*Clupea harengus*
Hydrobia	Mollusca: *Hydrobia ulvae*, *H. ventrosa*
Kelp Fly	Diptera: *Coleopa frigida*
Leather-jacket	Diptera: Tipulidae (larva)
Limpet	Mollusca: *Patella vulgata*
Freshwater	*Ancylus* spp
Lizard	*Lacerta* spp
Lugworm	Annelida: *Arenicola marina*
Mackerel	*Scomber scombrus*
May Fly	Ephemeroptera
Microtine Rodent	Cricetidae: Microtinae
Midge	Diptera: Nematocera
Mole	*Talpa europaea*
Mosquito	Diptera: Culicidae
Mouse, Wood	*Apodemus sylvaticus*
House	*Mus musculus*
Mussel	
Common (Blue)	Mollusca: *Mytilus edulis*
Zebra	*Dreissena polymorpha*
Newt	*Triturus* spp
Perch	*Perca fluviatilis*
Periwinkle	Mollusca: *Littorina* spp
Plant Bug	Hemiptera
Polychaete Worm	Annelida: Polychaeta
Prawn	Crustacea: *Palaemonetes varians*
Rabbit	*Oryctolagus cuniculus*
Ragworm	Annelida: *Nereis diversicolor*
Rat, Brown (Common)	*Rattus norvegicus*
Roach	*Rutilus rutilus*
Salmon	*Salmo salar*
Salmonid	Salmonidae
Sand-eel	*Ammodytes marinus*
Sand-hopper	Crustacea: *Talitrus saltator*
Sand-mason Worm	Annelida: *Lanice conchilega*
Sawfly	Hymenoptera: Symphyta
Sheep	*Ovis* (domestic)
Shrew	*Sorex* spp
Shrimp, Common	Crustacea: *Crangon vulgaris*
Opossum	Crustacea: Mysidacea
Simuliid	Diptera: Simuliidae
Spider	Arachnida
Spireshell	Mollusca: *Potamogyrus jenkensi*
Sprat	*Sprattus sprattus*
Springtail	Collembola
Squid	Mollusca: Cephalopoda
Squirrel, Red	*Sciurus vulgaris*
Stickleback	*Gasterosteus/Pungitius* spp
Stoat	*Mustela erminea*
Stonefly	Plecoptera
Tick	Arachnida: Acarina
Tipulid	see Leather-jacket
Trout, Brown	*Salmo trutta*
Vole, Bank	*Clethrionomys glareolus*
Field	*Microtus terrestris*
Water	*Arvicola amphibius*
Whiting	*Trisopterus luscus*
Weevil	Coleoptera: Curculionidae
Winkle	Mollusca: *Littorina* spp
Whale	Cetacea
Woodlouse	Crustacea: Malacostraca

Appendices

The essential information needed for the interpretation of the maps is given on pp. 15–19. These appendices describe the several stages in the development and running of the project and some expansion on the reasons why certain of the decisions were taken.

Planning and Pilot Survey

A full scale Pilot Survey for the *Winter Atlas* was conducted in the winter 1980/81 with two main aims. First and foremost, to establish a method of assessing abundance; and secondly, to learn more about movements between November and March in order to define the limits of the 'winter'.

There are several points to keep in mind when deciding on the methods for a survey like this.

(1) The methods must be scientifically valid and useful.

(2) The methods must be acceptable in the field to the largely amateur observers. For such a mass-participation survey the methods have to be straightforward and not too complex, and this applies especially to any necessary paperwork. Observers will take part in a project only if they enjoy it. Most people hate paperwork in general, and particularly anything involving calculations.

(3) The methods should be the same for all species.

(4) All data must refer to birds actually recorded. Observers must not be able to send in data based on what they 'know' to be present.

(5) The methods must be able to incorporate casual observations. If such observations cannot be incorporated a great deal of potentially usable information will be lost, especially for the rarer and more elusive species.

(6) Two or more observers will sometimes be working independently in the same area. The methods must not involve a subjective decision as to which observations are to be used.

For the Pilot Survey we wanted to assess several possible methods, and two quite distinct projects were carried out. About 100 observers were asked to participate in each, and both groups were widely spread across Britain and Ireland, so that information from a variety of habitats and observers would be obtained. In addition to sending in the results of their trials, observers were asked to comment on the methods tried and make any suggestions for improvements.

The first group were mainly people who were already working on BTO Common Birds Census or Waterways Bird Survey plots. They were asked to census a particular fixed route each fortnight from early November to mid March. This spanned the possible period of the survey. Several points emerged from these censuses and details are given in Lack (1983). Those which were important in deciding the methods to be used in the main survey are repeated here.

One possibility for the quantative element was to superimpose contours of abundance, generated by a computer from a series of fixed sites, onto a map showing presence or absence of each species on the 10-km square grid. The main point that ruled this out was that each site would necessarily be on a rather restricted area or in only a particular habitat type. Therefore several counts would be needed to obtain a reliable assessment of the abundance of a species, although this could be either several on one site or several on different sites. A restricted area also generally means a restricted species list and any numbers counted might be atypical. Also an observer who is going to visit a site regularly is likely to choose one which is good for birds but this is not necessarily going to be typical of the surrounding area.

These trials also showed that counts in early November and mid March were very different from those made at dates in between. In early November the counts which were most affected were those of some migrant species such as Fieldfare *Turdus pilaris* and Redwing *T. iliacus*. These birds were evidently still moving extensively in early November and it was also known that several waders and wildfowl (groups not covered by this trial) were still moving then. It was therefore decided not to start the field season until the middle of November.

The problems with the mid March count were most noticeable in some small passerines, *eg* Robin *Erithacus rubecula*, Dunnock *Prunella modularis* and Wren *Troglodytes troglodytes*. For these species there were markedly higher numbers recorded at this mid March count than at one a fortnight earlier. For some species the increase could be due to immigration but Dunnock and Wren, at least, are almost entirely resident. The increase in numbers seems likely to be due to the fact that the birds had begun to sing more intensively, making them more conspicuous and therefore more easily recorded and counted. Obviously such a major increase in conspicuousness would make a nonsense of comparisons with areas counted only earlier in the winter. It was therefore decided to finish the survey period at the end of February. It is true that some birds start to sing and display during February, or even January in some instances, but in the most northerly areas, in mid winter, the amount of daylight available to do useful fieldwork is very limited. On cloudy days there may be only three or four hours at the most. So all of February was needed to enable the fieldwork to be completed.

In choosing the end of February it was also accepted that some early breeding species, such as the Tawny Owl *Strix aluco* and Raven *Corvus corax*, would be back on their breeding grounds before the end of the survey period. The two species mentioned are completely resident as far as is known, but there were a very few cases of a species being recorded in late February in areas where they breed but do not spend the winter. Where this appears to affect the maps it is discussed in the relevant species accounts, and see p. 22.

The second group of observers for the Pilot Survey were mainly BTO Regional Representatives. They were asked to do two things:

(1) To go into their 10-km square with the object of recording all the species which occurred, although it was not necessary to try to see all on every visit. They were to count all the birds they saw, to note how long they spent looking, and how many 2-km squares (tetrads) they visited. This last would be used as a crude measure of the amount of ground covered.

(2) At the end of each month, using their counts as a guide, they were asked to estimate the total number of each species present in their square, on an order of magnitude scale 1–10, 11–100, 101–1,000, 1,001–10,000, 10,001+.

A full discussion of the results of these trials is given in Lack (1983) but the main points affecting the decisions taken are repeated here. The second part of this trial in particular was found to be very unpopular with observers and for several reasons. The calculations involved were universally disliked and, having done them, many observers did not believe or trust the resulting estimates. Problems also arose when two or more observers worked in the same 10-km square. Such observers often estimated a species abundance in different orders of magnitude, and this obviously would later require a subjective decision by someone. Furthermore it was not simply differing estimates: over a range of species some observers consistently arrived at higher orders of magnitude than others.

For several reasons, it would be preferable to estimate the total numbers present or the density on the ground (a measure of absolute abundance). Any measure using an index of relative abundance immediately excludes easy comparisons between species, although those species that are similar, morphologically, behaviourally and ecologically can be compared to a greater or lesser degree. But in view of the problems encountered with such estimates during the Pilot Survey the idea of using a measure of absolute abundance was, somewhat reluctantly, abandoned.

For all their counts observers recorded both the time spent in the field and a measure of the area covered, and when the results were analysed it was found that the time spent in the field was a more reliable predictor of number of birds seen. A more complicated measure of area covered was considered but this would have involved detailed map reading and/or calculations, neither of which would be popular with the observers. Time, though, is very easy to measure. A time-based relative abundance assessment was therefore chosen.

It was decided to use the number of birds seen on any one day as the unit, and the day was standardised as six hours (see below). Where multiple counts were available for a square, the highest was used. This simplified the decisions involved with calculation of means or medians caused by the incorporation or not of casual records. Observers would probably not send in a casual record of, for example, 5 Blue Tits, and there are particular difficulties with zero counts. It is impossible to distinguish between:

(a) there were no birds on that day, and (b) the observer did not visit the right habitat or site on that day.

References

LACK, P. C. 1983. Some results from different methods of censusing birds in winter. Pp. 5–12 in PURROY, F. J. (ed.) Bird Census and Mediterranean Landscape— Proceedings of VIIth Int. Bird Census Committee Conf. University of Leon, Leon.

Organisation in the field

For many years the BTO has had a network of Regional Representatives who co-ordinate BTO field activities, and often other natural history activities as well, in their areas. For many surveys these Representatives are essential for the distribution and collection of record cards to and from observers, and in the checking of the quality and reliability of data from their areas. Also, observers often prefer to work through someone who is local and who may be known to them, rather than through an unknown person at BTO headquarters. It is also easier for a National Organiser to deal with a hundred or so Regional Representatives rather than the many hundreds or on occasions, thousands of observers.

At the start of the planning of the Winter Atlas, BTO Regional Representatives were therefore contacted and asked if they would act as Regional Organisers for their area. About 80% agreed and of the remainder the majority found substitutes. The Regional Representatives have traditionally organised activities for a county or, in the case of larger areas, a part of a county, and they usually do this in conjunction with the local bird club. Since the Breeding Atlas, most boundaries of Representatives' areas have ceased to be the county boundary as such and have become the nearest equivalent on a 10-km square basis. Where a county boundary splits a 10-km square, the whole square is normally allocated to one of the Representatives involved. However, there are a few 10-km squares on the border of two counties with, for example, no bridges across the river which marks the boundary, so that access to the complete square is difficult. For the Winter Atlas such squares and a few others were covered from both sides independently.

The number of squares covered by each Regional Organiser varied from one to several hundred (this last with some help!). Figure 16 shows the area covered by each organiser, and their names are listed below.

SCOTLAND
1   B. Marshall
2   N. Riddiford
3   C. J. Booth
4   N. E. Buxton
5   D. Macdonald (assisted by Miss S. Read)
6   Mrs P. Collett
7   A. Currie
8   D. McAllister
9   B. Etheridge
10   R. A. Broad

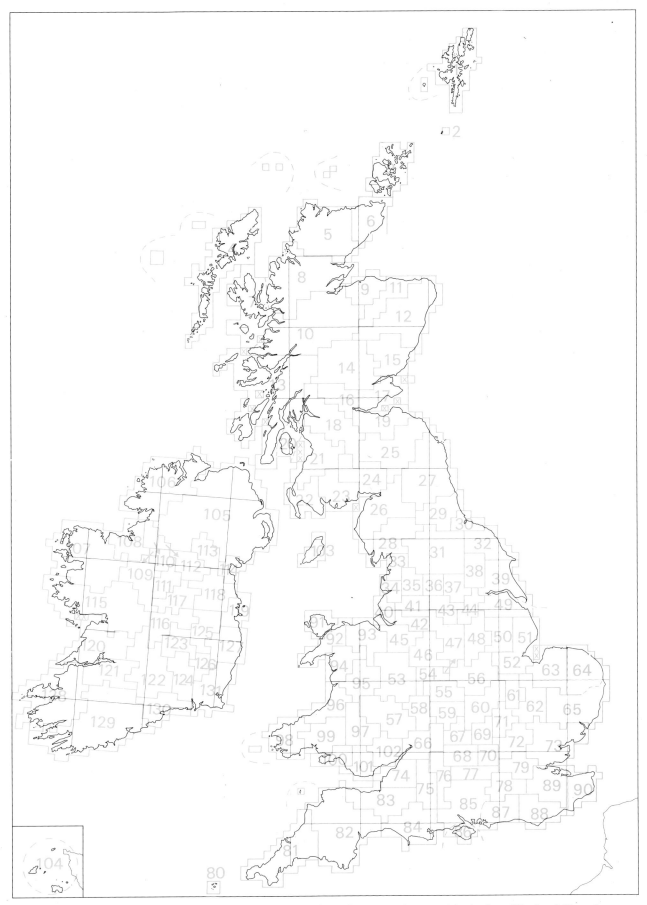

Fig. 16   The areas covered by Regional Organisers. The numbers are those used in the list of Regional Organisers on p. 432.

11 M. J. H. Cook
12 S. T. Buckland
13 R. F. Coomber
14 E. C. Cameron
15 N. K. Atkinson
16 W. R. Brackenridge
17 Mrs W. Mattingley (Isle of May, B. Zonfrillo)
18 I. P. Gibson
19 A. W. and L. Brown
20 J. A. Gibson
21 A. G. Stewart
22 G. Sheppard
23 Mrs H. S. C. Halliday
24 M. Wright
25 R. J. Robertson

ENGLAND

26 G. Horne
27 L. G. Macfarlane (1981–83), Mrs M. A. Macfarlane (1983–85)
28 M, Hutcheson
29 D. Sowerbutts
30 D. Summers-Smith (1981–82), R. McAndrew (1982–85)
31 P. A. Luker
32 R. Leslie (1981–82), S. Cochrane (1982–85) assisted by K. Watts (1983)
33 C. Clapham
34 W. J. Clift
35 A. A. Cooper
36 I. H. Dillingham (1981–82), C. Shields (1982–85)
37 S. P. Singleton
38 P. Hutchinson
39 A. Grieve
40 A. S. Duckels
41 J. T. Sutton
42 B. Martin
43 A. B. Gladwin (1981–82), A. H. V. Smith (1982–85)
44 M. Densley (1981–82), K. J. Hayhow (1982–85)
45 D. Elphick (1981–82), F. R. Walley (1982–85)
46 F. C. Gribble
47 G. P. Mawson
48 E. Cowley
49–52 P. J. Wilson (1981–82), Mrs A. Goodall (1981–82)
49 Mrs A. Goodall (1982–85)
50 Miss J. Garlick (1982–85)
51 R. Lambert (1982–85)
52 R. and K. Heath (1982–85)
53 C. E. Wright
54 P. K. Dedicoat
55 R. and A. Normand
56 R. A. O. Hickling
57 A. Marchant
58 G. H. Green
59 J. A. Hardman
60 P. Richardson
61 M. E. S. Rooney
62 M. J. Allen
63 A. L. Bull
64 M. P. Taylor
65 B. J. Brown
66 R. Goater
67 R. Knight
68 R. Knight (1981–83), Mrs C. Ross (1983–85)
69 P. C. Lack (1981–82), N. H. F. Stone (1982–85)
70 P. C. Lack (1981–82), J. Knight (1982–85)
71 A. J. Livett
72 K. W. Smith
73 G. Smith (assisted by G. Edwards)
74 R. L. Bland
75 R. Turner

76 A. Lowe (1981–82), S. Edwards (1982–85)
77 G. Wilson
78 D. Parr (1981–82), K. J. Herber (1982–85)
79 K. Betton
80 D. Hunt
81 R. Butts (1981–82), S. Jackson (1982–85)
82 F. D. Holmes
83 W. J. Webber
84 C. M. Reynolds
85 C. R. Cuthbert
86 J. Stafford
87 R. Lord
88 M. Banks
89 G. F. A. Munns
90 G. F. A. Munns (1981–82), A. C. B. Henderson (1982–85)

WALES

91 I. Wynmclean
92 R. W. Arnold
93 J. Birch
94 D. J. Brown
95 K. E. Stott
96 R. Bovey
97 R. J. Haycock
98 G. H. Rees
99 D. H. V. Roberts
100 R. J. Howells
101 I. Smith
102 P. N. Martin

ISLE OF MAN

103 E. D. Kerruish

CHANNEL ISLANDS

104 I. J. Buxton

NORTHERN IRELAND

105 I. Forsyth (assisted by C. Bailey (1981–82))

REPUBLIC OF IRELAND

S. Fleming (1981–83), C. J. Wilson (1983–85)

The following checked data cards
106 R. Sheppard
107 A. Whilde
108 D. Cotton
109 J. Early
110 D. Cotton
111 D. Scott
112 J. Lovatt
113 D. Scott
114 J. Fitzharris
115 G. Young
116 G. Duane
117 B. Carrick
118 W. Stuart-Mills
119 F. Fitzgerald (1981–82), K. Grace (1982–85)
120 P. Brennan
121 E. Jones (who also checked all Supplementary Record Sheets)
122 C. Wilson
123 T. Wood
124 R. Goodwillie
125 B. King
126 D. O'Connor
127 S. Fagan
128 F. King
129 K. Preston
130 D. McGrath
131 O. O'Sullivan

In some parts of Britain and Ireland there were worries about whether full coverage was feasible. At the outset of the project the Working Group privately kept open the option of using a fourth winter to complete the survey if it became necessary; and in the Republic of Ireland, for the first winter, a system of priority squares was selected to ensure an even scatter of coverage. The selection was done by taking at random one of the four 10-km squares within each 20-km square, with the proviso that the selected square contained some land. This resulted in a sample of about 27% of squares being listed. By the end of the first winter, however, it was apparent that full coverage was possible by the end of the three winters and so the system of priority squares was dropped. The fourth winter was not necessary.

In some counties, Regional Organisers had a system of 'stewards', who co-ordinated work for each 10-km square for the BTO and all other surveys. This system was however only practicable in well populated areas.

The instructions for the survey were printed as a special 6-page Supplement to *BTO News*. This was sent out to all members of the BTO with the September issue and to members of the IWC with the October issue of *IWC News* in 1981, 1982 and 1983. Regional Organisers also had a further supply to distribute to field workers as required. A revised Supplement was printed for each field season and the 1982 and 1983 Supplements included preliminary maps.

Field methods and recording cards

The methods in the field have been described briefly on p. 15. What follows, here, are some explanatory notes on the design of the recording cards, and on some aspects of the field methods.

For a timed visit observers filled in a Visit Card, a specimen of which is illustrated on p. 15. The information required was kept to a minimum. To identify the 10-km squares the system of two letters (one in Ireland) and two numbers was used rather than the all-number system, mainly because it is much easier to remember and would lead to fewer errors. As a check, observers were asked to name an identifying feature of the square such as the largest town, a precaution which led directly to the detection of several errors.

Dated records were wanted so that shorter periods within the survey could be analysed separately (see p. 15). Also records from outside the period of the survey could be easily deleted. Each winter's intake of cards contained three or four hundred cards which gave dates in early November or March, and even a few from October or April.

To qualify as a 'visit' at least one hour had to be spent in the field but there was no upper limit. Most observers recorded the time to the nearest five minutes.

Observers were asked to record the number of species they saw during a visit as an aid to checking. When the data were typed, one of several checks made was to verify that the number of species input agreed with the observer's total. Most discrepancies were typing errors but in some cases the observer had mis-counted.

On the majority of cards the box labelled 'Comments' was left blank. However, some observers filled it with all kinds of comments and notes. The most frequent were brief details of the weather and the habitat or habitats visited. Sometimes a specific site or sites were noted as being visited; sometimes notes of hard weather movements were recorded; or a note that certain birds were feral; or that the counts were exceptional or otherwise; sometimes that recent changes had occurred in the local habitat; and sometimes there were witticisms or signs of frustration! From these comments it was evident that most visits were done in reasonable, if cold, weather conditions (one comment—next time you organise a Winter Atlas please make arrangements to do the fieldwork in summer!), but it was extraordinary what miserable conditions were faced by some people. A coded version of some of these comments was entered onto the computer but no analyses have been attempted.

On the card was a list of 187 'species' expected to occur. Feral Pigeon and Rock Dove *Columba livia*, and Carrion, Hooded and Hybrid Crows *Corvus corone* were given individual entries, but other subspecies were not separated. It would have been preferable to have kept the Rock and Water Pipit *Anthus (s.) petrosus* and *A. (s.) spinoletta* as separate entries, though in this case many observers did note where appropriate that the Water Pipit was involved. There was some space left at the end of the card for observers to write in any extra species they noted. The printed list included some introduced birds, *eg* Mandarin Duck *Aix galericulata* and Ring-necked Parakeet *Psittacula krameri*, but several others were added by observers. After the start of the project observers were specially requested via *BTO News* to record all truly feral birds they encountered but to omit individuals known to have escaped from captivity.

It was emphasised on the instructions that each visit must record only the observations of one person, or of a group working together. If two or more people (or groups) surveyed different parts of a square on the same day each group was requested to fill in a separate card. Composite cards were not wanted.

The object of the visits was to record all the species that occurred in the square during the winter. This would involve visiting all the habitats present, although not necessarily all on each visit. The practice of visiting all of one habitat on one day, and all of another habitat on a separate day was actively discouraged. However, this inevitably happened regularly with large water bodies, either because there was often only one lake in a square or all such water bodies in a square occurred in the same area. For land habitats it happened rarely.

The vast majority of timed visits were carried out on foot, but a few observers were on a bicycle or in a vehicle. Normally a count from a vehicle overemphasises the numbers of some larger birds and underemphasises those of smaller birds, but as such counts were rather rare and randomly distributed it is very unlikely that they had any significant effect.

Observers were encouraged to visit their squares whenever they wished. A few did so nearly every day, but any observers who asked were told that a visit every two or three weeks was an adequate sample. However, even in well-covered areas some species were rarely encountered on special visits, hence the need for Supplementary Records.

A sample Supplementary Record Sheet is shown on p. 16. Data requested were much as before, ie 10-km square, date, species and number of birds seen. The column headed 'Locality' was included so that people passing through a square could note where they were and work out the 10-km square later. The entry could also be used as a check for correct 10-km square designation. In retrospect, it would have been preferable to have kept to 'identifying feature' or 'nearest large town'. Virtually all these square numbers were checked against locality by Regional Organisers, and the checking would have been much simplified if the locality had always been a village or other large feature, which appeared on road atlases. In several cases observers wrote the name of a farm or wood, some of which were very difficult to identify. In a few cases the locality was never found on any map, and the records were accepted or rejected depending on the likelihood of the observation being correct. This in turn was influenced by whether all other squares on that observer's sheet were correct, and if all the records were in the same area etc.

The majority of Supplementary Records were sent in on such sheets. However, particularly if an observer had more than about ten records from one square on one day, he or she could fill in a card instead, and put zero time in box 4 of the card. Timed counts of less than one hour were also put into this category. In retrospect again, it would have been better not to have had this facility and to have put all such records onto Supplementary Record sheets. They were treated as such in analyses.

In general all birds seen using the square could be counted and noted on the *Winter Atlas* records. There was very little problem in deciding this, even with flying birds.

The National Wildfowl Counts and counts for the Birds of Estuaries Enquiry continued through the three winters, and observers did not necessarily send in a duplicate set of data to the *Winter Atlas* as Supplementary Records. However, if they did a Wildfowl or Estuary Count as part of a timed visit, or if the count spanned more than one 10-km square, they were asked to send in the data to the *Winter Atlas* as well as to the other survey. In the event, a high proportion of *all* such counts came in to the *Winter Atlas* directly. As a great deal of extra computer processing of mainly duplicated data would have been necessary to incorporate these data, it was not attempted.

At the start of the survey it was thought that roosts, especially large ones attracting birds from a wide area, might cause difficulties of interpretation. Counts made at roosts were therefore kept separate. After the first winter it was apparent that this problem was far less than had been anticipated. Indeed roosts did not seem to be counted very often, or, if they were it was not specifically mentioned. In the first winter it was requested that all counts at roosts should be sent in as Supplementary Records, whether nocturnal

roosts, pre-roost gatherings or the daytime roosts of some waders, even if the roosts were met during the course of a timed visit. In practice, during the first winter, particularly with diurnal roosts, there was a certain amount of confusion. So, for the second and third winters the instructions were slightly modified—to conform with what was generally happening in the first winter. If an observer encountered a roost during a timed visit the relevant birds should be included, just as if they were feeding or loafing, or otherwise using the square. Special visits to roosts were, however, still to be retained as Supplementary Records.

The majority of records were of live birds seen or heard by the observer. Records of recently dead birds were also accepted, as were records of species such as owls obtained on hearsay from farmers, gamekeepers and other informed persons. All could be accepted at the observer's discretion.

For the Pilot Survey the card included some group species to allow for partially unidentified birds eg 'duck sp.', 'gull sp.', 'tit sp.'. However, it was soon realised that these would be impossible to analyse so the option was dropped. The only exception was for crossbills in Scotland, if an observer was unsure whether the birds were Common Crossbill *Loxia curvirostra* or Scottish Crossbill *L. scotica* (see p. 400).

In a few instances large blocks of habitat spanned the borders of two or more 10-km squares. This was particularly the case with major reservoirs and estuaries. Each was dealt with individually but, in general, if the greater part of a lake was in one 10-km square and only a small area in another, the whole feature was recorded as in the one square. In the case of larger estuaries it was recommended that boundaries of squares should be decided by natural points near to the real boundary rather than an arbitrary boundary line.

Most data were sent in during the spring and summer following the winter fieldwork but some continued to come in much later. The maps do not include data submitted after the end of 1984, ten months after fieldwork was completed.

Computing, checking and data storage

The majority of Visit Cards and Supplementary Record Sheets were sent by observers to their Regional Organisers. Most organisers scanned the records quickly to check for obvious errors or doubtful entries that should be queried.

At the end of each winter the Regional Organisers sent their cards and sheets to the National Organiser. Some cards and sheets were also received direct from observers. A few of the 'Comments' were coded and, in a few cases some action was required as a result of a 'Comment'. The cards representing counts of less than one hour were put into a separate batch. The cards received direct from observers were sorted into organiser's region and put into batches accordingly. All cards were given a serial number.

Rather more preparation was required for the Supplementary Record Sheets. The main task was to write in the two character species codes on each line. At the same time any errors noticed were corrected and a serial number was given to each sheet.

After initial attempts to input all the data at BTO headquarters, it was decided that the job was too large and that it would be quicker and, in the long run, cheaper if the initial typing could be done externally. All subsequent data cards and sheets were sent to Alpha-Numeric Ltd of Maidenhead to be typed.

The data were returned on magnetic tapes, in a mutually agreed format. The tapes were then read into the BTO computer and the data were converted to a more suitable format for subsequent use. Data were not verified after typing; this was considered unnecessary in view of the checks the data would receive subsequently. All data were then run through a checking program, which did two major checks. First, that all entries were legal (eg that species codes existed) and internally consistent (eg on cards, that the number of species entries was correct). Second, the program compared the count of birds of each species against a predetermined upper limit. Entries which exceeded that limit were specifically marked for checking. The upper limit for each species was arbitrarily designated and was fixed so that only the top few per cent of the counts would be marked. For example the 'limit' for Bewick's Swan *Cygnus columbianus* was 50 but counts at the main wintering sites such as Slimbridge and the Ouse Washes would exceed this. Anywhere else, a count over the 'limit' might well have been wrong. In practice most marked counts had been typed correctly but the system successfully trapped some errors. The computer files of the cards were then corrected as necessary after checking against the original data cards.

The corrected files were run through a program which printed out copies of the original data cards or sheets. On these print-outs any remaining high counts were marked with two identifying asterisks. The print-outs and the original cards were returned to the Regional Organisers for checking. Organisers were asked particularly to check the grid square numbers against the largest towns or localities given, and to check any asterisked entries. They were also told to delete any records which had not been accepted by local recorders; likewise any doubtful records, whether of identification or of numbers seen.

The Regional Organisers sent back the cards and print-outs, and the computer files were corrected as necessary and put into their final form. The cards and sheets are stored at BTO headquarters.

A last check was made, after the fieldwork had been completed, by producing master cards for each 10-km square. Printed copies of these were sent to Regional Organisers for verification. Any record which appeared to be 'out of place' on the species maps was specifically queried at this stage. This process also eliminated several errors which had slipped through earlier checks.

Producing the maps

The original data files were processed and the data separated into files containing all the records of each species. For each species a regression coefficient of

'number of birds seen' on 'time spent in the field' was calculated and it was computed with both axes on a logarithmic scale. The resulting coefficient for a species was used to standardise the counts of that species only if it was statistically highly significant ($P < 0.001$). The coefficients are listed in Table 4. Subsequently all counts resulting from timed visits of more than one hour were standardised by multiplying the count by $(6/T)^b$ where 6 is the standard six hours, T the actual time spent on that count and b the regression coefficient calculated above. All counts of all species from visits of less than one hour, and those sent in as Supplementary Records, were used without adjustment.

Preliminary working maps were produced on the BTO computer's line printer and sent to authors who were to write the species texts. Interim maps which were published (such as those in *BTO News* and *IWC News*) were drawn by hand. The final maps were produced by Laser-Scan Ltd, Cambridge.

Table 4 The regression coefficients used to standardise the counts

Red-throated Diver *Gavia stellata*	0.00
Black-throated Diver *G. arctica*	0.00
Great Northern Diver *G. immer*	0.00
Little Grebe *Tachybaptus ruficollis*	0.24
Great Crested Grebe *Podiceps cristatus*	0.24
Red-necked Grebe *P. grisegena*	0.00
Slavonian Grebe *P. auritus*	0.00
Black-necked Grebe *P. nigricollis*	0.00
Fulmar *Fulmarus glacialis*	0.00
Gannet *Sula bassana*	0.00
Cormorant *Phalacrocorax carbo*	0.33
Shag *P. aristotelis*	0.00
Bittern *Botaurus stellaris*	0.00
Grey Heron *Ardea cinerea*	0.21
Mute Swan *Cygnus olor*	0.23
Bewick's Swan *C. columbianus*	0.00
Whooper Swan *C. cygnus*	0.00
Bean Goose *Anser fabalis*	0.00
Pink-footed Goose *A. brachyrhynchus*	0.00
White-fronted Goose *A. albifrons*	0.00
Greylag Goose *A. anser*	0.00
Snow Goose *A. caerulescens*	0.00
Canada Goose *Branta canadensis*	0.00
Barnacle Goose *B. leucopsis*	0.00
Brent Goose *B. bernicla*	0.00
Egyptian Goose *Alopochen aegyptiacus*	0.00
Shelduck *Tadorna tadorna*	0.00
Mandarin *Aix galericulata*	0.00
Wigeon *Anas penelope*	0.00
Gadwall *A. strepera*	0.34
Teal *A. crecca*	0.30
Mallard *A. platyrhynchos*	0.40
Pintail *A. acuta*	0.00
Shoveler *A. clypeata*	0.00
Red-crested Pochard *Netta rufina*	0.00
Pochard *Aythya ferina*	0.22
Ring-necked Duck *A. collaris*	0.00
Ferruginous Duck *A. nyroca*	0.00
Tufted Duck *A. fuligula*	0.17
Scaup *A. marila*	0.00
Eider *Somateria mollissima*	0.00

437

Long-tailed Duck *Clangula hyemalis*	0.00	Great Black-backed Gull *L. marinus*	0.26
Common Scoter *Melanitta nigra*	0.00	Kittiwake *Rissa tridactyla*	0.00
Velvet Scoter *M. fusca*	0.00	Guillemot *Uria aalge*	0.00
Goldeneye *Bucephalus clangula*	0.20	Razorbill *Alca torda*	0.00
Smew *Mergus albellus*	0.00	Black Guillemot *Cepphus grylle*	0.00
Red-breasted Merganser *M. serrator*	0.00	Little Auk *Alle alle*	0.00
Goosander *M. merganser*	0.00	Puffin *Fratercula arctica*	0.00
Ruddy Duck *Oxyura jamaicensis*	0.00	Rock Dove/Feral Pigeon *Columba livia*	0.30
Red Kite *Milvus milvus*	0.00	Stock Dove *C. oenas*	0.40
Marsh Harrier *Circus aeruginosus*	0.00	Woodpigeon *C. palumbus*	0.92
Hen Harrier *C. cyaneus*	0.00	Collared Dove *Streptopelia decaocto*	0.40
Goshawk *Accipiter gentilis*	0.00	Ring-necked Parakeet *Psittacula krameri*	0.00
Sparrowhawk *A. nisus*	0.10	Barn Owl *Tyto alba*	0.00
Buzzard *Buteo buteo*	0.27	Little Owl *Athene noctua*	0.12
Rough-legged Buzzard *B. lagopus*	0.00	Tawny Owl *Strix aluco*	0.10
Golden Eagle *Aquila chrysaetos*	0.00	Long-eared Owl *Asio otus*	0.00
Kestrel *Falco tinnunculus*	0.26	Short-eared Owl *A. flammeus*	0.15
Merlin *F. columbarius*	0.00	Kingfisher *Alcedo atthis*	0.10
Peregrine *F. peregrinus*	0.00	Green Woodpecker *Picus viridis*	0.16
Red Grouse *Lagopus lagopus*	0.38	Great Spotted Woodpecker *Dendrocopos major*	0.18
Ptarmigan *L. mutus*	0.00	Lesser Spotted Woodpecker *D. minor*	0.00
Black Grouse *Tetrao tetrix*	0.00	Woodlark *Lullula arborea*	0.00
Capercaillie *T. urogallus*	0.00	Skylark *Alauda arvensis*	0.47
Red-legged Partridge *Alectoris rufa*	0.28	Shorelark *Eremophila alpestris*	0.00
Grey Partridge *Perdix perdix*	0.15	Meadow Pipit *Anthus pratensis*	0.40
Pheasant *Phasianus colchicus*	0.43	Rock Pipit *A. (s.) petrosus*	0.20
Golden Pheasant *Chrysolophus pictus*	0.00	Water Pipit *A. (s.) spinoletta*	0.00
Lady Amherst's Pheasant *C. amherstiae*	0.00	Grey Wagtail *Motacilla cinerea*	0.15
Water Rail *Rallus aquaticus*	0.00	Pied Wagtail *M. alba*	0.33
Moorhen *Gallinula chloropus*	0.43	Waxwing *Bombycilla garrulus*	0.00
Coot *Fulica atra*	0.00	Dipper *Cinclus cinclus*	0.13
Oystercatcher *Haematopus ostralegus*	0.53	Wren *Troglodytes troglodytes*	0.58
Avocet *Recurvirostra avosetta*	0.00	Dunnock *Prunella modularis*	0.54
Ringed Plover *Charadrius hiaticula*	0.00	Robin *Erithacus rubecula*	0.62
Golden Plover *Pluvialis apricaria*	0.00	Black Redstart *Phoenicurus ochruros*	0.00
Grey Plover *P. squatarola*	0.00	Stonechat *Saxicola torquata*	0.14
Lapwing *Vanellus vanellus*	0.58	Blackbird *Turdus merula*	0.78
Knot *Calidris canutus*	0.00	Fieldfare *T. pilaris*	0.53
Sanderling *C. alba*	0.00	Song Thrush *T. philomelos*	0.51
Little Stint *C. minuta*	0.00	Redwing *T. iliacus*	0.53
Purple Sandpiper *C. maritima*	0.00	Mistle Thrush *T. viscivorus*	0.41
Dunlin *C. alpina*	0.47	Cetti's Warbler *Cettia cetti*	0.00
Ruff *Philomachus pugnax*	0.00	Dartford Warbler *Sylvia undata*	0.00
Jack Snipe *Lymnocryptes minimus*	0.00	Blackcap *S. atricapilla*	0.00
Snipe *Gallinago gallinago*	0.28	Chiffchaff *Phylloscopus collybita*	0.00
Woodcock *Scolopax rusticola*	0.00	Goldcrest *Regulus regulus*	0.33
Black-tailed Godwit *Limosa limosa*	0.00	Firecrest *R. ignicapillus*	0.00
Bar-tailed Godwit *L. lapponica*	0.00	Bearded Tit *Panurus biarmicus*	0.00
Whimbrel *Numenius phaeopus*	0.00	Long-tailed Tit *Aegithalos caudatus*	0.25
Curlew *N. arquata*	0.47	Marsh Tit *Parus palustris*	0.25
Spotted Redshank *Tringa erythropus*	0.00	Willow Tit *P. montanus*	0.20
Redshank *T. totanus*	0.43	Crested Tit *P. cristatus*	0.00
Greenshank *T. nebularia*	0.00	Coal Tit *P. ater*	0.28
Green Sandpiper *T. ochropus*	0.00	Blue Tit *P. caeruleus*	0.68
Common Sandpiper *Actitis hypoleucos*	0.00	Great Tit *P. major*	0.60
Turnstone *Arenaria interpres*	0.33	Nuthatch *Sitta europaea*	0.25
Mediterranean Gull *Larus melanocephalus*	0.00	Treecreeper *Certhia familiaris*	0.21
Little Gull *L. minutus*	0.00	Great Grey Shrike *Lanius excubitor*	0.00
Black-headed Gull *L. ridibundus*	0.74	Jay *Garrulus glandarius*	0.32
Ring-billed Gull *L. delawarensis*	0.00	Magpie *Pica pica*	0.63
Common Gull *L. canus*	0.41	Chough *Pyrrhocorax pyrrhocorax*	0.00
Lesser Black-backed Gull *L. fuscus*	0.00	Jackdaw *Corvus monedula*	0.62
Herring Gull *L. argentatus*	0.30	Rook *C. frugilegus*	0.67
Iceland Gull *L. glaucoides*	0.00	Carrion Crow *C. corone corone*	0.66
Glaucous Gull *L. hyperboreus*	0.00	Hooded Crow *C. corone cornix*	0.55

Raven *C. corax*	0.17	Scottish Crossbill *L. scotica*	0.00
Starling *Sturnus vulgaris*	0.90	Bullfinch *Pyrrhula pyrrhula*	0.33
House Sparrow *Passer domesticus*	0.70	Hawfinch *Coccothraustes coccothraustes*	0.00
Tree Sparrow *P. montanus*	0.28	Lapland Bunting *Calcarius lapponicus*	0.00
Chaffinch *Fringilla coelebs*	0.90	Snow Bunting *Plectrophenax nivalis*	0.00
Brambling *F. montifringilla*	0.00	Yellowhammer *Emberiza citrinella*	0.47
Greenfinch *Carduelis chloris*	0.42	Cirl Bunting *E. cirlus*	0.00
Goldfinch *C. carduelis*	0.24	Reed Bunting *E. schoeniclus*	0.33
Siskin *C. spinus*	0.00	Corn Bunting *Miliaria calandra*	0.00
Linnet *C. cannabina*	0.29		
Twite *C. flavirostris*	0.00		
Redpoll *C. flammea*	0.19		
Common Crossbill *Loxia curvirostra*	0.00		

NOTE: This list includes only those species in the main map section. All other species had a coefficient of zero.

Index of birds mentioned in text

(Compiled by Malgosia Trojanowska, Caroline Stockley and Rita Gray)

The British Trust for Ornithology

Founded in 1933, the British Trust for Ornithology has throughout its history been deeply committed to the idea of membership participation. Often it is difficult, or even impossible, to evaluate the findings of a single observer, but let 500 or 1,000 pool their results and the broad picture starts to emerge. There could be no more convincing demonstration of this than the maps which form this *Atlas*.

Among its many functions the BTO administers the national Bird Ringing Scheme and organises a Common Birds Census, designed to detect changes in the population levels of commoner species breeding in Britain. For similar reasons, estuary birds are regularly censused by Trust members, as is the population of Heronries, while a Nest Records Scheme measure, year by year, the breeding success of our birds.

Thus, the theme common to all BTO studies is that the observations of individual members, guided and co-ordinated by a small research staff, supply information vital to the task of conservation. A measure of this usefulness is that much of the research is done at the request of, and with financial support from, the Nature Conservancy Council.

The members of the Trust come from all walks of life, and the keen beginner is as welcome as the expert. The postal lending library operated by the Trust is unparalleled in any country, while the many conferences it organises are a happy amalgam of information and enthusiasm. For details of membership write to: Membership Secretary, BTO, Beech Grove, Tring, Herts HP23 5NR.

The Irish Wildbird Conservancy

The Irish Wildbird Conservancy is the largest voluntary organisation in Ireland concerned solely with wildlife conservation. Formed in 1968 the IWC is a recognised charity supported by over 4000 members.

The IWC owns or manages an increasing number of nature reserves which protect threatened habitats for birds. Among the best known are the Wexford Wildfowl Reserve and Little Skellig. The IWC carries out research and surveys on birds and their habitats which form the basis of its conservation policies.

Most of the surveys are carried out on a voluntary basis by IWC members. Co-operation with the BTO is close especially for joint projects such as this Atlas and its predecessor *The Atlas of Breeding Birds in Britain and Ireland*. Particular species such as the chough and the terns, which have special conservation requirements, have been the subject of recent surveys.

The IWC has a network of branches throughout the country each one providing a programme of film shows, lectures and outings. The annual journal *Irish Birds* is published by the IWC and members receive the quarterly newsletter *IWC News*. For details of membership write to: Irish Wildbird Conservancy, Southview, Church Road, Greystones, Co. Wicklow, Ireland. Telephone 01-875759.